Economic Systems, Markets and Politics

Christian A. Conrad

Economic Systems, Markets and Politics

An Ethical, Behavioral and Institutional Approach

Springer

Christian A. Conrad
htw Business School, University of Applied Science
Hochschule für Technik und Wirtschaft
Saarbrücken, Germany

ISBN 978-3-031-10365-0 ISBN 978-3-031-10366-7 (eBook)
https://doi.org/10.1007/978-3-031-10366-7

This Springer imprint is published by the registered company Springer Nature Switzerland AG
The registered company address is: Gewerbestrasse 11, 6330 Cham, Switzerland

Preface

This book is the culmination of my research stay at Georgetown University and the EC Commission and my time as an assistant professor in the Department of Economics at the University of Tübingen, Germany. I have also amassed more than 12 years of professional experience in a large German bank, where I often worked with the management of international companies as a business consultant. The time period of this experience included the boom and crash at the beginning of the new millennium and the financial crisis. As a result, I have held seminars on political economy in the bachelor's and master's degree programs at the University of Applied Science HTW in Saarbrücken. This teaching experience as well as an extensive literature study has been incorporated into this book.

Finally, I would like to thank Ms. Danica Webb (USA) for the translation of the major part of this book and Prof. Starbatty, Prof. Hartherz, and the asset manager Dr. Markus Stahl for their support.

Saarbrücken, Germany
August 2022

Christian A. Conrad

Introduction

A weakness in many current theories of economics is a lack of detailed behavioral understanding and the moral aspects of human behavior. Moreover, economics analyzes the isolated individual in an economic environment but not in a group.

In this book, we take a new approach to economics with its behavioral and ethical orientation. The basics of institutional economics are our starting point, which we then combine with insights from business ethics and behavioral science. We then analyze human behavior in order to discover incentives for economic agents to behave in a welfare-maximizing way. We will analyze the impact of human behavior and morality on economic systems, markets, and politics.

Within the book, we will refer to new research results from behavioral economics, but also from other disciplines such as psychology and sociology, thus leading to new conclusions for economic science. How people behave and how such behavior can be guided towards moral welfare for everyone will be examined within this context. The knowledge relevant to the students is derived scientifically and the results are summarized. Each chapter has a behavioral and ethical summary. Students are also introduced to economic behavior using behavioral games where the results of the behavioral experiments are presented. This book is important for advanced students and researchers of economics as well as policy makers and business executives due to its focus on applications.

We will answer the central question of economics of whether and how the state should intervene in the economy to increase the welfare of society. We are primarily concerned with the interplay between a democratic society and the economy. Which incentives have a political and economic impact and influence the outcome of economic policy? This is where the findings of behavioral science and new institutional economics are to be incorporated into economics.

We will also analyze the extent to which ethics plays a role in the economic processes and the achievement of optimum welfare. Moral values and concepts of justice are closely linked to this analysis, and theories of justice will be used to explain questions of distributive justice such as taxation. In our efforts to understand how people are behaving ethically or unethically and how this affects the economy, we will apply research findings from economics, psychology, and behavioral economics. As part of behavioral economics, this book analyzes also economic behavioral dispositions with the help of models (behavioral modeling) in order to identify mistakes that actors make in groups.

Chapter 1 starts with an analysis of economic policy goals given certain weaknesses in economics and economic education. Modeling the image of man is Chap. 2. Here we will deal with man and his behavior. What motivates him? To what extent is it ethically oriented? Is there a sense of justice? This is the background for deriving economic incentives.

The task of economics is to explain the market economy, how markets and competition function, as well as centralized economies and social market economies. Chapter 3 analyzes the functions of market and competition. What can be deduced from behavioral science? Which rules apply in the so-called market economy? How are human behavior, culture, and human performance related? Are humans hard-wired for competition?

Given the behavior of people, what might be a fair economic system? Given the same behavior and the functioning of market and competition, what might be a fair and functional economic system? What are the pros and cons of the two alternative economic systems, market economy and central administrated economy? Most economies in the real world are hybrids of these two alternatives. Is a social market economy the optimal economic system? What does behavioral science say about the necessary institutional framework to stimulate the welfare enhancing behavior? We will answer these questions in Chap. 4 using institutional economics to design the economic framework.

Market economy has established itself as the global economic system, but this does not mean that the market is infallible. Market failure occurs whenever market functions do not deliver socially desired results. Ethical misconduct like corruption leads to market failure. What are the reasons for this? If the market does not work properly, the state must intervene, which is why market failure gives rise to the need for political interventions. When does human behavior cause market failure? This is the focus of Chap. 5. Individual policy areas such as environmental policy and labor market policy are a product of market failure.

After we address market failure, we want to investigate the question of whether politics makes economic decisions in a pareto-efficient or socially maximizing way in Chap. 6. How does the political system work and how do politicians behave? One reason for failures is the political voting procedure. The behavior of politicians and the voting procedures necessary for decisions form the political decision-making framework for economic policy. Politics manages democracy and must remedy the market failure and provide goods. To do this, it needs a bureaucracy to implement political decisions about the production of public goods. Here, too, we want to analyze the motives behind a bureaucracy and, in particular, whether it can efficiently implement political decisions. With discourse ethics we will analyze the basis for a legitimate democratic decision-making process.

In Chap. 7, we will deal with the international financial markets and analyze the reasons for the latest financial crisis which nearly caused a depression like the one of

1929. How can special behavioral traits trigger a financial crisis? Are the reforms sufficient or is a crisis still possible? Is speculation normal for a market economy and what are the economic effects? What are the institutional requirements for a sound financial order?

Economic fluctuations, particularly those of demand, are a major economic and business problem that political economy can influence only to a very limited extent. Chapter 8 analyzes the economic phenomenon of business cycles and its effects on the economy. How do psychological factors affect cyclical fluctuations? The reasons behind cyclical fluctuations are explained using the leading economic theories. Chapter 9 is the concluding chapter, which sums up the findings of the book to give the reader a bigger picture.

Contents

Chapter 1
Goals of Economic Policy and Weaknesses in the Approach of Economics

What Follows Why?
As an introduction, the first chapter represents the goal of economics policy. Then we will discuss the problems of economics to reach these goals. Quantitative oriented economics up to this point has described the behavior of economic agents and the development of the economy as a process by means of models. Quantitative models presuppose deterministic behavior. The results must be reproducible. In order to preserve such scientific accuracy, economics chose homo oeconomicus to represent human behavioral patterns. This assumption has since been refuted in numerous experiments. There might be good reasons for these assumptions, but how close to realitity and applied politics can economics be on the basis of these assumptions? In the following chapter we want to ask to what extent the quantitative economics can grasp the economic reality and thus come to the right conclusions.

Learning Goals
Readers should be able to explain the goals of economic policy and assess the limitations of quantitative economics in describing reality.

1.1 Goals of Economic Policy and the Welfare Optimum

Originally, the economy and ethics were interconnected. According to Aristotle, the purpose of economics as an art of household management was to provide the means to enable a happy life. Economics should solve the problem of scarce resources, which means to ensure their efficient use so that welfare could be maximized, thus enabling a life to unfold human potential. This was the ethical purpose, and thus the goal of economics. Prosperity was not an end in itself.[1] The long-term maximization

[1] See Aristoteles (1991), pp. 22 or 1258a, b, 1059b and Aristoteles (1960), pp. 5 or 1094a, b, 1095a.

C. A. Conrad, *Economic Systems, Markets and Politics*,
https://doi.org/10.1007/978-3-031-10366-7_1

of profit was the first step towards the development of business economics as a separate discipline. Added to this was the maximization of the shareholder value. It was thus left to the remaining national economics (national economy) to ensure that the maximization of profits also leads to welfare maximization. According to Aristotle the "art of gainfulness" and "the pursuit of maximum wealth" explicitly do not belong to economics.[2] Aristotle does not see the goal of "increasing money to the infinite"[3] as a meaningful, happy, human goal.[4]

What should be the goal of an economic policy? What goals should a state achieve for its citizens? To maximize people's happiness would be the obvious answer, because our happiness is the ultimate goal of our lives. Everybody strives for this all their lives and thus this would also be the maximum goal for a state. This is where modern happiness research comes in. It tries to measure the subjective happiness of people through questioning and medical tests. The problem with this approach, however, is that human happiness is highly volatile and exposed to many influencing factors, of which economics can only affect some.[5]

It is generally assumed that maximizing gross domestic product, ie growth, will lead to a corresponding increase in income and hence also to a "happiness profit". But that does not have to be like the Easterlin paradox. In the last fifty years, real national product has risen in the United States, but population satisfaction has remained constant as American average happiness has remained almost constant. This relationship has been reviewed by other studies. It is undisputed that satisfaction increases with increasing income, but with decreasing intensity.[6] There are many explanations for this result. For example, income distribution may have become more unjust, environmental pollution or job risk may have increased, but also non-economic influences such as lower internal or external security or reduced social contacts could be the root cause. Objectively, people are better off in terms of size of GDP. Is relative income in relation to fellow citizens more important than the absolute income? This is called a status effect. Luttmer showed that finding happiness is most likely when the income of neighbors decreases.[7]

Or are we just not built to be permanently happy? We know that the moment of happiness from the consumption of goods is brief. This seems true for income as well. We feel better and happier in the short term, but we get used to it, so we need even more income to maintain the sense of happiness. Studies have shown that lottery winners do not have a permanently higher feeling of happiness compared to non-lottery winners.[8] Clark, Frijters, Shields, found that the

---

[2] See Aristoteles (1991), p. 27 or 1258b.

[3] See Aristoteles (1991), p. 26 or 1258b.

[4] See Aristoteles (1991), pp. 22 or 1257b and 1258b.

[5] See Diener (1984). Subjective well-being. Psychological Bulletin, 95, 542–575.

[6] See Deaton (2010), pp. 235–263.

[7] See Luttmer (2005).

[8] See Brickman et al. (1978).

increased happiness from an increase of income was just approx. 40% and beyond that just 13% of the feeling of happiness lasted long-term.[9]

The Kingdom of Bhutan has introduced a gross national happiness index with 33 weighted indicators in nine different areas to capture the well-being of its citizens.[10] Bhutan does exaggerate its efforts to make some of its citizens happy, however. For example, the sale of tobacco and smoking in non-smoking areas is prohibited and punished with up to three years in prison.[11] There is thus a risk that a "happyness dictatorship" will occur, in which the lucky researchers and the state will decide what makes the citizens happy.[12]

It should also be remembered that happiness as an exclusive goal for civilization and and evolution is not appropriate. In order for us to evolve there must be an urge for change and, therefore, a degree of dissatisfaction. In the short term, happiness as a political goal can even be dangerous if long-term, important unpopular reforms are omitted, and here, as behavioral economics shows, man is naturally inclined not to think about the future, but rather of his short-term happiness. And who doesn't want to look back at their life and things they have done that demanded self-sacrifice with a sense of pride? The meaning of life is more than happiness. Ultimately, everyone has to find their own happiness over a life span while taking the happiness of others into consideration. A feeling of happiness is subjective. Only usefulness is objectively verifiable, which we will discuss later. Thus happyness remains too diffuse of a measurement for economics.

Consider: What is the fundamental human problem in this world?

Answer: The Earth's resources are limited and we humans have unlimited needs. Even when we are no longer concerned about securing our survival, we will always find new needs. We can often find ourselves trying to decide what we want to have next once the first object of our desire has been obtained. We humans are not programmed to be content. On the up side, we never stop improving our existence by developing our technology and civilization.

- Allocation (Latin: place): Allocation of scarce resources to the various uses in production. (Definition)
- Distribution: Distribution of goods directly or indirectly to individuals via incomes

Human economic activity is necessary because we must try to produce as many high-quality goods as possible from the scarce resources available. To maximize welfare we must also create products that maximize the benefits of society. Our goal is allocative efficiency, which we understand as the use of resources in the form that brings the highest benefit to society.

---

[9] See Clark et al. (2007), p. 19.

[10] See Ura et al. (2012).

[11] See Wangdi (2011).

[12] See Ura et al. (2012).

Let us consider the following questions:

⇒ 1. Which and how many products should be produced for whom? (Allocation and distribution problem)
⇒ 2. How can we produce as many high quality goods as possible? (Production problem)
⇒ 3. How do we get maximum benefit for the whole society? (Goals in all economic systems or social systems)

The term "economical" refers here to the optimal use of resources. We define economically (efficient):

(a) achieving a specified goal with minimum effort or
(b) realizing a maximum goal with a specific level of effort.

We maximize production output using given resources to maximize the benefits for society. This productive efficiency is the goal of human effort regardless of the state form or era.

How do we measure social benefit?

Our goal must be to increase the benefits for everyone up to the point that they cannot be further increased without impinging on the benefits to others. This is the Pareto efficiency that we are striving for.

Definition: A situation is pareto-efficient when benefits cannot be increased any further for one person without reducing the benefits to others. This is as far as we go as economists. Increasing the value of some people at the expense of others is a societal decision, not for market economics with its system based on choice.

Allocative efficiency (definition) is the use of resources in such a way that they provide maximum benefit.

The following figures illustrate allocative economic production.

The convex maximized transformation curve in Fig. 1.1 shows the efficient economics of production. The transformation curve represents the maximum possible production quantity of goods X or Y under optimal, thus efficient, use of the

Fig. 1.1 Efficient production

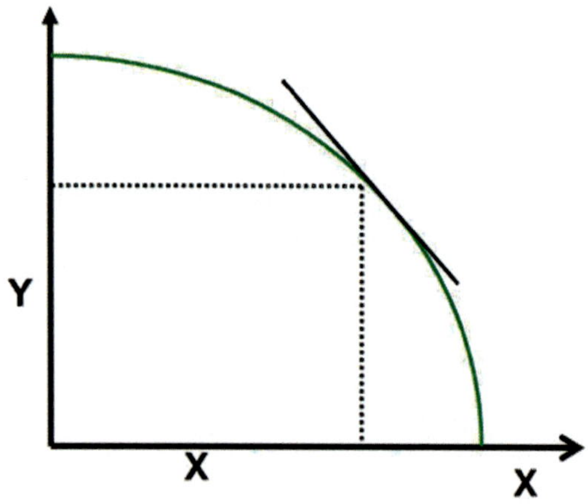

available resources. In such cases resources are optimally distributed to companies and optimally used in production. As an example one could take the products wine for Y and beer for X. Starting from the origin, the green curve represents the maximum possible combination of wine and beer, signaling that it is produced efficiently. In the tangent, the marginal rate of the transformation dY/dX results as a negative slope, indicating how much Y I have to give for an X. The angle of the curve shows that the more you want from one product, the less you will have from the other, meaning the negative marginal rate of transformation increases.

In the next graph (Fig. 1.2) I1 and I2 are indifference or isoquant curves of A.

For A, the question arises: which goods combination provides the highest benefit?

All goods combinations of X (e.g., beer) and Y (e.g., wine) on the indifference curves are equivalent for A, with I2 being more valuable for A because it has more of X and Y at each point.

In the market economy welfare is achieved through voluntary exchange. People exchange their goods or services through markets, until no one can increase their own benefit without reducing the benefit of another. This is how Pareto efficiency is achieved. Exchange continues until the pareto-efficient state has been reached. When it will be reached depends on the initial distribution of income and wealth. The more income or wealth a person has, the more goods they can acquire. If you buy a good for money, the benefit from this good must be higher than the alternative benefit from the consumption of another good (opportunity benefit).

Fraud is reduced by way of the welfare system, because the benefit expected by the exchange partner being deceived is not gained after the exchange, and thus Pareto efficiency is not achieved. Moral behavior, on the other hand, would guarantee Pareto efficiency.

In Fig. 1.3, A and B have different goods combinations so they can be found on indifference or isoquant curves that are different from the original. ❶ The utility of B can be increased with the same benefit to A, if A of good X is B, and B gets more Y. This will lead to an exchange. In ❷ there is a pareto-efficient state, since the utility of A cannot be increased without decreasing that of B and vice versa. This makes for

Fig. 1.2 Indifference curve

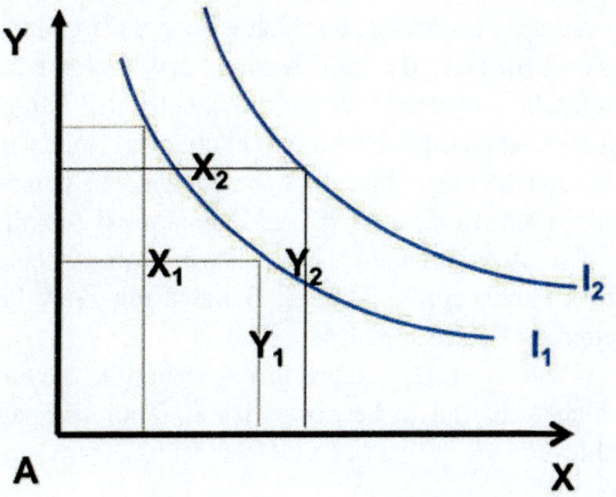

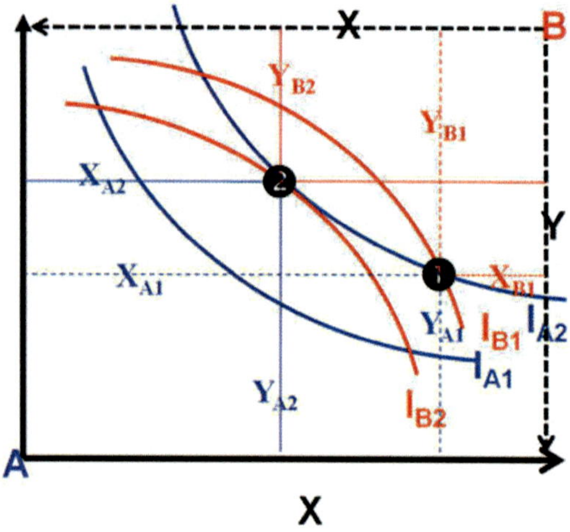

Fig. 1.3 Exchange optimum in the Edgeworth box

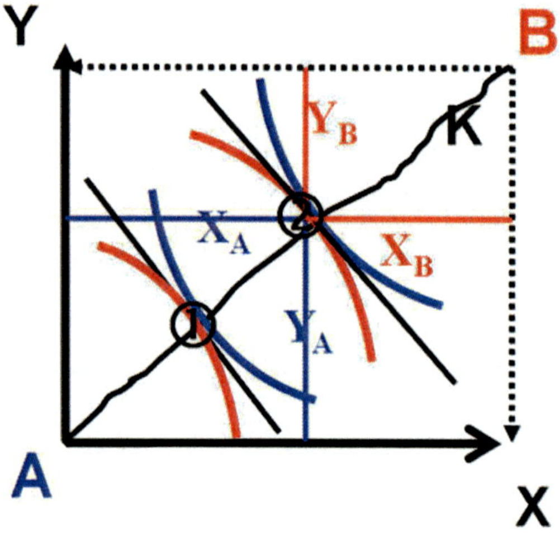

Fig. 1.4 Pareto-efficient Optima

a voluntary exchange: both have benefits (free lunch) until the pareto-efficient state is reached. Here the indifference curves of A and B are affected. The utility of A cannot be increased without the benefit of B being reduced. This corresponds to an efficient exchange: both have exchanged goods for as long as both can no longer gain an advantage through an exchange. The tangent at the point of intersection then has the substitution dY/dX and the slope is the marginal rate of the exchange.

This does not address the distribution of benefits between A and B, however. From Pareto combination 1, B has a relatively higher benefit than for A and 2 is better for A (see Fig. 1.4).

Fraud is a deceptive promise of benefit to the other party in a voluntary exchange, which turns out to be non-existent. Thus the pareto-efficient optimum cannot be achieved.

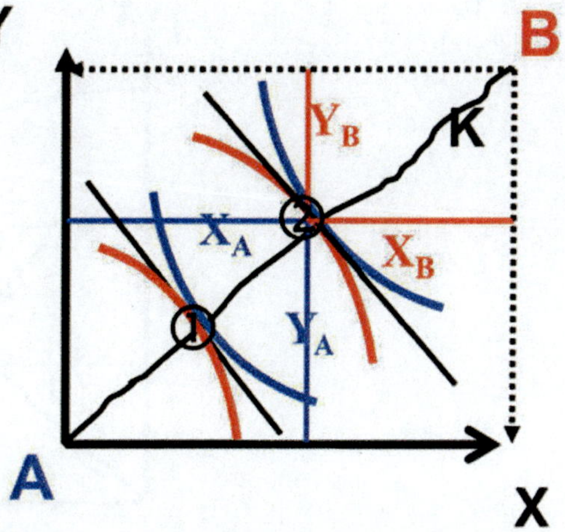

Fig. 1.5 Pareto-efficient exchange points
K = contract curve: all pareto-efficient exchange points

Results from the last graphic: Pareto efficiency indifference curves for A and B are tangents. The benefits of A cannot be increased without reducing the benefits of B. This reflects an efficient exchange: both have exchanged goods until neither can gain an advantage through further exchanges.

The slope of the tangent at the intersection indicates the marginal rate of exchange, the substitution dY/dX, yet this says nothing about the distribution of benefits (distribution) between A and B. Let's take a look at Fig.1.5. B has a relatively higher benefit than A from Pareto combination ❶ while ❷ is better for A than ❶, and vice versa for B. This is due to the different initial distribution of the goods X and Y. Asset and income distribution varies within our economy as well. For example, A could be a worker in a Russian vodka factory and B the owner of the factory. K is the contract curve with all possible Pareto-efficient exchange points.

In Fig. 1.6 an arbitrary Pareto-efficient state has been created. No further benefit is to be had through exchange. The curve has a different slope at each point. Only if the slope of the tangent of the transformation curve is equal to the slope of the tangent of the indifference curves, will exactly the amount required for X and Y be produced. The societal allocation optimum or welfare optimum (allocative efficiency, overall economic efficiency) is thus present if the limit of the ❶ exchange dY / dX is equal to the marginal rate of the ❷ technical production transformation dY / dX, because then the ratio of X and Y is produced as X2 and Y2 that meets the needs of A and B, making it pareto efficient. The Pareto-optimal amount will be produced. It can neither be better produced nor better exchanged. The benefits of society can no longer be increased. This optimum level of exchange and production is provided by the market, as we will see in the next chapter.

Although the combination of X1 and Y1 may produce efficiently, it is not the amount A and B need to realize their pareto-efficient exchange optimums. In such a case a company would offer a lot on the market that does not meet the needs of Demand A and B and could not sell it. There would be, for example, too much beer and too little wine.

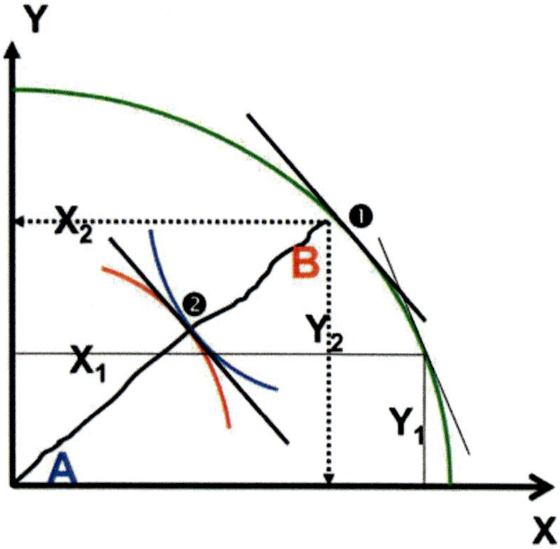

Fig. 1.6 The welfare optimum

Why does the state have to intervene in the economic process or set and optimize a business environment at all? The realization that the market cannot be left to its own devices was the result of trial and error through history. Social problems became apparent in the labor market early on in the Industrial Revolution. The first stock market crashes and economic fluctuations we already happening in the nineteenth century. By the end of the nineteenth century there was already a strong concentration of economic power in trusts (a contractually agreed merger of several companies), which showed the importance of political economy.

The biggest global crisis occurred in the twentieth century, with the Great Depression of 1929, which demonstrated global interdependence and the political effects of economic upheavals. In fact, governments were able to draw on these experiences and the resulting Keynesian theory to prevent an economic collapse like in 1929 during the next global economic crisis in this century. Historical experiences are always an occasion to revise and expand economic theory.

One of the last great realizations of the twentieth century, which still needs to be better understood, was that the economy is having a strong negative impact on the environment. This has caused environmental theory and the resulting political economy to become environmental policy.

While economic theory seeks to disclose cause-and-effect relationships, political economy makes statements about target/means relationships. It has a direct application reference and is therefore the more pragmatic part of the economic disciplinesPolitical economy complements the business administration in the macroeconomic issues and the international and inter-enterprise approach.

Economic policy (Political Economy) can be subdivided into institutional policy and process policy. Institutional policy includes all state measures to influence economic conditions, in particular the maintenance, adaptation and improvement of the economic order (**definition**). Political goals can only be achieved by legal regulations that provide incentives.

	Economic Policy	
	Institutional Economics	**Process policy**
Objective	shaping the framework of the economy	controlling the economic process by interventions
Goals	qualitative	quantitative
Actor	parliament	government
Instruments	Economic constitution like the monetary order, company laws, social and environmental laws, financial market regulation, trading law such as GATT	budgetary policies like taxes, subsidies, government bonds, social policy, social benefits infrastructure policies like investments, competition policies like maximum prices for monopolies, labor market policies like minimum wages, monetary policies like key interest rate, open market policy

Fig. 1.7 Structure of economic policy

Process policy is for direct intervention in economic processes to achieve political goals directly (definition). Social benefits to disabled citizens are an example of process-related measures that correct the market mechanism, since these people are not able to receive market income from the labor market. Process policy is implemented primarily by the government, while institutional policy is implemented by the legislature (see Fig. 1.7).

The state tries to influence the quantitative results of the economic process in the given economic order according to its goals. Governments, authorities, central banks, antitrust authorities, etc. as the main process-policy makers usually operate with a short to medium time frame. They attempt to exert influence by locking in or varying quantitative measures such as key interest rates, tax and customs duties, subsidy payments, fixed prices or production quotas, which cause changes in individual economic planning.

Economic policy must define its objectives in such a way that it is possible to test whether or not they have been achieved. Success must be verified to make the costs and benefits of the policy transparent. Politicians who prefer to avoid scrutiny tend not to follow these value judgements, by making statements that are unclear or impractical. The following discussion exercise illustrates this point.

Groupwork Goals for Modern Democracies

Imagine that a politician promises voters the following: (1) Freedom, (2) Equality, (3) Security, (4) Prosperity and (5) Justice. Would you vote for them? What do you understand each of these goals to mean? How would you define them for yourself?

Results
One way to define the goals would be as follows:

Freedom = self-determination. The freedom of the individual is limited by the rights of others.
Prosperity = material freedom to choose actions
Security = no changes, no risk
Justice = equality? What is justice? As a rule, people always demand justice when they feel worse than others. The reverse is rare.

Conclusion These ideals make great campaign promises because they are universally desired but are not clearly defined. Everyone has their own understanding of the terms making them near meaningless. This means a politician can promise these things without having to worry that they must prove their achievement of the goals.

Conflicting Goals
Differing goals will come into conflict with each other whenever the achievement of one goal is possible only at the expense of others. The solution to this conflict is often only possible through economic policy compromises.

Groupwork
Discuss the following conflicting goals:

1. Equality versus justice
2. Security versus wealth
3. Freedom versus security
4. Justice based on merit versus justice based on needs

Solutions

to 1. Neither are all people nor their economic outputs the same. Therefore, equal pay would not be fair.

to 2. Without change and the willingness to take risks there is security, but no growth from technical progress and generally no improvements. If you try new things you run the risk of failure. The entrepreneur who invests in a new product or a new production process runs the risk of losing his capital but also of achieving wealth.

to 3. Freedom means taking responsibility for oneself, but then you lose the security guarantee of third parties. Think about when you were still living at home with your parents. Did you have security? – Yes. Did you have freedom? – Only very limited, because your parents were only willing to take responsibility for you if they could tell you what you were allowed to do (for example, not to stay out later than 2 am).

to 4. Should one be paid according to their needs or their performance?

Conclusion: Economic policy takes place somewhere between the economic and political spheres

1.2 Cultural and Institutional Factors in Economics

An article in the German newspaper Handelsblatt titled, "Economic Culture Revolution." describes the self-recognition that economics "was ignorant for a long time about cultural factors." Representing the ignorant "traditional" economy, the assertion of Nobel laureates George Stigler and Gary Becker was quoted often from the end of the 1970s: "Economists who argue with cultural factors are just disguising the failure of their analysis." According to the article this verdict remained the dominant opinion until the late 1990s. American researchers were able to prove the influence of culture with a valid methodological effort.

Professor Raquel Fernández from New York University, together with her colleague Alessandra Fogli, was able to separate cultural factors from classical economic factors of influence. They made use of a medical research approach called the epidemiological approach. When American doctors want to filter out environmental influences as the cause of, for example, heart attacks in Japanese, they compare the heart attack rates for Japanese patients who have emigrated to the USA with their genetically similar counterparts living in Japan. The economic scientists compared the tendency to engage in a particular profession for women born in the USA, but whose parents came from different countries. The political and economic conditions were the same for all subjects, yet they showed great occupational differences. The greater the participation in employment of the family's original country, the more likely the daughters born later in the USA were working.[13] Another research group, Guiso, Sapienza and Zingales were able to prove that the normative, positive formation of thriftiness was just as important in explaining country-to-country differences in thriftiness as the economic factors of influence.[14] Another study by Andrea Ichino and Giovanni Maggi confirmed that regional culture differences formed the economic behavior of people. They investigated for a large Italian bank why southern Italians took more sick leave than their northern counterparts. They discovered that the place of birth had a significant influence on calling in sick. Italians born in the south had significantly higher absentee rates, even if they worked for years in the north.[15]

What conclusions can be drawn from these new revelations of economics? First of all, they are not new revelations, they are at best merely statistic confirmation. The sociologist Max Weber had already shown the importance of culture in economic development in "The Protestant Ethic and the Spirit of Capitalism" in 1905.[16] Before that there were already references made to the idea. Cultural influences were, and are, the basis for cultural sciences such as sociology or behavioral research. Many of

---

[13] See Fernández and Fogli (2005), pp. 552–561.

[14] See Guiso et al. (2006), pp. 23–48.

[15] See Ichino and Maggi (1999), p. 1057–1090 and Handelsblatt dated 19.02.07, p. 9.

[16] See Weber (1905). For the critique of scociology on the onesidedness of economics see Maurer and Schmid (2010), pp. 194.

the new statistic revelations made with such effort can be derived logically through common sense and may even be called banal.

What is in fact new is the alarming admission of economics to having ignored cultural factors for decades. It shut out all of the influencing factors in its observable world that it could not examine and prove with quantitative factors. It simply ignored their existence and all economists who wanted to include them despite their incalculability were denounced and banned, as was expressed in the statement of the two Nobel laureates.

In the modern, free society, everyone should have the chance to develop however they desire. Everyone should at least have the chance to work their way up to being a millionaire, which is a central incentive for performance in the market economy. National wealth is then not statically in the hands of the few. According to the enlightenment all people are equal, at least in their basic rights, which makes the solution relatively simple in that the freedoms of one individual end where those of the others begin. If we were to leave it at that, this would be an idealistic illusion, leading neither to a functional nor a humane society. There would only be individualists who maximize their benefits and freedoms within the limits determined by the rights of others. Each person would create their own island of freedom and benefits. The result would be just millions of little islands of freedom and egoists. Society as a continuous entity, a community, would not exist. No one would do anything useful to others for the common good. No one would sacrifice himself for his family; no one would care for their parents in old age out of gratitude, or care for their children. Volunteer work necessary for a community would no longer be performed. Politicians would use their positions just to maximize their own benefit. No one would engage themselves for the good of the community, society, state or nation.

All modern societies have institutions and organizations, giving them order, and instilling discipline in their citizens to behave in the manner socially desired. As we have already shown however, this is not sufficient. For a society to function and for productive forces to develop, the appropriate social capital for the type of system order and economic stage of development must be available. This depends greatly on the attitudes of people required for societal or community cooperation. Norms, values and morality are important here, including attitudes towards the political and economic system.

It is clear that it really must be the opposite, and that the more freedom individuals have, the greater their morality must be. When political leaders and church no longer sanction people in relation to their moral behavior or missteps and when there are few predetermined rules, people must have already internalized socially desirable behavior, possessing inner values and social capital. The more modern the economy, the more important morals and values are for the development of productive forces.

The Sociologist Max Weber had already noted in 1905 that the source of a positive economic development in Switzerland, the Netherlands, England and parts of Germany was a Protestant or Calvinist influence.[17] The attitudes of people in a society

[17] See Weber (1905), Ulrich (1993), pp. 1168 and Noll (2002), p. 166.

towards economically relevant activities have been paid as little attention by economic science as the existence of general economic knowledge. What does it help in the case of Russia that a market economy system was introduced, if the people still behave as they did in the communist, planned economy? What does it help if a framework, such as a legal system with legislative and executive branch, if the judges can be bribed because they are not remunerated adequately? What does it help if a democratic framework is created, as in Russia at the end of the 1980s and in Germany in the 1920s, if people are politically passive and desire a strong leadership that takes care of their problems? If a system of order is neither accepted nor understood it has no future.

Cultural terms are not always exact, and are surely not solely responsible for economic development. There are many cultural values that influence productivity, and on the other hand institutional framework conditions, or political order, play a role just as much as do macroeconomic variables such as monetary and human capital. One must therefore avoid normative conclusions from quantitative investigations and statements such as "the labor productivity of people A is greater than that of people B because people A are more willing to make an effort or work harder." The universal applicability claimed by this kind of statistic must be questioned, even if there is significance for a factor. Many factors are usually ignored, and it is meaningful to know how many people were questioned over what time frame. Associations are also problematic, since "not willing to perform" can be equated with "lazy," for example.

Ultimately the goal is to recognize the importance of such soft facts, bringing the qualitative factors into a logical connection with other factors to affect higher productivity. Company management and state government must implement morals and ethics, as well as propagate and exemplify values for each individual. Opinion surveys can offer an indication, but no more than that, although they do show where improvement is needed. This should be easier for companies than a national economy. Economics is not an exact science, but we may hope that at least more value will be place on ethics, morals and norms. This hope may be deceiving, however. Because a quantitative proof was provided it has now been admitted that cultural values have an effect on the economy, but which values exactly and how the values coincide will remain unknown based on purely quantitative analysis. With even the most refined quantitative analysis there will always be many influential factors and connections, ethics in particular, that will not be included. Thinking and deriving in contextual forms remains impossible.[18]

[18]"Business scholars could take a lesson from their colleagues in the discipline of psychology, which was stifling under the scientific model three or four decades ago. Psychological research then was dominated by rigorous, but ultimately unproductive, studies of reaction time. As long as psychology professors labored within a small area, they learned little that was of value to anyone. It was only after they began to apply their imaginations – and rigor – to much boarder problems that psychology began to make enormous strides. Not until respected psychologists dared to ask questions that mattered, whether or not they could be quantified in traditional ways, were groundbreaking studies undertaken, such as the Nobel Price – winning work of Daniel Kahneman and the late Amos Tversky on how people make financial decisions". Bennis and O'Toole (2005), p. 4.

The significance of a legal framework has often been discussed. Without ethical rules, thus the laws or the norms of a society, we have anarchy which allows now economic productivity. We call these ruels institutions. They have evolved over time to overcome social dilemma structures. Institutions are made up by the society and thus have a strong cultural infuence. They regulate interpersonal coexistence, in which they place appropriate incentives, for example laws and penal sanctions in the event of an offense. Economists like Marshal have stated that the institutional structure exerts an important influence on economic behavior. There has been a renaissance of institutional thinking with the New Institional Economic in the nineties but its meaning in economics is still much to low. The reason migth be simple as some economists tried to transform the social science economics to a hard science.[19]

> In the project of turning economics into a hard science could succeed, it would be worth doing . . . Ther are, however, some reasons for pessimism about the project.[20]

1.3 Economics as a Natural Science or Behavioral Science?

The most striking thing about mathematics is that it always delivers precise results from the model assumptions and the model construction, and these results are evidence. The first economic pioneer to develop economic science into a scientific/mathematical discipline such as mechanics or hydrodynamics was Léon Walras (1834–1910) with his general theory of equilibrium. After the Second World War the later American Nobel laureates Paul Samuelson, Gérad Debruie and Kenneth Arrow ensured the breakthrough of mathematics in economics. This seemingly scientific precision was apt for a social science and continued to prevail in the following years. The mathematical trend was perfected in the USA in the following decades. With the gigantic further development of computer computing, enormous amounts of numbers were processed. It also allowed statistics as so-called econometrics to move into the economics sciences. In 1940, in the prestigious "American Economic Review" 3% of the pages were filled with mathematical formulas, today it is about 50%.[21] This did not, however, increase the practical significance of the essays. A well-respected CEO described the economics publications as a "vast wasteland."[22] Meanwhile even in the USA, the pioneers of this orientation are critical. For Alan Binder, professor at the famous Princeton University, economics has become more mathematical than physics and the Nobel laureate for economics, Roland Coase, considers economic science to have been degraded to

[19]See Furobotn, Erik G. and Richter, Rudolf (2005), p. 1.

[20]Solow, R. M. (1979), p. 331.

[21]See Wirtschaftswoche vom 9.02.2006, p. 31.

[22]Quoted from Bennis and O'Toole (2005), p. 90.

> "a theoretical system floating in the air with hardly any connection to what is happening in the real world."[23] Or "As a method of economic analysis, econometrics are a childish game with figures that does not contribute anything to the elucidation of the problems of economic reality."[24]

This is where economic science strives to conceal its socio-scientific roots and to give itself the appearance of an exact science. Whatever is not measurable and calculable does not exist. Factors of influence such as qualitative soft facts are usually ignored. There is no gray area, just black or white. A lack of new discoveries, or only imprecise insights, is not something that can be marketed. What science wants to be constantly displaying its limits or inabilities? Professorships are not awarded for saying that one does not know. Whoever is searching for economic realities, for the truth, has a hard time of it on the job market for economic scientists. Technicians who show an exact science are in demand. Here it becomes clear how economic science attempts to hide its social science roots and appear as an exact natural science. Bennis and O'Toole talk of a "scientific model" that the social scientific economic science has borrowed from the natural sciences due to its "physics envy."

> The scientific model, as we call it, is predicated on the faulty assumption that business is an academic discipline like chemistry or geology. In fact, business is a profession, akin to medicine and the law, and business schools are professional schools – or should be.[25]

This is why the economic scientists think that the more complicated and complex the arithmetic model the better. The spread of computers and their calculation capacities has only augmented the trend. Meanwhile a verbal, logical, deductive thought process has no place in economic science and is scorned as unscientific. The increasing complexity has caused increased specialization. In order to present something new the models must be more complex. In order to achieve and to process this complexity, the new generation of economic scientists is forced to concentrate

---

[23] See Wirtschaftswoche vom 9.02.2006, p. 31, translated into English.

[24] "Deluded by the Idea that the science of human action must ape the technique of the natural sciences, host of authors are intent upon a quantification of economics. They think that economics ought to imitate chemistry, which progressed from a qualitative to a quantitative state. Their motto is the positivistic maxim: Science is measurement. Supported by rich funds, they are busy reprinting and rearranging statistical data provided by governments, by trade associations, and by corporations and other enterprises. They try to compute the arithmetical relations among various of these data and thus to determine what they call, by analogy with the natural science, "correlations" and "functions" do not describe anything else than what happened at a definite instant of time in a definite geographical area as the outcome of the actions of a definite number of people. As a method of a economic analysis econometric is a childish play with figures that does not contribute anything to the elucidation of the problems of economic reality." Mises, Ludwig van (1978): http://antipositivist.blogspot.com/2007/02/correating-nonsence.html.

[25] And further: "Like other professions, business calls upon the work of many academic disciplines. For medicine, those disciplines include biology, chemistry, and psychology; for business, they include mathematics, economics, psychology, philosophy, and sociology." Bennis and O'Toole (2005), p. 2.

on a very narrow subject area and to present it repeatedly in minute variations. There has been no place for generalists at universities for a while now, in particular verbal generalists.

> In fact, management professors seem to have an almost morbid fear of being damned as popularizers. Do they believe that the regard of their peers is more important than studying what really matters to executives who can put their ideas into practice? Apparently so. … Today it is possible to find tenured professors of management who have never set foot inside a real business, except as customers.[26]

In the meantime economics as a science has increasingly excluded the uncountable, qualitative implications of economic action because of the strong model orientation, and has separated itself from society as a self-contained discipline. There is little room for non-quantitative business ethics. Weber already criticized this tendency as a "fiction useful for theoretical purposes," which can not be made "the basis of practical evaluations of real facts." The economic instruments are multifaceted and, as a rule, "in another respect which is potentially important for human interests."[27]

Numbers are facts. However, this does not correspond to economic reality, since the economy is made by people. As we have seen, people do not always behave rationally, often emotionally and sometimes wrongly. Economic science is therefore not an exact deterministic science, but a spiritual and social science. Also, the inclusion of non-rational behavior in models does not alter the non-predictability.

Here follows one example of misinterpretation and judgement problems due to economic calculation methods. Much empirical research has already been conducted in order to analyze how speculation affects commodity and especially food prices. According to the scientists of the Raiffeisen Association the majority of empirical studies show no verifiable connection between stock volumes and the price increase.[28] The NGO WEED disagrees and lists over 100 empirical studies that are critical of speculation.[29] The economic ethicist Pies examined 35 studies and concluded that no negative effect from commodity speculation could be proven.[30] WEED accuses Pies of not examining important studies critiquing speculation and

---

[26] Bennis and O'Toole (2005), p. 4.

[27] See Weber (1968), p. 529…

[28] "Ganz im Gegenteil kommt die weit überwiegende Mehrzahl der bis dato zu diesem Thema verfassten empirischen Arbeiten – allerdings ebenfalls auf dem Boden der suboptimalen Terminmarktdatensätze – zu dem Ergebnis, dass kein nachweisbare Kausalzusammenhang zwischen Anlagevolumina und Preisanstiegen besteht." Translation: "Quite the opposite, the large majority of papers written on this topic to date – though also based on suboptimal futures market data sets – come to the conclusion that there no causal connection exists between stock volumes and price increases." Petersen, V. J., Herlinghaus, A., and Menrad, M. (2012). http://www.raiffeisen.de/wp-content/uploads/downloads/2012/11/DRV-Brosch-Risiko_10_02.pdf, p 14.

[29] See http://www2.weed-online.org/uploads/evidence_on_impact_of_commodity_speculation.pdf (Stand 26. November 2013, 04/01/2014).

[30] See Pies, Ingo, Prehn, Sören, Glauben, Thomas, and Will, Matthias Georg (2013).

having biased criticism against the methodology used in studies critical of speculation.[31]

Within the discussion both sides criticize one another's methodological weaknesses in econometric studies based primarily on Granger. Irwin and Sanders' results are criticized based on the fact that the Granger test is not an appropriate method with highly volatile variables, thus distorting results.[32] The problem is of a more fundamental nature, however. If causal variables are not eliminated, false correlations can show up in Granger tests (spurious regression). The same is true for purely coincidental correlations, which can show up particularly in short time periods of observation.

As we have already shown, many speculation proponents argue that the greatly increased demand for commodities from China, India and other emerging economies, interruptions in oil production, less consumer demand elasticity and US monetary policy were all responsible for the price increases. Increased biofuel production and weather were considered to have caused the price increases.[33] If so many factors were truly affecting prices the Granger test would not have been applicable due to multi-causality. The same is true for the effects of weather, since the required consistency of variables would not be given.[34] Highly volatile variables such as stock prices or commodities were also determined to have insufficient covariant stationarity, thus the requirement for the regression of time series is not met.[35]

Both positions are in fact supportable using the empirical studies that have been conducted. One part of the studies shows that speculation has influenced commodity prices and the other part proves the opposite. We see here the dilemma of econometric research. There is no proof of causality, as there can be many factors behind a correlation.[36]

Therefore the Popper criterion is not fulfilled. According to Karl Popper, who founded the Critical Rationalism school of thought, the universal validity of scientific hypotheses must be refutable, thus falsifiable. The original purpose of Popper's falsificationism was to provide a demarcation criterion for which of the actual activities of investigation count as real, empirical sciences.[37] Also the Popper criterion is also not fulfilled if the assumptions are not in line with reality.

---

[31] See Henn, Markus (2013), http://www2.weed-online.org/uploads/kommentar_literaturueberblick_agrarspekulation.pdf.

[32] For a critique of Irwin and Sanders see Frenk et al. (2011), 43–49.

[33] See Irwin, Scott H. and Sanders, Dwight R. (2010), p 4+.

[34] See Schulze, Peter M. (2004), p 17+ and Hassler, Uwe (2003), p 813.

[35] See Pagan, A. and Schwert, C. (1990), Phillips, P. and Loretan, M. (1990), p 45 and http://www.matthias-schlecker.de/kointegrationsanalyse-stationaritaet-und-augmented-dickey-fuller-test (04/04/2014).

[36] See Conrad, Christian A. (2014).

[37] See Popper, Karl (1958) and Suikkanen, Jussi (2017), 7. https://helda.helsinki.fi/bitstream/handle/10138/21756/ethicsof.pdf?sequence=2&isAllowed=y

With the model-based statistics, called econometrics in economic science, many connections can be calculated with a great degree of effort and make a grand impression, depending on the sample with its respective probability. It does not matter if there is no real economic sense from these calculations. The senselessness is sometimes apparent: "the level of beauty in high schools has an effect on criminal propensity 7–8 years later."[38] In 1929, Yule found a correlation of 0.95 between the ratio of marriages in the Church of England to all marriages and the death rate for the years 1866 to 1911. Henry developed was he later jokingly referred to as a new theory of inflation in 1980, in which he showed the correlation between rainfall in the UK and development of price levels.[39]

The obviously false conclusions of these models are much more dangerous, however. They can originate in a sequence of numbers that lead to false correlations, incorrect model assumptions or unrealistic model constructions, or just forgotten factors of influence. These weaknesses can also have mathematical model constructions. Here is one example from the German economic newspaper Handelsblatt about economic models.[40]

> Economists show with a theoretical model that it can make sense for a company owner to do without strict controls on managers. When a manager is constantly kept under watch his risk of losing his job increases. He must also give up some of his authority. In compensation he demands more money and is tempted to manipulate his information to the supervisory board. [Authors of the model: Benjamin Hermalin (University of California) and Michael Weisbach (University of Illinois)[41]]

Let us discuss the logical content of this model. Too strict of controls (whatever that means) is not possible unless the company owners follow a manager's every move. Controls per se have nothing to do with a manager's risk of losing his position unless the manager is bent on cheating the company. The authors of this model also assume that managers are bad people in principle. Why else would they assume that managers would react to controls by manipulating information? Manipulation of company information in such a case is not created by the controls, it is made more difficult. Why should the "bad" managers demand the maximum salary independent of their authority? It is more likely that managers find it easier to obtain advantages (salary and other benefits) when they are controlled less.

In addition, the results can be influenced not only in the selection of assumptions, but also through the construction of the models, but this is not obvious to non-statisticians, such as journalists.[42] Other researchers have simply miscalculated. Results may be considered scientifically proven for years if other researchers do not

[38] See Mocan and Erdal (2006) and Fedako (2007), http://antipositivist.blogspot.com.

[39] See Zorita (2006).

[40] Handelsblatt dated 04/03/06, p. 11, translated into English.

[41] See Hermalin and Weisbach (2007), pp. 1–26.

[42] Anyone who would like to see an example of this can take a look at the website http://timlambert.org/2003/09/0910/. Here the author of a statistical model proving that broad ownership of guns leads to less crime is accused of manipulation.

decide to follow the calculations in detail, which would otherwise have made the errors known. Harvard professor Martin Feldstein showed in 1974 in the renowned "Journal of Political Economy" that the increases in social benefits in the USA since 1937 had displaced the tendency to save money in private persons. Six years later Dean Leimer and Selig Lesnoy showed that Feldstein had miscalculated.[43] The thesis from Levitt and Donohue from 2001 suffered a similar fate. They had said that the main reason for a drop in criminality rates in USA since the early 1990s was the legalization of abortion in 1973. They maintained that unwanted children are raised in conditions that increase the probability that they will become criminals. Four years after the publication in the renowned Quarterly Journal of Economics, in 2005, two economists of the Federal Reserve Bank of Boston discovered their mistaken calculations.[44]

The worst thing about mathematics is that it almost always provides exact and clear results, thus proof, based on the model assumptions and design. Business science seems to have given in to the same temptation as economic science with the increasing popularity of financial mathematics. Numbers are facts. This is not economic reality however, since people make up the economy. People do not always act rationally; they are in fact often emotional and sometimes wrong. "Figures are facts, but people are not." Economic science cannot be an exact, deterministic natural science, but a social science. Including irrational behavior in model does not change the incalculable nature. There is a good reason why the economists often argue in public over the best method, which encourages some people to participate even if they have no background in economics. The progress made in academics through economic science and progress applicable in practice has been very slight in comparison to the natural sciences. It is very difficult to objectively evaluate the value of research contributions in a social science. Alfred Nobel most likely considered economic science as part of the social sciences, and therefore did not make a separate prize for it. The prize often called the Nobel Prize for Economics, awarded at the same time as the Nobel Prize, is from the Swedish National Bank. The attempt by economics to conduct experiments like those in the natural sciences at great expense have failed through their lack of comparability between situations, and the interchangeability of actors. Let us remember that the innumerable environmental influences that are constantly changing and the incalculable factor of humans only allow the identification of economic development trends. Hayek recognized this, and said that only pattern predictions can be seriously considered.[45] The future us never like the past. National economies and companies are not calculable. In the best case central factors such as money, and conditions such as state and competition can be

[43]"This paper uses an extended life-cycle model to analyse the impact of social security on the individual's simultaneous decision about retirement and saving Economic evidence, using an estimated time series of "social security wealth," indicates that social security depresses personal savings by 30–50 percent." Feldstein (1974), p. 90.

[44]"We offer evidence that legalized abortion has contributed significantly to recent crime reductions" Donohue and Levitt (2001), p. 379 see also Handelsblatt dated 04/30/07, p. 9.

[45]See Hayek (1974).

observed and regulated, but the rest happens of its own accord through the human productive forces. We don't need so many calculations for this; it is sufficient to train and educate the humans so that they can work within the framework (economic order) with the right incentives, and to structure the framework so that the human productive forces can develop for the good of the community.

This book makes clear that incentives for better institutions and morality are a prerequisite for economic efficiency. The economy can only work with people if the person is the center of attention. Economic laws and human characteristics must both be taken into account, with the economy as the sum of man-made, economically relevant institutions and organizations serving the human being. It is only in this way that it can be useful and gives meaning.

Ultimately the goal is to recognize the importance of soft facts, bringing the qualitative factors into a logical connection with other factors to affect higher productivity. Company management and state government must implement morals and ethics, as well as propagate and exemplify values for each individual. Opinion surveys can offer an indication, but no more than that, although they do show where improvement is needed. This should be easier for companies than a national economy. Economics is not an exact science, but we may hope that at least more value will be placed on ethics, morals and norms. This hope may be deceiving, however. Because a quantitative proof was provided it has now been admitted that cultural values have an effect on the economy, but which exact values and how the values coincide will remain unknown based on purely quantitative analysis. With even the most refined quantitative analysis there will always be many influential factors and connections, ethics in particular, that will not be included. Thinking and deriving in contextual forms remains impossible.[46]

Economics has isolated people and reality with its envy of hard sciences. To deny academic disciplines such as law and to discard interdisciplinary cooperation leads to economics becoming less relevant and economists less likely to be heard. The British Queen's accusatory question about the reasons for the failure of economics in the financial crisis has put the company's doubts in a nutshell. If there is no opening up of economics, fewer students and financial contributions must be expected.

The legitimacy of economics through elaborate mathematical or statistical methods is a mistake, as long as it does not lead to more economic insights. Scale must be the economic reality and not the maximum degree of abstraction and

[46]"Business scholars could take a lesson from their colleagues in the discipline of psychology, which was stifling under the scientific model three or four decades ago. Psychological research then was dominated by rigorous, but ultimately unproductive, studies of reaction time. As long as psychology professors labored within a small area, they learned little that was of value to anyone. It was only after they began to apply their imaginations – and rigor – to much boarder problems that psychology began to make enormous strides. Not until respected psychologists dared to ask questions that mattered, whether or not they could be quantified in traditional ways, were groundbreaking studies undertaken, such as the Nobel Prize-winning work of Daniel Kahneman and the late Amos Tversky on how people make financial decisions". Bennis and O'Toole (2005), p. 4.

formalization as evidence of apparent scientific accuracy. It might make sense that theorists make in special exceptions assumptions which are not accurate descriptions of reality but economics should not loose its meaning for reality.

Abstract and isolated models of thought are fine in principle. They make it possible to take the complex economy apart into separate connections and thus to allow discoveries about economic processes. Econometrics is thus a valuable ancillary science for economics. There is also nothing to be said against using mathematics, as long as the effort remains proportional to the usefulness of knowledge gained. Most of the models have unfortunately become so complex however, that they are no longer useful for teaching purposes. And a lot of the models have unfortunately so many seldom or unrealistic assumptions however, that they are no longer useful for explaining the economy. The effort required to learn them is greater than the knowledge gained. It is problematic when econometrics, thus the statistics applied to the economy with economic mathematics, are taught as exclusive representation of the only true economics. Economics deals with people. How they behave is the topic of behavioral science.

Behavioral science is a relatively new approach, which uses scientific experiments with human beings in order to deduce or test hypothesizes about general behavior. It is the investigation of human behavior through observation. The behavioral approach is represented mostly by behavioral economics, sociology, social psychology and psychology.[47]

What happens if the market players systematically make mistakes because they are not behaving rationally or because they do not know all the information, such as capacity increases of their competitors? As part of behavioral economics, this book analyzes economic behavioral dispositions also with the help of models (Behavioral Modeling[48]) in order to identify mistakes that actors make in groups (Collective Error Hypothesis [49]). The models are intended to outline the economic framework for the behavior of many actors, but do not claim to depict reality and the models should only contain factors relevant to the decision being made. The models then examine the interaction of many actors from a sociological perspective. Behavioral hypotheses are formulated, which are then tested on subjects within the framework of the models. When the structure of the experiment is explained the tests can be simulated by other scientists. According to Popper,[50] the hypotheses apply until they are falsified by experiments with the opposite result. The determined behavioral dispositions can then in turn be used for theories and economic policy strategies. In the longrun a Collective Error Theory could be the outcome.

---

[47] See https://www.merriam-webster.com/dictionary/behavioral%20science; http://www.businessdictionary.com/definition/behavioral-sciences.html and Beck (2014), pp. 1.

[48] See the Sect. 7.2.2.4. The Importance of Risk Adequate Compensation, Sect. 8.2.7.3. The effects on investment behavior of zero interest rate policy, evidence from a behavioral experiment; Sect. 8.2.8. The effects of money supply and interest rates on stock prices, evidence from two behavioral experiments and Conrad (2015, 2019, 2021).

[49] We could call these approaches in contrast to the Efficient Market Hypothesis "Collective Error Hypothesis". Therefore the New Behavioral Finance would also belong to this approach.

[50] See Popper (1958).

1.4 Ethics in Economic Education

Business ethics (definition) is the science of morality and ethos in the economy (definition). The aim of this science, as part of philosophy, is to understand the rules of the world, and in particular the behavior of human beings, which includes not only the being of man, but also his normative expectations. In the case of business ethics as a science, the aim is to analyze the causes and effects of ethical and unethical economic behavior and to develop approaches to improve productivity with the help of ethics in order to provide recommendations for action for companies and policies.

A common feature of the financial crises and others was the immoral enrichment of managers at the expense of their companies and the system and thus the society. But the way the world is viewed is also influencing people's behavior. Ideas and attitudes, including moral values, must be demonstrated and educated. The early socialization phase plays an important role in the moral behavior of a person. For example, schooling has had a great influence on the ethical-cognitive development of human beings as has been empirically proven.[51] In this respect, economic academies have a special responsibility.

There are those who blame management training for catastrophes such as Enron, the subprime crisis etc. Thomas Lindsay, once Dean of the University of Dallas, points to studies before Enron that prove managers rarely fail economically or morally because of a lack of professional knowledge. What they are generally missing is what Aristotle calls "wisdom," to be understood as interpersonal capabilities and practical knowledge. In Lindsay's opinion the American education for managers is excessively subject-oriented, and the moral capabilities of the students is almost completely lost through unadulterated profit maximization. Aristotle said that true leadership is based on the ability to recognize and serve the good of the community. To train these abilities one needs much more than a professional education, one needs instruction in history, philosophy, literature, theology and logic.[52]

In this context, international criticism of economic education at universities is increasing. Göbel, for example, argues that it is all too often suggested that "one can put oneself on a purely economic standpoint and hide everything else."[53] At universities, therefore, a rethink is necessary. Ethical considerations must not be excluded from the economic education.

With this background the internationally renowned business schools are in the defensive. Students, companies and the media blame the university for their graduates no longer being able to solve the complex, multidisciplinary problems of today's economy due to the wrong education. The universities fail to equip their students with useful abilities, to prepare them adequately as future managers and give them norms for ethical behavior, they say. Critique comes from within the university staff

---

[51] See Lind (1989), p. 311.

[52] See Bennis and O'Toole (2005), p. 95.

[53] Göbel (2010), p. 256.

as well, such as from the Dean of the renowned Kellog School of Management at Northwestern University. Professor Mintzberg from the Canadian McGill University accuses the business schools of lesson plans unconnected to practical needs. According to Warren G. Bennis and James O'Tool from the Marshall School of Business at the University of Southern California, number games and simulations are used more in the universities to give the education a scientific touch, and simultaneously neglects a broad, practical training.[54] The columnist David Brooks thus complains:

> ...our universities operate too much like a guild system, throwing plenty of people with dissertations at students, not enough with practical knowledge. Why aren't there more scholars ... who teach students to be generalists, to see the great connections?[55]

As early as 1988, a commission of the American Economic Association for the assessment of the graduate education program feared that the programs would produce "idiot savants" who had no knowledge of the real economic problems.[56]

Behavioral Economics experiments show that economics students are less cooperative from the beginning. In Ultimatum Game, they spend less and accept smaller amounts, so expect less cooperative behavior from the others.[57] As early as 1993, Frank, Gilovich and Regan found out from the economics study they examined that economics lessons in particular, which are based on the economic self-interest model, have cooperation-reducing effects.[58, 59]

The economics theory chose homo oeconomicus as a simplified model of thought. The Homo Oeconomicus, like the computer, is like the machine a purely rational being. Starting from a given information level, this creature always decides for the benefit-maximizing action and can thus be mathematically calculated. This gives students the impression that they have to maximize their own benefits, in order to be good, socially desirable. If households maximize their benefits and companies profit, this behavior is at the same time economically efficient and is therefore also a benchmark for economic education. Subcontractors always behave to maximize profits. Anyone who wants to become a successful entrepreneur should behave accordingly. Households make choices that follow benefit maximizing, as microeconomics teaches us. So this is the normal behavior as a private person.

This is the world that conveys economic science to young students in the Western industrialized countries. Many will say the world, and the people, are recklessly

---

[54] See Bennis and O'Toole (2005). See auch Mintzberg and Gosling (2004).

[55] Bennis and O'Toole (2005), p. 5.

[56] See Hodgson (2009), p. 1210.

[57] See Carter and Irons (1991), pp. 171–177, Marwell and Aimes (1981), pp. 306.

[58] See Frank et al. (1993), pp. 159–171. Beck (2014).

[59] It was interesting to see that in the ultimatum games students who had the course microeconomic before and therefore knew the experiment for showing not rational behavior gave only one of the ten chewing gums to the second person. Their argument was that they wanted to behave rational and the other person should be grateful to receive anything.

benefit maximizing. But what if men are neither good nor bad, and they are told to behave badly? Then the world would be worse than it could be.

Bad examples also corrode morals as well. It can be dangerous to continue to preach utility maximization with model thinking and to represent this as the only rational behavior. The consequence will be that people orient themselves towards these maxims of action and suppress their positive human qualities, such as compassion, willingness to help, general sacrifice and selflessness. Management education in particular must therefore ask whether it did not create these immoral managers, even indirectly, perhaps not even adversely affecting social development as a whole.

Many organizations are now active in the field of business ethics. For instance the Netzwerk Wirtschaftsethik (Network Economic Ethics) was founded in 1993, in which the churches, as well as representatives of business, politics and science, took part.[60] On the part of the students the demand for business ethics has intensified. This development is due to the immoral developments in the economy, which have been highlighted in the Enron scandal and the financial crisis. The Student Network for Ethics in Economics and Practice was founded by the students. The aim is to promote economic and business ethics in society and science, as well as to promote sustainable economics in theory and practice.[61] Sneep would like to encourage students, doctoral candidates, apprentices, as well as apprentices of all kinds, to think outside the boundaries of a "classical economy" and thus to show opportunities for business in the 21st century. Sneep called on the rectors of the German business schools to add business ethics as a compulsory lecture in the curriculum. The UN (Global Compact) launched an initiative in 2007 to stimulate research and teaching on business ethics, which has already signed nearly 500 universities around the world, with its Principles for Responsible Management Education (PRME).[62]

Harvard Business School formulates their community values:

> At Harvard Business School we believe that leadership and values are inseparable. The teaching of ethics here is explicit, not implicit, and our Community Values of mutual respect, honesty and integrity, and personal accountability support the HBS learning environment and are at the heart of a school-wide aspiration: to make HBS a model of the highest standards essential to responsible leadership in the modern business world. Our values are a set of guiding principles for all that we do wherever we are and with everyone we meet.[63]

Despite all these initiatives, business ethics is still not an integral part of economic science education.

What about management training in companies? Can an ethical behavior be created here? The mediation of ethical knowledge and awareness of the consequences of one's own actions are possible within the framework of seminars. Analytic capacity is not the problem among executives and the majority of

[60] See http://www.dnwe.de/Ueberblick.html (3.05.2013).

[61] http://www.sneep.info/sneep (3.05.2013). (author's translation)

[62] See http://www.unprme.org (5.05.2013).

[63] https://www.hbs.edu/mba/student-life/Pages/community-values.aspx (03/07/2018).

employees.[64] It is questionable, however, whether the ethical motivation can be changed or produced. A problem arises from the market economy. The market only knows the do-it-yourself mentality, i.e. reciprocity and a demand-driven efficiency or market fairness. According to the Kohlberg scheme, this corresponds to the second stage. The market is partly immoral. In the case of external effects, market failures occur, and the effects of economic trade on the welfare of an uninvolved third party. In addition to this, many companies have a strong hierarchy on the basis of orders and obedience, as well as a social appreciation of the company in the hierarchy. Against this background, Oppenrieder considers that it is possible for individuals to become negatively socialized with the entry into professional life and to re-develop in their moral consciousness.[65] A quotation from a board shows the discrepancy between ethical claim and reality:

> But inside the executives are aware of their ethical values, but they are often no longer able to get them out through the appliances. The companies have become appliances. The managers ... are often driven by their system.[66]

This quotation also shows that, from the point of view of leadership, that the economic environment has become more unethical. From this point of view, the current problem of ethics cannot be solved with ethics seminars alone. It requires the use of all ethics tools in the company, an ethically oriented legislation and jurisprudence as well as a critical public. The companies are part of the nation. Politicians, too, must therefore be aware of their ethical social role.

Conclusion

Economic policy tries to implement social goals by using economic theories and taking economic conditions into account. This places it right between business and politics. Happiness is inappropriate as a civilizing and evolutionary goal because only added benefit is objectively verifiable.

All modern societies have institutions and organizations, giving them order, and instilling discipline in their citizens to behave in the manner socially desired. As we have already shown however, this is not sufficient. For a society to function and for productive forces to develop, the appropriate social capital for the type of system order and economic stage of development must be available. This depends greatly on the attitudes of people required for societal or community cooperation. Norms, values and morality are important here, including attitudes towards the political and economic system. The attitudes of people in a society to the economically relevant activities have been paid as little attention by economic science as the existence of general economic knowledge.

---

[64] See Göbel (2010), p. 259.

[65] See Oppenrieder (1986), p. 38 and Göbel (2010), p. 256.

[66] Statement in the framework of an empirical study on the value propositions of top managers. See Buß (2009).

The way the world is viewed also influences people's behavior. Ideas and attitudes, including moral values, must be demonstrated and educated. The early socialization phase plays an important role in the moral behavior of a person. For example, schooling has had a great influence on the ethical-cognitive development of human beings, as has been empirically proven. In this respect, economic academies have a special responsibility.

Questions of Comprehension

1. What is the fundamental human problem in this world?
2. Explain the welfare optimum. What conditions must be fulfilled?
3. What is meant by the Easterlin paradox and the status effect?
4. Why is happiness unsuitable as a civilizing and evolutionary goal?
5. What are the limitations of quantitative economics in describing reality?
6. Why are social aspects often not taken into account by economics?
7. Have moral aspects been sufficiently taken into account in your business education?
8. What would you suggest to foster ethical behavior of managers?

Literature

Aristoteles. (1991). *Politik I, Werke (Bd. 9/I)*. Wissenschaftliche Buchgesellschaft.

Aristoteles. (1960). *Nikomachische Ethik, Werke Band* (2. Aufl.). Darmstadt. www.linke-buecher.de/texte/. . ./Aristoteles%2D%2DNikomachische%20Ethik.pdf. Accessed 19 Apr 2015.

Beck, H. (2014). *Behavioral economics: Eine Einführung* (1ed.). Springer.

Bennis, W. G., & O'Toole, J. (2005). Was ist die Managementausbildung noch wert? *Harvard Business Manager, 27*, 8–97.

Brickman, P., Coates, D., & Janoff-Bulman, R. (1978). Lottery winners and accident victims: Is happiness relative? *Journal of Personality and Social Psychology, 36*(8), 917–927.

Buß, E. (2009). Die soziale Kennkarte und Moral der deutschen Top-Manager. Befunde einer empirischen Erhebung. Vortragsmanuskript, Eugen Gutmann Gesellschaft. www.eugen-gutmann-gesellschaft.de/upload/vortrag_buss.pdf. Access 26 März 2009.

Carter, J. R., & Irons, M. (1991). Are economists different, and if so, why? *Journal of Economic Perspectives, 5*(1991), 171–177.

Clark, A. E., Frijters, P., Shields, M. A. (2007, June). Relative income, happiness, and utility: An explanation for the Easterlin Paradox and other puzzles (Discussion Paper No. 2840). Institute for the Study of Labor (IZA).

Conrad, C. A. (2014). Commodity and food speculation, is there a need for regulation? A discussion of the international research. *Applied Economics and Finance, 1*(2), 58–64.

Conrad, C. A. (2015). Incentives, risk and compensation schemes: Experimental evidence on the importance of risk adequate compensation. *Applied Economics and Finance, 2*(2), 50–55. https://doi.org/10.11114/aef.v2i4.1053

Conrad, C. A. (2019). The effects on investment behavior of zero interest rate policy, evidence from a roulette experiment. *Applied Economics and Finance, 6*(4), 18–27. https://doi.org/10.11114/aef.v6i4.4272

Conrad, C. A. (2021). The effects of money supply and interest rates on stock prices, evidence from two behavioral experiments. *Applied Economics and Finance (Open Access Journal), 8*(2), pp. 33–41.

Deaton, A. (2010). Income, aging, health and well-being around the world: Evidence from the Gallup World Poll. In D. A. Wise (Ed.), *Research findings in the economics of aging* (pp. 235–263). The University of Chicago Press.

Diener, E. (1984). Subjective well-being. *Psychological Bulletin, 95*, 542–575.

Donohue, J. J., & Levitt, S. D. (2001). The impact of legalized abortion on crime. *The Quarterly Journal of Economics, CXVI*(2), 379–420.

Fedako, J. (2007, February 18). *Correlating nonsense*. http://antipositivist.blogspot.com

Feldstein, M. (1974). Social security, induced retirement an aggregate capital accumulation. *The Journal of Political Economy, 82*, 905–926.

Fernández, R., Fogli, A. (2005). Fertility: The role of culture and family experience. *Journal of the European Economic Association*, *4*(2–3), S. 552–561.

Frank, R., Gilovich, T., & Regan, D. (1993). Does studying economics inhibit cooperation? *Journal of Economic Perspectives, 7*, 159–171.

Frenk, D. et al. (2011). Review of Irwin and Sanders 2010 OECD Report. In Institute for Agriculture and Trade Policy (Ed.), *Excessive Speculation in Agriculture Commodities, Selected writings from 2008–2012* (pp. 43–49). http://www.iadb.org/intal/intalcdi/PE/2011/08247.pdf

Furobotn, E. G., & Richter, R. (2005). *Instituions & economic theory* (Second ed.). The University of Michigan Press.

Göbel, E. (2010). Unternehmensethik (UTB, Stuttgart, 2010) G. Lind, Moralische Entwicklung in betrieblichen Organisationen, in Unternehmensethik, ed. H. Steinmann, A. Löhr, (Schaeffer Poeschel, Stuttgart, 1989), pp. 299–314

Guiso, L., Sapienza, P., Zingales, L. (2006). Does culture affect economic outcomes? *Journal of Economic Perspectives, 20*(Spring 2006), No. 2, pp. 23–48.

Hassler, U. (2003). Zeitabhängige Volatilität und instationäre Zeitreihen. In *Wirtschaftsdienst Nr* (Vol. 12, pp. 811–816).

Hayek, F. A. V. (1974). *The Pretence of Knowledge*. Lecture to the memory of Alfred Nobel, December 11, 1974. https://www.nobelprize.org/nobel_prizes/economic-sciences/laureates/1974/hayek-lecture.html (12/31/2017).

Henn, M. (2013). *Kommentar zum Literaturüberblick zur Spekulation mit Agrarrohstoffen* von Will et al., WEED, 14.

Hermalin, B. E., Weisbach, M. S. (2007). *Transparency and corporate governance* (pp. 1–26). http://ssm.com/abstract=958628

Hodgson, G. M. (2009). The Great Crash of 2008 and the reform of economics. *Cambridge Journal of Economics, 33*(2009), 1205–1221.

Ichino, A., & Maggi, G. (1999). Work environment and individual background: Explaining regional shirking differentials in a large Italian firm. *Quarterly Journal of Economics, 115*, 1057–1090.

Irwin, S. H., & Sanders, D. R. (2010). *The impact of index and swap funds on commodity future markets, OECD food, agriculture and fisheries*. Working Papers, No. 27, Paris 2010.

Lind, G. (1989). Moralische Entwicklung in betrieblichen Organisationen. In H. Steinmann & A. Löhr (Eds.), *Unternehmensethik* (pp. 299–314). C.E. Poeschel.

Luttmer, E. (2005). Neighbours as negatives, relative earnings and well-being. *Quarterly Journal of Economics, 120*(3), 963–1002.

Mai. (2013). http://www2.weed-online.org/uploads/kommentar_literaturueberblick_agrarspekulation.pdf

Marwell, G., & Aimes, R. (1981). Economists free ride, does anyone else? *Journal of Public Economics, 15*, 295–310.

Maurer, A., Schmid, M. (2010). *Erklärende Soziologie* (1. ed.). Spinger.

Mintzberg, H., & Gosling, J. (2004). Die fünf Welten eines Managers. *Harvard Business Manager, 26*, 46–59.

Mises, L. van. (1978). *The ultimate foundation of economic science*. Correlating nonsense. http://antipositivist.blogspot.com/2007/02/correating-nonsence.html.

Mocan, N., & Erdal, T. (2006). *Ugly criminals*. NBER working paper no. 12019, Issued in February 2006. http://www.nber.org/papers/w12019.

Noll, B. (2002). *Wirtschafts- und Unternehmensethik in der Marktwirtschaft*. Kohlhammer Verlag.

Oppenrieder, B. (1986). *Implementationsprobleme einer Unternehmensethik*. Diskussionsbeiträge, Heft 34 des Lehrstuhls für allgemeine Betriebswirtschaftslehre und Unternehmensführung der Universität Erlangen-Nürnberg, Prof. Dr. Horst Steinmann, Nürnberg.

Pagan, A., & Schwert, C. (1990). *Testing for covariance stationarity in stock market data: Economics letters, 33*(2), 165–170. http://schwerts.com/el90_ps.pdf. https://doi.org/10.1016/0165-1765(90)90163-U.

Petersen, V. J., Herlinghaus, A., & Menrad, M. (2012). *Risikomanagement auf globalen Agrarmärkten, Deutscher Raiffeisenverband e.V.*, DZ Bank 2012. http://www.raiffeisen.de/wp-content/uploads/downloads/2012/11/DRV-Brosch-Risiko_10_02.pdf

Phillips, P. & Loretan, M. (1990). *Testing covariance stationarity under moment condition failure with an application to common stock returns*, Discussion Paper No. 947, Cowles Foundation for Economic Research at Yale University New Haven Conneticut 1990, p 45.

Pies, I., Prehn, S., Glauben, T., & Will, M. G. (2013). *Kurzdarstellung Agrarspekulation*. Diskussionspapier Nr. 2013–2, des Lehrstuhls für Wirtschaftsethik an der Martin-Luther-Universität Halle-Wittenberg, hrsg. von Ingo Pies, Halle 2013.

Popper, K. (1958). *The logic of scientific discovery* (pp. 34–39). Harper Torchbooks.

Schulze, P. M. (2004). *Granger-Kausalitätsprüfung – Eine Anwendungsorientierte Darstellung, Institut für Statistik und Ökonometrie*. Johannes Gutenberg-Universität Mainz, Arbeitspapier Nr. 28(August 2004).

Solow, R. M. (1979). Economic history and economics. In *AmericanEconomic Review, Papers and Proceedings 75* (pp. 328–331).

Suikkanen, J. (2017). *Ethics of justification a defence of contractualism*, (Philosophical Studies from the University of Helsinki 17). https://helda.helsinki.fi/bitstream/handle/10138/21756/ethicsof.pdf?sequence=2&isAllowed=y

Ulrich, P. (1993). Unternehmerethos, in: Enderle, u.a. (ed.), Lexikon der Wirtschaftsethik, Freiburg 1993, Sp. 1165–1175.

Ura, K., Alkire, S., & Zangmo, T. (2012). Case study: Bhutan. Gross National Happiness and the GNH Index. In J. Helliwell, R. Layard, & J. Sachs (Eds.), *World Happiness Report*. Columbia University.

Wangdi, K. (2011). Do Bhutan's anti-smoking laws go too far? *Time Magazine*, http://content.time.com/time/world/article/0,8599,2057774,00.html (11.05.2019).

Weber, M. (1905). Die protestantische Ethik und der „Geist" des Kapitalismus, Tübingen 1905. (Faksimile-Ausgabe der in Tübingen erschienenen Erstausgabe), Düsseldorf 1992.

Weber, M. (1968). Der Sinn der „Wertfreiheit" der soziologischen und ökonomischen Wissenschaften, in Gesammelte Aufsätze zur Wissenschaftslehre, 3. Aufl., ed. M. Weber, (Tübingen, 1968), pp. 489–540.

Zorita, E. (2006). *Interactive comment on "On the verification of climate reconstructions" by G. Bürger and U. Cubach*. https://www.clim-past-discuss.net/2/S153/2006/cpd-2-S153-2006.pdf

Chapter 2
The Image of Man

What Follows Why?
The following chapter analyzes human behavior in the economy. Here we will examine the image of man in the economic sciences, along with recent interdisciplinary research. First we will analyze the economic science postulation of Homo Oeconomicus as a benefit-maximizing selfish individual, and challenge Adam Smith's "Invisible Hand" assumption of selfish utility maximization. Subsequently, recent experimental findings describe humans as social beings and we will then challenge both the economic-scientific behavioral assumption of egoism and benefit maximization.

Learning Goals
You should be able to describe the fundamentals of human behavior in your own words.

2.1 The Classical View of Man: Homo Economicus

Macroeconomics uses a simplified model of humanity to represent economic actors, namely homo economicus, an egoistic creature.[1] According to F. A. Hayek the term homo economicus goes back to John Stuart Mill[2] and Utilitarianism.[3] Homo

---

[1] Weber explains the reduction to rational goal-oriented action as simplified behavioral assumptions by giving examples of exceptions to rational behavior, such as stock market panic. See Weber (1922), p. 16.

[2] "It is concerned with him solely as a being who desires to possess wealth, and who is capable of judging of the comparative efficacy of means for obtaining that end. It predicts only such of the phenomena of the social state as take place in consequence of the pursuit of wealth. It makes entire abstraction of every other human passion or motive;" Mill (1844), See p. 38.

[3] See Hayek (1971), p. 77.

C. A. Conrad, *Economic Systems, Markets and Politics*,
https://doi.org/10.1007/978-3-031-10366-7_2

economicus is like a computer, or a being that only acts rationally (principle of rationality) as a machine would. This ideal actor is attributed preferences, and thus a constant utility function. Such assumptions have the advantage that human behavior would change only if the basic parameters for a decision changed.[4] Assuming a given degree of information, they would always choose the option that maximizes their gain (principle of the individual), making their decisions mathematically predictable.[5] On the other hand, it means that homo economicus not only leaves the benefit to others out of the equation but that he would even commit amoral acts to achieve his goal of maximizing his own advantage, including lying, betraying and other immoral acts.[6]

The theoretical homo economicus is a shallow image. When societal influences are not part of the equation, such an actor is represented as being purely psychological, not sociological. Mill considered people sociological, however.[7] If we take societal mores for human behavior into consideration, the resulting decisions change. These mores are societal norms that dictate to the members of a society how they should act in order to benefit the society and not harm it. Societal norms and values can be chosen consciously by the individuals or inculcated socially. Societal sanctions in the case of norm infractions can make certain decision alternatives seem to be more utility maximizing even if they bring fewer individuals more advantage than others.[8] The term gain is to be understood as net individual advantage, in other words profitable gain reduced by losses from social sanctions. On the flip side, sanctions prevent decision alternatives that would maximize the individual's gain at the cost of society. Sociology refers to motive/norm conflicts in this context, because an individual's need conflicts with the norm. Societal norms have rarely been taken into consideration by economic science, if at all.

The same is true for ethical values, although the term "gain" applies even less. The need that many people feel to do good for other people only indirectly provides a gain, by satisfying an existing subjective need. Everything that a person wants and gets could be described as a gain,[9] but additional benefit must also be objectively

---

[4] See Franz (2004) and Göbel (2010), p. 52.

[5] See Erlei et al. (1999), pp. 2. Current economic thinking handles market failure as a human failure only marginally, if it means rejecting the Rationality Theory of homo-oeconomicus. But even then human behavior is deterministic based on the assumptions of how they behave irrationally.

[6] See Milgrom and Roberts (1992).

[7] "The deeply rooted conception which every individual even now has of himself as a social being, tends to make him feel it one of his natural wants that there should be harmony between his feelings and aims and those of his fellow creatures. If differences of opinion and of mental culture make it impossible for him to share many of their actual feelings- perhaps make him denounce and defy those feelings- he still needs to be conscious that his real aim and theirs do not conflict; that he is not opposing himself to what they really wish for, namely their own good, but is, on the contrary, promoting it. This feeling in most individuals is much inferior in strength to their selfish feelings, and is often wanting altogether. But to those who have it, it possesses all the characters of a natural feeling." Mill (1863), pp. 267.

[8] See Föhr and Lenz (1992), p. 153.

[9] See Hausmann and McPherson (2006), pp. 79.

comprehensible to a third party. The fairy tale "Hans in Luck" by the Grimm Brothers[10] illustrated how a person can feel better subjectively, even though their objective gain has diminished. The term "gain" in this context is really too restrictive, as one can really only speak of fulfilling a need. Economic decision-making theory needs to be expanded to include this concept. To sacrifice something for others may be rare, but it is a very well known human phenomenon. To sacrifice would then indicate following the dictates of a need to help others, even if it reduces one's own objective advantage. This is exactly what earns our admiration and what many religions, including Christianity, demand of people; "It is better to give than to receive." The moral of the fairy tale is that Hans minimizes his objective gain and maximizes his subjective benefit, or better his happiness. We need to speak more generally of happiness maximization when examining human motivations. The idea that having goods from the economy alone does not bring happiness is clear once goods have been acquired. That happy feeling does not usually last very long, and in the end the goods only fulfill material needs.

Jeremy Bentham, James Mill and his son John Stuart Mill, the main founders of Utilitarianism, grew apart over time. Utility maximization is now understood exclusively in relation to material gain. Happiness is closer to Bentham's thinking, as he considered pain and pleasure.[11] For Bentham, happiness could arise from things such as sensory pleasure, a good reputation, wealth, power, or charitableness, but also negatively connoted traits such as malevolence. Pain might result from privation, a bad reputation, enemies, but potentially also from charitableness, piety or malevolence. John Stuart Mill includes not only desire in the pursuit of happiness but also the pursuit of honor, duty, and morality. Whoever rejects Utilitarianism because they reject the pursuit of happiness underestimates humanity. People search for happiness through their desires, but also through dignity.[12] A person's self interest, thus the basis for being happy, can be found in the pleasure derived from understanding and morality. According to Mill, there are moral and immoral pleasures or perceptions of happiness, which is why people must question their interests and adjust their motives to their ethical views.[13] Utility maximization must therefore be

[10] See http://www.authorama.com/grimms-fairy-tales-2.html

[11] "Nature has placed mankind under the governance of two sovereign masters, pain and pleasure. It is for them alone to point out what we ought to do, as well as to determine what we shall do. On the one hand the standard of right and wrong, on the other the chain of causes and effects, are fastened to their throne. They govern us in all we do, in all we say, in all we think: every effort we can make to throw off our subjection, will serve but to demonstrate and confirm it. In words a man may pretend to abjure their empire: but in reality he will remain subject to it all the while. The principle of utility recognizes this subjection, and assumes it for the foundation of that system, the object of which is to rear the fabric of felicity by the hands of reason and of law." Bentham (1789), first chapter.

[12] "... but its most appropriate appellation is a sense of dignity, which all human beings possess in one form or other, and in some, though by no means in exact, proportion to their higher faculties, and which is so essential a part of the happiness of those in whom it is strong..." Mill (1863), p. 10. See Mill (1992), pp. 86.

[13] See Mill (1992), pp. 86 and 90.

understood as pleasure maximization and not solely as the maximization of material gain.

As opposed to the economic theory of homo economicus the information processor, social psychology considers people to be decision-making problem simplifiers. To this end people use patterns, created from their impressions and experiences. Social psychology has used several interesting experiments to show the influence of patterns. Pre-determined thought structures and ways to solve problems (behaviors) help to call up patterns and information quickly. Overconfidence can also be an issue with thinking. It has been shown that people do not have the abilities of a homo economicus.[14] New Behavioral Finance agrees.[15]

The Prospect Theory of Kahnemann and Tversky provides an empirical approach for measuring subjective benefit based on decision-making behavior under uncertainty. The problem, however, is the different risk behavior of humans, which is why no clear reproducible utility function can result. Human behavior is not deterministic.[16]

The simplified human model of homo economicus is legitimate. Rational, informed and balanced action generally does bring advantages. The assumptions behind homo economicus become problematic when economic science forgets that they are dealing with a model[17] and treat it as reality.[18]

2.2 Falsely Understood Egoism

Perhaps the lack of ethics and morals of many managers comes from a false understanding of the economic bible "Wealth of Nations," by Adam Smith, or at least a very abbreviated and thus misleading representation of his ideas as presented in economic education. The brilliant idea of Adam Smith was how human self-interest is directed toward the common good through the "invisible hand" of the market. Even bad people thus serve the common good, as Hume commented. The law of the market functions as an ethical guideline thus:[19]

---

[14] See Jonas et al. (2007), pp. 374; Fehr and Fischbacher (2003), p. 786 and Fehr et al. (2001); Frank (2004); Frank (1988) and Gürerk and Rockenbach (2006).

[15] See Conrad (2010), pp. 391.

[16] See Kahneman and Tversky (1979) and (1984).

[17] "Not that any political economist was ever so absurd as to suppose that mankind are really thus constituted, but because this is the mode in which science must necessarily proceed." Mill, John Stuart (1844), V 38.

[18] An interesting neurological experiment was conducted in 2003 that showed *homo-economicus* to be a fiction, and the press gave its conclusions much attention. The ultimatum game was conducted in the laboratory of Princeton University by Alan Sanfeys. See Sanfey, Alan et al. (2003) and Handelsblatt vom 03/23/06, p. 11.

[19] See Starbatty, Joachim (1999), pp. 17.

> . . .it is not from the benevolence of the butcher, the brewer, or the baker, that we expect our dinner, but from their regard to their own interest.[20]

> By pursuing his own interest he frequently promotes that of the society more effectually than when he really intends to promote it[21]

It almost seems as though many managers take this as a free pass to limitless pursuit of their own interest, as though they understood it as egoism at the cost of others. The second central work of the Scottish moral philosopher Adam Smith, "Theory of Moral Sentiments" is almost never mentioned. Here we find quite different quotes:

> How selfish soever man may be supposed, there are evidently some principles in his nature, which interest him in the fortune of others, and render their happiness necessary to him, though he derives nothing from it except the pleasure of seeing it.[22]

According to Smith, people have a highly developed conscience that functions as an internal moral judge. Like Schopenhauer and Hume,[23] he accords people the capacity of compassion and sympathy with other people. They can empathize with the interests and needs of their fellow humans, and must therefore weigh them in their conscience against their own self-interest. They are helped in this by an imaginary, objective third-person opinion derived from the question of how an impartial third party would decide. The principle of rational thinking is the basis for weighing the various interests. This capacity of a human conscience is generally credited to God or generally to human rationality. The individual is part of the natural whole and responsible for his or her own decisions. Responsibility and freedom are natural and God-given. Smith believes a truly uninvolved and objective third party's opinion is necessary to determine whether an action is morally and ethically acceptable. This impartial observer takes on the task of social corrective, which is comparable to Immanuel Kant's categorical imperative. Always act in such a way, that the basis for decisions could be the principle behind a general rule, the behavior could always be acted upon by all people and for the good of society.[24]

Empathy has meanwhile been detected as human compassion in the region of the brain called the insula. As a rule, it also leads to altruistic helpfulness.[25]

---

[20] Smith, Adam (1776), Paragraph I, p. 82. The idea of an invisible hand can be traced back to Mandevilles bee fable. "The worst of all the Multitude Did something for the Common Good." Mandeville, Bernard de (1732) p. 9. Mandeville had already seen the danger than self-interest can pose to society: "So vice is beneficial found, when it's by justice lopt, and bound; Nay the people would be great; as necessary to the state; As hunger is to make them eat; Bare virtue can't make nations live; In Splendor; they, that would revive A Golden Age must be as free For Acorns, as for Honesty." Mandeville, Bernard de (1732) p. 24

[21] Smith, Adam (1776), Book IV, Chapter II, p. 489.

[22] Smith Adam (1759), Part I, Chapter I.

[23] "We are certain, that sympathy is a very powerful principal in human nature." Hume, David (1739), p. 667. See Schopenhauer, Arthur (1840), § 15–18.

[24] See Nass, Elmar (2003), p. 47.

[25] See Singer, T., & Lamm, C. (2009), pp. 81–96.

Adam Smith was aware that the invisible hand is not sufficient to protect the common good from damage done by an individual. He stressed the need for an economic and structural system that included protection for the common good. Enrichment of the individual at the expense of the common good cannot be tolerated by a society for various reasons. Besides the damage sustained by the national economy, such behavior supplants the system. According to Smith, trade can develop via markets to the benefit of all people, thus creating wealth, only when the legal system is functional and there is trust in the supremacy of the state.[26]

2.3 Conclusion and Summary

What motivation for ethical behavior do we have? There are many people who selflessly do good deeds and feel better for doing so, not worse. This gives us a selfless motivation that contradicts the theory of utility maximization, or the concept of homo economicus. The fact that selfless, or even self-sacrificing, acts exists shows that such an ethic is not unrealistic. Volunteer work and individuals like Mother Theresa are clear examples. This behavior can be explained by a more general theory of maximizing happiness, which is behind theories like the Happiness Theory from Bentham and Mill. Many people are generally good, which is to say they have an ethical disposition.

Selfless acts generally garner prestige in a society, presenting another motivation for ethical behavior. Both motivations are bases for behavior relevant to the satisfaction of a person's basic needs, according to Maslow's[27] hierarchy of needs. Beyond maximizing one's advantage, people need to feel a purpose in life. There are people who measure their benefit or value as a person by how beneficial they are to others. Behavioral theories have given too little consideration to intrinsic motivations until now. Here we are looking at an enlightened human ethos. People consciously behave ethically because they understand the importance of such behavior to society, or because they empathize with other people. Normally these motivations only become meaningful after all of one's basic needs have been met, and they cannot be presupposed for every person. Nonetheless, such ethical motivations must not be disregarded. Our representative democracy in fact demands altruistic behavior from people as a prerequisite to allowing delegates to represent the voter's interests. This expanded theory allows us to explain altruism, helping others and sympathy.

Man is a social being. Social rewards have a positive effect in the brain (dorsal or ventral striatum).[28] Withdrawal of social inclusion, recognition and empowerment causes pain and even damage to health. Even a hormone that promotes trust and

[26] See Smith, Adam (1776), chapter III, first paragraph.

[27] See Maslow, A. H. (1943).

[28] See Fehr, E., & Camerer, C. F. (2007).

social bonds has been discovered in the human body. Neuropeptide oxytocin caused subjects to clearly prioritize social risk over equal monetary risk.[29]

The economics, with their focus on a pure objective utility maximization, are far from human reality. Although an exclusively objective benefit allows for measurability and thus the use of deterministic decision-making models, they lead to the wrong results. There are three systematic errors:

1. Economic sciences are exclusively individually oriented. People decide in a social environment, which is why sociology is at least as important for behavior as psychology. Motives such as social rewards or sanctions are not taken into account. For instance is acceptance by others is a very important behavioral incentive.2. Taking the objective as the basis for human decision-making, the influence of the group (the company) or society must also be taken into account. Norms that are sanctioned reduce payouts and are critical to decision-making.3. Finally, the objective benefit is not decisive but the subjectively perceived. However, this is difficult to measure from the outside. However, decision models that build on only objective material utility are misrepresentative and cannot explain many human motives, such as emotions, envy, sense of justice, and compassion. Man is stunted with the homo oeconomicus. It would therefore be more realistic to base the explanation of human behavior on the maximization of happiness as on benefit maximization.

People should be motivated to work happily and efficiently in such a way that they use their skills to maximize the company's participation in the production process. That's how they benefit others. This is best ensured by freedom and competition in decentralized decision-making and market coordination. Quantitative economics should be supplemented in this book by the findings of behavioral sciences.

If irrational behavior is not the exception, models based on rational behavior can no longer be a rule, but can at best describe optimal behavior or average behavior by which the irrational behavior shows deviations. If people do not behave predictably like natural laws, then at best we can set a framework to direct behavior with incentives and sanctions. The economy then consists mainly of institutional regulations, a regulatory framework.

The Prospect theory[30] complements the previous behavioral models based on rational behavior and thus moves a step closer to reality. However, as expected, this increases the complexity of the models. This was the very reason for the simplistic assumption of the homo oeconomicus. The problem, however, is the different risk behavior and irrational behavior of humans, which is why no clear, reproducible utility function can result. Human behavior remains not deterministic.

Why should markets be rational if their human participants are not?

If irrational behavior is not the exception, models based on rational behavior can no longer be a rule, but can at best describe optimal behavior or average behavior by which the irrational behavior shows deviations. If people do not behave predictably

[29] See Kosfeld, M., et al. (2005).

[30] See Kahneman and Tversky (1979) and (1984).

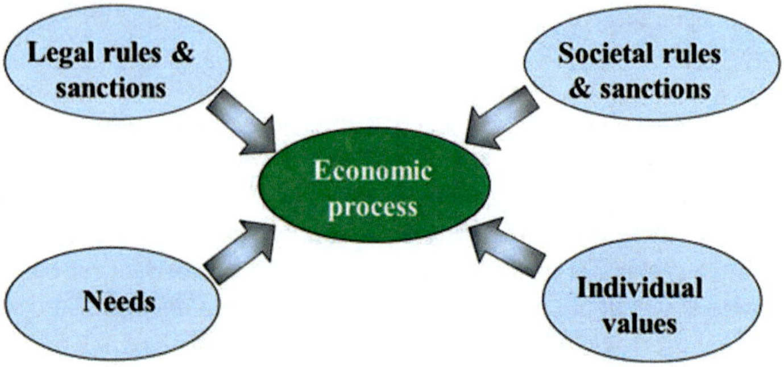

Fig. 2.1 Framework as an institution for economical optimal behavior

like natural laws, then at best we can set a framework to direct behavior with incentives and sanctions. The economy then consists mainly of institutional regulations, a regulatory framework (See Fig. 2.1). One goal of this book is to create a state control framework as an institution for economical optimal behavior.

Ethical Summary
Behavioral experimental findings describe humans as social beings and we will then challenge both the economic-scientific behavioral assumption of egoism and benefit maximization. There is selfless motivation that contradicts the theory of utility maximization, or the concept of homo economicus. However, decision models that build on only objective material utility are misrepresentative and cannot explain many human motives, such as emotions, envy, sense of justice, and compassion. It would therefore be more realistic to base the explanation of human behavior on the maximization of happiness as on benefit maximization.

Behavioral Summary
Man is a social being. Social rewards have a positive effect in the brain (dorsal or ventral striatum). Withdrawal of social inclusion, recognition and empowerment causes pain and even damage to health. Even a hormone that promotes trust and social bonds has been discovered in the human body. Neuropeptide oxytocin caused subjects to clearly prioritize social risk over equal monetary risk. Economic sciences are exclusively psychologically oriented. People decide in a social environment, which is why sociology is at least as important for behavior as psychology. Motives such as social rewards or sanctions are not taken into account. For instance is acceptance by others is a very important behavioral incentive. If irrational behavior is not the exception, human behavior remains not deterministic. Markets can only be as rational as their actors behave. If people do not behave predictably like natural laws, then at best we can set a framework to direct behavior with incentives and sanctions.

Comprehension Questions

1. Describe the characteristics of homo oeconomicus. Is that image of human beings realistic? Draw your own image of man.
2. Why is it not realistic if Economic sciences are exclusively psychologically oriented? What might be the consequences?
3. What are the pros and cons of the assumption of objective utility maximization as goal of men? How realistic is this?

Literature

Bentham, J. (1789). *Introduction to the principles of morals and legislation* (1780, published 1789) (J. H. Burns & H. L. A. Hart., eds.). (The Collected Works of Jeremy Bentham) (2nd ed.).

Conrad, C. A. (2010). *Morality and economic crisis – Enron*. Subprime & Hamburg.

Erlei, M., Leschke, M., & Sauerland, D. (1999). *Neue Institutionenökonomik*.

Fehr, E., & Camerer, C. F. (2007). Social neuroeconomics: The neural circuitry of social preferences. *Trends in Cognitive Sciences, 11*, 419–427.

Fehr, E., & Fischbacher, U. (2003). The nature of human altruism. *Nature, 425*(23), 785–791.

Fehr, E., Gächter, S., & Fischbacher, U. (2001). Are people conditionally cooperative? Evidence from a public goods experiment. *Economics Letters, 71*, 397–404.

Föhr, S., & Lenz, H. (1992). Unternehmenskultur und ökonomische Theorie. In W. H. Staehle & P. Conrad (Eds.), *Managementforschung* (pp. 111–162). Berlin.

Frank, R. H. (1988). *Passion within reason. The strategic role of the emotions*. WW Norton & Co.

Frank, R. H. (2004). *What Price the Moral High Ground?* Princeton.

Franz, S. (2004). *Grundlagen des ökonomischen Ansatzes: Das Erklärungskonzept des Homo Oeconomicus*, Working Paper der Universität Potsdam. 2004–02. www.uni-potsdam.de/u/makrooekonomie/docs/studoc/stud7.pdf

Göbel, E. (2010). *Unternehmensethik*.

Grimm, B. (1819). *Hans in Luck*. http://www.authorama.com/grimms-fairy-tales-2.html

Gürerk, Ö. I., & Rockenbach, B. (2006). The competitive advantage of sanctioning institutions. *Science, 312*(April), 108–111.

Hausmann, D. M., & McPherson, M. (2006). *Economic analysis, moral philosophy, and public policy* (2nd ed.).

Jonas, K., Stroebe, W., & Hewstone, M. (2007). *Sozialpsychologie, Eine Einführung* (5th ed.).

Kahneman, D., & Tversky, A. (1979, March). Prospect theory: An analysis of decision under risk. *Econometrica, 47*(2), 263–292.

Kahneman, D., & Tversky, A. (1984). Choices values and frames. *American Pschologist, 39*(4), 342–350.

Kosfeld, M., et al. (2005). Oxytocin increases trust in humans. *Nature, 435*, 673–676.

Mandeville, B. de (1732). The fable of the bees; or, private vices, public benefits, London 1714 (first edition 1714).

Maslow, A. H. (1943). A theory of human motivation. *Psychological Review, 50*(4), 370–396.

Milgrom, P., & Roberts, J. (1992). *Economics, Organization & Management*.

Mill, J. S. (1844). *Essays on Some Unsettled Questions of Political Economy*, London. http://www.econlib.org/library/Mill/mlUQP5.html (25.04.2015).

Mill, J. S. (1863). Utilitarism. In Mill, John Stuart (2010). *The basic writings of John Stuart Mill: On liberty, The Subjection of Women and Utilitarianism*, New York.

Mill, J. S. (1992). Utilitarismus. In O. Höffe (Ed.), *Einführung in die utilitaristische Ethik, Klassische und zeitgenössische Texte* (pp. 84–97). Edition.

Nass, E. (2003). *Der mensch als Ziel der Wirtschaftsethik: Eine finalethische Positionierung im Spannungsfeld zwischen Ethik und Ökonomie*. Schöningh.

Sanfey, A. G., Rilling, J. K., Aronson, J. A., Ny. Auflstrom, L. E., & Cohen, J. D. (2003, June). The neural basis of economic decision-making in the ultimatum game. *Science, 300*(13), 1755–1758.

Schopenhauer, A. (1840). *Preisschrift über die Grundlage der Moral*. Hamburg.

Shiv, B., Loewenstein, G., & Bechara, A. (2005). The dark side of emotions? When individuals with decreased emotional reactions make advantageous decisions. *Cognitive Brain Research, 23*, 85–92.

Singer, T., & Lamm, C. (2009). The social neuroscience of empathy. *Annals of the New York Academy of Sciences, 1156*, 81–96.

Smith, A. (1759). *The theory of the moral sentiments*. Edinburgh.

Smith, A. (1776). An inquiry into the nature and causes of the wealth of nations. *Edinburgh, 1776*. http://www.econlib.org/library/Smith/smWN8.html

Starbatty, J. (1999). Das Menschenbild in den Wirtschaftswissenschaften. *Tübinger Diskussionsbeiträge der Wirtschaftswissenschaftlichen Fakultät*, 176. https://publikationen.uni-tuebingen.de/xmlui/handle/10900/47437

von Hayek, F. A. (1971). *Die Verfassung der Freiheit*. Mohr (Siebeck).

Weber, M. (1922). *Wirtschaft und Gesellschaft, Grundriss der verstehenden Soziologie*. Edition. Tübingen.

Chapter 3
Market and Competition

What Follows Why?
After familiarizing ourselves with the image of man and the basic tenets and societal objectives, we will now analyze the functions of the market and competition as the basis of our market system. We will show that the market and competition provide an allocation-efficient result and thus a welfare optimum. Which rules apply in the so-called market economy? How are human behavior, culture and human performance related? Is man made for competition? We will address these questions in the following.

Learning Goals
You should be able to

1. Explain why the market and competition provide an allocation-efficient result and
2. Explain the competition functions by means of examples.

3.1 Behavior and Economic Performance

3.1.1 Culture and Performance

Does culture influences performance of man? Culture is all norms, values and attitudes that define the behavior of people as a group (**definition**).

Culture unites the members of a social system in terms of the meaning and interpretation of what is going on around them, which encourages similar behaviors. Culture thus gives identity to the group members. The concept of culture can be applied to families, teams, organizations and countries. Culture develops society as a group when society tries to respond to external influences using optimal adaptation. Climate, landscape and natural resources all lead to economic activities such as agriculture, hunting and mining. Conflicts with other groups often lead to to military actions. This results in social best practices in family structure, intergroup

C. A. Conrad, *Economic Systems, Markets and Politics*,
https://doi.org/10.1007/978-3-031-10366-7_3

relationships, gender roles that are conveyed through socialization processes such as parenting, schooling, and occupational socialization, which in turn leave behind psychological footprints such as cognitive styles, values, beliefs, and behaviors as a culture that binds society together.[1]

Empirical studies confirm a familiar basic principle of raising children, or human socialization in general. Social, or more exactly, moral and ethical behavior can be taught and learned.[2] The reverse conclusion is that moral behavior weakens whenever it is no longer taught or demonstrated. For this reason there is a duty to educate children and socialize members of a society in all areas. If this does not take place, or only poorly, the effects will be felt in all areas, in companies and in national economies. The effects are gradual, noticeable only over the longer term, similar to the effects of pollution in the environment. It often pays off for individuals to violate social rules as long as others keep to them. There is also the fact that socialization as a practiced social behavior and moral values can be lost. Like a young cat dependent on the role model of its mother to catch mice despite its hunting instinct, humans need role models, guidelines and education, including punitive measures for moral transgressions. This allows them to become functional members of the human community in a positive sense. If values are not passed on and socialization does not occur, this human capital, the experiences of living together, is lost and cannot be given to the next generation.

Morality and customs of managers are also products of each respective society. Morality of the individual is partially inherent and partially trained through the social and familial socialization process.[3] According to David Hume, Stinchcombe and Friedrich A. von Hayek there is also a cultural development process. Sociology calls this the process of natural selection. The unsuitable behavioral patterns and rules (institutions) die out with the groups that have selected them. Cultural development is a process of trial and error, with uncertain results. Legal constructs (institutional rules) such as private property, money and credit, even the market economy itself, are discoveries that brought benefits to groups that initiated them. Forms of social life and societal organization are tried out and taken on if they provide economic success and social acceptance, and rejected if they do not. If a society does not behave in this manner, it risks going under in the competition with other societies with its poorer organization, which is the explanation for such a developmental process.[4] One could argue, for example, that when the Socialist and Communist systems collapsed, private property had instituted itself. The process of natural selection takes place through a very slow process of selection. The decisive factor is selection through human thought and learning from experience (trial and

[1] See Smith et al. (2006) and Smith (2014), pp. 569.

[2] One study was conducted in Germany with craftsmen and one in the USA with students (lecture "business ethics"). See See Steinmann and Löhr (1994), pp. 174, 190 and Noll (2002), p. 144.

[3] See Wiswede (1985), p. 195.

[4] See Wiswede (1985), p. 195, von Hayek (1976), p. 39, 40 und 59; von Hayek (1979), pp. 154 and 167 and Noll (2002), p. 29.

error). This applies especially for the creation of economic order and in general of social order.

The social evaluation of good and evil is also subjected to this principle of cultural selection. A society defines what is good and bad for itself, just as does every individual. Society develops norms for its protection and welfare. If it develops the wrong norms it can cause its destruction. This awareness is very broad and is not applicable only to moral norms, but to all behavioral guidelines.

People orient themselves by other people. If traditional values are rejected, in youth for example, or by influential social classes, first a trend is created as a new mainstream culture. We may refer to this as the zeitgeist, which represents the temporary nature of this trend. A regeneration is then already almost impossible, if the old values no longer reflect common sense in the society. If the moral values are no longer common sense, or dominant, there are no longer sanctions from the society for moral missteps. At some point the values are forgotten. The respective social culture is then lost forever; it dies out, like so many cultures of the native peoples in earlier colonies during the European socialization. We are not talking about the natural questioning of parental values during one's youth and the process of constant rejuvenation that results for social orientation and values, but of massive cultural ruptures. A rupture of this kind can be brought about by exceptional events, such as a war. Families are torn apart in war, which impedes the natural process of passing on values. Social values are particularly called into question when a war is lost and the dominant social and power structures collapse. Not only is an authority vacuum created, but there seems to be a tendency to take on the social norms and values of the superior, victorious society.

How does culture affect the economic behavior of people?

Henrich, Joseph, et al. noted that the willingness to contribute was culturally different in the public good games and the ultimatum games.[5]

In the early 1980s, Hofstede described the connection between the general culture of a country and the behavior of the people in the company by interviewing IBM employees in 71 countries with a questionnaire on their behavior for 10 years. He showed that the behavior of managers is strongly influenced by their culture, which is particularly reflected in their leadership and the organization of the company process.[6]

From the answers Hofstede developed four cultural dimensions for describing cultures:

1. an individualistic versus a collectivist culture, in which the American corporate cultures are given an individualistic character and the Japanese a collectivist.
2. a different acceptance of status differences (power-distance)

---

[5] See Henrich et al. (2005), p. 814.

[6] See Hofstede et al. (2010).

3. a different risk assessment or uncertainty avoidance (uncertainty avoidance)
4. More male or female dominated cultures (masculinity/femininity)

Schwartz conducted similar transnational studies in 1994 and 2004, which essentially confirmed Hofstede's findings.[7] Bond and Smith (1996) applied Asch's Conformity Experiment to those countries that also examined Hofstede and Schwartz and found higher conformity in collectivist countries.[8]

Many more studies have been done, but they did not give a consistent picture of other properties. It is very difficult to find further significant and stable differences between national cultures.[9] However, further distinctions can be deduced from the difference between cultures oriented towards collectivist or individualist styles.

Earley tested the collectivist and individual orientation of 45 Israelis, 60 Mainland Chinese and 60 Americans and then tested their performance individually and within groups, whereby one group would seem homogeneous and similar to the participants (self group) and the other group would be different (foreign group). Then all test subjects were asked to solve tasks on their own, whereby the individual task was to solve a box filled with 20 tasks and the two other groups were said to have a total of 200 tasks to solve. The individualists were predominantly Americans and solved significantly fewer tasks in one of the seemingly collective conditions as opposed to individually. Conversely, the collectivists – mostly Chinese – were much more productive when they thought they were working in an in-house group.[10]

Weber described the economic ascent after the Reformation as a result of a Protestant ethic, which enhanced performance motivation by permanently shaping the attitudes of entrepreneurs and workers. This is a form of one

> gets nothing out of this wealth for himself, except the irrational sense of having done his job well[11]

McClelland was inspired by Weber and suggests that Protestant values in education have promoted the achievement motive. Values such as personal responsibility and hard work lead to more entrepreneurial activity and thus to an economic upswing.

McClelland developed a performance index in 1961 by evaluating historical textual sources of various kinds for performance motives (eg fairy tales, poems, speeches or textbook texts) and compared them to the economic development of the respective cultures. For ancient Greece, late medieval Spain, England in the fifteenth to nineteenth centuries, and the United States for the period between 1800 and 1950, he was able to show that periods of economic upturn had been preceded by an increase in the national index of performance indices, whereas an economic decline was preceeded by a decrease. This is a connection but not necessarily proven a

[7] See Schwartz (1994), pp. 85–119 and Schwartz (2004).

[8] See Bond and Smith (1996).

[9] See Smith (2014), pp. 574.

[10] See Earley (1993), pp. 319–348 and Smith (2014), p. 591.

[11] See Weber (1905).

causality.[12] In 2009 there was a comparable analysis in relation to two German states, which confirmed the result of McClelland.[13]

Conclusion
Culture is a productive factor as the identity of society. In collectivist cultures, incentives work differently than in individualistic cultures. Max Weber (Protestant Ethics) was correct. Cultural achievement motives (eg fairy tales, poems, speeches or textbook texts) influence economic development.

Economic policy should be geared towards positively assessing performance in society or as a group norm. On the one hand, there are limits to individual freedom and, more generally, to the human rights of the individual to be respected. On the other hand, social recognition and identity, which a society can give as a group, are contrasted with negative group actions in the case of standard infringement.

3.1.2 Economic Behavior Motivation and Performance

What motivates living beings to become economically active and perform well?

Perin and Williams explored this in rats. The longer they were deprived of their food (between 3 and 23 h) and the more often they had to press a lever to get food (incentive) (between 5 and 90 times), the stronger their resistance to giving up (reaction potential) when there was no longer a reward for lever pressing. It was measured how often the lever was pressed until the test animals persisted for at least 5 min without any reaction in the experimental apparatus.[14]

This means that living beings are motivated by deprivation of their basic needs, which would explain that cultures that had suffered very hard deprivations were subsequently very economically engaged. Provided they have had the positive experience of economic behavior that they can alleviate their misery.

Based on the experiments of Perin and Williams, Hull found in 1952 that the motivation is also positively dependent on the quality of the reward offered as an incentive. The behavioral theory of Hull determined a behavioral tendency as follows:[15]

$$\text{Behavioral tendency} = \text{habit} \times \text{drive} \times \text{incentive}.$$

Need-induced instincts generate a pressure to act (push), while situational incentives created by the environment of the individual trigger a certain behavior in order to satisfy the pressure to act and to bring about satisfaction (pull).[16]

---

[12] See McClelland (1961) and Brandstätter et al. (2018), pp. 35.

[13] See Engeser et al. (2009).

[14] See Perin (1942) and Williams (1938).

[15] See Hull (1952), pp. 140.

[16] See Brandstätter et al. (2018), pp. 18.

The economy can influence incentives. The rules of the game that lead to rewards or sanctions form the institutional framework for behavior.

There are three incentive classes, which can be assigned to three motivational topics and are treated separately in later chapters. These incentive classes are

1. Achievement motive, that is, to master challenges. In behavior that is oriented towards achievement, the actor's goal is to be economically productive (definition). Performance motivation reflects the need for fair performance competition in the market economy.
2. Affiliation motive, ie socializing and maintaining social contacts.[17] The pursuit of interpersonal satisfying relationships (definition of connection motivation) was of great importance in evolutionary biology. Bonding with peers and coexistence in groups was central to ensuring the survival of individual.

   This poses a special challenge in the computer age. The workplace of humans should still allow social contacts to meet the needs of the people.
3. Power Motivation, the Ability to Influence or Impress Other People

   The power motivation is defined as the tendency to draw satisfaction from the physical, mental or emotional influence on others.[18] This plays a role in the motivation of politicians and managers.

In motivational research, it was shown that motivations measured by pictorial stories and those recorded via self-reporting did not correlate with each other.[19] This is because there are conscious (intrinsic) and unconscious motives "self-imposed motives" (explicit motives or self-attributed motives) for human action.[20] The implicit motives arise from past affective experiences (affect-driven needs) that enter the subconscious mind, whereas the explicit motives consciously question the advantageousness of one's own action, even though they are less spontaneous. Here social structures in the form of social incentives flow into this.

In the power motive, the positive affective experiences are decisive as the feeling of being able to empower others to feel strong. The attachment motivation comes from the feelings of social harmony, if one experiences affection and sympathy from other people. From these experiences, preferences for certain actions form.[21]

In addition, one distinguishes between intrinsic and extrinsic motives. In the case of intrinsic motives, the incentive for action is internal, whereas stimuli such as rewards or sanctions are behavior-inducing for external motivation.[22]

---

[17] For the affiliation motive see the study of Atkinson et al. See Atkinson et al. (1954), pp. 405–410.

[18] See Schultheiss, O. C. (2008).

[19] See deCharms, R., Morrison, H. W., Reitman, W., & McClelland, D. C. (1955) and McClelland, D. C., Atkinson, J. W., Clark, R. A., & Lowell, E. L. (1953).

[20] See McClelland, D. C., Koestner, R., & Weinberger, J. (1989) and Brandstätter, Veronika/Schüler, Julia/Puca, Rosa Maria/Lozo, Ljubica (2018), pp. 81.

[21] See Schultheiss (2008); McClelland et al. (1989) and Brandstätter et al. (2018), p. 81.

[22] See Brandstätter et al. (2018), pp. 113 and Deci and Ryan (2000), p. 233.

The theory of basic needs explains how intrinsic motivation arises. It distinguishes three basic psychological needs: autonomy, competence and social inclusion. These were universally proven for different types of people (women, men, workers, managers, etc.) and cultures (individualistic Western and collectivist Eastern cultures).

- Autonomy can be characterized as self-determination. It is defined as need. Man wants to experience himself as autonomous in his actions so that he can adapt them to his values and interests. Studies show that extrinsic motivational tools such as control, sanctions, rewards, but also more subtle manipulations such as controlling language ("Thou shalt" rather than "You can") and the generation of guilt, reduce intrinsic motivation.
- Competency experience means the need to experience onesself as competent and effective in the pursuit of goals. This includes the need for clear structures that reveal the effect of one's own actions.
- Social inclusion is the need not only to be socially recognized, but also to be associated and connected with other people or groups (partners, family, friends, work colleagues).

To achieve social inclusion, a warm and inclusive social environment is important. A distant and indifferent environment causes the opposite. Received emotional social support has a positive effect because it stimulates behavior oriented towards reinforcing that support.

Basic needs are basic human needs such as eating and sleeping. When they are met one has intrinsic motivation, well-being and personal development. If they are not satisfied, the result is demotivation and malaise.[23]

Economic goals can be derived from these needs: the state must guarantee the economic freedom of the individual, but must also make social contact possible. In addition, the state structures, in particular those with direct citizen contact must remain small enough to be personal.

Meyer et al. tested the theory of basic needs of professional fashion and photo models with two studies. Their hypothesis was that they would have to be dissatisfied because they have little influence on their success (competence), they are judged (autonomy) on superficial values (of their beauty) and they have relatively few opportunities for deep interpersonal relationships due to work-related travel. The models reported low life satisfaction, low emotional well-being, and low self-esteem.[24]

Conclusion

Living beings are motivated by deprivation of their basic needs, which would explain why cultures that had suffered very hard deprivations were subsequently very economically engaged.

---

[23] See Deci and Ryan (2000), 227–268 and Brandstätter et al. (2018), pp. 117.

[24] See Meyer et al. (2007), pp. 2–17.

The motives of autonomy and competence show that people actively deal with the challenges of life and want to understand the effects of their actions. Freedom of design and achievement motivation are central human needs. They are thus overarching goals of the state, which the state must take into account in its organization and institutions. This inevitably leads to the desire for free-market freedom and a decentralized organization of the economy. The goal of the individual to be economically productive reflects the need for fair competition in the market economy.

Need-induced drives generate a push of action, while situational incentives created by the environment of the individual trigger a certain behavior.

The economy can influence the incentives. The rules of the game that lead to rewards or sanctions form the institutional framework for behavior. The state must guarantee the economic freedom of the individual, but must also enable social contact in order to take account of the attachment motivation (motive of social inclusion). In addition, the state structures, especially for the authorities with citizen contact, must be kept accessible and be able to waive regulations and taxation, insofar as they complicate the economic processes for the actor and thus make processes opaque (social inclusion).

The tendency to draw satisfaction from physical, mental or emotional influence on others (power motivation) must be taken into account when assessing the behavior of politicians.

3.1.3 Human Intelligence and Social Performance

What abilities are decisive in life? What makes it possible for people to cope with the challenges from their environment? What makes people successful and which kind of intelligence do we need for social cooperation thus altruism and ethical behavior? These are questions about human intelligence. Today intelligence is mainly defined as the correctness and speed with which unknown tasks are solved.[25] There used to be three forms of intelligence identified. The ones necessary here are the mathematical, spatial and linguistic intelligence, whereby the mathematical is the most well known. Mathematics is understood here to be the pure form of abstract and logical thought. People gifted with this intelligence are able to use chains of proof and rules that can be recorded with figures. Mathematics is considered nature's blueprint because many laws of nature can be represented mathematically. The most famous of those with this feature of intelligence was Albert Einstein, the founder of the Theory of Relativity. The second, spatial intelligence, allows three-dimensional comprehension and processing of the environment as forms, spaces or objects. The embodiment of this form of intelligence is considered to be Michelangelo Buonarotti with his statue of David and the images in the Sistine Chapel with perfect perspective. The third traditional form of intelligence is a gift with languages. This

[25] See http://wirtschaftneudenken.blogspot.de/2010/09/abschied-vom-iq.html

allows hearing through words, written and verbal expression and independent reflection through writing. An example here would be Johann Wolfgang von Goethe with a vocabulary of around 90,000 words. The average person has between 2000 and 5000 words. These three traditional forms of intelligence have determined the way human capabilities are perceived and perhaps their valuation for decades. The explanatory power of these gifs for success in solving tasks in life is quite limited, however. According to the Harvard Professor for Psychology Howard Gardner, in the best case these three traditional forms of intelligence could only predict scholastic success to a certain extent. According to Gardner there are some careers whose demands are concentrated in these forms of intelligence, such as lawyers through formulations and verbal arguments, physicists who work with mathematical formulas or pilots who must think spatially. For most other careers however, such as managers, politicians, musicians etc., these criteria are not suited to determining potential. This fact caused the Gardner to investigate other forms of intelligence. In the 1980s he developed his radical concept of multiple types of intelligence, in which he included four additional gifts. In the meanwhile, research has identified a total of ten forms of intelligence.

First there are the special forms of intelligence, such as the naturalist, musical and kinesthetic intelligence. Naturalist intelligence refers to a particular comprehension of nature and its products. Foresters, biologists, veterinarians and top chefs would be careers for this group. Alexander von Humbolt, who discovered and explained many interconnections with his field research would a prime example of naturalist intelligence. The first example to come to mind for musical intelligence is the genius Wolfgang Amadeus Mozart. Kinesthetic intelligence is relatively unknown. Science considers it to be the ability to use one's body to complete tasks. A famous kinesthetic genius would be the silent film actor Charlie Chaplin.

The four most important forms of intelligence to have been recently identified are the existential, interpersonal, intrapersonal and emotional intelligence. Relationships between people, social competence or soft-facts had been completely neglected by the traditional forms of intelligence. Interpersonal intelligence allows one to recognize and understand the motives and desires of other people. In particular teachers, politicians and sales people need this kind of empathic ability. Only someone who can put him or herself in the shoes of others can motivate and recognize both strengths and weaknesses to then best apply, encourage and demand them, developing them optimally, as an ideal manager does. Another example is politicians who must recognize the desires of their voters in order to be successful.

The transitions between the abilities are fluid however, and there are many overlaps depending on the type of demands made. Thus rhetorical abilities belong to linguistic abilities as well as to interpersonal intelligence, since a good speaker must gauge what the listeners are receiving and react rhetorically to their reactions. Overlaps are particularly numerous for interpersonal relationships. This is how the American Daniel Goleman developed the concept of emotional intelligence in the mid-90s. He considers this to be not only recognizing and dealing with the feelings of others, but applies this to one's own feelings as well. Emotional intelligence is thus located between the interpersonal and intrapersonal intelligence as the capacity to deal with human emotions. Mahatma Gandhi represents an excellent example of emotional intelligence. He was able to judge the feeling of his compatriots, influence them and channel them into passive resistance as well as to control his own feelings in an exemplary manner, making him an excellent leader. He was a model for his compatriots in suffering. The nickname Gandhi translates as "large spirit." The intrapersonal capacity to understand one's self makes it possible to differentiate between realistic goals and personal dreams, an ability not to underestimated, as it is then possible to achieve an inner balance at live with inner harmony. In 1896 Sigmund Freud described scientifically for the first time how self-knowledge is the basis for human existence on earth, and inner peace. Internal balance and finding the right relationship between reality and a person's capacities and desires is the basis for internal force and perseverance, and thus for a person's long-term success.

The last three forms of intelligence for social competence are not only determining factors for managers, but also for the successful integration in a team. Only he who knows himself and understands others can offer his strengths and weaknesses to the team in a way that increases the team's ability to perform. The last of the new forms of intelligence is the existential intelligence. It is attributed mostly to philosophers, priests and authors, because they are capable of addressing the fundamental questions about the world and humanity. Immanuel Kant is our example here, who significantly contributed to modern thinking with his work "Critique of pure reason" (1781) and his categorical imperative,[26] as well as his thoughts on enlightenment. This intelligence can generally be characterized as the capacity to get to the source the past and future of things, or to put social or environmental observations into a larger perspective. This form of intelligence is therefore important when addressing that big picture of human structures. This also applies for economic science as the science of people in economic interconnections.[27]

For the question of the extent to which man behaves ethically, compassion, that is, sympathy with other people, plays an outstanding role. This is an emotion. In principle, it is therefore necessary to distinguish between a rational impact assessment and emotion-driven compassion. This also occurs in two separate brain areas, as the case of the railway worker Phineas Gage showed. In an accident, an iron rod, 1 m long and 3 cm wide, had been shot through his head. He survived this and, surprisingly, the basic cognitive basic functions were unaffected as perception (except for the loss of an eye), intelligence, memory and speech. Only his social intelligence seemed to be impaired. Before, he was a popular, prudent and successful personality, after the accident he had problems, long-term decisions and social contacts. It turned out in a later investigation that especially brain regions had been damaged, which are added to the processing of emotions.[28] As in experiments where the brain activity was measured by means of functional magnetic resonance

[26] People need to select maxims to guide their actions, which can simultaneously function as general laws.

[27] See Gardner (1983); Gardner et al., (1996); Gardner (1999) and Schlesinger (2006).

[28] See Holzmann (2015), p. 117.

tomographs (fMRI), emotional inhibitions occurred in subjects especially when: (1) a personal responsibility (ME) was (2) for direct physical damage (HURT) (3) A physically present or alive person (YOU) was present (MeHurtYou).[29]

Haidt et al. succeeded in demonstrating the influence of emotions caused by norms, in particular, on moral decisions by placing people before decision – making alternatives which did not result in objective harm but were morally problematic, such as the eating of the deceased dog before the Background that dog meat should taste good or use a bust American flag to wipe the toilet.[30]

Where do we place the character of morality with the background described above? Morality, like all characteristics, is partially inherent and can be helpful in solving unknown tasks in life, just like the forms of intelligence. It belongs to the social abilities, or more exactly to interpersonal intelligence. As we have already shown, morality is the basis for trust and thus also for productive human social existence. Repeated moral behavior inspires others to do the same, to compromise in transactions, to invest for example, and to trust in the later reciprocal action of a business partner, which leads moral people to experience more interpersonal success than immoral people. There is a negative form of interpersonal intelligence, which we call cleverness. We understand cleverness to be the ability to enrich one's self immorally at the cost of others, to gain advantages, without being discovered. This ability is unfortunately often a key to success in life. From the perspective of the society, this success should be prevented because it damages individuals and the system as a whole.

Pure altruism can be associated with empathy (empathy-altruism hypothesis). Batsons u.a. experimented with pity in 1981 using an electric shock experiment. They tested the extent to which the subjects were willing to accept the electric shocks as substitutes for a subject Elaine, if this signaled extreme suffering. The subjects were divided into four groups, for one group a similarity to Elaine was established and then it was open as to wheter the subject could leave after two rounds of watching the electric shock or if they had to watch even longer. The possibility of leaving was only entertained by subjects who did not identify with Elaine. If the test subjects were very similar to Elaine they stayed and were in large part ready to receive the electric shocks on her behalf.[31]

It seems that people can empathize with the suffering of other people (empathic emotion) when they take on the perspective of a suffering person or they perceive themselves as similar to the other person. Then they want to improve the other's situation. This behavior shows man as a social being. Since this behavior has asserted itself through evolution, it must not only have produced benefits in the group, but also favored the individual in reproduction at the very least.[32]

---

[29] See Greene et al. (2004).

[30] See Haidt et al. (1993).

[31] See Batson et al. (1981) and Batson and Shaw (1991), pp. 107–122.

[32] See Campbell (1965) and Brewer and Caporael (2006), pp. 143–161 and Kessler, Thomas/ Fritsche, Immo (2018), pp. 99.

Studies showed that altruistic behavior is associated with specific intrinsic rewards, as various studies have shown that charitable donations are activate areas of the brain that exhibit a high degree of overlap with areas (e.g., strata) that are activated when people receive positive social or financial rewards.[33]

Conclusion

The conclusions on can draw from these new findings are quite reassuring. When someone has not scored well in the traditional three forms of intelligence, it neither means that they will be unsuccessful, nor that they are dumb. Intelligence as the capacity to be successful in life is as complex and diverse as the challenges of life itself.

The types of intelligence show us the diversity of human abilities. With cooperation people can realize as society gains from division of labor, economies of large scale and specialization. Organized group work allows to combine the strength of each individual and thus to overcome the weaknesses of each individual (see the function of organizations in Sect. 5.4).

Analysis and problem simplification can be trained with a study in an orchestra score. In order to be successful in a group, one needs both interpersonal and emotional intelligence. There are many overlapping abilities, so that it seems almost impossible to definitively classify a person's intelligence or to evaluate someone in relation to their chances in life. Everyone has strengths and weaknesses that are often balanced, even at extremes. All too often we find engineers who cannot use their ingenious inventions because they lack the ability to sell it. Intelligence can also be learned to a certain degree. The fundamental abilities are inherited, but they can be increased by around 15% through training.

From the various forms of intelligence one can conclude that people are able to understand the effect of their behavior on the welfare of third parties and to feel compassion. Furthermore, they show that human nature goes far beyond the homo oeconomicus.

On the whole, it may be doubted that all the intelligentsia worked out by Gardner can be proved empirically. Up to now, social intelligence has been isolated and empirical proof has been given of a connection with the success of personal influence on people. In addition, links between the academic degree as well as age and social intelligence were identified.[34]

Comprehension Questions

1. What are the central motivations for human behavior?
2. How could be explained why cultures that had suffered very hard deprivations were subsequently very economically engaged?

---

[33] See Moll et al. (2006); Harbaugh et al. (2007); Fehr and Camerer (2007), pp. 419–427 and Levine and Manning (2014), p. 392.

[34] See Eshghi et al. (2013). Zur Diskussion See Gardner and Moran (2006).

3. Which forms of intelligence are important for moral thinking and decision-making?
4. Which forms of intelligence are important for a successful life?

3.1.4 Distribution and Performance

How do people react on distribution differences affecting themselves and others? Is there a sense of justice? And is there a relation between distribution and the willingness to perform?

Alan Sanfeys conducted the "ultimatum game" in the laboratory at Princeton University.[35] Two subjects are told to divide $10 amongst themselves. The first (proposer) get the whole amount and can decide how much he gives the other. The second (responder) can then decide whether he accepts or rejects the portion he is offered. If he rejects the offer, neither gets anything. At universities one can play the game with chewing gums.

Game 1: Ultimatum Game
Two students are to split 10 pieces of chewing gum. The first one receives everything and can determine how much he gives to the second. The second can then decide whether to accept or reject the gift. If he does not accept the money, they both get nothing.

Rational behavior would dictate that the second subject agree to any amount offered. Regardless of how much he is given, he would still be better off than if he were to reject it and both get nothing. People apparently behave quite differently, however. If the offer is seen as too low, many subjects rejected the offer completely and preferred to have nothing.[36] Brain activity values (MRT) showed that the lower the offer was, the more the prefrontal cortex (PFC), responsible for rational thinking, was overshadowed by the Insula, responsible for emotions. The interpretation of this experiment indicates that the positive decision to gain money was increasingly superimposed by the negative feeling of being treated badly by the other subject.[37]

This interesting neurological experiment from 2003 was lauded by the press for the realization that homo economicus is a fiction, yet the experiment can be

[35] See Sanfey et al. (2003).

[36] The ultimatum game was adapted and executed under competitive conditions with a proposer and several responders. Only the first responder to accept the proposer's offer received a payout. The responders accepted even very low offers in this situation. See Holzmann (2015), p. 130 and Roth et al. (1991). Such a something or nothing situation is not comparable to the competition based on performance as per the do-ut-des principle of the markets.

[37] See Sanfey et al. (2003). The ultimatum game has existed since the 1980s. See Güth et al. (1982).

interpreted differently if we take into account that humans are social animals, as Aristotle suggested.[38] We can interpret the second subject's rejection of an offer felt to be too low as an expression of the sense of fairness. It seems obvious that $10 should be split evenly among equals with $5 each. If we assume that humans are social animals descended from apes, we can call the behavior of rejecting a low offer irrational, yet goal-oriented and effective. How would such a group experiment play out in real life? By rejecting the offer, the second subject signals that he rejects the social behavior of the first subject as unfair. He is also showing the proposer that his behavior can have negative consequences for him in the group if the other members agree that he has violated a social norm, namely how sustenance is divided within a group. This behavior is programmed into us as humans and could not be denied in another experiment with different parameters. The refusal to accept the amount could alternatively mean that the second subject wishes to signal the first that he is not willing to be disparaged in the group with a lesser share of sustenance, and that the first subject has maneuvered himself into a conflict situation with his offer and the second subject will get him back at the next opportunity regardless of the experiment.[39]

Therefore, the Proposer's knowledge of the distribution is also crucial to the Responder. It has been shown that the responder accepts lower bids if he believes the Proposer unconsciously treats him unfairly.[40] In contrast, the amount of the amounts to be distributed has no influence on the behavior of the subjects since the same experiments in poorer cultures did not lead to substantially different results. Rather, the contributions depended on the civilizational development of the cultures. The more interactive, dependent and the more divided the labor of society was, the more was given`.[41]

Therefore, the Proposer's knowledge of distribution is also crucial for the Responder. It has been shown that the Responder accepts lower bids if he believes the Proposer unconsciously treats him unfairly.[42]In contrast, the amounts to be distributed have no influence on the behavior of the subjects.[43]

A variant of the ultimatum game is the dictator game.

Game 2: Dictator Game

Two students are to split 10 pieces of chewing gum. The first one receives everything and can determine how much he gives to the second. The second has to accept the offer.

In this game the second subject has no influence on the final distribution, rather he must accept what the first subject gives him. Here it would rationally maximize one's

---

[38] See Aristoteles (1944), 1253a.

[39] See Conrad (2010), pp. 125 and Fehr and Fischbacher (2003), pp. 785.

[40] See Kagel et al. (1996), pp. 100–110.

[41] See Henrich et al. (2005) and Beck (2014), pp. 279.

[42] See Kagel et al. (1996), pp. 100–110.

[43] See Henrich et al. (2005) and Beck (2014), pp. 279.

utility for the first subject to keep everything. The dictator game is normally played with 10$ instead of chewing gum. The experiment shows however, that on average about 30% is given to the second subject, again showing an altruistic sense of justice.[44]

Research on primates has also concluded that fairness is a central principle for creating cooperation in a group. Frans de Waal and Sarah Brosnan at Emory University in Atlanta conducted experiments with capuchin monkeys, in which different rewards – a grape or a cucumber – were given for the same effort. The monkeys refused the cucumber as a lesser reward for the same effort, leading De Waal and Brosnan to conclude that primates have an innate sense of fairness that has evolved to develop cooperation. Susan Perry from the Max Planck Institute for Evolutionary Anthropology in Leipzig also did experiments with capuchin monkeys and arrived at similar conclusions.[45]

The experiment also shows the influence of group behavior on economic decisions, which has been heretofore neglected in economic science. Fairness as an ethical value has concerned people as long as they have existed. Fairness, or justice, is the objective of the basic normative principle of human co-habitation (principle of social behavior).[46] This is the prerequisite for an individual to participate in the division of labor of a group. The individual will only adapt to group's demands and work cooperatively if his share from the labor distribution is felt to be fair. Without fairness there is no added value from labor distribution for our society and civilization (emergence). That means for a company as the group with which he earns his livings the employee will adapt to supervisors demands and work cooperatively if his share from the labor distribution is felt to be fair. If not he will stop cooperation, which is important information for leadership theory. To be successful the leader has to explain this distribution share to each individual in order to create motivation to work in a group.

The same must be true for the society as a group with which the individual earns his livings the he will work cooperatively if his share from the labor distribution is felt to be fair.

Yaari and Bar-Hillel[47] had young volunteers distribute 12 grapefruits and 12 avocados between Jones and Smith. The only important factor is how many vitamins both can gain from the fruits. Due to their differing nutritional predispositions, the doctors say that Jones can gain 100 mg of vitamins from each grapefruit but none from avocados, but Smith can get 50 mg from each fruit. If you wanted to maximize welfare, Jones would have to get all Grapefruits and Smith all of the avocados (Jones): 1200 mg + Smith 600 mg = 1800 mg of vitamins. Only 2% decided to do so while 82% of the subjects wanted to give the same benefits to both: Jones gets

[44] See Holzmann (2015), p. 129 and Kessler and Fritsche (2018), p. 101.

[45] See Brosnan and de Waal (2003); Perry (2003) and Brosnan and de Waal (2014).

[46] See Höffe (1992b), pp. 91.

[47] See Yaari and Bar-Hillel (1984).

8 grapefruit (800 mg) and Smith 4 grapefruit and all 12 avocados (800 mg, so together 1600 mg of vitamins).

People do not seem to strive for welfare maximization, but for equal distribution. As a compromise, the primary economic policy objective is to maximize gross domestic product in order to have a greater amount for redistribution via the secondary income distribution.

The desire for justice is so strong in people that they are willing to make sacrifices for it. Fehr and Fischbacher's third-party punishment game demonstrates this idea. A gets a sum and should divide it between herself and B. C also gets a sum and can use it to correct the division by three units downwards if he thinks that A did not split up fairly. He can thus reduce A's self-assigned amount by 3 if he is ready to give up one unit. Roughly 60% of the subjects make use of it in unfair distribution and thus sacrifice for the benefit of others for the sake of justice. However, this sacrifice for B tends to decrease sharply if C is included in A's original distribution. Above all, what counts is what C receives.[48]

There are further developments of the Ultimatum Game and the Dictator Game, which explore the human notions of fair distribution in more detail. Bolton and Ockenfels hereby determine an orientation of the subjects to an average payout, namely that people do not want to be worse off than the average. Fehr and Schmidt as well as Engelmann and Strobel determined that any kind of deviations of the distributions is not accepted.[49] Other studies have shown that the Unltimatum Game depends on the relative proportion of the amount to be distributed. The more the amount approaches half, which is considered fair, the more positive reactions can be detected in the brain (ventral striatum).[50] The Ultimatum Game shows sanctions for unequal distribution and the Dictator Game the willingness to surrender. Everyone preferred equal distribution.[51] These games, however, all refer to arbitrary distributions among objectively equal persons.

Fershtman, Gneezy and List test the tendency to equal distribution based on the dictator game. The dictator should decide if he gives himself $11 and the second player $2 or if each player gets $8. 75% preferred equal distribution, although they waived $3. This could be interpreted as needs-based, since the candidates had to assume the same needs.

Fershtman, Gneezy and List then introduced a performance and competitive component. The subjects had to do a GMAT test or tick off individual letters from a series of letters. If the dictator won the test, he got $11 and the second player only two dollars, if he lost, each player got back the same $8, so he would have equalized without effort. However, the participants struggled to win and get the $11, thus

---

48 See Fehr and Fischbacher (2004) and Beck (2014).

49 See Bolton and Ockenfels (2000); Fehr and Schmidt (1999), p. 275 and Engelmann, Dirk; Strobel, Martin (2000) and Beck (2014), pp. 275.

50 See Golnaz et al. (2007), pp. 339–347.

51 See Bolton and Ockenfels (2000), pp. 166–193; Fehr and Schmidt (1999), pp. 817–868 and Engelmann and Strobel (2000) and Beck (2014), pp. 275.

declining an equal distribution without effort.[52] To make sure that the reward incentive and not the fun of competitive play was the motivation, Fershtman, Gneezy and List turned the pay rule into a control group, giving the dictator, like the second player, $8 if the dictator won, but then the participants no longer made an effort. Apparently they refused an equal distribution on the basis of different performance. Yamagishi already showed the idea of performance justice in 1987. Thus, unequal distributions are considered to be acceptable if the payouts for all depend on the total service provided, but not if they are independent of the service.[53]

Fershtman, Gneezy and List explain the behavior as social norms, one for equal distribution and one for performance-based pay. The results in anonymous dictator games would seem to confirm their hypothesis. If the players know that neither the teammates nor the game leaders know how much they are giving away, the sharing rate drops to 10.5% (from 23.3%).[54]

List simulated the behavior in markets conducted as Gift Exchange Game. He first ran the sale of baseball cards in the lab and then on an anonymous market. The sellers were expected to deliver the lowest quality for profit maximization and the buyers were expected to maximize their gain by paying the lowest price. In the laboratory the participants could be observed, but not in the market. The result was that sellers in the lab offered better quality and customers paid more. In the markets they felt unobserved and sold the customers low quality at high prices.[55] We are generally born with this social behavior preprogrammed, as even small children share more when they feel they are being watched.[56] In spite of everything, equality remains a human need, albeit a minor one. It has been shown that rising inequality leads to less happiness, but more so in Europe than in the US.[57]

Whether one had to earn the money is decisive for the willingness to share, apart from the observation by third parties. Cherry, Frykblom and Shogren distributed $10 and $40 at first without work, and then the dictators made them work for it. Then the dictators were again asked if and how much they would give to the second player who had not worked. Only the administrator knew how much they gave, not the players. The dictators that gave nothing rose from 19% (or 15% at $40) to 79% (70% at $40) percent. Now, when not even the person administering the test knew whether the dictator shared, the percentage of dictators sharing nothing rose to 95% at 10€ and 97% at $40.[58]

Levine et al. tested to what extent group affiliation plays a role in helping to emphasize different social identities. Manchester United's football fans wrote one essay on how they like to be fans of Manchester United and another on why they like

[52] See Fershtman et al. (2012), pp. 131–144 and Beck (2014), pp. 277.

[53] See Yamagishi (1987).

[54] See Smith (2002).

[55] See List (2006) and Beck (2014), pp. 283.

[56] See Leimgruber et al. (2012).

[57] See Alesina, A.; Di Tella, Rafael; MacCulloch, Robert J. (2004), Beck (2014).

[58] See Cherry et al. (2002) and Beck (2014), pp. 277.

being football fans. Then they let the fans help injured spectators and found that after the first essay they were more likely to help the spectators with Manchester united jerseys and after the second essay people in all jerseys with club names were helped, including Liverpool fans, whereas spectators with jerseys not bearing a team name were helped less. So social identity is crucial and it can be influenced.[59]

Hein et al. found that willingness to help someone of one's own group correlated with activation in the anterior insula, a brain region activated by empathy, whereas the nucleus accumbens was activated when those outside of the group was not helped. This part of the brain is known to be activated when people enjoy the misfortune of others. Hein et al. also noted that the empathy-based insula was activated (identification) when an outsider was seen positively, making it likely that they would receive help despite belonging to another group.[60]

Singer et al. tested subjects' responses to fair and unfair behavior in connection with punishment. Punishments of fair individuals produced empathy (compassion) in the corresponding brain areas (fronto-insular and anterior cingulate cortices), whereas this pity greatly diminished for the punishment of people being unfair in males and activated brain hemispheres responsible for rewarding revenge feelings. This confirms the empirical studies on altruistic punishers (strong reciprocators). Other studies using fMRI brain scanners also showed neural rewards for punishing unfair behavior.[61]

The greater the identification, the more likely and more strongly one is to adopt group behavior and to favor one's own group members in resource distribution. According to Tajfel, identification with a group is defined as social identity is "that part of an individual's self-concept which derives from his knowledge of his membership of a social group (or groups) together with the emotional significance attached to that membership“.[62]

Conversely, an identification increases the willingness to work for the group and to share with the group members. This should be taken into account in taxation and redistribution within national groups. A country where citizens identify strongly with each other can redistribute more because the willingness to share with other group members is greater. Thus it can be assumed that in states such as the USA, which have a relatively heterogeneous society, the willingness to co-finance a social system through taxes will be lower.

Conclusion

Altruism and compassion do exist. A limited amount of redistribution can thus be justified, because it enhances welfare. As the differences between public and non-public behavior show, here too the social norms that can also differ culturally are decisive. If there is no income, people tend to regard equal distribution as fair. However, the willingness to pay something from earned income is much lower and

---

[59] See Levine et al. (2005), pp. 443–453.

[60] See Hein et al. (2010), pp. 149–160; Singer and Lamm (2009); Singer et al. (2006) and Levine, M., & Manning, R. (2014), pp. 393.

[61] See DeQuervain et al. (2004) and Singer, T., et al. (2006) and Fehr and Camerer (2007).

[62] See Tajfel (1978), p. 69.

there is a conflict of interest regarding willingness to perform. The willingness to work with equal distribution for income is very low.

Subjectively, fairness is understood as an ethical value. The classical world considered it a fundamental virtue as well as a guiding principle for action, which prevented any overreaching one's fellow humans. Even though there are no sanctioned norms, a righteous person behaves ethically by not taking advantage of others even when he has the opportunity; he in fact gives others their share.

People strive for equal distribution, especially when they identify with other group members. But they reject an equal distribution with different performance of the group members. The performance motivation decreases with equal distribution, which redistributive policy must take into account. It is therefore not advisable to compensate for income differences caused by performance. The purpose of this is to maximize the gross domestic product as a distribution mass. A progressive income tax must not reduce the achievement motivation so much that welfare losses occur. Not only would this not be considered fair, it would also reduce the redistributive mass.

In the company, management must consider the employees' strong sense of justice. The distribution of income in the company must be explained to the employees so that it is accepted and the employee remains motivated. In addition, a key task of management is to ensure that the company is also justified among the employees. The same is true for the distribution of income in the society.

Comprehension Questions

1. What function do fairness and justice have for the cooperation of humans?
2. Which experiments prove altruism and compassion?
3. How can one explain altruism and compassion? What are the requirements for this?
4. Which distribution do people consider fair? What influences her attitude? Justify your assessment with the experiments presented above.
5. Why are rules with sanctions important for human co-operative living?
6. What is the function of strong reciprocators?

3.2 Behavior and Competition

Groups are economically relevant both as companies and as societies of states. Competition can take place between these kinds of groups and within the groups.

Groups arise when several people feel that they belong to each other (definition).

Only a common stay such as in a waiting room is not enough. However, if it comes to a delay of an aircraft, but there may be a solidarity effect through the shared delay. Groups have similar knowledge, describe themselves in a similar way and follow similar rules, norms.[63]

Norms are social behavioral guidelines (definition). For instance: Do not smoke if others are eating. Respect the property of others, etc. The elementary norms are incorporated into the laws of a society. Empirical studies show that apart from the damage caused by an action, the social norms, or the ethical consensus, are decisive for whether a person behaves ethically or unethically.[64]

For sociology, norms are the unwritten rules that make the conflict-free coexistence of many people in a society possible. Unclear or missing norms lead to anomie-producing situations, meaning a lack of social integration. Too much or too restrictive of norms cause special stress situations and contradictory norms create norm conflicts. If a society has many different groups or sub-societies (pluralistic society), it will also have many different and conflicting norms, as each sub-society has its own norms. If a person moves in different sub-groups he must inevitably violate the behavior norms of the sub-groups. This applies not only to immigration but also between generations. A youth must behave according to the rules of his age group in order to be recognized there, but he is also dependent on the acceptance of his parents. And there are other norms of behavior. In contrast to norms, conventions are voluntary agreements between people, for instance the terms for objects in a language, or shaking hands with greetings.

According to Darwin's theory of evolution, the sociobiological concept emphasizes the adaptive value, thus the value-generating value of group formation. In the group, people could hunt better, raise children and support each other in emergencies. The evolutionary advantage favored people who could socialize in groups, and as a stimulus created the need for group affiliation. They survived and reproduced and the group orientation has been passed on. And indeed, group orientation is found in all human cultures, which is an indication of an evolutionary context.[65]

As early as 1954, Berkowitz showed in an experiment that the enforcement of norms in this case specifically motivates and thus the performance depends positively on the group feeling of belonging, the so-called group cohesion. Four groups were to produce ashtrays with three tasks in a division of labor (cutting, painting and pasting together). He manipulated the group affiliation feeling by suggesting to the groups that the psychological tests had shown that they fit well or not well together and measured the performance after 12 min each. In the next step he faked messages from group members to establish norms. There were standards with high performance standards: "Let's try to set a new record!", "Let's keep up a fast, steady clip!" And weak performance standards: "You are getting way ahead of me relax", "Take it easy, I'm tired!". Both types of norms affected group performance relative to

[63] See Kessler and Fritsche (2018).

[64] See Singhapakdi et al. (1996); Frey (2000) and Butterfield et al. (2000).

[65] See Bowlby (1958); Baumeister and Leary (1995) and Nijstad, B. A., & Van Knippenberg, D. (2007), p. 441.

baseline performance, but only if the group was highly cohesive. With low cohesion there was no influence.[66]

The stronger the identification with a group, the more members conform in their behavior. This is called self-stereotyping. Individuals are at least partially absorbed in the collective by behaving in accordance with the prototypes of the group that demonstrate the group's characteristics, rules, standards, and ideals. Addressing a group membership reinforces this behavior, as demonstrated by psychologists who became more empathic when they were reminded of their professional orientation.[67]

Initiation rites can enhance the identification of individuals with the group. Gerard and Mathewson divided four groups. Two were given weak electric shocks and two were given strong shocks. Half of the group was also told that the electric shocks are a condition to be included in a discussion group. It turned out that the subjects who received strong jolts to join the discussion group rated them the most positive and found the other members most attractive.[68] The harder or more expensive admission into the group is, the higher the individual rated the group affiliation. Gangs or religions, therefore, usually have tough induction rituals because they want to achieve strong group cohesion and subordination of the individual to group norms. Rituals, shared prayers and dance also reinforce the sense of community among religions and the coordination of the group. The higher the identification of the individuals with the group, the smoother the coordination of joint actions will be. Expectations as reliance on the behavior of the other group members are stabilized.[69,70]

What sanctions can groups use to force an individual to comply with the group norms? They range from the withdrawal of recognition by the group, to mobbing to exclusion. Exclusion is the hardest sanction. During simulated exclusion, reactions in the pain center of the brain have been detected.[71]

People rely on social contact to be happy. Everyone needs social acceptance. According to various studies the presence of other people contributes to a feeling of wellbeing, especially if they are familiar people with whom a social relationship already exists. Everyone needs social belonging. There are several studies showing that positive social relationships even promote good health. Berkman and Syme, for example, used a random sample of the population (nearly 7000 inhabitants of Alameda, California) or people with positive social relationships and found a survival probability two to three times greater (2.3 in men and 2.8 in women) after

---

[66] See Berkowitz (1954).

[67] See Turner et al. (1994) and Hogg and Turner (1987) and Kessler and Fritsche (2018), pp. 117.

[68] See Gerard, H. B., & Mathewson, G. C. (1966), pp. 278–287.

[69] See Platow et al. (2012).

[70] See Kessler, Thomas/Fritsche, Immo (2018), pp. 119.

[71] See Richman and Leary (2009), pp. 365–383; Eisenberger et al. (2003), pp. 290–292 and Kessler and Fritsche (2018).

9 years.[72] This is currently justified in the literature by an evolutionary advantage. People who could rely on the support of others have survived and have been able to reproduce.[73] Here one differentiates between emotional and instrumental social support.[74]

Schachter simulated group socialization processes by inserting dissenters. Since they did not adapt their opinion to the group, they were first marginalized, no longer talked to and ignored. Finally, they were excluded.[75]

What pay best motivates groups? Rosenbaum et al. (1980) showed that competition within small groups can be counterproductive. They had teams of three build towers with building blocks and varied the payoffs from cooperative (everyone gets the same amount) and only the best gets a reward. The amount of blocks built was decisive. With cooperative reward the group members got the same amount and in the case of pure competition the best member was rewarded for all built blocks. An intermediate solution would be, for example, that 50% of the bricks are credited to all and 50% to the best. It showed that as more competition was brought into the group, the result became worse and worse. The group members did not cooperate anymore by taking turns in setting the blocks and got negative attitudes towards the other group members. Finally, the towers collapsed more often as competition increased.[76]

In the case of individually identifiable and non-interdependent tasks, however, a productivity-increasing competition was also identified. The individuals try to outdo each other in group performance (social competition, interpersonal competition).[77] Hüffmeier and Hertel showed this on the basis of the relay swimming. Here, the individual performance is very transparent and their importance increases the later they start in the group. It turns out that thanks to this motivational effort, the group performance is well above the sum of the individual performances.[78] In terms of transparency of performance, there is also the Köhler effect, in which the weaker group members work harder to not be responsible for poor group performance.[79] Finally, there is social compensation where the stronger group members try to compensate for the lower performance of the weaker group members. Social compensation occurs when the group goals are accepted by everyone, as Williams and Karau have shown.[80]

James and Greenberg, however, showed that competition between groups increases performance. They allowed groups of different universities to solve

[72] See Berkman and Syme (1979) and Karremans, Johan C./ Finkenauer, Catrin (2014), pp. 403.

[73] See Baumeister and Leary (1995), p. 499.

[74] See Karremans, Johan C./ Finkenauer, Catrin (2014), pp. 403.

[75] See Schachter (1951) and Karremans and Finkenauer (2014), p. 451.

[76] See Rosenbaum et al. (1980), pp. 626–642.

[77] See Stroebe et al. (1996).

[78] See Hüffmeier and Hertel (2011).

[79] See Köhler (1926), pp. 274–282 and Witte (1989).

[80] See Williams, K. D., & Karau, S. J. (1991) and Schulz-Hardt, Stefan/Brodbeck, Felix C. (2014), pp. 478.

anagram problems, once independently and again by emphasizing direct comparison and group affiliation. The group performance without this emphasis was much lower.[81] This corresponds to the market competition between companies as groups. Businesses can thus increase their productivity by increasing group cohesion and ensuring the acceptance of corporate goals.

The presence of other people can be performance enhancing (so-called social relief) or inhibiting. As studies have shown, this depends on whether there is a valuation expectation, and whether the actor thus feels dependent on the judgment of others. If the work is difficult, observation by others tends to be detrimental to performance but more stimulating in simple activities.[82]

The performance of groups is influenced by coordination and motivation. In addition to the sense of group cohesion (see above), motivation is influenced by the awareness of one's own significance for group performance. Thus, a football team classified clearly lower can win against the favorites, because here the players think that their performance contributions are necessary (free-riding). On the other hand, social loafing is when the group members limit their performance because they can hide in the group. Decisive here is to make the individual's contribution in the group transparent and to sanction free riding as shown in the public good games (see above). Coordination losses occur when the performance of the individual group members cannot be optimally aggregated, such as in tug of war, if not all use their power simultaneously.

However, the nature of the group performance is also crucial to the optimal organization of the group. There are tasks with a positive interdependence of group performance, because you can only succeed together as a group, such as in a football team (one wins or loses together). This promotes cooperation, whereas being negatively interdependent means the contribution of the individual without the team is what brings success.

For example, in tug-of-war or building a tower of building blocks as discussed above, we have an additive performance, while in team tasks the weakest group member determines group performance (eg mountaineering). Here it is advisable as far as possible not to form a single large group, but several small ones. For example, a group of powerful mountain climbers could push ahead. In disjunctive tasks, the performance of the best group member is the most important, such as for solving math problems.[83]

It is easy to describe the impact on group performance using the example of brainstorming groups. According to Osgood and others, groups should be able to generate more effective ideas than individuals because they creatively stimulate each other. However, experiments showed that the group members can generate about twice as many ideas individually as in the group. Diel and Stroebe showed that performance reduction is multi-causally conditioned by both motivation and

[81] See James and Greenberg (1989), pp. 604–616.

[82] See Kessler and Fritsche (2018), pp. 123.

[83] See Kessler and Fritsche (2018), pp. 125 and Karremans and Finkenauer (2014), p. 474.

coordination. To show this function they told one group that only the group performance for an exercise counted and compared those results with a group told that the individual performance was recorded. They also examined the influence of rating anxiety by filming a group in brainstorming and announcing that they would be showing the film to fellow students. The filmed group created far fewer ideas than the unfilmed ones. Diel and Stroebe then studied coordination effects by gradually adjusting the conditions of the individuals (nominal group) to those of the brainstorming group by using microphones. When participants had to wait to contribute their ideas until the others had made their contributions the results were very similar to that of the brainstorming group, which shows that the contributions of the group ultimately interfere with each other and brainstorming should be a phase with individual idea generation before discussing the results in the group. Diel and Stroebe discovered that brainstorming gives the impression of a high level of mutual creative stimulation because the group members themselves in the discussion also take the ideas of others into account.[84]

Moods and emotions are transmitted in groups. Barsade had an actor in a group transmit moods through facial expressions and accents. When communicating positive emotions, the group behaved more cooperatively, and there were fewer conflicts. Sy, Coté, and Saavedra came to the same conclusion, letting a group leader transmit emotions. Here the group performance increases when the group leader exhibits positive emotions.[85]

How does competition affect the relationship between groups? Sherif and Campbell developed the theory of realistic group conflict. This theory is based on maximizing utility and rational behavior in individuals, but more on the specific characteristics of individuals. In order to maximize its utility for public goods, division of labor (emergence), or in conflicts, individuals need groups. The achievement of goals depends on other individuals (interdependence).

There is a positive interdependence when other individuals contribute positively or are necessary to achieving one's goals, and negative when others are against one's goals because they pursue other conflicting goals. Attitudes to the other individuals and groups are developed from these interdependencies. Anyone who can be used to further ones's goal becomes the object of positive feelings, while those who are not helpful are seen negatively.

Sheriff and others tested the theory of realistic group conflict as part of vacation camps for children ages 10–12. They formed groups of children who did not know each other or where influences of origin, personality, or interpersonal attraction would not be factors. Group norms, structures, loyalty, and positive attitudes quickly developed among the group members. In the best-known Robbers Cave study, they engaged the groups in competitive situations with a prize awarded for the best group. Thus, all actions that contributed to the success of one's own group were bad for the

[84] See Osgood et al. (1957); Diehl and Stroebe (1987); Stroebe and Diehl (1994) and Kessler and Fritsche (2018), pp. 127.

[85] See Barsade (2002), pp. 644–675; Sy et al. (2005), pp. 295–305.

success of the other groups. The tensions between the groups became so strong that the groups yelled at each other and threw apples at each other or tore the tents of the other group. Then the game leaders gave the groups tasks that they could only solve together, cooperatively. For example they were to pull out a truck with food that was allegedly stuck in the mud, or repair the pipes for water supply. As a result, the conflicts and negative attitudes between the groups diminished and even friendships between the groups developed.[86] This shows the importance of common economic interests and projects in international understanding. Global trade, and customs and economic unions in particular, can reduce the negative attitudes between national groups. Here it is important that the benefits are shared with the group members as well. European integration would be an example of such an approach to international understanding.

Henri Tajfel et al. studied group relationships without interdependence by arbitrarily forming groups randomly and not providing group members with information about the other group members. There was also no interaction between the group members. The subjects should now distribute money among the trial participants. The subjects preferred the members of their own group. Even the knowledge of belonging to a group leads to behavioral changes, by favoring one's own group members. The subjects were even willing to give up money for their own group, if they could distinguish their group from the other group. Giving rewards to the subjects was not influenced by the profit for all participants, but only based on group success.[87]

Experiments showed that people have a need for self-determination. They want the freedom to take their destiny into their own hands and react to restrictions of this freedom with resistance (so-called reactance).[88]

In 1974 Zanna and Cooper had a group of students voluntarily write an essay against freedom of expression, and forced another group to do so. The assessment of a ban on freedom of expression was much more positive for the voluntary group, thus the resistance (reactance) to write something that was not their own opinion was lower because they were willing to do it. There was cognitive dissonance involved in writing the essay, so participants adapted their attitude to avoid an unpleasant feeling about acting contrary to their own opinion. A group that had been given a placebo tablet that supposedly caused negative emotions did not adjust their attitudes because they attributed the negative sense of cognitive dissonance to the tablet.[89] The state must therefore guarantee the freedom of its citizens. Freedom also becomes an independent value in economic activity.

[86] See Sherif (1966), pp. 71; Sherif et al. (1961).

[87] See Tajfel et al. (1971), pp. 149–178 and Kessler and Fritsche (2018), pp. 161.

[88] See Brehm and Brehm (1981).

[89] See Zanna and Cooper (1974), pp. 703–709, pp. 140.

Conclusion

Groups are economically relevant both as companies and as societies of states. People take on roles within groups that influence their behavior. Individuals adapt to the group in order to gain social recognition (social comparison process or aspiring to conformity). Norms create moral behavior, as has been shown in experiments.[90]

As early as 1954, Berkowitz showed in an experiment that the enforcement of norms in this case specifically motivates and thus the performance depends positively on the group feeling of belonging, the so-called group cohesion. The stronger the identification with a group, the more members conform in their behavior and the smoother the coordination of joint actions. Expectations as reliance on the behavior of the other group members are stabilized. The knowledge of belonging to a group leads to behavioral changes, by favoring one's own group members.

People rely on social contact to be happy. Everyone needs social acceptance.

The sanctions to force an individual to comply with the group norms range from the withdrawal of recognition by the group, to mobbing to exclusion. Exclusion is the hardest sanction. Studies showed that if dissenters not adapt their opinion to the group, they are first marginalized, no longer talked to and ignored and finally excluded.

Competition within small groups can be counterproductive. In the case of individually identifiable and non-interdependent tasks, however, a productivity-increasing competition was also identified. The individuals try to outdo each other in group performance (social competition, interpersonal competition). It turns out that thanks to this motivational effort, the group performance is well above the sum of the individual performances. In terms of transparency of performance, there is also the Köhler effect, in which the weaker group members work harder to not be responsible for poor group performance. Finally, there is social compensation where the stronger group members try to compensate for the lower performance of the weaker group members. Social compensation occurs when the group goals are accepted by everyone.

Competition between groups increases performance. This corresponds to the market competition between companies as groups. Businesses can thus increase their productivity by increasing group cohesion and ensuring the acceptance of corporate goals.

The performance of groups is influenced by coordination and motivation. In addition to the sense of group cohesion (see above), motivation is influenced by the awareness of one's own significance for group performance. On the other hand, social loafing is when the group members limit their performance because they can hide in the group. Decisive here is to make the individual's contribution in the group transparent and to sanction free riding as shown in the public good games (see above). Coordination losses occur when the performance of the individual group

---

[90] See Hewstone, M. und Martin, R. (2007), pp. 374; Jonas et al. (2007); Fehr and Fischbacher (2003), p. 786 and Fehr and Fischbacher (2001); Frank (1988, 2004) and Gürerk and Rockenbach (2006).

members cannot be optimally aggregated, such as in tug of war, if not all use their power simultaneously. However, the nature of the group performance is also crucial to the optimal organization of the group. Moods and emotions are transmitted in groups. When communicating positive emotions, the group behaved more cooperatively, and there were fewer conflicts, thus productivity increased.

The theory of realistic group conflict shows with its studies the importance of common economic interests and projects in international understanding. Global trade, and customs and economic unions in particular, can reduce the negative attitudes between national groups. Here it is important that the benefits are shared with the group members as well. European integration would be an example of such an approach to international understanding.

Experiments showed that people have a need for self-determination. They want the freedom to take their destiny into their own hands and react to restrictions of this freedom with resistance (so-called reactance).

Comprehension Questions

1. When do people orient their behavior to groups?
2. What remuneration criteria work in and between groups?
3. How to prevent social loafing (free riding) in groups?
4. Why does brainstorming reduce group performance?

3.3 Competition Versus Cooperation

Role Game Individualism Versus Collectivism

Each participant gets seven clothespins. The goal is to attach as many clothespins as possible to the other participants. After 30 s play stops and clothespins are counted. Round 2 follows with the aim of removing as many clothespins as possible from the others. The participants fight for the clothespins. After 30 s again play is stopped and clothespins counted. The game host now asks the participants why they fought against each other. He never said anything about competition. Through cooperation, they would have progressed much further (The game was explained in a talk by Dirk von Vopelius at the IHK in Nuremberg on June 10th 2015).

With cooperation people can realize gains from division of labor, economies of large scale and specialization. Organized group work allows to combine the strength of each individual and thus to overcome the weaknesses of each individual. However, it is even more rewarding to let the others work for oneself and to benefit from the group work. The same is true for economic transactions. It is more rewarding to defraud the business partner by withholding the promised quid pro quo. If this is common the welfare enhancing effect of trading (the free lunch) could not be realized.

The dilemma of social cooperation for a functioning social cooperation is as follows (see Fig. 3.1): The best case for A is if A behaves uncooperatively, but B

Fig. 3.1 Payoff matrix dilemma of social cooperation. * Nash equilibrium is the worst case for all (Nash: No one can unilaterally improve through another strategy)

	B behaves cooperatively	B does not behave cooperatively
A behaves cooperatively	5, 5	0, 6
A does not behave cooperatively	6, 0	1, 1*

does not. This is the free rider position. The worst case for a person A is if he behaves cooperatively, but the other person B does not. B is in the same decision-making situation. The result is the combination in which both persons operate uncooperatively, thus the worst case for all (Nash equilibrium). The gains from cooperation cannot be realized.

Cooperative behavior in practice is a public good in economic terms. The benefits of cooperative behavior of a society benefit all who are a part of it. The benefit is arbitrarily divisible, so not rival, and no one can be excluded. This also applies to teamwork. There is a free-rider problem, however (see Fig. 3.1). There is an incentive not to participate in the group performance because one cannot be excluded from the group's success.

Rational utility maximization, however, does not necessarily mean harm to third parties. For example, in game theory multi-round games show that decision-makers learn from their decisions and take into account the other's harmful counter-reaction, which is why they no longer maximize their usefulness in the short term. From a game theory point of view, games over several rounds have shown behavior to be profit-maximizing if one behaves first cooperatively and only if the other does not cooperate, to counter this with a likewise uncooperative behavior (trigger or tit-for-tat strategy).

The trigger or tit-for-tat games describe the underlying conflict between individual and collective rationality. In the prisoner's dilemma, maximizing individual utility at the cost of third parties is in direct opposition to collective benefit through social gains, e.g. access to collective goods such as a clean environment. In the 1960s, Anatol Rapoport and Albert Chammah used experiments to show that cooperation begins if games such as the prisoner's dilemma are played repeatedly. Based on computer simulations, Robert Axelrod later analyzed the conditions under which cooperation comes into being. In this context the tit-for-tat strategy suggested by Rapoport maximized results. This strategy has its strengths and weaknesses. The strategy says to play fair and never fleece or injure your opponent. Only if your opponent behaves uncooperatively, should you do the same. This strategy maintains the possibility for opponents to gain more only as long as they behave cooperatively, and to gain less if they are uncooperative. The motivation is thus to be cooperative and receive sanctions if you are not. The regulated sanctions would be the norms of the game. Exploitative strategies harm one's self and the other, because the gains from cooperation disappear. In the end, maximizing individual gain at the cost of another party means less net utility. Rapoport calls the principle behind this strategy "in weakness is strength," and recommends it as a leitmotif in his studies on arms races and conflict avoidance.[91] But this is only true for smaller groups. The more players are in the game the less they can see the connection between their (un-) cooperative behavior and the reaction of the others.

The issue of cooperation benefits from public goods can also be illustrated with a game. A **public goods game** consists of say five people who must each pay $10 into a pot. If everyone pays in, the money in the pot doubles, which is meant to represent the added value of public goods. If not everyone pays in, the public good is not created and the sum is divided by five and paid back out. In the worst case scenario a player could pay in $10 and get back $2.

Game 3: Public Goods Game
Play the public goods game with chewing gum.

Give at least three people two pieces of chewing gum each. Tell them if they all put the chewing gum in a pot or in a cap below the table then you will give them an additional chewing gum each. If there are not two from each person in the pot all the chewing gum is distributed equally between the players.

The experiment shows that in the case of public goods made available, the initial trust decreases over several rounds of play because of the free-rider issue.[92] The player does not know how the others behave. Best case: he does not pay but he gets 1.3 pieces of chewing gum (3 players) and does not risk anything. Worst case: he gives 2 pieces and all others do not, then he gets 0.30 pieces back.

In a public goods game, 40–60% of players are cooperative at the beginning. This behavior decreases when they notice that they are hurting themselves and the cooperative good is not being created. They then play up to ten rounds of anonymous play cooperatively and then become uncooperative.[93] There is always a base group of players who insist on being uncooperative and try to maximize their gain to the detriment of the other players. These free riders make up about one third of players. Altruistic rewards and punishments, which are also at the cost of the participants, can discipline the free riders into more cooperative behavior, which can allow the public good to be created to everyone's benefit.[94] The public good stands for every advantage human beings gain from cooperation.

With cooperation people can realize gains from division of labor, economies of large scale and specialization. Organized group work allows to combine the strength of each individual and thus to overcome the weaknesses of each individual. We find

[91] See Rapoport and Chammah (1970); Axelrod (1987) and Schwaninger (2008).

[92] See Holzmann (2015), p. 131.

[93] See Fehr and Fischbacher (2003), p. 786.

[94] See Fehr and Fischbacher (2003), p. 786 and Fehr and Fischbacher (2001). Fehr and Gächter (2000), pp. 980–994.

these gains from cooperation in the economy and in companies. In the first case the government has to form an institutional framework that prohibits fraud and in the second case the manager has to punish free riding in the company.

Fehr, Fischbacher, Gürerk et al. emphasize the role of so-called "strong reciprocators," meaning players that punish uncooperative free riders even though it is to their detriment.[95] Emotions motivate the strong reciprocators to set the norms despite the loss they may suffer. Altruistic sanctioning of uncooperative behavior can be motivated by gratefulness, or a desire for retaliation. Without emotions no one would punish another to their own detriment. Getting upset over uncooperative behavior creates a sense of gratification and thus a net benefit for inflicting the punishment, which makes altruistic punishments possible.[96] Fehr and Fischbacher showed that over 60% of neutral third parties will intervene in the case of game behavior perceived as unfair and uncooperative to impose fairness and cooperation even if it puts them at a disadvantage.[97] We are talking about the sense of justice that makes us human. The sense of justice is why cooperative behavior in a group gets enforced. There are sanctions meted out, even though doing so requires effort and the sense of justice unites the group in its behavior.

The strong reciprocity goes far beyond the reciprocal altruism, because no countervailing countermeasures can be expected in the future, but the individual harms himself for the system. The group interest is placed above the individual interest.

These games also show the importance of societal sanctions (norms) and learning/socialization. The great majority of players enter the game in a spirit of cooperation, but they are willing to change that behavior if the advantages of cooperating turn to disadvantages. Such an experience is also part of the learning process, such as the role that reputation plays. If there is an option to switch to a game where sanctions are possible, it will be taken in order enjoy public goods. With time the players are able to establish norms, allowing punishments to diminish greatly.[98] The tit-for-tat strategy was observed during these games as well. Thus most players saw their cooperative contribution increase along with that of the other players.[99]

It maximizes one's advantage to be uncooperative when playing just one round of the game, yet cooperative if playing several rounds. In other words, if the other players can neither defend themselves nor retaliate it is advantageous to fleece one's opponents, behaving unethically to the detriment of others, but not if they are able to defend their interests.

---

[95] "Strong reciprocators bear the cost of rewarding or punishing even if they gain no individual economic benefit whatsoever from their acts." Fehr and Fischbacher (2003), p. 785. See Gürerk and Rockenbach (2006). In the games they can pay for the punishment of the freerides.

[96] See Föhr and Lenz (1992), pp. 153 and Frank (1988, 2004).

[97] See Fehr and Fischbacher (2003).

[98] See Fehr and Fischbacher (2003).

[99] See Falk (2003), p. 147 and Fehr and Fischbacher (2001).

It is therefore not surprising that many ethical misdeeds have taken place within the finance sector within the last few years, since the games are generally played with just one round. No one even knows their business partner on the stock market. The bad subprime credits were mostly sold through the stock markets. If the buyer could have prosecuted the seller, the worthless sales would never have reached such a level because it would not have maximized utility to do so. Anywhere there is a long-term business relationship, or legal damage compensation is easy to obtain, it is not utility maximizing to injure a business partner.

We can observe however, that business is sometimes conducted such that this utility-maximizing strategy is contradicted. There are fields of u-pick flowers, and self-serve newspaper kiosks in the city, where one can cut flowers or take a paper without paying for it. Not paying would be the rational utility maximization strategy, since the "buyer" would not fear any reprisal. These offers exist nonetheless, which means that many people behave ethically and socially, instead of rationally utility-maximizing.

There have been several studies on human behavior using errant pieces of mail. Letters with postage were tossed into a mailbox at a rate of almost 80%. If the letter contained money, still more than 50% were forwarded.[100] In an experiment in which a wallet was placed in the letter, passersby in New York forwarded untouched wallets at a rate of almost 50%.[101] Gneezy's sender-receiver game experiment using students showed[102] that many people tend towards the truth, even if they do worse because of it. Asymmetrical information is thus not always used to one's advantage.

The results of these experiments can be explained by altruism, honesty as a human character trait or by corresponding social norms. That the addressees of the letter were unknown, and thus the finder could not identify with them, speaks for the explanation that moral behavior derives from norms.[103] On the other hand, there are no sanctions in this example that would create the norms, since the behavior was believed to be unobserved.

The individual becomes part of the collective as soon as he or she assumes a social role. The deindividuation through role assignments and social norms is made clear in the "Stanford Prison Experiment" by Haney, Banks and Zimbardo.[104] Stanford University researchers built a prison in the basement of the Psychological Institute and assigned 24 "normal, average and healthy" students the roles of prison guards and inmates. The experiment took 2 weeks but had to be stopped after 6 days because the guards tortured the prisoners too much.

---

[100] See Lück and Manz (1973).

[101] See Hornstein et al. (1968).

[102] See Gneezy (2005), p. 387.

[103] See Hausmann and McPherson (2006), p. 86.

[104] See Haney et al. (1973), pp. 69–97; Zimbardo (2006), pp. 47–53 and Zimbardo et al. (2000), pp. 193–237.

Guards and prisoners wore different clothes and got so deep into their roles that the sense of individual identity and responsibility got lost (deindividuation). New behavioral norms developed, although there had been no explicit influence from the experimenter. The experiment recalls the treatment of Iraqi prisoners in Abu Ghraib prison in 2003.[105]

In 1955 Solomon E. Asch showed through an experiment in which individuals must say which of three lines is the longest that approx. 37% opted for the wrong group opinion if it was presented sufficiently strongly and dominantly. With the Asch Conformity Experiment, Asch proved that individuals can adapt to wrong group opinions if the group is self-assured.[106]

According to social psychology, cultural/societal influences inform human behavior, which deviates from the homo economicus stereotype. Examples include various gestures and the strongly self-centered Western cultures as opposed to Asian cultures. It is also important to know how people adapt to cognitive dissonance, which might be created by an immoral environment. The Ash Conformity Experiment proved that individuals even adopt a false group opinion if the group presents its view with self-confidence. We humans therefore tend to over evaluate the way something is being presented. This also explains why managers who are so self-confident that they do not question themselves and never admit mistakes are more successful than those that correct themselves. However, this also results in more mistakes.

The larger the group, the stronger its influence on opinion if it represents the majority. Asch later showed that the pressure to conform wears off as soon as the majority opinion is contrasted with a contradictory opinion. Having social support for correct judgment is not the crucial factor, but whether there are other opinions at all. For example, Asch had an assistant give a second false opinion, which led to more subjects being willing to stand up for their correct opinion.[107]

Allen and Levine noted that influencing opinion also depends on the acceptance of opinion leaders in the group (social support), and Bond and Smith (1996) found in a meta-study that collectivist cultures tend to be more opinion-conformant than individualistic cultures.[108]

Three reasons are given to explain the tendency of individuals to adjust their assessment to that of the group opinion. First, only the group can effectively pursue a goal, so the group members must agree in their assessment. Second, due to uncertainty, the individual may question their opinion (informative influence) and correct it, and thirdly adapt to be accepted by group members (normative influence).[109]

---

[105] See Hewstone and Martin (2014), p. 278.

[106] Vgl. Asch (1951) and Jonas et al. (2014a, b), pp. 9 and Levine and Manning (2014), p. 379.

[107] See Asch (1987), p. 477.

[108] See Allen and Levine (1971) and Bond and Smith (1996).

[109] See Hewstone and Martin (2014), p. 283.

All the influences on group decisions that lead to an informative exchange being compromised, so that informational rather than normative decisions will be made, are called groupthinks. The group members strive for conformity at the expense of a realistic appraisal of alternative courses of action.[110]

Conclusion
Based on the examples, we can see that an individual can be in conflict with the collective, or other people, and yet that individual is dependent on others in the pursuit of their own interests, if those interests must be realized in a group. Dependency on other people does automatically limits one's freedom, however. Group-dependent goals cannot be achieved without considering the interests of other group members, which to a certain extent subordinates the individual to the collective, in order to benefit from the group goods. The desirability of the goods, as well as the necessity of individual adaptation, will tend to increase along with the cultural division of labor (emergence).

Group adaptation behavior can become market-relevant if market participants have social contact and identify themselves as a group. This is possible in financial centers or online chat platforms, where market participants can exchange their opinions and adapt them to each other. Here too, in the sense of groupthink, false dominant market opinions can arise. This is so called herding behavior (see Sect. 7.1).

However, the presented behavioral studies also show that human beings are not social oriented enough for economic altruism at a level that a socialist or commun.

Comprehension Questions

1. What importance do societal norms have for society?
2. Why does the individual subordinate to the collective?
3. Why have many ethical misdeeds taken place especially within the anonymous finance sector?

3.4 Economy and Freedom – A Historical Overview

What did economy and society look like a few hundred years ago? In the middle ages the economic and social form of organization was feudalism. These two forms were interdependent even then, whereby the technological-economic developments determined the social form. The societies that adapted to these new developments applied the technological progress and the subsequent productivity advantages the best.

In feudalism the society was hierarchically centrally organized corresponding to the economic structure. The economy was particularly determined by the agrarian sector. Simple tasks were required for agriculture and the distribution of labor was slight. There were few products that had to be produced. The simple tasks to be

[110] See Hewstone and Martin (2014), p. 302.

executed were easy to supervise. Whether or not a laborer picked the fields was easy to see. The aristocracy and the church had power concentrated in their hands. The prince assured internal order and external security and there was no separation of powers. The same person held legislative and executive powers. The individual had to subjugate himself and submit. In the towns the people were unconditionally at the mercy of the prince. In addition to the harsh early rules of the prince, there were also strict moral rules from the church. The punishment for disobedience could reach all the way to eternal hellfire. Life for people at that time was very constricted; there was hardly any individual freedom. The fact that these societal structures were determined by the economy is clear in the saying of the time that "city air makes you free by year and day."[111]

In the so-called free cities it was at least possible to work as an independent handyman or salesman, allowing a certain amount of self-determination in life. The amount possible was determined by the guilds, the self-government of the cities. The guilds embodied the economic order of the time. Within their framework the individual could move freely, be active in the guilds and even participate in determining the city policies depending on one's fortune, such as in a city council. The cities were created with the development of differentiate crafts and the blossoming of trade. Later the manufacturers came and with them a new economic level with the corresponding power. The level of welfare that could then be obtained created power, which the princes repeatedly tried to obtain for themselves over the next few centuries, but which they never could. On the contrary, the new bourgeoisie demanded with the economic power increasing distribution of power in feudalism and ended up stripping the power of aristocracy.[112] The technology determined the economy, and the economy determined the society.

The economy continued to develop. With technological progress people were increasingly replaced by machines for simple tasks. The people were needed for planning, building and operating. Fewer and fewer people were needed in agriculture. The labor saved by technological progress could then be used to produce new products, which increased the general welfare or could be used as leisure time. The time this freed up allowed a broad populace to achieve a basic education. With the shift in the national economic production from agriculture to the continual industrial manufacturing of new goods, the rules of a market economy gained new importance. Whereas the agricultural system allowed centralized, top-down planning, implementation and supervision, more complex production of an increasing number of goods had to be coordinated. This was only possible through the decentralized price mechanism of the market. More and more markets for more and more products and preliminary products were created and controlled the production, sales, investment and consumption plans of people. The structure of the products and thus their production process were increasingly complex, and the variety of products increased

[111] See Mitteis (1976) and Hühns and Hühns (1963), p.123.

[112] See Schäfer (2009).

as well. Thus the distribution of labor and specialization also increased. This trend is very visible in new training and study courses.

The tendency towards more complex structures demanded an increasing level of self-responsible behavior from people, thus an increasing level of freedom. The strong incorporation of the individual in the village community and extended family as well as the subjugation to the power of the prince and the church were replaced over time with more freedom for the individual. After the industrial revolution the service sector rose to the fore, and then came the computer age, which brought new demands for the people in the economic process once again. The tendency moved away from physical activities towards metal activities. If there were still many simple tasks in industry before the computer age, now the manufacturing robots have taken over the simple assembly line jobs. The machines were mostly controlled by calculating machines, the computers. With the progressing industrialization not only the market economy but also the individual had a completely different value. The actions that were simple for supervisors to control, within the hierarchy, became fewer, while being a self-starter and having self-responsibility became more important. The computer age increased this trend. The companies had to grant their employees more space and responsibility. The strictly hierarchical control through supervision of the employees was not as well suited to assure optimal manufacturing processes. Instead, the companies increasingly turned to setting targets and a sliding scale for wages. Technical progress determined the economic and thus the political development. Thus if an economic system of market and competitive freedom is to function with the level of technology we have today, the individual must be free. A system that tries to separate economic from political freedom will not last, as history as shown. Over the long term economic power has always acquired political power. In the end the economic power makes decisions about the options to politically assert itself. This applies to countries as well. Economically developing countries have always demanded political power abroad over the long or short term. One could compare the foreign policy power of the USA now with 200 years ago.

The decentralized economic activity of the market economy on the other hand, has remained just as important, with a high level of individual freedom. This is why democracy and market economies are interdependent, since democracy promises the maximum possible political influence for the individual as a form of political freedom. For a modern market economy system to function the individual must be free. Technological development determines the economic structure, which in turn determines the societal structure. The stages of economic development and the political system are interdependent if the strengths of the respective economic system are to be realized.

The agrarian sector does not need the individuals involved to develop independently. A feudalistic social system is thus possible and fitting for the organizational needs. Cultivation of fields can be planned and controlled centrally. The optimal economic system appropriate for the modern production technology is the market economy and the appropriate political system is democracy. A centralized, dictatorial system would be contradictory. Considering this the USSR could never have won the arms race because the political system did not fit the economic requirements of the second half of the twentieth century. It was destined to lose for evolutionary reasons. This does not necessarily mean that the society must unconditionally subordinate itself to the economy. The law of economy must be used for the good of humanity, just like the law of nature. Freedom is connected to the possibility for individuals to gain property through their performance in the market. Owning property is the central motivation in a market economy, although it also contains the respective power of disposal over the resources and thus rights and power.

Market economy needs self-determined entrepreneurs as a personality type, like Schumpeter's pioneer entrepreneur.[113] This type of person must be able to develop freely. It is not sufficient to liberate those who are not free. When people grow up in bondage of any kind, no one can expect them to behave creatively and self-responsibly when they suddenly gain freedom. Even if people have a basic tendency to be entrepreneurial, they must reorient themselves to the new freedom and the new market system. Experience in a market economy is only gained through trial and error, which needs time.

For instance there is a great gap between the economic and the political freedom in China, which historically always let to a political emancipation of the citizens.

The tendency towards the separation of the individual from society induced through technology, thus the tendency towards increasing freedom of the individual from social constraints, still exists. The enlightenment with its freedom and participation demands the consequences resulting from the technological developments that have changed economic and social structures. The consequent application of the market economy rules is also the consequence of the optimal adaptation to the predetermined technical conditions.

How does this tendency affect individual freedom?

In 1989, Kerber found that the young leaders were inclined to opportunism and accepted immoral and often criminal behavior when material success was achieved. Slogans like "Everyone is the next one", "One hand washes the other" or "To achieve a higher goal, sometimes wrong can not be circumvented" were popular. Kerber summarized the trend as follows:

> The tendency seems to be a stronger ego-orientation and more attention to success, material goods and enjoyment.[114]

At the beginning of the 1990s there was a trend away from duties such as order, discipline, loyalty, thoroughness and reliability to so-called unfolding values such as independence, self-responsibility, participation and creativity.[115]

A tendency towards individualization has been confirmed by the consulting company Hay Group – in a joint study ("Leadership-2030") with the company Z-Punkt. They also refer to the impact on employee motivation:

---

[113] See Schumpeter (1911).

[114] Kerber (1989), p. 280.

[115] See Dahm (1993), p. 4 f.

> Individualization has a strong impact on the loyalty and willingness of employees, who often attach greater importance to 'soft factors' such as recognition, self-development, self-responsibility, value-driven commitment and work-life balance than traditional factors such as payment and promotion.[116]

Many authors see the way into the "post-material evolutionary development" not only positively. They point out that a society can not exist without obligations. Many problems cannot not be solved through self-realization, pleasure, and embarrassment, but would only be talked away.[117]

In modern free society everyone should have the opportunity to develop as he wishes. Everyone should at least have the chance to work their way up to become a millionaire, which is the central stimulus of the market economy. According to the Enlightenment, all human beings are at least equal to their basic rights, which is why a problem-solving approach suggests that the freedom of the individual ceases where the other begins. If left aside, this would be a very idealistic illusion which would lead neither to a functioning nor a humane society. There were only individualists who would maximize their usefulness, their freedom within the boundaries defined by the rights of others. A society as a coherent whole, a community would not exist. No one would do something useful, something charitable, for others. No one would sacrifice himself for his family, no one would nurture or support his parents in old age, or strive to educate his children. Socially necessary honorary offices would no longer be accepted. Politicians would only use their offices to maximize their own benefit. For the benefit of the community, society, the state, or the nation, no one would stand.

Conclusion and Summary

The view that honesty is stupidity seems not only to have established itself in the economy, but throughout the society. "You have to be able to afford morality" and "you have to watch out for your own," are common phrases. Public spirit and a willingness to make sacrifices have been replaced by thoughtless benefit maximization. Social education is subject to variations, which we called zeitgeist. If there were ideologies at the beginning of the twentieth century that demanded self-sacrifice for the supposed general good, today the individual and its benefit maximization is the dominant idea. People had the same predispositions over the past few centuries as they do today. Immorality was always rife, and after a time a cultivated civilization developed morally, then often fell back into the middle ages.[118] Still, there were other, more moral times and societies. How can these moral changes be explained? Morality is above all a social problem, and has always been so, at least since people have been dependent on one another in groups. The church had a monopoly on interpreting morality for the last 2000 years, or at least until the enlightenment. Whether the result was morally irreproachable is another issue. According to Immanuel Kant, enlightenment is a person leaving the nonage they themselves are

[116] See Hay Group (2011), p. 8.

[117] See Leisinger (1997), p. 144.

[118] Such as in Germany during the time of National Socialism.

responsible for. This sounds well enough, like freedom and escaping moral slavery, but it is also like a second expulsion from the Garden of Eden. A shortcoming of the modern age is that people are left to their own conscience, and must make the choice between good and evil on their own. It is the "you mayest" of the American author John Steinbeck, who expresses the ability to choose even as the meaning of life. For an average person this balancing act between good and evil is almost impossible without help from outside. Leaving the self-imposed nonage has led to a certain loss of orientation.

This disorientation is not unproblematic. It is probably the tree of knowledge in fact, from which Adam and Eve ate the apple. They can distinguish between good and bad actions, which means they have the fundamental aptitude of conscience. The right path is not handed to people without their own effort, however. They must work for it, or to put it another way, people are not born good, but they can improve. This can take place internally through increasing mental maturity or externally. This phenomenon is called socialization, and is the forming of human behavior patterns through rewards or negative sanctions and role models. We could also call this one's upbringing. Parents are not the only ones to educate their children, rather the whole society influences people through these mechanisms.

On the way to total freedom, more and more rules and norms are abandoned; more and more taboos are broken. This trend, however, should be questioned by society, because it is also a way to total individualism. Does this route offer more advantages than disadvantages for society? Does the trend have to be steered into the socially desired pathways? It becomes clear that due to the technically driven economic and social changes, we can assume less and less duty ethics combined with social control. To this extent, we agree to the statement of Homann, but we arrive at other conclusions than the moral economy. It must be the other way round: the greater the freedom of the individual, the greater the morality of man. If the prince and the church no longer sanction men for moral misconduct, if there are little or no pre-determined rules, then the individual must have internalized the socially desirable behavior by inner values, so called ethos. The more modern the economy is, the more important are morality and values for the development of the productive forces.[119]

A total state control of human behavior is both impossible and undesirable, because individual behavioral freedom should be abandoned. This also applies to the control of employees in companies. This gap must close moral, ethical behavior, and business ethics also applies to the economic sector. It has to influence the behavior of the people in the economy in such a way that the company productivity and the common good are maximized.

In conclusion, many authors point to a tendency towards individualism and materialism. It is a question of a "change in values", a neglect of the classical class

[119] See auch Dahm (1993), p. 8.

and profession ethos, as well as an erosion of traditional values such as honesty, justice and solidarity.[120]

The genetic predisposition to cooperative behavior we have described is not sufficient on its own, however. Hobbes recognized that cooperative behavior must be worthwhile for the individual, who must also be able to count on it from others, since we would otherwise have anarchy. Luhmann considers trust to be a tool used to reduce the complexity of social interactions.[121] Trust can only be ensured by a society rewarding cooperative behavior and punishing non-cooperative behavior. Without controls and sanctions there is no guarantee of fair, thus economically ethical, behavior.

Comprehension Questions
1. What is meant by so-called individualization?
2. What are the reasons for this?
3. What is the significance of this development for business ethics?

3.5 Basic Conceptions of the Market

The worldview that stressed individual freedom and responsibility, and encouraged individuals to pursue their own self interest made its way into economics via Adam Smith (1723–1790). A division of labor increases productivity, and a strict system of competition prevents monopolies. The unifying idea of the classical school, its liberalism influenced by the Enlightenment, is that self-interest within the context of competition works in the interest of the economy as a whole (Invisible Hand).

The socio-political, legal and economic concepts of liberalism are:

1. Democracy
2. Rule of law
3. Market economy

In the so-called free market economy, self-determined, self-responsible individuals with private property act in their own interest and pursue individual goals (pursuit of happiness). Everyone is trying to increase their own welfare. If there is competition in the market, this can only be achieved by above-average performance at below-average costs. If man wants to improve his fate, he must work hard to provide the market with a desirable product. This is how the self-interest of people through the market as an institution becomes a productive force for the community.

According to David Hume, Stinchcombe and Friedrich A. von Hayek, there is also a cultural development process.[122] Sociology calls this the process of natural

---

[120] See Pritzl and Schneider (1999), p. 327.

[121] See Luhmann (2000).

[122] See Wiswede (1985), p. 195, von Hayek (1976), p. 39, 40 and 59; von Hayek (1979), p. 154ff and 167 and Noll (2002), p. 29.

selection. Unsuitable patterns of behavior and rules (institutions) will fail along with the groups that have chosen them. Cultural development is thus process of trial and error with an uncertain outcome. Legal constructions (institutional arrangements) such as private property, as well as money and credit, and even the market economy itself have benefited the groups that introduced them. Forms of social coexistence and social organization are tried out and adopted if they garner economic success and social acceptance, and are otherwise discarded. If a society does not choose its structure this way it risks losing in competition with the other societies, which also describes a cultural development process. For example, one could argue that with the collapse of socialist and communist systems, the private property form of ownership prevailed. However, the process of natural selection by elimination is very slow. More crucial is the selection through human thinking and learning from experience (trial and error). This is especially true for the design of economic systems and general social order.

Group Work Transfer the economic thinking of Adam Smith into our time:

- Which political party in your country best represents the position of liberalism?
- What do you understand by democracy and the rule of law?

Solution
A democracy includes freedom of expression, freedom of the press, and freedom of assembly. Policy is largely determined by the people (demos), be it directly through voting or in representative democracy through elected representatives.

The rule of law requires a legal system, laws to which everyone is subject, including the state. Citizens must be protected against encroachments from the state by a constitutional organ, in our case the Federal Constitutional Court. The judges must be independent and incorruptible. In addition, there must be a separation of powers (concept of the French philosopher Montesquieu), independent judiciary, legislative and executive. In Germany, the division of authority by the appointment or promotion of judges by the Ministry of Justice is slightly limited.

→ Give examples of countries where all three criteria exist and countries where this is not the case?

We sum it up. The basic ideas of the free market economy are that self-determined, self-responsible individuals enjoy private ownership, act in their self-interest and pursue individual goals (pursuit of happiness), while their decisions are coordinated anonymously and powerlessly over markets where contractual freedom prevails (definition). In general, the polypol is cited as a perfect market. Here special conditions apply.

Assumptions of a polypol as the perfect market:

1. Homogeneous goods.
2. Perfect information.
3. Prices adjust with infinite speed.
4. Suppliers and buyers are not able to influence the price (price taker).

→ The supply of companies will be extended until the price equals the marginal cost.

The market coordinates the plans of supply and demand. Price is the controlling instrument. It signals shortages as profit potential and overproduction as loss potential (information function) and thus enables companies to make the desired offer available.

The equilibrium prices, as marginal cost prices, reflect the efficiency of the market and the competition. As a social benefit they lead to the maximum social surplus in the form of producer and consumer surpluses. As long as there is competition, the market mechanism produces equilibrium prices and quantities. These are pareto and production efficient because at the equilibrium price in a polypoly the marginal utility is equal to the marginal cost. It is then not possible to produce goods cheaper or more efficiently (see Fig. 4.1). All economic subjects have exchanged and reached a pareto optimal state. Households either exchanged their products with each other by means of money or bought the products of companies and therefore have maximum benefits. The companies are at the profit maximum, the profit representing a benefit maximum for the company owner.

Prices set too high lead to an oversupply. As companies compete for customers the price drops until it just covers the extra cost per product, and consumer surplus rises at the same time. The equilibrium price is equal to the marginal cost of the last company offering. If the company sold cheaper, it would lose money. For the household, the same applies. If the price is too low, not all buyers will get a product. However, the marginal utility of the buyers is higher, so they will offer a higher price in order to obtain the goods. They increase the price until it is equal to their marginal utility. If they were to buy more products, the benefit from the price of the good would be higher than the benefit of the purchase. With the money for the purchase, the household could have bought a good with a higher benefit. Outbidding raises the price and thus the producer's income (see Figs. 3.2 and 3.3), which maximizes consumer and employee benefits as well. The plans of vendors and buyers are matched by p, which is also a signal for the new plans.

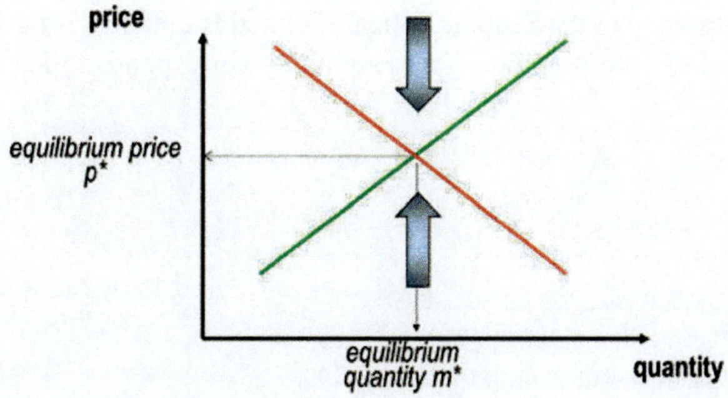

Fig. 3.2 Stable market clearing at the equilibrium price. For p * applies: limits of buyer's willingness to pay = price in monetary units = marginal production costs

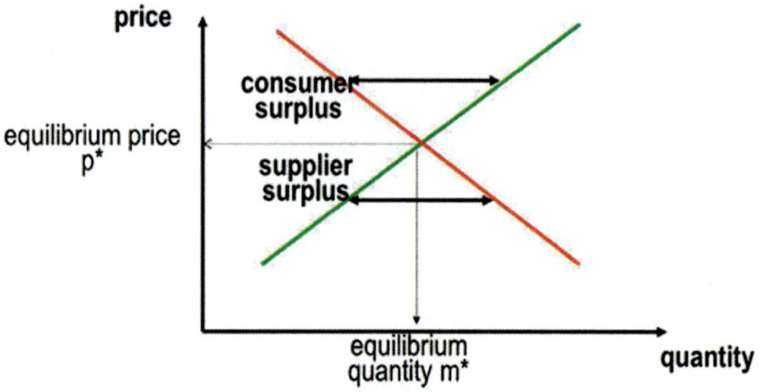

Fig. 3.3 The Marshall Supply and Demand Cross

3.6 How Does the Market Economic System Work?

The market economy is described by many authors as being driven by common sense, using morality, social values and even solidarity. Starbatty contradicts Dietzfelbinger that morality and market economy have different rationalities, that is, the market can be immoral, but he believes that these are two ethical designs. Molitor sees the market economy as a moral institution, because it has the prosperity of all as its goal and it achieves best results. Here, he compares the pure market economy with the central administration economy. For him the higher productivity and the higher degree of freedom for the individual are an ethical advantage of the market economy. He sees the central social ethical justification in its orientation to the wishes of the consumers, as the prosperity of all. The market economy is considered to be ethically superior to alternatives such as a planned economy (central administration).[123] In principle, the Catholic Church is in favor of this assessment:

> At the national level of the individual nations as well as those of international relations, the free market appears to be the most effective instrument for the creation of resources and for the best satisfaction of needs.[124]

However, the Catholic Church does not see the market economy as sufficient to satisfy all human needs. For a Christian ethic, the basic statement of the pastoral autonomy of the Second Vatican Council is that man is the author, the center and the goal of all economics. This essentially corresponds to Kant's rules for reasoning.

[123] See Molitor (1989), p. 71ff.

[124] See Max and Wulsdorf (2002), p. 290.

3.6.1 Functions of Competition

What comprises the system as a whole? What rules apply in the so-called market economy? What does market economy have to do with morality? Or, to ask it a different way, do market forces encourage or hinder moral and ethical behavior? We examine these questions in the following sections.

Because of its various forms, there is no generally accepted definition of "competition."[125] The core of the market economy competition could be seen as at least two market participants who compete with each other on the supply side and the demand side. In a market economy the decentralized decisions are made by individuals and coordinated via the market. Each participant is responsible for their own economic plans and decisions, and is then rewarded or punished by the market. The strength of the market economy is that all the productive forces of individual people are stimulated and coordinated. The limit is only human potential and their creativity or inventiveness and their level of education. The basic prerequisite for the development of market economic forces is competition with transparency in what is offered on the markets. Private property and the improved economic situation it brings for the individual is the main incentive of the market economy. Markets and competition fulfill various functions together.

The ethical result of the market economy can be attributed to competition functions.[126] The market provides the basis for the elementary competition functions with the price signals and the market mechanism. Prices indicate scarcity, costs, profit potentials and benefits (opportunity utilization). Without market competition, however, the market does not provide any allocation-efficient results.

There is no universally accepted definition of competition because of the many forms it can take.[127] The basic character of competition in a market economy can be understood as the contention between at least two participants on the supply side and those on the demand side.

Static Competition Functions

Static competition functions have a short-term effect, dynamic competition functions long-term. If you want to get a rough idea of the length of this short term, you could imagine a period of up to 2 years.

1. **Steering function**

Competition forces companies to adjust their supply to correspond to the wishes and needs of their consumers (Consumer sovereignty). A supplier who is not oriented to the wishes of the customer will sell nothing, thus fail in the market.

[125] See Herdzina (1999), p. 9.

[126] See Conrad (2005), pp. 23.

[127] See Herdzina (1999), p. 9.

2. **Incentive function**

The reward (profit) in competition is the motivation to perform well, which is the basic requirement for productivity. This reflects Adam Smith's idea that people perform for the market in competition to improve their own lives, their well-being.

3. **Sanction function**

Competition ensures that only those companies that use their resources efficiently (productive efficiency) and are guided by market requirements can remain in the market. The entrepreneur who does not produce what the market (consumers) wants or who does not use resources efficiently in production is sanctioned. Here, the sanctions emphasize loss of income or even exclusion from the market, which is the livelihood and wealth of the company. Here the liability for misconduct in the market has the greatest effect.

Incentive and sanction function are the two sides of competition; reward for market orientation and punishment for long-term disregard. A monopolist exists outside of these rules, however. If he wants to increase profit, he only has to increase prices depending on the price elasticity of demand.

4. **Distribution function**

Competition leads to fair market remuneration and thus provides motivation for good performance, which is in turn the basic requirement for productivity.

Competition leads to a marketable, performance-based pay. The market, and more specifically the people as market participants, reward performance via their willingness to pay and through the conditions of competition.

5. **Allocation function**

In a national economic system, the desire to maximize profit produces the dynamic in which the raw materials with the best value are used in production. As we have already seen, striving to maximize profit guarantees that the raw materials to offer the best quality for the lowest price are the ones used (*first allocation function*). In addition, the most cost-effective company has the highest demand and can attract more production because it has the most room to maneuver with its prices (*second allocation function*).[128]

Companies achieve optimal success when their costs equal the profits from an additional unit of production. When they have enough influence, in other words a lack of competition such as in a monopoly, entrepreneurs will set a price far above their costs. Competition forces prices down towards the production costs through dispersed market power. Lower prices are then charged for a higher quality product, both for finished products and raw materials. This increases consumer profit in the case of finished products and the international competitiveness of a country for raw

[128] According to empirical estimations, in a polypoly – as opposed to a monopoly – the static welfare gains in one period alone constitute 10% of the GDP. This is assuming there are no secondary effects. See Scherer (1997), p. 11.

materials, thus indirectly also affecting employment. Competition guarantees that over the longer term only companies using their resources efficiently (*productive efficiency*) can stay on the market (*sanctioning function*). Trying to keep a step ahead of one's competitors prevents resources from being wasted and encourages relative prices to be corrected for production factors.

6. **Freedom function**

Competition provides a lot of leeway for those participating in the market to develop their potential. Companies can decide how to make profit but also take responsibility for their decisions, workers can change their employment, and consumers have the freedom to choose between many different offers.[129] Everybody is free to make their own decisions but also responsible for them.

As we discussed in this chapter, freedom for people is a value in itself. Behavioral experiments showed that people have a need for self-determination. They want to have the freedom to take their destiny into their own hands and react to restrictions of this freedom with resistance (so-called reactance).

7. **Control function**

The competition of many players for buyers or suppliers automatically ensures a limitation of economic power. Dominant positions cannot exist in competition and thus have no power over market participants.

Dynamic Competition Functions

1. **Adaptation function**

The competition we have described thus far is in reference to a point in time and is thus referred to as static competition. The dynamic character of competition is especially important for the growth process of an economy, however.[130] Successful companies must also continually try to gain a competitive advantage over their competitors by offering new products and new production techniques (*adaptation function*).

If companies do not continuously adjust their production to market requirements in response to changing demand structures, optimal international division of labor or other external influences, they will be sanctioned by the market. For example, labor-intensive products such as textiles or toys are manufactured today in Eastern Europe or Asia. The reason for this is the lower labor costs there and the sharp drop in transport costs in recent decades. German companies that did not relocate their production to these countries lost their market position and with it the sales of these products.

Friedrich August von Hayek portrayed dynamic competition as a process of search and discovery, through which things are discovered that would otherwise

[129] See Berg (1999), p. 233. The Freiburger School sees the equivalent of democracy in individualistically oriented competition, and thus the prevention of a dictator.

[130] See Heuß (1980), pp. 29 for the importance of competition for the growth process.

have remained unknown or at least not made use of. Competition is evolutionary for Hayek,[131] which applies to both product and process innovation. Innovation can be understood in this context as the economic application of a discovery, in other words invention. In the expectation of above-average rewards from the market an entrepreneur is always searching for cost-effective methods of production and new products for which there is a potential market demand. The entrepreneur conducts risk assessment at their own cost or analyzes external research results. The market decides the success of an innovation and thus in the end the consumer or producer that further refines a product has the last say (*innovation function*). Should an entrepreneur decide not to bother with innovation and invention, they will be pushed off the market by their competitors (see adaptation and sanction function). It is clear that the functions of competition and adaptation are closely connected with each other. If companies fail to adapt their products to the demand structures on the market and international division of labor, they will also be sanctioned by the market.

2. **Innovation function**

According to Friedrich August von Hayek, dynamic competition is a process of search and discovery.[132] Hayek characterizes competition as a process for the discovery of facts (process or product innovations) that would either remain unknown or at least not be used if there were no competition. These facts enable pioneer profits and a place in the competition.

The successful innovation of the pioneering entrepreneur gives him a competitive advantage in the marketplace over the entrepreneurs who have retained their old production structure. For Hayek, competition is above all evolutionary. At some point, all products and production processes were once an innovation. For example, Apple's iPhone was launched as a product innovation on the market. This was the combination of known techniques to create a new product. Traditional cell phones like those from Nokia did not have the iPhone features. Apple was a pioneer and got the monopoly profits as a reward for the market for innovation. When Samsung phones came out with their smart phone, prices fell. Here the imitation function starts as a competition function.

3. **Imitation function**

According to Joseph Schumpeter,[133] competition is a process of innovation and subsequent imitation (*imitation function*). The successful innovation on the part of the pioneering company proves a competitive advantage over other companies on the market that have maintained their old production structures. Above-average profits are won from this advantage, which in turn makes other companies want to copy the invention, or even forces them to do so if they do not want to be pushed off

---

[131] See von Hayek (1969), p. 249 and Starbatty (1987), p. 164.

[132] von Hayek (1969).

[133] See Schumpeter (1911).

the market. This is how the new, resource saving methods of production come about, and thus brings about widespread technological progress and production growth.[134] Innovation and sanction functions thus support each other in dynamic competition.

Having explained the central static und dynamic functions of competition we can now derive the **criteria of market conformity,** which has been developed by ordoliberalism (see Sect. 3.6.2). All market interventions of governments have to be market conform, thus they must not impede the functions of competition. Otherwise the productivity-enhancing impact of the functions is reduced. We will apply these criteria to the central administration economy in Sect. 4.9 and to the industrial policy in Chap. 9.

From the perspective of the individual companies it would be positive to restrict competition. For one thing, when a company profits from an increase in its market power, such as those from a monopoly, it reaps the benefits without having to work for it. Competition is also a nuisance, in that it forces companies to constantly better their performance. If they do not adapt to the market and innovate they must face losses or may even have to withdraw from the market altogether.[135] The state must protect competition in order to make sure that companies cannot elude the competition functions. Are these functions applicable at the international level, though?

The competition forces companies to continually try to gain competitive advantage through new products or production processes, or at the very least to catch up with the competitors' competitive advantages. On the one hand, this reduces the use of resources and, on the other hand, adapts to changes in the relative prices of production factors,

This principle must be the same internationally,[136] though there are country-specific absolute and comparative cost advantages (Ricardo's Theory of Comparative Cost Advantage). According to Ricardo even a unilateral liberalization of foreign trade would give the importing country an advantage. Scarce production factors in individual countries would balance out internationally, which would in turn lead to higher total productivity.[137]

The largest part of world trade takes place intersectorally, which means within a branch and between the western industrial nations that have similar cost and demand structures such as capital and labor provisions. How does foreign trade come about even when there are identical cost and demand structures? This can be explained by the specialization of the producers to various demands. Foreign trade as cross-border competition forces the suppliers to orient themselves to the international demands and or to qualify themselves for a market niche. The broad pallet of products to result

[134] For an explanation of "Schumpeterschen Unternehmers" See Dürr (1987), pp. 245 and Vickers (1994), p. 17.

[135] See Drude (1991), p. 7.

[136] Empirical proof of the positive effects from import competition on productivity can be found in MacDonald, Porter, Baily, and Gernsbach as well as in the studies from the EU-Commission on gains in welfare within the European domestic market. See Baily and Gernsbach (1995); EU-Commission (1988); MacDonald (1994); Porter (1990) and Scherer (1997).

[137] See Conrad (2003).

from this process is also a gain in welfare. Gains are also possible digressively, in other words with a reduced amount of production within the framework of international specialization. With the increased demand corresponding to the world market, production amounts increase and thus unit costs decrease.[138]

In principle then, globalization as national markets growing closer together into one national market leads to an overall higher level of welfare. How the benefits are distributed is another question. This is mostly because with changes in international production the jobs are shifted and cause short-term structural unemployment.

Unfortunately the advantages and functions of the market and competition are not public goods, which is surely the main source of the rejection and hate directed at the market, and at the international market in particular. The willingness of states to explain and educate is desperately needed.

Can the market process really regulate everything based on human egotism? Does the market really need morality? Is it really true that the more profit companies make, the more immorally they behave? Do the laws of the market even allow companies to act morally?

3.6.2 A Free-Market Without Social Rules?

An extreme free-market orthodoxy is considered as one of the causes for the subprime crisis. A spoke word of the investment bankers is "rules are for fools". Greenspan and many U.S. politicians such as Reagan were against rules for the economy. Rather, they wanted to unleash the market forces in order to create more growth. Continental Europe, however, demanded stronger regulation of financial markets. The reason are different conceptions of economics. As Fox points out:

> Europeans tend to be less hostile to government as regulator and more skeptical of private cooperation as servant of the public interest.[139]

In Continental Europe the most spread economic concept is the Ordoliberalism. It does not share the optimism that the market would develop perfectly without state intervention, however, since it might be in the interest of companies to rid themselves of irksome competition, such as price agreements, mergers, vertical restraints etc., and secure profits through a monopoly.[140] The individual freedom in the market is a competition policy goal for ordoliberalism inasmuch as the assumption holds that companies will try to abuse their freedom at the cost of others within competition processes.[141] Thus a strong state is necessary to channel the behavior of market

[138] See Conrad (2005) and Bender (1992), pp. 419–448.

[139] See Fox (1986), p. 983.

[140] See Starbatty (1983), pp. 570.

[141] See Starbatty (1983), p. 569 and Hildebrand (2002), p. 160.

participants through laws and prevent or remove restrictions to competition through intervention.

Adam Smith was aware that the invisible hand alone is not sufficient to protect the common good from damage by individuals. He stressed the necessity of an economic system and a system to keep order, which did not exclude intervention to protect the common good. An individual enrichment at the cost of the common good cannot be tolerated by a society for several reasons. Besides the damage that is done to the national economy, such behavior has a degenerative effect on the system. Only if the legal system functions well and there is "trust in the sovereignty of the state" can trade on markets develop to the advantage of people, according and create welfare. Smith also identifies the most important components of order to be internal security, jurisprudence, infrastructure, educational institutions and national defense.[142] Adam Smith had already differentiated between an economy and an economic system. The economic system must set the framework for economic behavior in such a way that the invisible hand of the market and competition can develop optimally, meaning that the actions of people determined by their own interests are channeled for the common good. The economic system has the task of setting and implementing the rules for competition and the markets. Adam Smith was thus the first theoretician of order. Unfortunately, he did not analyze the importance of the framework for economic order in depth.

The opposite view is represented for instance by Milton Friedman. An extreme belief in the market is expressed for instance in the answer Friedman gave in reaction to the balance sheet scandal in the USA at the beginning of this decade. He said, "Don't do anything, the market will regulate itself!"[143] Is that really the case?

3.6.3 *Moral Goals and Market Economy*

The market cannot solve all human problems. The solution that the market has developed is that each person pays for the performance they want. The problem creates a demand that creates its own supply. The market only knows the principle "due ut des" as the principle for trade. This mechanism often functions, but not always. The reach of market forces is limited. Superordinate and subordinate relationships have always exited. In every group of apes or humans there is a social order. There are also different mental and physical capabilities and different access to resources, especially in humans, which determines power, dependencies and hierarchies. For example, the resource distribution in Latin America and many developing countries cripples their economic development. Whoever was able to grab something now owns it. Lands and assets have often been inherited within the same family for centuries. Like noble titles, the children of these families have

[142] See Smith (1776), chapter III, first paragraph.

[143] See Schwarz and Vaughn (2002), p. 1672.

inherited the fortunes of these families without any effort of their own. They have the capital for worthwhile investments, however. Distribution of assets and welfare are therefore set, just like the hierarchical relationships. Anyone without land must work for the others as a dependent employee. In order to change anything in the order and the distribution of wealth, one must have power and even use violence. If this is the case, power through strength or access to resources is a central factor in the social order, which is much stronger than the market mechanism. The given factors of power make the question of whether spontaneous market mechanisms and their ability to fix themselves are sufficient, or whether the state must provide an additional framework with its order and even directly intervene in the market mechanism obsolete. The voluntary, mutual, advantageous exchange of goods is more of the exception. The market mechanism can only ever control a small part of the societal exchange process, so it is more of a question really of how much and which system of order, and when the market mechanism is appropriate and when it is not. This question is settled to a large degree by the social framework conditions, as will make clear with the example of Russia.

A lack of property means dissatisfaction, since threatened survival means having to enter into dependent employment, or the rental of one's own time and labor. The distribution of income in a market economy is only oriented towards performance to a certain extent, since the initial distribution of wealth is differently inherited. However a market economy system with the correct conditions provides for a distribution of income based on performance, and thus leads to a more balanced equity distribution with time.

Business ethics places people above the economy, and assumes that the economy should serve the people. There are other perspectives on this, whereby economic success justifies the means. Economics would then be placed above morality. According to Calvinism, economic success is s sign of God's benediction. Economic success is thus not only morally legitimized, but those with success have been chosen by God. There can hardly be a greater incentive to strive to earn more. Hard work and asceticism are then the fundamental characteristics of a successful Calvinistic enterprising personality.[144]

This idea contradicts the original Christian belief of justified wealth. This has been expressed in sayings such as "it is easier for a camel to go through the eye of a needle, than for a rich man to enter the kingdom of heaven."[145] Theologians from the middle ages demanded that no Christian work as a salesman, since breaches in loyalty, honor and virtue would result from exchange with the promise of profit in the spirit of greed.[146] Market prices were felt to be unfair (Thomas von Aquinas (1224/25–1274 A.D.) or generally the income distribution of the market, because it was not based only on performance and it completely neglected human needs. The

[144] Max Weber had already recognized the source of the positive economic developments in Switzerland, the Netherlands, England and parts of Germany as being from the Protestant or Calvinist influence. See Ulrich (1993), Sp. 1168f and Noll (2002), p.166.

[145] See Schwarze (2007).

[146] See Wilkening (2004), p. 61.

Christian economy was to be a responsible and thus free proposition and establishment of as many individuals as possible for the good of everyone.[147] Adam Smith (1723–1790), shared this view with his "invisible hand" of the market that led to the benefit of everyone.

The moral expectations confronting economy is ancient. Aristotle (384–322 B. C.) had already differentiated between the art of naturally acquiring or procuring and the art of enrichment (chrematistic), which he condemned because it did not naturally occur but was rooted in the weakness of mankind. Striving after money becomes an end in and of itself, which distances man from his natural purpose, namely satisfying the elementary needs for a good life. Aristotle places virtue above economics because man can only achieve happiness by exercising his virtues. The perfect virtue for Aristotle is justice, which serves as a norm for the economy. He does not understand distributional justice as the equity of needs as did Socialism, but rather equal for the equal and unequal for the unequal. According to this principle from Aristotle there must also be a redistributive justice, which balances out unjust distribution results such as those from fraud.[148]

Moral Property

The human factor as individuals is the central actor in the market economy. In a market economy the market mechanism coordinates the plans of individuals through the market price that matches supply and demand. The basic prerequisite for a total economy to develop optimally is that competition dominates the markets. Private property and its augmentation are the main incentive for individual economic activity. More is required than just the free interaction of supply and demand for such a complex system to function, however. For example, to transform a socialist planned economy into a market economy, allowing free price-setting and creating private property is not sufficient. What good is property if it is not protected or acquiring it is not regulated? The market economy conditions are thus much more extensive than those according to the theory of order from Walter Eucken, and include a functional legal system, among other things. Insufficient attention was given to the necessary conditions in the consultation for the countries leaving Socialism or Communism, as we saw in the example of Russia. With the currently dominant mathematical and quantitative perspective being taught, the market is assumed to function ideally. The human factor is systematically ignored because it cannot be put into deterministic models due to its often irrational nature. People are equal in their rights, but not in their behavior. Thus the market economy could not be successfully established in Russia. People are formed and socialized by their environment from birth. Market economy behavior must be practiced. The market economy demands a different behavior from individuals than planned economies do, such as individual responsibility. An abrupt changeover from planned to market economy is like suddenly demanding a spoiled housecat go catch its own dinner. It is

[147] See Beutter (1989), 56–75.

[148] See Schefold (1989), pp. 19–55.

not possible to just switch from a feudal agrarian system or a tribal or clan system to a market economy with individuals that can hardly be controlled without going through an adjustment process.

For the mendicant from the Dominican order, Thomas von Aquinas, all goods are God-given. They are only entrusted to people for their earthly use. Like Aristotle he rejects ownership as an end in itself. Property should serve the good of humankind. He rejects common property as well, since no one would feel responsible for it. According to the idea that "property binds," those who have possessions should give some to those in need. Property is generally to be used with consideration for others.[149]

Even without using God as an argument the question of justifying the use of property arises. Property can serve a single individual or the community. If an economy is to serve the good of the community, property may only be obtained through participation in the economic process. Performance on the market, thus evaluated by other people, contributes the most to the general good via the rules of the market and competition. Deceit or theft is obtaining services or property from others without reciprocation, which is usually only possible through devious means or the use of force.

Moral values are expressed e.g. through "fair competition". This includes the moral demand that the fruit of the market, income, should only be received by those who contribute, in other words those who outdo their competition through an exchange of effort on the market and open competition and not through advantages. Whenever assets are not earned through effort, the community will not accept an unequal distribution. In extreme cases assets are immoral, when they are obtained through theft and fraud. Societal approval as a motivation to perform well disappears in such cases. The motivating model of the American dishwasher who worked his way up no longer has any effect, since effort does not pay off. Property is therefore above all a motivation to perform well. Adam Smith was the one to recognize its importance the most comprehensively. On the other hand, as Smith considers the cause, or driving force, behind the development process to be the constant striving of people to improve their material situation, those who are "satisfied" and those who are hungry but cannot amass assets are hardly motivated to make an effort. The development of productive forces thus requires equitable rewards for performance as the distribution principle for income and assets, which the market evaluates as the location of all material needs of the community.

It is of no importance for the market and the general good whether the performance comes from the necessity to meet one's basic needs or from limitless greed, glamour and power. The market is only interested in the performance, not the motivation. The individuals bear the consequences, not the community. Each person has just one life and must decide how to invest his energy during his lifetime and for what ends, insofar as conditions allow. However, for the community it can be a

---

[149] See Beutter (1989), 56–75.

problem if too many individuals make egotistical economic gain their life goal, seeing ruthless property maximization as an end in and of itself.

Independent of subjective assessments, the economy may not be its own end, which applies for all instruments used by people to survive since they have existed. The economy must serve people, not the other way around. This statement is always universally valid, including this era of globalization.

What role should money play in a market economy as property? Money functions as an exchange and value retention device, as well as a unit of calculation with all of the price signal and competition functions connected with it. Money is of central importance in a market economy. Because of its value retention function, money represents purchasing power and thus power. The market mechanism consciously relies upon egotism and the human striving to enrich themselves, and money is the means to do so. Money makes it possible for the market economy incentives and thus Smith's invisible hand to function fully. Money should always be a means to an end however, not as a dominant societal goal in and of itself that replaces other important goals including social morality. For example, if we assume that the end justifies the means, it would mean that every damaging action for other people or the community would be justified. A top manager who sold his stock to others even though he knew his company would do poorly would be a societal role model just because he got rich. Social morality is thus an important corrective in a market economy. If a market economy works for the advantage of the community, the community must condemn immoral, damaging behavior through legal punishments or social exclusion.

For Kant, the market has its limits where dignity is at stake and therefore there can be no price:

> In the realm of purposes, everything has either a price, or a dignity. What has a price, in its place can be put something else as equivalent; which, on the other hand, is superior to all price, and therefore does not allow any equivalent, that has a dignity.[150]

Property is therefore primarily a means of motivation. This was recognized as early as Aristotle.[151] Adam Smith recognized its importance most extensively. Conversely, when Smith sees the cause or driving force that determines the process of development in the constant striving of man to improve his material situation, people who are "full" and people who are hungry, but cannot acquire property, are little motivated to perform. The unfolding of productive forces therefore presupposes a fairness of the distribution of the income and wealth. It has been shown in this chapter that people demand a fair distribution of the collective gains in order to participate in group performance.

What forms of justice are there? We differentiate between (1) Justice of performance, (2) Justice of exchange, (3) Justice of distribution, (4) Justice of needs and (5) Social justice.

---

[150] See Kant (1785), p. 434.

[151] See Aristoteles (1991), p. 17 or 1263a.

1. **Justice of performance**

The basis for remuneration is productivity in the company. What added value does the employee provide? Here the result decisive, not the effort. If the results of individual employees cannot be measured, as in large corporations, the effort and willingness to commit (commitment) are often chosen as a reward criteria. It can be advantageous for the employee to stay longer in the office, even if he does not do any productive work.

2. **Justice of exchange**

Is assumed for voluntary exchanges as both parties agree only if the exchanged benefits are beneficial for both and seen as fair.

3. **Justice of distribution**

Distribution is a relative measure and refers here to income and other rewards. There is a distribution within the company and a distribution of income in the economy. Both distributions are perceived as being justified only if they are transparent and their criteria are recognized.

4. **Justice of needs**

Justice based on need is different from just exchange because entitlement to benefits based on need or urgency is considered just.

Karl Marx proposed the quality of necessity ("each according to his needs"). This is about the urgency with which an individual needs an income. For example, a single-parent unemployed mother is in a state of emergency. In this respect, it would be more appropriate to give more to her than to a high-income woman without family obligations.

5. **Social justice**

The goal here is that all individuals in society have the same income chances. For example, Workers are to waive wage increases in order to employ others.

The market distribution is not just based on performance. The market determines remuneration for value (also called market fairness), such as when the market compensates scarcity. Here it is not based on effort, but on the result and the evaluation by the market. The reward is based on competitive conditions and people's preferences in the marketplace. This becomes clear in fashion and art objects. Here, the performance can be completely irrelevant if everyone wants to own the output of a popular painter or fashion designer.

Competition can only assure a fair outcome in the markets if it is not limited, for example by monopolies, cartel agreements, or corruption. The same applies to the cases that are regulated in the law against unfair competition, such as misleading buyers about product characteristics, exploitation of inexperience, and other forms of fraud.

Justice of exchange is often assumed in market transactions to be voluntary. If both improve their position in the exchange, the welfare of all is improved (Pareto efficiency or overall economic optimum, see Sect. 1.1). However, consideration must be given to whether there were dependencies or power positions. Rawls speaks of procedural justice in this context. Economic procedures should lead to fair distribution results. For example, competition on the markets as a procedure ensures a fair result only if it is not limited by monopolies, cartel agreements or the like, or eliminated by corruption.[152] The competition thus legitimates the market economy as an ethical process. In order to ensure fair competition, there are competition authorities and laws regulating how unfair competition law is regulated, such as misleading buyers about product properties, fraud, and exploiting inexperience, etc.

For example, if the employee is dependent on the employer to ensure his/her survival, it can not be assumed that the "voluntarily" accepted wage is just because it corresponds to the employee's performance. In this context, the unions are important in order to establish a fair method. They have the task of bundling the interests of employees into a negotiating position, thus balancing the unequal distribution of the economic power of many "small" workers (suppliers) against a large monopolist labor market (bilateral monopoly).

The justice of needs is a contrast to the justice of exchange, since a claim is regarded as just if it is based not on a performance but on a need. For example, Pope Leo XIII said in the social encyclica "Rerum novarum" that a worker must be able to earn with his wages, his livelihood.[153] But we do not find any need for justice in the market economy.

In the case of the justice as regards performance, remuneration is based on the performance as assessed on the market. Productivity is the basis for this assessment. The value added is generated by the employee or the company. This does not depend on the effort made, but on the result and the evaluation by the market, which is measured as demand.

Ultimately justice is considered very subjective. For example, the East German workers demanded equal pay for equal work after reunification. Objectively, however, due to the old economic system the East German workers were less productive than the West German workers. The well-known principle of equality by Aristotle is therefore: "The same is to be treated equally and unequal unequally."

Despite evaluations being subjective, one thing must be said about the economy that applies to all the instruments that have been used by man since his existence to secure his survival. The economy is not self-serving; it has to serve man and not vice versa. This statement is always and universally applicable.

Conclusion

Market and competition together provide an allocation-efficient result. While the market provides the information, the competitive features ensure the best possible involvement of the market players. At first glance, competition is a zero-sum game: one person can only increase their degree of achievement if the target achievement of

[152] See Rawls (1999), pp. 73 and 240.

[153] See Papst Leo XIII (1891), No. 34; Höffe (1992a), p. 93; Schmidt (1982), p. 225 and Göbel (2010), pp. 152.

at least one other person decreases, It's just like a sport in which everyone struggles to finish ahead of the other competitors.

The winner gets the prize and maybe there will be a reward for the second and third places. It has been shown that as a whole society profits from the competition of companies. Yet competition also encourages individuals to perform and rewards them, making competition worthwhile for the individual as well as companies. There are losers in competition too, in which cases society is obliged to secure at least the survival of the losers using welfare gained by the competition. This will be shown later in the chapter on Social Market Economy.

Ethical Summary
Morality of the individual is partially inherent and partially trained through the social and familial socialization process. According to Sociology this the process of natural se-lection. The unsuitable behavioral patterns and rules (institutions) die out with the groups that have selected them. Cultural development is a process of trial and error, with uncertain results.

Altruism and compassion do exist. Pure altruism can be associated with empathy (empathy-altruism hypothesis). Interpersonal intelligence allows one to recognize and understand the motives and desires of other people. Morality, like all characteristics, is partially inherent and can be helpful in solving unknown tasks in life, just like the forms of intelligence. It belongs to the social abilities, or more exactly to interpersonal intelligence. As we have already shown, morality is the basis for trust and thus also for productive human social existence. For the question of the extent to which man behaves ethically, compassion or sympathy with other people, plays an outstanding role. This is an emotion. In principle, it is therefore necessary to distinguish between a rational impact assessment and emotion-driven compassion. It seems that people can empathize with the suffering of other people (empathic emotion) when they take on the perspective of a suffering person or they perceive themselves as similar to the other person. Studies showed that altruistic behavior is associated with specific intrinsic rewards. Fairness is understood as an ethical value. Management and the government must consider the humans' strong sense of justice.

The market economy is seen as a moral institution, because it has the prosperity of all as its goal and it achieves best results. The higher productivity and the higher degree of freedom for the individual are an ethical advantage of the market economy. However, the market cannot solve all human problems. The solution that the market has developed is that each person pays for the performance they want. The market only knows the principle "due ut des" as the principle for trade. The market knows only the justice of exchange and the justice of performance but not the justice of needs. Markets are not social.

Behavioral Summary
Groups are economically relevant as companies and economies. In order to maximize its benefits through public goods, through the division of labor (emergence) or in the event of conflicts, the individual needs groups. Here, the achievement of goals depends on other individuals (interdependence). Motivation and thus performance depend positively on the group's sense of belonging, known as group cohesion. For interdependent tasks, competition reduces performance. In the case of individually

identifiable and non-interdependent tasks, however, competition was found to increase productivity. The individuals try to outdo each other in group performance (social competition). In collectivist cultures, incentives work differently than in individualistic cultures.

Group tasks that the group members could only solve together, i.e. cooperatively, reduced the group conflicts (application example EU). All beings are motivated to action when deprived of their basic needs, which would explain why cultures that had suffered very severe deprivation were very economically committed afterwards. The productive importance of social capital as shared group knowledge was demonstrated. Public goods, joint projects do not work without rules and sanctions, about 30% free riders have to be sanctioned by "strong reciprocators", with a strong sense of justice as the individual sacrifices for group performance.

Max Weber (Protestant ethics) was confirmed. Cultural achievement motives (e.g. fairy tales, poems, speeches or textbooks) influence economic development.

Exercises

1. What is meant by the sanction function?
2. Describe the allocation function.
3. Why are the three dynamic competitive functions important? Explain briefly how it works.
4. Assign the examples below to the respective competition functions. The examples may fit several competition functions.

    4.1. The invention of the assembly line and serial production by Henry Ford at the beginning of the previous century (Ford model-T) lowered production costs and allowed Ford to make so-called pioneering profits. He was the first to use process innovation, which allowed him to undercut the competition. The competitors were also forced to introduce series production. Ford was not able to hold on to its pioneering profits thanks to the existing competition and had to lower prices in favor of its customers. A broad range of people could then afford a car.

    4.2. An entrepreneur produces 2 million pink rubber boots for the German market but nobody wants them.

    4.3. Consumers do not have to buy the pink boots, but the producer can offer them if they want to. People are free in their decisions, but they have to bear the consequences.

    4.4. Competition allows independence for supply and demand. If there are several competing textile producers, the textile workers can apply elsewhere if they are treated badly.

    4.5. A textile producer buys his yarn from his brother in Germany. The market for textile products is opened to foreign competition. The foreign price is about 20% below the German price. Competition forces the textile producer to purchase the cheaper yarn from abroad.

    4.6. The textile producer who cannot sell the pink rubber boots suffers a loss and must leave the market.

4.7. Steel was the most important raw material until the 1970s. In addition, after the Second World War there was an over-demand for steel to rebuild European industry. The market price showed this through a high profit margin on the manufacturing costs, which is why many companies invested in the expansion of their steel capacities. There was a massive overproduction crisis in the Seventies and the price of steel fell drastically. Many steelworkers lost their jobs, and some companies had to close or merge. In this adjustment process, capacities were adjusted to demand again.
4.8. A textile producer uses a computer-controlled fabric punching machine to produce shirts with less fabric than the competitors, making them 20% cheaper. As a result, they undercut their competitors by 10%, allowing them to sell more shirts cheaper.
4.9. Our company succeeds in turning the pink rubber boots into a lifestyle product within the framework of a skillful advertising campaign and thus generating demand that far exceeds supply. The entrepreneur could thus sell the entire lot far above production costs.
4.10. A dynamic young entrepreneur sells his house to build his idea of a recruitment agency on the Internet. He works proverbially day and night and is very successful and after 3 years can buy a new house twice as big.
4.11. A manager takes over an ailing company (management buy-in) from his boss. He works day and night and creates a turnaround.

Literature

Alesina, A., Di Tella, R., & MacCulloch, R. J. (2004). Inequality and happiness: Are Europeans and Americans different? *Journal of Public Economics, 88*, 2009–2042.

Allen, V. L., & Levine, J. M. (1971). Social support and conformity: The role of independent assessment of reality. *Journal of Experimental Social Psychology, 7*, 48–58.

Aristoteles. (1944). *Politics*, http://www.perseus.tufts.edu/hopper/text?doc=Perseus:text:1999.01.0058:book=1:section=1253a

Aristoteles. (1991). *Politik II, Werke Band 9/II*. Darmstadt.

Asch, S. E. (1951). Effects of group pressure upon the modification and distortion of judgments. In H. Guetzkow (Ed.), *Groups, leadership and men; research in human relations* (pp. 177–190). Oxford University Press.

Asch, S. E. (1987). *Social psychology*. Oxford University Press.

Atkinson, J. W., Heyns, R. W., & Veroff, J. (1954). The effect of experimental arousal of the affiliation motive on thematic apperception. *Journal of Abnormal and Social Psychology, 49*, 405–410.

Axelrod, R. (1987). *Die Evolution der Kooperation*. Munich.

Baily, M., & Gernsbach, H. (1995). Efficiency in manufacturing and the nature of competition. In *Brookings papers on economic activity, microeconomics, S* (pp. 307–358).

Barsade, S. G. (2002). The ripple effect: Emotional contagion and its influence on group behavior. *Administrative Science Quarterly, 47*, 644–675.

Batson, C. D., & Shaw, L. L. (1991). Evidence for altruism: Toward a pluralism of prosocial motives. *Psychological Inquiry, 2*, 107–122.

Batson, C. D., Duncan, B. D., Ackerman, P., Buckley, T., & Birch, K. (1981). Is empathic emotion a source of altruistic motivation? *Journal of Personality and Social Psychology, 40*, 290–302.

Baumeister, R. F., & Leary, M. R. (1995). The need to belong: Desire for interpersonal attachments as a fundamental human motivation. *Psychological Bulletin, 117*, 497–529.

Beck, H. (2014). *Behavioral Economics: Eine Einführung*. 1 Aufl. Springer.

Bender, D. (1992). Außenhandel. In D. Bender (Ed.), *Vahlens Kompendium der Wirtschaftstheorie und Wirtschaftspolitik* (5th ed., pp. 419–477).

Berg, H. (1999). Wettbewerbspolitik. In Bender, Dieter u.a. (Ed.), *Vahlens Kompendium der Wirtschaftstheorie und Wirtschaftspolitik,* Vol. 2, 7. ed., Munich 1999, pp. 299–362.

Berkman, L. F., & Syme, S. L. (1979). Social networks, host resistance, and mortality: A nine year follow-up study of Alameda County residents. *American Journal of Epidemiology, 109*, 186–204.

Berkowitz, L. (1954). Group standards, cohesiveness, and productivity. *Human Relations, 7*, 509–519.

Beutter, F. (1989). Thomas von Aquin. In J. Starbatty (Ed.), *Klassiker des ökonomischen Denkens* (pp. 56–75). Beck.

Bolton, G. E., & Ockenfels, A. (2000). ERC: A theory of equity, reciprocity, and competition. *American Economic Review, 90*(1), 166–193.

Bond, R., & Smith, P. B. (1996). Culture and conformity: A meta-analysis of studies using Asch's (1952b, 1956) Line Judgment Task. *Psychological Bulletin, 119*, 111–137.

Bowlby, J. (1958). The nature of the child's tie to his mother. *International Journal of Psychoanalysis, 39*, 350–373.

Brandstätter, V., Schüler, J., Puca, R. M., & Lozo, L. (2018). *Motivation und emotion*. Springer.

Brehm, S. S., & Brehm, J. W. (1981). *Psychological reactance. A theory of freedom and control.* Academic.

Brewer, M. B., & Caporael, L. R. (2006). An evolutionary perspective on social identity: Revisiting groups. In M. Schaller, J. A. Simpson, & D. T. Kenrick (Eds.), *Evolution and social psychology* (pp. 143–161). Psychology Press.

Brosnan, S. F., & de Waal, F. B. M. (2003). Monkeys reject unequal pay. *Nature, 425*(September), 297–299.

Brosnan, S. F., & de Waal, F. B. M. (2014). Evolution of responses to (un) fairness. *Science, 346*(6207), 314–320.

Butterfield, K. D., Treviño, L. K., & Weaver, G. R. (2000). Moral awareness in business organizations: Influences of issuerelated and social context factors. *Human Relations, 53*, 981–1018.

Campbell, D. T. (1965). Ethnocentric and other altruistic motives. In D. Levine (Ed.), *Nebraska symposium on motivation* (Vol. 13). University of Nebraska Press.

Cherry, T. L., Frykblom, P., & Shogren, J. F. (2002). Hardnose the dictator. *American Economic Review, 92*(4), 1218–1221.

Conrad, C. A. (2003). Strategies to reform the regulations on international competition. *World Competition, 26*(1), 101–121.

Conrad, C. A. (2005). *Die Notwendigkeit, die Möglichkeiten und die Grenzen einer internationalen Wettbewerbsordnung – Reformansätze vor dem Hintergrund derzeitiger außenwirtschaftlicher Problemfelder und der Doha-Welthandelsrunde*. Dunckner & Humblot.

Conrad, C. A. (2010). *Morality and Economic Crisis – Enron, Subprime & Co.*, disserta Verlag.

Dahm, K.-W. (1993). „Management of Values" Ethikseminare für Führungskräfte, part 1 in: *Forum Wirtschaftsethik*, 1993, No. 2, pp. 4–9, part 2 in: Forum Wirtschaftsethik, 1994, No. 2, pp. 3–11.

deCharms, R., Morrison, H. W., Reitman, W., & McClelland, D. C. (1955). Behavioral correlates of directly and indirectly measured achievement motivation. In D. C. McClelland (Ed.), *Studies in motivation* (pp. 414–423). Appleton-Century-Crofts.

Deci, E. L., & Ryan, R. M. (2000). The "what" and "why" of goal pursuits: Human needs and the self-determination of behavior. *Psychological Inquiry, 11*, 227–268.

DeQuervain, D., et al. (2004). The neural basis of altruistic punishment. *Science, 305*(5688), 1254–1258.

Diehl, M., & Stroebe, W. (1987). Productivity loss in brainstorming groups: Toward the solution of a riddle. *Journal of Personality and Social Psychology, 53*(3), 497–509. https://doi.org/10.1037/0022-3514.53.3.497

Drude, M. (1991). Walter Eucken – Ein Wegbereiter des „Deutschen Wunders". Industrie- und Handels kammer Nordschwarzwald (Pforzheim): Informationen für die Wirtschaft, No. 4.

Dürr, E. (1987). Der Schumpetersche Unternehmer in der Theorie der wirtschaftlichen Entwicklung. In *Markt und Wettbewerb : Festschrift für Ernst Heuss zum 65*, (pp. 245–263). Geburtstag. - Bern: Haupt, ISBN 3–258–03822-8.

Earley, P. C. (1993). East meets West meets Mideast: Further explorations of collectivistic versus individualistic work groups. *Academy of Management Journal, 36*, 319–348.

Eisenberger, N. I., Lieberman, M. D., & Williams, K. D. (2003). Does rejection hurt? An fMRI study of social exclusion. *Science, 302*, 290–292.

Engelmann, D., & Strobel, M. (2000). *An experimental comparison of the fairness models* by Bolton and Ockenfels and by Fehr and Schmidt, Discussion Papers, Interdisciplinary Research Project 373: Quantification and Simulation of Economic Processes, No. 2000, 28, urn:nbn:de:kobv:11–10047345. http://hdl.handle.net/10419/62222

Engeser, S., Rheinberg, F., & Möller, M. (2009). Achievement motive imagery in German schoolbooks: A pilot study testing McClelland's hypothesis. *Journal of Research in Personality, 43*, 110–113.

Eshghi, P., Arofzad, S., & Hosaini, T. A. (2013). Relationship between social intelligence with effective influence among physical education expertise in Isfahan education organizations. *World Applied Science Journal, 28*(12), 2177–2181.

EU-Commission. (1988). *Research on the "costs of non-Europe": Basic findings*. Publications Office of the European Communities.

Falk, A. (2003). Homo oeconomicus versus Homo recipocans: Ansätze für ein neues Wirtschaftspolitisches Weltbild? *Perspektiven der Wirtschaftspolitik, 4*(2003), 141–172.

Fehr, E., & Camerer, C. F. (2007). Social neuroeconomics: The neural circuitry of social preferences. *Trends in Cognitive Sciences, 11*, 419–427.

Fehr, G., & Fischbacher, U. (2001). Are people conditionally cooperative? Evidence from a public goods experiment. *Economics Letters, 71*, 397–404.

Fehr, E., & Fischbacher, U. (2003). The nature of human altruism. *Nature, 425*(23), 785–791.

Fehr, E., & Fischbacher, U. (2004). Third party punishment and social norms. *Evolution and Human Behavior, 25*, 63–87.

Fehr, E., & Gächter, S. (2000). Cooperation and punishment in public goods experiments. *The American Economic Review, 90*, 980–994.

Fehr, E., & Schmidt, K. M. (1999). A theory of fairness, competition and cooperation. *Quarterly Journal of Economics, 1999*, 817–868.

Fershtman, C., Gneezy, U., & List, J. A. (2012). Equity aversion: Social norms and the desire to be ahead. *American Economic Journal: Microeconomics, 4*(4), 131–144.

Föhr, S., & Lenz, H. (1992). Unternehmenskultur und ökonomische Theorie. In W. H. Staehle & P. Conrad (Eds.), *Managementforschung* (pp. 111–162).

Fox, E. M. (1986). Monopolization and dominance in the United States and the European Community: Eficiency, opportunity, and fairness. *Notre Dame Law Review, 61*(5), 981–1020.

Frank, R. H. (1988). *Passion within reason*. The strategic role of the emotions.

Frank, R. H. (2004). What Price the moral high ground?.

Frey, B. F. (2000). The impact of moral intensity on decision making in a business context. *Journal of Business Ethics, 26*, 181–195.

Gardner, H. (1983). *Frames of mind. The theory of multiple intelligences*. Basic Books.

Gardner, H. (1999). *Intelligence reframed. Multiple intelligences for the 21st century perseus*. Books Group.

Gardner, H., & Moran, S. (2006). The science of multiple intelligences theory: A response to Lynn waterhouse. *Educational Psychologist, 41*(4), 227–232.

Gardner, H., Kornhaber, M. L., & Wake, W. K. (1996). *Intelligence*. Multiple Perspectives.

Gerard, H. B., & Mathewson, G. C. (1966). The effects of severity of initiation on liking for a group: A replication. *Journal of Experimental Social Psychology, 2*, 278–287.

Gneezy, U. (2005). Deception: The role of consequences. *American Economic Review., 95*(1), 384–394.

Göbel, E. (2010). *Unternehmensethik*. UTB.

Golnaz, T., Satpute, A. B., & Lieberman, M. D. (2007). The sunny side of fairness: Preference for fairness activates reward circuitry. *Psychological Science, 19*(4), 339–347.

Greene, J. D., Nystrom, L. E., Engell, A. D., & Darley, J. M. (2004). The neural bases of cognitive confict and control in moral judgment. *Neuron, 44*, 389–400.

Gürerk, Ö. I., & Rockenbach, B. (2006). The competitive advantage of sanctioning institutions. *Science, 312*(April), 108–111.

Güth, W., Schmittberger, R., & Schwarze, B. (1982). An experimental analysis of ultimatum bargaining. *Journal of Economic Behavior and Organization, 3*(4), 367–388.

Haidt, J., Koller, S., & Dias, M. (1993). Affect, culture, and morality, or is it wrong to eat your dog? *Journal of Personality and Social Psychology, 65*, 613–628.

Haney, C., Banks, C., & Zimbardo, P. (1973). Interpersonal dynamics in a simulated prison. *International Journal of Criminology and Penology, 1*, 69–97.

Harbaugh, W. T., Mayr, U., & Burghart, D. R. (2007). Neural responses to taxation and Voluntry giving reveal motives for charitable donations. *Science, 316*, 1622–1625.

Hausmann, D. M., & McPherson, M. (2006). *Economic analysis, moral philosophy, and public policy* (2nd ed., p. 2006). Cambridge University Press.

Hay Group. (2011). *Führungskräfte für eine neue Welt. Was die Zukunft von Führungskräften verlangt*. www.haygroup.com/.../de/Leadership_2030_Whitepaper_DE_web.pdf.

Hein, G., Silani, G., Preuschoff, K., Batson, C. D., & Singer, T. (2010). Neural responses to ingroup and outgroup members' suffering predict individual differences in costly helping. *Neuron, 68*, 149–160.

Henrich, J., et al. (2005). "Economic man" in cross-cultural perspective: Behavioral experiments in 15 small-scale societies. *Behavioral and Brain Sciences, 28*(2005), 795–855.

Herdzina, K. (1999). *Wettbewerbspolitik* (5th ed.). UTB.

Heuß, E. (1980). Wettbewerb. In Albers, Willi u.a.(Hrsg.), *Handwörterbuch der Wirtschaftswissenschaft (HdWW)*, Bd. 8, Stuttgart u.a.

Hewstone, M., & Martin, R. (2007). Sozialer Einfluss. In K. Jonas, W. Stroebe, & M. Hewstone (Eds.), *Sozialpsychologie* (5th ed., pp. 359–408). Springer.

Hewstone, M., & Martin, R. (2014). Sozialer Einfluss. In K. Jonas, W. Stroebe, & M. Hewstone (Eds.), *Sozialpsychologie, 6., vollständig überarbeitete Auflage* (pp. 269–314). Springer.

Hildebrand, D. (2002). *The role of economic analysis in the EC competition rules*. The Hague (Kluwer Law International).

Höffe, O. (1992a). *Utilitarismus* (2nd ed., pp. 84–97). Francke Verlag.

Höffe, O. (1992b). Einleitung. In O. Höffe (Ed.), *Einführung in die utilitaristische Ethik, Klassische und zeitgenössische Texte* (pp. 7–54). Edition.

Hofstede, G., Hofstede, G. J., & Minkov, M. (2010). *Cultures and organizations – Software of the mind: Intercultural cooperation and its importance for survival*. McGraw-Hill Education.

Hogg, M. A., & Turner, J. C. (1987). Intergroup behaviour, self-stereotyping and the salience of social categories. *British Journal of Social Psychology, 26*(4), 325–340. https://doi.org/10.1111/j.2044-8309.1987.tb00795.x

Holzmann, R. (2015). *Wirtschaftsethik*. Wiesbaden.

Hornstein, H. A., Fisch, E., & Holmes, M. (1968). Influence of a model's feeling about his behavior and his relevance as a comparison other on observers' helping behavior. *Journal of Personality and Social Psychology, 10*(3), 222–226.

Hüffmeier, J., & Hertel, G. (2011). When the whole is more than the sum of its parts: Group motivation gains in the wild. *Journal of Experimental Social Psychology, 47*, 455–459.

Hühns, E., & Hühns, I. (1963). *Bauer, Bürger, Edelmann: Leben im Mittelalter*. Verlag Neues Leben.
Hull, C. L. (1952). *A behavior system: An introduction to behavior theory concerning the individual organism*. Greenwood Press.
James, K., & Greenberg, J. (1989). In-group salience, intergroup comparison, and individual performance and self-esteem. *Personality and Social Psychology Bulletin, 15*, 604–616.
Jonas, K., Stroebe, W., & Hewstone, M. (2007). *Sozialpsychologie, Eine Einführung* (5th ed.). Springer.
Jonas, K., Stroebe, W., & Hewstone, M. (Eds.). (2014a). *Sozialpsychologie* (6th ed.). Springer.
Jonas, K., Stroebe, W., & Hewstone, M. (2014b). Einführung in die Sozialpsychologie. In K. Jonas, W. Stroebe, & M. Hewstone (Eds.), *Sozialpsychologie, 6., vollständig überarbeitete Auflage* (pp. 1–29). Springer.
Kagel, J. H., Kim, & Moser, D. (1996). Fairness in ultimatum games with asymmetric information and asymmetric payoffs. *Games and Economic Behavior, 13*, 100–110.
Kant, I. (1785). Grundlegung zur Metaphysik der Sitten, (A). In W. von Weischedel (Ed.), *Werksausgabe Band VII*. suhrkamp. 1974, first edition 1785 Internet-edition (B) (1785), http://www.korpora.org/kant/aa04.html. Access: 17. April 2015
Karremans, J. C., & Finkenauer, C. (2014). Affiliation, zwischenmenschliche Anziehung und enge Beziehungen. In K. Jonas, W. Stroebe, & M. Hewstone (Eds.), *Sozialpsychologie* (vollständig überarbeitete Auflage) (6th ed., pp. 401–438). Springer.
Kerber, W. S. J. (1989). Zum Ethos von Führungskräften, Ergebnisse einer empirischen Untersuchung. In H. Steinmann & A. Löhr (Eds.), *Unternehmensethik* (pp. 273–283).
Kessler, T., & Fritsche, I. (2018). *Sozialpsychologie*. Springer.
Köhler, O. (1926). Kraftleistungen bei Einzel- und Gruppenarbeit. *Industrielle Psychotechnik, 3*, 274–282.
Leimgruber, K. L., Shaw, A., Santos, L. R., & Olson, K. R. (2012). Young children are more generous when others are aware of their actions. *PLoS ONE, 7*(10), e48292. https://doi.org/10.1371/journal.pone.0048292
Leisinger, Klaus M. (1997), Unternehmensethik, Globale Verantwortung und modernes Management.
Leo XIII, P. (1891). *Über die Arbeiterfrage, Enzyklika RERUM NOVARUM*. www.christusrex.org/; www1/overkott/rerum.htm. Access: 4. April 2015.
Levine, M., & Manning, R. (2014). Prosoziales Verhalten. In K. Jonas, W. Stroebe, & M. Hewstone (Eds.), *Sozialpsychologie, 6., vollständig überarbeitete Auflage* (pp. 357–400). Springer.
Levine, M., Prosser, A., Evans, D., & Reicher, S. D. (2005). Identity and emergency intervention: How social group membership and inclusiveness of group boundaries shape helping behavior. *Personality and Social Psychology Bulletin, 31*, 443–453.
List, J. A. (2006). The behavioralist meets the market: Measuring social preferences and reputation effects in actual transactions. *Journal of Political Economy, 114*(1), 1–37.
Lück, H. E., & Manz, W. (1973). Die Technik der verlorenen Briefe – Ein neues Instrument verhaltensbezogener Einstellungsmessung? *Zeitschrift für Soziologie, 2*(4), 352–365.
Luhmann, N. (2000). *Vertrauen: Ein Mechanismus der Reduktion sozialer Komplexität*. Stuttgart.
MacDonald, J. M. (1994). Does import competition force efficient production? *The Review of Economics and Statistics, MIT Press, 76*(4), 721–727.
Max, Reinhard & Wulsdorf, Helge (2002), Christliche Sozialethik, Paderborn.
McClelland, D. C. (1961). *The achieving society*. Van Nostrand.
McClelland, D. C., Atkinson, J. W., Clark, R. A., & Lowell, E. L. (1953). *The achievement motive*. Appleton-Century-Crofts.
McClelland, D. C., Koestner, R., & Weinberger, J. (1989). How do self-attributed and implicit motives differ? *Psychological Review, 96*(4), 690–702.
Meyer, B., Enström, M. K., Harvstveit, M., Bowles, D. P., & Beevers, C. G. (2007). Happiness and dispair on the catwalk: Need satisfaction, well-being, and personality adjustment among fashion models. *The Journal of Positive Psychology, 2*(1), 2–17.
Mill, J. S. (1844). *Essays on some unsettled questions of political economy*, London 1844, http://www.econlib.org/library/Mill/mlUQP5.html (25.04.2015).

Mitteis, H. (1976). Über den Rechtsgrund des Satzes "Stadtluft macht frei". In: Erika Kunz (Ed.), Festschrift Edmund E. Stengel zum 70. Geburtstag am 24. Dezember 1949 dargebracht von Freunden, Fachgenossen und Schülern. Böhlau, Münster u. a. 1952, pp. 342–358, (Auch in: Carl Haase (Ed.), Die Stadt des Mittelalters. Vol. 2: Recht und Verwaltung. 2. Auflage, Darmstadt 1976, ISBN 3-534-04680-3, (= Wege der Forschung 244), pp. 182–202 Berlin, 1963).

Molitor, Bruno (1989), Wirtschaftsethik.

Moll, J., et al. (2006). Human fronto-mesolimbic networks guide decisions about charitable donation. *Proceedings of the National Academy of Sciences of the United States of America, 103*, 15623–15628.

Nijstad, B. A., & Van Knippenberg, D. (2007). Gruppendynamik. In K. Jonas, W. Stroebe, & M. Hewstone (Eds.), *Sozialpsychologie* (6th ed., pp. 439–468). Springer.

Noll, B. (2002). *Wirtschafts- und Unternehmensethik in der Marktwirtschaft*. Kohlhammer.

Osgood, C. E., Suci, G., & Tannenbaum, P. (1957). *The measurement of meaning*. University of Illinois Press.

Perin, C. I. (1942). Behavior potentiality as a joint function of the amount of training and the degree of hunger at the time of extinction. *Journal of Experimental Psychology, 30*, 93–113.

Perry, S. (2003). Social conventions in wild White-faced capuchin monkeys: Evidence for traditions in a Neotropical primate. *Current Anthropology, 44*(2), 241–268.

Platow, M. J., Foddy, M., Yamagishi, T., Lim, L., & Chow, A. (2012). Two experimental tests of trust in in-group strangers: The moderating role of common knowledge of group membership. *European Journal of Social Psychology, 42*, 30–35. https://doi.org/10.1002/ejsp.852

Porter, M. (1990). *The competition advantage of nations*. Free Press.

Pritzl, R. F. J., & Schneider, F. (1999). Korruption. In W. Korff (Ed.), *Handbuch der Wirtschaftsethik, Band 4: Ausgewählte Handlungsfelder, Gütersloh* (pp. 310–333).

Rapoport, A., & Chammah, A. M. (1970). *Prisoner's dilemma – A study in conflict and cooperation* (2nd ed.). University of Michigan Press.

Rawls, J. (1999). *A theory of justice*. Harvard University Press (revised edition 1999). www.univpgri-palembang.ac.id/.../John%20Rawls%20-%20A%20Theory%. Access: 4. Mai 2015.

Richman, L., & Leary, M. R. (2009). Reactions to discrimination, stigmatization, ostracism, and other forms of interpersonal rejection: A multimotive model. *Psychological Review, 116*, 365–383.

Rosenbaum, M. E., Moore, D. L., Cotton, J. L., Cook, M. S., Hieser, R. A., Shovar, M. N., et al. (1980). Group productivity and process: Pure and mixed reward structures and task interdependence. *Journal of Personality and Social Psychology, 39*, 626–664.

Roth, A. E., Prasnikar, V., Okuno-Fujiwara, M., & Zamir, S. (1991). Bargaining and market behavior in Jerusalem, Ljubljana, Pittsburgh, and Tokyo: An experimental study. *American Economic Review, 81*(5), 1068–1095.

Russo, J. E., & Schoemaker, P. J. H. (1992). Managing overconfidence. *Sloan Management Review, 33*, 7–17.

Sanfey, A. G., Rilling, J. K., Aronson, J. A., Nystrom, L. E., & Cohen, J. D. (2003). The neural basis of economic decision-making in the ultimatum game. *Science, 300*, 1755–1758.

Schachter, S. (1951). Deviation, rejection, and communication. *Journal of Abnormal and Social Psychology, 46*, 190–207.

Schäfer, M. (2009). *Geschichte des Bürgertums*. Köln.

Schefold, B. (1989). Klassiker des ökonomischen Denkens, ed. J. Starbatty. Platon (428/427–348/347) und Aristoteles (384–322) (C.H. Beck, Munich, 1989).

Scherer, A. G. (1997). Spirale nach unten? Zur Verantwortung multinationaler Unternehmen bei der Etablierung weltweiter Sozial- und Umweltstandards. *Forum Wirtschaftsethik, 5*(3), 11–13.

Schlesinger, C. (2006). Abschied vom IQ. *Die Wirtschaftswoche, 52*, 124–130. (2007) *Applied Psychology, 90*, 295–305.

Schmidt, H. (1982). *Philosophisches Wörterbuch*, ed. von G. Schischkoff, 21st edition (Kröne, 1982).

Schultheiss, O. C. (2008). Implicit motives. In O. P. John, R. W. Robins, & L. A. Pervin (Eds.), *Handbook of personality: Theory and research* (3rd ed., pp. 603–633). Guilford.

Schulz-Hardt, S., & Brodbeck, F. C. (2014). Gruppenleistung und Führung Stefan Schulz-Hardt und Felix C. Brodbeck. In K. Jonas, W. Stroebe, & M. Hewstone (Eds.), *Sozialpsychologie* (6th. ed.). Springer.

Schumpeter, J. A. (1911). *Theorie der wirtschaftlichen Entwicklung. Eine Untersuchung über Unternehmergewinn, Kapital, Kredit, Zins und den Konjunkturzyklus* (München und Leipzig, Duncker & Humboldt, München, 1911).

Schwaninger, M. (2008). Anatol Rapoport (May 22, 1911–January 20, 2007). Pioneer of systems theory and peace research, mathematician, philosopher and pianist. *Wiley Online Library Systems Research and Behavioral Science, 24*(6), 655–658.

Schwartz, S. H. (1994). Beyond individualism and collectivism: New cultural dimensions of values. In U. Kim, H. C. Triandis, Ç. Kağitçibaşi, S. C. Choi, & G. Yoon (Eds.), *Individualism and collectivism: Theory, method and applications* (pp. 85–119). Sage.

Schwartz, S. H. (2004). Mapping and interpreting cultural differences around the world. In H. Vinken, J. Soeters, & P. Ester (Eds.), *Comparing cultures: Dimensions of culture in a comparative perspective* (pp. 43–73). Brill.

Schwarz, N., & Vaughn, L. A. (2002). The availability heuristic revisited: Ease of recall and content of recall as distinct sources of information. In T. Gilovich, D. W. Griffin, & D. Kahneman (Eds.), *Heuristics and biases: The psychology of intuitive judgment* (pp. 103–119). Cambridge University Press.

Schwarze, G. (2007). *Gibt es gerechten Reichtum? oder Wie kommt das Kamel durch's Nadelöhr?* Von einer Tagung in Brandenburg, Morgenandacht (2007, März 11), www.oekonomie-und-kirche.de/diskussion/Kamel.pdf

Sherif, M. (1966). *In common predicament. Social psychology of intergroup conflict and cooperation.* Houghton Mifflin.

Sherif, M., Harvey, O. J., White, B. J., Hood, W. R., & Sherif, C. W. (1961). *Intergroup conflict and cooperation. The robbers cave experiment.* University of Oklahoma Press.

Singer, T., & Lamm, C. (2009). The social neuroscience of empathy. *Annals of the New York Academy of Sciences, 1156*, 81–96.

Singer, T., et al. (2006). Empathic neural responses are modulated by the perceived fairness of others. *Nature, 439*, 466–469.

Singhapakdi, A., Vitell, S. J., & Kraft, K. L. (1996). Moral intensity and ethical decision-making of marketing professionals. *Journal of Business Research, 36*, 245–255.

Smith, A. (1776). *An inquiry into the nature and causes of the wealth of nations, Edinburgh 1776.* http://www.econlib.org/library/Smith/smWN8.html

Smith, V. (2002). *Constructivist and ecological rationality in economics*; Nobel Prize Lecture, December 8, 2002; printed in THE AMERICAN ECONOMIC REVIEW JUNE 2003, pp. 465–508. https://s3.amazonaws.com/academia.edu.documents/39690274/Constructivist_and_Ecological_Rationality_in_Economics.pdf?AWSAccessKeyId=AKIAIWOWYYGZ2Y53UL3A&Expires=1557228716&Signature=JGGEiHTSNscHsGWEJZ94uSZIHLc%3D&response-content-disposition=inline%3B%20filename%3DConstructivist_and_Ecological_Rationalit.pdf

Smith, P. B. (2014). Sozialpsychologie und kulturelle Unterschiede. In K. Jonas, W. Stroebe, & M. Hewstone (Eds.), *Sozialpsychologie* (6th ed., pp. 565–606). Springer.

Smith, P. B., Bond, M. H., & Kağıtçıbaşı, Ç. (2006). *Understanding social psychology across cultures: Living and working in a changing world.* Sage.

Starbatty, J. (1983). Ordoliberalismus. In *Wirt schaftswissenschaftliches Studium* (Vol. 12).

Starbatty, J. (1987). Die ordnungspolitische Dimension der EU-Technologiepolitik. *ORDO (Jahrbuch für die Ordnung von Wirtschaft und Gesellschaft), 38*, 155–180.

Steinmann, H., & Löhr, A. (1994). *Grundlagen der Unternehmensethik* (2nd ed.). Schäffer-Poeschel Verlag.

Stroebe, W., & Diehl, M. (1994). Why groups are less effective than their members: On productivity losses in ideagenerating groups. *European Review of Social Psychology, 5*, 271–303. https://doi.org/10.1080/14792779543000084

Stroebe, W., Diehl, M., & Abakoumkin, G. (1996). Social compensation and the Köhler effect: Toward a theoretical explanation of motivation gains in group productivity. In E. H. Witte & H. Davis (Eds.), *Understanding group behaviour: Small group processes and interpersonal relations* (Vol. 2, pp. 37–65). Erlbaum.

Sy, T., Coté, S., & Saavedra, R. (2005). The contagious leader: Impact of the leader's mood on the mood of group members, group affective tone, and group processes. *Journal of Applied Psychology, 90*, 295–305.

Tajfel, H. (1978). Social categorization, social identity and social comparison. In H. Tajfel (Ed.), *Differentiation between social groups: Studies in the social psychology of intergroup relations* (pp. 65–93). Academic.

Tajfel, H., Billig, M. G., Bundy, R. P., & Flament, C. (1971). Social categorization and intergroup behaviour. *European Journal of Social Psychology, 1*, 149–178.

Turner, J. C., Oakes, P. J., Haslam, S. A., & McGarty, C. (1994). Self and collective: Cognition and social context. *Personality and Social Psychology Bulletin, 20*, 454–463.

Ulrich, P. (1993). Unternehmerethos. In Enderle, u.a. (Ed.), *Lexikon der Wirtschaftsethik, Freiburg* (pp. 1165–1175).

Vickers, J. (1994). *Concepts of competition, an inaugural lecture delivered.* University of Oxford. On 2 Nov 1993.

von Hayek, F. A. (1969). Der Wettbewerb als Entdeckungsverfahren. In F. A. von Hayek (Ed.), *Freiburger Studien*. Mohr-Siebeck.

von Hayek, F. A. (1976). *Law, legislation and liberty, the mirage of social justice* (Vol. 2). University of Chicago Press.

von Hayek, F. A. (1979). *Law, legislation and liberty, the political order of free people* (Vol. 3). University of Chicago Press.

Weber, M. (1905). *The protestant ethic and the spirit of capitalism*, chapter 4. https://www.marxists.org/reference/archive/weber/protestant-ethic/ch02.htm. Deutsches Original: Weber, M. (1904). Die protestantische Ethik und der Geist des Kapitalismus. Archiv für Sozialwissenschaft und Sozialpolitik.

Wilkening, H.-R. (2004). Competitiveness und Ethik, Herausforderungen an das Management, Schriftenreihe der Graduate School of Business Administration Bd. 11, ed. R. Berndt et al. Wirtschaft und Ethik – aktueller denn je! (Zurich, 2004), pp. 59–75.

Williams, S. B. (1938). Resistance to extinction as a function of the number of reinforcements. *Journal of Experimental Psychology, 23*, 506–521.

Williams, K. D., & Karau, S. J. (1991). Social loafing and social compensation: The effects of expectations of co-worker performance. *Journal of Personality and Social Psychology, 61*, 570–581.

Wiswede, G. (1985). *Soziologie* (1st ed.). Verlag Moderne Industrie AG.

Witte, E. H. (1989). Köhler rediscovered: The anti-Ringelmann effect. *European Journal of Social Psychology, 19*, 147–154.

Yaari, M. E., & Bar-Hillel, M. (1984). On dividing justly. *Social Choice and Welfare, 1*(1), 1–24.

Yamagishi, T. (1987). Interpersonal conflicts in reward allocation and their resolution. *Japanese Journal of Psychology, 58*, 78–83. (in Japanese).

Zanna, M. P., & Cooper, J. (1974). Dissonance and the pill: An attribution approach to studying the arousal properties of dissonance. *Journal of Personality and Social Psychology, 29*, 703–709.

Zimbardo, P. G. (2006). On rethinking the psychology of tyranny: The BBC prison study. *British Journal of Social Psychology, 45*, 47–53.

Zimbardo, P. G., Maslach, C., & Haney, C. (2000). Reflections on the Stanford prison experiment: Genesis, transformations, consequences. In T. Blass (Ed.), *Obedience to authority: Current perspectives on the Milgram paradigm* (pp. 193–237). Erlbaum.

Chapter 4
Economic Systems

What Follows Why?
This chapter is about the economic institutions. Given the behavior of men and the functioning of market and competition, what might be a fair and functioning economic system? After discussing the functioning of markets and competition and showing that they achieve our desired welfare optimum, let us now turn to the institutional framework of the two alternative economies within market economy and central administration. What are the building blocks of a market economy? How does the central administrative economy work? What are the Pros and Cons? Most economies in the real world are hybridized to these two alternatives. Is the so called social market economy the optimal economic system?

Learning Goals
You should be able to explain the functions, advantages and disadvantages as well as the essential differences between the two systems in your own words.

4.1 Theories of Justice

What ideas were there to regulate social coexistence and economic activities and the distribution of the resulting goods? What is meant by a just social order?

It was Thomas Hobbes who defined justice in 1651 independently of God and thus provided the first scientific theory of justice in his main work "Leviathan". He imagines a natural state of people without state order. The consequence would be anarchy as a state without property and legitimacy. His image of man is not just a utility maximizer, but a wolf. "Homo homini lupus est",[1] so that the abolition of the state order would result in war of everyone against everyone, "Bellum omnium contra omnes". Man is not fair, because he pursues only his own interests, with

[1] Hobbes Widmung in seinem Werk „De Cive"an William Cavendish, den Grafen von Devonshire.

C. A. Conrad, *Economic Systems, Markets and Politics*,
https://doi.org/10.1007/978-3-031-10366-7_4

which he comes into conflict with the interests of others. For reasons of humanity, therefore, man decides to restrict his natural freedom by, in the context of a social contract, entrusting to a sovereign the task of enforcing peace and justice by force. Justice is then expressed through the treaties and the legislature of the sovereign.[2]

For David Hume, 1748, justice is not logically grounded, but a value-judgment that has emerged as a habit. But justice is also the virtue that ensures order in human life. Extreme deficiency leads to a collapse of social justice, because only those who act egoistically can survive. Based on a shortage of everyday necessities, there can be no need-based justice. Only in a land of milk and honey can everyone get what they want. Like Adam Smith, he sees equality of justice as central justice, because it best promotes society's well-being.[3] He rejects the original natural state described by Hobbes as false, because the family stood as a community before the state formation by larger groups. There were already rules and education, but also a caring love that can not be transferred to larger groups. States can only be formed if there are already social orders.[4]

In contrast to Hobbes, in 1823 John Locke developed the idea of a divine right of nature that was given to man by the Creator. These are life, freedom and possessions. Citizens assign the task of enforcing or protecting natural law to the state. Unlike Hobbes, the articles of association can be recalled at any time if the state does not adequately represent the will of the citizens. Locke developed law enforcement (Judiciary, Executive and Legislature) as an instrument to control the power of the government. The legislature is elected by the people and is bound by a constitution. The government is also bound by the laws.[5]

Rousseau also starts from a natural state. Man was not originally selfish, but peaceful, self sufficient, and compassionate. The fruits of nature belonged to all humans and the soil to no one. Only through the development of agriculture did property become property. Labor-acquired property is beneficial to Rousseau, but not the property that enhances inequality, for the rich as through agriculture, because it increases wealth through the work of the poor. Freedom and equality are lost and greed and domination gain the upper hand. A way out of this unjust society is only offered by a social contract (contrat sociale) in which citizens transfer their rights to the state. It then has to represent the interests of the community. The interests of the community are not identical with the sum of the individual interests, since these are

---

[2] See Hobbes (1651), Chapter 13–31 and Ebert (2015), pp. 130.

[3] See Hume, David (1748).

[4] See Ebert (2015), pp. 143.

[5] See Locke, John (1823).

only for themselves. Starting from his postulate of equality,[6] he calls for social redistribution by the state in order to restore social justice.[7]

> *Enlightenment is man's release from his self-incurred tutelage. Tutelage is man's inability to make use of his understanding without direction from another. Self-incurred is this tutelage when its cause lies not in lack of reason but in lack of resolution and courage to use it without direction from another. Sapere aude! 'Have courage to use your own reason!'- that is the motto of enlightenment.*[8]

For Kant equality, freedom and respect for the rights of others result from reason. The personality and dignity of man must be respected. Through reason, for example, he develops the categorical imperative, which can be regarded as an essential basis for human coexistence and thus also for jurisprudence.[9]

The categorical imperative:

> Only act according to the maxim that you can make a universal law.[10]

For Kant, maxims are guidelines that people give themselves. In addition, there are generally applicable human laws, which therefore absolutely apply categorically.[11] And the practical imperative:

> Act in the way that you use humanity, both in your person and in the person of each other, at any time not just as means but also as a purpose.[12]

How do my actions affect people? The purpose of my action should be to do good, or at least not to harm anyone.

The sociological institutional theories go back to Durkheim and Weber. Because man is free in his actions, social rules are needed to avoid damaging others. Therefore, even interests cannot lead to stable social relationships or orders. For this purpose, the morality of a group (Durkheim) requires legitimate systems of order (Weber).[13] "I can only be free to the extent that someone else is prevented from

---

[6] „*"L'homme est né libre, et partout il est dans les fers."Rousseau, Jean-Jaques (1762), Du contracts social ou principles du droit polititiques, Livre 1, capitre 1.1., https://www.rousseauonline.ch/pdf/rousseauonline-0004.pdf, english:* "Man is born free and everywhere he is in chains".

[7] See Rousseau (1755), p. 117 and Rousseau (1762b).

[8] Kant, Immanuel (1784), p. 481–494.

[9] See Ebert (2015), pp. 177.

[10] See Kant (1797), (C), p. 421.

[11] See Schmidt (1986), p. 47 and Schmidt (1982).

[12] Kant (1797), (C), p. 429.

[13] See Weber, Max (1980/1922), pp. 16; Weber, Max (1981/1920), and Maurer, Andrea (2017), 135.

exploiting his physical, economic, or other superiority, which he holds in order to suppress my freedom; only social rules can prevent abuse of power."[14]

Karl Marx sees the dependence of labor on capital, that is, the ownership of factories, as the reason for the injustice in income distribution. Only when property belongs to everyone in communism can one say: "Everyone according to their abilities, each according to his needs."[15]

For Hayek, there is a legal and political equality of people, but not economic. Hayek emphasizes that the rules of the game are given by the market and that changing the rules of the game only worsens productivity. If the game's rules are followed, the result is fair. Hayek is, however, in favor of a social security at subsistence level. It is therefore possible to have an adequate life, but no distribution justice in the sense of equal distribution. A social policy that conforms to the market does not change the rules of the game, but it can increase the satisfaction and security of society and thus the productivity of the economy.[16]

For Rawls, a social order has the task of overcoming conflicts and harmonizing citizens' interests. The social institutions are formed according to the social ideas of justice. Institutions such as the rule of law, private property, competition rules, etc. enable welfare profits for all involved. There is a primitive state in which the members of the society, who are entitled to equal rights, commit themselves to a basic order which everyone considers to be just. They do this to benefit from the collaborative gains (e.g., Prisoner's Dilemma Game). These are therefore the public goods which only a state as an organized community can make available to the individual. In doing so, a veil of ignorance helps to establish the principles in which no one knows what role he will play under what conditions and qualifications. According to Rawls, those involved will then agree on basic human rights such as equality before the law, democratic freedoms, the rule of law, human rights, and so on. Central to all concerned is equality of opportunity. Inequalities are only allowed if they bring about an advantage for the least favored person (principle of difference). Rawls is therefore committed to a market economy with a welfare state with a social redistribution, especially in the education sector (egalitarian liberalism). A high savings rate should increase the fairness between the generations.[17]

In 1986 Gauthier developed a morale based on utility-maximizing rationality. Moral behavior is chosen when it benefits the individual. According to this, moral behavior of not cheating one's competition, that is to say cooperation, brings cooperation gains over several rounds in the theoretical prisoner's dilemma. Prerequisite for a stable cooperation solution is mutual trust, because otherwise people would protect themselves from cheating by non-cooperation. In addition, imperfect

---

[14] See Durkheim (1988) and Büttner (2017), pp. 47.

[15] See. Marx, Karl 1973, p. 31. http://www.mlwerke.de/me/me19/me19_013.htm and Ebert, Thomas (2015), pp. 230.

[16] Vgl. Hayek, Friedrich August von (1971), 361; Hayek, Friedrich August von (1981), S. 112 and Ebert, Thomas (2015), p. 327.

[17] Vgl. Rawls, John (1971) and Ebert, Thomas (2015), pp. 291.

market conditions must be replaced by a fair, negotiated solution. For this it is important that fair starting conditions for negotiations are created. There must be enough rationality that the negotiated solution does not fail due to unrealistic maximum demands. Everyone has to be better off with the negotiated solution and it is optimal if the cooperation achieves a maximum result with minimum concessions that are the same for each one (justice as a minimax principle).[18] This approach thus corresponds to the image of man of homo oeconomicus and of economics[19] as a justification for morality.

Scanlon takes up the rationality of Kant and derives principles of justice from a universal balance. In terms of content, the postulates must be recognized by other persons, in other words the society, as undeniable (**contractualism**). On this basis, he advocates egalitarianism. Gross status differences lead to humiliation, which is why human equality should be improved. In what he calls equal opportunity, power should be limited in the economic system, as it leads to an unequal income distribution. Economic freedom limits economic power. Redistribution is intended to improve the situation of people in great need, but people have to shape their own lives and are responsible for their own quality of life.[20]

Habermas rejects legal positivism, natural law and reason as justifications for societal regulations, i.e. institutions such as law. Laws cannot be derived from higher principles, because the complexity of society would cause them to fail. Since religious and metaphysical legitimacy are no longer effective in modern society, social norms must be accepted by society. Law and morality as social ideas belong together and are subject to social change. For this purpose, the individual must be convinced of the correctness of the rules, consider them to be just because he was involved in their determination, understands himself as a "reasonable author of these norms". The law thus obtains legitimacy through a social discourse on the structure of the rules, in which all concerned must be involved. Democracy, the rule of law and public free opinion forming an important basis for this.[21]

Starting from Hegel, Honneth develops a theory of justice that emphasizes intersubjective relationship, social interaction and recognition. It is not about isolated individual ideas of freedom of the liberal justice theories, but about equal rights in the form of recognition of equal rights by the other fellow citizens. Justice is thus not primarily the distribution of goods, but the distribution of rights and duties among each other. In this way, Honneth sees distributive justice and needs-based

[18] See Gauthier (1986); Heil (2005), pp. 197 and Herlinde (2015), pp. 75.

[19] A moral framework should be designed in such a way that self-interest becomes socially productive. Homann transfers the utility maximization from Adam Smith to all spheres of life, referring to the economist G. S. Becker. See K. Homann, pp. 335 and Conrad, Christian, A. (2018), pp. 32.

[20] See Scanlon, Thomas M. (1998); Wallace, R. Jay (2002), pp. 429–470; Scanlon, Thomas M. (2018) and Weisshaar, Kenneth R. (2018).

[21] See Habermas, Jürgen (1992), Mazouz, Nadia (2009), S. 263ff and Goppel et al. (2016), pp. 236.

justice derived from charity, as well as the performance justice derived from the fair division of labor and an expression of social esteem.[22]

For Sen, prosperity is less about material wealth, but about freedom of design, which allows people to shape their lives according to their own needs. Freedom is thus a value in itself. A society is fairer the more self-realization opportunities it offers people. Sen includes political and economic freedoms, equal opportunities, freedom of expression and the press and social security, such as social assistance in such opportunities. For Sen, the social institutions must promote justice. Sen has developed this approach together with the UN, which has been an international standard for capturing the evolution of states.[23] He sees utilitarianism and Kant's ethics of reason as an approach to global justice. Global justice in terms of equal opportunities could – as Sen critically notes – only be enforced by a world government, which he considers unrealistic.[24]

Conclusion

Kant's principles of reason, democracy, and the separation of powers have largely prevailed. Equality, freedom and respect for the rights of others arise from reason. The personality and dignity of man are reflected in human rights. Hume is right to say that the scarcity of goods requires economic activity in the form of labor, which goes hand in hand with deprivation. It is not the desire for organized work that determines occupations, but the shortages or the needs of the people. There can therefore be no need-based justice, but a compensatory social redistribution that protects against unfair acts of fate and makes possible a humane life in the interest of human dignity. Others who are willing to do so must make the redistribution, otherwise they will emigrate.

As we discussed in Sect. 3.1.4 on the topic of fairness, people on a non-performance based income tend to regard equal distribution as fair. However, the willingness to give up earned income is much lower. And there is a conflict of interest regarding willingness to perform. The willingness to work in equal distribution for income is very low.

This requires a social discourse that weighs the balances sacrifices and needs against each other and a democratic decision-making process, which is supported by all citizens. However, this does not require a veil of ignorance, but the recognition of one's own position in the common system. It must be made clear to what extent the individual benefits from the state and what he has to do for it. For this purpose, trust of the citizen in the machinations of the state with its rights and contributions is required. In order to finance social compensation and livelihood security, it is

[22] See Honneth (2007); Axel Honneth (2011); Baschek (2012) and Horn (2018), pp. 16–40.

[23] See Sen, Amartya (2000); Sen, Amartya (2009); Sen, Amartya (2003), pp. 41–58. http://morgana.unimore.it/Picchio_Antonella/Sviluppo%20umano/svilupp%20umano/Sen%20development.pdf; Sen, Amartya (2001). https://them.polylog.org/3/fsa-de.htm

[24] See Sen, Amartya (2001). https://them.polylog.org/3/fsa-de.htm; Böhler, Thomas (2004) and Dierksmeier, Claus (2013).

necessary for citizens to realize that they themselves can get into such a situation, then they would see the contributions as an insurance premium. As the presented behavioral studies on groups have shown, it is additionally beneficial for citizens to identify with each other, since compassion favors the willingness to make a donation.

Justice thus results from social discourse. Inheritance tax increases equality of opportunity when used to finance a public education system.

Civilization is the central strength of humanity. By sharing work in a large group, productivity benefits can be realized. For the organization of this division of labor states were founded and the "natural rights" were transferred to the state. The financing and provision of public goods is the central task of the state. These benefits are for anyone who submits to the rule of the state.

Even Durkheim and Weber see the need for rules. Recognized institutions must be enforced by the state to protect the individual and enable civilization. Society must agree on morality and give itself group rules.

Following the rules of the market maximizes the social return from the division of labor. Imperfect market conditions must be supplemented socially or corrected by the state. Competition limits power and increases freedom. Freedom is seen by humans as a value in itself. The state institutions must provide the framework for economic and social freedom.

Justice is an order that is socially accepted. Prerequisite is the freedom to choose between the social roles, ie duties and rights. Changes can often be brought about only by revolutions. According to Hayek, society evolves evolutionarily. Social market economy increases productivity and the technical development of the economy determines social roles.

Global justice in the sense of equal rights can only exist in public goods, to which all people have the same claim. All other goods were taken over by the settlement and agriculture and historically fought or defended. Global justice will therefore only be able to refer to behavior towards each other. In the sense of universal human rights, the rights of others must be respected. Help in times of need will therefore always be voluntary.

Social decisions are not unproblematic as group decisions. They do not automatically lead to the best decision for a society. The influences on group decisions that cause the informative exchange to be impaired, leading to decisions that are normative based instead of informationally based (groupthink), must be prevented. In addition, even public good games have shown that group interests and individual interests can diverge. Only if everyone participates in the financing of a public good such as a legal system or infrastructure, the public goods come about. Individual interests can also directly oppose this, if, for example, a highway is to be built for the community, but to do so a property must be expropriated or lose its value due to external effects. For this reason, no social rules can arise from individual interests. Individual interests would always try to achieve personal gain, but never weigh the personal interests up with conflicting other individual interests and they would never represent the overriding group interests. So you need a social discourse about the common rules and the form of fairness that the group wants and enforces against individual interests. The result is democracy as the rule of the group. Alternatively, you can hire a third party to represent the common interests, a monarch, but then the group must control the pursuit of common interests.

Comprehension Questions

1. What is meant by "homo homini lupus est"?
2. Why is there no need for justice, according to Hume?
3. What problems does Rousseau associate with property?
4. Why cannot there be economic equality, according to Hayek? What does he offer as a solution?
5. From what does Honneth derive performance justice and needs justice?
6. Why are the self-development opportunities of people so important to Sen?

4.2 Constitutional Economics

Constitutional economics examines the rules, the constitution of the economy in its functioning, with the aim of shaping them so that they serve the interest of the affected individuals. The consent of the individual applies as an objective evaluation criterion. The order is considered legitimated when all individuals agree (methodological individualism).[25] What is problematic here is that individuals agree on their own with regard to their preferences and goals, with which the subjective interests of individuals become the basis of legitimation (normative individualism). Objective function criteria or superordinate common interests are not considered.

> The critical normative presupposition on which the whole contractarian construction stands or falls is the location of value exclusively in the individual human being.[26]

However, an agreement of all individuals means unanimity, whereby a design or change of the rules only succeeds if all individuals have the same interests and a decision is organizationally possible.[27] Vanberg deduces the constitutional economic importance of consumer sovereignty from the precedence of the citizen's interests where individual benefit is greatest. Entrepreneurial interests are then subordinate. Consumer sovereignty is best supported by a performance competition that comes from the school's public policy free school.[28]

---

[25] See Vanberg, V. J. (1997), p. 713; Vanberg, V. J. (1998), p. 70.

[26] Brennan, G., & Buchanan, J. M. (1985), p. 25.

[27] See Vanberg, V. J. (2004), p. 4; Vanberg, V. J. (1997), pp. 713.

[28] See See Vanberg, V. J. (2004): 721f; Feld, L. P., & Köhler, E. (2011). 173–195. https://nbn-resolving.org/urn:nbn:de:0168-ssoar-349165, pp. 180.

Buchanan broadens economics by the rules that bring people economic and political benefits.

> My argument was that economics, as a social science, is or should be about trade, exchange, and the many and varied institutional forms that implement and facilitate trade, including all of the complexities of modern contracts as well as the whole realm of collective agreement on the constitutional rules of political society.[29]

According to Buchanan, traditional economics deals with the voluntary relationships between economic agents. Constitutional Economics examines the institutional framework in the form of rules that organize economic and social coexistence. People subject themselves to rules, thus voluntarily restricting their freedom in order to benefit from those rules. While traditional economics examines and attempts to optimize the behavior of economic agents within the given institutional framework, Constitutional Economics addresses the effects and optimization of the institutional framework, including the political framework.[30]

Constitutional economics, like the Freiburg School, places the shaping of the economic order in the foreground and looks for optimal rules, but more specifically, voluntariness places citizens' approval of the rules in the foreground.[31] The Freiburger Schule, however, saw welfare maximization of the population as a central goal. If one supplements the main principles of competitive order as per Eucken with the principle of the ability to assent and adds consumer sovereignty to citizen's sovereignty, Order Theory becomes Constitution Theory.[32]

4.3 Parts of a Market Economic System

What constitutes an economy? How is everything related? Let's begin with the building blocks of a market economy.

1. **Legal protection of private property**

Property is the basis of a market economy and must therefore be anchored in the constitution of a country. Without ownership there can be no incentive function from competition. Without ownership of the means of production, there is no pursuit of profit and no liability for errors in competition, thus eliminating all competitive functions but the freedom and control functions. The Invisible Hand cannot fulfill its role. Ownership of goods is also the basis for the purchasing power of money and thus for capital and thus also for saving and investing.

---

[29] Buchanan, James M. (1991): pp. 31.

[30] See Buchanan, James M. (1991): pp. 81; Buchanan, James M. (1979), pp. 17 and Vanberg, V. J. (2004): pp. 5.

[31] See Vanberg, V. J. (1988): S. 27.

[32] See Feld, L. P., & Köhler, E. (2011). S. 182.

2. **Constituent and formative company laws**

Business laws are necessary, such as bankruptcy law, competition law, HGB,

Stock Corporation Act etc. They are the basis for liability and contractual freedom.

3. **Tax Law**

To finance the state or community you also need a tax law.

4. **Institutions or organizations for law enforcement**

An executive is necessary to enforce the law; a multi-level legal system with independent judges is required to ensure legal certainty. Defendants must be able to have a judgment reviewed by another judge to prevent arbitrariness and dependency. Of course the judges must not be corrupt, so that fair judgments are given. Here again, separation of powers is a necessary condition. The judiciary and the executive should be separate and there should be no dependencies between them. Seen in this way, it is not in the interest of a meaningful separation of powers that the judges are not appointed by the Ministry of Justice in Germany. Other necessary enforcement bodies are the police and competition oversight (see Chap. 8).

Secure framework conditions for business transactions reduce the risk, and hence the hedging costs, of business transactions (see Sect. 6.6 Transaction Costs). This is one competitive advantage of the FRG compared to other countries. Transactions are safer in Germany than in many other countries.

5. **Financial system**

We also need a two-tier banking system with profit-driven private banks and a non-profit independent central bank (e.g. ECB). The role of private commercial banks is to ensure efficient capital allocation as financial intermediaries. Banks must look for profit-driven investment opportunities in the economy that offer high returns relative to risk. This function can only be carried out by commercial banks. They collect the capital (capital collection points) and thereafter ensure the efficient allocation of that capital. They are liable for mistakes they make even if this means the bankruptcy of one's own company, which is associated with a high loss of assets. If there is no liability, there are moral hazard issues. As in the financial crisis, there is a risk that profits will be privatized and losses will be socialized. An efficient supply of capital also requires a scarce supply of money. If money is made abundantly available by the central bank, it will not be carefully distributed and efficient capital allocation will not be achieved. For this purpose, a potential-oriented monetary policy is required, which means that only so much money may be circulated by the central bank since the production potential develops as a measure of the quantity of goods. If the money supply rises faster than the quantity of goods it causes inflation (see also the equation of quantity in Chap. 10).

The value retention function of money must be unimpaired in order to preserve confidence in the currency. The ban on financing public deficits and the independence of the central bank are important prerequisites in this context in order to create confidence in a policy of the central bank aimed at price stability. For this reason, a central bank is not allowed to work for profit, but can only be committed to the goal of price stability. A central bank makes profits primarily by providing liquidity. The central bank or another independent organization also has the task of supervising the commercial banks. It must monitor the implementation of financial market laws and prevent excessive risk positions (cluster risks).

From an institutional order perspective the central bank is part of the governmental system, which is why it is not allowed to buy private or state bonds on the capital market or even worse shares in private companies.

(a) The state must decide on an exchange rate system, such as flexible or fixed exchange rates. If necessary it can fix its currency to another or join the European Monetary System.
(b) Finally, domestic and foreign convertibility must be defined. This means that domestic and foreign parties can buy or sell unlimited currencies of any origin at the existing (fixed or floating) exchange rate (monetary convertibility). Restrictions may relate to a specific group of persons (national/foreign convertibility) as well as to the underlying transactions (performance/capital transactions).

4.4 Institutional Economics: Elements of the Economy

- What is the economy made of?
- How is everything related?
- Why are there companies and contracts?

From the perspective of institutional economics, economic actions are not just technical processes of production or the transfer of goods. Rather, they are transactions, thus transfers of property rights on goods.

Transaction cost theory[33]: Representatives: Oliver E. Williamson (1975–1996) and Ronald Coase (1937).

Economic decisions are implemented by market participants through transactions. Definitions for transaction:

> Transactions are all transfers of property rights for goods and services (**definition**). The transfer of services also includes, for example, the employment activity in a company. Under transaction costs we understand all costs that are directly or indirectly caused by the transactions (definition). The transfer of goods and services is associated with many costs: information, negotiation, control and enforcement costs and, in a broader sense, transport costs. For example, inspection and enforcement costs can be caused by the lack of a legal system in the buyer country for exports.

According to transaction cost theory, transaction partners choose the contractual relationship that best minimizes transaction costs. The reason for institutions like

[33] See Williamson (1979), pp. 18 and Williamson (1985) and Furubotn and Richter (2005), p. 47.

contracts is then to minimize the transaction costs if the market solution is more expensive.

For a company, the question is: make-or-buy? Also called insourcing or outsourcing. Three criteria of the transaction influence the optimization calculus according to Williamson:

1. frequency (is it worth it),
2. uncertainty (i.e. the risk to the company associated with the price management) and
3. specificity (of investment) or complexity (increase with adaptation). The more specific, regular, and uncertain a transaction is, the more it speaks for an internal, "hierarchical" coordination. According to the respective combination of transaction frequency and specific investments, one can differentiate between three types of contracts:

1. **Classic contracts**

The interaction is clearly defined by scope and time. The risk of poor execution of the contract is limited. No party expects a subsequent adjustment to the contract. For example, buying a newspaper in the supermarket is a classic contract.

There is no risk or complexity associated with the transaction of acquiring a newspaper for either transaction partner. It is only when the buyer decides to buy the newspaper every day that it is worthwhile for both parties to conclude a long-term contract in the form of a subscription. A subscription contract minimizes transaction costs.

2. **Long-term contracts**

A contract cannot include all possible conditions for a transaction, so some adjustment is to be expected. Security, adjustment and warranty clauses serve this purpose. For example, building a home is a complex transaction that also carries some risks. The buyer cannot be sure that the transaction will be implemented to his satisfaction. During the construction, adjustments and changes to the transaction may occur. Some defects show up only long after the completion of the house. Guarantee clauses are just as necessary here as they are for long-lived assets such as machines. The more frequently a transaction takes place, the more it pays off to hire employees for this and to promote them in the company. Employee contracts are long-term contracts, but frequency has an effect on transactions outside the company as well.

3. **Relational contracts**

Relationship-based transactions are long-term and complex. Common decisions and adjustments are expected, such as occurs throughout a project, which is why the work takes place in organizations such as companies. For example, the production or distribution of complex products is best handled internally. The quality and development of the product cannot be controlled and monitored by other companies. In sales, the commitments and negotiations must be tailored to the product. The company is not only liable for mistakes, but the customer relationship is also endangered.

Here is an example scenario: a bank outsourced its securities settlement for cost reasons but the implementation was very flawed, and customers complained. They could not submit their tax return. The board explained the problem to the head of the company, but he did not have any influence on the operation because it had not taken place within the company. The available options would be to terminate the contract with the outside company or sue for damages, but neither would directly improve the situation.

In addition to the transactions, there are relationships between people, the actors who work together. Optimization approaches have evolved over time for this as well. In the next section of this chapter we will look at organizations, institutions cooperative networks and human capital. We will then be able to answer the following questions:

- What is the economy made of?
- How is everything related?
- Why are there companies?

4.5 The Economic Division of Labor

The decisive question is thus which soft facts are relevant for productivity in a company and national economy and how they can be used. To be more exact, how can the natural tendencies, motivations and desires of employees be applied for the good of the company and other employees? What would this kind of management or company approach look like? First we want to define a company more precisely however, what its functions and special features are. Let us consult academic science. Institutional economics defines a company as "a coalition of resource owners bound by a nexus of contractual relations that is governed by a contract decision and monitory agent – the entrepreneur."[34] This definition describes the composition of a company, but does not really address its core. According to Coase, the function of a company is to avoid transaction costs. This would make companies a unit that regulates repetitive transactions internally and externally through relational long-term contracts, which would then save transaction costs. Adam Smith recognized companies as a means of organizing labor distribution and thus taking advantage of the learning process, which simplifies production and using the individual strengths of the employees. Alchian and Demsetz later stress this aspect and identify team production as the main function of a company, as did Wieland.

An important task of a company is thus to enforce cooperative behavior in the context of prisoner mentality and thus to prevent free riding.[35]

[34] Quoted from Nowak (1997), p. 22.

[35] See Alchian and Demsetz (1972); Nowak (1997), S 19ff and Wieland (1999), pp. 54.

The decisive characteristic of a company is neither long-term contracts nor team production, but organization in and of itself. A company does not have to produce in a team to make profits. A bus company for example, is made up of many individually operating transportation units that are completely independent of one another. There is no team production here. The important value creation in this case is the organization of buses or bus routes. We define organization as the systematic assignment of functions into a whole capable of action (definition). In our example this would be the assignment of routes to the individual buses and drivers, thus assigning functions to people and machines. Within the framework of the company organization the employees receive tasks and decision-making powers. This organization of productive forces provides productivity, from which comes the added value of the organizational form "company." The art is thus in an optimal assignment of functions to employees and machines. The productive force of the company is hidden here. For example this is why job descriptions in a company (tasks and abilities) must be matched with the capabilities of the employees.[36]

Why is there human culture? Only because the mathematical principle of $A + B + C = 1 \times (A + B + C)$ is disproved by life in human communities. If a group of people join forces for a common task the result of the common action is greater than the sum of the individual actions (emergence). The sum is greater than its parts, which is a human wonder because it contradicts mathematical law. In the end organizations are nothing else but societal solutions to problems that they have developed in answer to external demands and conditions. Over time social constructs come into being, which create added value through the cooperation of different people. With cooperation people can realize gains from division of labor, economies of large scale and specialization. Organized group work allows to combine the strength of each individual and thus to overcome the weaknesses of each individual.

For these people to create an added value cooperatively, several challenges must be overcome. Suitable rules for potential conflicts must be found. In companies this often takes the form of the long-term contracts mentioned. Not only do they reduce transaction costs by regulating performance and compensation between the employer and employee of the long term, which encompasses the social inclusion of the actors in team production, but they also regulate the power to make decisions and thus all internal rights and duties including the distribution of added value created in the company as income.

Social rules are called institutions in Sociology. In contrast to the organization, an institution does not create direct added value, but it is an important requirement to do so. Institutions have been created over time to overcome societal dilemma structures, such as the state legal system. A social dilemma comes from the fact without a state framework for order, it would be worth enriching one's self at the cost of others. For example, not even a bridge could be built with the guarantee of ownership, because the construction site would be constantly plundered. If only the law of the strongest applied, property would not be obtainable through labor, or at least one could not

[36] See Vahs (2001), p. 62 and Conrad (2010).

keep it, which removes a central motivation to work. Without institutions many added social values would not be obtainable.

Another social construction that creates added value is cooperative networks. These are practiced forms of cooperation or generally supportive interactions amongst many people, which create added value. Every team is a cooperative network; repetitive labor is delegated within a team and practiced in cooperation together, for example. Every team member knows what output is received from each partner. The decisive factor is the added value possible through this cooperation. The cooperation between the network members can also include the exchange of information. The added value then comes from decisions made that are more in touch with reality.

Companies are generally made up of several interactively cooperating networks that are included in the organization as an assignment of functions. Cooperative networks also exist outside of companies however. The first such networks was probably founded in hunting groups in the Stone Age. Only together was it possible to herd wild animals or kill a large beast. A soccer team is another example of a cooperative network that is not a company. A soccer team can be created spontaneously, which makes clear that long-term contracts are not imperative for cooperative networks. An informal, mutual agreement is sufficient. Since most cooperative networks are designed to be long term, such contracts are the rule. For all social constructs based on mutuality, at least an informal agreement is required for cooperation. Otherwise the members of the network would not agree to advance concessions with their cooperation, since they are usually expecting compensation. Let us resume: Cooperative networks are social constructs, just like institutions and organizations that have been created in the society over time to create more added value through group cooperation. Cooperative networks are the first level of cooperation if measured by complexity. Organizations give structure to cooperation, putting the cooperative networks in a more complex order and hierarchy, so that more complex processes can be structured securely over the long term. Long-term contracts are necessary for this. Institutions make cooperation possible as rules that provide a framework. In principle this is nothing more than the best possible application of all productive forces, the combination of humans and machines. With this background the necessity for hierarchies is given for purely functional reasons, to coordinate processes from above and to bundle the flow of information from below upwards.

There is no corresponding example in nature for the differentiated labor distribution in human culture. Take the comparison with ants. Ants do not have differentiated possibilities for communication, nor do they have a central decision-making body that can collect and evaluate information in order to make decisions for the group. Despite these differences, the following has been observed in ant colonies: (a) they raise and milk aphids, (b) they grow trees suitable for their housing by destroying the seedlings of other trees (c) they collectively build bridges over rivers and (d) together they build living rafts in case of a flood. These are also repetitive behaviors, yet they are not consciously designed and then practiced. They must be the product of evolution. Certain inborn behaviors offered survival advantages over other species, and with this programming they were able to solve problems in a decentralized manner and were able to gain the evolutionary advantage compared to other insects. All of the estimated ten trillion ants, including 12,000 species, amount to as much biomass as the humans living on earth.[37] Recent observations have even led to the supposition that ants have at least a certain degree of cognitive abilities. There is one species of ants for example, in which it was observed that the older ants showed the younger ants the way to food sources.[38] We can conclude from this that decentralized solutions to complex tasks, or decision-making at lower levels taking superior company goals into consideration is indeed possible without consulting a higher instance. This assumes however, that the employees have a character like that of the ants. This would include knowing the goals of the company and the morality, or better said the willingness to follow them without supervision.

We have now worked out two important components of companies, first cooperative networks that are, second, embedded in an organization. Another important component is the human capital of the employees. If one put together a company with just any employees without paying attention to their characteristics, it would not be functional. Human capital can be understood here as all of the prerequisites and potential for added value creation in which people are involved and incorporated as productive forces. We can differentiate here between social capital and individual capital.

Social capital is all of the prerequisites for productivity a person has, but only in a group, thus social in the sense that they can only be realized within a society. The practiced cooperative and informative behavior of members in cooperative networks is social capital, because it can only provide an added value through the interaction with other people. Another example for social capital is practiced social behavior, including virtues, morals and politeness.[39] The social added value that is only created with others comes from a reduction in the transaction and control costs of all social activities. The so-called honorable salesman used to know the basic principle of "good faith." If everyone behaved perfectly morally, most legal costs and other expenses created by the implementation of rights would be done away with. Of course the problem of defining correct moral behavior and delimitation of individual rights would not be solved. The most extensive certainty of the law coming from moral behavior from individuals would stimulate many economic decisions, in particular investment decisions that would otherwise not be made due to insecurity about the behavior of others and the rights to investment profits. More productive forces would be developed and social product and welfare would increase. Morality as social capital makes decisions that are good for everyone possible, and thus increases the productivity of the company and national economy. For instance researchers at the University of Bern in Switzerland found out that rats selflessly help even unknown members of their species if they had been helped in

[37] See Handelsblatt dated September 14th 2006, p. 9.

[38] See Handelsblatt dated January 26th 2006, p. 15.

[39] For the impact of social capital as norms on crime rates see Buonanno, Paolo; Montolio, Daniel; Vanin, Paolo (2009), pp. 145–170.

their own past. This allows us to assume that a willingness to help proved beneficial to evolutionary goals. The more help the rat had experienced, the more help it was willing to give.[40] Individual capital on the other hand is all of the prerequisites the individual has in order to produce added value, creating value without the community or third parties. Education as a goldsmith is an example of individual capital.

Each person has various abilities as a social being and individual. An efficient business organization seeks to combine these useful qualities through a structured assignment of function – through the inclusion of real capital, for example by bringing together machinery and patents – to create a greater synergistic whole and thereby the optimal creation of value. Human capital (through individual and social capital) and real capital create for the firm the maximum benefit, or greatest possible combined interaction of assets.[41]

Is social capital created without costs? Of course not. Just like for individual capital, it needs investments over longer time periods. Cooperation for networks must be practiced, for example. This means that every member practices their function in the network and learns who can give them what information or performance, and who to delegate to. Organizations, such as companies whose design and continuation create costs, are also social capital because they assign functions and structure a whole unit capable of making decisions and taking action, including practicing processes. Except for the costs of company excursions, the costs of social capital are not included in the controlling and national economy calculations. In fact, the labor time to create cooperative networks, in other words training cooperation, should also be measured and evaluated. Forgetting this fact, and because it is perhaps only difficult or quite costly to capture it in detail, a value estimate of this capital is neglected. Unfortunately the benefits reaped from the social capital are not attributed to social capital. In general only a small part of human capital is registered, with the corresponding distortions in the allocations of resources. With the costs to build up human capital, just the costs for education or training is registered, but even so, the value created or the individual and social capital do not appear as an asset. An employee who has been trained for a task in a company has human capital, be it more individual or social capital depending on the task envisioned. If the employee is incorporated into the company for this task, additional social capital is created. His "value" for the company is realized when applied for the good of the company, just like for a machine, and corresponds to the cash value of the added value from production minus the wage expenses and the expenses of the job. Human capital in positions filled is taken all too seldom into consideration, although the company is interested specifically in the optimal development of productive forces. Analyses of employee potential, in which the companies identify the maximum contribution an employee can make to value creation are thus invaluable in order to avoid poor resource allocation.

---

[40] See Weltkompakt dated July 3th 2007, p. 25.

[41] See Conrad (2010).

The costs of the cooperative networks and a large part of the organizational costs for a company are recorded just as little as the company added value, which means that there is de facto no value approach. How can one explain the difference between the liquidation value of a company, thus the value of the net assets (value of the non human capital minus the liabilities) and the present value of the cash flow (or the shareholder value) as the net value creation of a company? Only through the added value that the organization, institutions and cooperative networks create via the productive combination of human and non-human capital. Alternatively formulated, if the cash value of the cash flow drops below the net asset value, it is often because of a poor combination of productive forces. The same applies of course in general for national economic systems as a whole and even for states. The state is also an organization, comparable to a company with branches with a systematic assignment of functions into a functional whole. Organizations, institutions and cooperative networks create added value in states as well, through the productive combination of human and non-human capital. Just like in companies, this added value is the difference between the value of a national economy's capital stock, or assets, and the cash value of the future GDP.

There are studies on the importance of social capital as common group knowledge, the so-called transactive memory. Moreland and Myaskovsky had three different types of groups assemble a radio. The groups were trained differently for this. In the first group the members were only individually trained, in the second the individuals were given information about the task-related knowledge of others and in the third group the members were trained together as a group. The result of the last two groups was significantly better than that of the group in which the members were individually trained. The most productive (measured by the number of errors) was the group with shared group training. In the experiment, the implementation was additionally evaluated according to the three criteria for a transactive memory: specialization, coordination and trust. Specialization was understood as the application of one's own expert knowledge, coordination as an optimal assignment of tasks to the respective abilities of the group members and trust in the expert knowledge of the other as fewer disputes about the assignment of tasks.[42]

Improving productive forces is about the best possible assignment and structuring of organizations, institutions and cooperative networks. This is a science of order. Seen in this light it is possible to compare order using business science and economic science to find out what combinations of organizations, institutions and cooperative networks have had the best results or which deficits have been found. Human capital varies from country to country and is difficult to capture. This is a decisive factor to develop productive forces however, and therefore for the development of a country as well. These factors are more qualitative than they are quantitative. Despite the unpredictability, at least tendencies can be identified. An ideal order like a blueprint

[42] See Hollingshead, A. B. (1998), 254–280; Moreland, R. L. (1999), pp. 3–31; Moreland, R. L., & Myaskovsky, L. (2000), pp. 117–133 and Nijstad, B. A., & Van Knippenberg, D. (2014), pp. 459.

to guide companies or the national economy does not exist, and will never exist. The most that can be hoped for is the optimization of order as a framework for a company or economy and for a certain point in time.

The Incomputability is also the main reason for the previous neglect of qualitative factors. Despite this unpredictability however, there is not only an influence from these factors, this influence is so lasting that it would be negligence not to include it in calculations. Quantitative economic science does not explain why, for example, many Asian countries that were at a similar level of affluence to African countries were able to achieve economic prosperity in the last few centuries and many African countries have been fighting starvation despite development aid. The limited ability to predict and plan macroeconomic indicators is generally made clear by the different development in planned and market economic systems. The differences in the development between West and East Germany or North and South Korea after the war can only be explained qualitatively, thus by comparing the systems of order. On the other hand, Communism and Socialism were able to get many people to work until physically exhausted or to sacrifice themselves. Wages do not exist in these cases as an incentive, and the willingness to sacrifice oneself cannot be explained only through the threat of totalitarian measures of oppression. There must therefore have been an immaterial, intrinsic incentive. Why are there countries that develop into prosperous and dominant countries seemly out of nothing, increasing their capital stock many fold, just to then become meaningless and poor again without outside influence? Human capital is not a static factor. Also the institutions and organizations change.

Communism and Fascism are ideologies. Like religions, they give people clear moral values and behavioral guidelines. They give actions a purpose. Human behavior is given a value that goes above and beyond the material value, and it thus becomes a value in and of itself. Apparently many people want to believe in something good, something they can apply themselves to. They want to feel they are part of something bigger than themselves. One's personal benefit is at least partially subjugated to the greater good because individuals define benefit differently, and they feel better because of their activities for the group. Of course ideologies and religions are often abused and there tends to be a danger of being manipulated. We do not wish to preach an economic ideology, just to determine the importance of moral values as motivations for actions and behavior, and thus for the development of productive forces. Values as human capital can also advance societies as well as in particular companies and national economies by stimulating the productive forces of its people.

Humans aren't machines, and almost all of them question the sense in their existence either consciously or unconsciously. Considered in this way moral values are like the oil in the machinery, if we want to stick with the machine metaphor. If the values are lost, the engine grinds. The gears no longer catch for the functioning of the system as a whole, and take on a life of their own. People maximize their own benefit at the cost of the whole system. Such behavior was one reason of the Enron crisis and the subprime crisis. This is not the maximization of one's interests that encourages general welfare, as Adam Smith had in mind. The invisible hand cannot do anything against corruption and embezzlement. Profit and morality are not in conflict, as is often assumed. There can be no profit without morals, either in companies or national economies.

A survey of 400 German executives showed that the majority of problem-solving competencies are seen in self-organizing networks. Because of the collective intelligence, more creative impulses, higher innovative power, acceleration of processes and reduction of complexity can be expected by this organizational form than by others.[43]

Conversely, immoral behavior diminishes the added value of organizational forms. Let us assume that employees are distrustful and do not help each other anymore. If they do not exchange information among themselves or inform themselves wrongly, the added value they can reach through division of labor and cooperation will decrease.

Immoral behavior from top managers has the greatest negative effect on stakeholders and shareholders. The company's success is endangered by immoral behavior. Moral, ethical behavior is thus very important for companies, and the same applies among the companies and in competition. As we have already described, only fair competition for performance assures an optimal allocation of resources and thus an efficient economic production. Immoral behavior damages the society as a whole, beginning with market process, internal company processes and all the way down to interpersonal relationships.

The genetic disposition towards cooperative behavior we have already described is unfortunately insufficient. Hobbes had already recognized that cooperative behavior must be worth it for the individual, and that he must be able to trust in it, because otherwise we would have anarchy. How can this be achieved? Only if society encourages cooperative behavior by rewarding it and by sanctioning uncooperative behavior. Economic laws, courts and supervision are absolutely necessary for this reason. They have the task of acting as referee for behavior in accordance with competition, so they must be able to control competitive actions and sanction missteps. Without controls and sanctions there is no assurance of fair, thus economically ethical behavior. Cooperative behavior is the same as moral/ethical behavior. People will only trust the cooperative behavior of others if they can presume moral/ethical behavior, thus morality as a social standard to measure actions that must be practiced and trained (socialization).

The disparity described somewhat provocatively at the beginning between private, rewarded morality on the one hand and societal and politically unsanctioned immorality on the other hand is a basic evil that need not exist. The society must find appropriate conditions for moral behavior, which must be worth the effort in politics and economics. This is even true for a community of apes, where deceit, such as stealing bananas or beating weaker apes in the group is addressed and usually punished.[44]

---

[43] See Initiative Neue Qualität der Arbeit (2012), p. 7.

[44] See Handelsblatt, dated 8th December 2005, p. 8.

Conclusion
Morality complements the positive effects of the market. The results of the market correspond only partially to our ideas of what is right. In case of market failure, morality ensures that third parties are not harmed. Against this background, the social market economy intervenes in the market and changing the distribution results. Social morality is an important corrective factor in the market economy. If a market economy is to be an advantage for society, society must discourage immoral, damaging behavior through legal penalties or social exclusion. In addition, it must promote voluntary ethical behavior through the provision of values.

In order for a society to function and to develop its productive forces, the ethics of social capital has to be aligned with the orders, the system, and the economic stage of development. In this context, the attitudes of the people are particularly important for society, thus the community, and social cooperation. The norms, values and morality as well as the attitudes to the political and economic system are important.

Comprehension Questions
1. Define a company. What makes a company and what creates added value?
2. Define organization, institution, human and social capital.
3. To what extent is morality necessary for the functioning of an organization?

4.6 Institutional Challenges in Specific Game Situations

4.6.1 The Ethical Prisoner Dilemma

If all competitors behave morally it creates a fair performance competition from which all parties profit. It has already been established that the economic order has to exhibit moral behavior. If it is advantageous for a company to behave immorally, it may be forced to do so in order to remain competitive. Market advantages can result from unfair competition such as deceptive advertising, libel, etc. At the very least the trust of the consumer in the product is lost. Due to a lack of transparency he will not buy the product from any company. This is a prisoner's dilemma.[45] Even if the company were to behave morally, it does not know how the other companies will behave, and therefore must assume immoral behavior and behave immorally in order to ensure its survival. There is a risk of an unfair predatory competition by means of concealed immoral means. The economic welfare potential cannot be achieved. The problem of ethical imprisonment always arises when no moral rules are enforced. The ethical prisoner dilemma is not just true for companies in competition but also for companies with unethical business cultures and for the employees themselves. This also applies to the internal competition of employees within the company. Here an employee can gain a career advantage by lying. Unethical companies cannot

[45] See Kirchgässner (1991), pp. 51.

Fig. 4.1 Payoff matrix of fair competition in the ethical prisoner dilemma. (* Nash equilibrium is the worst case for all (Nash: No one can unilaterally improve through another strategy)

	B behaves morally	B does not behave morally
A behaves morally	5, 5	0, 6
A does not behave morally	6, 0	1, 1*

realize the collective best case with high productivity if the employees do not behave morally. Like with the company Enron, the employees compete internally and do not cooperate. The return of teamwork cannot be realized.

The ethical prisoner dilemma for a fair competition is as follows (see Fig. 4.1). The worst case for a company manager A is if he behaves morally, but the company manager of another company B does not and the best case for A is if A behaves immorally, but B does not. B is in the same decision-making situation. The result is the combination in which both companies operate unfairly, thus the worst case for all (Nash equilibrium). Without ethical rules, such as law enforcement when the ethical prisoner dilemma arises, a company finds itself in the worst-case situation if it behaves ethically.

In the context of such a distorted situation, companies have the opportunity to approach the government and request a change to the regulatory framework. Unfortunately, such attempts to change regulations are rarely successful. Rather, many companies try to delay ethically motivated regulations for as long as possible. For example, Ford's self-defeating lobbying delayed Ford's security measures for 8 years to avoid the additional $11 of the plastic buffer on the petrol tank. Accident victims were accepted as a liability.[46] The egg industry, which defends the agonizing mass management of laying hens, is another good example.[47] This is due to the fact that the decision-making structure for A and B changes as a result of the company having to bear only a part of the costs of a decision in the case of decisions made at the expense of third parties (external effects, see Sect. 5.2). The payouts for third parties are therefore listed separately in Fig. 4.2. In the case of the environment, the cost of pollution is borne by the public, whose health and quality of life are adversely affected (negative external effects). In the case of work safety, the company can save costs at the expense of employees. In our examples above, the health risk affected Ford's customers or laying hens.

An empirical study has shown that managers are only willing to stick to moral standards when they believe their business partners are sticking to them. If this is not so, they are not willing to behave morally, even if they consider the rules to be

[46] See Wörz (1994), p. 22.

[47] See Göbel (2010), p. 183.

Fig. 4.2 Payoff matrix; Decisions on third parties in the ethical prisoner dilemma. (* Nash equilibrium is equivalent to the worst case for all. The morphological/moral combination is pareto-efficient)

A/B/third parties	B behaves morally	B behaves immorally
A behaves morally	1, 1, 0**	0, 5
A does behaves immorally	5, 0	1, 1, (-10)*

important and meaningful.[48] In the case of the prisoner's dilemma, there is uncertainty about the conduct of the other companies. Even if they all wanted to behave ethically, they could not, because there was then the risk of coming into the worst-case situation. The solution to this problem is:

1. Educating A and B about the added value of moral behavior so that the incentive to behave morally is increased. One can, for example, appeal to the altruistic conscience or use-oriented arguments. In game theory, it could be shown in games over several rounds that it is result-maximizing if one behaves cooperatively at first, and only if the other does not behave cooperatively to counter this with an equally uncooperative behavior (trigger or tit-for-tat- Strategy, see Sect. 3.3). With many players, however, this reciprocity goes under. Here it depends on the so-called "strong reciprocators" to punish unfair behavior. Motives for the altruistic punishment of uncooperative behavior are emotions such as gratitude, desire for revenge and the pursuit of retribution. Without the feelings, no one would punish others to their own disadvantage. Getting angry about uncooperative behavior brings satisfaction and thus also a benefit if punishment has been carried out. This is the only way to succeed in altruistic punishments because there is a positive net benefit. However, this behavior can only be assumed for family businesses. In public companies, shareholders will not accept personal goals such as altruistic punishment for unfair behavior.
2. Moral behavior is rewarded by incentives (morality must be worthwhile) z. B. An ethical consumer awareness leads to increased sales of ethical products. Immoral behavior must not pay off for companies. Moral violations must be made known so that the actors can be socially sanctioned. This is where the non-governmental organizations (NGO) come in. The media also have a special responsibility here.
3. Binding contracts with sanction options: laws, state control and sanctions in the event of misconduct (institutions).

[48] See Blickle (1996), p. 116.

Fig. 4.3 Payoff Matrix Gender Struggle

Woman / Man	Soccer	Theatre
Soccer	3, 1	0, 0
Theatre	0, 0	1, 3

4.6.2 *Games of the Gender Struggle Type*

There are also gender-based games where there is no reward for cooperative behavior in the first round, but only a dilemma (see Fig. 4.3). The woman wants to go to the opera and the man to a soccer game. Only when the two go together do the benefits come from the evening together. Here, however, cooperative behavior is the prerequisite for any additional benefit to be achieved. The solution is that the spouses take turns fulfilling the other's wishes.[49]

This game represents the compromise. Only if you give, do you get something. Such games are always found in mutual dependence without dominance in the pursuit of different goals in politics, which is why a vote exchange takes place.

Mutual dependence is the basis of human coexistence. The gains are realized in organizations like companies or states, which use regulations to organize the do ut des (institutions). People accept these institutional arrangements as compromise in order to get the gains.

4.6.3 *Insurance or Trust Game*

Rousseau already used another variant of the game for the derivation of the necessity of social contracts. Two persons A and B can form a hunting group to kill a deer (see Fig. 4.4). Each can also kill a hare alone. Now they both want to meet in the forest, but do not know if the other one is going to keep the meeting or has killed a hare to be on the safe side. There are two Nash balances as positions from which one cannot improve one-sidedly.[50] The players can contractually agree in advance to take a deer

[49] Vgl. Kirchgässner (1991), S. 52 f.

[50] See Rousseau, Jean-Jacques (1988/1755), pp. 233; Maurer, Andrea/Schmid, Michael (2010), pp. 221.

Fig. 4.4 Payoff matrix Stag Hunt

B A	Stag	Hare
Stag	4, 4*	0, 3
Hare	3, 0	3, 3*

together. To enforce this penalties are required. Or they can observe the behavior of the other, and if it repeatedly comes to stag hunting, the game stabilizes, as trust is created. Like the gender struggle and the prisoner mentality, this game is the starting point for international cooperation in specific policy areas. Only together can they take down a deer, thus achieving added value. The EU Treaties are an example of this.

Which distribution results will arise from these games? With the same distribution of power, the same results tend to be had, while unequal distribution of power tends to create unequal results, which is also accepted by the players.[51] However, it will not be the case that the losing position gets nothing. This is shown by the ultimatum games. If there is too much deviation from the equal distribution, the weaker players react irrationally and the result is rejected so that the superior player receives nothing.

Conflicting Strategies, the Chicken Game, Negative Payouts

The Chicken Game (see Fig. 4.5) belongs to the Hawks and Doves Games and deals with conflict situations. The situation became known through the film "Rebel Without a Cause" with James Dean. Two people want to find out who of them is the "chicken", or the coward. They drive towards each other with two cars and whoever swerves first is the "chicken". In the narrower sense, there is nothing to gain here, since it involves a relative change in the positions between two players (see chart).[52]

Players can strengthen their position by bluffing or self-restriction. These would be threatening gestures to display aggression and irrationality in order to make conflictual action credible. Self-restraint would be like tying a rope to the steering

[51] See Maurer, Andrea/Schmid, Michael (2010), pp. 253.

[52] Vgl. Dawkins, R. (1978), pp. 83; Gramms, T. (1999); Presteich K. N. (1999); Theodor W. May (1983) and Maurer, Andrea/Schmid, Michael (2010), pp. 218.

Fig. 4.5 Payoff matrix Chicken Game

	A behaves cooperatively	A behaves conflictory
A behaves cooperatively	-100, -100	10, -10
A behaves conflictory	-10, 10	0, 0

wheel while driving. There is also a time pressure to be the first to take the superior conflictual position to force the other to the lower position. As a solution to conflict games, it is a good idea to involve a third party as a mediator, who provides a stable distribution compromise. However, credibility enhancement from the conflicting strategy can be used by both parties, increasing the potential for maximum damage to both. Conversely, in multi-round games there is a risk of yielding, or cooperative behavior, such as a lasting position in a game of chicken, in which aggressive behavior no longer seems credible to the other player.

Application examples would be warlike conflicts, such as between the US and North Korea. Here, North Korean dictator Kim Jong-un managed to connect an irrational image with nuclear weapons, bringing the US to the negotiating table even as an insignificant state. The chicken game leads to divorce in many marriages, if irrationally no one wants to yield to the other. Divorce is the crash with maximum loss for both sides. This is also the peculiarity of the game. In the non-cooperative situation there are extremely negative payouts for both players. You can win if you simulate the conflict behavior in order to bring the other player into the worse position of the "chicken". In marriage, that would be: "I will get a divorce if you do not give me that and that". Of course, this inevitably leads to the loss of a basis of trust and makes cooperation profits difficult. Therefore, in the end, such a strategy is only advisable if there are no joint cooperative gains. In the economic area, a competitor could threaten to introduce a product to prevent the introduction of a competitor's product, or threaten to penetrate into competitor's markets with both a ruinous dumping competition. An employer might face dismissal, although it is legally difficult and involves high costs to force the employee into desired behavior or wage loss.

How should the distribution of income within a company be organized? Labor and capital benefit from division of labor as a product of the company as an organization because the assignment of functions creates an actionable whole. The employee must be able to harm the employer to avoid pushed to a disadvantageous position. If there is no coordination of all workers through unions, no strikes are possible and the worker must accept an inferior position in the distribution or leave the company (see Sect. 5.10).

Both players can avoid a negative game like in the game of chicken, in which they convince themselves to behave cooperatively, thus not to play the game. Alternatively, a third party can enforce cooperative behavior, so for example, the state can prohibit conflict behavior. And finally, morality and ethics can prevent damaging behavior, thus creating cooperative play.

Conclusion

As a social solution to conflictual and non-conflictual games, institutions have established themselves as social rules that are enforced through sanctions. Another solution is morality, as the players would not want to harm the opponent. Stabilizing behavioral expectations can prevent damage in conflictual games, while cooperation gains can be safely realized in non-conflictual games. The resulting benefits move the individual to join society and submit to the institutions, at least as long as the benefits outweigh the disadvantages. As the public good games without sanction show, the willingness to behave cooperatively decreases greatly after a few negative distribution experiences, which is why the games then collapse without sanctions. Switching to other games with sanction options, i.e. standards, are used by the players to increase their own benefits.[53] We have analyzed several types of markets, which are summed up in the overview below (Fig. 4.6).

Two players

Transparency /numbers of rounds	**Symmetric information**	**Lack of information: asymmetric**	**Lack of information: bilateral**
Anonymous=One round	Betrayal unlikely	Betrayal likely	Welfare reducing market results
Several rounds finite	Public good instable and unlikely	Betrayal possible	Welfare reducing market results
Several rounds infinite	Stable public good, Trigger strategy, no betrayal possible	no betrayal possible	Welfare reducing market results

Several players

Transparency /numbers of rounds	**Symmetric information**	**Asymmetric -unilateral (with sanctions)**	**Lack of information Asymmetric, multilateral**
Anonymous=One round	Betrayal unlikely, Public good likely	Betrayal likely (Betrayal unlikely)	Welfare reducing market results
Several rounds finite	Betrayal unlikely, Public good unlikely	Betrayal likely (Betrayal unlikely)	Welfare reducing market results
Several rounds infinite	Betrayal unlikely, Public good unlikely	Betrayal likely (Betrayal unlikely)	Welfare reducing market results

Fig. 4.6 Outcome of market constellations

[53] See Falk (2003), p. 147; Fehr and Fischbacher (2003) and Fehr et al. (2001).

Comprehension Questions

1. Explain the ethical prisoner's dilemma in fair competition and at the expense of third parties. What are the possible solutions?
2. Why is the insurance or trust game a starting point for international cooperation?
3. Why is the chicken game so dangerous? What can be done against the negative outcome?

4.7 Ethical Institutions and Organizations

The significance of an ethical framework has often been discussed. Without an ethical rule enforced with laws, an ethical problem arises in which the company comes into the worst-case situation, which is then unethical. Of course, positive incentives such as environmental subsidies can also help escape the ethical prisoner dilemma. After all, the state can counteract unethical behavior by trying to develop social morality and thus shape employees either before they enter the company or create a more ethical environment for the company. Ultimately, all citizens are asked to act ethically in their environment (duty ethics).

Institutions have evolved over time to overcome social dilemma structures, such as the state legal system. Institutions are made up of people who serve people. They regulate interpersonal coexistence, in which they place appropriate incentives, for example laws and penal sanctions in the event of an offense. Ethics, which is concerned with moral institutions, is called institutional ethics, social ethics, or even order ethics.[54]

Insofar as we are not dealing with a dictatorship, institutional ethics derives from collective ethics. All social regulations are developed and implemented by the community. An institution such as the legal system must be morally recognized by society. It is only through compulsion and control that institutions cannot go against the will of the individual. The institutions also shape the individuals who live with them. Together with non-legislative collective ethics (norms) and parents, institutions determine the socialization of individuals. Ultimately, the institutions, such as the legal system, determine the consequences of moral actions and thereby set the incentives to behave in certain ways. If there is no employment law and a prohibition of association, the employee is not only at the mercy of the employer (institutional ethics), but another employer is also hard-pressed to make concessions to his employees, as he has to fear competitive disadvantages. Moral behavior is thereby made more difficult. Institutions such as democracy, with all the legal regulations on

[54] See Göbel (2010), p. 34.

the division of powers, make it possible to exercise equitable, and thus moral, discourse ethics.

In a study that investigated why people obey laws, it turned out to be crucial for most people that they are convinced that the laws are ethical and legitimate. Furthermore, most people feel a strong commitment to follow laws that address education and protect the environment. Penalties are necessary for a minority, but excessive penalties in case of violation of regulations can have a counterproductive effect.[55]

Social moral norms and values emerge in a trial and error process: a cultural evolution. They express what behavior is desired by society because it benefits society and its members. This behavior that a company considers positive is rewarded by social recognition. Conversely, negative and thus societally damaging, behavior is sanctioned by social exclusion or even by the judiciary as a social organization. We refer to people as good when they are positive for others and vice versa. Ultimately, the categorical imperative of Kant expresses exactly this: always act so that your action could be the basis of a general law, or as per the saying "what you do not want done to yourself, do not do to others." Ultimately, laws are valid for everyone and represent a social rule that should be valid for all. Equality before the law should always apply.[56]

Legitimacy derives from what reason, conscience, and public discourse recognize as justifiable interests. Legitimacy does not necessarily follow legality. Laws can also be immoral, such as the laws on racial segregation in the US and South Africa. Economic activities can be legal but unethical, such as child labor in some countries. Finally, many unethical practices are not punishable, because a court action is often not worthwhile or the injured parties lack the necessary financial resources.

An example of the difference between legality and legitimacy from the company's point of view is the case of the 1991 Salomon Brothers. Four top managers were reported for legally non-conformist behavior at the trading table for government bonds. They had their legal department check whether they were obliged to publish the lapse, and they were not. However later, when the incident came to the public, their silence led to a massive breach of trust that led to an estimated loss of one billion US dollars due to customer or contract losses and higher legal and refinancing costs.[57]

The state regulates the company's dealings with its stakeholders through laws and regulations. Of particular importance are the following:

(A) Employee protection rights
(B) Protection of consumers (starting with the general terms and conditions of business, the regulation of prices, the food regulation and the Unfair Competition Law).

---

[55] See Tyler (1990) and Paine (1994), p. 111.

[56] See also Habermas (1975), p. 72

[57] See Paine (1994), p. 110.

(C) Investor protection (from the Investment Protection Act to the Securities Trading Act)
(D) Environmental protection legislation (covers waste disposal, noise protection, air pollution, water protection and landscape protection)
(E) Animal welfare laws and regulations

4.8 Is the State of Law Sufficient?

The economy produces goods for the community to consume and invest in. This is necessary for the survival of the community, but there are also other products that the community needs. These include inner stability, including internal security, low crime rates, a general harmony amongst its members and thus a smooth functioning of societal and economic processes. There are many prerequisites for this to happen, including societal rules and laws and thus institutions and organizations to implement them. These alone are not sufficient, however. Social morality, good behavior and politeness are additional prerequisites for societal processes to run smoothly. The state as an organization cannot control, monitor and implement everything. Even if one were to attempt to do so, the expense would be enormous. On the other hand, if social rules were not adhered to by anyone the social system would collapse. Machiavelli had already realized this in his Discorsi: "Just as... laws are necessary to maintain manners, good morals are necessary to respect the laws."[58] This interconnection also applies to the economy, since the economy is part of the society, but we will address this in more detail later on. Good manners, morality or more generally, behavior in conformance with the community, is mostly transmitted through social education. This basis for behavior is another good needed for the society to survive, and which the people themselves must produce. It is not just a question of rules and control. For instance, you cannot make a functioning company out of a prison full of criminals. Even if the criminals are controlled as well as possible, the outcome will be miserable without motivation and morality.

Market failure would occur without these laws. For example, some companies in Germany use the fact that the packaging sizes are no longer regulated by law. Price increases are hidden by a smaller packaging content. The consumer only sees that the packaging costs the same as before. Such packaging tricks are unethical because they change the exchange to the disadvantage of the customer, without informing them about what is actually fraud in the broader sense.[59]

Laws are a necessary prerequisite for the functioning of an economic and social system but not sufficient. Without morality it does not work. Laws can be ignored because either control is incomplete or the punishment is not dissuasive. Thus, it becomes worthwhile for long-haul drivers not to comply with legally prescribed rest

---

[58] Machiavelli (1977), p. 64.

[59] See Göbel (2010), pp. 287.

periods and to accept a fine. And in the construction industry the legal minimum wages are undermined. Laws can be circumvented. Since children's programs are not allowed to show advertising blocks, the channels broadcast the programs as a "family program." Laws are inaccurate or leave a great deal of room for interpretation because they must be universal and cannot anticipate every individual case. For example, there are interpretable terms such as "faithfulness and faith," "carefulness," or "reasonable compensation." The Act on the Appropriateness of the Management Board Remuneration (VorstAG) merely states that the remuneration of the Management Board should be proportionate to the tasks and performance of the Management Board, the Company's position and the usual remuneration.

There is, for example, a problem of law enforcement in the economy. Economic deprivation is seldom uncovered in comparison with other illegal acts, and even more rarely punished. In relation to the consequences and the likelihood of being discovered, the penalties for economic crime are far too small. For a long time economic science has been calling for a tightening of economic criminal law. For example, the economist Gary S. Becker claims that the penalties are based on the consequential damages and the probability of discovery. The aim is that the expected value of the sentence is not less than the consequential damages for society. For example, if the impact of an action is €1 million and the probability of detection is 10%, the penalty would be €10 million.[60]

In order to comply with these laws, the acting norms and customs also need their own morality. Furthermore, society, economy and technology are developing, so that laws have yet to be enacted for many immoral acts. An example is the Internet and the mobile phone sector with new possibilities to take advantage of customers. Laws usually end at the borders of a country, which is why regulatory arbitrage occurs. By way of example, shipping companies bypass the safety regulations of their home countries by sailing under the flag of a country without regulations.[61] In general, morality or ethical awareness is the prerequisite for the emergence of laws and jurisprudence. In the case of legislation, the judge is bound to his conscience, as is the judge in case law. There can be no laws and no jurisprudence without morality.

You can also see it reversed. It is not the order that matters, but what people make of it. Here Johann Heinrich Pestalozzi can be cited as a representative of the people who believe that people can be influenced by education: "He has learned that all forms of government are of no use when people are no good".[62]

Conclusion

The economy produces consumer goods and capital goods for society. This is vital for society, but there are also other products that society needs. This is above all inner stability, which is to be understood not only as internal security, but above all a low crime rate, in general the harmonization of the citizens and thus the smooth

[60] See Becker and Becker (1998), pp. 173.

[61] See Göbel (2010), pp. 289.

[62] http://haus-des-verstehens.ch/tagebuch-blog/636-johann-heinrich-pestalozzi-und-rosa-luxemburg.html

running of social (also economic) processes. For this, there are many prerequisites: above all, social rules, laws and institutions, and the organizations to enforce them, but these prerequisites are not enough. Social morality, good manners or courtesy are further prerequisites for the smooth running of social processes. The institutions and organizations cannot control, monitor and enforce everything. If, on the other hand, no social rules were respected by anyone, the social system would collapse immediately. Where laws and control cease, morality begins. Morality regulates human behavior so as to prevent social harm.

Comprehension Questions

1. Why is there a difference between legality and legitimacy?
2. Explain the extent to which morality is necessary for the functioning of a legal system.
3. Discuss: should every social rule be enforced by sanctions?

4.9 Central Administration Economy (or Planned Economy)

In principle, there are two ways to organize an economy: decentralized via markets or centrally via a planning authority. We call these two basic forms of economic systems the market economy and central administration economy.

Definition of central economy (planned economy in colloquial language: the economy is planned ex ante (from the earlier point of view) centrally (a plan).

$\neq$

Definition of the market economy: People plan themselves ex ante decentrally and the plans are coordinated via markets ex post (from a retrospective perspective) (many plans).

Historical examples of states in which the central administration economy was used are the GDR (German Democratic Republic), the USSR and China. They still exist in North Korea and Cuba. In times of war intermediate forms often developed, in which the state determined who produced what, however there was still private property.

Characteristics of the Central Administration Economy

1. Only ex-ante planning, no ex-post coordination of the plans. An extensive, hierarchically organized bureaucracy aggregates people's needs in the form of one to five-year plans (bottom-up) and then determines production, including resource allocation, giving top-down specifications, Companies are asked what capacity they have and what resources they need for production.
2. Planning via production balances, adjustment of plans by force

   Then they are assigned the production of end products and delivery of pre-production materials to other companies by the central planning office. A bureaucracy must organize the production and distribution of goods and services. To this end, the authority must be able to assess people's needs and control the optimal use of resources. Property rights must be severely encroached upon to get this control.

3. No private ownership of the means of production

   That means that there can be no private property. Companies belong to the state. In this sense, all people work for the state and, in the communist sense, for the community, i.e. only indirectly for themselves.

4. Prices are only politically assigned values

   There are no markets and no market prices. The prices for production are planned in such a way that they should cover the costs for the companies or are determined according to political criteria. For example, books and housing were subsidized by the state in the GDR.

This was touted to have led to advantages over the market economy solution. The main criticism of capitalism was that goods or asset distribution was seen to be unjust.

Advantages of the Central Administration Economy Compared to the Market Economy

The industrial revolution led to extreme income differences between workers and factory owners, the so-called capitalists. The market mechanism led to extremely low wages and thus to the so-called "impoverishment of the proletariat" with the excess supply of labor caused by the population explosion (see Sect. 6.10). Ownership of the means of production was considered problematic. The market only pays for things when there is a demand (and perhaps values enhanced by scarcity). The market as an institution is neither humane nor social.

The distribution of goods according to need and diminishing the power of capital was seen as a solution to this problem (see the writings of Karl Marx, and as precursors of the state designs Plato or the book Utopia by Thomas More). We saw this idea after the October Revolution in Russia first and then implemented the USSR, which led to a social form of communism in which private property no longer existed.

If the state, in other words society, owns the means of production, there are theoretically some advantages.

1. Planning security for companies and workers, no unemployment

   If all production is planned with the available workers, there is no unemployment. If there are no planning errors, there are also

2. No business cycles or economic crises.
3. Theoretically there are also no problems with microeconomic conflicts of interest, such as pollution from production, since all business decisions are ultimately made by the state, and thus welfare-oriented.

How was this approach implemented in practice?

To answer this question, let's look at the example of the GDR.

Case Study Life in the GDR

Group work: Read the article about the GDR. What do you notice? What are the advantages and disadvantages compared to your experience with the market economy?

1. **article: Impressions of the GDR central administration economy**

Conversation with Marion Blumeyer, saleswoman

For years, Marion Blumeyer was a meat specialist in the deli of a consumer department store.

MDR: Ms Blumeyer, was everything delivered that you ordered?

Marion Blumeyer: No. Pork fillet, pork chops, roulades were barely delivered, the items we sold with "no". Schnitzel, pork belly and offal were always available – but who always wanted to eat those? In order to avoid misunderstandings: In the GDR nobody had to starve. If there were no pork chops, then there was schnitzel on the lunch table – if asparagus didn't happen to be in season. Not the quantity, but the selection was rather small.

How often did people come to your department store and ask, "Do you have…?"

That happened all day long. It was really like families sending their grandma out to find out where there was something to be had. So this grandma came to us four or five times a day and asked. So we also knew our regular customers well and could set our clocks by their visits. This did not work for bananas and the like, because they were given only against the presentation of an identity card, on which the number of children was noted. The more children, the more bananas. But the few bananas were never enough for all the customers anyway. Customers stood in line forever and when it was finally their turn there were no bananas left. There were always short tempers.

Speaking of scarce goods like bananas, how about "under the counter"?

When coveted goods arrived, usually a quarter was withheld and distributed among us buyers. Our boss, on the other hand, even had a store room of her own, and when canned peaches or pineapples came at Christmas, everything went straight to her stocks, and even we saleswomen could only beg to see if we could get a can. We put the rest in small bags with price tags, so it did not stand out. But I think every customer knew exactly what was in the bags.

Who did you hold those things for?

On the one hand for acquaintances and relatives. For example, my grandfather got a bottle of brandy every Friday and three boxes of filter cigarettes of a certain brand. I always gave him that in a bag. On the other hand, our customers approached us: "We're having a party and would like to have cooked ham or bacon, and if you need an anorak, then you come to me." One knew their clientele.

Have you never had problems with customers who came away with nothing?

Of course. Some customers were sad, while others became aggressive. They then shoved each other's shopping carts into each other's heels and got into fistfights over certain rare things. Every Saturday morning we sold the remnants of the Friday delivery and when we opened at 7 am, the customers were already in a really long queue at 6:30 waiting for us to open. Everyone wanted to be first and they shoved and jostled until it got ugly. If there were any bananas, people were queuing up in front of the empty fruit stand before we knew a delivery was on the way.

They saw the car and they all ran to us. Then they knocked on the window and got downright pushy. They never actually robbed the trucks or anything, but the people have always stood in a disciplined line.

Did the supply situation improve over time or not?

It got steadily worse. In the seventies we were still able to sell fruit, but later we had it almost exclusively on public holidays. In the last few years before the wall fell, we had to stretch our product supply further and further just so that we could fill the shelves. In other words, we were always expanding the space for jam, flour, rice and pasta because we no longer had enough baking mixes, peas, lentils, waffles or even ketchup bottles.

Given the constant worsening, would you have called yourself a saleswoman or a distributor?

I was a saleswoman! Despite the shortage, we had a set sales target and to achieve this we had to talk up our goods, to make people want the unpopular items. There were also real billboards or special events such as "in-house slaughter days" or the like. None of our stuff ever spoiled.

Were you happy in your job?

Yes, I was a happy saleswoman for twenty years.

(Conversation with Marion Blumeyer, saleswoman, 2013, translation by the author)

2. **Article: Economy of the GDR**

Consumption Policy | Shortage economy | Economic policy

War damage in the production plants, reparation payments to the Soviet Union and the economy destroyed throughout Europe – after World War II and well into the 1950s, the main goal of the GDR's economic policy was to reach the pre-war levels of food supply and consumer goods.

It was not until 1958 that the last rations on everyday commodities could be abolished (meat, butter, shoes, etc.). The political system bore most of the responsibility for the "long post-war period" in comparison with West Germany and the "stable" lack of critical goods. From the very beginning, competition between economic reason and political-ideological maxims impeded economic development.

Economically necessary measures were regularly prevented or weakened to maintain the ruling party or its main convictions.

Stable prices through subsidies

Attempting to achieve social justice, consumption for all, and stable prices with a central plan instead of cautiously directing the free market required so much state intervention that it overburdened the administration and hampered economic productivity. Thus the predetermined stable and low prices for basic foodstuffs, housing rents, heating led to increasingly horrendous subsidy amounts, which could only be financed by over-taxing other products (such as technical devices and "luxuries") or by lending. At the end of its history the GDR faced bankruptcy, unable to meet its financial obligations either internally or externally.

Although the population, the "ruling class of workers and peasants", was otherwise rarely asked their views, the concerns of ordinary people as regarded living standards were watched attentively. What the disappointed and enraged people were capable of when cheated out of their wages had been demonstrated on June 17, 1953.

"How we work today, we will live tomorrow"

Ever new initiatives and solutions were created from the activist movement following Adolf Hennecke (from 1948). To get the people to increase production with promises of a rosy future as a reward for current deprivations, easy explanations for the permanent lacks there were formulas such as "How we work today, we will live tomorrow" and propaganda lies of sabotage by enemy forces.

(Source: Central German Broadcasting, http://www.mdr.de/heute-im-osten/index.html and http://www.mdr.de/damals/lexikon/artikel75416.html, Economy of the GDR, translation by the author)

The example of the GDR shows that the central administration economy did not work in some areas. In the following, we will analyze these areas to explain what these problems are.

Phenomena of the Central Administration Economy

1. **Long lines**

   How can you explain so many lines? Lines are an expression of scarcity. People are not getting the goods they want. Due to low productivity, too little was produced or the wrong products were produced, which nobody wanted. There has to be store guards. In the market economy the market mechanism balances supply and demand. If there are too few goods, the price increases and with it the profit margin of the producers. Production is expanded to increase profits and it becomes worth importing goods from abroad. In a central economy prices are fixed, which is why the market mechanism cannot work. On the contrary, black markets with flexible prices form and offer the desired goods at higher prices.
2. **Black markets**

   The black markets are expressions of good shortages, wrong prices and bad money. There was too much currency in Ostmark in relation to goods. Some goods were scarce, so you could not buy it at the government-fixed prices in the shop, but only on the black markets. On the black markets, therefore, foreign exchange was usually used or a much higher price in Ostmark than the state-fixed one.

3. **Money surplus (hidden inflation)**

   Money surplus is an expression of money overproduction, lack of productivity or lack of value to customers. Money has to be scarce, so that the money has purchasing power and supply aligns to demand (for example, German currency reform in 1948 led to supply.). The money surplus led to hidden inflation. The people hoarded their earned money because they did not find the products they wanted, or there were just too few goods. However, the companies continued to pay wages. If they did not sell their products they took a loss, but this was offset by the state, which printed more money. This was called soft budgets for the companies. The people were all busy and no one was unemployed, at least not in the sense of not being assigned to a company as a worker.
4. **Hidden unemployment** means a lack of productivity. Although everyone had jobs, they were not all productive. Unemployment is also an expression of a delayed adaptation to structural change. This was also a reason for the low productivity of East Germany. Structural change was delayed, especially in heavy industry, i.e. coal and steel.
5. **Hidden goods distribution** according to the access to power. Not every East German citizen suffered the shortage of goods. Heads from supermarkets always had a full range of food choices. They had the right of first access. Those who could get to the goods first did so in the shops and in the companies. Even more important was the political power that allowed production to be channeled and used. Politicians used the system to their advantage and took advantage of what they wanted.

The increasing diversification of the economy (products and production) was increasingly difficult to control centrally despite the use of computers. Why was it that the central administration economy failed, especially economically?

Systemic Errors of the Central Administration Economy

1. Welfare losses due to extensive bureaucracy

It is obvious that the planning of an entire economy is laborious down to the last detail. More elaborate than when people plan decentrally because the plan does not have to be brought together and aggregated through a bureaucracy. In addition, as a result of product innovations, there were more and more products that needed to be planned. The increasing diversification of the economy (products and production) was increasingly difficult to control centrally despite the use of computers.

In order to analyze the malfunctioning of the central administration economy, we will now go into the question of how competition functions in the central administration economy, thus how functions are performed.

Disadvantages of a Central Administration Economy

A. **Static competitive functions**

The authorities have an information deficit (from Hayek, von Mises[63]), as there are no market prices (**information function**). If many consumers want a product, the price goes up. The increased price signals an increased profit margin for companies, which is why they expand production. Conversely, low prices for primary products and production processes signal increased profit margins. The producers optimize production and make the desired offer available. Since prices are fixed in the central administration economy, the planning authority lacks this information.

The authorities cannot know everyone's needs. The bureaucracy of planning is time-consuming and inflexible, which is why they can't react to short-term changes, in needs or scarcities, for example. Lack of competition for demand and lack of incentive leads to lower quality and wasted resources. Plan fulfillment through quantity, because quality is not measurable. (Control function).

Neither can the authorities know the abilities of people, all production methods, or availabilities of resources, nor do they have profit incentive (allocation function). Without flexible prices, even the cheapest supplier cannot attract the most demand (second allocation function) and would not be interested in it without ownership and profit.

Without ownership, competition and existential risk, there is a lack of significant performance incentive, which reduces productivity. Absolute control does not exist. Corruption and laziness are frequent. Community ownership belongs to everyone and no one. Nobody cares about the property because it belongs to nobody in particular, but to everyone. The same phenomenon can be observed in the shared ownership of student dormitories. Everyone wants to use the dishes, but nobody wants to wash them. Lack of liability and a lack of property rights lead to waste (**incentive function**).

Since companies do not have to fear bankruptcy, there is no incentive to operate efficiently (**sanction function**). The state must be responsible for losses of the companies. To finance this, it prints more money (alimentation by government money supply, soft budgets).

The authorities must determine the needs of people, their labor input and the distribution of goods, which is why the consumer sovereignty of the market economy becomes the political sovereignty of the planned economy (**freedom function**). Central administrations must therefore be dictatorships. The need-oriented distribution (**better political allocation**) of the goods is ultimately no fairer than the performance-oriented in the market system. Politicians can maximize their own

[63] See von Hayek (1975) and Mises (1920).

benefits in the system by having access to the means of production through political power. (**Distribution function**).

As a rule, the state combined the production of goods in order to exploit the economies of scale. Without competition, companies will behave like monopolists and artificially tighten supply in order to impose higher prices on the planning authority. They will try to hide capacities in order to have production for themselves and reserves for the fulfillment of the plan (**control function**).

B. **Functions of dynamic competition**

Lack of competition and lack of incentive lead to less technical progress, because innovations are not worthwhile (**innovation function**). The dynamic entrepreneur (Schumpeter) cannot develop within the rigid planning bureaucracy. Imitating innovations is not worthwhile for lack of ownership (profit) and is not necessary due to the soft budget (**imitation function**).

There is no further incentive to adapt quickly to other economic conditions (adjustment function) when companies do not have to fear bankruptcy because of the soft budgets. The many identified functional disadvantages of the central administration economy caused the cultural and social advantages of communism to be replaced by inefficiencies and statism; everyone was equally poor. The economic situation of the population deteriorated more and more and the distance to the western market economy systems increased. The population wanted a system change that politicians could not stop from happening. Russia opted for a market economy.

Is it possible for a society to develop without any social values, democratic knowledge or economic understanding? If we are looking for an example to analyze this question we can look at Russia. There can hardly be a more fascinating country than Russia, an empire that determined world politics in the last few decades together with the USA and which is an example for the attempt to find an alternative to the market economy system through socialism and communism. In the end Russia decided to return to a market economy. This transformation policy made Russia in the nineties into an example of an unsocial and badly constructed market economy ("predatory capitalism").

From November 1991 to January 1994, Åslund worked with Jeffrey Sachs and David Lipton as a senior advisor to the Russian reform government under President Boris Yeltsin.

4.10 Russia's Transformation into a Market Economy with a Poor Economic System

After Glasnost and Perestroika and after Yeltsin and part of the army held off the communist putsch, there was a historically unique chance for Russia at the end of the 1980s to make a fresh start economically and politically. Russia called in one of the most internationally renowned economic scientists, such as the American Geoffrey Sachs, and thus representatives of the quantitative research trend of the period. The

USSR was economically finished for good, not least of all because of the arms race with the USA, and discredited morally as a totalitarian system among a large portion the Russian population. Russia thus seemed to be a unique chance to apply economic theory in a practical setting and to create a flourishing landscape with the market system the theorists had dreamt up. Using a quantitative model Sachs found it reasonable to apply the elementary point of departure to Russia, and thus the functional prerequisites of the model, namely private property, contractual freedom and free prices all introduced overnight as a so-called shock therapy. The Russian economy did not develop as the model had predicted however, but fell apart visibly with the raw material sector being the only exception. Per capital real income fell to a third of its previous value. Unemployment, which had not occurred directly in socialism, became a mass phenomenon, and those who were lucky enough to have a job were often not paid. Many of the proud middle class in the USSR, the intellectual elite such as researchers, teachers, engineers and doctors were poverty-stricken or emigrated, as did the employees of the state such as judges and police officers. The educational system, social system and internal security all collapsed, including basic medical care for the population, all of which were quite obviously a public good in the USSR. The UN Human Development Report placed Russia in the early 1990s among the developed nations with a high standard of living. The system collapse after the shock therapy threw Russia back to the dark ages in a catastrophe of biblical proportions. The average life expectancy for the population dropped from 69.3 years in 1986 to 63.4 in 1994, being just 57.6 years for men. Illnesses that had been long forgotten, such as tuberculosis and cholera appeared again. Alcoholism and other diseases of addiction also spread. More than two million children were homeless, much more than during the Russian civil war and World War II. Another two million children did not attend school. Criminality increased dramatically, with politically and economically motivated murders a daily occurrence. 10–15% of the population clearly benefited from the reforms, but 60% were made poor. What happened? It had nothing to do with the expected adjustment process to the new market economy framework. Were these the promised benefits of a market economy? Were these the flourishing landscapes?

Surely not. Where then, was the mistake? There were two elementary mistakes. The first mistake was that the shock therapy destroyed the existing economic and social institutions and organizations without creating new ones. The reforms were purely quantitative, which means that the specific qualitative conditions in Russia were not taken into consideration. The second grave mistake was to conduct the privatization from a regime that was not democratic. The two mistakes together meant that assets were distributed according the law of the fittest. Power and influence in the political cadres and access to resources combined with unscrupulous brutality set up the new distribution. 40–45% of the capital used to acquire assets is thought to have been from criminal activities.[64] The public legal and security systems were overwhelmed, incapacitated or were corrupt or disorientated due to a lack of political guidelines. New democratic or market economy structures such as

[64] See Yurlov (1999); Åslund (2007) and Weigl (2008).

institutions and organizations were nonexistent. According to the Analytical Center of Russian Academy of Science, 55% of company capital and 80% of voting rights in the public companies were acquired by Russian and foreign criminals. 85% of public property was sold at a low nominal value. In the end the American consultant Geoffrey Sachs distanced himself from the Russian market reform. In his opinion the Russian leadership had exceeded the worst prejudices of Marxists about the capitalistic system by understanding their function or goal as achieving private enrichment at the cost of the general population. The criminal circles did not hesitate to engage in murder in order to remove adversaries and resistance. We must fear that in the meanwhile large portions of the Russian economy and politics are in their hands. The illegal economy was neither recorded by the state nor controlled by the official economy, and probably accounted for around 40% of GDP at that time. It was impossible for an independent, innovative middle class to develop in this environment. Performance was never established as a criterion for economic success. Within 7 years between $300 and 400 billion in private funds was transferred to foreign banks. With this background it is not a surprise that in 1997 only 8% of Russians said they were better off than before the economic reform. When asked what was responsible for the "new Russians" doing so well, 39% was speculation, 34% theft from state assets and 17% the use of criminal funds.[65] This is what one would call predatory capitalism, an anarchistic capitalism at its extreme.

Tests for the success of the market economy reforms thus came back with disastrous results. The market economy system and so-called neoliberalism have not only been discredited, but have a negative association and not just since the subprime crisis. As a result of the unethical und disastrous Russian transformation they have been equated with social injustice, mass poverty, exploitation, hunger and impoverishment. Russia's experiences with a market economy were not seen in isolation, but have been transferred to the discussion on globalization. The idea that the market, competition and liberalism are able to bring welfare to everyone was doubted. Their new critics have dubbed the representatives of liberalism market fundamentalists.[66]

Of course it is easy to criticize something after the fact. On the other hand, we would always be repeating the same mistakes if we were not prepared to learn from them. One of the main reasons for the failure of market economy reforms is the lack of attention given to the initial cultural and social situations, in other words the qualitative factors. What was the qualitative situation? Firstly, a functional market economy was as nonexistent in Russia as was democracy. There was thus neither a middle class that had arisen out of the enlightenment and industrial revolution, nor was there practiced market economy and democratic behavior available as human capital, which would have come from knowledge of market economic functions and individual behavior optimally adapted to market economic conditions or social capital[67] such as the function and practice of common behavior among supply and

---

[65] See Lapidus (1995), Åslund (2007), Marsh (2005) and Yurlov (1999), p. 5.

[66] See Yurlov (1999), p. 5

[67] For the expressions individual capital and social capital see Sect. 6.4.

demand on markets. This may sound banal, but is it not banal in any way. When one must present themselves to an employer in competition with others, the way one must strive to attract customers, what customers should expect from a seller, that one must compare and deal over prices and quality are not abilities one is born with. A moral code for delivery and payment must also be learned. Paying bills on time is in principle a difficult thing for any customer, but he must learn that if he does not pay on time he will have to pay additional fees or face a lawsuit. This is necessary in the market economy system, since the supplier would otherwise have liquidity costs or might even go bankrupt, leaving other creditors all the way down to the employees without compensation. All of these examples are human experiences, rules of behavior that must be learned through practice in the market economy. These games must be played over several rounds so that people can see how they must behave in the market economy. The invisible hand of Adam Smith must be practiced. Behavior in economic freedom must be learned as much as behavior within political freedom.

The same applies for the system of political freedom, democracy. Market economy and democracy presuppose the existence of active, self-confident and responsible citizens, and democracy also demands an active, selfless political participation. Those people driving the economy and citizens must be informed and know what they want and actively work towards achieving it based on that information. Even an optimal market economy and democratic system as institution and organization will not inspire the desired behaviors in people, at least not at the beginning. First people have to learn the rules of the game in order to follow them, and they will not immediately behave in such a way in the newly created organizations that they would carry out their assigned functions optimally. To fully develop the productive forces the human capital in a market economy is required beyond just the organizations and institutions. Democratic human capital is necessary for a functioning democracy. There was no human capital (social capital) for the market economy in Russia, which is why the transformation to a market economy had to fail as shock therapy. The same applies to the transformation into a democracy.

Because Russia was lacking both political and economic frameworks as well as human capital, the old social structures have taken hold in a new guise, the same structures that formed people during the time of the Czars, and which only nominally changed power holders during Communism. A small group of beneficiaries surrounded a dominant leader who got rich ruthlessly at the cost of the Russian people. At least under Communism the people received basic provisions. This is still no longer provided and the difference in wealth gets constantly larger. If this continues a new socialist revolution may result. Neither is the social situation endurable for the population, nor the distribution of assets acceptable, since it is based on immoral behavior instead of performance. The only chance for the new upper class, the so-called "new Russians" would be to create a new social market economy based on the existing property distribution and hope that the people forget the where the distribution originated. A functional tax system without a shadow economy, with which public goods such as education could be socially redistributed and financed would be a basic prerequisite.

To bring it all together we want to look for the lessons to be learned from the greatest national economic experiment of all time. A much-discussed and fundamental question of transformation theory is whether shock therapy or gradualism is preferable. The question can now be answered. A shock therapy, the short-term changes to all institutions and organizations from planned to market economy, or Socialism to Capitalism, can only work in exceptional cases such as after German reunification where an economically and politically stable country economically controls and socially cushions the change of a smaller country. In all other cases only gradualism is an option, as seen in the context of Russia's example. In fact Russia's experiences may well have moved China to decide in favor of a gradual release or changeover in its economy and ownership structures. The social capital as common economic group knowledge about the functioning and distribution of work in a market economy was lacking. Russia would have been better off importing human capital, in particular executives on a large scale from a country in considered suitable, as Peter the Great did in his reforms. This human capital, appointed to the most important political and economic functions, would have provided a gradual but constant dissemination and implementation of the necessary knowledge behind market economies and democratic systems.

If Geoffrey Sachs had predicted this development he would have given a different consultation, or perhaps none at all. Admittedly a consultant cannot be held responsible for a development over which he has no influence. Be he is responsible for the advice he has given. The project to transform Russia will always be connected to his name. A consultant always has the option of distancing himself from the project if his advice is not followed, but this only applies if the action is not taken at the important crossroads. The quantitative American line of research was simply overwhelmed due to its simplicity and was not qualified for a consultation on a practical economic and political order.

Geoffrey Sachs is a phenomenon that represents the current state of national economic science. He was and is one of its largest figureheads. At 30 he was already a Professor at Harvard and meanwhile receives a salary from three departments at Columbia University in New York. Having been brought up and educated in a mathematical form of thought, it was easy for him to reach clear statements and recommendations. The models have another advantage in that they can be applied to any countries. Mathematics and econometric models are universally applicable and transferable. A model has variables, which can take on the respective quantitative country values. This is how Sachs managed to advise at least 75 countries. Did he know any of them? In Russia he later said that the corruption "was surprising" for him and that he had underestimated how much Russia was hindered by the lack of a functioning citizenry. Today he expresses doubt about the dominant economy, the standard education "has little use" and hardly any connection to the public.[68]

[68] See Heuser (2003).

Admittedly the economic performance has improved in Russia. From 1999 to 2005 Russia's economy experienced an average rate of 5.5% real growth and the per capita income more than doubled from 2001 to 2005 to around $5250. Be that as it may, it could have been quite a different story. This economic growth is mostly due to the significant increase of raw material prices. The raw material price index CRB increased by around 81.6% from 2001 to 2005 and the price of oil by around 90%. Distortions caused by ruble to dollar conversions mean that we can only make approximations for the share raw material price developments had in Russia's economic upswing. For example, the oil price increased by 40% in 2005, but real oil production only by 2.2%. The CRB increased by around 23% in 2005, and Russia's exports in dollars increased by around 33% to approx. $241 billion, whereby raw materials comprised 67% of this, or around $161 billion. The exports minus imports were $36.8 billion, which increased GDP by around 4.8% to $766 billion. If we also consider the multiplier effects for the Russian domestic demand due to increased income from the higher raw material prices, we may conclude that the Russian growth is at least mostly due to the raw material price increases.

What is more, the majority of the population has barely profited from the positive development. We may hope that Russia finds a way to use the billions earned from raw materials for social security and education for the general population, which would provide a step towards long-term stabilization of a modern national economy.[69]

Conclusion

As the example of Russia shows, the twentieth century was the century of competition between systems. Different economic systems were attempted. The market economy was able to establish itself as the basic principle of order. Socialism seemed to be the answer to many ethical problems created by the industrial revolution at first. Here we should mention the pauperization of the working class or the lower classes that were poorly educated or impoverished. Market and morality were considered opposites. Socialism considered the basis of the evil to be distribution of wealth via the central function of capital in the market economy as well as market mechanisms felt to be unfair and held responsible for the inequity of needs met. By removing private property and with the central coordination of production plans in the planned economy, a method was devised to better satisfy the needs of the society. Socialism, or Communism, was unable to develop the productive forces. The gulf in the standard of living between the capitalistic and socialist countries grew until it caused the socialist system to collapse. What remains however, are several questions about the market economy system that have gone unanswered. We have examined company crises and the errors in company organization. A lack of moral values or a code of ethics was determined to be a central cause for the crises as much as the one-sided focus on figures or quantitative facts. We have also analyzed Russia as an example

[69]For details about the Russian transformation see Weigl (2008); Åslund (2007); Lapidus (1995); Grabrisch and Holscher (2007); Javlinskij (1994), Der Spiegel, no. 39 (2007), p. 82 and Yurlov (1999), p. 7.

for an unethical market economy and an example of quantitative economic consultation. The transition of Russia to a functioning market economy failed due to a lack of institutional regulations and a lack of social capital as common economic group knowledge about the functioning and distribution of work in a market economy.

The example of Russia has shown that a market system without rules and controls cannot function. Although capitalism or better to say the market economy is responsible for many crises, it remains with its growth and individual freedom the best of all possible economic systems. Crucial is much more that rules and controls exist to prevent damaging individual behavior. The regulatory concept of ordoliberalism has prevailed against the laissez-faire liberalism. Additionally the society has to implement moral responsibility in order to get a functioning market system.

4.11 Social Market Economy

The market and competition offer great advantages, expressed in the market functions already described. Other social or humanitarian goals such as a margin of subsistence or the compensation of market power between employer and employee cannot be explained through the market and competition, however. Other institutions and organizations are necessary for such goals, and are incorporated into the economic order. The market only considers interests important if they have market power. An employee who cannot find a demand for his skills on the labor market because of an overabundance of competitors with his job qualifications will not receive compensation from the market. On the other hand, the employer can afford to treat the employees he already has poorly, since they are so easily replaceable, a behavior that would otherwise be punished via the market.

Market sanctions are moody and sometimes unfair. The market rewards luck, such as those who already have a scarce resource with market condition profits, or a scarcity benefit. Real estate speculators for example, count on the real estate supply being limited with an increasing demand. Hard work itself is not a value for the market. Hard work is rewarded only if labor leads to something others are willing to pay for. In other words, without a product for which there is a demand, there is no reward from the market, which can mean starvation. There is no such thing as compensation according to need in the market system. The criticism from Karl Marx regarding the market economy system is thus justified. Charity and sympathy are foreign concepts to the market. Market and competition are instruments to achieve only some of humanity's goals, and they must be supplemented by other social regulations. This is where the social market economy comes in. It differentiates between primary and secondary income distribution, which closes the gap between economic and social goals. Since there is no intervention in the primary income distribution of the market, such as price or competition-distorting subsidies, the market and competition continue to function. The subsequent control of income created allows a certain amount of social goals to be realized, such as securing a margin of subsistence. Social market economy does not mean interfering in the market mechanisms for social purposes, as it is often misunderstood. Social means societal, not socialist. Applied correctly, the concept of a social market economy is preferable to all other forms.

This statement may cause objection at first, but it will be understandable when we remember all of the things that the market cannot provide. We already identified securing a margin of subsistence. What would the advantages of this be? The first may be the avoidance of social unrest. A person who fears for their existence may be prepared to do anything, including criminal activities. The willingness of market participants to take risks may well be much higher if they know that should their investment or founding of a company fail, their physical survival will still be secure. This would encourage enterprising or innovative behavior. Securing a level of subsistence also guarantees human capital for the economic process. A policy of financed education through redistribution can be justified economically as an investment in human capital. The productivity of those who have been supported increases, thus increasing economic power and income through taxes for the country. A good basic education also strengthens democracy, since citizens no longer believe unbalanced, one-sided arguments so easily. On the other hand, support for primary and university education exclusively through private scholarships will not provide a broad system of human capital. Procuring external knowledge is an alternative for the national economy and for companies. The international competition between states and companies for resources is not just over capital, but also over human capital.

It would be a fallacy to think that the community, the state, could provide for all the responsibilities in caring for people and perhaps even raising children. It must intercede where there are no family members, but the idea that people only behave egotistically and hand over all duties and responsibilities to the state is contrary to human nature and is simply impracticable. Not even the Socialism that existed went so far.

How can we explain that in reality countries that call their form of economy a social market economy, e.g. Germany, are not necessarily superior in economic productivity to exclusively market economies such as the USA? Most countries have a mixed form. Even the arch-capitalistic USA often demonized by socialists is not a purely market economy, since it has social security, even if not very much. An active social education policy is not implemented, but they do use clever lures for human capital, in particular through the elite American universities. Germany refuses to take this path in the belief that an active educational policy is sufficient. Most European universities are no competition for American universities in the international human capital market due to the lower salaries.

Under a social market economy we understand the combination of free market with social compensation (**definition**). This is where the concept of the social market economy begins. It distinguishes between primary and secondary distribution of income, thus balancing between economic and social goals. Since the primary income distribution of the market is not influenced, for example through subsidies that distort prices or distort competition, the market and competition remain functional. The subsequent taxation of income generated can be influenced to a certain extent by social objectives, such as securing the subsistence minimum.

Ludwig Erhard, who was the first Federal Minister of Economics of the Federal Republic of Germany from 1949 to 1963, introduced the term "social market economy". The term was first mentioned by Erhard's comrade-in-arms Alfred Müller-Armack, who was head of the Economic Policy Department in the ministry of economic since 1952, in his book "Wirtschaftslenkung und Marktwirtschaft".[70]

Social market economy, therefore, does not mean to enter the market mechanism socially, as is often misunderstood. Social is not socialist but societal. Properly implemented, the concept of social market economy must be superior to all other economic contexts because it balances the disadvantages of market and competition through additional regulations.[71]

This statement is likely to produce a contradiction, but becomes understandable when one realizes what the market cannot afford. We have already mentioned the protection of the subsistence minimum. What is the benefit of this? We first think of the prevention of social unrest. A person who has to fear for his existence is willing to do anything in order to survive and will likely not shy even from criminal acts. However, the risk attitude of the market participants is also likely to be higher if they know that in the event of a failure of their investment or business start-up, at least their physical continuity is guaranteed. This should encourage entrepreneurial or innovative behavior. In addition, by simply safeguarding livelihoods the human capital for the economic process is preserved. An education policy financed by redistribution can also be justified economically as an investment in human capital because the productivity of the beneficiaries increases, thus also the economic power and tax revenue of the country. Good general education also strengthens democracy, because citizens are no longer so easily exposed to unbalanced one-sided arguments. An exclusive promotion of school and university education with private scholarships will not be able to guarantee a broad range of human capital. An alternative here is the acquisition of external knowledge for the national economy as well as for companies. The international competition of states and enterprises for resources includes not only capital, but also human capital.

The main structural building blocks of a social market economy are social, pension, unemployment and health insurance, a free educational system and a progressive tax system.[72] This results in ethical advantages, inasmuch as a benefit

[70] See Müller-Armack (1947), p. 88; Zweynert (2008) and Bundesministerium für Wirtschaft und Technologie (2013).

[71] In a sense, Aristotle already foresaw the social market economy in which he wished to make use of the advantages of private property but also wanted to make private property available to the community: "On the other hand, an order of property which follows the custom and which is characterized by habitual behavior and the Order of proper laws is a great advantage: it should combine the advantage of both orders-by this I mean the advantage of common property and of private property."

Aristoteles (1991), pp. 17 or 1263a. (author's translation)

[72] See Bundesministerium für Wirtschaft und Technologie (2013).

is generated for people. A secure existence and health care regardless of income, as well as equality of opportunity through free education, are important prerequisites for a good and meaningful human life according to Aristotle. However, there are also economic advantages. Social market economy pays off. The main economic advantages are:

1. Development of human capital through a government financed education system.
   Educating the population increases productivity. Employees with better skills earn more. Due to technical progress the demands on the qualification of workers are increasing. A high human capital is once again the prerequisite for innovations, i.e. technical progress. And innovations increase the productivity, competitiveness and profits of the industry of a country. Well-paid jobs are created. This all leads to significantly higher tax revenues. Investment in the human capital of the population thus pays off in many ways.
2. Greater equality of opportunity and thus better economic use of human capital.
   The education that a person receives should not depend on the income of his parents, but on his abilities. If education has to be paid for, there will always be people whose skills could not be developed because they could not afford the training.
3. Preservation of human capital by statutory health insurance.
   It makes little sense to invest in human capital and then let it be destroyed by illness. Even well trained workers can become unemployed. If they can no longer pay for their health care, the human capital is lost.
4. Social peace through a state guarantee of the subsistence minimum and redistribution in the form of progressive taxation.
   Anyone afraid for his existence is ready for violence. A market economy is more likely to be accepted as an economic form if the inequality of the distribution results is mitigated. Not least of all, the distribution results of the markets are not just based on performance and are sometimes perceived as unjust.

The principle of assistance for self-help applies. This principle of subsidiarity derives from Catholic social doctrine.[73] The social market economy also corresponds to Rawl's principle of justice. Everyone can be freed from their interests by moving into a primitive state, without social differences, in order to ensure procedural fairness when establishing social institutions. Out of a veil of ignorance the citizens do not know their fate and must fend for themselves in the worst case.[74] However, if they do not know whether they are born poor or rich or have health problems, they need social security and basic care. They would, therefore, opt for a social market economy with social redistribution as an insurance against the worst-case scenario.

[73] See Schulte (2000) and http://www.uni-muenster.de/Geschichte/SWG-Online/sozialstaat/glossar_subsidiar.htm

[74] See Rawls (1979), p. 158ff and 341, and in the original Rawls (1971), p. 10ff, 12, 139 f.

But how do we explain that in reality, countries that characterize their economic form as a social market economy, such as Germany, are not necessarily superior to the other almost exclusive market economies, such as the US, in the productivity of the economy? Most countries are mixed forms. Even the US is not a pure market economy, but has a social security, albeit a small one. An active social education policy is not being pursued, but the skillful abolition of human capital, especially by American elite universities. Germany, for example, renounces this in the belief that an active education policy alone is sufficient. However, due to lower salaries for professors, most European universities are not able to compete with the US in the international competition for human capital. The term "socialized market economy" also applies to Germany as a "social market economy". On the one hand, a large number of economic sectors were directly involved, with the result that competition and market functions were disrupted. On the other hand, taxation and social protection have been exaggerated to the point where the incentives have been adversely affected. This was at least partly corrected by the Agenda 2010 of the Federal Chancellor Schröder.

As we saw in Sect. 3.5. on the issue of fairness, people tend to look at an equal distribution as fair with unearned income. However, the willingness to give up earned income is much lower. And there is a conflict of interest regarding willingness to perform. The willingness to work for income equal distribution is very low.

The level of wealth positively influenced the amount given to the public good, however.

Studies have shown that social acceptance of taxation as a norm can be crucial to tax evasion.

Thus, the possibility of making tax evasion public also generated emotional distress among subjects at the moment of evasion, such as high penalties.[75]

As seen in Sect. 3.5. identification increases the willingness to work for the group and share with the group members. This should be taken into account in taxation and redistribution within national groups. A country where citizens identify strongly with each other can redistribute more because the willingness to share with other group members is greater. Acceptance for unequal distribution differs culturally from country to country. A study examining Norwegians, Italians and Americans on their attitudes towards income redistribution showed that everyone wants redistribution but differently. Norwegians demanded a much higher redistribution in performance-related and non-performance income differentials, while Italians accepted income differentials based on benefit differences the most. The Americans interviewed were in between.[76]

[75] See Coricelli et al. (2010), pp. 226–247 and Beck (2014), p. 290.

[76] See Gianluca Grimalda, Francesco Farina, Ulrich Schmidt, Preferences for Redistribution in the US, Italy, Norway: An Experiment Study, Kieler Discussion Papers No. 2099 January 2018, Kiel Institute for the World Economy.

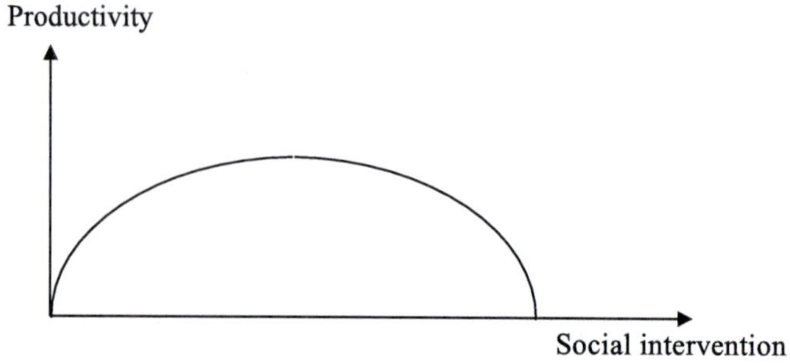

Fig. 4.7 Social intervention and productivity

Higher productivity as well as social peace arises through the building blocks of the social market economy. In general, therefore, a correlation can be drawn with the Laffer curve[77]: the productivity of an economy initially increases sharply with an increase in the social intervention of the state, but the increase lessens and then decreases from a maximum with increasing rapidity. This is a semicircular-like functional relationship (see Fig. 4.7).

Conclusion
The twentieth century was the century of system competition as the example of Russia illustrates. Various economic systems were tried, but the market economy won the system competition. At first socialism seemed to offer an answer to the many ethical problems that arose during the industrial revolution. In this context, we should mention the impoverishment of the working class or the lower poorly trained and simply poor population strata. Market and morality were perceived here as a contrast. Socialism saw the ethical basis for the unjustly perceived prosperity distribution in the central function of capital in the market economy and in the market mechanism, which was blamed for the lack of justice in needs and distribution.

Conclusion
The market economy is considered to be ethically superior to alternatives such as a planned economy (central administration economy) because it achieves the moral goal of adequate prosperity with a higher degree of individual freedom. The competition functions lead to an ethical result in the sense of a justice for performance. The social market economy is the ethical expansion of the market economy. It combines the productivity advantages of the market economy with ethical aspects, which can increase the productivity of a pure market economy when properly applied. However, there is a risk that overriding social interventions can severely limit competition and lead to the same problems as in the central administration economy.

[77] The Laffer curve describes the relationship between tax rates and tax revenues.

Planned economy considered the abolition of private property and the central coordination of production plans to be two tools to better meet the needs of society. But socialism, or even communism, could not unleash productive forces. The prosperity gap between the capitalist and socialist states became ever greater until the socialist systems collapsed. Nonetheless, the social market economy cannot eliminate all ethical weaknesses in the market economy. The greatest damage is caused by market failures, as we shall see in the next chapter.

Although capitalism, or the market economy, is responsible for many crises with its growth and individual freedom, it remains the best of all possible economic systems. It is much more crucial that rules and controls exist to prevent damaging individual behavior. The regulatory concept of constitutional economics has prevailed against the laissez-faire liberalism. Additionally, society has to implement moral responsibility in order to get a functioning market system.

Ethical Summary

The example of Russia shows that a market economy without social rules leads to unsocial, unjust and thus unethical results. Morality complements the positive effects of the market. The results of the market correspond only partially to our ideas of what is right. In case of market failure, morality ensures that third parties are not harmed. Against this background, the social market economy is entering the market and changing the distribution results.

Another social solution to conflictual and non-conflictual games is morality, as the players would not want to harm the opponent. Stabilizing behavioral expectations can prevent damage in conflictual games, while cooperation gains can be safely realized in non-conflictual games.

Social morality, good manners or courtesy are further prerequisites for the smooth running of social processes. The institutions and organizations cannot control, monitor and enforce everything. If, on the other hand, no social rules were respected by anyone, the social system would collapse immediately. Where laws and control cease, morality begins. Morality regulates human behavior so as to prevent social harm.

Behavioral Summary

As a social solution to conflictual and non-conflictual games, institutions have established themselves as social rules that are enforced through sanctions. Stabilizing behavioral expectations can prevent damage in conflictual games, while cooperation gains can be safely realized in non-conflictual games. The resulting benefits move the individual to join society and submit to the institutions, at least as long as the benefits outweigh the disadvantages. A reason for the problems of Russia during the transition to a market economy was the lack of common economic group knowledge as social capital.

The knowing of belonging to a group changes the behavior of the members by giving preference to the own group members. Identification with the group and the individual is crucial. People strive for equal distribution, not for the maximization of welfare. Rising inequality leads to less happiness, but more in Europe than in the

USA. An equal distribution on the basis of different performance is rejected, equal distribution leads to a lower willingness to perform. The economics cannot achieve distributive justice directly, but only indirectly after the gross domestic product maximization within the framework of market and competition. The fairness of performance stands in the conflict of goals with equal distribution as a human goal. From this, the social market economy has developed into a successful model in Germany.

Social decisions are not unproblematic as group decisions. They do not automatically lead to the best decision for a society. The influences on group decisions that cause the informative exchange to be impaired, leading to decisions that are normative based instead of informationally based (groupthink) must be prevented.

Comprehension Questions

1. What are the advantages of the market economy as a system?
2. Name and explain the competition functions.
3. Is there a conflict between market and ethics?

Literature

Alchian, A. A./Demsetz, H. (1972), Production, information costs and economic organisation: American Economic Review, 62, pp. 777–795.

Apolte, T. u.a. (2007). *Vahlens Kompendium der Wirtschaftstheorie und Wirtschaftspolitik – Währung und Internationale Finanzmärkte, Smeets*. Vahlen Verlag, 1 Band, 9 Auflage.

Aristoteles. (1991). Politik II, Werke Band 9/II, Darmstadt 1991.

Asch, S. E. (1987). *Social psychology*. Oxford University Press.

Åslund, A. (2007). *How capitalism was built: The transformation of Central and Eastern Europe, Russia and Central Asia*. Cambridge 2007.

Baschek, N. (2012). *Diese Welt anerkennen – Axel Honneth geht mit seinem zweiten Hauptwerk „Das Recht der Freiheit" auf Abstand zur Kritischen Theorie*. https://literaturkritik.de/id/16187.

Beck, H. (2014). *Behavioral Economics: Eine Einführung*. 1 Aufl. Springer.

Becker, G. S., & Becker, G. N. (1998). *Die Ökonomik des Alltags*. UTB.

Bender, D., Berg, H., Cassel, D., Claasen, E.-M., Gabisch, G., Hübl, L., et al. (2003). *Vahlens Kompendium der Wirtschaftstheorie und Wirtschaftspolitik* (Bd. 1). Verlag Franz Vahlen GmbH.

Blickle, G. (1996). Argumentationsintegrität: Anstöße für eine reflexive Managementethik? In D. Wagner & H. Nolte (Eds.), *Managementbildung* (pp. 113–123). Hampp.

Böhler, T. (2004). *Der Fähigkeiten- Ansatz von Amartya Sen und die „Bevorzugte Option für die Armen" in der Befreiungstheologie – Zwei Ansätze auf dem Weg zur ethischen Begründung von Armutsforschung und Armutsreduktion* (Working Paper, facing poverty, No. 6). University of Salzburg/Austria Poverty Research Group. https://uni-salzburg.at/fileadmin/multimedia/Zentrum_fuer_Ethik_und_Armutsforschung/documents/Working_Papers/Facing_Poverty/Böhler-FähigkeitenSenUndBefreiungstheologie.pdf

Brennan, G., & Buchanan, J. M. (1985). *The reason of rules*. Cambridge University Press.

Buchanan, J. M. (1979). *What should economists do?* Liberty Press.

Buchanan, J. M. (1991). *The economics and ethics of constitutional order*. The University of Michigan Press.

Bundesministerium für Wirtschaft und Technologie. (2013). *Soziale Marktwirtschaft.* http://www.bmwi.de/DE/Themen/Wirtschaft/soziale-marktwirtschaft.html 30 Oct 2015.

Buonanno, P., Montolio, D., & Vanin, P. (2009). Does Social Capital Reduce Crime? *Journal of Law and Economics, 52*(1), 145–170.

Büttner, S. M. (2017). Émile Durkheim: Über soziale Arbeitsteilung. In K. Kraemer & F. Brugger (Eds.), *Schlüsselwerke der Wirtschaftssoziologie* (pp. 47–S. 54). Springer 2017.

Conrad, C. A. (2010). *Moral und Wirtschaftskrisen.* dissert Verlag.

Conrad, C. A. (2018). *Business ethics – A philosophical and Behavioral approach.* Springer International.

Coricelli, G., Joffily, M., Montmarquette, C., & Villeval, M. C. (2010). Cheating, emotions, and rationality: An experiment on tax evasion. *Experimental Econonmics, 13*(2010), 226–247.

Dawkins, R. (1978). *Das egoistische gen.* Springer.

Dierksmeier, C. (2013) *Ökonomische Freiheit und Verantwortung bei Amartya Sen.* https://webcache.googleusercontent.com/search?q=cache:_Y5vVMJCrisJ:https://www.weltethos-institut.org/uploads/media/Antrittsvorlesung_20130517.pdf+&cd=2&hl=de&ct=clnk&gl=de

Durkheim, É. (1988). *Über soziale Arbeitsteilung. Studie über die Organisation höherer Gesellschaften.* 2. ed., Frz. Orig. v. 1893. Suhrkamp.

Ebert, T. (2015). Soziale Gerechtigkeit, Ideen • Geschichte • Kontroversen, Bundeszentrale für politische Bildung, Schriftenreihe Band 1571, 2. ed., Bonn 2015.

Falk, A. (2003). Homo oeconomicus versus homo recipocans: Ansätze für ein neues Wirtschaftspolitisches Weltbild? *Perspektiven der Wirtschaftspolitik., 4*, 141–172.

Fehr, E., & Fischbacher, U. (2003). The nature of human altruism. *Nature, 425*(23), 785–791.

Fehr, E., Gächter, S., & Fischbacher, U. (2001). Are people conditionally cooperative? Evidence from a public goods experiment. *Economics Letters, 71*, 397–404.

Feld, L. P., & Köhler, E. (2011). Ist die Ordnungsökonomik zukunftsfähig? *Zeitschrift für Wirtschafts- und Unternehmensethik, 12*(2), 173–195. https://nbn-resolving.org/urn:nbn:de:0168-ssoar-349165

Furubotn, E. G., & Richter, R. (2005). *Institutions and Economic Theory.* University of Michigan Press, 2005.

Gauthier, D. (1986). *Morals by Agreement.* Oxford University Press; Auflage: Revised (23. September 1999).

Giorgio, C., Joffily, M., Montmarquette, C., & Villeval, M. C. (2010). Cheating, emotions, and rationality: An experiment on tax evasion. *Experimental Econonmics, 13*(2010), 226–247.

Göbel, E. (2010). *Unternehmensethik.* UTB.

Goppel, A., Mieth, C., & Neuhäuser, C. (2016). *Handbuch Gerechtigkeit.* Springer.

Grabrisch, H., & Holscher, J. (2007). *The successes and failures of economic transition: The European experience.* New York 2006.

Gramms, T. (1999). *Von Helden, Feiglingen und anderen.* http://www2.hs-fulda.de/~grams/OekoSimSpiele/Helden.html

Habermas, J. (1975). *Strukturwandel der Öffentlichkeit* (7th ed.). Luchterhand.

Habermas, J. (1992). *Faktizität und Geltung. Beiträge zur Diskurstheorie des Rechts und des demokratischen Rechtsstaates.* Suhrkamp.

Heil, J. (2005). *Philosophie und soziale Gerechtigkeit: Eine Ringvorlesung.* Turnshare Ltd. – Publisher.

Herlinde, P.-S. (2015). *Das Andere der Gerechtigkeit: Moraltheorie im Kontext der Geschlechterdifferenz.* Walter de Gruyter.

Heuser, U. J. (2003). Die Wandlung des Jeffrey Sachs. In *Die Zeit* (Vol. 38).

Hobbes, T. (1651). *Leviatan, London, printed for Andrew Crooke, at the Green Dragon in St. Pauls Church-yard* 1651.

Hollingshead, A. B. (1998). Group and individual training: The impact of practice on performance. *Small Group Research, 29*, 254–280.

Homann, K. (1999). Die Relevanz der Ökonomik für die Implementation ethischer Zielsetzungen. In W. Korff (Ed.), *Handbuch der Wirtschaftsethik. Band 1: Verhältnisbestimmung von Wirtschaft und Ethik* (pp. 322–343). Gütersloher Verlagshaus.

Honneth, A. (2007). Gerechtigkeit und kommunikative Freiheit. Überlegungen im Anschluss an Hegel Published 17 January 2007 Original in German First published in Barbara Merker/Georg Mohr/Michael Quante (ed.): *Subjektivität und Anerkennung*. mentis: Paderborn 2004. Re-printed with the editors' kind permission in Critique & Humanism 22 (2006) (German and Bulgarian versions) Downloaded from eurozine.com. https://www.eurozine.com/gerechtigkeit-und-kommunikative-freiheituberlegungen-im-anschluss-an-hegel/. 8 Feb 2019.

Honneth, A. (2011). *Das Recht der Freiheit. Grundriß einer demokratischen Sittlichkeit.* Suhrkamp Verlag, 2011.

Horn, A. (2018). Anerkennung und Freiheit: SubjekttheoretischeGrundlageneiner Theoriedemokratischer Sittlichkeit. *Archiv für Rechts- und Sozialphilosophie (ARSP), 104*(1), 16–40.

Hume, D. (1748). *Treatise on human nature, III.* Book, Part 2, Section 1 and 2.

Initiative Neue Qualität der Arbeit. (2012). *Führungskultur im Wandel Kulturstudie mit 400 Tiefeninterviews*, Berlin. https://www.inqa.de/SharedDocs/. . ./fuehrungskultur-im-wandel-monitor.pdf?

Javlinskij, G. A. (1994). *Laissez- faire versus policy-led transformation: Lessons of the economic reforms in Russia*. Moskau 1994.

Kant, I. (1784). Beantwortung der Frage: Was ist Aufklärung? In: *Berlinische Monatsschrift*, 1784, H. 12, S. 481–494.

Kant, I. (1797). Werkausgabe, Bd. VIII, ed. von W. Weischedel. Die Metaphysik der Sitten, Zweiter Teil: metaphysische Anfangsgründe der Tugendlehre (suhrkamp, Frankfurt a. M, first edition 1794).

Kirchgässner, G. (1991). *Homo Oeconomicus (Tübingen).* https://www.mohr.de/buch/homo-oeconomicus-9783161523274?createPdf=true

Klump, R. (2011). *Wirtschaftspolitik – Intrumente, Ziele und Institutionen* (2 Ausg.). Pearson Studium.

Kraemer, K., & Brugger, F. (Hrsg.) (2017). *Schlüsselwerke der Wirtschaftssoziologie* (S. 47–54). Springer

Lapidus, G. W. (1995). *The new Russia: Troubled transformation.* Boulder, Colo [u.a.] 1995.

Locke, J. (1823). *Two treatises of government, London.* file:///C:/Eigene%20Dateien2016/Political%20Economy/Material/Locke.pdf.

Machiavelli, N. (1977). *Discorsi: Gedanken über Politik und Staatsführung, Deutsche Gesamtausgabe* (2nd ed.). Kröner.

Marsh, C. (2005). *Unparalleled reforms: China's rise, Russia's fall, and the interdependence of transition*. Lanham, 2005.

Marx, K. (1972). *Randglossen zum Programm der deutschen Arbeiterpartei*. In: Karl Marx & Friedrich (Eds.), MEW, Bd. 19, Dietz, Berlin (pp. 15–32). Engels – Werke. (Karl) Dietz Verlag, Berlin. Band 19, 4. ed. 1973, first edition 1962, Berlin/DDR. pp. 13–32. http://www.mlwerke.de/me/me19/me19_013.htm

Maurer, Andrea/Schmid, Michael (2010), Erklärende Soziologie, 1. Aufl. : Springer.

Maurer, A. (Ed.). (2017). *Handbuch Wirtschaftssoziologie* (2nd ed.). Springer.

May, T. W. (1983). *Konfliktspielen*. Lang.

Mazouz, N. (2009). *Aspekte einer deliberativen Theorie des Guten und Gerechten.* https://elib.uni-stuttgart.de/bitstream/11682/5348/1/veroeff_diss_2009_final.pdf

Mises, L. (1920). Die Wirtschaftsrechnung im sozialistischen Gemeinwesen. *Archiv für Sozialwissenschaft und Sozialpolitik, Bd., 47*(1920), S. 86–S.121.

Moreland, R. L. (1999). Transactive memory: Learning who knows what in work groups and organizations. In L. Thompson, D. Messick, & J. Levine (Eds.), *Shared cognition in organizations: The management of knowledge* (pp. 3–31).

Moreland, R. L., & Myaskovsky, L. (2000), pp. 117–133 and Jonas, Klaus /Stroebe, Wolfgang / Hewstone, Miles (Hrsg.), Sozialpsychologie, 6., vollständig überarbeitete Auflage, Springer-Verlag Berlin Heidelberg, pp. 459.

Müller-Armack, A. (1947). *Wirtschaftslenkung und Marktwirtschaft*. Verlag für Wirtschaft und Sozialpolitik.

Nijstad, B. A., & Van Knippenberg, D. (2014). Gruppendynamik. In K. Jonas, W. Stroebe, & M. Hewstone (Eds.), *Sozialpsychologie* (6th ed., pp. 439–468). Springer.

Nowak, E. (1997). *On investment performance and corporate governance*. Verlag Paul Haupt.

Paine, L. S. (1994). Managing for organizational integrity. *Harvard Business Review, 72*(2), 106–117.

Picot, A., Dietl, H., Franck, E., Fiedler, M., & Royer, S. (2012). *Organisation – Theorie und Praxis aus ökonomischer Sicht* (6 Ausg.). Schäffer-Poeschel.

Presteich, K. N. (1999). *Explanation of the hawks and doves game*. http://college.holycross.edu/faculty/kprestwi/behavior/ESS/HvD_intro.html

Rawls, J. (1971). *A theory of justice*. Harvard University Press (Revised edition 1999).

Rawls, J. (1979), *Eine Theorie der Gerechtigkeit*. Frankfurt a.M. 1979.

Rousseau, J.-J. (1755). *Diskurs über die Ungleichheit* (Hrsg. Heinrich Meier). Reclam, 2017.

Rousseau, J.-J. (1762a). *Der Gesellschaftsvertrag oder Prinzipien des Staatsrechts*. marixverlag, 2008.

Rousseau, J-J. (1762b). *Du contracts social ou principles du droit polititiques*. Livre 1, capitre 1.1. https://www.rousseauonline.ch/pdf/rousseauonline-0004.pdf

Rousseau, J.-J. (1988/1755). Aufgabe der Akademie zu Dijon: Welches ist der Ursprung der Ungleichheit unter den Menschen, und ist sie durch das natürliche Gesetz gerechtfertigt? In *Jean-Jacques Rousseau, Schriften* (Vol. 1). Fischer Taschenbuch Verlag.

Scanlon, T. M. (1998). *What we owe to each other*. Harvard University Press.

Scanlon, T. M. (2018). *Why does inequality matter?* Oxford University Press.

Schmidt, H. (1982). In G. Schischkoff (Ed.), *Philosophisches Wörterbuch* (21st ed.). Kröne.

Schmidt, W. (1986). *Führungsethik als Grundlage betrieblichen Managements*. Springer.

Schmidt, I. (2012). *Wettbewerbspolitik und Kartellrecht* (2 Ausg.). Oldenburg.

Schulte, B. (2000). Das deutsche System der sozialen Sicherheit. Ein Überblick. In Allmendinger, Jutta/Ludwig- Mayerhofer, Wolfgang (Eds.), *Soziologie des Sozialstaates*. München, 2000, S. S. 15–38.

Sen, A. (2000). *Ökonomie für den menschen. Wege zu Gerechtigkeit und Solidarität in der Marktwirtschaft*. Hanser.

Sen, A. (2001). Globale Gerechtigkeit Mehr als internationale Fairness, polylog. In *Forum für interkulturelle Philosophie* (Vol. 3). https://them.polylog.org/3/fsa-de.htm

Sen, A. (2003). Development as a capability expansion. In S. Fukuda-Parr et al. (Eds.), *Readings in human development* (pp. 41–58). Oxford University Press. http://morgana.unimore.it/Picchio_Antonella/Sviluppo%20umano/svilupp%20umano/Sen%20development.pdf

Sen, A. (2009). *The idea of justice*. Belknap Press of Harvard University Press.

Tyler, T. E. (1990). *Why people obey the law*. Yale University Press. http://www.psych.nyu.edu/tyler/lab/Chapters_1-4.pdf

Vahs, D. (2001). *Organisation: Einführung in die Organisationstheorie und –praxis*. Schäffer-Poeschel.

Vanberg, V. J. (1988). 'Ordnungstheorie' as constitutional economics. The German conception of a 'social market economy'. *ORDO –Jahrbuch für die Ordnung von Wirtschaft und Gesellschaft, 39*, 17–31.

Vanberg, V. J. (1997). Die normativen Grundlagen von Ordnungspolitik. *ORDO – Jahrbuch für die Ordnung von Wirtschaft und Gesellschaft, 48*, 707–726.

Vanberg, V. J. (1998). Constitutional political economy. In J. B. Davis, D. W. Hands, & U. Mäki (Eds.), *The handbook of economic methodology* (pp. 69–75). Edward Elgar. S. 70.

Vanberg, V. J. (2004). Market and state: The perspective of constitutional political economy. *Freiburger Diskussionspapiere zur Ordnungsökonomik, 10*, S. 4.

von Hayek, F. A. (1945). The use of knowledge in society. *The American Economic Review, 35*, 1945.

von Hayek, F. A. (1971). *Die Verfassung der Freiheit, Tübingen: J.B.C. Mohr* (Paul Siebeck), pp. 100–110ff, 299-310ff, 328/329, 361.

von Hayek, F. A. (1975). Die Anmaßung von Wissen. *ORDO (Jahrbuch für die Ordnung von Wirtschaft und Gesellschaft), 26* (1975), pp. 12–21.

von Hayek, F. A. (1981). *Die illusion der sozialen Gerechtigkeit.* Verlag Moderne Industrie.

Wallace, R. J. (2002). Scanlon's Contractualism, symposium on T. M. Scanlon's. *What We Owe to Each Other, Ethics, The University of Chicago Press Journals, 112*(3), 429–470.

Weber, M. (1980/1922). *Wirtschaft und Gesellschaft. Grundriß einer verstehenden Soziologie* (5. ed.). J.C.B. Mohr (Paul Siebeck).

Weber, M. (1981/1920). Die protestantische Ethik I. Eine Aufsatzsammlung. In J. Winckelmann, München, et al. (Eds.), (6th ed.). Siebenstern Taschenbuch Verlag.

Weigl, T. (2008). *Strategy, structure and performance in a transition economy: An institutional perspective on configurations in Russia.* Wiesbaden 2008.

Weisshaar, K. R. (2018). *Scanlon's contractualism and its critics.* City University of New York (CUNY) CUNY Academic Works. https://pdfs.semanticscholar.org/83c5/534b06ae731c71b3f9c05caa6364ceca5e89.pdf

Wieland, J. (1999). *Die Ethik der governance.* Metropolis.

Williamson, O. E. (1979). *The economic institution of capitalism.* Free Press, 1985, 1979.

Williamson, O. E. (1985). Transaction cost economics: The governance of contractual relations. *Journal of Law and Economics, 12*(2), pp. 233–261.

Wörz, M. (1994). *System und dialog. Wirtschaftsethik als Selbstorganisation und Beratung.* Verlag Michael Wörz Beratung.

Yurlov, F. N. (1999). Russia: A lost decade. *World Affairs, 3*(No. 3) (Jul.–Sept. 1999). http://www.ciaonet.org/org/olj/wa/wa_ 99yuf01.html

Zweynert, J. (2008). Die Soziale Marktwirtschaft als politische Integrationsformel. *Wirtschaftsdienst, 5*(88), 334–337.

Chapter 5
Market Failure and Economic Policy

What Follows Why?
In the first chapter we saw that the market economy, the combination of market and competition, realizes the economic-policy objective of welfare optimum. Despite the benefits of the market mechanism, it cannot be used everywhere. In the following, we will analyze the areas in which there is so-called market failure and discuss the countermeasures.

Market failure is when the market does not provide allocation-efficient (socially enhancing) results (definition).

In this context rent seeking[1] is a subform of market failure because it describes cases in which individuals enrich themselves at the expense of the common good, such as by redirecting pensions to themselves. The market result from such behavior is suboptimal because it does not achieve allocation-efficient (socially enhancing) results. In this chapter different cases of rent-seeking are presented, such as corruption and asymmetrical information. The problem of anti-competitive behavior was already discussed in Chap. 3. Political rent-seeking is discussed in Chap. 6. In order to prevent rent-seeking, a strong economic system with the organizations and institutions presented in Chap. 4 is an important prerequisite.[2]

Learning Goals
After this chapter you will be able to give examples of market failures, explain their causes and show possible solutions. The market mechanism does not provide efficient solutions for.

[1] See Krueger (1974).

[2] See Chakraborty and Dabla-Norris (2006).

C. A. Conrad, *Economic Systems, Markets and Politics*,
https://doi.org/10.1007/978-3-031-10366-7_5

5.1 Market Failure Due to External Effects

External effects are the consequences of economic action on the welfare of an uninvolved third party whose interests are not expressed in market prices (**definition**), which is why they have an ethical dimension. Negative external effects are immoral because they cause harm. If the state wants to prevent others from being harmed, it must internalize negative external effects through taxes or positive external effects through subsidies.

External effects are effects that originate from economic subjects and are not internalized by the market mechanism, which distorts the incentive system. Negative effects (negative external effects) are not sanctioned by the market and positive effects (positive external effects) are not remunerated, resulting in a suboptimal resource allocation. For example, environmentally damaging products, such as plastics, do not share the welfare costs that their disposal creates, which is a negative external effect.

Negative external effects (social costs) harm a third party. Some examples are exhaust gases, noise, wastewater, damage to the environment and to the welfare of third parties. The injury is not included in the production costs and thus does not compensate the victim. Positive external effects (social benefits) favor third parties. For example, a park in a large city or the maintenance of buildings increases the value of neighboring buildings. In this case, the positive effect is measurable because it manifests itself in the appreciation of the land value.

External effects cause misallocations because not all costs or benefits are reflected in the market prices. Since the suppliers and consumers in the market only take individual advantage into account in their decisions, the market profit is not efficient from an economic point of view.

Exhaust gases, mostly CO_2, are produced during the operation of airplanes, damaging the ozone layer. Layers of the atmosphere are destroyed and the level of noise makes life near airports almost impossible. These effects are not included in the operating costs of the aircraft, which leads to a misallocation. Due to the high negative external effects, the flight prices would have to be substantially more expensive. The price does not cover the cost, which is why too many flights are in the air.

The education of the population, on the other hand, has positive external effects. In the long run, education leads to a higher productivity of the population and thus to higher tax revenues, which is why the free education system pays off for the state. Furthermore, as already shown in the social market economy, an educated population is not as vulnerable to opinion manipulation and unilateral extremist slogans, which stabilizes democracy. Overall, there is a higher welfare of the population through education.

When operating aircraft exhaust gases, such as CO_2 are produced, which damage the ozone layer. Atmospheric layers are destroyed and the high noise level makes life close to airports almost impossible. These effects are not included in the operating costs of the aircraft, which causes a misallocation. Due to the high negative

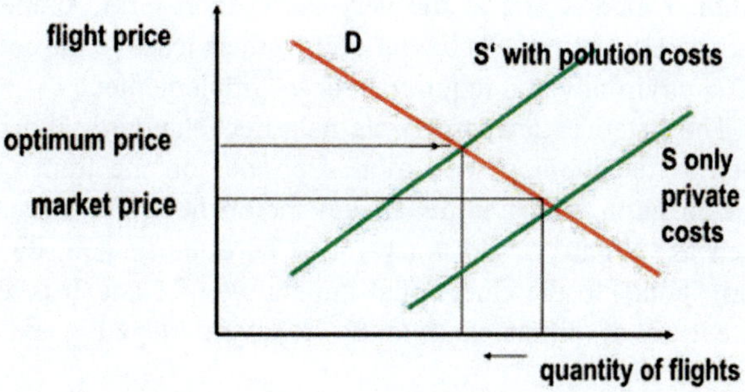

Fig. 5.1 Negative external effects during production

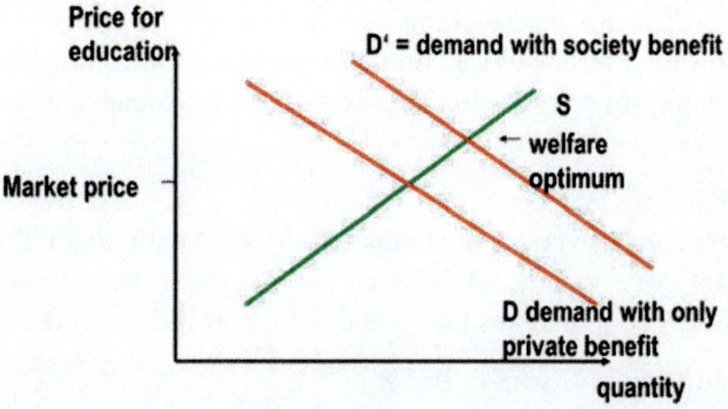

Fig. 5.2 Positive external effects from education

externalities, the fares would actually have to be much more expensive (see S', Fig. 5.1). The price does not cover the cost, which is why too many flights are booked.

The education of a population also causes external effects. Education (see Fig. 5.2) leads in the long term to higher productivity of the population in the economy and thus to higher tax revenues, which is why the free education system and the BAFÖG make financial sense for the state. Furthermore, as already shown in the framework of the social market economy, having an educated population stabilizes democracy because citizens are not as vulnerable to opinion manipulation and one-sided extremist slogans. Overall, the welfare of the population is increased by education.

Solutions for External Effects
Ethical Solutions

People can take others into consideration and try to avoid external effects out of helpfulness, solidarity or compassion as well. There are ethical solutions for external effects. Moral behavior requires that third parties not be harmed. Thus an ethically oriented company would either have to stop the production with negative external effects or at least compensate for the resulting damage. However, if there is no internationally binding regulatory framework, moral behavior is associated with major drawbacks, because it entails competitive disadvantages. This places the national governments in a prisoner's dilemma. Environmental pressures in the national market are, at the very least, short-term competitive disadvantages. The uncertainty about the behavior of the others leads to the collective worst case, insofar as no environmental requirements are implemented.

The state has developed external effect standards and sanctioned external effects such as telephoning with mobile phones on the train or smoking in restaurants. Socialization and parenting are key factors here. There are also behavioral guidelines such as "What you do not want to be done to you, do not do to others", which corresponds to the categorical imperative of Kant. It is also possible for people to take care of others, and to try to avoid negative externalities and to support positive ones.

Education and Socialization
There are private solutions for external effects. Society has developed norms for external effects and sanctions for them such as talking on cell phones in a train or smoking in restaurants. This is also where socialization and parenting show their effect.

Codes of Conduct
There are also codes of conduct such as "Do not do unto others what you would not want done to yourself" which is in keeping with Kant's categorical imperative: "Only act on maxims that you can support if they were to become a universal law."

Bundling of Business Deals
Finally, business deals can be pooled to realize mutual externalities. For example, a beekeeper could team up with an apple plantation owner. The bees would pollinate the flowers as external effects and in return produce honey from the nectar to the beekeeper. Shopping malls are also based on the principle of positive externalities. The many shops side by side allow the consumer to save time. Due to these positive externalities, more customers shop in malls than in individual locations.

The Coase Theorem
Internalization of External Effects Through Trading in Property Rights

The Coase Theorem starts with compensation for damage by allowing the injured party to sell the right to harm to the perpetrator. By commercializing the damage, the external effects are internalized. For this, the state must first assign rights of disposition to the injured party. Perpetrator and injured party negotiate allocation. The polluter must pay damages. The goal is to enter into negotiations and to achieve compensation for damages. Ronald H. Coase received the award of the Swedish Central Bank in memory of Alfred Nobel in 1991. However, the Coase Theorem is bound by a few conditions:

1. no transaction costs when trading with property rights,
2. clear ex-ante distribution of property rights,
3. no restriction on the transfer of property rights and
4. no transaction costs on the capital.

In practice, the Coase theorem is rarely feasible, because the conditions cannot be met, since the number of participants is usually high and thus so are the negotiation costs (transaction costs). Often, the perpetrator and the injured party are unknown or the cost of the damage cannot be quantified.

It works between two neighbors, who agree that the tree of each neighbor may reach into the other's garden. Here the injured parties are known and the damage can be detected, limited and compensated.

The situation is different in the case of broad or diffuse damage. Let's say that all residents of the Rhine sell their right to claim damages from factories located there and receive some compensation. A negotiation in the spirit of the Coase Theorem is not feasible because either the injured parties are unknown or there are too many of them. How should rights be assigned? Should the residents that live within a 1 or 2 km radius of the Rhine receive damages? And what if no damages are awarded or the price is unrealistically high. How should the injured party determine the price? Is the injured party aware of the damage and can health damages be compensated in monetary terms?

In general, private solutions often fail because of

- existing prejudices on both sides,
- transaction costs too high (* negotiating with all injured parties is unrealistic),
- misjudgments of negotiating positions,
- coordination costs too high (with a large number of participants *)

For this reason, the state must intervene in the market. The aim is to get the missing costs and benefits into market prices, to internalize them (internalization).

Measures to Internalize External Effects

1. Regulation by requirements e.g. catalytic converters on cars, obligations, prohibitions, standards e.g. Requirements for desulphurization plants for blast furnaces
2. Taxes to internalize negative externalities (Pigou tax) or subsidies for positive externalities
3. Assignment of property rights (New Institutional Economics, such as Emission Rights Trading)

The central problems remain however:

1. The damage is often not measurable.
2. The damage is not attributable to the person responsible (for example, cancer).
3. The connection between emission (exhaust) and immission (isolated effect of pollutants) is often ambiguous.
4. In general, many economic transactions have both positive and negative externalities. If these concern a person, they can decide for themselves whether the positive effects outweigh the negative ones offering a net benefit. This results in distributional effects. An example of this is an expansion of the airport with the associated flight movements. The noise and exhaust fumes from aircraft taking off and landing cause significant health hazards when flying over densely

populated areas. In addition to the health effects, there is an effect on property value, which can reach total loss.

Economic, non-external effects are higher profits for the airport, the airlines and the higher direct tax revenues of city and state. Of course, there are also positive external effects that are not included in the prices. For example, both passengers and the regional economy benefit from the improved transportation. Finally, there may be economic growth due to the lower transport costs. Companies that want to use these transportation benefits settle near the airport, which in turn brings higher tax revenues and jobs. It becomes obvious that the profiteers and the injured parties will be at odds. In terms of infrastructure measures, the state has the task of recording, assessing and balancing all effects in order to determine the social benefits. This decision-making process should be transparently documented for all concerned.

If the damage is justifiable, compensation must be paid if the damage is massive. Ideally, this would be done through redistribution from the profit-earners to the injured parties, so that the externalities are compensated. However, in practice this will often not be feasible if e.g. the persons are unknown or the group is too big, which also means that the transaction costs are too high. Then, compensation is to be financed from tax revenue. If there are unacceptable damages, e.g. to health, which cannot be compensated, the project is rejected. The decisive factor is that the state determines the **net benefit of the society** and, if necessary, ensures that negative externalities are compensated. Otherwise, there may be a reduction in societal benefits and distributional problems. Objectivity must be ensured. As a rule, the state benefits from most infrastructure projects. In addition, the negative external effects often particularly affect a minority group and a majority profits slightly, as in the case of airport expansion. In a democratic vote, the result could be that the project gets a political majority, although the disadvantage to the minority is greater than the majority benefit.

In such a case of imbalanced interests, politics would not be a suitably objective way to make a decision. It would be the task of the courts to review the decision of the policy makers and ensure the minority group has protection. In practice the courts are often consulted only when the building permit has already been granted and the construction is practically completed. A problem in this context also arises when the government, as in Germany, can exercise influence over the courts through the allocation of jobs and promotion.

A concept derived from the property rights approach to internalize the external effects of CO_2 emissions is emissions trading.

Emissions Trading

In general, emission trading is the trade in industrial pollution rights. This model is based on the so-called Kyoto mechanisms, which were discussed for the first time at the climate protection conference in Kyoto in December 1997.

What are the Kyoto mechanisms? The term "Kyoto mechanisms" has recently been used to summarize emissions trading (see above), joint implementation and the

Clean Development Mechanism.[3] The background is the greenhouse gas effect, which is caused in large part by the CO_2 emissions. The objective of emissions trading is therefore to reduce CO_2 emissions in industry. For this purpose, certificates that entitle issuance are distributed to the originating companies and then reduced annually. Missing emission rights must be bought from others (incentive to reduce emissions). If you save more emissions than you need, you can sell the rights.

The approach of emissions trading has so far been largely ineffective because.

1. The certificates have been issued so far for free. This means that there is no transfer of private wealth to the state to eliminate the environmental damage.
2. Nevertheless, an emission-avoidance effect would have occurred if the initial equipment with usage rights had been scarce. So far, however, too many rights have been issued, which is why the rights have only a small value.
3. The emission limits are generally too high to reverse the greenhouse gas effect. There are political reasons for this. In general, politics wants to avoid too high costs for the economy. In addition, this is not a global approach, which is why European Union policy fears competitive disadvantages.

Conclusion
The defining characteristic of external effects is that they are not included in market prices. This results in a divergence between individual and societal calculations when making market decisions. This causes market failure. The state must then intervene with measures of internalization in the market. The internalization creates costs and can only balance the external effects.

Comprehension Questions
1. Give examples of positive and negative external effects.
2. Explain what consequences these effects have on the market.
3. Which political economy measures would you recommend to internalize these effects?

5.2 Market Failure Due to Non-exclusion, Public Goods

Public goods are goods in the national economy whose benefits for society (public utility) exceed the individual, because the utility is freely available and the market participants cannot be excluded from its use. For this reason, public goods are offered in small quantities or not at all through the market mechanism. The fact that the market fails here is widely accepted. Let's take clean air. Clean air can be produced not just for one person, but everyone in the same environment also profits from it. However, using the air does not make is scarce, so there need not be rivalry to use it. Examples of other public goods from which individuals cannot be excluded

[3] See http://www.foes.de/themen/oekologische-steuerreform/lexikon/ (11. 03.2013).

would be internal and external security. There is an acknowledged market failure in all of these goods. Since no one can be excluded from their use, many would not want to participate in the cost and hope others finance its procurement. In addition, there are high transaction costs and the impossibility of an individually agreed financing, which is why the state has to provide these goods to society through compulsory contributions (taxes).

There are also public goods in the private sector, where there is the problem of free riding. Whenever several people want to purchase an item where the usage cannot be made exclusive, there is an incentive not to participate in the cost and still use the item. Let's take the acquisition of a common television in a student hostel as an example. Moral behavior would preclude such parasitic behavior and every student would honestly admit that he wants to use the television and participate in the cost.

Social morality or better ethics as practiced moral behavior is itself a public good. Everyone benefits by cooperative, considerate, and courteous behavior. Social morality is a public good. The benefit is arbitrarily divisible, thus not competitive and no one can be excluded.

The methods described in Sect. 3.4 Individualism versus collectivism of public goods showed the importance of social sanctions (norms) and learning or socialization.

Only outputs for which the **exclusion principle** can be applied are able to be traded via markets, otherwise there will be a market failure because people only pay for goods that are not freely available. The exclusion principle is only applicable if it is possible to restrict access to a good until a contract exists between supplier and consumer. On the other hand, if those who don't wish to pay cannot be prevented from accessing the goods free rider behavior will prevent the creation of a market. In 2007 Leonid Hurwicz and Eric S. Maskin, Roger B. Myerson received the economics award from the Swedish National Bank for the analysis of these relationships.

The term "public good" is intended to indicate that the goods or services in question must be provided under collective or governmental administration because the market fails to deliver them. Public goods are things like sun and air.

The use of the exclusion principle for **private goods** is indisputable (see Fig. 5.3), since rivalry to secure them must exist among consumers. **Rivalry to consume** occurs when the use of a good by one consumer precludes the use of this good by others. If one person eats a candy bar, no one else can eat it. However, there is no rivalry for the protection a dyke offers against flooding because it does not diminish individual protection by allowing others to enjoy the same protection. In so-called pure public goods there is neither exclusion nor rivalry for consumption (e.g. air, lighthouses, dykes, public security). A clean environment is a pure public good. To what extent and what quality public goods are provided by the state is a political decision. The decision problem, in particular the choice of voting procedures, will be dealt with later (see Chap. 6 Political System).

The combinations of exclusion and rivalry result in four types of property. Private and public goods have already been described. In addition, there are so-called club goods where exclusion is possible, but rivalry is not present. These goods are very

	rivality	no rivality
exclusion	privat goods	club goods (toll roads, pay-TV or public beach, for example)
no exclusion	common goods e.g. exclusion too expensive (fish stocks in the sea) or crowded streets	pure public goods (clean air, roads, lighthouses, dikes)

Fig. 5.3 Types of goods

interesting in the private economy, because they can be sold endlessly at no extra cost. A current example is pay-tv. For most club goods, however, rivalry eventually occurs with intensive use, which is why it then becomes a private good, such as overcrowded toll roads. If exclusion is impossible or too costly, but there is rivalry it becomes a common good. For example, pure public goods become common goods when rivalry occurs with excessive use. The fish stock in the sea were originally a public good but due to overfishing rivalry has now occurred, so we unfortunately have to consider them common goods. They could become private goods if property rights can be attributed, like the hunting and fishing rights on shore.

How should public goods be financed? Here we can use the **Samuelson condition**. State provision of the public good is pareto-efficient if the sum of individual willingness to pay is greater than the costs of provision (marginal utility). The access costs can determine the policy, but problems occur in regards to the willingness to pay. Politicians cannot ask every citizen and often do not get an honest answer because many want to free ride.

For example, if the students of a shared flat wanted to purchase a television, they would have to vote on the funding. A TV in the common kitchen, however, is a pure public good. The utility is arbitrarily divisible (until the kitchen is full) and no one is excludable, since the kitchen is accessible to all. If you ask roommates for their opinions on whether to buy a device together, most will probably say that they do not watch TV so they would not have to contribute to the cost of purchase, but could still use the purchased TV, thus being free riders. The individual benefit increase is not transparent and thus ignored, which is why an individual gains the most advantage by downplaying their benefits and thus their contribution. The free-rider phenomenon is thus a problem in the financing of public goods.

There is no viable and unambiguous solution for optimally delivering public goods, since costs and benefits are often indeterminate. However, private provision of public goods is more likely the smaller the group (organizational costs) and the greater the benefit, since then some are willing to pay the costs to attain the good (see Fig. 5.4).

Fig. 5.4 Private provision of public goods

Need intensities	Large group (i.e.100)	Small group (i.e..5)
equal	very unlikely	Not determined
not equal	determined	very likely

Example of unequal need intensity groups: in a small group of 5 students looking for a TV. it is likely that if there is an unequal distribution of needs, students with a high level of need will give in and pay for the others, otherwise they would not be able to enjoy a television.

The likelihood of those with a greater need being willing to cover the costs for something others can also use is much lower in a large group. It is not unlikely that voting on public goods and how to finance them is either impossible or too difficult in large groups. If voting is not possible, the question remains of whether the result reflects the needs of the population.

For example, in a community, the question is whether a kindergarten with a playground or a swimming pool should be built. Not all citizens of a community have children. A majority decision could lead to the construction of no playgrounds if, for example, the majority of voters have no children (see also Sect. 6.5 on voting procedures). A survey is complex and the willingness to pay difficult to determine. Even in the community there are free riders. There will hardly be enough parents willing to pay for the playground alone because the costs are too high. The pool is similar. The community needs to recognize the needs of others and implement the most useful project for the citizens. A public kindergarten with a playground will be built and the costs will be allocated to the community.

The problem of public goods can be replayed within the framework of game theory as we saw in Sect. 3.3. There are dynamic behavioral adjustments in multi-round games.

Summary

There are no markets for public goods (market failure due to no exclusion)
- due to missing exclusion technology (external security),
- due to lack of legally enforceable property rights or ownership (ozone depletion measures) or
- because the costs exclusion are too high (toll road)

} No exclusion

Supply is then only assured if the state takes over production, regulates distribution and finances it by compulsory levies (taxes, duty etc.). The term public goods is derived from these tasks.

5.3 Market Failure Due to the Prisoner's Dilemma

Allocative problems arise when individual rational utility maximization, as in the case of the Prisoner's Dilemma (see Fig. 5.5), leads to ineffective outcomes:

Two captured criminals in custody are to be interrogated. If both confess they will go to prison for 5 years. If only one person confesses, they will be released and the other will receive a 6-year sentence. If neither of them confesses, they little evidence against them and they only have to go to prison for 1 year, which would be the best outcome for both together (maximum collective benefit). The dominant decision strategy however, is for each player to try and confess first. Both players confessing leads to the Nash equilibrium in which no party can improve through deviating behavior. The situation of the Prisoner's Dilemma is used in the form of the Leniency Notice. Whoever confesses gets a drastic reduction in prison time, while the others are punished more severely.

The worst case for an A is if he does not confess, but B does, and the best case is if A does not confess but B does. B is in the same decision situation. The incentive for A and B is to avoid a prison sentence. Each player is under pressure to confess first. The worst-case creates a fear of sanction; because both are interrogated separately and the opponent may have already confessed, either one could get the longer imprisonment. The incentive to confess (best case) and the prison sentence as a sanction (worst case) are both known. Because of the uncertainty about the other's behavior, both must assume the worst case, in which both confess (Nash equilibrium*). Only then can both strive for the best case and avoid the worst case. This is called dominant strategy.

Fig. 5.5 Payoff Matrix Prisoner's Dilemma
* Nash equilibrium represents the worst case for all
** Best case for A
*** Worst case for A

years of prison	B confesses	B does not confess
A confesses	5, 5*	0, 6***
A does not confess	6, 0**	1, 1

Fig. 5.6 Payoff matrix: decision situation of global environmental policy
** Free rider position (free rider), as the environment is a public good, including non-exclusion

n states state A\	(1) environ-mental regulations	(2) no environ-mental regulations
(1) environ-mental regulations	(2, 2)	(- 2, 0)
(2) no environmen-tal regulations	(4, 2)**	(0, 0)*

From the Nash equilibrium, one decision maker cannot improve with the given behavior of the other (definition).[4]

The uncertainty surrounding the behavior of the other player is the cause of the Prisoner's Dilemma. The solution to this is binding contracts with sanction options. The sanctions must be tougher than the worst case of the dilemma situation. Thus, in the world of the mafia, confession is sanctioned with death. As a countermeasure there is the witness protection program, however.

Environmental Policy

In December 2012, a long extension of the Kyoto Protocol was discussed in Doha and the following minimum target was reached: representatives of 200 countries agreed to extend the Kyoto Protocol until 2020. However, the contract only affects 15% of global CO_2 emissions.[5] The balance of the previous global climate policy is worse than bad. The world is looking at a global climate crisis.

Environmental Policy Case Study

The following sentence was uttered at the Durban World Climate Summit in 2011: "Meanwhile, other important countries, such as Japan, Canada and Russia, are refusing to introduce new binding CO_2 targets for the period after 2012 unless India or China go along with it."[6] This shows the Prisoner's Dilemma in Global Environmental Policy (see Fig. 5.6).

Payoff Matrix

While all countries would benefit from global environmental regulations, it would reduce CO_2 emissions and improve the global climate for all. There would be a

[4]In games with several rounds, the prisoner's dilemma results in special dynamic behavioral adjustments (see Sect. 3.3).

[5]Spiegel Online vom 8.12.2012. http://www.spiegel.de/wissenschaft/mensch/klimagipfel-in-doha-kyoto-protokoll-bis-2020-verlaengert-a-871780.html (11.10.2016).

[6]See Schwägerl and Traufetter (2011).

welfare gain of 4 in our payout matrix. There is uncertainty for each state as to how other states will behave. Every state faces n states, the rest of the world. The worst case for any state A is if it introduces environmental regulations for its economy, but the other n states do not. Then it would have to bear the costs of environmental regulations and the deterioration of the competitiveness of his industry in the amount of 2, but would get no welfare increase, because this would require almost all countries to accept environmental regulations. The best case is if all other states were to enforce environmental regulations, but A did not. A could thus save the cost of environmental regulations and still enjoy the welfare of a clean environment (free rider position). Every state finds itself in the situation of A. They will strive for the best case and want to avoid the worst case. All states behave this way, which is why no environmental regulations are implemented. One must wonder why states India and China even participate in the summits.

There should be a world government to enforce compliance. However, there is no parent state that represents the common good and the prisoner's dilemma prevents the provision of a clean environment as a public good. This problem does not exist at the national level, which is why Germany has a working environmental policy. Environmental regulations are enforced by the state. We know that mandatory prison sanctions are needed to resolve the prisoner's dilemma. The environment is a global problem and a public good. The Kyoto agreements have been non-binding self-regulating commitments of the states without sanctions for non-compliance. Contracts should no longer be non-binding, and there should be monitoring and sanctions for non-compliance.

But there is hope that the countries will learn to cooperate for a better global environment. As we saw in Chap. 4, rational utility maximization does not necessarily mean damage to third parties. For example, in game theory multi-round games show that decision makers learn from their decisions and take into account the opponent's damaging counter-reaction, which is why they no longer maximize their advantage in the short term. According to game theory, in games over several rounds being cooperative maximizes positive results and only when the opponent is not cooperative do players counter with uncooperativeness (trigger or tit-for-tat strategy).

The trigger or tit-for-tat games describe the fundamental conflict between individual and collective rationality. Individual benefit maximization at the expense of third parties contrasts with the collective benefit of community income, such as the provision and use of public goods (such as the clean environment) in the Prisoner's Dilemma. In the 1960s', Anatol Rapoport and Albert Chammah showed experimentally that cooperation occurs in prisoner's dilemma games. On the basis of computer simulations, Robert Axelrod later analyzed the conditions for the occurrence of cooperation. The tit-for-tat strategy proposed by Rapoport proved to maximize earnings. This strategy is weak and strong at the same time. The strategy is to play fair and benefit or at least never harm your opponent. Only if they behave uncooperatively first, then you behave likewise. This strategy always gives the opponent the opportunity to gain more by cooperating and less by behaving uncooperatively. It therefore provides incentives for cooperative behavior and sanctions for uncooperative behavior. The regulated sanctions would then be the norms of the game. Exploitative strategies harm oneself and the other, because the profits from cooperation are lacking. The individual benefit maximization at the expense of third parties in the end brings less net benefit. Rapoport also calls the principle of the strategy "In weakness is strength" and recommends it as a leitmotif in his studies on arms race and conflict prevention.[7]

In the prisoner's dilemma the problem is that we have too many states as players for a tit-for-tat strategy. A solution would be to coordinate the environment problem in blocs like the EU before the problem is addressed at a global scale. Then we would have fewer players with a higher probability of mutuality and strong reciprocators leading to a cooperative outcome.

Summary
Market failures in public goods and prisoner's dilemma market failure in public goods is mainly attributable to non-exclusion. Pure public goods also have non-rival consumption. Thus, government provision of public goods is beneficial when the costs are less than the social benefits. When provided by the state through an economic transaction, the positive externalities are realized. If there is no parent state that represents the common good, prisoner's dilemmas can make it difficult or prevent the provision of public goods.

Exercises
1. Give examples of the different goods and explain the applicable criteria on the basis of the examples.
2. According to which criteria should public goods be provided by the state?
3. Explain the Prisoner's Dilemma in Global Environmental Policy Using a Payout Matrix.

5.4 Market Failure Due to Lack of Rationality

John Stuart Mill, Utilitarianism, 1806–1873, introduced the Homo Oeconomicus image of humanity to economics. Homo Oeconomicus is a rationally acting individual whose only goal is its own utility maximization (definition). What does rational mean in this context?

Actions are rational if they maximize results by using all available information, and do not contradict one's own goals (definition).

The model of the perfect market assumes rational behavior (Homo Oeconomicus). In reality, however, we are dealing with "limited rationality". George Akerlof, Michael Spence and Joseph Stiglitz were awarded the 2001 Nobel Prize for this concept. However, Homo Oeconomicus was originally a simplified model of

[7] See Rapoport and Chammah (1970), Axelrod (1987) and Schwaninger (2008).

thought, as shown in Sect. 2.1. Homo Oeconomicus is like the computer, which is a purely rational being. Based on a given level of information, this being always decides on the utility-maximizing action alternative and thus becomes mathematically calculable. Since almost all qualitative relationships of human complexity are not quantifiable, they usually fall through the cracks. What cannot be calculated is not suitable for an exact science and is repressed. We will analyze in the following the main reasons for market failure due to a lack of rationality.

5.4.1 *Meritorious and Demeritorious Goods*

Meritorious goods are private goods whose usefulness (merits) are not properly appreciated by the private economic subjects (in the view of the state) (definition). This means that the benefits of these goods are subjectively underestimated. There is therefore no rational behavior. Since the social (state) benefit assessment is higher than the benefit assessments according to individual preferences, the state provides the meritorious goods. For example, young people often underestimate the need for care when they are older. They think they will stay young for a long time. They overvalue present needs and underestimate future needs for an old age period, in which they will not be fit for work. Therefore, there is a pension insurance obligation in Germany. Other examples include compulsory education, unemployment insurance and health insurance.

Demeritorious goods are private goods whose harmfulness (demerits) is not sufficiently appreciated by private economic subjects (in the view of the state) (**definition**). This means that the harmfulness of these goods is subjectively underestimated. There is therefore no rational behavior. In the case of harmfulness the state increases purchase costs (tobacco tax, alcohol tax) or prohibits a market for demeritorious goods from forming (such as drugs). Addiction is an irrational behavior; man is no longer master of his own will because he is dependent. The citizens therefore behave to their detriment when they consume such substances.

How can one explain such a behavior and can people be influenced to make the best decision for themselves? People do not have all the information to choose the best alternative. Heuristics are simplified rules of behavior that people use to respond quickly and easily. They are mainly based on experience. One could speak of prejudice, for example. People are more likely to recognize events when they can remember or see things more often, which is called availability heuristics. Also, the effort to get to the information affects the assessment. For example, Schwarz and Vaughn et al. found that respondents rated themselves as less assertive when they had to write down 12 situations in which they succeeded instead of just 6. They then felt the situations they were able to remember were too few.[8] In response to this observation, the concept of bounded rationality was developed, implying limited

[8] See Schwarz and Vaughn (2002) and Schwarz et al. (1991).

information processing capacities as opposed to complete rationality. A decision is then rationally limited if, taking account of information access and processing effort, the decision that maximizes utility is chosen.[9] From this, the so-called **Nudges** were derived as an instrument for influencing decision-making behavior (definition). The decision makers are to be directed towards higher benefit using simplified access, in which, for example, healthy food is placed at eye and grasp level and unhealthy food is to be located on the bottom of the shelf in supermarkets.[10]

5.4.2 Risk-Averse or Risk-Taking Behavior

Risk-averse behavior (fear of risk) or risk-taking behavior (opportunities are rated higher than risk, opportunity-oriented) is also not rational. Rational behavior would only be given with risk neutrality. Decisions with the same expected value but varying payouts would have to be rated the same for risk neutrality. However, risk-averse decision-makers will choose alternatives with the same expected value, which have a lower probability but higher payouts. They are opportunity-oriented, which is irrational behavior. For example, playing lotto is irrational, because the expected value is much lower than the stake. However, playing lotto would become rational again if one were to value the joy of playing (tension) or even hope for the opportunity to escape from a poor life. Risk-averse decision-makers will choose alternatives with the same expected value, but with fewer losses.

The Prospect Theory of Kahneman and Tversky not only provides an empirical approach on how to measure subjective benefit, but also incorporates irrational behaviors. After using heuristics, various irrational behaviors are included that have been empirically determined. Probabilities and payouts are not valued linearly. Thus, the valuation of profits and losses is distorted by previous gains and losses as reference points. The perceived gain or loss decreases with its amount, which means decreasing marginal utility or damage.

In 1992, Kahneman and Tversky determined loss aversion. Losses are thus rated more heavily than comparable profits. They also found a non-linear probability estimation. Small probabilities are rated higher than large ones. Kahneman and Tversky also found, in addition to the loss average and the reference points, that the presentation and formulation of questions affects the decision of subjects. Influencing decisions through representation of the problem of decision-making has since been called **framing** (definition).[11]

[9] See Simon (1959), p. 262.

[10] See Thaler and Sunstein (April 8, 2008); Thaler et al. (2010); *Sunstein, Cass (2009); Wright, Joshua; Ginsberg, Douglas (2012).*

[11] See Kahneman and Tversky (1981); Kahneman and Tversky (1982); Kahneman and Tversky (1984). Kahneman and Tversky (1986). Kahneman et al. (1991), pp. 193–206.

The best way to explain framing is the Asian disease problem of Kahneman and Tversky. There is an epidemic and 600 vulnerable people. Subjects should choose between two alternative therapies that are presented in different ways:

1. Presentation

In therapy A, 200 people die. In therapy B, 600 people are treated with a 1/3 chance of survival. There is a 2/3 chance that no one will be saved.

2. Presentation

In therapy A, 400 people are saved. In therapy B, there is a probability of 33% that nobody will die. There is a 66% chance that 600 people will die. Although both representations are equivalent in their result, in presentation 1 the majority (72%) chose A and in the second presentation a majority (78%) opted for B.

Kahneman and Tversky explain this with a positive reference point in the first presentation, because it puts in the foreground that people are saved. In the positive area people are risk-averse. They do not want to endanger the rescued people and opt for safe rescue. In the second presentation, both times the loss is emphasized. Here people want to minimize the loss (loss aversion), avoid alternative A as a worst case reference point and are prepared for higher risks.

Framing can be used to manipulate decisions to the benefit or disadvantage of the decider. For example, you may be more likely to encourage people to take a health check-up by telling them the risks of illness if they fail to get a check-up than by emphasizing the opportunities for early discovery and recovery.[12]

The Prospect theory has since been relativized. Thus, the decision of the subjects in the Asian Disease Problem is also due to incomplete information. Kühberger showed that the decisions are balanced, so the framing effect disappears, if you supplement the missing information in alternative A: "200 people are saved, 400 people are not saved" for variant A and "400 people will die and 200 people will not die "for variant B. Kühberger changed the wording in the first version of A to "400 people are not saved" for variant A and in the second presentation to "200 people will not die" for variant A. Now the subjects decided exactly vice versa. In the first representation B was preferred and in the second representation A. The framing effect reversed. There was willingness for risk with the profit formulation and risk aversion in the loss formulation. What remains is the framing effect in general, since the decision alternatives were still equivalent.[13]

However even with the Prospect Theory of Kahneman and Tversky human behavior remains not predictable and not deterministic.[14]

Behavioral Economics derived the so-called liberal paternalism. If a person cannot decide rationally to their advantage, the state must help them make their decision by favoring the decision alternatives that are more favorable to the citizen.

---

[12] See Meyerowitz and Chaiken (1987) and Beck (2014), p. 154.

[13] See Kühberger (1995), pp. 230–240 and Beck (2014), S. 162.

[14] See Kahneman and Tversky (1979) and Kahneman and Tversky (1984).

The aim is a governmental behavioral control for the benefit of the citizens, a kind of paternalism without coercion.[15]

For example, you can use the status quo bias to set the better option as the default. If the citizen wants to deviate from that, then he must actively do so. One could prescribe appointments for preventive examinations, which the citizen would then have to cancel themselves, if they do not want to accept them.

Representatives of Asymmetric Paternalism go one step further by calling for the better option to be mandatory in order to rule out irrational behavior. For example, a second doctor should be consulted prior to surgery in order to ensure the correct therapy or to avoid unnecessary surgeries. In addition, state information campaigns should prevent irrational behavior, for example by lotto in which people vividly explain the low probability to others, because otherwise they tend to overvalue small probabilities. Asymmetric paternalism proposes decision-making breaks, so-called cooling-off periods, to prevent short-term emotional and therefore not rational decisions. For example, only being allowed to commit to buying very expensive goods after a period of delay or have a right of withdrawal from the contract. Such things already exist, for example, in the consumer laws in door-to-door sales. Tobacco taxes, alcohol taxes, and entertainment taxes are also advocated for asymmetric paternalism, as time inconsistency poses short-term benefits over long-term damage. It is important that the consumer still has a choice.[16]

5.4.3 *Emotions*

Fear, envy and courage are emotions. They are not always controllable and influence our actions, so rational action is not possible. This is particularly the topic of psychology and Behavioral Economics.

Evolutionary theory assumes that emotions have a function because they have prevailed and been passed on. They have an adaptive function in enabling adaptation to the environment, thus ensuring their survival and reproductive success. Emotions are a genetically rooted position that a being has to its environment. Situations are evaluated and serve the preparation of action and communication. The fear of unknown situations may have helped survival just as much as positive feelings from social confirmation and the pride of coping with a challenge or important task. Emotional evaluations occur unconsciously in the amygdala, situated in the deeper brain regions, whereas the conscious emotional evaluations happen in the cerebrum. The unconscious emotional assessment is faster than the conscious and

[15] See Thaler and Sunstein (2003) and Beck (2014), p. 372.

[16] See Camerer et al. (2003), pp. 101–144; Whitman (2006).

initiates physiological responses before the assessment becomes conscious and thus controllable.[17] Emotions such as fear or anger usually set in quickly and uncontrollably, allowing a quick reaction to new environmental impressions. Here the most important advantage is speed. Since the emotional center of the brain causes the action, often without allowing a rational check of the action, it can also lead to wrong behavior.

Emotions have a negative connotation for us because they are not rational behaviors, but they can be efficiency enhancing. Damasio tested people with damage to the prefrontal cortex compared to people without damage in the emotional center. They were asked to draw from four piles of cards, with two stacks holding poor cards that caused a corresponding loss. The emotionally-responsive candidates behaved irrationally, because they had negative emotional reactions from repeatedly pulling from the poor pile. The emotionally injured behaved just the opposite. They had no emotional reactions and continued to move evenly from all four piles, resulting in corresponding losses. The same applies vice versa. It has been observed that in lotteries with a positive expectation the subjects with functional emotion center play too little due to loss aversion and then perform worse.[18] Emotions like fear superimpose thinking in order to escape quickly. This will have proven beneficial in evolution. Seen in this light one can differentiate between short-term and long-term human decisions, according to Kahneman. Short-term decision-making behavior is about speed. Heuristics and emotions are dominant. Only when we consciously think about problems does rational thinking dominate.[19] Neuroscience speaks of controlled and automatic brain processes.[20] Most thinking as knowledge, i.e. processing information until a decision is made, takes place in the subconscious.[21]

McClure et al. determined that different areas of the brain were activated depending on the time horizon and complexity of the decision. For short-term simple decisions and rewards, the beta region (ventral striatum, medial orbifrontal cortex, medial prefrontal cortex) and, in the case of difficult decisions, the delta region (prefrontal and parietal cortex, lateral prefrontal cortex and posterior parietal cortex) were used.[22]

For short-term decision-making behavior, one can also count the so-called good feeling (somatic marker hypothesis). The somatic marker is an emotion that unconsciously gives us the green light in our decisions or warns us of negative consequences.[23] Emotions strongly influence our decisions, but they are difficult to

[17] See Schneider (1992), p. 407 and Brandstätter et al. (2018), p. 169.

[18] See Shiv Baba et al. (2005) and Damasio (2006), p. 212.

[19] See Kahneman (2011).

[20] See Camerer et al. (2005).

[21] See Zaltman (2000).

[22] See McClure et al. (2004).

[23] See Damasio (2006) and Pham (2007).

measure and explain because people react differently in the same situations and everyone reacts differently.

Conclusion

Actions are rational if they maximize results by using all available information, and do not contradict one's own goals. The harmfulness of the demeritorious goods is subjectively underestimated. If the goods are too dangerous they must be forbidden. For the other goods **nudges** might be a legitimate instrument for influencing decision-making behavior in favor of the individual as long as the individual is free to decide against them.

Framing goes one step further. It manipulates the people in a way that information is not presented in a balanced manner. As long as one persuades people with horrible pictures of sick people not to smoke or get a check-up, the purpose may justify the means, but there are the limits to such manipulation of free will. We will discuss that in the Chap. 7 political failure. The problem is after all that the decision must lie finally at the individual. So, everything which enables him to increase his information to find the objectively best decision for him is an advantage but he must have the freedom to decide. Asymmetric Paternalism is different to framing transparent to the decision maker. Therefore, framing cannot be justified. And strict rules with sanctions to protect the health of the individual presuppose a democratic decision making process.

Emotions have a negative connotation for us because they are not rational behaviors, but they can be efficiency enhancing. Emotions like fear superimpose thinking in order to escape quickly. This will have proven beneficial in evolution. Seen in this light one can differentiate between short-term and long-term human decisions. Short-term decision-making behavior is about speed. Heuristics and emotions are dominant. Only when individuals consciously think about problems does rational thinking dominate.

Comprehension Questions

1. Explain framing and nudges.
2. Is framing dangerous? Discuss the advantages and disadvantages.
3. Why do people use heuristics?
4. What functions have emotions?
5. Is irrational behavior a disadvantage in terms of economic success?
6. What is the somatic marker hypothesis?

5.5 Market Failures Due to Asymmetrical Information

The model of the perfect market assumes complete market transparency. Market participants have all the information relevant to their decisions.

One speaks of asymmetric information when the parties have unequal knowledge about:

A. the properties of the product to be exchanged (Hidden Characteristics).
B. the behavior of the partner after conclusion of the contract (Hidden Actions) and/or.
C. the intentions of the partner in the Hidden Intentions.

The economic participants have different knowledge and one party can exploit this unethically to the detriment of the less informed. This party then has less value than expected, which leads to a non-pareto-efficient situation.

A. Asymmetric information concerning the properties of the product to be exchanged (Hidden Characteristics)

If, prior to the conclusion of the contract, the exchange partners have different information on the objective characteristics of the goods to be exchanged (for example in the market for consumer goods), this favors the process of negative selection. For example, there is a lot of information on the goods on the used car market, which can be unethical to the advantage of the buyer.

The problem of the hidden characteristics is found particularly in anonymous markets, in which buyers and sellers do not know one another, and are not dependent on one another because they will not do business again. The seller can thus deceive the buyer because of the asymmetric information, without having to fear retaliation if the buyer has identified the fraud. One thinks of the itinerant vendors who went from village to village, and so were never accessible. In decision theory, this corresponds to the game with one round. Anonymous markets can be financial markets, but also in big cities people do not know each other and often do not see each other again after buying. This is why, as a rule, crime is higher in an anonymous city than in a village. Despite the cliché of the country bumpkin who gets rolled in the big city, he is not more naive than the city inhabitant; he has simply not had bad experiences and is therefore more trustful.

The perfect market model assumes perfect market transparency, where market participants have all the information relevant to their decisions. One speaks of asymmetrical information when the parties have different levels of knowledge in their economic transactions. This can then be used by the better-informed party, giving them an advantage over other parties. After the transaction the less-informed party has less benefit than expected, which leads to non pareto-efficient situations. The welfare optimum from Chap. 1 cannot be reached.

Examples

1. *Medical services*

The services of a physician correspond to a supplier-induced demand: physicians define which illnesses the consumers have and which services are as necessary. In doing so, they indirectly determine their income as well. Here, a solution is only possible through control by health insurance and the state, and patients are recommended to get several offers. However, there is an incentive problem if the patient does not have to pay for the costs, rather the health insurance. In this case, it helps to incentivize patients by applying deductibles or controlling the medical services provided by patients and third parties.

2. *Auto Repairs*

If you bring a car into the workshop, you often cannot exactly understand if the repair is really necessary and what was billed. Here it is advisable to obtain several offers.

3. *Food*

When it comes to food, you can not exactly understand how the animals are kept or how the foods affect our bodies.

In this case, the state must ensure better market transparency and prevent harmful production through controls and sanctions.

Case Study Used Car Market
(G: good car, S: bad car)

1. **Situation with Complete Information (see Fig. 5.7)**

With complete information good and bad cars are sold (here: 50% each). With incomplete information buyers form expectations (here: "medium quality" m), buyers do not know the condition of the car, good and bad cars seem the same. The negative experiences happen after the purchase. Dealers know the condition, which is why they still try to sell good cars more expensively than bad cars.

2. **Situation of Incomplete information Part 1 (see Fig. 5.8)**

Same demand curve, but different supply curves.

Contemplation of the Dm line.

M: Medium quality because the quantity is uncertain.

With incomplete information:

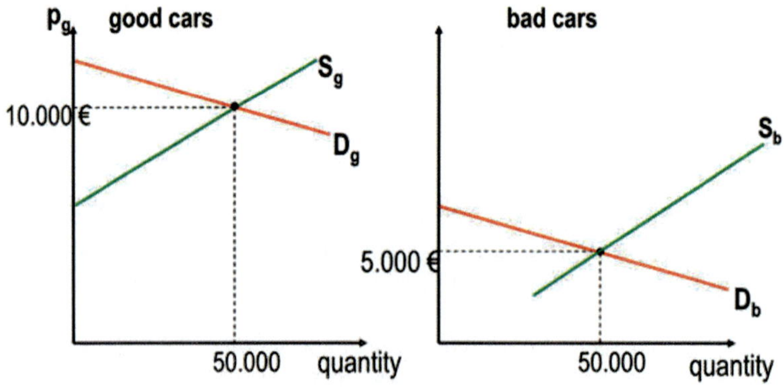

Fig. 5.7 Used car market situation 1 complete information

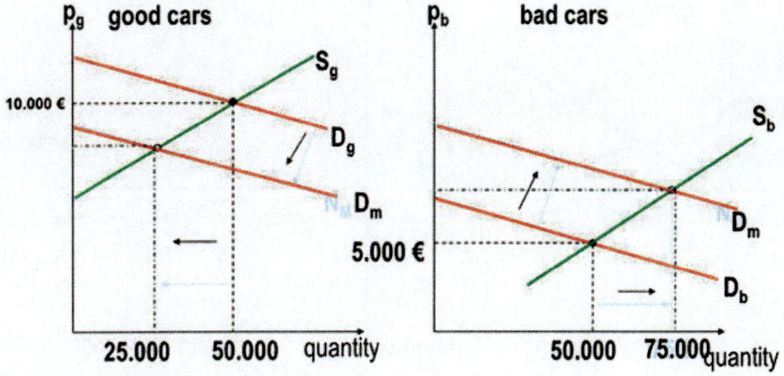

Fig. 5.8 Used car market situation 2

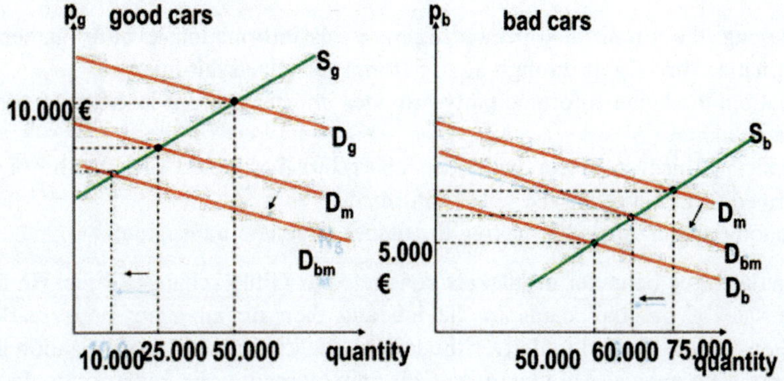

Fig. 5.9 Used car market Situation 3

- 75% bad cars are sold and 25% good cars.
- Shoppers are downgrading their mid-range expectations, which is why they are less willing to pay for the cars and therefore buy more bad cars because dealers are willing to sell them cheaply.

3. **Situation of Incomplete information Part 2 (see Fig. 5.9)**

After renewed adjustment of expectations (see Fig. 5.10):

- Fewer cars are sold; 86% are bad and 14% are good cars.
- Buyers continue to adjust their expectations.

Conclusion

The consequences of this process of negative selection are that poor quality supplants good quality and fewer cars are sold. Producer and consumer pensions (i.e. social welfare) fall.

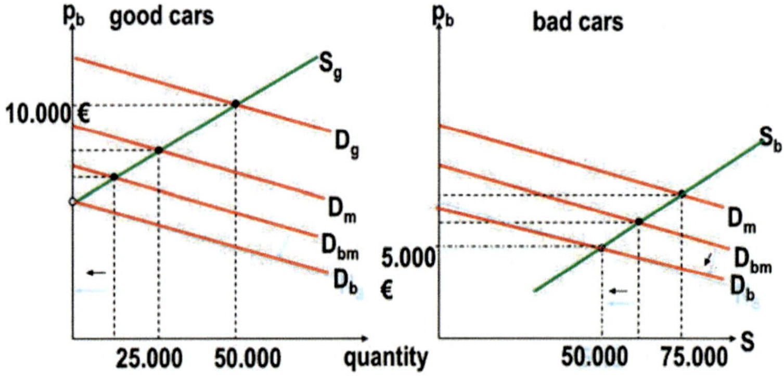

Fig. 5.10 Used car market Situation 4

Market failures can be countered by:

- Screening: the uninformed person improves his information level by gathering information directly or through advice from specialized third parties.
- Signaling: the better-informed party provides information, for instance by offering a guarantee.[24]
- Morality: Ethical behavior in hidden characteristics would prevent the better informed from betraying the worse informed.
- De-anonymize markets by making the names of sellers transparent.

List simulated the behavior in markets conducted as Gift Exchange Game. He first ran the sale of baseball cards in the lab and then on an anonymous market. The sellers were expected to deliver the lowest quality for profit maximization and the buyers were expected to maximize their gain by paying the lowest price. In the laboratory the participants could be observed, but not in the market. The result was that sellers in the lab offered better quality and customers paid more. The reputation seems to have played a role in the behavior of the buyers. In the markets they felt unobserved and sold the customers low quality at high prices.[25]

Another area with the problem of hidden characteristics is personnel management.[26] For example, when a new employee is hired, the quality of that person is not directly identifiable. Hidden characteristics are the qualities of the applicant, which are unknown to the employer when hiring, such as the actual degree of qualification, the integrity, the working attitude and loyalty. Hiring external employees therefore entails a high risk of failure assessment due to the hidden characteristics, associating it with high risks. It can only be recommended if no one is available internally at the

[24]See Dillerup and Stoi (2011), p. 24; Welge and Al-Laham (2008), p. 52 and Fritsch et al. (2011), p. 263.

[25]See List (2006).

[26]See Berthel and Becker (2013), p. 48.

time of hiring, or if external knowledge can be brought into the company that the company has no other way to access.

Ultimately, the importance of the corporate identity and, in particular, the emotional attachment of the employee to the company has decreased over the last decades. This has aggravated the principal agent problem. In the past, it could be expected that a company's management would have worked hard or at least learned about the most important value-added stages and corporate identity. This not only had the advantage that managers could better assess the impact of their decisions on the company, and they had a stronger identification with the company. Furthermore, the risk of failure due to hidden characteristics was less, because the management had to prove itself in the company for many years. However, the problems of hidden characteristics, hidden information, and hidden actions exist on every level of leadership down to the subordinate decision-making units.

In German literature, there is still the distinction between trust and experience goods. In the case of experience goods, the customer knows the characteristics of the goods after the purchase, not in the case of trust goods. The commercial audit is, for example, cited as the trust good. In the case of trust goods, self-policing is an effective solution, such as by offering a guarantee.[27]

B. Hidden actions

Since in general the one partner does not know how the other will behave after signing the contract, this favors possible hidden actions. The contract is then not implemented to the advantage of both sides, but the one side betrays the other and the allocation optimum is not achieved.[28]

This problem of moral risk (moral hazards) is seen particularly often in the insurance industry. The behavior of the insured person may change after the conclusion of the contract at the expense of the insurer, because he will no longer be liable for his property. After completion of the insurance policy, the insured person may, under certain circumstances, influence the probability of the loss occurring without the insurance having any influence on this. For example, the owner of a fully insured luxury car might hope that he can order a new car if he parks it in a dangerous area. Incentives such as refunds can be used to prevent market failures. Self selection is a solution for health insurances if the client knows his health risks. If his health is poor he will choose health insurances rates with no co-pay.

Moral hazards are an incentive for individuals to act against or at the expense of many, society or their company (**definition**). One of the causes of the financial crisis was, for example, was paying the sales agents by the volume of house loans provided to the sub-prime borrowers. They were not liable when a loan failed, which gave them an incentive to lend to bad borrowers. Another example is the awarding of bonuses to the managers of a company based on short-term share price increases.

[27] See Ballwieser and Clemm (1999), p. 414.

[28] See Weisser (2012), p. 53 and Alparslan (2006), p. 22.

This creates an incentive to do everything in the short term to increase profits. This can be done by less investment. In the long term, this jeopardizes the company's success, however.

There are hidden actions with rental, since the landlord does not know how the tenant will deal with the object after the conclusion of the lease. To reduce the risk, the tenant must provide a deposit. With moral behavior this would be superfluous and he could trust the tenant.

C. Hidden intentions

The difference between the hidden intentions and the hidden actions is the intention. A contract partner has performed first and now depends on the other for the fulfillment of the contract. There is a one-sided dependency after conclusion of the contract.

Ignorance of the contractor's "covert intentions" can lead to the exploitation of contractual scope for interpretation by the economically stronger person to the detriment of a contract partner dependent on him (hold-up behavior).

This possible exploitation or blackmail could be attempted with a strategy of interest harmonization (incentives, such as profit sharing). Hidden intentions exist not only in leases, but also advance payment. The one-sided dependency is counteracted here with deposits and guarantees. Risks from Hidden Intentions are also present in joint ventures for market closure, where a company has the know-how. The other partner could try to build his own company as soon as he has acquired the know-how. Here, harmonization of interests can be achieved by a very high participation of the partner in the joint venture. The participation must be so high that it is no longer worthwhile for the partner to build a second company. Again, it helps if one can trust in moral behavior.[29]

Another example would be so-called "rent nomads". They never intend to make rent payments except the deposit when moving in. Years can pass until the landlord has kicked out the rent nomad. Here it is advisable to be particularly careful when choosing tenants and perhaps to obtain a landlord referral in addition to proof of income. The current landlord might have a biased view. If tenant is already resident at the property, it is often advisable to offer the tenant a termination payment to leave rather than to enter into a drawn out legal process.

[29] See Dillerup and Stoi (2011), p. 25 and Welge and Al-Laham (2008), p. 53.

5.6 Market Failure Due to Transaction Costs

If market transactions fail because of their transaction costs, one can also speak of market failures in a broader sense.[30] Transactions can be understood as all transfers of rights to dispose of goods and services.[31] The transfer of services includes the internal sale of work through an employment contract. The transfers incur costs, such as information, negotiation, control and enforcement costs, as well as transport costs in a broader sense.

We distinguish between direct and indirect transaction costs.

1. **Direct transaction costs**

Over the past few decades direct transaction costs have fallen very sharply, leading to the formation of numerous new markets. Some factors in cost reduction have been the Internet, new transport techniques and English as an international business language. All together, globalization has been a key factor affecting costs. The world has become smaller because the paths have become shorter and more cost-effective. The invention of the Internet increased market transparency with reduced transaction costs. Prices and services can be compared faster and more cost-effectively. Innovations have been made in the transport techniques like container shipping, large oil tanks and reduced flight costs. The implementation of English as an international business language is comparable to the introduction of a uniform standard (e.g., metric or DIN). Translation costs are thus obsolete as people trade with other cultures, e.g. German and Chinese in a common foreign language. They have to learn only one language through the common standard in order to be able to do business.

2. **Indirect transaction costs**

If, as with the asymmetric information presented, the fulfillment of the contract is uncertain, there is a risk of loss. This is always the case if behavior after contract conclusion cannot be controlled absolutely. This is relevant for all forms of transactions, which include long-term contract fulfillment, thus also employment contracts. The higher the advance performance and the longer the contract duration, the higher is the risk of a lower counter-performance. This applies in particular to investments by companies in new production facilities, for example. Here, the investment is high but the return is distributed over many periods. These indirect transaction costs can be reduced by an objective and rigorous legal system. A written Code of Law also reduces the risk and is better than a case law because case law builds on precedents. Countries that do not have a reliable law enforcement system have difficulties in attracting direct investment.[32]

[30] See Williamson (1979), p. 18 and Williamson (1985) and Furubotn and Richter (2005), p. 47.

[31] See Gabisch (2003), p. 56.

[32] See See Steinherr et al. (1997), p. 1.

The indirect transaction costs can be reduced by strong morals. Luhmann also sees trust as a means of reducing the complexity of social interactions. If the culture of a country is moral, the contracting party can trust in the implementation of its treaties.[33] There is no longer a risk of fulfillment resulting from being taken advantage of.

Transactions are completed when the indirect transaction costs are reduced, which can be considered its own business approach. Phrases like "A good name is worth its weight gold" and "My word is my bond" as well as the legal concept "good faith" illustrate this approach. The reputation of a person or a company includes everything associated with its name: poor or good performance, moral or immoral behavior, etc. A reputation is formed by acts that are observed and interpreted by people, by the market. This means that every company is responsible for its own reputation.

The honor of the merchant also derives its significance from the elimination of the risk of contract settlement. This honor was institutionalized by merchant guilds. They introduced codes of ethics and sanctioned corresponding rules. Grievous violations were punished with exclusion from the guild, which was equal with the abolition of the entrepreneur's livelihood, because he lost the trust of his business partners.[34] Even in Mafia circles there is an honorary code within the criminal organization and their business partners. Thus even criminal circles need a minimum of morality to deal with their business transactions. They also need mutual trust.

Trust

After the Enron crisis confidence in the company's balance sheets was shattered, and as a result of the financial crisis (subprime crisis) no one trusted the banks, while the banks trusted themselves least of all. Confidence was lost, which almost collapsed the global economy. What role does trust play for people?

A survey of 500 employees of European companies showed the great importance of trust in ethical behavior. If employees can trust their executives, they are more ethical. Empirical behavioral experiments also confirm this.[35] The gift exchange game or trust game, which builds on the ultimatum game:

Game 4: Gift Exchange Game or Trust Game

Two students are to split 10 pieces of chewing gum, as they did in the ultimatum game. The first (proposer) receives everything and can determine how much he gives to the second. This amount is then tripled. The second (responder) can then decide how much he will give the proposer.

The Gift Exchange Game or Trust Game is normally played with $10 instead of chewing gum. Rational behavior presupposes that the proposer should keep all money because, as a rational actor, he also assumes that the responder will give

---

[33] See Luhmann (2000).

[34] See Beschorner and Hajduk (2011); Albach (2003) and Lin-Hi (2014), p. 10.

[35] See van den Akker et al. (2009).

him something afterwards. After all, it is a game with one round. In the games, however, only a small proportion has chosen this strategy. Most of the proposers had confidence in the unknown responder and were rewarded because of the strong correlation between the amount of money transferred and the subsequent responses of the responder.[36]

Trust is nothing more than believing that someone will behave as expected without sanctions. Trust exists in relation to good performance, moral behavior, help etc. Ethical behavior is an elementary prerequisite for human cohabitation. If one wishes to pursue common goals in a marriage for example, such as providing for each other and raising children together, the basis must be mutual trust. Without ethical, moral behavior there can be no trust between the spouses. Behaving ethically in this context, according simply to our definition, means not to damage the other party, or to be of use. Trust in companies is also important. Companies enter into transactions with new, unknown business partners because they have a good reputation. A good reputation engenders trust. As we saw in Chap. 3, if transactions occur only once, and so anonymously that damage to one's reputation is not expected, it would maximize one's advantages to fleece the business partners. The reputation of a person or company includes everything associated with them. Good or bad performance, moral or immoral behavior, etc. A reputation is made up of actions that both people and the market observe and interpret. Every company is thus responsible for its own reputation.

If the human being is descended from the monkey, similar group behaviors may also be applied to man. A solitary existence is a rare exception in the life of monkeys. They have to adapt themselves to predetermined hierarchical levels and rely on the favor of the other group members; this political behavior has even been observed in chimpanzees. The only monkey able to dominate the group must be able to unite the strongest group of supporters, a relative democratic majority. A minimum of cooperative behavior must therefore be applied to monkeys and thus also be a genetic attribute in humans. Otherwise no groups would form, and both monkeys and man would be observable in nature only as solitary individuals.[37]

Reality shows that predetermination is by no means sufficient to ensure cooperative behavior. The incentive to behave non-cooperatively must therefore be correspondingly large. One of the reasons for this is that many decision-making situations in everyday life have a dilemma structure, such as the prisoner's dilemma presented above.[38] The dilemma is that although the overall benefit from cooperative behavior is greatest for the individual, the uncertainty about the cooperative behavior of others makes non-cooperative behavior the best choice for the individual. The worst result for the individual is if he is the only cooperative player and all others uncooperative. Vice versa, the profit-gain is greatest for the individual if all others behave cooperatively. Since the insecurity in the situation is about everyone's behavior, they all opt

[36] See Holzmann (2015), p. 129.

[37] See Windeler (2014), p. 175.

[38] See Kirchgässner (1991), p. 51.

for non-cooperative behavior, which is the worst result for everyone (ethical prisoner dilemma, see also Sect. 4.6.1). Here is an example from a decision-making situation on the market: The buyer buys a product that he has not yet been able to try out, or does not know. The vendor will rely on the buyer to pay for it later, after the delivery of goods. If neither one trusts the other, they will have to assume that they are going to be cheated. The consequence will be that they are also cheating, in order not to suffer from the purchase, so the business transaction is not concluded or high hedging costs arise. For example, in transactions with unknown foreign business partners, it is customary to carry out the transactions step by step with guarantees from a bank.

Dilemma and asymmetrical information are problematic, especially if the persons who are acting are not familiar with one another (on anonymous markets), cannot vote, or if they are dealing with a one-sided dependency in which uncooperative behavior cannot be sanctioned later (play with one round). It is even better, then, to trust the active man directly. In the case of morality as a social basis for trust, cooperative behavior can be assumed, which is why these values are productivity-enhancing.

Citizens can trust in laws, courts and the executive branch. But as we have already mentioned, no system can control and implement the rules 100%, no matter what efforts are undertaken. Rules help in particular when they are clear and transparent, known by all actors, and everyone involved assumes a consistent application of the rules. Absolute control is impossible, which means that unethical behavior can pay off. Why then, do people generally behave fairly and ethically? How can we explain this "irrational" behavior? Is it deterrence or are people as social animals programmed that way? Both answers are elementary for moral behavior, but there is also the element of socialization, which teaches us how to live in our communities. Socialization as practicing behaviors and beliefs takes place mostly in childhood, but continues throughout our lives as long as people are in groups where they are at least partially in a dependent relationship. Behavior in conformance with the group is demanded of individuals. Sanctions are applied here as well. They can range from a refusal of recognition to exclusion from the group. People generally continue the behavior they have practiced even if the sanction is removed. Moral behavior must be practiced just like driving a car. The traffic laws provide the framework of behavior, and for interpersonal interaction there must also be rules with sanctions. The continued learning of the correct, or socially desirable, behavior begun in childhood creates a conscious value system in people as the foundation of their own goals and actions, which enters into the subconscious through constant repetition. Based on this subconscious set of values, we act as unconsciously as we drive a car, without having to reflect anew. Sanctions become superfluous. For the community this means that values must be passed on and socialization must take place in the youth. Role models are also important. They communicate beliefs that offer an explanation for behaviors. The disposition towards certain types of behavior are inherited, varied and cannot be influenced. If we want to influence people positively with business ethics, we must start with social, economic or business role models for socialization and communicating beliefs and attitudes.

Trust is an absolutely central economic factor both at the level of the individual and the whole economy. Who would want a business partner they cannot trust? How does it help a customer to be consulted by the best bank, the market leader, and have the feeling that all this intelligence and experience is working against him in order to empty his pockets, perhaps even recommending investments that will permanently damage him? The bank could recommend poor stocks still on the books from an IPO that made it a lot of money, and which the bank now wants to get rid of. Or someone could sell him life insurance with large fees hidden in small yields later on. Let's say the customer had already taken out two life insurance policies. What he cannot know is that the bank forces its consultants to sell at least five life insurance policies regardless of whether the customer needs them or not. Loyalty and confidence, or morality and ethics, are thus an important part of any service and a competitive advantage for companies on transparent markets. Once a customer's trust has been violated, if he acts rationally he will change banks, and as soon as he finds a bank he can trust he will stay there. For the bank that lost his trust he is lost forever, making the profits from the strategy with short-term success much less over the long term. The ethics campaign of Citibank, once the largest and most profitable banks, thus makes sense not just because of the imposed fines, but because the bank recognized that it went too far with its sales methods. It went so far in fact that the damage to its reputation and customer satisfaction could damage its future market position.

We have already discussed the importance of moral values for national economic development. The same applies at the microeconomic level for each company. A company that must operate in an immoral environment (such as in Russia) will have higher transaction costs. It must monitor and protect itself more. This causes inefficiency, since many economic transactions are lost to higher costs and risks. A company acts in a given social framework and recruits its employees from this society. Suppliers, customers, the legal system... everything comes from this society. The possibility for a company to influence a society is very limited, the opportunities for influence are trade associations, thus politics or advertisement. The most important thing for the company is to acquire morally suitable employees, and to hold them to moral behavior, whereby management focused on qualitative goals plays an important role, as we will show later on.

The importance of moral values for economic development has already been demonstrated. The same applies microeconomically to each individual company. An enterprise that has to operate in an immoral environment (as in Russia, for example, due to the uncertain legal situation) will have higher transaction costs. It must control more and secure more. Efficiency suffers, and many economic transactions are avoided because of higher costs and risks. A company moves in a given social context. It recruits its employees from this company. Suppliers, customers, legal order – everything comes from this company. The possibility for a company to influence society is only very limited by economic associations, such as politics or advertising. In the short term, it is also important for the company to acquire morally responsible employees and to educate employees on moral behavior, whereby a quality-oriented management plays an important role, as will be shown later.

Conclusion Missing Rationality and Asymmetric Information
Asymmetrical information may favor the informed contractor over the uninformed and allow the uninformed contractor to benefit. Reputation, trust, morality (culture) have emerged as social solutions to this problem. In the case of irrational behavior, the state can intervene only in cases in which there are massive health impairments, since irrationality belongs to human nature. Only rarely can a restriction of human freedom be justified.

Comprehension Questions
1. Give two examples of irrational behavior from economic agents.
2. (a) Give an example of both meritorial and demeritorial goods and explain the criteria to be applied on the basis of the examples.
   (b) How should the state behave here?
3. (a) Give an example of hidden characteristics, hidden actions and hidden intentions. (b) What is the problem here? (c) What do you suggest as a solution?
4. What is asymmetric information?
5. What effects can this have on business relations?
6. Give examples of the economy in which asymmetric information exists and possible tools to prevent unethical effects.

5.7 Market Failure Due to Corruption

The market economy generally has a system of rules for playing the game that must be learned and controlled. Immoral behavior in particular can damage the system in this context. The most famous example of immoral behavior and negative systemic behavior is corruption.

Case Study: Does Corruption Pay? The Example of Siemens[39]
1. Discuss the following article in the group. Why is there always corruption and why does it not pay off in the long term? Why is corruption harmful? What measures would you recommend to a company to prevent corruption?

   Siemens, as one of the largest exporters of industrial equipment and train systems, maintained a widespread system of corruption. It was decentralized with the tacit approval of the group headquarters. There were a multitude of opaque transactions, insider cliques, and hundreds of accounts abroad in the many

[39] Sources: http://www.faz.net/aktuell/wirtschaft/unternehmen/bestechende-grossunternehmen-korruption-rechnet-sich-nicht-12050962.html?printPagedArticle=true#pageIndex_2; http://www.zeit.de/online/2008/51/siemens-korruption-strafe; http://www.sueddeutsche.de/wirtschaft/korruptionsaffaere-siemens-akzeptiert-millionen-dollar-strafe-1.372394; http://www.manager-magazin.de/unternehmen/industrie/siemens-zehn-jahre-nach-dem-siemens-skandal-a-1118197.html; http://www.handelsblatt.com/unternehmen/industrie/der-fall-siemens-sec-klopft-bei-staatsanwaltschaft-muenchen-an/2805400.html

divisions and countries of the world conglomerate. The investigations of the American lawyers commissioned by the Siemens Supervisory Board, as well as the Munich public prosecutor's office, showed that between 2001 and 2006, bribe payments of at least 1.3 billion euros had flowed through those bank accounts. The recipient and the purpose of the payments are partly unknown to date.

It turned out that many orders, apparently acquired with bribes, were unprofitable. The Italian energy supplier Enel was responsible for the kick-off of Siemens, although the turbines were scarce and had to be allocated. In Argentina, the governments of Menem and de la Rúa were bribed. However, the announced, and in some cases contractually agreed, major contracts did not come about. Instead, there was blackmail on the part of the Argentinians who were involved in the distribution of orders, as they demanded money for the silence on the bribe payments. Siemens employees in Argentina reported life-threatening difficulties. Thus the seemingly lucrative business became a nightmare and a loss in business.

The US SEC initiated a corruption case against Siemens in the United States, as Siemens is listed on the US stock market. The Siemens Supervisory Board had then instructed a law firm in the US to investigate the Group and pass the findings directly to the US stock exchange supervisor. It turned out that there were far more questionable payments than the board had initially reported. In the middle of November 2006, the Munich Public Prosecutor's Office carried out a big raid at Siemens. In 2007, Siemens was threatened with the exclusion of public contracts on the world's most important markets, huge image damage and billions in penalties. Siemens decided to make uncompromising reconnaissance and practically exchanged its entire management. At the same time, a comprehensive compliance system was set up. Siemens came away with an asset loss of an estimated 2.5 billion euros, of which were 1.2 billion euros in punitive payments. In 2008, the SEC imposed a fine of $1654 million on Siemens for the bribery of public authorities in several countries on the basis of the American Foreign Corrupt Practices Act (FCPA), of which $350 million went to the SEC, $450 million to the US Department of Justice, and $854 million went to the German prosecutor's office. The CEO of Siemens von Pierer maintained he had not known anything about the bribes. Pierer stepped down from his post. He was not prosecuted under criminal law, but had to pay damages of €5 million. A prosecution against him for neglecting the duty of supervision was suspended for a fine of €250,000. He then worked as an honorary professor and served on a supervisory board.

Private corruption is the abuse of a position in a private organization by using the position for one's own purposes and under public corruption we understand the abuse of a public office (definition).[40]

---

[40]See Pritzl and Schneider (1999), p. 312.

The advantage is difficult to detect and can be hidden behind apparent powers, such as consultancy fees or excessively high prior-day auditors.[41] Personal contributions are used to influence an individual in his market decisions. Market economy as a system generally has rules, which must be learned and their implementation must be monitored. Immoral behavior can damage the system in this context, and the most well known example for immoral and system-damaging behavior is corruption. The individual is influenced in his market decisions by personal benefit. The corrupted individual no longer makes decisions according to objective market criteria, which cancels out the market and competition functions, including the invisible hand. The person no longer optimizes in the interest of the whole system, and can thus damage the system and others.[42] If, for example, a worse and more expensive supplier bribed the buyer for a company he would damage the company, the market economy system and thus the entire community. The company would then have to pay out more for the same amount in preliminary production than if it had bought the objectively better product on the market, the result is production of fewer goods. As a whole the company then produces more expensive preliminary products of a poorer quality and fewer goods. This is damaging for the company, the national economy and the community. Research in 97 countries in 1997 showed a negative statistical connection between corruption and GDP as well as between corruption and growth of the GDP.[43]

There are authors who regard corruption as a voluntary bargaining act, in which both sides win, whereby the redistribution cannot be assessed at the expense of the principal.[44] The bribe money as so-called Speed-Money attests to corruption advantages. An inefficient situation created by slow bureaucracy uses the money as an incentive to get involved, thus making the situation more efficient. It is either assumed that the bureaucracy is ineffective or that efficiency is increased by corruption.[45] This implies that the bureaucratic rules are either nonsensical, inefficient, or that the officials would not apply the rules without corruption. Then the state apparatus would be an obstacle to the economy and thus better off done away with entirely. If one presupposes meaningful activity however, corruption creates an incentive to act corruptly. The decisions of the bureaucracy are at least no longer objective when corruption is involved.[46] They no longer represent the interest of the state or they give preference to companies that pay more, which leads to distortions in competition. We then have to ask who is paying the price of corruption. Bribery

---

[41] See Göbel (2010), p. 300.

[42] See Graeff (2002), p. 295 and Homann and Blome-Drees (1992), p. 163.

[43] Corruption gross domestic product correlation coefficient: – 0.80, statistically significant with a t-ratio of −13.2. Corruption gross domestic product growth correlation coefficient: – 0.32, statistically significant with a t-ratio of −3.2. See Jain (2001), p. 90 = .

[44] See Homann (2003), p. 242.

[45] See Graeff (2002), p. 296.

[46] See Pritzl and Schneider (1999), p. 322.

only pays off when it offers a greater advantage. As a rule, the damage is much greater than the benefit of bribery. Thus the damage to a bribed official who allows a drug that harms the general public is many times higher than the benefit to the pharmaceutical company.

It is in fact likely that bribery will make bureaucracy more expensive and will not make it more efficient because a corrupt official will try to get the maximum out of an administrative monopoly. A saying from China is "official and rich" and in the Philippines an official was paid up to $ 75,000 for an item that was valued at $ 10,000.[47]

Corruption is also partly classified as a voluntary contract, and therefore considered positive. However, the price and the bribe are, as shown above, at the expense of others, which is why corruption is unethical. While it is pointed out in the literature that a relationship of trust is established between the briber and the bribee of the exchange contract, this trust in the benefit, the maximization of the utility, is limited by the bribery. The briber cannot usually prove that he has paid for something, and the bribery contract is not enforceable. The immorality in the abuse of trust that the bribed man commits is much easier to prove. A third party (state or company) has entrusted him to carry out a task, paid for it and yet was harmed. The fact that the payment offered was not enough cannot be used an argument, unless bribing was open to the contract between the principal and the agent. The bribee has voluntarily entered into the contract. Corruption is, therefore, first and foremost a breach of trust, and therefore repels many people. For Kant it would be dishonesty, a defeat, and a significant weakness of personality or character. Corruption violates all three Kantian rules of reasoning (categorical and practical imperative as well as publicity rule). Someone who breaks a trust at the expense of the one who trusted him to maximize his financial advantage, can no longer be trusted.

As already described, corruption is the misuse of a position in a private or public organization for one's own purposes. This includes nepotism, the abuse of the position for relatives or friends. Using relationships for advantageous deals or even name-dropping sound familiar and unproblematic, but the effect can be the same as with financial corruption. It depends on whether the relationship provides an information advantage, a higher transparency for the principal because it gets a person or a product that is better, or whether the person or the product is worse, and can only be accepted because of the relationship. Then there is no advantage for the principal, but a disadvantage through the relationship.

The greatest negative effects of the development of corruption are found in the social impact on the society. Performance is no longer the decisive factor in improving one's own situation, but rather relations allowing nepotism and bribery in daily life, including the purchase of offices. Objective private or state decisions are made impossible by personal advantage and outside influence, which also has a long-term effect by lowering economic power. Foreign investors shy away from

[47] See Pritzl and Schneider (1999), p. 322.

countries with strong corruption because they no longer have legal certainty.[48] Corrupt politicians and officials promote the uneven distribution of wealth as money leads to political power and vice versa. Money becomes the greatest factor in the system, thus displacing democratic decisions at the expense of the population who are excluded from the decision-making process. The distribution of wealth becomes more unequal.[49] In the Bible, bribery is severely condemned not only by a sense of justice, but also as a purely egoistic behavior against divine human dignity. The individual is enriched at the expense of the public.[50]

The unethical effects of corruption lead to the disintegration of the common system. If the acts are not punished, they will soon be imitated. It is always worthwhile for two parties to engage in corruption if they can benefit to the disadvantage of a third party. The incentives of corruption are quite strong and without sanction. There are plenty of arguments that play down damage to the third person and make it easier to avoid a bad conscience. This business, in which both parties profit greatly without much effort, finds imitators and, according to Kant's categorical imperative, multiply until the common system no longer works. That is, the culture is eroded as a basis for a productivity-enhancing division of labor. The damage to third parties is borne by the public through bribed state officials, the expense to the owners of companies as well as indirectly at the expense of all employees, insofar as the company is weakened. Overall, the company has less profit to be distributed.

Corruption is also unethical in the sense that it undermines the advantages of the market economy in the function of competition. The distribution becomes unfair because equals are given unequal reward. Performance is no longer crucial to success.

Since corruption not only affects the national economy, but also the companies themselves, Transparency International has compiled recommendations for companies on corruption prevention.[51] Transparency generally recommends companies involved in bribery to be listed in an anti-corruption register and to exclude them from the award of public contracts for several years.[52] However, this sanction would affect only a part of the companies, since not all of them participate in public contracts.

Internationally, there is a trend towards a tightening of corruption regulations. In response to the Watergate scandal, the U.S. issued the Foreign Corrupt Practices Act (FCPA) in 1977, which punished the bribery of foreign public officials by American corporations and citizens internationally. Since other countries did not follow, and

---

48 See Graeff (2002), p. 298 and Lambsdorff (2002).

49 See Pritzl and Schneider (1999), p. 322.

50 See Pritzl and Schneider (1999), p. 324.

51 See http://www.transparency.org/whatwedo/pub/assurance_framework_for_corporate_anti_bribery_programmes, http://www.transparency.de/fileadmin/pdfs/Themen/Wirtschaft/Checkliste_Self-Audits_TID.pdf (4.04.2013).

52 See http://www.transparency.de/Stellungnahme_Entwurf-Gesetz-S.2338.0.html

Germany partly promoted the bribery of foreign companies to support exports, the FCPA initially had a negative effect on the competitiveness of American companies. In addition, all companies listed in the US are obliged to adjust their accounting to the anti-corruption rules of the FCPA.[53]

In 2008, the SEC imposed a fine of $1654 million on Siemens for the bribery of public authorities in several countries on the basis of the American Foreign Corrupt Practices Act, a settlement of which is $350 million went to the SEC and $450 million to the Ministry of Justice. $854 million went to the German government. The profit from these transactions, however, amounted to $1.1 billion for Siemens.[54]

In 1997, the OECD adopted a "Convention on Combating Bribery of Foreign Public Officials in International Business Transactions" signed by all 29 states with an obligation to incorporate the content into national law. This law, however, only regulates the bribery of foreign officials and presupposes that a breach of service duty can also be proven. This law was only ratified in Germany.[55]

The United Nations Declaration against Corruption entered into force on 16 September 2005. It is the first international treaty to fight corruption. The contracting parties undertook to punish various forms of corruption against officials and international cooperation. After persistent public criticism, the Bundestag passed a tightening of the rules of parliamentary deputies in 2014. A convicted deputy will be punished with up to five years imprisonment.[56]

Corruption is punishable for individuals, but not for companies. The introduction of criminal liability for legal persons and associations of persons failed to take hold in 1998. If a company commits a criminal offense, this is treated as an administrative offense.[57]

Bribery or attempted bribery in private business transactions is punishable for instance in Germany according to StGB §299 with imprisonment up to 3 years or with a monetary penalty. It also punishes whoever is trying to bribe employees or agents of a business enterprise. StGB §344 stipulates the punishment of the bribery or attempted bribery with an imprisonment of 3 months to 5 years.

Since corruption is not public, it is difficult to measure. Transparency International uses the Corruption Perceptions Index (CPI) to measure the corruption perceived in the public sector. However, this is not a direct, comprehensive measurement, but an aggregation of various studies from a number of independent and well-known institutions. The countries are listed according to the degree of corruption in the public sector. According to Transparency International, the CPI is the most widespread corruption indicator in the world.[58]

---

[53] See Pritzl and Schneider (1999), p. 329 and http://www.justice.gov/criminal/fraud/fcpa/

[54] See http://www.sec.gov/news/press/2008/2008-294.htm

[55] See Elsner (2012); Keuchel (2002); Göbel (2010), p. 300 and http://www.gesetze-im-internet.de/intbestg/BJNR232729998.html#BJNR232729998BJNG000100305

[56] See http://www.transparency.de (4.04.2013) and Deutscher Bundestag Drucksache 18/476.

[57] See Bundesrechtsanwaltskammer (2013).

[58] See http://www.transparency.de (4.04.2013).

What does behavioral science say about corruption? Is corruption just a part of human behavior? How honest are human beings? Do they cheat on every occasion if they can increase their benefit?

In terms of the willingness of people to obey the law, evidence suggests that people assess the legitimacy of the legal demands. Research shows that people generally comply with the law if it is accepted as just and fair, and if they assume that the law has been established in a legitimate manner.[59] The legitimacy of social demands is important for compliance. If the social demands are not accepted individually or by the prevailing corporate culture, the compliance rates drop.[60] Consequently, it has been shown that compliance in companies can be increased if the employees are informed about the procedural fairness of organizational rules.[61]

As we have seen, in a public goods game there is always a base group of players who insist on being uncooperative and try to maximize their gain to the detriment of the other players. This can be seen as a behavior similar to corruption, since someone maximizes his benefits at the expense of a third party. These cheating free riders make up about one third of players. Altruistic rewards and punishments, which are also at the cost of the participants, can discipline the free riders into more cooperative behavior, which can allow the public good to be created to everyone's benefit.[62]

However, it can also be demonstrated that people do not cheat to maximize their benefit. A computation test is conducted one with a group that is externally judged and one group where the subjects judge themselves. Both groups are rewarded with real money. The externally judged group scores around four out of ten on average whereas the self-controlled group claims six out of ten on average. Thus the not controlled subjects do not maximize their utility by maximizing cheating.[63]

We can observe that many people prefer to be honest. Business is sometimes conducted such that the utility-maximizing strategy is contradicted. There are fields of u-pick flowers, and self-serve newspaper kiosks in the city, where one can cut flowers or take a paper without paying for it. Not paying would be the rational utility maximization strategy, since the "buyer" would not fear any reprisal. These offers exist nonetheless, which means that many people behave ethically and socially, instead of rationally utility-maximizing.

There have been several studies on human behavior using errant pieces of mail. Letters with postage were tossed into a mailbox at a rate of almost 80%. If the letter contained money, still more than 50% were forwarded.[64] In an experiment in which a wallet was placed in the letter, passersby in New York forwarded untouched

---

[59] See Kahneman and Tversky (1986), pp. S285–S230, p. 285 and p. 299 and Tyler (1990), p. 5.

[60] See Tyler et al. (2008), pp. 31–51; Feldman (2014) and Langevoort (2015), p. 10.

[61] See Feldman and Oren Perez (2012), pp. 405–442, p. 405; Feldman and Orly Lobel (2009), pp. 1151–1152; and Feldman and Tyler (2012), p. 46.

[62] See Fehr and Fischbacher (2003), p. 786 and Fehr et al. (2001).

[63] See Ariely (2012), pp. 11–22 and Langevoort (2015), p. 3.

[64] See Lück and Manz (1973).

wallets at a rate of almost 50%.[65] Gneezy's sender-receiver game experiment using students showed[66] that many people tend towards the truth, even if they do worse because of it.

The public goods games also show the importance of societal sanctions (norms) and learning/socialization. The great majority of players enter the game in a spirit of cooperation, but they are willing to change that behavior if the advantages of cooperating turn to disadvantages. Such an experience is also part of the learning process, such as the role that reputation plays. If there is an option to switch to a game where sanctions are possible, it will be taken in order enjoy public goods. With time the players are able to establish norms, allowing punishments to diminish greatly.[67] The tit-for-tat strategy was observed during these games as well. Thus, most players saw their cooperative contribution increase along with that of the other players.[68] Therefore, corruption must be sanctioned directly by the company and the society. It seems to be particularly important that corruption not become a socially accepted behavior. The public good games show that cooperative behavior is abandoned if it does not pay. That explains why cheating is contagious. If others observe cheating it makes it more likely the observer will also cheat.[69]

Immoral behavior intensifies immoral attitudes in a culture. Judson Mills checked the attitude of the students toward cheating at a primary school and then they had to take an exam that was so difficult it could only be passed by cheating. He explained to the students that they cannot be caught while cheating, but this was not correct. Some students did not cheat, while others did. Then the students were questioned again about their attitude to cheating. The students who had cheated had a more lenient attitude to cheating than before, and those who had not cheated rejected cheating even more strenuously.[70]

Compliance is fostered by the corporate culture. The employees work together in the company group every day and internalize the norms and values of their company (socialization). The norms become an internal benchmark against which the employees compare their own behavior. They serve as a normative-actual value comparison, otherwise known as a conscience. Compliance is internally rewarded by good feelings, whereas noncompliance leads to negative feelings. This can be proved indirectly by brain imaging studies, which show activities in the same primary reward centers in the brain for altruistic punishment or social cooperation as external benefits such as preferred food, drinks, and monetary gains (the nucleus accumbens and caudate nucleus).[71]

---

[65] See Hornstein et al. (1968).

[66] See Gneezy (2005), p. 387.

[67] See Fehr and Fischbacher (2003).

[68] See Falk (2003), p. 147 and Fehr et al. (2001).

[69] See Ariely (2012).

[70] See Aronson et al. (2008), p. 171.

[71] See Mazar et al. (2008), pp. 633–644.

Most people see themselves mostly as honest with a very strong belief in their own morality. Moreover, people want to remain true to their self concept. To behave unethically is not easy because it results in sanctions like negative feelings or requires rationalization.[72] People stick to their ethical internal standards even if this means exerting themselves or sacrificing financial gains.[73] This struggle can be used to generate compliance,. If people are reminded of their honesty standards, they generally behave more ethically.[74]

Research shows that a code of ethics only influences manager behavior positively when the code includes a certification choice because signing a code increases moral reasoning in the manager.[75] Certification choice indicates that the employee recognizes the rules and adopts them as their own with their signature. Only when the employee has accepted the rules as their own do they feel obliged to comply. The employee must read the rules but not be forced to sign them. They will identify with the ethical rules in the sense of ethos as long the decision to do so was freely made. Thus, employees should sign an agreement to uphold specific ethical standards and then be reminded of these standards regularly as they work.

Ethical nudges can be used as an effective instrument to enhance ethical behavior in the firm. Whereas normal nudges help the people to choose the right decision in their own self-interest, ethical nudges are designed to make people make choices that are good for third parties. For instance, it has been shown that signing an ethical code of conduct reduces unethical decisions significantly, or can even eliminate it.[76]

People generally behave less ethically if they are more motivated in their actions by how they will affect a third party than themselves.[77] In Kouchaki's research the subject's misbehavior increases if the profit goes to the employer and not to the employees.[78] Thus altruism can increase corruption and misconduct. Research shows that it makes it easier for people to act unethically if they do it in the name of the corporation and for its interests, and not for their own interest.[79]

People find it easier to act unethically if they share the results of their misconduct with others and are less willing to act unethically if they are the only profiteer.[80] A lack of social responsibility increases unethical behavior. They cheat more if they can use an agent or institutions to carry out unethical behavior. Acting through third parties reduces responsibility and therefore guilt and the likelihood of punishment.

---

[72] See Griffin and Ross (1991), p. 319; Sanitioso et al. (1990), pp. 229–241. –359; Greenwald (1980), pp. 603–618 and Josephson Institute of Ethics (2006, October 15).

[73] See Aronson and Carlsmith (1962), pp. 178–182 and Harris et al. (1976), pp. 123–135.

[74] See Mazar et al. (2008), pp. 633–644.

[75] See Ariely (2010), p. 28.

[76] See Shu et al. (2011), p. 330 and Shu et al. (2012), pp. 15197–15200.

[77] See Gino et al. (2013), pp. 291–292.

[78] See Kouchaki (2013).

[79] See Feldman and Kaplan (2019), p. 6.

[80] See Wiltermuth (2011), p. 168 and Feldman and Kaplan (2019), p. 6.

Compensation schemes might also encourage corruption, and influence cheating. Gilla, Prowseb and Vlassopoulosc show that exposing workers to a compensation scheme based on random bonuses makes them cheat more but has no effect on their productivity.[81]

The employees react to the way the company sets guidelines. If the earning goals cannot be reached with ethical work, unethical methods are applied, as the example of Sears shows. Sears – a leader in auto work – was under pressure as its competitors Wal-Mart and K-Mart destabilized the retail marketplace through cost cutting. In order to survive the company set unfeasibly high profitability goals in combination with tough variable compensation schemes like incentive-compensation programs for service advisers and the elimination of product-specific sales quotas. In order to reach the goals the employees cheated the customers and repaired more than necessary.[82]

Most people justify their actions to themselves and are blinded to the fact that they are doing so, which can foster non-compliance and illegal conduct in the company, both of which are a severe compliance problem. For instance, it has been shown that people can more easily justify stealing small items from the workplace to themselves than any even a small sum of cash from their employer.[83]

Motivated reasoning taking perspective can help the employees to identify which choice benefits them most by being ethically superior.[84] Ethics seminars are important to explain ethical judgment.

Conclusion

Corruption acts as a reward for an expected risk, such as moral hazards, thus as incentives directed against the interests of the company or the community. Only a fair competition of performance ensures an optimal allocation of resources and thus an efficient overall economic production. Immoral behavior harms society generally, from market processes, internal business processes and the erosion of culture.

In public good games cheating free riders make up about one third of players. Altruistic rewards and punishments, which are also at the cost of the participants, can discipline the free riders into more cooperative behavior, which can allow the public good to be created to everyone's benefit. We can observe that many people prefer to be honest. Gneezy's sender-receiver game experiment using students showed that many people tend towards the truth, even if they do worse because of it.

The public goods games also show the importance of societal sanctions (norms) and learning/socialization. Therefore, corruption must be sanctioned directly by the company and the society. It seems to be of special importance that corruption becomes not a socially accepted behavior. The public good games show that the cooperative behavior is abandoned if it does not pay. This explains why cheating is

---

[81] See Colesa et al. (2006), pp. 431–468 and Gilla et al. (2013), pp. 120–134.

[82] See Schmeltzer (1992) and Driscoll (1992).

[83] See Hollinger and Clark (1983), p. 398.

[84] See Underwood and Moore (1982), p. 143 and Kunda (1990), p. 480.

contagious. Compliance is built up by the corporate culture. Compliance is internally rewarded by good feelings, whereas noncompliance leads to negative feelings.

Comprehension Questions.

1. What is corruption?
2. Why is corruption harmful?
3. To what extent is corruption punished?
4. Identify the forms of market failure and explain to what extent morality is necessary here.

5.8 Market Failure Due to Lack of Market Transparency

In contrast to the market failure due to asymmetric information, the information may also be incomplete or wrong. Market transactions are not carried out if there is no transparency about the services and risks or costs. If they are carried out because wrong assumptions about the contents of the transaction are the basis of the decisions, this leads to misallocations. For example, food ingredients and their effects are unknown or transparent so we cannot choose the right foods. Labeling the goods with an organic label helps to increase transparency. Stocks are the least transparent of all. The companies are so complex that not even the managers as insiders could value stocks properly. The time required to obtain the information far exceeds the expected benefits of better market transparency. For this reason, even if all the information were available, we would still have to live with a lack of market transparency.

5.9 Market Failure Due to Natural Monopolies

Definition: A natural monopoly is when an individual company can provide a given good to the whole market at a lower cost than two or more companies in a competitive situation.

This case sometimes occurs:

1. high transport costs; the so-called spatial monopolies,
2. increasing economies of scale

and always with indivisibility of production.

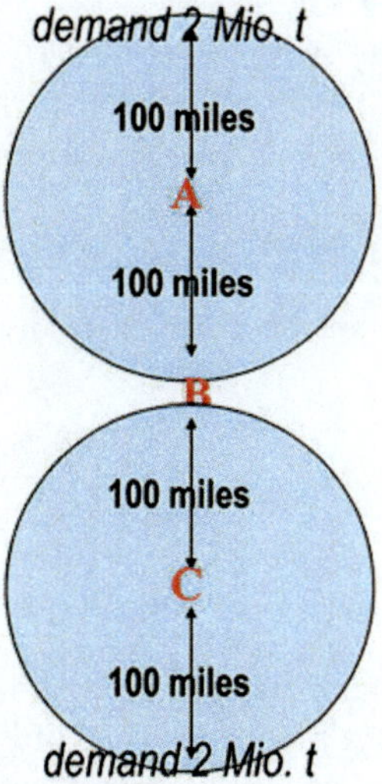

Fig. 5.11 Spatial monopoly

5.9.1 Spatial Monopoly

Spatial monopolies give a company competitive advantage due to its location, making it the sole supplier (definition).

High transport costs result in price advantages for local suppliers and represent market entry barriers for third parties. The steel industry serves to illustrate a spatial monopoly. The transport costs for a ton of steel are 100 €/100 km. As a result, two markets will emerge (see Fig. 5.11). The competitor company 2 would have to be able to offer cheaper prices to penetrate the market of the other and in fact be 200 €/t cheaper to be able to supply both markets completely on the same terms as company 1. There are many spatial monopolies. Everyone knows a typical food shop in a village. But even in the refectory of a university chocolate bars can be sold more expensively, because the nearest supermarket is far away.

5.9.2 Natural monopoly Due to Falling Unit Costs

With a high fixed cost burden (especially for large-scale plants), a significant reduction in unit costs only occurs with very large batch sizes. Examples: large-scale power generation plants, integrated steelworks, etc.

Example: Integrated steelworks

At 80% utilization, the production costs with a two million ton furnace are 500 €/t. With only 50% utilization, they increase to 800 €/t (degressive unit costs).

Fig. 5.12 Ruinous competition Initial situation

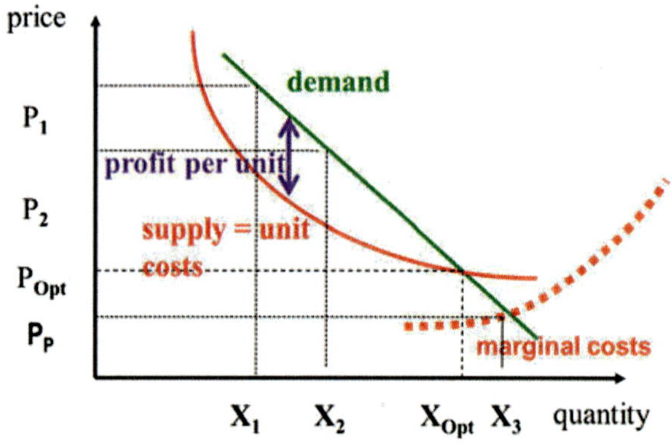

Alternatively, an oven with only a one million ton production capacity would also have production costs of € 800/t. Optimum furnace size is therefore two million tons.

Large production plants generate high fixed costs. If only one ton of steel were produced, the cost of this ton would be the fixed costs plus the variable costs. The same applies to the capacity utilization of the two million t furnace. With a capacity utilization of only 50%, the allocation of fixed costs to the lower number of units results in significantly higher unit costs of € 800 / t. As a result, the market in Fig. 5.12, taking into account the transport costs, is served by a company at point B with a two million t furnace and not by two companies with one million t each. It is a natural monopoly. The company that occupies this position first will prevail in the competition. In the following, we will analyze this competitive process of ruinous competition under the assumption of complete competition.

PP (polypol price): The competition price does not cover the unit costs, ruinous competition!! P < costs

Assumption: Two companies each with two million tons of steel production capacity X1 and X2 can serve the entire market. U1 offers P1 and U2 P2 and thus steals some of the sales. Due to the falling unit costs U1 will follow suit. The lower price limit of this price competition is the variable cost. Everything above that brings additional marginal returns for the fixed costs (breakeven analysis), which is why these prices are offered. This would still be within the loss range, however. In addition, the other company is offering the same product, so that the expected sales will not be reached. The production made at the low unit cost cannot be sold, resulting in overproduction, which further increases sales pressure.

That means: Falling unit or average costs lead to price undercutting and a simultaneous increase in supply. The company left standing after a ruinous price competition becomes a monopolist and the only supplier. But not Xopt to Popt!

Xopt and Popt

Highest welfare in the form of the consumer pension, because customers can buy at favorable but still cost-covering prices.

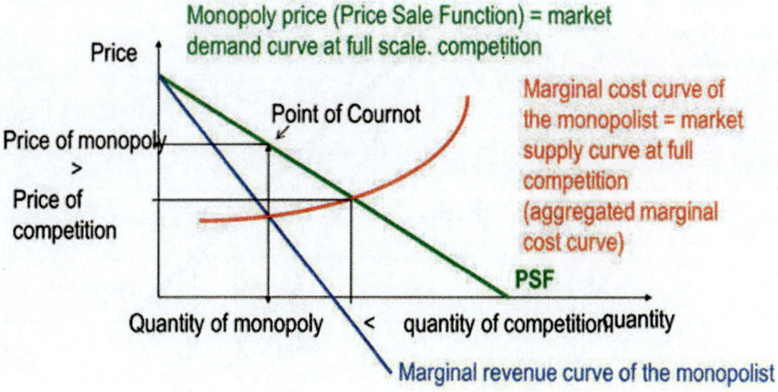

Fig. 5.13 Ruinous competition Final state monopoly

X3 = PP = K '.

The willingness to pay of the buyer is equal to the marginal cost but below the unit cost. Thus, the gain in benefits lies below the economic effort. If one were to produce and offer here, the result would be a negative welfare, a waste of resources.

The price optimum is undercut until only one supplier can survive on the market. This becomes a monopolist. The condition is that a company can supply the market more favorably than several companies in the competition. The cost advantage lies in this form of natural monopoly in production: a company produces twice that amount with decreasing unit costs. However, an economic problem arises as soon as the company has reached the monopoly position, because it can then determine the price. How will he set the price?

Pricing in Monopoly as per Cournot at Normal Cost

The monopolist controls the entire market through the quantity offered only by him and can thus control the market price by the amount offered. This characterizes the behavior of a so-called Cournot monopolist. It is assumed here that the monopolist knows the course of total demand (price-sales function) (see Fig. 5.13).

Marginal cost curve of the monopolist K' = market supply curve with perfect competition (aggregate marginal cost curve), price monopoly function (PAF) logo CNRS logo INIST.

Market demand curve with perfect competition.

The monopolist reaches his profit maximum in the quantity where the marginal costs correspond to the marginal revenue. He achieves the monopoly price for the monopoly quantity. Compared to the complete competition, the amount provided is too small and the price of the goods is too high. The highest welfare in the form of the consumer pension is not achieved, because customers cannot buy cheap but still cost-covering prices. This form of monopoly pricing is associated with static welfare losses.

Fig. 5.14 Overview of natural monopoly with declining unit costs

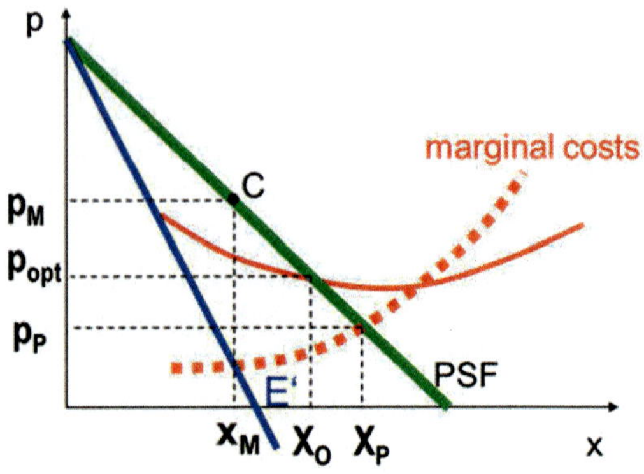

With decreasing average costs, there is a natural monopoly that fixes the maximum output at the point where the marginal cost is equal to the marginal revenue. Natural monopolies are the opposite of the welfare optimum and are the result of price competition. This relationship is shown in Fig. 5.14.

XM: monopoly quantity,
XM: monopoly price,
XO: optimum quantity,
PO: optimum price.

Consider Fig. 5.14 and the quantities and prices recorded here. The monopolist makes the biggest profit in point C, but the price is too high and the amount too low. There is a market failure and thus a loss of welfare in the form of the consumer pension.

Here the price covers the unit cost, i.e. for the resulting costs are correspondingly high benefits of consumers. The maximum consumer surplus and thus welfare is realized. This is optimal for the economy, but suboptimal for the individual company due to the lack of profit.

XP: Polypol Quantity,
PP: Polypol Price.

The willingness to pay of the buyer is equal to the marginal cost but below the unit cost. Thus, the gain in benefits lies below the economic effort. The costs are no longer covered by the willingness of the customers to pay. So there is no benefit to the costs of the same amount. If one were to produce and offer here, there would be a negative welfare, i.e. a waste of resources.

Conclusion

The company, which survived ruinous price competition, will offer the monopoly price and the monopoly price as a monopolist. This leads to welfare losses. There is a market failure because the market does not provide the socially desired results. Natural monopolies always lead to market failure. The state has to intervene in the market. There are basically two options. The state itself can offer the product, and produce and offer the optimal quantity at the optimal price or he can supervise the monopolist.

5.9.3 Natural Monopoly on Internet and Software

High development costs and low duplication costs are specific to the production of software. The high development costs represent high fixed costs, which are at the same time market entry barriers. Before software can be sold and proceeds can be realized, programming must be completed. After that, almost no variable costs arise in the production, because the software can be selectively reproduced. As a consequence, the fixed cost degression is very high. In the meantime, software can even be purchased and copied directly over the Internet. If a software application succeeds in becoming the market standard, it meets the requirements of a natural monopoly. In principle, no second software is necessary. An enterprise can supply the whole market more cheaply than two companies in a competitive situation. However, this is only static as a snapshot. Over time, the natural monopoly will have to do far less research, depending on the market entry barrier, than in a competitive situation. Constantly new products need not be associated with a benefit for the user. The monopolist can also use the standard to force users to purchase updates, if the old versions are not compatible. Software monopolies also want their programs to be incompatible with competing applications to maintain market entry barriers.

Microsoft thus has a monopoly due to its lack of compatibility with other programs and the market entry barriers resulting from high software development costs. A new word processor would have too high of development costs and must be compatible with MS-Word, otherwise no one would use it. In addition, Microsoft could undercut a new market participant at any time with the using price to push it out of the market. The same applies to the Windows operating system. Free programs such as Open-Office and Java have been developed by programmers to break the heavy dependency.

Such standard setting also occurs on Internet platforms. The more users there are, the more interesting the platform is for other users. It is not worthwhile, for example, to offer your car on a second platform, if all those interested in buying are looking at the offers of the market leader anyway. The investment for programming is very complex, with high fixed costs and market entry barriers. For network goods and network services, the greater the number of players on the supply and demand sides, the more attractive the offer (positive network effects). Of course, this also applies to application programs that finance themselves via advertising and advertisers such as Google or Facebook.

Natural monopolies in the software and Internet sector also have a tendency to ruinous price competition. Positive feedback loops between economies of scale and positive network effects show their effects here. Price cuts attract more users, leading to further economies of scale and network effects. The more favorable cost structure due to the economies of scale and positive network effects allows the dominant supplier to win any price war. Competition policy must therefore monitor the natural monopolies in the Internet and software sector for abuse of their dominant position.

5.9.4 Indivisibility of the Factors of Production

Indivisibility of the factors of production is when a single production capacity suffices to serve the entire market. A second supplier would have to build up a second production capacity. Not only is this inefficient, it would be worthless if the supplier were to withdraw from the market (irreversibility of costs). This applies, for example, to the rail network of Deutsche Bahn (german railway). Building a second rail network would be pointless as long as the capacity of the other is sufficient. New trains from another provider would not increase competition, because there would not be an increase in train passengers; rather the rail network of Deutsche Bahn would no longer be as full.

The phenomenon of the indivisibility of the factors of production mainly affects pipeline-related supply networks, such as power lines, railways, roads, airfields or telecommunication cables, i.e. goods whose supply is linked to a specific infrastructure (electricity, gas, water, telecommunications, postal services, transport).

Of course, monopolies result in profit maximization at the expense of the consumer. The state must therefore intervene in the market to correct this failure. In principle, there are three political economy options available: nationalization, state supervision and the separation of networks.

Political Economy Concepts for Natural Monopolies

A. **Nationalization = transfer of business to public ownership**

Nationalization offers many advantages. The state-owned company can produce the quantity and offer it at the price that covers the unit cost. This is how welfare optimum can be achieved. The state then maximizes welfare rather than profit. Needs can be completely met by the supply. In this way, the state can apply infrastructure policy with a state railway, thus making economically weak areas attractive as a production location through good infrastructure. It can institute social policies, for example by offering cheaper train tickets for families. Environmental policy also becomes possible by subsidizing rail travel. Environmentally damaging car trips and flights are then replaced by train journeys.

Example: Deutsche Bahn was to be privatized via an IPO. To do this, unlike a state-owned company, it had to be profitable. To achieve this, investments have been postponed and staff laid off. Delays increased as a result.

State-owned companies also have many disadvantages. State influence can lead to inefficiencies, for example by awarding posts to politicians. A bureaucratization, thus inflated administration can also be the result (see political failure).[85] A lack of work ethic and cost awareness is also attributed to state-owned enterprises due to lack of profit pressure. That is, the disadvantages of nationalization are comparable to the problems of the central administration economy. On the other hand, a private monopolist only has an interest in maximizing profits. Why should they behave better when there is no competition?

Alternative: B. Privatization & Regulation.

The second option to avoid the welfare disadvantages of a natural monopoly is state price control. Private monopolies in Germany are controlled by state regulatory authorities (BKartA, BNetzA) in their economic activities. The price control is still the prohibition of discrimination. In other words, natural monopolies must serve all consumers equally and are not allowed to use their market position to force their suppliers to lower their prices disproportionally, which is in line with the competitive approach to abuse control. We differentiate between price regulation, so-called **cost-plus regulation** and **price cap regulation**. In the cost-plus regulation the monopolist must provide unit costs and approve mark-up. In price cap regulation, a price is set by the regulator as an upper limit. This exists currently for letter postage.

There is an information deficit with the regulator in price cap regulation. The regulatory authority does not know the cost structure of the monopolist. There is asymmetric information in favor of the monopolist that can be exploited. The control authority lacks information on production costs. Even when comparing similar markets, e.g. comparing the German electricity prices with the lower French prices there are production differences that relativize the comparison. In France there is a proportionate increase in nuclear power from outdated and thus already depleted nuclear power plants (such as Cattenom). Also, utilities can artificially raise prices, even if they include fictitious costs such as future demolition or disposal costs.

Alternative C: Separation of the nets.

The third alternative is to force monopolists to make their networks available to other providers. This is called a throughput compulsion. The monopolists have to separate their networks as their own societies (so-called unbundling) so that they can objectively determine network costs. This process, and in particular the discrimination ban on access to the network, must be monitored by a governmental agency (network agency). This is in turn linked to price regulation. For example, there is a network transmission requirement for electricity, telephone, Internet and railway networks. The implementation is supervised by the Federal Network Agency for Electricity, Gas, Telecommunications, Post and Railways.

---

[85]Thus, the former chancellery chief Pofalla became CEO of Deutsche Bahn and then replaced the longtime chief environmental officer with his former office manager Gehlhaar.

See Spiegel Online vom 29.04.2016. http://www.spiegel.de/wirtschaft/unternehmen/deutsche-bahn-ronald-pofalla-schmeisst-einen-nach-dem-anderen-raus-a-1090019.html

Excursus: Competition Through Additional Providers?
Work in Groups

1. Discuss the advantages and disadvantages of competition for Deutsche Bahn from long-distance buses. Will this make Deutsche Bahn's offer cheaper and qualitatively better? Solution: Competition by private long-distance buses has since been approved. People waited for a better and cheaper offers from Deutsche Bahn due to the competition in long-distance transport. But the question is, how does competition between private companies and governments work? Deutsche Bahn will have to cut prices on long-haul routes, which is an advantage for its customers. However, taxpayers' earnings will have to offset the loss. As long as Deutsche Bahn still has the public service mission of the population as a state-owned company, and does not have to offer any profitable routes, it will not be able to cover its costs.
2. Discuss the advantages and disadvantages of competition from other railway providers on the rail network of Deutsche Bahn. Deutsche Bahn will be forced to make its rail network available to other railway service providers for a fee. The fee collection and the rail access are monitored by the state. Will this make Deutsche Bahn's offer cheaper and qualitatively better?

   Again, it is questionable whether a welfare-enhancing competition will come about. For example, it is not profitable to drive a second train at only half capacity 5 minutes after the ICE of Deutsche Bahn has passed. In addition, connections would have to be coordinated with Deutsche Bahn to allow passengers to change trains. Will trains wait if the train of a competitor is late? Just due to the fact that regional traffic is not organized by the German Federal Railways, but the federal states, there are currently coordination problems and thus missed connections.
3. **Group work:** Discuss the advantages and disadvantages of competition through private mail services for Deutsche Post. Will this make Deutsche Post's offer cheaper and better in quality?

Solution The admission of private postal services should also be questioned. As long as the performance is the same, nothing changes in the natural monopoly. If now two letter carriers each bring one letter, instead of one carrier with two letters nothing has been gained in efficiency. Assuming that every household receives at least two letters per day, it is more efficient for one carrier to bring the two letters instead of two letters one at a time. In the long term, therefore, only one supplier should prevail after a ruinous cutthroat competition.

Experience in Practice
What are the experiences of these approaches in practice? In the telecommunications sector, unbundling, i.e. the separation of networks, could be achieved without any major deterioration in quality. Deutsche Telekom's obligation for competitors to conduct competitions led to significantly lower prices and the same quality.

Meanwhile, Telecom has separated from their networks. Negative experiences resulted in the privatization of the British railway. In Great Britain, there was a private rail operator for eight years (railtrack, from 1994 to 2002). Before that there was the state-owned British Rail and since 2002 the infrastructure belongs to the state-owned, non-profit Network Rail. The private company railtrack had previously suffered serious accidents, which are attributed by market observers to a lack of maintenance. Energy supply was not affected by the desired price decrease as a result of competition, even though the power grids were separated from the compulsory transmission companies. To prepare for the IPO, the new railway chief Mehdorn was hired. After the plans were postponed, and there was a change in leadership, the new railway manager Grube a few years later found an investment backlog of tracks, switch points and switch towers amounting to € 30bn.[86]

Conclusion

Transaction costs and lack of market transparency hamper the market mechanism. Either the transactions do not materialize or they lead to inefficient results. For natural monopolies, market failure is mainly due to the indivisibility of the factors of production, such as rails. Nationalization is usually the better alternative because the information is lacking for regulation and oversight. Technical progress in the IT sector has created new natural monopolies that must monitor competition policy.

Comprehension Questions

1. Give two examples of market transactions that cannot be achieved due to excessive transaction costs, and identify the costs.
2. Give two examples in which the market mechanism is hampered by a lack of transparency of benefits.
3. Which invention has both reduced transaction costs and increased market transparency in recent decades? Explain your assessment.
4. (a) Discuss the advantages and disadvantages of nationalization and regulation of natural monopolies.
   (b) Give an example of a natural monopoly.
   (c) Explain your assessment.
   (d) What economic measures do you propose?

[86] See Handelsblatt vom 3.11.2013. http://www.handelsblatt.com/unternehmen/handel-konsumgueter/investitionsstau-im-schienennetz-bahn-chef-fordert-staatliche-milliarden-spritze/9020654.html

5.10 Market Failure on the Labor Market

What Follows Why?
The labor market is a central market that determines economic development and on which the welfare of the population depends. Again, there is market failure. Unemployment has far-reaching social and political consequences, which is why the state intervenes here and tries to prevent market failure.

Learning Goals
You should be able to explain the market failure in the labor market, how unemployment is measured and why unemployment is such a big economic and social problem.

Historical Development
Industrialization led to the creation of labor markets where day laborers offered their work. As a rule, they came from the countryside, meaning that they were unskilled workers who, due to the lack of transportation, were dependent on the labor demand of the local employer. Work was the only source of income for the whole family. In addition, there was strong population growth. There were many workers for only a few employers. The workers in the labor market and their families were impoverished. The pay was not enough to feed families and send children to school. In order to survive, the children also had to offer their labor under demeaning conditions. Due to the peculiarities of the labor market, market failure also occurs here. Why is this?

Neoclassical Labor Market Model
Even the neoclassical model for a macroeconomic labor market, developed under very rigid model-theoretical assumptions, proves that under certain circumstances the laws of supply and demand do not provide a stable equilibrium solution.

This is mainly due to the sometimes atypical developments of the job offer function.

Assumptions of the Neoclassical Model
1. Labor is a homogeneous factor,
2. there is complete competition in the goods and factor markets,
3. companies work with profit-based production functions,
4. employees have no other factors (no assets),
5. they cannot resort to state or equivalent income protection (no social assistance or family support) (original market – survival of the fittest), everyone is on their own and.
6. they must individually negotiate the wage level with companies (no collective bargaining agreements and no trade unions → each employee must negotiate individually with the employer).

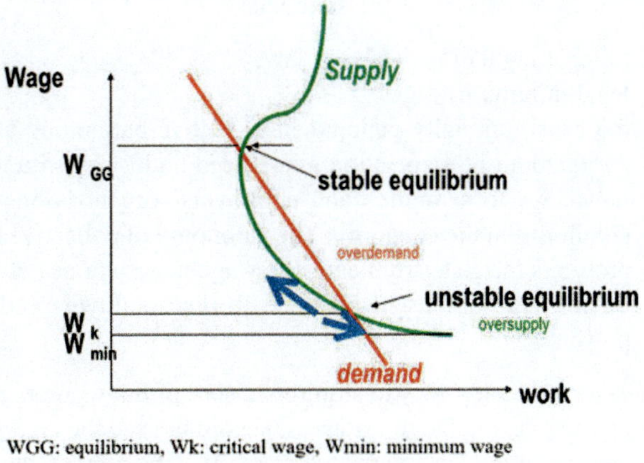

Fig. 5.15 The abnormal response of the work supply *WGG* equilibrium, *Wk* critical wage, *Wmin* minimum wage

Consider Fig. 5.15. In the normal situation of neoclassicism, salary is sufficiently high. Then a rising wage leads to an increased supply of labor, because the suffering of the labor is overcompensated by the increased wage. The worker views the job as a sacrifice because it is exhausting and it costs him free time. On the other hand, the reward is added value. If the wage decreases, the employee reduces his offered labor. He is always balancing job sacrifice and compensation for wages. The loss of benefit (suffering) from 1 h of overtime is equal to the benefit from the purchase equivalent of the hourly wage.

An unstable balance is created in the labor market when wages are so low that workers cannot live off their earned income. They must take a second or even third job to survive. This increases the job supply. This is called an abnormal reaction of the work offer.

As long as wages on the labor market are lower than wk., there is an overabundance of work, which means that the incomes of workers drop again and again to the minimum (w_{min}) = "iron law of wages" by Ferdinand Lassalle. Only when it is possible to raise the wage level above wk., does a wage drift set in, since the demand for labor is greater than the supply. The over-demand leads to the stable balance in W_{GG}. If the wage rises above Wk, the labor supply reduces, because the money is enough to live on, the job is too exhausting, 14 h is too long compared to 8 h, and there is no more child labor. Wages above this equilibrium wage rate cause unemployment.

One consequence of the impoverishment of industrial workers was the strengthening of socialism and communism: Marx regarded private property as the core problem. By the capitalists' ownership of the means of production, in his opinion, the "proletariat" was depended on and exploited. For this reason, in the socialist states after the forcible expropriation of the factory owners, the community property was introduced within the framework of the central administrative economy. In order to avert the exploitation and misery of workers, the state also intervened in the labor market in market-based systems, as the structural weaknesses of workers resulting from the lack of wealth could not be eliminated in the short and medium term.

The interventions of the state led.

1. to legal regulations of labor law,
2. legal minimum wages.
3. the constitutionally guaranteed collective bargaining autonomy. On the basis of the freedom of association guaranteed under Constitutional Law, employees can nowadays form unions and employers' organizations to regulate labor market conditions in the economy. The autonomy of collective bargaining enshrined here prohibits the state from entering wage negotiations between employers and trade unions. The unions negotiate with the employers and so there is a balance of power.

Marx saw the only way to stop the misery of the workers in the expropriation of the capitalists, i.e. the factory owners. He did not see the emergence of trade unions as a suitable solution, in contrast to Lasalle. The job of the unions is to absorb the imbalance between labor demand and labor supply. Before unions existed, there was a monopoly of demand, and the formation of unions now provides for a bilateral monopoly. Lasalle should be right. It is not just the trade unions that have achieved a social balance between work and capital, and the market economy has been accepted by society, but also that purchasing power has been redistributed to workers, with sufficient demand for the products generated.

Conclusion
Growth and unemployment are of political and social importance. It can be assumed that the declared unemployment is understated. On the other hand, unlike in the 1930s, there is social security at the subsistence level and, as a consequence, voluntary unemployment. Due to the compulsion to secure the subsistence minimum, an abnormal supply curve (market failure) arises in the labor market. The intervention of the state is not only welfare promoting, but also indispensable to ensure social preservation and stability as morality is not sufficient to stop the employers from abusing their strong bargaining position.

Comprehension Questions
1. Explain why there is an abnormal supply curve on the job market and what consequences it has.
2. What is the economic function of trade unions?
3. Why was Marx wrong with his predictions for the labor market?

5.11 Conclusion of the Chapter Market Failure

Market failure is when the market does not provide allocation-efficient (socially enhancing) results. There are ethical solutions for external effects. Asymmetrical information may favor the informed contractor over the uninformed and allow the uninformed contractor to benefit and corruption favors two actors at the cost of a third. Reputation, trust, morality (culture) have emerged as social solutions to this problem. Moral behavior requires that third parties are not be harmed. Thus, an ethically oriented company would either have to stop the production with negative external effects or at least compensate for the resulting damage. However, morality alone is not sufficient for a functioning economy as there is a conflict of individual and collective interests or third party interests. Institutional provisions have to punish unethical behavior. On the labor market morality is also not sufficient to stop the employers from abusing their strong bargaining position. Thus the intervention of the state is not only welfare promoting, but also indispensable to ensure social preservation and stability. Humans are must be rational if there should be allocation-efficient decisions or decisions with the best outcome for the individual. Behavioral science shows, that this is not the case. Here also the state has to provide institutional arrangements, which help the citizens to make the best decision for themselves and others. In the case of irrational behavior, the state can intervene only in cases in which there are massive health impairments, since irrationality belongs to human nature. Only rarely can a restriction of human freedom be justified.

Ethical Summary

There are ethical solutions for external effects. Moral behavior requires that third parties are not be harmed. Thus an ethically oriented company would either have to stop the production with negative external effects or at least compensate for the resulting damage. However, if there were no binding regulatory framework internationally, it would mean that moral behavior is associated with major drawbacks, because it entails competitive disadvantages. This places the national governments in a prisoner's dilemma. Environmental pressures in the national market are, at the very least, short-term competitive disadvantages. The uncertainty about the behavior of the others leads to the collective worst case, insofar as no environmental requirements are implemented.

The state has developed external effect standards and sanctioned external effects such as telephoning with mobile phones on the train or smoking in restaurants. Socialization and parenting are key factors here. There are also behavioral guidelines such as "What you do not want to be done to you, do not do to others", which corresponds to the categorical imperative of Kant. It is also possible for people to take care of others, and to try to avoid negative externalities and to support positive ones. Ethical behavior in situation with hidden characteristics would prevent the better informed from betraying the worse informed or hidden actions like moral hazards would not occur. An incentive for individuals to act against or at the expense of many, society or their company would be seen as unethical and thus be suppressed by the decider.

Dilemma and asymmetrical information are problematic, especially if the persons who are acting are not familiar with one another (on anonymous markets), cannot vote, or if they are dealing with a one-sided dependency in which uncooperative behavior cannot be sanctioned later (play with one round). It is even better, then, to trust the active man directly. In the case of morality as a social basis for trust, cooperative behavior can be assumed, which is why these values are productivity-enhancing.

With morality there would be also no corruption. The public goods games also show the importance of societal sanctions (norms) and learning/socialization. Therefore, corruption must be sanctioned directly by the company and the society. It can be proved indirectly by brain imaging studies, that compliance is internally rewarded by good feelings, whereas noncompliance leads to negative feelings. It seems to be of special importance that corruption becomes not a socially accepted behavior. The public good games show that the cooperative behavior is abandoned if it does not pay. This explains why cheating is contagious. Immoral behavior harms society generally, from market processes, internal business processes and the erosion of culture.

We can observe that many people prefer to be honest. Moreover, people want to stick to their self-concept. To behave unethically is therefore not easy respectively results in sanctions like bad feelings or needs efforts like motivated reasoning. However, people stick to their ethical internal standards even if this means efforts or sacrificing financial gains. For compliance, this can be used. If people are remembered of their honesty-standards, they behave more ethically. Thus, employees should sign ethical standards and should be remembered of them during their work. Ethical nudges are designed to make people choose decisions, which are good for third parties. Ethical nudges can be used as an effective instrument to enhance ethical behavior in the firm.

On the labor market the intervention of the state is not only welfare promoting, but also indispensable to ensure social preservation and stability as morality is not sufficient to stop the employers from abusing their strong bargaining position.

Behavioral Summary

Market failure is when the market does not provide allocation-efficient (socially enhancing) results. Humans are not must be rational why there are no allocation-efficient decisions or decisions with the best outcome for the individual. The harmfulness of the demeritorious goods is subjectively underestimated. If the goods are too dangerous they must be forbidden. For the other goods nudges might be a legitimate instrument for influencing decision-making behavior in favor of the individual as long as the individual is free to decide against them. Framing goes one step further. It manipulates the people in a way that information is not presented in a balanced manner. Important is after all that the decision must lie finally at the individual. So everything which enables him to increase his information to find the objectively best decision for him is an advantage but he must have the freedom to decide. With framing this is not the case. Asymmetric Paternalism goes one step further by calling for the better option to be mandatory in order to rule out irrational behavior. But Asymmetric Paternalism is transparent to the decision maker. Therefore, framing cannot be justified. Also strict rules with sanctions to protect the health of the individual presuppose a democratic decision making process.

Emotions have a negative connotation for us because they are not rational behaviors, but they can be efficiency enhancing. Emotions like fear superimpose thinking in order to escape quickly. This will have proven beneficial in evolution. Seen in this light one can differentiate between short-term and long-term human decisions. Short-term decision-making behavior is about speed. Heuristics and emotions are dominant. Only when individuals consciously think about problems does rational thinking dominate.

In public good games cheating free riders make up about one third of players. Altruistic rewards and punishments, which are also at the cost of the participants, can discipline the free riders into more cooperative behavior, which can allow the public good to be created to everyone's benefit. We can observe that many people prefer to be honest. Gneezy's sender-receiver game experiment using students showed that many people tend towards the truth, even if they do worse because of it.

The public goods games also show the importance of societal sanctions (norms) and learning/socialization. Therefore, corruption must be sanctioned directly by the company and the society. It seems to be of special importance that corruption becomes not a socially accepted behavior. The public good games show that the cooperative behavior is abandoned if it does not pay. This explains why cheating is contagious. Compliance is built up by the corporate culture. Compliance is internally rewarded by good feelings, whereas noncompliance leads to negative feelings.

Comprehension Questions

1. What is market failure?
2. Name the types of market failure and explain why there is no welfare-enhancing outcome.
3. What are the problems of governmental market regulations? Discuss the Pros and Cons. How far should the freedom of the individual be restricted?

Literature

Albach, H. (2003). Betriebswirtschaftslehre ohne Unternehmensethik! Z. *Betriebswirtschaftslehre, 75*, 809–829. (2005).

Alparslan, A. (2006). Strukturalistische Prinzipal-Agent-Theorie, Wiesbaden.

Ariely, D. (2010). Predictably irrational: The hidden forces that shape our decisions.

Ariely, D. (2012). *The (Honest) Truth about Dishonesty* (pp. 11–22). Harper.

Aronson, E., & Carlsmith, J. M. (1962). Performance expectancy as a determinant of actual performance. *Journal of Abnormal and Social Psychology, 65*(3), 178–182.

Aronson, E., Wilson, T. D., & Akert, R. M. (2008). *Sozialpsychologie* (6th ed.). Pearson Studium.

Axelrod, R. (1987). *Die Evolution der Kooperation.* Munich.

Baba, S., George, L., & Antoine, B. (2005). The dark side of emotions? *When individuals with decreased emotional reactions make advantageous decisions, cognitive brain research, 23*, 85–92.

Ballwieser, W., & Clemm, H. (1999). Wirtschaftsprüfung. In: W. Korff (ed.), *Handbuch der Wirtschaftsethik*, Vol. 3: Ethik wirtschaftlichen Handelns, Gütersloh 1999, pp. 399–416.

Beck, H. (2014). *Behavioral Economics: Eine Einführung* (1st ed.). Springer.

Berthel, J., & Becker, F. G. (2013). *Personalmanagement, Grundzüge für Konzeptionen betrieblicher Personalarbeit* (10th ed.). Schäffer Poeschel.

Beschorner, T., & Hajduk, T. (2011). Der Ehrbare Kaufmann – Unternehmensverantwortung „light"? *CRS Magazin 3*, 6–8. http://www.alexandria.unisg.ch/export/DL/206603.pdf

Brandstätter, V., Schüler, J., Puca, R. M., & Lozo, L. (2018). *Motivation und emotion*. Springer.

Camerer, C., Loewenstein, G., & Prelec, D. (2005, March). Neuroeconomics: How neuroscience can inform economics. *Journal of Economic Literature, XLIII*, 9–64.

Camerer, C., et al. (2003). Regulation for conservatives: Behavioral economics and the case for "asymmetric paternalism". *University of Pennsylvania Law Review, 151*, 101–144.

Chakraborty, S., & Dabla-Norris, E. (2006). Rent seeking. *IMF Staff Papers, 53*(1), 1. Palgrave Macmillan.

Colesa, J., Danielb, N. D., & Naveenb, L. (2006). Managerial incentives and risk-taking. *Journal of Financial Economics, 79*(2), 431–468.

Damasio, A. (2006). *Descartes' error: Emotion, reason and the human brain*. Vintage.

Dillerup, R., & Stoi, R. (2011). *Unternehmensführung, 3*. ed.

Driscoll, P. A. (1992). Sears settles allegations of shoddy and unnecessary auto repairs. In *AP News*, September 3, 1992. https://apnews.com/0b3e6ba776bd41ff03180ccfc6f5dc85

Elsner, U. (2012). *Korruption sollte auch für Ärzte strafbar sein*. http://www.vdek.com/magazin/ausgaben/2012-0708/politik-einwurf.html.

Falk, A. (2003). Homo oeconomicus versus Homo recipocans: Ansätze für ein neues Wirtschaftspolitisches Weltbild? *Perspektiven der Wirtschaftspolitik, 4*(2003), 141–172.

Fehr, G., & Fischbacher, U. (2001). Are people conditionally cooperative? Evidence from a public goods experiment. *Economics Letters, 71*, 397–404.

Fehr, E., & Fischbacher, U. (2003). The nature of human altruism. *Nature, 425*(23), 785–791.

Fehr, G., Gächter, S., & Fischbacher, U. (2001). Are people conditionally cooperative? Evidence from a public goods experiment. *Economics Letters, 71*, 397–404.

Feldman, Y. (2014). Behavioral ethics meets behavioral law and economics. In E. Zamir & D. Teichman (Eds.), *Oxford handbook of behavioral economics and the law*. Oxford University Press.

Feldman, Y., & Kaplan, Y. (2019). Behavioral ethics as compliance. In B. van Rooij & D. D. Sokol (Eds.), *Cambridge handbook of compliance* (Faculty of Law Research Paper No. 19–18). Bar Ilan University. https://papers.ssrn.com/sol3/papers.cfm?abstract_id=3458582

Feldman, Y., & Lobel, O. (2009). The incentives matrix: The comparative effectiveness of rewards, liabilities, duties, and protections for reporting illegality. *Texas Law Review, 88*(6), 1151–1212.

Feldman, Y., & Perez, O. (2012). Motivating environmental action in a pluralistic regulatory environment: An experimental study of framing, crowding out, and institutional effects in the context of recycling policies. *Law & Society Review, 46*(2), 405–442.

Feldman, Y., & Tyler, T. R. (2012). Mandated justice: The potential promise and possible pitfalls of mandating procedural justice in the workplace. *Regulation & Governance, 6*(1), 46–65.

Fritsch, M., Ewers, H.-J., & Wein, T. (2011). *Marktversagen und Wirtschaftspolitik: Mikroökonomische Grundlagen staatlichen Handelns*. Verlag Franz Vahlen.

Furubotn, E. G., & Richter, R. (2005). *Institutions and economic theory*. University of Michigan Press.

Gabisch, G. (2003). Unternehmen und Haushalte, Vahlens Kompendium der Wirtschaftstheorie und Wirtschaftspolitik. In H. Berg, D. Cassel, & K.-H. Hartwig (Eds.), *Unternehmen und Haushalte* (Bd. 2). Vahlen.

Gilla, D., Prowseb, V., & Vlassopoulosc, M. (2013). Cheating in the workplace: An experimental study of the impact of bonuses and productivity. *Journal of Economic Behavior & Organization, 96*(December), 120–134. http://ftp.iza.org/dp6725.pdf

Gino, F., Ayal, S., & Ariely, D. (2013). Self-serving altruism? The lure of unethical actions that benefit others. *Journal of Economic Behavior & Organization, 93*, 291–292.

Gneezy, U. (2005). Deception: The role of consequences. *American Economic Review, 95*(1), 384–394.

Göbel, E. (2010). *Unternehmensethik*. UTB.
Graeff, P. (2002). Positive und negative ethische Aspekte von Korruption. *Sozialwissenschaften Berufspraxis 25*(3), 291–302. http://nbn-resolving.de/urn:nbn:de:0168-ssoar-37838. accessed 8. Mai 2015.
Greenwald, A. G. (1980). The totalitarian ego. Fabrication and revision of personal history. *American Psychologist, 35*(7), 603–618.
Griffin, D. W., & Lee, R. (1991). Subjective construal, social inference, and human misunderstanding. In M. P. Zanna (Ed.), *Advances in experimental social psychology* (Vol. 24, p. 319). Academic.
Harris, S. L., Mussen, P. H., & Rutherford, E. (1976). Some cognitive, behavioral, and personality correlates of maturity of moral judgment. *Journal of Genetic Psychology, 128*(1), 123–135.
Hollinger, R. C., & Clark, J. P. (1983, December). Deterrence in the workplace: Perceived certainty, perceived severity, and employee theft. *Social Forces, 62*(2), 398–418. https://doi.org/10.1093/sf/62.2.398
Holzmann, R. (2015). *Wirtschaftsethik*. Springer Gabler.
Homann, K. (2003). Anreize und moral. In C. Lütge (Hrsg.), *Unternehmensethik und Korruption* (S. 233–267). LIT.
Homann, K., & Blome-Drees, F. (1992). *Wirtschafts- und Unternehmensethik*. Vandenhoeck.
Hornstein, H. A., Fisch, E., & Holmes, M. (1968). Influence of a model's feeling about his behavior and his relevance as a comparison other on observers' helping behavior. *Journal of Personality and Social Psychology, 10*(3), 222–226.
Jain, A. K. (2001). *The political economy of corruption*. Routledge.
Josephson Institute of Ethics. (2006, October 15). Report card on the ethics of American youth. Available at http://www.josephsoninstitute.org/reportcard/
Kahneman, D. (2011). *Thinking, fast and slow*. Allen Lane.
Kahneman, D., & Tversky, A. (1979). Prospect theory: An analysis of decision under risk. *Econometrica, 47*(2), 263–292.
Kahneman, D., & Tversky, A. (1981). The framing of decisions and the psychology of choice. *Science, 211*, 453–457.
Kahneman, D., & Tversky, A. (1982). The psychology of preferences. *Scientific American, 146*, 160–173.
Kahneman, D., & Tversky, A. (1984). Choices, values and frames. *American Pschologist, 39*(4), 342–350.
Kahneman, D., & Tversky, A. (1986). Rational choice and the framing of decisions. *Journal of Business, 59*(4), 5251–5278.
Kahneman, D., Knetsch, J., & Thaler, R. (1991). Anomalies: The endowment effect, loss aversion and status quo bias. *The Journal of Economic Perspectives, 5*(1), 193–206.
Keuchel, J. (2002). Aufseher nehmen Exportwirtschaft ins Visier. In *Handelsblatt vom*. http://www.handelsblatt.com/archiv/schmiergeldzahlungen-ins-ausland-nicht-mehr-absetzbaraufsehernehmenexportwirtschaft-ins-visier/2203170.html. Zugegriffen: 14. Okt. 2002.
Kirchgässner, G. (1991). Homo Oeconomicus (J. C. B. Mohr (Paul Siebeck), Tübingen, 1991).
Kouchaki, M. (2013). Professionalism and moral behavior: Does a professional SelfConception make one more unethical?. Edmond J. Safra working papers 4. https://doi.org/10.2139/ssrn.2243811.
Krueger, A. O. (1974). The political economy of a rent seeking society. *American Economic Review, 64*(June), 291–303.
Kühberger, A. (1995). The framing of decisions: A new look at old problems. *Oragnizational Behaviour and Human Decision Processes, 62*(2), 230–240.
Kunda, Z. (1990). The case for motivated reasoning. *Psychology Bulletin, 108*, 480–498.
Lambsdorff, J. G. (2002). Korruption – Ausmaß und ökonomische Folgen. *Wirtschaftsdienst, 31*(9), 544–547.

Langevoort, D. C. (2015). *Behavioral ethics, behavioral compliance*. http://scholarship.law.georgetown.edu/facpub/1507 http://ssrn.com/abstract=2651101

Lin-Hi, N. (2014). Der Ehrbare Kaufmann. In Hrsg. Industrie und Handelskammer Nürnberg für Mittelfranken. Der Ehrbare Kaufmann: Tradition und Verpflichtung. Nürnberg.

List, J. A. (2006). The. *Behavioralist Meets the Market: Measuring Social Preferences and Reputation Effects in Actual Transactions, Journal of Political Economy, 2006, 114*(1), 1–37.

Lück, H. E., & Manz, W. (1973). Die Technik der verlorenen Briefe – Ein neues Instrument verhaltensbezogener Einstellungsmessung? *Zeitschrift für Soziologie, 2*(4), 352–365.

Luhmann, N. (2000). *Vertrauen: Ein Mechanismus der Reduktion sozialer Komplexität*. UTB.

Mazar, N., Amir, O., & Ariely, D. (2008). The dishonesty of honest people: A theory of self-concept maintenance. *Journal of Marketing Research, 45*(6), 633–644. Available at SSRN. https://ssrn.com/abstract=979648

McClure, S., Laibson, D. I., Loewenstein, G., & Cohen, J. (2004). Separate neural systems value immediate and delayed monetary rewards. *Science, 306*, 503–507.

Meyerowitz, B. E., & Chaiken, S. (1987). The effect on message framing on breast-self-examination attitudes, intentions and behavior. *Journal of Personality and Social Psychology, 52*(1987), 500–510.

Pham, M. T. (2007). Emotion and rationality: A critical review and interpretation of empirical evidence. *Review of General Psychology, 11*(2), 155–178.

Pritzl, R. F. J., & Schneider, F. (1999). *Korruption*, In Handbuch der Wirtschaftsethik, Vol. 4: Ausgewählte Handlungsfelder, edited by. W. Korff. , Gütersloher Verlagshaus, S. 310–333.

Rapoport, A., & Chammah, A. M. (1970). *Prisoner's Dilemma – A study in conflict and cooperation* (2nd ed.). University of Michigan Press.

Sanitioso, R., Kunda, Z., & Fong, G. T. (1990). Motivated recruitment of autobiographical memories. *Journal of Personality and Social Psychology, 59*(2), 229–241. –359.

Schmeltzer, J. (1992). Sears settlement seeks to fix car-repair image. In C. Tribune, 3. September 1992. https://www.chicagotribune.com/news/ct-xpm-1992-09-03-9203200288-story.html

Schneider, K. (1992). Emotionen. In H. Spada (Ed.), *Lehrbuch allgemeine Psychologie* (2. ed., pp. 403–449). Huber.

Schwägerl, C., & Traufetter, G. (2011). Klinisch tot. In *DER SPIEGEL 42/2011*. http://www.spiegel.de/spiegel/print/d-81015403.html

Schwaninger, M. (2008). Anatol Rapoport (May 22, 1911–January 20, 2007). pioneer of systems theory and peace research, mathematician, philosopher and pianist. *Wiley Online Library Systems Research and Behavioral Science, 24*(6), 655–658.

Schwarz, Norbert; Vaughn, Leigh Ann (2002), The availability heuristic revisited: Ease of recall and content of recall as distinct sources of information, in: Thomas Gilovich, Dale W. Griffin, Daniel Kahneman (eds.) Heuristics and biases: The psychology of intuitive judgment; Cambridge University Press, pp. 103–119.

Schwarz, N., Bless, H., Starck, F., Klumpp, G., Rittenauer-Schatka, H., & Simons, A. (1991). Ease of Retrieval as information: Another look at the availability heuristic. *Journal of Personality and Social Psychology, 61*(2), 195–202.

Shu, L. L., Gino, F., & Bazerman, M. H. (2011). Dishonest deed, clear conscience: When cheating leads to moral disengagement and motivated forgetting. *Personality and Social Psychology Bulletin, 37*(3), 330–349.

Shu, L. L., Mazar, N., Gino, F., Ariely, D., & Bazerman, M. H. (2012). Signing at the beginning makes ethics salient and decreases dishonest self-reports in comparison to signing at the end. *Proceedings of the National Academy of Sciences, 109*(38), 15197–15200.

Simon, H. A. (1959). Theories of decision-making in economics and Behavioral science. *The American Economics Review, 49*(3), 1.

Steinherr, C., Steinmann, H., & Olbrich, T. (1997). Die US-SentencingCommissionGuidelines, eine Dokumentation, Diskussionsbeitrag Nr. 90 des Lehrstuhls für Allgemeine Betriebswirtschaftslehre und Unternehmensführung der Universität Erlangen-Nürnberg (Nürnberg, 1997).

Sunstein, C. (2009). *Going to extremes: How like minds unite and divide*. Oxford University Press. ISBN 9780199793143.

Thaler, R., & Sunstein, C. R. (2003). Libertarian paternalism. *American Economic Review Papers and Proceedings, 92*(2), 175–179.

Thaler, R. H., & Sunstein, C. R. (2008, April 8). *Nudge: Improving decisions about health, wealth, and happiness*. Yale University Press. ISBN 978-0-14-311,526-7. OCLC 791403664.

Thaler, R. H., Sunstein, C. R., & Balz, J. P. (2010). *Choice architecture* (April 2, 2010). https://doi.org/10.2139/ssrn.1583509. SSRN 1583509

Tyler, T. E. (1990). *Why people obey the law*. Yale University Press. http://www.psych.nyu.edu/tyler/lab/Chapters_1-4.pdf

Tyler, T., Dienhart, J., & Thomas, T. (2008). The ethical commitment to compliance: Building values-based cultures. *California Management Review, 50*, 31–51.

Underwood, B., & Moore, B. (1982). Perspective-taking and altruism. *Psychological Bulletin, 91*(1), 143–173.

van den Akker, L., Heres, L., Lasthuizen, K., & Six, F. (2009). Ethical leadership and trust: It's all about meeting expectations. *Int. J. Lead. Stud., 5*(2), 102–122. www.regent.edu/. . ./IJLS_vol5_iss2_akker_ethical_1

Weisser, J. (2012). *Pfand und Anreizsysteme, 1*. ed.

Welge, M., & Al-Laham, A. (2008). Strategisches Management (5th ed.). Wiesbaden: Springer.

Whitman, G (2006), Against the new paternalism. Internalities and the economics of self-control. Cato Institute, Policy Analysis No.563 (February 2006).

Williamson, O. E. (1979). *The economic institution of capitalism*. Free Press. 1985.

Williamson, O. E. (1985). Transaction cost economics: The governance of contractual relations. *Journal of Law and Economics, 12*(2), S. 233–261.

Wiltermuth, S. S. (2011). Cheating more when the spoils are split. *Organizational Behavior and Human Decision Processes, 115*(2), 157–168.

Windeler, A. (2014). *Kompetenz: Sozialtheoretische Perspektiven* (VS Verlag für Sozialwissenschaften).

Wright, J., & Ginsberg, D. (2012, February 16). Free to err?: Behavioral law and economics and its implications for liberty. *Library of Law & Liberty*. https://www.lawliberty.org/liberty-forum/free-to-err-behavioral-law-and-economics-and-its-implications-for-liberty/

Zaltman, G. (2000). Consumer researchers: Take a hike! *Journal of Consumer Research, 26*(4), 423–428. https://doi.org/10.1086/209573

Chapter 6
Traits of the Political System

What Follows and Why?
Now that we have dealt with the market failure, we want to investigate the question of whether politics makes economic decisions in a pareto-efficient or socially maximizing way. The behavior of politicians and the voting procedures necessary for decisions form the political decision-making framework for economic policy. Politics manages democracy and must remedy the market failure and provide goods. To do this, it needs a bureaucracy to implement political decisions about the production of public goods. Here, too, we want to analyze the motives behind a bureaucracy and, in particular, whether it can efficiently implement political decisions. With discourse ethics we will analyses the basis for a legitimate decision making process.

Learning Goals
After this chapter you should be able to explain the voting procedures with their advantages and disadvantages and be able to portray the essential theories about the behavior of politicians in your own words.

6.1 The New Political Economy

An explanation for the decision-making behavior of political decision-makers is provided by the approach of the "New Political Economy".[1] According to the approach of the New Political Economy (NPE), which emerged in the early seventies, a politician does not maximize the common good, but predominantly

[1] The behavioral theories of Smith and Schumpeter have picked up on Downs in the USA and Herder-Dorneich in Germany, thus founding the New Political Economy. See Starbatty (1985), S.40; Schumpeter (1993), S. 427ff; Andel (1990), S. 48; Downs (1957) and Herder-Dorneich (1957).

C. A. Conrad, *Economic Systems, Markets and Politics*,
https://doi.org/10.1007/978-3-031-10366-7_6

his own benefit. Political offices provide benefits in the form of power, prestige and income. In order to achieve the desired office, the politician must collect as many electoral votes – one speaks of maximizing votes (homo politicus). This behavioral orientation is called "political rationality" (assumption utilitarianism = utility maximization).[2] There is thus a divergence between political rationality (own benefit) and social rationality (social benefit), and there may be conflicts of interest between the benefits of the policy and the social benefits,[3] but politicians should represent the social interests. For this reason, the influence of other interests on politicians must be prevented. Donations to parties and politicians as well as additional income have to be disclosed and limited.

The New Political Economy is confirmed by psychology.[4] Motivation for power, as the goal to influence or impress other people, is an act of maximizing utility and making it more difficult to act altruistically in the interests of society. People motivated by power are particularly attracted to political offices. The tendency to draw satisfaction from the physical, mental or emotional influence on others is harmful for third parties and thus also unethical. It is the tyrants who must fear democracy.

People shy away from change when they cannot assess how they are affected. The status quo is preferred over another alternative (status quo bias). Samuelson and Zeckhauser also identified an advantage of the incumbent in political elections.[5] Fernandez and Rodrik state a status quo bias in trade liberalization reforms in developing countries. At first the population was against it, later when she realized that she benefited.[6]

Thaler showed that people discount inconsistent time because they value things that happen in the short term more than events in the future. There is a present-day preference. Experiments show that the future benefit does not decrease continuously. This is called hyperbolic discounting.[7] Politicians can take advantage of the underweighting of long-term events by making voter elections unpopular after the elections and popular pre-electoral decisions, as in the Nordhaus economic model. And they can combine underweighting of long-term events with the status quo bias by making unpopular decisions, such Establish the introduction of the euro in Germany as a jam today, but only follow the implementation in the long term. This reduces the political resistance as political costs.

---

[2] An empirical verification of further parts of the New Political Economy was carried out by Meyer-Krahmer. See Meyer-Krahmer (1979). See also *Franke.* See Franke (1996), Downs (1968), Andel (1990), S. 47ff; Braybrooke and Lindblom (1963) and Lindblom (1965).

[3] See also the trade-offs between economic and political objectives presented in Chap. 2.

[4] See Brandstätter, Veronika, Schüler, Julia, Puca, Rosa Maria, and Lozo, Ljubica (2018) and Schultheiss, O. C. (2008).

[5] See Samuelson and Zeckhauser (1988) and Beck (2014), p. 165.

[6] See Fernandez and Rodrik (1991), pp. 1146–1155 and Beck (2014), p. 165.

[7] See Thaler (1981) and Frederick et al. (2002), p. 360 and Beck (2014), p. 215.

Moral hazards are an incentive for individuals to act against or at the expense of many, society or their company. Politicians also have moral hazard, and politicians are not liable for the long-term damage to their policies. Only the short-term disadvantages of their policies are relevant as long as they affect reelection.

Example: It is politically rational to finance the pensions with debt, because the future generation is not entitled to vote. The funding hits the successor, so it's good for the politician. The Italian politician Berlusconi has promised tax gifts in the election campaign and funded this debt. This led Italy into the debt crisis. Berlusconi promised a tax relief for the citizens, as it brought him a large number of votes. The intergenerational contract for pensions in Germany was also paid out of the budget, and now the pension contributions are rising, but the expected pension of the next generation continues to decline. Politicians in all democracies have increased indebtedness to the detriment of future generations.

Especially in this regard, the press has the special task to point out the long-term policy consequences. The press is not allowed to be dependent on advertising or a private owner. It must analyze the work of politicians also independently and unprejudiced and explain it to the public. Freedom of expression and the press must not be impaired.

If there are hardly any altruistic (disinterested, unselfish) politicians, they need to be even more controlled. In the context of democracy, the division of powers is of particular importance in this context. The politicians must be subject to the law. In practice, political decisions by courts must be controllable. If the state is not subject to the courts, it can lead to arbitrariness and massive discrimination against minorities due to the lengthy legislative periods and the principle of a simple majority. In this context, it is also problematic if the government can exert influence on the courts via the allocation of employment and promotion. Constitutional judges, like all other judges, should be appointed from within their own ranks.

Politicians are servants of the citizens. They are instructed by you to represent your interests in government. They are similar to the principals in the principal agent theory. For this reason, an incentive (incentivization) would be conceivable as it is for managers: future pensions depend on indicators such as debt, GDP. Principal agent for politicians could be that the payout of their pension depends on a good financial management in the form of low new borrowing.

However, already Adam Smith realized that politicians in exceptional national situations could move from a pure benefit maximizer ("man of the system") to an altruistic statesman ("man of the state").[8] While the vote-maximization hypothesis greatly simplifies the behavioral motives of politicians, it is imperative for national politicians reliant on reelection. Downs' vote-maximization model shows interesting interrelations in this respect.

[8] See Smith (1985), pp. 394.

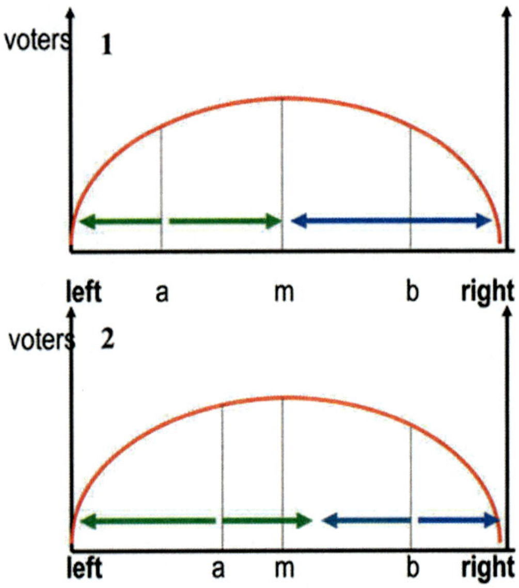

Fig. 6.1 Downs model Situation 1 and 2

6.2 The Vote Maximization Model from Downs

Assumptions:[9]

1. Two parties provide public goods such as social assistance, schools, etc. as electoral promises and compete for the votes of the voters for a government election.
2. Voters have different preferences and choose the politician who maximizes their utility, that is, the election program that comes closest to their wishes. Example: Socialist voters choose the politician who works for the increase in social welfare. Conservative voters choose the politician who works for the reduction of social welfare.
3. The political options can be arranged in a scheme from left to right (extreme: socialist to conservative). The voter distribution for these options corresponds to a normal distribution with m as median

Situation 1 (see Fig. 6.1): Party A (left) represents option a and party B (right) point b, m stands for the median.

Situation 2 (see Fig. 6.2): If party A moves to the right, it can win all voters to the left and half the voters to their right and Party B's point of view.

Situation 3: B has to go to the left to regain votes. A must then react as well and continue to the right. This process continues until both meet at the median

[9] See Downs (1957).

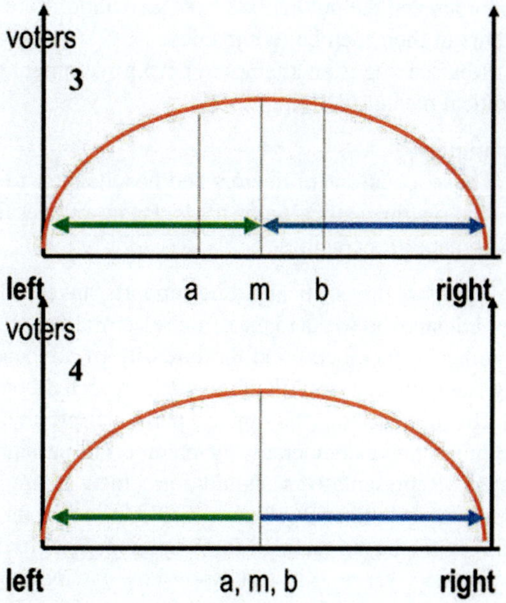

Fig. 6.2 Downs model Situation 3 and 4

position. This is the dominant strategy, since any other strategy will result in losing the election if the other party behaves rationally.

Conclusion

The Downs model confirms the political thesis that the elections are won in the middle. This result is also called median voter theorem. Grand coalitions are more widely accepted by the public during their reign because they represent more voters in the center than middle-margins coalitions. However, the same dominant strategy also creates problems. The party programs are congruent in the middle. In the view of the voters, voting is no longer worthwhile because the electoral programs hardly differ anymore. Voter turnout declines. The members of the parties are becoming increasingly dissatisfied as the parties move away from their original positions towards the center. The edges are no longer politically covered. At some point, new parties form, covering the margins left and right again.

6.3 Interest Groups (Lobbying)

Lobbying, bribing and personal ties also distort the decision-making process of politicians. Through lobbyism (lobbying), companies, associations and interest groups seek to influence government and parliamentary decisions.

The groups affected by the decision of the politician can increase their political influence by organizing themselves into advocacy groups and trying to influence the politician and the public. Business associations are trying in this way to increase the profits of their member companies.

Rent seeking is an attempt to get a government grant without reciprocating, i.e. a political payout (definition).

Examples

- The associations of doctors and hospitals try to receive higher compensation.
- The pharmaceutical industry is trying to meet fewer requirements for the development of medicines.

The more the political public supports stakeholders, the greater their influence on a politician who seeks to maximize electoral votes. A group's degree of organization (number of members) and the intensity of advocacy will be greater, the lower the organization costs and the higher the expected benefit for the individual.

The influence of lobbying is a particular problem of democracy. In countries with a representative democracy, the members of parliament shall represent the will of the voters. Representatives should form their opinions objectively so that they best represent the citizens without considering other interests. They should use objective sources for information to form opinions. Lobbying is actually not permitted in a democracy, yet we must question how far lobbying influences political decisions. There will be no clear answer to this question however, because influence is not transparent. Lobbying is so dangerous precisely because it does not make it clear to the citizen how far a politician's decision reflects their interests or that of a lobbyist.

Lobbying is at least successful enough at influencing policymakers' decision making that it pays off for the industry to make the effort. We can thus conclude from the mere existence of a strong lobby representation that they have influence. Secondary income of politicians and election campaign sponsors are also problematic in this context. A politician and the political parties who, like civil servants, perform sovereign tasks should be financially provisioned so that they do not need additional revenue. If a member gives a speech, it must be assumed that he is doing so in the context of his official duties and therefore does not need to be paid extra. Secondary employment is also to be approved by the employer in the economy because of possible conflicts of interest both in content and time. Otherwise, lobbying will become capitalism's open door to democratic institutions. This undemocratic influence can be strengthened by the election donation dependency of the parties. The financial lobby is one of the largest campaign donors. In addition, numerous public offices have been occupied by former employees, for example, by Goldman Sachs.[10]

Group task: Discuss the political influence of lobbyists. What do you suggest as a solution to the problem?

[10] So did the former Secretary of State for Finance, Clinton Rubin, as well as the Bush Finance Minister Paulson of Goldman Sachs. See Conrad (Ed.) (2015).

Solution One could, for example, equate the profession of representative with that of a normal employee. Then the representative would have to have their other activities approved. You could ban paid additional activities generally or insist that any fees must be donated, for example.

6.4 Economic Theory of Bureaucracy

The employees of government ministries, the so-called bureaucrats, also pursue their own interests (income, prestige, number of employees, promotion, etc.) and are therefore interested in expanding their influence and budget. Bureaucrats have no profit target and therefore no efficiency target. This fosters interventionism and leads to bureaucracy growth and more regulation.

The bureaucrats have an information advantage (asymmetry) over the politicians and the voters about the costs and the production of public goods, which they can use to enhance their importance and budget needs. The quality of the goods provided by the bureaucracy is also difficult for politicians and citizens to assess due to the lack of comparable competitive products. Only quantity is objectively verifiable, which is why bureaucracy tends to produce quantity rather than quality. In this sense, we have the same initial problems as those already described in the bureaucracy of the central administration economy (see Sect. 3.4).

In order to increase their authority, bureaucrats depend on politicians. Politicians provide budgets (appropriation) to the bureaucrats for the production of public goods. Politicians should control the allocation of bureaucracy. However, the question arises whether the politicians have any interest in limiting the bureaucracy. Not as long as they can finance it without political voting losses. On the contrary, politicians are dependent on bureaucracy to fulfill their election promises and generally in implementing their policies. Without the bureaucracy, a politician cannot implement anything and because of the lack of specialist knowledge of the politicians, sometimes they are not even able to explain their policies and make decisions. The bureaucracy provides the public goods. Thus one can speak of a bilateral monopoly in terms of politicians and bureaucracy. Example: Greece's politicians increased the bureaucracy budget as long as it was financially viable. When Greece ceased to receive money from the capital markets, becoming insolvent, one in four Greeks was in government service.[11]

These laws also apply to the bureaucracy at the corporate headquarters of large companies. For example, if the head of a large bank assumes more and more responsibilities, he will be promoted to divisional director due to his many responsibilities and can thus earn a higher income. The quality of his work is difficult to measure, so quantity goes before quality.

---

[11] See http://www.spiegel.de/wirtschaft/soziales/griechische-beamte-superstars-ausser-dienst-a-787835.html

How is it possible to counteract the law of bureaucracy growth? The bureaucracy will always find reasons why they need for a higher budget. For example, a case-by-case examination and approval by Parliament hardly limits the growth of bureaucracy. Restriction can only be achieved through restrictive tax laws and debt limitations. There should be caps on indebtedness and on the tax burden of the citizens enshrined in constitutions. Exceptions to this would be very difficult to achieve, such as a two-thirds majority in parliament. Another way to limit the escalating costs of bureaucracy is to introduce competition in the provision of public goods by allowing private providers alongside public providers. Increased control of bureaucracy can also be achieved through external business consultants. And finally, as with managers, it is also possible to introduce performance and efficiency incentives for officials, for example, through indicators or benchmarks (in-quota).

Conclusion
If politicians do not put social benefits before their own interests they must be controlled and selected by society even more. In addition to an independent press, this requires voting procedures that aggregate the preferences of the citizens. There are also direct votes on economic policy or the provision of public goods such as referendums.

6.5 Voting Procedure

A social discourse does not automatically lead to the best result for the society. Thus we do not always get the best economic policy decisions in a democracy. We want to deal with the reasons in the following section. We already addressed one reason with the group behavior (groupthink) in Sect. 3.3.

Studies show that the group participants do not go into the discussions with an open mind, but try to form their own opinion based on their incomplete pre-information and try to enforce it in the discussion. The discussion participants do not enter the discussion to form an opinion. More shared information is exchanged, which is also more credible in the group because it is represented by several people. If the opinions are similar on the basis of incomplete information, the preconceived opinion will prevail in the discussion regardless of whether it is correct.[12]

[12] See Gigone, D., & Hastie, R. (1993); Stasser, G., & Birchmeier, Z. (2003); Mojzisch, A., Grouneva, L., & Schulz-Hardt, S. (2010); Larson, J. R., Jr., Foster-Fishman, P. G., & Keys, C. B. (1994); Dennis, A. R. (1996); Greitemeyer, T., & Schulz-Hardt, S. (2003); Mojzisch, A., Schulz-Hardt, S., Kerschreiter, R., Brodbeck, F. C., & Frey, D. (2008); Brodbeck, F. C., Kerschreiter, R., Mojzisch, A., & Schulz-Hardt, S. (2007); Mojzisch, A., & Schulz-Hardt, S. (2006); Chernyshenko, Miner, Baumann, & Sniezek (2003) and Schulz-Hardt, S., & Brodbeck, F. C. (2014), pp. 483.

Schulz-Hardt et al. formed, 135 three-person groups out of 405 female and male students and had discussions in various group constellations. The proportion of correct solutions increased with the diversity of opinion (dissent). Groups with the same opinion only made the right decision 7% of the time. When different but wrong opinions were presented at the beginning, at least a quarter of the groups chose the right solution and if one of the dissenting opinions preferred the right solution at the beginning, the success rate rose to 60%. Therefore, it is advantageous if there is a diversity of opinions at the beginning of the discussion. Here, the likelihood is much higher to make the right decision. It is therefore recommended to compile discussion groups with different opinions.[13]

If different opinions are important for a group to come to the right decisions through discourse, this means that marginal opinions and marginalized parties have a special significance in democracy. They should therefore not be perceived as disruptive, but enriching and included in the discussion. The problem is rather the formation of opinions in a few parties, because within the parties, the party hierarchy exerts a strong influence and thus suppresses marginal opinions.

Solomon E. Asch showed in 1955 with the Asch Conformity Experiment, that individuals can adapt to wrong group opinions if the group confidently represents them.[14]

The bigger the group, the stronger their opinion influence is if it represents the majority. Asch later showed that the pressure to conform wears off as soon as the majority opinion is confronted with a contradictory opinion. It is not the social support of the subject with his or her right mindset that is decisive, but that there are other opinions at all. For example, Asch had an assistant agreed with the false opinion, which meant that the subjects again dared to stand up to their correct opinion.[15]

Allen and Levine (1971) noted that influencing opinion also depends on the acceptance of opinion leaders in the group, and Bond and Smith (1996) found in a meta-study that collectivist cultures are more inclined to conform than individualistic cultures.[16]

All the influences on group decisions that hinder informative exchange, causing decisions to be made on a normative basis instead of an informational one, are called groupthink. The group members strive for conformity at the expense of a realistic assessment of alternative courses of action.[17]

---

[13] See Schulz-Hardt et al. (2006), pp. 1080–1093.

[14] Vgl. Asch (1951); Jonas et al. (2014), pp. 9 and Levine and Manning (2014), pp. 379.

[15] Asch, S. E. (1987), pp. 477.

[16] See Allen and Levine (1971); Bond, R., & Smith, P. B. (1996) and Hewstone, M. & Martin, R. (2014), pp. 287.

[17] See Levine, J. M., & Moreland, R. L. (1998) and Hewstone, M. & Martin, R. (2014), p. 302.

How should the provision of public goods be decided? How should decisions be made in economic policy conflicts of interest? For this we need voting procedures. We are looking for a voting procedure that aggregates the preferences of citizens directly or indirectly via representatives of the people, without contradictions and pareto-efficient or use maximizing (as long as one's own benefit increases, one can also take away something from others). Which voting procedures should be used to make economic policy decisions?

6.5.1 Unanimity Rule

At best, Pareto efficiency can be guaranteed by the unanimity rule, because everyone has to agree, and no one loses out (advantage). Decisions reached this way are satisfactory, because there is only a result if everyone agrees. It is thus the procedure with the maximum approval. But there are disadvantages:

1. The cost of decision-making is high because everyone has to agree. It therefore takes a long time to either convince everyone or find an acceptable compromise.
2. Implied right of veto, therefore often no decision is made.

Changes at the expense of everyone, but to the benefit of a decision maker cannot be corrected.

Example: EU treaty changes must be approved by all member states. This means that e.g. The Stability Pact, as a limit to the debt-equity ratio of the EU, can always be relaxed, but never tightened, because all the states concerned must agree to this treaty amendment.[18]

1. **Strategic Voting Process**

There is often a vote exchange called "**log-rolling**". This includes linking temporally successive votes, so that everyone agrees. Disadvantages, which would cause the decision makers to veto, are compensated in other votes: "I'll give my vote when I get yours" is the motto. Then there are the package deals where individual voting issues are agglomerated in a common vote, so that everyone agrees. This way if a decision maker wants to enjoy advantages, they must accept some disadvantages that are advantageous to other decision makers. A **package-deal vote**, in contrast to an exchange of votes, gives decision-makers the certainty that they will get their benefits, whereas in the exchange of votes one party always has to pay in advance. The individual decisions are then no longer pareto-efficient, but the package or the sum of all votes.

[18] See for instance https://www.welt.de/politik/ausland/article13758533/EU-Vertragsaenderung-mit-allen-27-Laendern-gescheitert.html (23.09.2016).

2. **Loss of emergence**

The problem with undermining unanimous decisions through vote exchange and package deals is that the synergy, the emergence is lost. The whole is no bigger than the sum of its parts, because each decision maker maximizes their utility but no longer creates benefits the superordinate organization, such as the EU. One consequence may be utility maximization, but socially sub-optimal voting results (unanimity paradox).[19]

Deals can undermine important economic policy rules (institutions), such as the EU subsidy code. The EU Subsidy Code was overturned by a vote exchange on coal, steel and trade subsidies. In principle, national subsidies were prohibited under Article 4c of the ECSC Treaty. Unanimity was required under Article 95 of the ECSC Treaty for an exception by the Council of Ministers. In 1994 the United Kingdom, Denmark, the Netherlands and Portugal demanded that all subsidy applications be voted on simultaneously (keyword: package solution). The German Economic Minister REXRODT agreed with the idea, pointing out that he could only vote for subsidy applications of the Italian steel company ILVA and the Spanish company CSI if the Council of Ministers approved the application for the German EKO-STAHL. Italy, for its part, made its voting behavior clear: It would agree to the coal subsidies in the Council of Ministers only if they also approved the subsidies for ILVA (keyword: vote exchange).[20] Finally, the Council of Ministers unanimously approved all subsidy applications. By means of package solutions and the exchange of votes, some member states were thus able to circumvent the prohibition on subsidies of the ECSC Treaty or the restrictive subsidy code.[21]

Another example would be a municipal council decision, assuming unanimity. One group wants approval for a swimming pool, another a children's playground and a third group a bypass. But the community can only afford one of these three projects. How will the vote go?

Answer: All three projects are approved because otherwise there is no unanimity (maybe no majority). Each party will agree with the other in a vote exchange to get their own project approved. The damage is borne by the community.

3. The unanimity rule does not aggregate social benefits. It is enough if a decision brings all users some benefit. If there are small disadvantages for a decision maker, they will not agree, although other people affected by the decision would very much benefit from a positive vote. A decision that could not achieve unanimity may be more useful than a unanimous decision, which can lead to socially suboptimal decisions. CONCLUSION: Pareto-efficient or societal benefit-maximizing voting results are unlikely.

[19] See Conrad (2003).

[20] The main interested parties in extending the coal subsidies were Germany and Spain.

[21] See Conrad (1997).

6.5.2 *Majority Rules (Absolute or Relative, Choice of Plurality)*

An absolute majority is reached when a decision gets at least 50% of the votes. With a relative majority the alternative with the most votes wins.

Above all, the advantage of the absolute majority decision is that the costs of the vote are lower than with the unanimity rule. Since there are only two voting points to choose from, there will almost never be stalemates. With the relative majority (choice of plurality), there will be stalemates even in the case of several votes only if there is a tie. The voting procedure is simpler than the unanimity rule. According to utilitarianism, majority voting maximizes the benefits of the majority, but the preferences of the minority get lost. Under certain circumstances, the net benefit for the majority is lower than that of the minority in the vote. There are even decisions at the expense of the minority with a benefit reduction that is greater than the benefit to the majority.

Example: Imagine that in your lecture room you put the decision to the vote that all blonds should give the brunettes 100 €. If there are more brunettes than blonds, you should get the majority for this decision.

An important principle of democratic voting is therefore that all parties involved in the decision must be involved in the vote, otherwise decisions are made at the expense of third parties (for example, the financing of government expenditure with debt at the expense of future generations). To include the future generations more intensively, one could discuss that parents have a separate right to vote on behalf of their children. Even if it would only count as half a vote and parents do not always know what their children want, at least the interests of future generations could be included in the vote.

Another Example German Gorleben was chosen for the question of nuclear waste disposal. The residents cannot win a vote against the rest of Germany, which is glad that the nuclear waste is not stored in their vicinity.

In a democratic vote, the result could be that the project receives a political majority, although the loss of value for the minority is greater than the benefit of the majority. Especially in this case, politics would not be a suitably objective decision-maker. Here it would be up to the courts to review the decision of the politicians and to ensure minority protection (see above). In practice, however, the courts are only consulted when the building permit has already been granted and the construction is practically completed. In this context, it is also problematic if the government can exert influence on the courts via the allocation of employment and promotion.

Condorcet or Arrow Paradox

There is still a problem of cyclical majorities in paired majority voting: If there are more than two alternatives for more than two voters and if the preferences are not unimodal, the order of voting is crucial to the outcome. There is no transitivity. Condorcet paradox was discovered by MARQUIS DE CONDORCET, French philosopher and mathematician, and occurs in pairwise voting at multi-modal preferences.

Example

Decision makers 1, 2 and 3 are to vote on alternatives A, B and C. The result is the following payoff matrix and preference matrix (Figs. 6.3 and 6.4).

The preference matrix shows that the preferences of decision maker 2 are multi-pronged.

Cyclic majorities.

1. vote: A ⇔ B: 1:2 ⇒ B > A } **C > B > A**

2. vote: B ⇔ C: 1:2 ⇒ C > B } **⇒ C > A**

3. vote: C ⇔ A: 1:2 ⇒ A > C

↑ **Control vote** — **contradiction!**

The order is decisive in the vote C > B > A or A > C, so there is no consistent aggregation of individual preferences and no correct solution.

Fig. 6.3 Payout matrix

decision maker\alternative	1	2	3
A	0	60	40
B	50	0	50
C	55	45	0

Fig. 6.4 Preference matrix

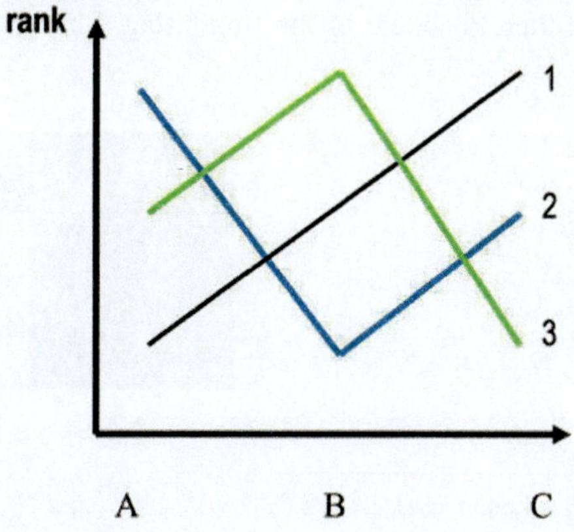

6.5.3 *Borda Rule*

The Borda Rule is a ruling rule that was named after the French mathematician J.C. Borda. In the Borda rule, the intensity of the preferences is weighted, e.g. for three alternatives each decision maker can give 1, 2 and 3 points. The alternative with the most points wins. The weighting makes the social benefits transparent and thus also the willingness to pay for the financing of public goods. Example: The Eurovision Song Contest. Each country can give each song from 1 to 12 points. By the distribution of the points one can weight something more, because 12 points are worth twelve times more than 1 point.

Problem

- If an alternative fails, the order of evaluation of the remaining alternatives changes. You have to re-vote.
- With so many alternatives, the process is too time-consuming, because the decision-maker has to be aware of the relative benefits of all alternatives: how much is this decision-making alternative better than the other.

Exercise Voting Rules

The economist Leininger reconstructed the vote on the German capitol in the Bundestag after the reunification.[22] Here he also took into account various proposals to estimate the preferences of MEPs (see Fig. 6.5). There was a difference in the number of Members' votes in the different ballots, as well as abstentions, which is why the figures do not always add up to 657. We wonder if the result of the vote would always have been Berlin, irrespective of the voting procedure. It is your turn: what is the result of the ballot when using the

1. majority rule,
2. relative majority rule and
3. the Borda rule

Historical Result

At the suggestion of the Council of Elders and after the approval of the Bundestag, the then President of the Bundestag, Süssmuth, had her first vote on the Bonn and

Fig. 6.5 Preferences of the 657 members

	1. preference	2. preference	3. preference
A:Bonn & Berlin	146	222	289
B: Berlin	222	265	170
C: Bonn	289	170	198

[22] See Leininger (1993).

Berlin compromise proposals. As a result, only MPs who had Alternative A as their first preferences chose A. Other MPs still hoped to have their first preference confirmed at the next vote. A was rejected by 489 votes to 147. Ballot B versus C then gave 338 for B and 320 for C, so Berlin became the capitol. This was because Berlin had more first and second preferences.

Conclusion

- Voting results depend on the choice of voting procedures.
- Aggregation of preferences can only be guaranteed through the Borda procedure (maximum social benefit).
- The unanimity criterion guarantees Pareto efficiency in the individual vote, but not in several decisions (due to vote exchange and package deals).
  - If politicians and bureaucracy pursue their own interests, and not those of the general public, the economic constitution must be immunized against the influence of the politicians, so the institutions should be designed so that they place the interests of society above the interests of the politicians,
  - "How can we organize political institutions in such a way that it is impossible for bad or incompetent rulers to inflict too much damage."[23] Elements of direct democracy are recommended here. They would also counteract the strong influence of lobbying and accommodate the argument of the constitutional economists that citizens should be given legitimacy in shaping the institutions.[24]

6.6 Discourse Ethics as Basis for a Legitimate Decision Making Process

What procedure is appropriate for a decision making in a society? Decision-making can also be distinguished from the starting point of the moral and thus legitimate evaluation. Does the individual, the public, a society or a public institution assess whether an action is moral? Individual ethics is understood to mean that man is both the object of ethics and the subject who decides on morality. This moral decision-making process is also referred to as monological ethics, in which the individual himself performs the moral evaluation.[25] Classical ethics, such as that of Kant, is an individual ethics. It is about a good life for the individual and the group. In this respect, the consequences of the actions are closely related. The consequences should be positive for the person and for other people. Ethics in this case is a part

[23] Popper, K. R. (1957), p. 157.

[24] See Feld, L. P., & Köhler, E. (2011). https://nbn-resolving.org/urn:nbn:de:0168-ssoar-349165, p. 179.

[25] See Göbel (2010), pp. 40.

of practical ethics that aims to provide assistance for the perfection of the individual and the wisdom of a group. The goal here is the happiness of all.

Discourse ethics sees the public as the starting point for moral evaluations. Thus Habermas is of the opinion:

> That only those norms which claim to be the consent of all parties concerned as participants in a practical discourse may apply.[26]

Habermas, in this sense, favors the principle of unanimity as a societal method of voting, since everyone can prevent a decision they would find damaging by vetoing. This would also create a kind of benefit maximum. The benefit of one person cannot be increased without decreasing the benefit of another. This Pareto efficiency can best be guaranteed by the unanimity rule, since everyone must agree so that no one is at a disadvantage (advantage). Reaching a decision by this procedure will be satisfying because it will only take effect if there is unanimity. It is considered the procedure with the maximum agreement, but there are also disadvantages, we have already discussed above. It takes a long time to either convince everyone or find an acceptable compromise. Changes that occur to the detriment of all parties, but to the advantage of one decider cannot be corrected. There are log rolling and package deals as a solution but the problem is that the synergy is lost. The whole is no longer greater than the sum of its parts, since each decision-maker maximizes their own utility, but no longer makes use of the utility of the superordinate organization, e.g. of the EU. One result may be that the individual politician can maximize their advantage, but at the expense of socially suboptimal reconciliation results (unanimity-paradox).

We depend on individual ethics in the community. A drowning person needs the help of others. Therefore, even though *according to* individual ethics it is extremely immoral not to help, a refusal to provide aid is additionally sanctioned by society as discourse ethics.

Individual ethics is also the starting point for discourse ethics, since the individual ethics of human beings are incorporated into discourse. Collective ethics can also be seen as a contrast to individual ethics. On the one hand, there is the aspect of control by society, which may be regarded as moral. In the context of public rules, Kant asserts that all actions relating to the rights of other people, with a maxim that is not compatible with public needs, are wrong. On the other hand, the legitimacy of a decision affecting the community makes it necessary for all to have the opportunity to participate in the formation of opinions. This is the basis of a democracy (demos). Public opinion determines the right policy and morality. The public should therefore discuss what it considers to be moral. Habermas and Ulrich are representatives of discourse ethics. However, for an objective opinion formation, Ulrich presupposes that citizens have to be publicly oriented, enlightened and rational. The representatives of discourse ethics also see that these presuppositions are rarely, if at all, given. Neither are all human beings, and therefore the community, adequately morally

[26] Habermas (1991), p. 12 (authors translation). See as one founder Apel (1973).

informed about the well being of the community. This is reflected in all the opportunities for participation in modern democracy. Although at the federal level all citizens are directly affected by decisions, the electoral participation is relatively low. At local level, this deficit of participation is even more evident. There will be not only a lack of interest, but also lack of time. The information necessary for the formation of opinion must also be procured and processed by everyone in discourse ethics.

In the modern western democracies, the task of opinion formation has been taken over the media, and indirectly the control of politics has been taken over by the public, so that we already speak of the fourth branch of government. Information media like television and the Internet are increasingly replacing newspapers, which leads to fewer resources for investigative journalism. A counterweight could be public television.

Habermas sees the modern media world as a hindrance to forming an objective opinion, since the mass media, and above all television, selects and evaluates information before the citizen can encounter it. They are more manipulative than informative. Discussions on public opinion are increasingly rare. As a solution, Habermas proposes that citizens organize themselves more intensively in internal public spheres, for instance parties, associations and interest groups, in order to have more influence on public opinion.[27]

Without a correlation to the usefulness or well being of other people, a distinction between good and evil can neither be made in individual ethics nor in discourse ethics. Schopenhauer already saw the basis for selfless and thus moral action in compassion with the fate of others (compassion ethics):

> "The truth now expressed, that compassion, as the only non-selfish one, is also the only genuine moral motive ..." and "All virtues flow from righteousness and love of mankind ..."[28]
>
> This presupposes, however, that I have certainly identified with the other, and consequently the barrier between myself and non-I, for the moment, is abolished: only then does the matter of the other, its need, its suffering, directly to mine: ....[29]

According to Mead, for example, in his approach as a prerequisite for collective moral decisions, the consequences of a decision should be weighed impartially for all parties concerned, and their interests, by taking the decisive role in the role of other stakeholders.[30]

Rawls developed a similar approach. Everyone is to be freed from his interests by moving into a primal state, without social differences, in order to ensure procedural justice. Proceeding from a veil of ignorance, citizens cannot know what destiny is for them. Their abilities, their origin, their health, their wealth, and their environment are

[27] See Habermas (1975), p. 292.

[28] Schopenhauer (1839), p. 270 (author's translation).

[29] Schopenhauer (1839), p. 269 (author's translation).

[30] See Mead (1968), p. 301.

unknown to them. They could therefore not represent any interests and put themselves into the role of all concerned and consider whether the norm would affect them in an unbiased manner. This impartiality guarantees that just rules for the state and society will be found. This role identification is to be applied when it comes to the design of institutions and social systems. This is the prerequisite for including all those affected by a decision in order to be able to judge the decision from every point of view. He uses this in order to examine the theory of social contract as per Hobbes, Locke, Rousseau, and Kant, the results of which are regarded as just and ethical by all concerned.[31]

Can the group or society in principle evaluate ethically better than the individual? From the approach of discourse ethics one might conclude that a group can better weigh the consequences for third parties or society than a private person affected by the action. From this point of view the victim of an unethical act would not be objective enough. The group or society is legitimized to evaluate actions that affect it, but it is not per se more ethical than an individual. For example, emotions in the group can mutually reinforce each other and lead to irrational, unethical actions. Unethical social trends can be dominant in society, as in National Socialism.[32] Ultimately, in Germany, serious ethical offenses are not left to a jury but to legally trained and ethically qualified judges.

But the discourse ethic is impaired as people prefer conformity and adapt to the political group opinion. To stick to an independent own will leads to suffering. Therefore it is unlikely that everyone's interest is taken into account. What sanctions can groups use to force an individual to comply with the group norms? They range from the withdrawal of recognition by the group, to mobbing to exclusion. Exclusion is the hardest sanction. During simulated exclusion, reactions in the pain center of the brain have been detected.[33]

People rely on social contact to be happy. Everyone needs social acceptance. According to various studies the presence of other people contributes to a feeling of wellbeing, especially if they are familiar people with whom a social relationship already exists. Everyone needs social belonging. There are several studies showing that positive social relationships even promote good health. Berkman and Syme, for example, used a random sample of the population (nearly 7000 inhabitants of Alameda, California) or people with positive social relationships and found a survival probability two to three times greater (2.3 in men and 2.8 in women) after 9 years.[34] This is currently justified in the literature by an evolutionary advantage. People who could rely on the support of others have survived and have been able to

[31] See Rawls (1979), pp. 158, 341 and in the original Rawls (1971), pp. 10, 12, 139.

[32] See also Habermas (1975), p. 279.

[33] See Richman and Leary (2009), pp. 365–383; Eisenberger et al. (2003), pp. 290–292 and Kessler and Fritsche (2018).

[34] See Berkman and Syme (1979) and Karremans and Finkenauer (2014), pp. 403.

reproduce.[35] Here one differentiates between emotional and instrumental social support.[36]

Schachter simulated group socialization processes by inserting dissenters. Since they did not adapt their opinion to the group, they were first marginalized, no longer talked to and ignored. Finally, they were excluded.[37]

In 1955 Solomon E. Asch showed through an experiment in which individuals must say which of three lines is the longest that approx. 37% opted for the wrong group opinion if it was presented sufficiently strongly and dominantly. With the Asch Conformity Experiment, Asch proved that individuals can adapt to wrong group opinions if the group is self-assured.[38]

The larger the group, the stronger its influence on opinion if it represents the majority. Asch later showed that the pressure to conform wears off as soon as the majority opinion is contrasted with a contradictory opinion. Having social support for correct judgment is not the crucial factor, but whether there are other opinions at all. For example, Asch had an assistant give a second false opinion, which led to more subjects being willing to stand up for their correct opinion.[39]

Allen and Levine noted that influencing opinion also depends on the acceptance of opinion leaders in the group (social support), and Bond and Smith (1996) found in a meta-study that collectivist cultures tend to be more opinion-conformant than individualistic cultures.[40]

Three reasons are given to explain the tendency of individuals to adjust their assessment to that of the group opinion. First, only the group can effectively pursue a goal, so the group members must agree in their assessment. Second, due to uncertainty, the individual may question their opinion (informative influence) and correct it, and thirdly adapt to be accepted by group members (normative influence).[41]

All the influences on group decisions that lead to an informative exchange being compromised, so that informational rather than normative decisions will be made, are called groupthinks. The group members strive for conformity at the expense of a realistic appraisal of alternative courses of action.[42]

However, the responsibility for group decisions is problematic. In principle, group ethics cannot replace individual ethics. Everyone must also be responsible for themselves and not just the group. Groups can thus even promote unethical behavior if the individual can hide in the group in order to escape the responsibility for unethical behavior. This is always observed in demonstrations where violent

[35] See Baumeister and Leary (1995), p. 499.

[36] See Karremans, Johan C., Finkenauer, Catrin (2014), pp. 403.

[37] See Schachter (1951) and Karremans and Finkenauer (2014), p. 451.

[38] Vgl. Asch (1951); Jonas, Klaus, Stroebe, Wolfgang & Hewstone, Miles (2007), pp. 9 and Hewstone, M. und Martin, R. (2007), pp. 379.

[39] See Asch (1987), pp. 477.

[40] See Allen and Levine (1971) and Bond and Smith (1996).

[41] See Hewstone and Martin (2014), p. 283.

[42] See Hewstone and Martin (2014), p. 302.

agitators attempt to get lost in the group to avoid prosecution. Criminals are looking for unjust systems to legitimize themselves by the group at the expense of others. Overall, it can be observed that the individual is not responsible for collective decisions. This was also a problem of the socialist or communist central administration economies. As a consequence, politicians should also be responsible for their individual decisions and not just as a group. Whatever parliament decides, each member must be able to justify his voting behavior.

In order to carry out an ethical assessment, the impact of behavior on the welfare of a third party must be assessed. Where to start?

Without individual ethics, an institutional or collective ethics, a prosperous discourse ethics cannot be created because all individuals pursue their own benefit and do not shrink from manipulating information or having conflicts of interest, in order to achieve their goals at the expense of others in the form of strategic bargaining. Thus, on the one hand, people need the right to vote and to regulate procedures by means of a discourse ethics, to grasp and weigh the views and interests of all parties involved in order to arrive at a morally balanced decision or to carry out a moral evaluation as a collective. In addition, they must first be consensus- and common-minded, and thus also morally oriented, and be able to put themselves into the position of other parties in order to develop a moral reconciliation result. Otherwise, suboptimal horse-trading will result in the enforcement of the stronger group or no decision will be made at all. Wiser heads must prevail by relenting. There must be a willingness to subordinate individual needs to the overall interest of the group. In the case of a discourse, the aim should not be to defend its positions against the arguments of the others, but to measure one's own arguments with those of the others in order to find the best solution. The purpose of the discussions is thus the discovery of truth and not pure self-presentation, as is often observed in talk shows.

Does publicity always produce the truth? Let people discuss their sex-life or stereotypes in public. The publicity will hinder people from saying certain things if they expect negative consequences by the public. On the other hand a public discussion, a discursive ethic will not always represent the desire and interests of the people.

How can this be applied to practice in companies? Collective decisions are also made in the economy. The board is a group of experts. In this case, the people representing the company are to aggregate information for uniform company decisions. Particularly in the case of risky decisions, for example credit decisions, a tendency has been observed in which as many employees as possible are asked to co-sign. This means that the responsibility for a wrong decision cannot be attributed to a single individual and liability is difficult to achieve. Without responsibility for the consequences, however, the risk of misjudgment increases, as decisions are made too easily or out of self-interest at the expense of the company (moral hazard).

In principle, group decisions are legitimate because all stakeholders have been involved. A supervisor is therefore well advised to present the decision alternatives of the group (the team) and to obtain statements from the affected parties in the case of important decisions affecting his subordinates. If the supervisor takes the decision and responsibility on himself, those concerned will more likely accept it, in particular those who are negatively affected, because they will at least assume that the supervisor was aware of their position and took it into account when making the decision. Conversely, if the supervisor had decided without the inclusion of the group, he might have turned the group against him. Thus, at least, he could describe his motivations and give the group the feeling of being heard and of their concerns being taking into account. If the group signals that a majority consents to a decision beforehand and their wishes correspond to that of the supervisor, the group is behind the decision, which gives its weight and backing to differing individual opinions.

Finally, the many opinions must be aggregated. Unfortunately, there is no voting procedure that can express the aggregate public opinion in a balanced way. The majority will always dominate the minority. There are also power and information asymmetries in public opinion. Depending on their influence and character, there will always be people who influence public opinion more than others.

What should be taken into account when making a decision? In order to make the right decisions, sufficient information about the effects and the expected results of the decision alternatives with their respective probabilities of occurrence (if available) is needed. But is this sufficient to get the best decisions?

In the democratic market economy there are incentives that promote immoral behavior. As a rule, this means there are advantages for companies through competition restrictions. Decision-making constellations that have a negative impact on society have so far received very little attention, which is why morality plays an important role. The damage and the injured parties from these decisions are often unknown, which is why they are very problematic. The agent will not suffer the damage caused by his decision. The negative consequences of the decision are borne by others. Take, for example, the inclination of politicians to pay for electoral promises through debt and thus shift the burdens from their electorates to the next generation. The next generation is not yet eligible to vote. The future generation is not involved in the decision-making process. Jurisprudence calls these contracts at the expense of third parties. Such negative decision-externalities arise whenever all the parties affected by the decision are not involved in the decision.

Adam Smith,[43] Joseph Alois Schumpeter,[44] and the approach of the "New Political Economy"[45] provide an explanation for the behavior of political decision makers based on these prophesies. For the politician, this behavior is designed to maximize the votes. According to the above already discussed approach of the New Political Economy, the politician is not an altruist maximizing the common good, but rather an individual utility maximizer. Political authorities grant these benefits in the form of power, prestige and income. In order to be able to reach the appointed

[43] See Starbatty (1985), p. 40.

[44] See Schumpeter (1993), pp. 427.

[45] The behavioral hypotheses of Smith and Schumpeter have taken up Downs in the United States and Herder-Dorneich in Germany, thereby establishing the New Political Economy. See Andel (1990), p. 48; Downs (1968) and Herder-Dorneich (1957).

offices, the collection of as many electoral votes as possible – so-called vote maximization – is decisive for the politician. This behavioral orientation can be described as "political rationality" in the sense of political functionality.[46]

Corrupting or manipulating lobbying distorts the political decision-making process and does not lead to democratically just decisions, because the advantage of the politician's decisions are gained at the expense of third parties. The parties concerned must be the central principle of decisions. Discourse ethics only works if all concerned can participate in the discourse.

Lobbying influences politicians' decision-making by convincing them that an expenditure is worthwhile for the industry and does so effectively to judge by the existence of such strong lobby representation. The side effects of politicians and their election campaign donations are also problematic. A politician and the political parties who, like officials, perform sovereign functions should be financially autonomous. If a representative makes a speech, it must be assumed that he does so in the course of his duties and therefore does not need to be paid extra. In the case of business, side jobs can also be approved by the employer both for content and time, due to possible conflicts of interest. Otherwise, lobbyism becomes the gateway of capitalism to undercut democracy. This undemocratic influence can be mitigated by the parties' choice of donor, as it is in the US. This is where the financial gambler appears as one of the largest campaign candidates. In addition, numerous public offices were occupied by former employees, from Goldman Sachs for example.[47]

How can man be morally controlled, and how is moral behavior supported? Incentive ethics (moral economy) emphasizes rules, the framework of action. A company cannot compete against unethical incentives in the competition. This applies equally to the individual in the company. Individual ethical appeal and postulation are regarded as obsolete and meaningless, so intentions and attitudes are not decisive for action.[48]

Discourse ethics focuses on the ethical process, in which the ethical solution is found through the introduction of many points of view and aspects. In this context the individual appears inappropriate.[49] Discourse ethics, however, only works if individuals can bring their own ethically based opinion into the discourse and can identify both ethical arguments and consequences. They must also be able to accept the arguments of the others as a whole for a consensus, and to evaluate their ethical meaning in order to come to a priority and ranking of the arguments.

---

[46] A comprehensive theoretical analysis of political ministerial rationality can be found in Frey, Bruno (1981). An empirical verification of further parts of the New Political Economy was carried out by Meyer-Krahmer.See Meyer-Krahmer (1979). The most comprehensive summary of the approaches of the "New Political Economy" is provided by Franke. See Franke (1996). A good theoretical analysis of political values can be found Downs (1968); Andel (1990), pp. 47; Braybrooke and Lindblom (1963) and Lindblom (1965).

[47] For example, the former Finance Minister of President Clinton Rubin, as well as Finance Minister Bush's Paulson, came from Goldman Sachs. See Conrad (Ed.) (2015).

[48] See Homann and Blome-Drees (1992), pp. 18, 22, 38 and Pies and Blome-Drees (1993), pp. 177.

[49] See Wittmann (1994), pp. 16.

Ultimately, institutional ethics and discourse ethics do not function without individual ethics. National Socialism made it clear that the individual, with reference to the laws, cannot be released from ethical responsibility. No order is comprehensive and no system can control people 100%. A total supervisory state would leave no room for individual freedom. This would also be a contradiction to the dignity of man and to his freedom to make self-responsible decisions. People without conscience are an aberration. This is also recognized by the moral economists and encourages the interplay of moral intentions and the institutional stabilization of moral codes of action.[50] An ethically oriented institutional order must provide the incentives for ethical action and serve as an orientation aid when the individual is overwhelmed by choosing between goods because, for example, he can not estimate all the consequences of his actions. Individual morality is the basis for the ethical order, which cannot exist without it. As already stated, individual morality is also needed as a continuous corrective for an ethical order.

Individual ethics is therefore the basis for ethical evaluations and institutional ethics; individual ethics and discourse ethics must work together.

Decisions are always made by individuals within companies. It is not the companies that can take ethical responsibility, but only the people. A conscience is also required for the ethical weighing of responsibilities. However, the responsibility of the individual must be seen in relation to his or her discretionary competence in the company.

Decisions taken by groups are generally better than individual decisions given unequal information (undivided information) between the members. Studies have shown however, that the group participants do not go into discussions unbiased. Rather, they have already formed their opinion on the basis of their incomplete information and then try to assert this opinion in the discussion. Participants do not enter a discussion to form an opinion, yet more shared information is exchanged, which has more credibility in the group because it is shared by more group members. If the opinions are similar based on the incomplete information, the preconceived opinion will prevail in the discussion, regardless of whether it is right or wrong.[51]

Conclusion

Politicians may make decisions at the expense of the citizens. It is therefore necessary to demand that at least the main interests concerned should be represented in decision making, or that the decisions be sanctioned by those concerned, if only in retrospect.

---

[50] See Enderle (1992), p. 15 and Homann and Blome-Drees (1992), p. 44.

[51] See Gigone and Hastie (1993); Stasser and Birchmeier (2003); Mojzisch et al. (2010); Larson et al. (1994); Dennis (1996); Greitemeyer and Schulz-Hardt (2003); Mojzisch et al. (2008); Brodbeck et al. (2007); Mojzisch and Schulz-Hardt (2006); Chernyshenko et al. (2003); Nijstad and Van Knippenberg (2007), p. 483 and Schulz-Hardt und Felix (2014), pp. 485.

6.7 Political Manipulations

Group Discussion
As we have seen in Sect. 5.4 Kahnemann and Tversky found, that the presentation and formulation of questions affects the decision of subjects. Influencing decisions through representation of the problem of decision-making has since been called framing. Framing can be used as a political instrument. As long as one persuades people with horrible pictures of sick people not to smoke or get a check-up, the purpose may justify the means, but where are the limits to such manipulation of free will? Discuss!

For example, as a politician one can take advantage of citizens' loss anxiety and represent a different taxation of citizens by emphasizing the lower taxation of a group as a benefit (benefit) rather than mentioning the taxation of the other group as a loss. This also leads to illusion of money: An increase of 5% in wages with an inflation rate of 12% is more likely to be accepted than an equivalent real wage reduction of 7%.[52]

Another possibility for manipulation is the so-called shaming. Shaming is the attempt to provoke feelings of guilt in people in order to prevent them from doing certain things.[53]

Shaming identifies emotions that are triggered in the individual in relation to the group. This does not necessarily have to be negative. On the contrary, they act as regulation in order to enforce collective behavior towards self-oriented utility maximization. One feels guilty about breaking the norms of the group and is proud to be fulfilled. So a group can also promote the productivity of their members.[54]

Shaming is voluntary insofar as it only works when the individual enters shaming and allows guilt to be generated. However, this happens predominantly in the area of the subconscious, which can control the individual only to a very limited extent consciously. Furthermore, shaming can lead to sanctions in the group (e.g., exclusion) and is associated with discomfort, so that it would be ethically justifiable on the basis of a social discourse that transparently legitimizes the shaming. However, this kind of manipulation is part of the political discourse, such as the so-called "political correctness",[55] which is why it is cited here, not least in order to create sensitivity in dealing with morals as a political instrument.

For a democratic discourse to be successful, it is also important to allow minor opinions and not to suppress them through shaming.

---

[52] See Kahneman and Tversky (1986).

[53] See Gopalan (2007).

[54] See Lindbeck and Nyberg (2006).

[55] Political correctness is understood here in a politically neutral way as an opinion stipulated by the group that dominates public opinion. Those who think differently are sanctioned by extreme moral exclusion from this group when they express their opinion. This is not a new phenomenon. The zeitgeist, i.e. the opinion of the group, and the dominant group change.

Schulz-Hardt et al. made up of 405 female and male students, 135 three-person groups were formed and discussions were held in various group constellations.

The proportion of correct solutions increased with the diversity of opinion (dissent). Groups with the same opinion only made the right decision 7% of the time. If different but wrong opinions were represented at the beginning, at least a quarter of the groups chose the right solution. And if one of the dissenting opinions preferred the correct solution in the beginning, the success rate rose to 60%. It is therefore advantageous if there are a variety of opinions at the beginning of the discussion. The probability of making the right decision is significantly higher here. It is therefore recommended to set up discussion groups with different opinions.[56]

Experiments show that the future benefit does not decrease continuously. This is called hyperbolic discounting. Thaler asked subjects what interest rate they demanded in order to accept a decrease in value of $15. It turned out that they required a much higher value for short periods of time than for long periods: For 1 month, they demanded $20 (345%), $50 (120%) and $1 for a year 10 years $ 100 (19%).[57] This explains why people renounce a benefit compensation for saving as a short-term consumption in the form of the interest demand.

You can also explain that people plan a lot of good things for the long term, but then do not implement them when the time comes. We want to lose weight, for example, but then when it's time to start the diet we weaken and eat the wrong things. To overcome this weakness, we develop self-imposed limitations. Beck cites as an example the so-called Christmas clubs in the US, where you can deposit money that is paid out again just before Christmas. This is meant to counteract temptation to spend it on other things.[58]

Political measures reflecting the hyperbolic discounting would be to announce unpopular decisions several years earlier so that voters underestimate their future impact. For instance the introduction of the Euro was made public with the Maastricht treaty in 1992 whereas the Euro was introduced in 2002. In several states – especially in Germany – people felt unhappy to quit the national currency. On the contrary, the politicians like German Chancellor Kohl were convinced and committed to introduce a single European currency.

Political manipulation has natural limits, however.

> You can fool all the people some of the time and some of the people all the time, but you cannot fool all the people all the time.[59]

Conclusion

Politicians, bureaucrats and citizens, according to the New Political Economy, like Homo Oeconomicus, maximize their own benefit first, not that of society. Politicians

---

[56] See Schulz-Hardt et al. (2006), pp. 1080–1093.

[57] See Thaler (1981) and Beck (2014), pp. 215.

[58] See Beck (2014), pp. 214.

[59] Abraham Lincoln on September 2, 1858, speaking in Clinton, Illinois, during the famous Lincoln-Douglas debates. https://historynewsnetwork.org/article/161924 (8.05.2019).

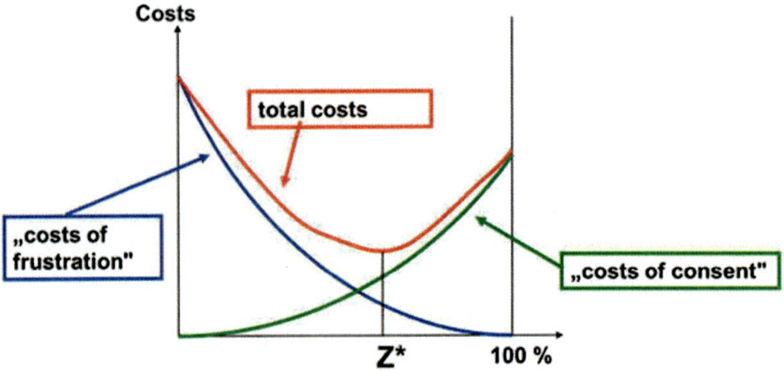

Fig. 6.6 Optimal approval requirement Z *

must therefore be controlled by independent bodies (Federal Constitutional Court) and by institutional guidelines as well as by the press. Each voting procedure has advantages and disadvantages. In addition, as the voting procedures influence the results, it is important to weigh carefully what procedure is chosen. Although the borda method best expresses the social benefits by taking preferences into account, it is surprisingly rarely used in practice. Aggregation of preferences can only be guaranteed by the BORDA criterion. Figure 6.6 shows the relationship between the costs arising from the consideration of all interests in a vote and the "frustration costs" of the voters because they are not sufficiently considered in the vote.

Framing as the manipulative representation of decision information as well as the use of hyperbolic discounting to enforce decisions to the detriment of citizens in the future are to be rejected. Rather, the press in a democracy has the special task of presenting the information so objectively that the citizen can make a decision that is not influenced from outside. Shaming is only justifiable on the basis of a social discourse that transparently legitimizes the shaming.

Ethical Summary

Power motivation, i.e. influencing or impressing other people, plays a major role in politics; it must be controlled institutionally. People shy away from change when they cannot assess how they are affected. The status quo is preferred over another alternative (status quo bias).

If there are hardly any altruistic (disinterested, unselfish) politicians, they need to be even more controlled. For this reason, the influence of other interests on politicians must be prevented. Donations to parties and politicians as well as additional income have to be disclosed and limited. The tendency to draw satisfaction from the physical, mental or emotional influence on others is harmful for third parties and thus also unethical. It is the tyrants who must fear democracy. In the context of democracy, the division of powers is of particular importance in this context. The politicians must be subject to the law. In practice, political decisions by courts must be controllable.

Discourse ethics is proposed as a solution to find a decision that comprises and the interests of all citizens, thus collective moral decisions. By taking the decisive role in the role of other stakeholders the consequences of the decision should be weighed impartially for all parties concerned, and their interests. This discourse has to take place in public and must be transparent. Everybody concerned by the decision must be able to participate in the decision making process. The decision alternatives and their probable outcome must be explained to the citizens by the press before the voting takes place. However, behavioral sciences shows that group decisions have their own rules that impede an equal representation of interests.

Behavioral Summary

The New Political Economy is confirmed by psychology. Motivation for power, as the goal to influence or impress other people, is an act of maximizing utility and making it more difficult to act altruistically in the interests of society. In addition there is a moral hazard problem as politicians are not liable for the long-term damage to their policies.

A problem is that people shy away from change when they cannot assess how they are affected. The status quo is preferred over another alternative. Thus, the incumbent has always an advantage in political elections. Moreover, with framing he has instruments to manipulate the political perception of the citizens. With hyperbolic discounting politicians can take advantage of the underweighting of long-term events by making voter elections unpopular after the elections and popular pre-electoral decisions. Shaming is only a political instrument if there is a dominant political mainstream of the same bent covered by the press. So a free press is not always a guaranty for the free will. As behavioral science shows people prefer conformity and adapt to the political group opinion. To stick to an independent own will leads to suffering. Therefore it is unlikely that everyone's interest is taken into account.

Comprehension Questions

1. Weigh the pros and cons of the voting procedures against each other. Which would you prefer and why?
2. What is meant by the Condorcet paradox?
3. (a) What is meant by package deals and the exchange of votes?
   (b) Explain the pros and cons.
4. Give an example from politics where political benefits and social benefits diverge. Justify your choice. What do you suggest to encourage the politician to pursue more of the social benefits?
5. Are you aware of examples where politicians have decided against their own benefit in order to pursue the social benefits? Explain your assessment. Is this the refutation of the New Political Economy?
6. What does the vote-maximization model of Downs show?

Literature

Allen, V. L., & Levine, J. M. (1971). Social support and conformity: The role of independent assessment of reality. *Journal of Experimental Social Psychology, 7*, 48–58.

Andel, N. (1990). *Finanzwissenschaft* (3rd ed.). Mohr.

Apel, K.-O. (1973). *Transformation der Philosophie, Das Apriori der Kommunikationsgemeinschaft und die Grundlagen der Ethik: Zum Problem einer rationalen Begründung der Ethik im Zeitalter der Wissenschaft* (K.-O. Apel, Ed., Bd. 2, pp. 358–435). Suhrkamp (Orig.: 1972).

Asch, S. E. (1951). Effects of group pressure upon the modification and distortion of judgments. In H. Guetzkow (Ed.), *Groups, leadership and men; research in human relations* (pp. 177–190).

Asch, S. E. (1987). *Social psychology*. Oxford University Press.

Baumeister, R. F., & Leary, M. R. (1995). The need to belong: Desire for interpersonal attachments as a fundamental human motivation. *Psychological Bulletin, 117*, 497–529.

Beck, H. (2014). Behavioral economics: Eine Einführung. Wiesbaden: Springer.

Berkman, L. F., & Syme, S. L. (1979). Social networks, host resistance, and mortality: A nine year follow-up study of Alameda County residents. *American Journal of Epidemiology, 109*, 186–204.

Bond, R., & Smith, P. B. (1996). Culture and conformity: A meta-analysis of studies using Asch's (1952b, 1956) line judgment task. *Psychological Bulletin, 119*, 111–137.

Brandstätter, V., Schüler, J., Puca, R. M., & Lozo, L. (2018). *Motivation und emotion*. Springer.

Braybrooke, D., & Lindblom, C. E. (1963). *A strategy of decision*. Free Press.

Brodbeck, F. C., Kerschreiter, R., Mojzisch, A., & Schulz-Hardt, S. (2007). Group decision making under conditions of distributed knowledge: The information asymmetries model. *Academy of Management Review, 32*, 459–479.

Chernyshenko, O. S., Miner, A. G., Baumann, M. R., & Sniezek, J. A. (2003). The impact of information distribution, ownership, and discussion on group member judgment: The differential cue weighting model. *Organizational Behavior and Human Decision Processes, 91*, 12–25.

Conrad, C. A. (1997). *Europäische Stahlpolitik zwischen politischen Zielen und ökonomischen Zwängen*. Nomos.

Conrad, C. A. (Hrsg.) (2015): Unternehmenssteuerung und Ethik – eine empirische und theoretische Untersuchung ausgewählter Fallbeispiele aus der Finanzbranche und anderen Branchen. Hamburg: Disserta.

Conrad, C. A. (2003). The dysfunctions of unanimity: Lessons from the EU steel cri-sis. *Journal of Common Market Studies, 41*(1), 157–169.

Dennis, A. R. (1996). Information exchange and use in small group decision making. *Small Group Research, 27*, 532–550.

Downs, A. (1957). *An economic theory of democracy. New York 1957 (deutsch 1968).* Ökonomische Theorie der Demokratie.

Downs, A. (1968). *Ökonomische Theorie der Demokratie*. Tübingen: Mohr.

Eisenberger, N. I., Lieberman, M. D., & Williams, K. D. (2003). Does rejection hurt? An fMRI study of social exclusion. *Science, 302*, 290–292.

Enderle, G. (1992). Aktuelle Probleme der Wirtschaftsethik. In K. Homann (Ed.), *Grundlegung einer Unternehmensethik: das Unternehmen als moralischer Akteur* (pp. S. 143–S. 158). Duncker & Humblot.

Feld, L. P., & Köhler, E. (2011). Ist die Ordnungsökonomik zukunftsfähig? *Zeitschrift für Wirtschafts- und Unternehmensethik, 12*(2), 173–195. https://nbn-resolving.org/urn:nbn:de:0168-ssoar-349165.

Fernandez, R., & Rodrik, D. (1991). Resistance to reform: Status quo bias in the presence of individual- specific uncertainty. *American Economic Review 1991, 81*(5), 1146–1155.

Franke, S. F. (1996). *(Ir) rationale Politik?* Metropolis.

Frederick, S., Loewenstein, G., & O'Donoghue, T. (2002). Time discounting and time preference: A critical review. *Journal of Economic Literature, 40*(2), 351–401.

Frey, B. S. (1981). *Theorie demokratischer Wirtschaftspolitik.* Vahlen.

Gigone, D., & Hastie, R. (1993). The common knowledge effect: Information sharing and group judgment. *Journal of Personality and Social Psychology, 65*, 959–574.

Göbel, E. (2010). *Unternehmensethik.* UTB.

Gopalan, S. (2007). Shame sanctions and excessive CEO pay. *Delaware Journal of Corporate Law, 32*, 757–797.

Greitemeyer, T., & Schulz-Hardt, S. (2003). Preference-consistent evaluation of information in the hidden profile paradigm: Beyond group-level explanations for the dominance of shared information in group decisions. *Journal of Personality and Social Psychology, 84*, 322–339.

Habermas, J. (1975). *Strukturwandel der Öffentlichkeit* (7th ed.). Luchterhand.

Habermas, J. (1991). *Erläuterungen zur Diskursethik.* Suhrkamp Verlag.

Herder-Dorneich, P. (1957). Theorie der Bestimmungsfaktoren finanzwissenschaftlicher Staatstätigkeit. Dissertation, Freiburg.

Hewstone, M., & Martin, R. (2007). Sozialer Einfluss. In K. Jonas, W. Stroebe, & M. Hewstone (Eds.), *Sozialpsychologie* (5th ed., pp. 359–408). Springer.

Hewstone, M., & Martin, R. (2014). Sozialer Einfuss. In K. Jonas, W. Stroebe, & M. Hewstone (Eds.), *Sozialpsychologie, 6., vollständig überarbeitete Aufage* (pp. 269–314). Springer- Verlag.

Homann, K., & Blome-Drees, F. (1992). *Wirtschafts- und Unternehmensethik.* Utb.

Jonas, K., Stroebe, W., & Hewstone, M. (2007). Einführung in die Sozialpsychologie. In K. Jonas, W. Stroebe, & M. Hewstone (Eds.), *Sozialpsychologie* (5th ed., pp. 1–32). Springer.

Jonas, K., Stroebe, W., & Hewstone, M. (2014), Einführung in die Sozialpsychologie, In J. Klaus, S. Wolfgang, H. Miles (Hrsg.), *Sozialpsychologie, 6. ed.* (pp. 1–29). Springer.

Kahneman, D., & Tversky, A. (1986). Rational choice and the framing of decisions. *Journal of Business, 59*(4), 5251–5278.

Karremans, J. C., & Finkenauer, C. (2014). Affiliation, zwischenmenschliche Anziehung und enge Beziehungen. In K. Jonas, W. Stroebe, & M. Hewstone (Eds.), *Sozialpsychologie* (6th ed.). Springer.

Kessler, T., & Fritsche, I. (2018). *Sozialpsychologie.* Springer.

Larson, J. R., Jr., Foster-Fishman, P. G., & Keys, C. B. (1994). Discussion of shared and unshared information in decision-making groups. *Journal of Personality and Social Psychology, 67*, 446–461.

Leininger, W. (1993). The fatal vote: Berlin versus Bonn, Finanz Archiv, Bd. 50, Nr. 1, S. 1–20.

Lindbeck, A., & Nyberg, S. (2006). Raising children to work hard: altruism, work norms, and social insurance, quarterly *Journal of Economics*, November 2006, 121(4), 1473–1503.

Lindblom, C. E. (1965). *The intelligence of democracy.* The Free Press.

Levine, M., & Manning, R. (2014). Prosoziales Verhalten. In K. Jonas, W. Stroebe, & M. Hewstone (Eds.), *Sozialpsychologie, 6., vollständig überarbeitete Auflage* (pp. 357–400). Springer.

Levine, J. M., & Moreland, R. L. (1998). Small groups. In D. T. Gilbert, S. T. Fiske, & G. Lindzey (Eds.), *Handbook of social psychology* (Vol. 1, 4th ed., pp. 415–469). McGraw-Hill.

Mead, G. H. (1968). *Geist Identität und Gesellschaft.* Suhrkamp Verlag.

Meyer-Krahmer, F. (1979). *Politische Entscheidungsprozesse und Ökonomische Theorie der Politik.* Campus Verlag.

Mojzisch, A., & Schulz-Hardt, S. (2006). Information sampling in group decision making. In K. Fiedler & P. Juslin (Eds.), *Sampling and adaptive cognition* (pp. 299–326). Cambridge University Press.

Mojzisch, A., Schulz-Hardt, S., Kerschreiter, R., Brodbeck, F. C., & Frey, D. (2008). Social validation in group decision-making: Differential effects on the decisional impact of preference-consistent and preference-inconsistent information. *Journal of Experimental Social Psychology, 44*, 1477–1490.

Mojzisch, A., Grouneva, L., & Schulz-Hardt, S. (2010). Biased evaluation of information during discussion: Disentangling the effects of preference consistency, social validation, and ownership of information. *European Journal of Social Psychology, 40*, 946–956.

Nijstad, B. A., & Van Knippenberg, D. (2007). Gruppendynamik. In K. Jonas, W. Stroebe, & M. Hewstone (Eds.), *Sozialpsychologie* (6th ed., pp. 439–468). Springer.
Pies, I., & Blome-Drees, F. (1993). Was leistet die Unternehmensethik? *Zeitschrift für Betriebswirtschaftliche Forschung, 47*, 175–179.
Popper, K. R. (1957). *Die offene Gesellschaft und ihre Feinde, Bd. 1, Der Zauber Platons, Francke, Bern; 7.* Auflage, Tübingen: Mohr Siebeck 1992.
Rawls, J. (1971). *A theory of justice*. Harvard University Press.
Rawls, J. (1979). *Eine Theorie der Gerechtigkeit*. Suhrkamp Verlag.
Richman, L., & Leary, M. R. (2009). Reactions to discrimination, stigmatization, ostracism, and other forms of interpersonal rejection: A multimotive model. *Psychological Review, 116*, 365–383.
Samuelson, W., & Zeckhauser, R. (1988). Status quo bias in decision making. *Journal of Risk and Uncertainty, 1*, 7–59.
Schachter, S. (1951). Deviation, rejection, and communication. *Journal of Abnormal and Social Psychology, 46*, 190–207.
Schopenhauer, A. (1839). Die beiden Grundprobleme der Ethik (Diogenes, Zürich) (1977).
Schultheiss, O. C. (2008). Implicit motives. In O. P. John, R. W. Robins, & L. A. Pervin (Eds.), *Handbook of personality: Theory and research* (3rd ed., pp. 603–633). Guilford.
Schulz-Hardt, S., Brodbeck, F. C., Mojzisch, A., Kerschreiter, R., & Frey, D. (2006). Group decision making in hidden profile situations: Dissent as a facilitator for decision quality. *Journal of Personality and Social Psychology, 91*, 1080–1093.
Schulz-Hardt, S., & Brodbeck, F. C. (2014). Gruppenleistung und Führung. In K. Jonas, W. Stroebe, & M. Hewstone (Eds.), *Sozialpsychologie* (6th ed., pp. 469–506). Springer.
Schulz-Hardt, S., & Felix, C. B. (2014). Gruppenleistung und Führung. In K. Jonas, W. Stroebe, & M. Hewstone (Eds.), *Sozialpsychologie*. Springer. (p. 469–506), pp. 485.
Schumpeter, J. A. (1993). *Kapitalismus, Sozialismus und Demokratie* (7th ed.). Francke.
Smith, A. (1985). *Theorie der ethischen Gefühle* (2nd ed.). First published von 1926.
Starbatty, J. (1985). *Die englischen Klassiker der Nationalökonomie*. Wissenschaftliche Buchgesellschaft.
Stasser, G., & Birchmeier, Z. (2003). Group creativity and collective choice. In P. B. Paulus & B. A. Nijstad (Eds.), *Group creativity* (pp. 85–109). Oxford University Pres.
Thaler, R. H. (1981). Some empirical evidence on dynamic inconsistency. *Economic Letters, 8*, 201–207.
Wittmann, S. (1994). *Praxisorientierte Managementethik*. LIT.

Chapter 7
Financial Markets After the Financial Crisis

What Follows Why?
The chapter about the financial markets is divided in three subchapters. We start with the most important research result of behavioral science about the behavior of humans in financial markets. Then we analyze causes of the financial crisis and the reforms made, and finally question to what extent speculation influences the financial markets.

Learning Goal
You should be able to explain the reasons for the financial crisis and to what extend the financial markets are influenced by specific human behavior and speculation in general.

7.1 Behavioral Research Results and Financial Markets

What Follows Why?
In this chapter we analyze the weaknesses of humans acting on financial markets. How can special behavioral traits trigger a financial crisis?

Learning Goal
You should be able to sum up the main insights of behavioral science concerning financial markets and the behavior of investors.

7.1.1 The Efficient Market Hypothesis

Until the mid-1980s, the efficient market hypothesis in financial market theory had an undisputed sole representation claim. Milton Friedman of the University of Chicago significantly influenced the Efficient Market Hypothesis. This hypothesis

C. A. Conrad, *Economic Systems, Markets and Politics*,
https://doi.org/10.1007/978-3-031-10366-7_7

assumes that all accessible price-relevant information of the past, present and future are included. If there were a fundamental price imbalance, arbitrageurs would use this source of income immediately and restore the fundamental price through counter-transactions. So-called "smart money" of funds and in the hands of professional arbitrageurs, supported by researchers who examine in which direction the fundamental market trend moves 24 h a day, guarantee the efficiency of the market. Since, in principle, rational investor behavior is assumed, irrational investor behavior or wrong decisions are not influencing the price. Non-fundamentally justified investment decisions are punished by the market immediately. Investors who behave irrationally lose money and have to withdraw from the market. Stock market prices therefore reflect the latest and best information. Course changes can only be caused by new information. Also, purchases and sales must not have any impact on prices, since the smart money is always ready to form the other side, so to buy or sell up to the fundamental price. According to the Efficient Market Hypothesis, investors can therefore not outperform the market by increasing their level of individual information.[1]

For a long time, the explanation of stock market bubbles was dominated by a clarification approach that assumed rational behavior among market participants. Representatives of this theory include Flood, Garber, Blanchard and Watson.[2] After this explanatory approach, investors know well that the prices are speculatively exaggerated and thus unrealistic. While the likelihood of a crash is greater than that of further bubble growth, the expected gains overcompensate for the likelihood of a crash, so that the expectation of a further rise in price is greater than that of a crash. Every investor assumes that he can get out in time, that is, before the others. This may apply to the individual but not to the whole of the investors. In that sense one could speak of rational errors. The bubble bursts when the price increases necessary to compensate for the crash probability are no longer expected for some reason. But do these explanatory approaches correspond to the course patterns of stock market bubbles that can be observed in practice?

7.1.2 *Review of the Efficient Market Hypothesis*

In the known crashes of 1929 and 1987, parallels can be observed in the price development. First there is a steep upward trend and then the growth rate decreases a few weeks before the crash. In this short phase before the crash, stronger price drops and strong growth in turnover can be observed relative to the upswing.[3] The stock

[1] See Sloan and Stern (1988), pp. 55–59; Shleifer (2000a, b), pp. 1 and Mankhoff and Röckemann (1994), p. 278.

[2] See Flood and Garber (1980), S. 746 ff and Blanchard and Watson (1982), and Jüttner (1989), p. 474.

[3] See Rasch (1993), p. 300.

market upswing takes several years. The downturn or price collapse usually takes place within a few days.[4] The sales and the subsequently falling prices induced new sales and price falls:[5]

> As **the 19th** wore on, investors witnessed symptoms of market failure and were frightened by rumors that the NYSE would close. They also worried that other investors had come to believe the market was overvalued. Fear fed upon fear as investors en masse rushed to sell their stocks.[6]

Here, psychology is one of the most important influencing factors of stock market development. An old stock market saying goes: "The stock market consists of 50% facts and 50% psychology." However, models based on the theory of rational behavior proved unsuitable for explaining or depicting the performance of the '87 crash, which is why economists were called upon to create new models:

> We need to build models of financial equilibrium which are more sensitive to real life trading mechanisms, which account more realistically for the information of expectations, and which recognize that, at any one time, there is a limited pool of investors available with the ability to evaluate stocks and take appropriate action in the market.[7]

Opinion polls on the causes of the crash were carried out after the 1987 crash. The most significant was performed by the Brady Group and gave the following picture:

Noticeable in Fig. 7.1 is the increased influence of psychological factors at the time of the crash. An old stock market saying goes: "50% of the stock market consists of facts and 50% of psychology." However, the models built on the theory of rational behavior proved unsuitable for explaining or reflecting the price development of the '87 crash. Why economists demanded new models:

> We need to build models of financial equilibrium which are more sensitive to real life trading mechanism, which account more realistically for the information of expectations, and which recognize that, at any one time, there is a limited pool of investors available with the ability to evaluate stocks and take appropriate action in the market.[8]

For example, Shiller pointed out that the historical evolution of stock market prices could not be explained solely by expectations of future profits and dividends. He calls this phenomenon "excess volatility".[9] Meanwhile, the assumption of rational investor behavior has been falsified. Investors generally behave irrationally and have similar patterns of behavior.[10] Where does the strong influence of psychological factors on the development of stock prices come from and how does it affect itself?

---

[4] The price display was several hours late in 1987, which is why the NYSE expanded its computer-aided automatic trading systems to a turnover of 1 billion shares per session. See Rasch (1993), pp. 282.

[5] Vgl. The Presidental Task Force (1988), p. V.

[6] Leland and Rubinstein (1988), p. 46.

[7] Leland and Rubinstein (1988), p. 50.

[8] Leland and Rubinstein (1988), p. 50.

[9] See Shiller (2000), pp. 180.

[10] See Shleifer (2000a, b), pp. 10.

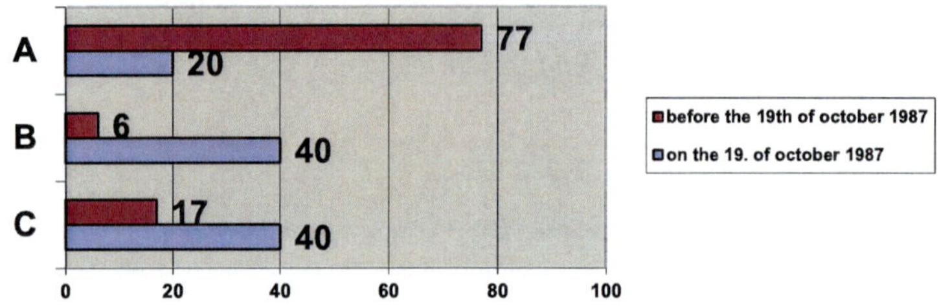

A: fundamental reasons, B: technical reasons, C: psychological reasons

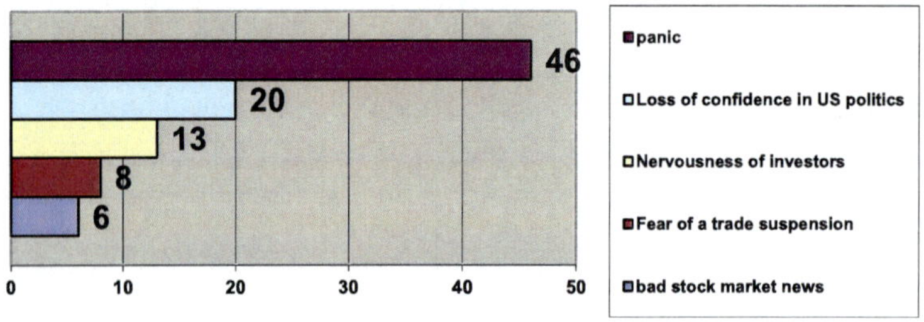

Fig. 7.1 The most important reasons for the price decline on the US stock exchange in 1987 (470 market participants (upper diagram 8.1) and 231 market participants (lower diagram) were surveyed Quelle: The Presidental Task Force (1988) and Jüttner, Johannes (1989), p. 475)

7.1.3 The New Behavioral Finance

Studies of the behavioral research direction New Behavioral Finance confirm the psychologically oriented, non-deterministic explanatory approach. It turned out that investors perceive and evaluate the information available to them in a very subjective way and in their decisions – contrary to the neo-classical model world – do not always maximize the expected benefits. The investor is more upset about losses than he is pleased about profits and behaves more risk-averse with losses than with profits, which is why he tends to let shares in the profit range go rather than in the loss range (disposition effect). He is upset about his "poor decision" and hopes to recover later on – a phenomenon that could usually be observed even in oneself. For example, investment decisions are also influenced by the presentation of the information (framing effect). If the historical yield development of a paper is shown, this leads to an undervaluation of future price volatility. The so-called splitting effect, on the other hand, causes security types with more investment options (for example, German and foreign shares) to be valued equally with better alternatives (for example, bonds). It can also be observed that investors tend to overestimate their level of information and skills. This is called overconfidence. Overconfidence causes an overestimation of the probability of success of one's own decisions. Behavioral finance researchers, for example, attribute the frequent, yield-reducing buying and selling of stocks to overconfidence, which would be comparable to the constant change of lane in a traffic jam. Investors tend to overvalue the information that they first hear over any later info. Conversely, older information is relegated to the background when people receive new information. The same can be observed with regard to information complexity. Investors are paying more attention to reports of takeovers, sales slumps and IPOs than information that they cannot classify or need to process, such as the release of balance sheet ratios. New information is processed and converted with a delay. This causes an overreaction on the exchanges in both directions (overreaction).[11]

De Bondt and Thaler (1985) showed overreaction on the US stock market on the basis of the 35 best and worst stocks. The worst stocks outperformed the overall market as much as the best 35 stocks underperformed it. It is obvious that the market has processed the information late. The bad stocks were not that bad and the good ones were not that good.[12]

Overvaluation and undervaluation happen because information contradicting the trend is taken into consideration too late in the decision-making process. Lastly, the value of the source of information is not properly ranked. The investor hardly considers the information coming from an investment adviser or a designated expert, but rather how determined they present themselves.[13]

However, if human behavior is not determinable and predictable because it is not rational, then the applicability of exact mathematical models is limited, as well as the universality of economic knowledge as a whole. This is best shown by the failure of the hedge fund LTCM co-founded by Nobel laureates Robert Merton and Myron Scholes. Merton and Scholes had been awarded the Nobel Prize for discovering a method of calculating the price of options. Based on this calculation approach, the LTCM fund operated primarily in the market-neutral bond arbitrage. However, the method of calculation is based primarily on historical volatilities and does not take into account irrational human behavior, such as panic, as was to some extent due to the Russian crisis. In the fall of 1998, the LTCM fund was finally close to bankruptcy. His open positions and loan commitments threatened the international financial system to such an extent that Alan Greenspan was forced to organize a rescue operation.

[11] See Behavioral Finance Group (2000), See Menkhoff, Lukas; Röckmann, Christian (1994), pp. 287 and Shleifer (2000a).

[12] See De Bondt, Werner F. M.; Thaler, Richard (1985), Beck (2014), p. 363.

[13] See Behavioral Finance Group (2000), p. 29.

The study was conducted by the Chair of Banking at the University of Mannheim, Prof. Martin Weber and Andreas Laschke. See Menkhoff and Röckmann (1994), pp. 287 and Shleifer (2000a, b).

Overconfidence is the human tendency to overestimate one's self that has been demonstrated in numerous experiments as early as the 1970s. Here one can establish a subjective, positive self-judgment. Subjects regularly overestimate their own knowledge, their control options, their abilities as well as their achievements.[14] Lichtenstein and Fischhoff found that the overestimation decreases as more tasks are solved correctly. The harder the tasks, the greater the overconfidence.[15]

Weinstein tested students and found that they overestimate their positive outcomes and underestimate their negative outcomes. They estimated the likelihood of earning more than $10,000 as their starting salary, 41.5% higher than their fellow students, and the likelihood of a heart attack before the age of 40, 38.4% lower than their peers.[16] Overconfidence increases with the difficulty level of the tasks. It is also subject to experts who feel that they are better informed.[17] This is also a problem in economic consulting, which Hayek called the presumption of knowledge. Confirmation bias reinforces the problem.

The confirmation bias describes how people process facts in a way that confirms their own opinions. Contradictory facts are not taken into account or are subordinate.[18] These include:

- Pseudo-diagnostics: Humans tend to favor their own hypotheses rather than weighing them objectively critically against others. Doctors should not commit themselves so early to their diagnosis, for example.[19]
- Belief Perservance: In order not to have to change their opinion, hypotheses are maintained even when they have already been refuted.[20]

When valuing goods, people tend to value the benefits higher than when they do not have them, which can make sales more difficult. This is called an endowment effect.[21] The effect is more pronounced in long-lived household goods which are rarely bought. The use of consultants (eg estate agents) can reduce this effect.[22]

[14] See Metcalfe (1998).

[15] See Lichtenstein et al. (1982).

[16] See Weinstein (1980).

[17] See Angner (2006) and Russo and Schoemaker (1992).

[18] See Wason, Peter C. (1960), Nickerson, Raymond S. (1998), and Beck, H. (2014).

[19] See Doherty et al. (1979).

[20] See Ross et al. (1975).

[21] See Kahneman, Daniel; Knetsch, Jack; Thaler, Richard (1991), Beck (2014), p. 171

[22] See Marshall et al. (1986).

Decisions are not always logically and rationally linked or their results connected to each other. In decision-making situations people form accounts in which they allocate losses and profits (mental accounting).[23]

Added to this is the illusion of control as an overestimation of one's own influence on processes, such as throwing dice to influence the outcome or selecting a winning ticket. Experiments showed that test takers overestimate their dice skills if they were lucky in the beginning[24] and that test takers are willing to buy the more expensive tickets if they can choose the numbers themselves.[25] Thus, there is a tendency to rate more expensive products as higher quality, although the correlation is very weak. And the willingness to pay a higher price for a product increases when it externally resembles a quality product.

People shy away from change when they cannot assess how they are affected. The status quo is preferred over another alternative (status quo bias). Samuelson and Zeckhauser found that the majority of test subjects do not change their investment portfolio in the case of inheritance. The subjects retained the shares they had inherited or did not buy any shares in cash.[26] In principle, sticking to the status quo can be a rational and efficient approach. Boxall, Adamowicz and Moon found that the status quo bias increases the more complex and time-consuming the decision-making process is.[27] Another explanatory approach is the regret aversion. To revise a decision that has already been made means, on the one hand, that one has to admit to having made a mistake. This generates regret and negative emotions.[28]

The status quo bias is reinforced by the omission bias.[29] People rate negative results from active actions higher than negative results resulting from non-actions, i.e. omissions. Kahneman and Tversky showed as early as 1982 that the losses on an equity investment are considered to be more negative if they were created through active buying than by neglecting to sell.[30] Ritov and Baron show that parents refrain from vaccination even if the risk of disease is 5/10,000 lower than that of non-vaccination at 10/10,000.[31]

---

[23] See Kahneman and Tversky (1984), p. 160.

[24] See Langer and Roth (1975).

[25] See Langer (1975).

[26] See Samuelson and Zeckhauser (1988), p. 12 and Kahneman et al. (1991), pp. 193–206. Beck (2014), p. 164.

[27] See Boxall et al. (2009) and Beck (2014), p. 167.

[28] See Bell (1982) and Loomes and Sudgen (1982), pp. 805–824.

[29] See Ritov and Baron (1992) and Spranca et al. (1991) and Beck (2014), p. 168

[30] See Kahneman and Tversky (1982), p. 173.

[31] See Ritov and Baron (1992).

7.1.4 Noise Trading Approaches

In return for Efficient Market Hypothesis, a series of psychologically-oriented explanatory approaches emerged called noise trading approaches, where "noise" stands for a disturbance (noise) that causes prices to deviate from the fundamental data, In their models, some noise trading approaches explicitly work with groups of investors who make their decisions on the basis of distorted probability distributions, thus unconsciously behaving irrationally.[32] For example, Shiller models an emotionally charged cyclical stock market demand, with speculative bubbles forming.[33] Bubbles can also be triggered by positive moods of the market participants (price euphoria), which are amplified by feedback (positive feedbacks) and can lead to a rectified mass behavior (so-called herd mentality).[34] An example of Shiller's "information cascade" illustrates the herd behavior.[35] Two restaurants, A and B, are identical to one another through a shop window. At first they are empty, then comes a hungry guest and has to choose one of the two restaurants. There is another hungry man coming. He has no additional information on the quality of the restaurants, but only sees that no one is eating in one restaurant and at least the first guest has arrived in the other restaurant A. He will probably trust the choice of the first guest and also choose restaurant A. The decision-making situation continues with other hungry guests until Restaurant A is overcrowded as the most popular restaurant, even though it is completely identical to B. Although this behavior leads to a distorted result, it is rational when considered from the point of view of the individual guests, and could have been quite successful if the assumption that those already dining have a higher level of information were correct. In general, human behavior is oriented towards learning through copying. First a person learns from his parents and trusts them blindly, and in his further development he gets his information from other people. This information often cannot be reviewed due to its complexity and limited decision-making time. Man has to create simplifying behavioral schemas. If people are fleeing, he will join them, though he does not know what they are fleeing from. In the Stone Age this behavior seems to have ensured survival, as the people who waited for the pursuing predator were killed. It has also proven worthwhile when enjoying berries to copy those that have eaten the same kind of berries and survived.

With herd mentality the sociological group orientation of man comes to the fore. In the typical stock market situation of uncertainty, the investor orients themself by the other market participants, which the stock exchange rewards with increasing prices – at least in the short term. In the approach of Shefrin and Statman bubbles build, then burst, when the irrational Noise Traders again adjust their distorted

32 See Blume and Easley (1992), p. 9–40.

33 See Shiller (1984), p. 457–498.

34 See Froot et al. (1992), p. 1461.

35 See Shiller (2000), S. 152.

expectations of the rational market participants.[36] The expectations of the market participants influence each other. For example, empirical studies show that the estimation of market developments by analysts and investors is influenced by previous valuations from other analysts.[37] Extrapolative expectation and technical analysis strategies also lead to share sales when prices rise. Herd behavior is intensified by the short-term speculative horizon. A crash seems less likely. This is especially true for professional investment managers who are subjected to a one-year performance evaluation.[38]

Individual market participants cannot oppose the development of herd behavior, even if they notice deviation from the fundamental price factors. If they speculate against such a strong market trend, they will lose as long as the bubble does not burst. On the contrary, in the upward process, there are self-reinforcing distribution effects that aid the creation of a bubble.[39] For example, suppose that in a given uncertain situation on the stock market there are investors with two risk positions, and that they have the same purchasing power. The optimists (bulls) expect the same level of information to lead to higher price or corporate profits than the risk-averse pessimists (bears). If new positive information is added that leads to a price increase, the long-term buyers (long position) have more purchasing power than the sellers (short position) that did not invest in the stock, but rather liquidity or a short position due to the previous price gains, and thus incurred losses.[40] The unequal purchasing power causes a demand surplus and thus favors the upward process. Since the bulls can bring about their own success in the form of higher prices due to the surplus, the upward process is self-reinforcing. On the other hand, the bears lose even more purchasing power because it is a zero-sum game. These effects are reinforced by the change in refinancing options. If the stock portfolio of the bulls wins, so do their credit lines with the banks. The same applies vice versa for the bears. The mirror image downward trend occurs when the new information is negative.

In addition, there is a psychological effect that unilaterally strengthens the stock market's upwards movement. The investor feels richer because of his increased equity portfolio, which will increase his purchasing position (wealth effect). Man adapts his behavior to his environment, more precisely to his experiences. If new price increases occur over a longer period of time, he will adjust his risk assessment. His own price gains reinforce this and make it rational to reinvest in equities. As a rule, capital investment will be greater in the second investment because the investor expects to repeat his successful initial investment.

[36] Quotes after Menkhoff and Röckmann (1994), p. 284.

[37] See De Bondt and Forbes (1999).

[38] See Shleifer and Vishny (1990), pp. 148–153.

[39] See Treynor (1998), pp. 69–74.

[40] A person who tends to be a seller (bear) does not have to be passive on the market by holding liquidity, but can also buy short positions (long-short futures or long-put options).

Conclusion

New Behavioral Finance Theory shows that investors tend to overestimate their level of information and skills. This is called overconfidence. Overconfidence causes people to overestimate the likelihood that their decisions will be successful. New information is processed and implemented with a delay. This causes an overreaction on the stock exchanges in both directions (overreaction). Price exaggerations and price understatements occur because the information that contradicts the trend is taken into account too late in the decision-making process.

The noise trading approaches implement this decision-making behavior in models. For example, Shiller models an emotional cyclical demand for equities with resulting speculative bubbles. Bubbles can also be triggered by positive moods on the part of market participants (price euphoria), which are reinforced by feedback (positive feedback) and can lead to mass behavior in the same direction (herding).

New Behavioral Finance shows that people can err collectively in a group. The group opinion dominates over the individual opinion. Individuals adopt the group opinion, as has been shown by social psychology and sociology (in chapter 3.1). This means that systemic crises such as the financial crisis can be explained by human error and the Efficient Market Hypothesis is falsified. For the state this means that it has to take institutional precautions in the form of financial market regulation in order to counteract and mitigate systemic crises.

Since the psychologically oriented approaches are not deterministic, their drawback is the lack of a uniform universal model conception and the possibility of verification independent of the situation. However, in view of the weaknesses of the classical theory based exclusively on rational behavior, they have considerably enriched financial market theory. The psychologically oriented approaches blame the over-interpretation of the assumption of rational behavior, which is always valid in reality, on the original abstract model approach of neoclassicism, which adopted the rational homo oeconomicus merely to simplify the complexity of human behavior.[41]

Comprehension Questions

1. What is the content of the Efficient Market Hypothesis?
2. Why does the New Behavioral Finance contradict the Efficient Market Hypothesis?
3. Give examples for overconfidence and herding.
4. Explain the status quo bias. How can it influence economic behavior?
5. Is the confirmation bias a problem for science? Should scientists control themselves? How could they do that?

[41] See Behavioral Finance Group (2000) and Conrad (2016).

7.2 The Financial Crisis and the Reforms to Stabilize the Financial Markets

What Follows Why?

The financial crisis led to the worst depression since 1929. Only by massive economic programs could worse be prevented. Here Keynesian theory came into play. Only through globally agreed massive credit-financed government spending increases could depression be prevented. The banks had to be saved with tax money, as many banks had invested in the government bonds of weak European countries whose solvency was called into question. The sovereign debt crisis has emerged from the financial crisis. Against this background, the question arises of state regulations that limit the risk of banks. Politicians and economists have urged such regulation of the financial markets since the onset of the 2007 financial crisis. What has happened in the meantime? Were the right reforms implemented or could there be another financial crisis? After analyzing the causes of the crisis, the main reforms are examined below.

Learning Goals

You should be able to explain the reasons for the financial crisis and the attempts to counteract it.

7.2.1 The Subprime Crisis, the Biggest Financial Crisis After 1929

In 2003, Warren Buffet said of the credit derivatives market that they were "financial weapons of mass destruction, carrying dangers that, while now latent are potentially lethal." Others also warned that credit based derivatives coupled with a lack of transparency were leading to a significant concentration of risk. Unfortunately, they were right.

Derivative products such as CDOs (Collateralized Debt Obligations) can be directly traced as being one of the major factors leading to the subprime crisis and the greatest financial crisis since the Wall Street crash of 1929. CDOs are structured financial products comprised of a variety of loans, bonds, mortgages and credit derivatives such as Credit Default Swaps or CDSs. For the most part the major Wall Street investment banks put together CDOs using home mortgages, which were then resold as investment products. These CDOs were structured to meet the requirements of the major US rating agencies, which based their risk calculations on complicated economic models and statistical analysis. Two apparently ingenious combinations of factors made it possible to create an innovative financial product with a combined calculated risk in the portfolio lesser than the sum of the individual risk associated with each element in the portfolio.

The basis for the evaluation of risk associated with these financial products as calculated by the rating agencies was based upon the historical default rate of US mortgages. As this data was not always available, it was necessary to draw upon estimates that fit within established portfolio theories and expectations and which would produce the desired reduction of risk between two comparative portfolios. Part of this process was to investigate the relationships and correlations between the individual elements of these portfolios to determine the probability that both or more elements could be eliminated from risk calculations. The complex statistical financial models used by the rating agencies were not always understood or even available to those in the market place as investors. This situation was not considered to be an issue at the time, as the capital markets had a great deal of trust and confidence in the ratings provided by the rating agencies. For decades, the ratings provided by the rating agencies concerning potential risk had been used to determine the terms for credit and loans to borrowers in the capital markets. As a consequence of the subprime crisis, the objectivity of these ratings agencies has now been called into question, most notably due to their previous relationships with the investment banks for which they provided the CDO ratings.

The second situation by which a portfolio rating could be improved was through the use and subordination of various "risk tranches". In the event of a default or failure of one of the elements or "tranches" in the portfolio, the most subordinated tranche (junior note) would be affected. This process would continue on up the scale to the tranches with AA to BB ratings, (mezzanine notes) and in the extreme case on up to the most senior tranches with AAA ratings.

For decades, the value of American real estate has steadily increased. After all, the USA has been a country of considerable growth both in terms of population and economic expansion. This growth has also been the basis for a historically low level of home mortgage defaults. For the most part, home values have been sufficient to cover outstanding mortgage balances in the event of a default. As a consequence, lenders were encouraged to offer ever-increasing mortgage loans based on the projected future value of homes in an ever-expanding market. As home values rose, lenders would offer homeowners access to their equity through refinancing or home equity lines of credit, which would support even further consumption. Much of the mortgage financing made available to borrowers by Freddie Mac and Fannie Mae was also supported by political incentives to encourage home ownership among socially and economically disadvantaged minority groups. This initiative originated in the mid-1990s with the Clinton administration as lending criteria were relaxed[42] and continued under the Bush administration. In 2003, Congressman Ron

[42]"... the Fannie Mae Corporation is easing the credit requirements on loans ... The action ... will encourage those banks to extend home mortgages to individuals whose credit is generally not good enough... Fannie Mae... has been under increasing pressure from the Clinton Administration to expand mortgage loans among low and moderate income people and felt pressure from stock holders to maintain its phenomenal growth in profits. In addition, banks, thrift institutions and mortgage companies have been pressing Fannie Mae to help them make more loans to so-called subprime borrowers whose incomes, credit ratings and savings are not good enough for

Paul warned that this relaxed lending policy would eventually lead to individuals borrowing to buy homes that they could ill-afford and eventually require financial intervention on the part of government. In 1994, the market for subprime mortgages made up only 5% of the total mortgage market and amounted to $35 billion dollars, and by 2006 it had increased to become 20% of the mortgage market for a total of approximately $600 billion dollars. This increase in lending volume was only made possible by ever more relaxed lending standards. Borrowers were able to obtain mortgage loans without showing any proof of income or employment or assets, the so-called "ninja loans" meaning "No Income, No Job, and No Assets". This situation was further encouraged by ever-falling interest rates as initiated by the Federal Reserve under the leadership of Alan Greenspan, with short-term rates reaching a low of 1% in 2004. Subprime borrowers were also offered ARMs, or Adjustable Rate Mortgages with low, interest-only payments required, as well as "teaser loans" with initial interest rates well below market rates that would dramatically increase or reset at a later date. Also available were payment option loans which made it possible for borrowers to set their own repayment schedule and thereby postpone repayment for as long as possible. Altogether, US mortgage borrowing rose from $680 billion in 1974 to $14 trillion in 2001. From a total of 8.8 million homeowners with mortgages, about 10.8% had no actual equity in their property or, in fact, owed more than their home was worth.

Average home values in the USA increased 126% from 1997 to 2006, while the relationship between home values and annual income changed from a ratio of 2.9 in 2001 to 4.6 in 2006. This dramatic change in home values, as compared with annual income, was not considered a problem as long as borrowers were able to service their debt and maintain their mortgage payments. The crisis only came about as a consequence of changing interest rates and the payment structures built into these loans.

Banks can, but in a limited manner, restructure loan intervals as needed to meet business requirements but if they require refinancing at a later date, then it will be necessary for them to draw upon their own liquidity. Therefore every banking student is taught the golden rule of lending, which is to restructure loans through refinancing at appropriate coverage intervals.

When restructuring loans, the risks associated with changing interest rates and refinancing are to be carried and collateralized by the banks themselves. These fundamental rules of finance were unfortunately ignored when it came to the issuance of CDOs by investment banks, which finally amounted to a market value of over $2 trillion dollars. Long-term mortgages were repackaged and sold by the investment banks as special purpose vehicles (conduits) and collateralized at fairly low capital ratios through the use of short-term commercial paper (CPs). In this way,

---

conventional loans... Fannie Mae is taking on significantly more risk... the government subsidized corporation may run into trouble... prompting a government rescue... the move is intended in part to increase the number of... home owners who tend to have worse credit ratings..." September 30, 1999 New York Times.

the CDOs could be refinanced at lower interest rates, which created more profitable margins for the banks. The CDOs in these "special purpose entities" did not surface on the bank's balance sheet. As was the case with Enron, these obligations were not listed as consolidated third party liabilities and therefore not readily apparent at first glance. On bank balance sheets these obligations were simply listed as possible liabilities in the comments section and often escaped notice. In the unlikely event that banks were unable to sell these securities on the market, they would be required to provide adequate liquidity to cover these obligations. High leveraging of stock purchases was also a reason for the financial crisis in 1929.

Deregulation further encouraged the direct and indirect use of leverage by investment banks. For example, in 2004 the SEC allowed investment banks to expand their use of leverage by lowering their capital margin requirement from 8% to 6%. By 2007, the five largest US investment banks had increased their borrowing for investment purposes to $4.1 trillion dollars, which equaled approximately 30% of the US gross domestic product. What motivated the investment banks to take on this level of risk? This was the era of the "shareholder value concept", of short-term gain and exceptional bonuses. The simplest way to increase shareholder value and therefore also stock value was to use leverage to boost returns on investment. Finally, in order for a bank to receive a rating of "excellent" from the rating agencies, they were required to show a 25% return on investment of capital and therefore a favorable rating for future refinancing. An attractive aspect of CDOs was that it was not required that they be rated as loans, but could be rated as a security product. This classification allowed the investment banks to realize additional profits by selling them on to other investors and not hold bank funds in reserve as collateral.

Using CDOs, investment banks were therefore able to boost their profitability on invested capital as well as their internal rate of return. Loans would be classified as CDO securities and therefore positively influence the banks balance sheet. As securities, these CDOs would appear to be without risk. In addition, the rating agencies would assign them AAA status, indicating that these "securities" were without risk. As securities, the CDOs were not subject to the strict federal regulations required for debt products nor would they have to be evaluated as debt obligations on the books of the already highly leveraged banks. Free from complying with external financial requirements and internal lending limits, investment bankers were able to secure profitable sources of revenue and therefore substantial bonuses as well. By repackaging US mortgages as investment products, bankers were able to realize approximately $23.9 billion dollars in bonus payments in 2006. In 2007, Swiss bank UBS paid out $10 billion Swiss Francs in bonus payments alone. The availability and easy access to credit for home mortgages encouraged not only dealers but also lenders who provided loans to ever less qualified borrowers. In the end, these lenders were selling these loans on to other investors and therefore did not have to contend with the risk. The relationship between the lenders issuance of credit and mortgages and the associated risk of default were distinctly separated from one another, which lead to a fundamental violation of the market (order) principles of accountability and transparency. The exceptionally complex structure of the CDOs also contributed to this lack of transparency. It only became clear later that it was all but impossible to separate the various problem loans within the CDOs from the total in the portfolio, and impossible to trace them back to the original borrowers. Also, the system of bonus payments made to bankers selling the CDOs appears to be in contradiction to principles of accountability, as their bonuses were based on short-term profitability while the potential long-term negative consequences of their actions were ignored.

The bubble in the US housing market burst in 2006. A contributing factor was the dramatic rise in short-term interest rates, which made it impossible for many mortgage borrowers to maintain their payments. This rise in interest rates lead to ever-greater defaults and bank repossessions and home prices fell. The consequences for the financial sector first became apparent in February 2007 as HSBC was compelled to write off loans repackaged as CDOs valued $10.5 billion dollars. While serious, the crisis seemed to be limited to the banking sector and did not pose a threat to the real economy. In November 2007, the volume of subprime mortgages was valued at $148 billion dollars. At this point, the extreme difficulty in placing an accurate value on the CDOs became all too apparent. The lack of transparency associated with the CDOs and the high level of risk they carried due to the subprime mortgages they contained made them all but impossible to sell or accurately value. The market for CDOs collapsed entirely, leading to a crisis of capital liquidity for those banks carrying them on their books. This issue leads to an unexpected reduction of liquidity at the banks. In December, the amount of subprime debt was corrected from $200 billion to $300 billion, and then finally in March 2008 from $350 billion to $600 billion dollars.

A rating of AAA was now considered worthless and all trust in the rating agencies had been lost. Without accurate and reliable ratings from the agencies, the capital markets were crippled. It soon became obvious that the crisis was not limited to just the US. As CDOs had been sold on the international market, the risk that they carried was now also an international problem. Swiss banks such as UBS, and German banks IKB and Sachsen Landes Bank had built up considerable portfolios filled with CDOs and as a consequence experienced severe liquidity problems. In addition, these banks required ever increasing amounts of fresh capital to cover the write-offs associated with CDOs and to support lines of liquidity. The banks that had invested too much of their client's capital were in danger of going bankrupt. US investment banks and larger banks such as UBS were able to raise additional capital on their own, while banks such as Germany's IKB and Sachsen Landes Bank had to be rescued by the German federal government. British mortgage lender Northern Rock experienced a run on the bank and had to be nationalized.

The crisis continued to expand. Two basic issues became apparent: increasing suspicion and mistrust between banks and ever further write-offs due to CDOs, which served to accelerate the crisis of liquidity and available capital. Banks felt that they could no longer trust one another and therefore stopped lending to each other. Without transparency and trust between banks, no one could be sure which banks were solvent and how much remaining debt had to be written off. Ratings given to the banks by the ratings agencies could no longer be relied upon. The inter-banking market collapsed. Banks without branch offices, and therefore without access to investors, found themselves short of liquidity. Central banks were compelled to provide infusions of capital into the marketplace and to lower interest rates. The quarterly reports by banks concerning their ever-increasing CDO related write-offs only served to further depress the already discouraged mood in the marketplace. As European banks primarily followed US-GAAP for accounting purposes as well as the internationally accepted IFRS standards, this lead to an even greater difficulty in accurately assigning a value to the CDOs. Following US accounting standards which tend to favor shareholder interests, securities and other financial products such as the CDOs must be "mark to market" to assign a current market value. In contrast to European accounting standards, the costs of acquisition are not included if a reduction in value is only temporary. Although home mortgages continued to operate for the most part unchanged, the market for CDOs had collapsed and banks were compelled to write down the market value of their CDOs by as much as 70%. This development culminated in the partial illiquidity of US investment bank Bear Stearns in March of 2008. The head of Germany's Deutsche Bank Josef Ackermann was quoted at this time as saying that "he no longer believed in the ability of the markets to self-correct and heal themselves".

Bankers called on the government to help them out of the situation. JP Morgan purchased Bear Stearns for $1.2 billion dollars after receiving a bailout loan of $29 billion from the US Federal Reserve. After this action by the Federal Reserve the financial markets seemed to settle down. The danger of collapse of further large financial institutions seemed to be over. At the beginning of 2007, market participants started to believe that perhaps the worst of the subprime crisis was over, only to have the crisis flare up again. But the worst of the crisis was yet to come. The crisis would continue as the banks CDOs increasingly lost value and were written down to comply with accounting regulations. Prices for homes on the US real estate market and the almost non-existent CDO market continued to fall ever further. A shortage of liquidity compelled the banks to sell additional securities, which lead to a vicious cycle of price declines. The mistrust of ratings assigned by the ratings agencies and the general uncertainty in the market lead to investors selling all forms of securities and to seek refuge in government bonds and treasuries.

In September 2008 the entire financial system came close to collapse. Only through a massive intervention by national governments up to and including the nationalization of many banks could the financial crisis be contained. Many newspapers compared the current financial crisis to that of the Wall Street crash of 1929. The US mortgage lender Silver State bank and many other smaller real estate lenders had to be closed and both major mortgage lenders Fannie Mae and Freddie Mac were nationalized. The growing crisis lead to the bankruptcy of Lehman Brothers, the 4th largest investment bank in the US. The CEO of a major German bank was quoted as saying "Lehman was the downfall that lead the financial crisis to a mass panic."

US Treasury secretary Paulson wanted to make an example of Lehman Brothers. Wall Street needed to realize that things could not continue as before, with the government prepared to bail out every bank facing insolvency... as if in keeping with the motto "Privatization of profit and nationalization of loss." This concerned the concept of "moral hazard" as versus the adage "too big to fail". The majority of

Americans were against the idea of using taxpayer money to bail out bankers on Wall Street. Paulson had drastically miscalculated the situation. Mohamed El-Erian, co-manager of the market's largest bond fund PIMCO made the case that, after the fall of Lehman Brothers all sense of trust and confidence was lost in the ability of financial institutions to be extricated from the crisis in an orderly fashion. In actuality, the collapse of Wall Street's 4th largest investment bank was an event beyond comprehension. All the major players in the financial markets had expected that the adage "too big to fail" certainly applied to Lehman Brothers, and that after the rescue of Bear Stearns by the federal government that Lehman Brothers could expect the same treatment.

That Paulson allowed the collapse of Lehman Brothers shook the financial world to its core. Nothing more seemed to be certain, and there was no longer any relying on a bail out. The danger for the financial system was that Lehman Brothers was one of the largest traders of derivatives and so its collapse would have profound consequences. The sword of Damocles, as wielded by George Soros in the form of billions of dollars of derivatives contracts, fell. After the bursting of the Internet bubble banks discovered derivatives as the next major source of almost unlimited revenue potential. Derivatives are a form of obligation with their value tied to the occurrence of specific events in the financial markets. Options, for example, give the investor or speculator the right to buy or sell a specific security at specific price during a pre-determined period of time. Options, however, do not belong to the classic form of derivative. A derivative is normally used to cover an exposure to risk as a hedge. For example, the owner of a share of stock would use a sell option (Put-option) to sell his shares at a pre-determined price, or for speculation. The attraction of options derivatives is that with relatively little money an investor can speculate on the movement of a stock price with greater leverage, and also greater risk, than if he had to actually buy and own the underlying stock. Especially risky were a fairly new form of financial innovation known as Credit Default Swaps or CDSs. They also were developed in the US at the start of the 1990s as a form of hedge against loan risk. If a bank, for example, desires to reduce the risk of default for a loan that it has with a borrower, it can hedge the risk of default by buying a CDS from a third party. With a CDS it was possible for banks to increase their rates of return on capital while avoiding the use of their own capital to cover loans. In contrast, those providing the risk coverage were not bound by any specific regulations. They were not required to put up any capital of their own, so the actual risk of default was not covered. Investment banks and highly leveraged hedge funds[43] were also partly involved in these transactions as contrarian speculators. In 2001, the nominal value of outstanding CDS contracts reached approximately $1 trillion dollars, and in 2005 it amounted to $10 trillion dollars. For the most part, this increase in CDS volume was due to speculation on the part of contrarian investors

[43] In 2000, warnings were issued as to the threat posed to the financial system due to the lack of regulation on Hedge Funds as counter-parties to derivative transactions. See Conrad and Stahl (2000a, b).

and not from actual transactions to hedge loan risk. The bankruptcy of auto parts supplier Delphi stands as a good case in point, whereby $5.2 billion dollars in loans and bonds were hedged by $28 billion dollars in CDS contracts. In 2008, the total value of all outstanding CDS contracts was approximately $62 trillion dollars. The degree of counter-party risk had become impossible to ignore.

After the collapse of Lehman Brothers complete panic broke out. The domino effect was enormous. It was not only that the banks no longer trusted each other or their level of solvency, but rather the entire financial system was called into question leading to worst-case scenario. The capital markets collapsed. The banks could no longer refinance or restructure the portfolios effectively. In addition, subprime securities such as corporate bonds were no longer marketable, or could only be sold at greatly reduced value. The consequences for the real economy were immediately apparent.

Lehman Brothers certificates had been sold to investors around the world. Now they were worthless. The media took advantage of the negative publicity by running dramatic headlines leading to widespread fear and uncertainty. In this way they helped to spread the panic. Everyone became convinced of a pending catastrophe and recession, and so reduced their investment and consumption. This became a self-fulfilling prophecy. People became fearful of potentially losing their jobs and stopped spending. As a consequence of reduced liquidity and a shortage of available capital, banks stopped making loans. The "credit crunch" had arrived. The greater economy became fearful of declining sales and liquidity problems and stopped investing. Due to the negative sentiments it came to the classical Keynesian case of underinvestment together with the liquidity-trap. Savers lost faith in banks and withdrew their deposits, which further exacerbated liquidity problems at the banks. In order to generate liquidity, the banks sold shares. Falling market prices lead to even further price declines as risk limits triggered computerized trading and stock sales at many hedge funds. Investment bank Merrill Lynch was taken over by the Bank of America. The US government set up a special fund of $700 billion dollars to buy up the bank's portfolios of non-performing loans. In a form of reverse auction process, banks were permitted to sell their portfolios of non-performing securities to federal funds offering the highest percentage of face value for the securities. The two remaining US investment banks, Goldman Sachs and Morgan Stanley had to give up their previous business model so as to be considered as universal banks and gain access to refinancing funds from the US Federal Reserve. Further access to capital was given to suffering banks by the federal authorities. The world's largest insurer AIG was partially nationalized through this process. AIG had been speculating as a counter-party to billions of dollars in obligations using CDSs and CDOs following a trading strategy based on the mathematical-statistical model of Yale Professor Gary Gordon. The probability of default as calculated by Gordon proved to be mistaken, however. Further banks were forced into bankruptcy or taken over. Hypo Real Estate in Germany was saved by a combination of private banks and the German federal government. Banks in England and elsewhere had to be nationalized to prevent the collapse of the financial system. Governments came to the rescue of banks through the use of bailout funds from taxpayers. By this time the world's stock markets had fallen from a peak in August 2007 by more than 50% and set the world on the path to recession. Between March 1st and June 18th 2008, the FBI arrested 406 individuals for loan and mortgage fraud, ranging from small mortgage brokers to bank presidents who were later charged with having deceived investors as to the risks of the subprime market.[44]

As with Enron, Merrill Lynch was insolvent. With approximately $9 billion dollars in losses, Merrill's CEO O'Neal was responsible for the worst financial results at the bank in its 93-year history. And in 2008, there were an additional $15 billion dollars in write-offs. Similar to Skillings at Enron, O'Neal was also possessed of an unusually overbearing management style and obsession with profit results. The consequences would soon become all too apparent. By taking on more risk, O'Neal could produce better profit results while the top management at Merrill cashed in on huge bonuses. At Citigroup, CEO Prince was also facing more than $20 billion dollars in write-offs. Here as well, in 2008 it was necessary to write off huge sums. Both Prince and O'Neal were not only responsible for billions in write-offs, but as senior management received exceptionally handsome compensation packages (Prince received $26 million dollars and O'Neal $48 million dollars in 2006), and a severance package in the $100 million range. O'Neal received about $160 million in cash and stock options while Prince received approximately $100 million.[45] Others would assume the losses, namely the shareholders who lost a portion of their investment in the banks while many employees lost their jobs. In other words, not only did the agents of disaster gamble away their investor's money but they were also well rewarded for it. With this disconnect between risk and compensation it's easy to understand why so many bankers took on such huge risks, which lead us to today's subprime crisis.[46]

With the crises described above, the general question arises as to what went wrong? What economic dysfunctions are responsible for this huge resource destruction?

7.2.2 *Some Causes of the Financial Crisis in the Light of Behavioral Theory*

7.2.2.1 Belief in the Self-Correcting Power of the Market

The first serious debate as to the infallibility of the capitalistic economic system arose in 2000 within the framework of the Enron crisis. By 2007, it was obvious that

[44] See Mayr (2007); Handelsblatt 23.10.08 and 10.1.08, p. 30; Süddeutsche Zeitung 17.11.08, p. 22, Neue Zuricher Zeitung 7.02.08; Zeit Online, 26/2008, p. 24, Der Spiegel, No. 47 (2008), p. 46–79 and Conrad (2010), p. 21.

[45] This income was exceeded by Goldman Sachs CEO Henry Paulson, who earned a bonus of $18.7 million along with realizing proceeds from the sale of $480 million in stock by exercising options issued prior to his becoming US secretary of the treasury. See Der Spiegel No. 8 (2009), p. 62.

[46] See also Shiller (2007); Gold and Feldmann (2007); Muolo and Padilla (2008) and Woods (2009).

the world economy was in a fundamental crisis with the emergence of the subprime crisis. The subprime crisis was seen as the epitome of the ethical failure of our modern economy. Everything came together and many saw in the crisis the final act of "turbo capitalism",[47] the limitless enrichment of the few at the expense of society, which almost lead to a total collapse of the financial system. The lack of regulation and belief in the self-correcting power of the market was used by a few to take advantage of the situation. Considered historically, financial crises have increased significantly in recent years. This is not the result of simple coincidence, but rather much more an indication of a massive weakness in the present economic system. The market economy has always placed the individual at the forefront for the economic creation of value, which provided him with an ever-growing range of opportunity. Through the pursuit of individual interests, it was believed that this motivation would also create the most beneficial results for society and the greater good. This appears to not be the case. Individuals exploited the absence of rules and the belief in the self-healing forces of the markets to their advantage.

Could the worst financial crisis since 1929 have been prevented? Naturally, in hindsight it would be easy to answer the question with a "yes", given what we know now about the causes and course of the crisis. Above all, the crisis can be traced back to a violation of market order principles through political intervention. Let's start with the inappropriate involvement of the US government in the financial markets. The crisis started in the early 1990s as a consequence of a misguided social program on the part of politicians. In 1995, Fannie Mae and Freddie Mack received a mandate from the office of Housing and Urban Development (HUD) to lend to subprime borrowers using funds to be provided by HUD at below market interest rates. These funds were to provide mortgages to subprime borrowers in what were considered to be economically disadvantaged social groups, so that they could buy homes that they normally could not afford. The volume of loans and the regulations concerning the classification of subprime loans were increasingly expanded. These cheap loans made it possible for both Fannie Mae and Freddie Mac to boost their profit margins. Executives at Freddie Mac reciprocated with illegal campaign contributions while mortgage lender Connie Wide offered low-interest loans to influential politicians in Washington. One could say the basis for the subprime bubble can be traced back to the US government. It's also worth mentioning that the low interest rate policies of Alan Greenspan played an important role. By making cheap money readily available and supporting deregulation, the Fed created fertile ground for the bubble to grow.[48] One can also blame the US government for an exceptional lack of financial oversight. US financial regulators were aware of the growing problem but chose not to act, so as not to influence competition in the markets.

Rather than acting to regulate and control the mortgage markets, they put their faith in the ability of the market to correct itself and deregulated. Without regulators,

[47] See Dahrendorf (2009).

[48] See the film "Inside Job" of 2010 by Charles Ferguson (Sony Pictures) and Conrad and Stahl (2002a, b).

it was possible for companies to hide the risk inherent in these loans from appearing on their balance sheets. Greenspan refused to act to control these new and innovative financial products. Despite the LTCM crisis,[49] Greenspan and the US government remained unconvinced that unregulated speculation by the hedge funds posed as serious threat to the financial system. Many governments, including the German government had been pushing for more regulation. Belief in the markets and the influence of financial lobbyists was more powerful, however. At no point during this phase of the crisis did financial regulators seem to be aware of the combined risk posed by CDOs and how it was spread among the banks.[50] With their complex mathematical models and AAA ratings, these deceptively secure financial innovations and the risk that they posed were able to escape the attention of over-worked federal regulators. National regulators, in the case of those in the US were divided and under-manned. At the federal level in the USA there were four uncoordinated regulating authorities and at the state level additional independent authorities. The most powerful authority, the SEC was considerably weakened and unable to deal with the problem due to massive reductions in personnel in their department for risk control and regulation.[51] These cuts in personnel occurred during a time in which a former head of Goldman Sachs acted as the head of the Office for Management and Budget, and while Henry Paulson, the future head of the Treasury department was CEO at Goldman Sachs. Later, for instance the head of the German banking regulatory authority admitted that his office was unable to come to terms with and regulate the rapid developments of these new financial products. Although they were aware of the problems posed by these unregulated financial products, they chose to not intervene. The banks had complete independence of action. Motivated by short-term profits and handsome bonuses, banking managers took on ever-greater levels of risk using ever-greater amounts of leverage. Many wanted to just get rich quick and gave little thought to the consequences of their actions. This actions lead as well to criminal activity. The most dangerous risk was kept off the balance sheets or allocated to unregulated, hidden offshore accounts. Also, the level of risk to counter-parties through the use of these innovative financial products seemed to be unknown to the regulating authorities. Due to the excessive use of leverage, many of

---

[49] In 1998 this hedge fund named Long Term Capital Management (LTCM) then lost the investors around 90% of the $4 billion invested, which threatened to trigger a chain reaction on the international finance markets. The issue here is not just the credit taken by LTCM, but also the derivative positions of LTCM as contracting party, with which other finance market actors had protected themselves. Only when the then US central bank president Alan Greenspan intervened personally and pulled together an emergency package of billions from several large banks could the capital market crisis be averted. See Conrad (2005).

[50] "What we have found over the years in the marketplace is that derivatives have been an extraordinarily useful vehicle to transfer risk from those who shouldn't be taking it to those who are willing to and are capable of doing so." "We think that it would be a mistake" to more regulate the contracts. Greenspan in front of the Banking Committee in 2003. New York Times, 20.10.2008.

[51] The chief controller of the SEC later spoke at a conference when questioned about "the systematic elimination of personnel from the regulatory office,.. so that became impossible for the office to perform any regulation whatsoever." Der Spiegel, No. 47 (2008), p. 78.

the hedge funds had also taken on considerable risk. Nonetheless, the hedge funds remained unsupervised.

Paulson seemed to be unaware that the collapse of Lehman Brothers would lead to an unstoppable chain reaction. With the bankruptcy of Lehman, US policy regarding the issue became unpredictable. For the financial markets, it seemed that the Fed was willing to allow for the collapse of some banks, and that an intervention to save those in crisis should not be expected. Market participants completely lost their trust and confidence. Permitting the collapse of Lehman was one of two major mistakes made by Paulson. The other was the failure to change financial accounting requirements for the balance sheet in a timely manner. The mark-to-market regulations concerning CDOs as securities was the main reason for the ongoing write-offs, along with continuous reductions in the value of CDOs due to an almost non-existent market for them. On-going earnings warnings and loss reports strained not only the existing capital of the bank, but also awakened in the mind of the public the perception that a huge, uncontrollable and uncontainable financial catastrophe was occurring. Unfortunately, we will never know how many mortgage loans could have been saved from default by quick government intervention, as the opportunity was missed to act quickly to prevent the financial crisis from spreading to the real economy. At least it's certain that if the banks had been permitted to balance the value of their CDO portfolios, taking into account the portion of the securities not affected by bad mortgage loans, the write offs could have been greatly reduced. In consideration of this remaining base value, the banks could apply to the Fed as a "lender of last resort" for refinancing with the CDOs acting as collateral. This funding conversion and extension of debt servicing could have been implemented at the beginning of the crisis, already in the middle of 2007 and not at the end of 2008. The banks and the US administration must have had great interest in keeping mortgage borrowers facing foreclosure in their homes. This could have kept the pressure off of the housing market and home prices. As this did not happen, many borrowers lost their homes and some even ended up living on the streets as the homeless, which raises the question of moral and economic responsibility. Many vacant houses were neglected and others were vandalized.

The banks' trading departments responsible for internal and external credit supervision withdrew their risky long-term loans and refinanced them as short-term securities. Any bank would realize that this was a violation of the golden rule of lending and would have significant consequences. This lack of control, the failure to implement responsible business practices and immoral behavior deserves critical review. It is beyond comprehension how bankers could be so misled by their statistical and mathematical models, as well as how many could have such unlimited trust in the rating agencies and their recommendations. Despite the ratings assigned by the rating agencies, we can expect senior management planning an investment of billions of dollars to perform at least some degree of due diligence to gain an understanding of the rating agency's procedures. To rely so completely on the judgment of what may be a biased third party is completely irresponsible. In the USA, the dramatic increase in home prices had become impossible to ignore and the easy access to subprime loans was often criticized. Warnings were sounded as to the impending bursting of the real estate and derivatives bubble.

The central problem of derivatives is that the leverage of the invested capital distorts the risk distribution between the speculator and the financial system. If the speculator is wrong he will lose only a portion of what is at stake for the system. The loan derivatives CDS did not have to be funded with equity, so banks earned much more than was appropriate on a risk adjusted basis in the good years. When the bad years came there was no capital to cover the losses so society had to bail out the speculators because they were too big to fail. Bonus payments had been made in the good years and there were no repayments in the bad years, when the bill was presented.

Speculators normally do not speculate against each other, but with each other. There is a familiar saying that "the trend is your friend". Only a stable trend facilitates speculation with nearly no risk. The biggest danger of derivatives is the leverage. If futures are used for speculative purposes for instance, the leverage multiplies artificially the effects of the derivatives on prices (via arbitrage and expectations)[52] and does not reflect an underlying real demand or supply. Therefore derivatives can distort the fundamental market functions. As a consequence, the price develops differently as it would normally to cover the needs of demand and supply. The price signals become distorted, which leads to wrong resource allocation. For instance, if prices of commodities like oil become too high because from derivative speculation, it increases the costs for the producing economy and for the consumers. Because of the high commodity prices the commodity sector invests to increase its capacities. The missing demand causes the speculation bubble to burst sooner or later. The new capacities are overcapacities and the commodity sector is in trouble.[53]

The economy worked well without derivatives. Either the risks of derivatives can be controlled or the use of derivatives should be restricted to a mere hedge against risks, their original purpose. An underlying transaction should be compulsory. At least the leverage of the derivatives should be reduced significantly and credit derivatives should be treated like credits so they have to be funded with equity. Otherwise the next financial crisis might be too big for the governments to bail out. The argument that regulations on financial markets cannot be implemented because the world is too divided might be true. Also, the incentive not to regulate is strong, since the free rider position is the most profitable.[54] But also the losses of a possible

[52] Empirical studies show that the spot prices follow the future prices. See Deutsche Bundesbank (2006), pp. 59.

[53] For the discussion of the effects of food and commodity speculation see Conrad (2014).

[54] Governments find themselves internationally in a dilemma, since the best outcome for a single state is if all other sates regulate their financial market and it is therefore with its unregulated market the most attractive location for financial institutions (Free-rider position). The worst result for the individual state is if it regulates its financial market while the others do not. Since everyone is subject to this situation of insecurity, everyone decides to behave uncooperatively, which provides the worst results for everyone, national and international not regulated financial markets. Such a dilemma is called in the Public Choice Theory "prisoner's dilemma". For the expression "prisoner's dilemma" see Brennan and Buchanan (1985), p. 3.

crisis are too big for each single state. An unregulated financial market is a risk for all other countries. This loss risk has to be paid for to avoid distortion. A tax on financial deals of individual states with unregulated institutions would be the right solution to avoid a free-rider behavior and it could be implemented by each state individually.

At least the current reforms on banking regulation go in the wrong direction as they increase the equity requirements to cover the systemic risk instead of decreasing the risks of derivatives. We will discuss that below.[55]

Can the financial crisis be explained by behavioral science? Heuristics are simplified rules of behavior that people use to respond quickly and easily. They are mainly based on experience. One could speak of prejudice, for example. People are more likely to recognize events when they can remember or see things more often, which is called availability heuristics. Also, the effort to get to the information affects the assessment. For example, Schwartz and Vaughn et al found that respondents rated themselves as less assertive when they had to write down 12 situations in which they succeeded instead of just 6. They then felt the situations they were able to remember were too few.[56] In response to this observation, the concept of bounded rationality was developed, implying limited information processing capacities as opposed to complete rationality. A decision is then rationally limited if, taking account of information access and processing effort, the decision that maximizes utility is chosen.[57]

Group adaptation behavior can become market-relevant if market participants have social contact and identify themselves as a group. This is possible in financial centers or online chat platforms, where market participants can exchange their opinions and adapt them to each other. Here too, in the sense of groupthink, false dominant market opinions can arise. This is what New Behavioral Finance calls herding behavior.[58] We can call this collective erring. In the case of the financial crisis this was the common belief in the self-correcting power of the market and the ongoing prosperity and housing price increases.

7.2.2.2 Exaggerated Belief in Figures

During her visit of the London School of Economics in November 2008 the British Queen asked: “Why did no one see it coming?”[59]

[55] See Conrad (2014).

[56] See Schwarz and Vaughn (2002) and Schwarz et al. (1991).

[57] See Simon, Herbert A. (1959), pp. 262 f.

[58] See De Bondt, W. F. M., and Forbes, W. P. (1999).

[59] See The Financial Times, November 25th 2008. https://www.ft.com/content/50007754-ca35-11dd-93e5-000077b07658.

Krugman responded: "As I see it, the economics profession went astray because economists, as a group, mistook beauty, clad in impressive-looking mathematics, for truth."[60]

> Several studies analyzed the risks management practices and came to the conclusion that there was an over-reliance on quantitative analysis (studies by the Financial Stability Forum, the Working Group on Risk Assessment and Capital, the Senior Supervisors Group, the Basel Committee on Bank Supervisions, the International Institute of Finance and the International Monetary Financial Committee) (Voinea & Anton, 2009).

As the Classic-Neoclassic theory after the Great Depression of 1929, today's economic theory has explanation and justification problems. Neither of the statistical models foresaw the crisis nor are they now able to explain it. Moreover, the econometric models based on historical figures pretended there was a safety where there wasn't one, which was itself one reason for the crisis. Nassim Nicholas Taleb wrote about the delusions of control and reliability held by Wall Street and many other businesses. He pointed at the dangers of trusting the "bell-curve" models used by many financial institutions to mitigate risks. He questions the reliance on past historical information and brings the example of the black swan, that nobody expected until its discovery in Australia, or the example of the turkey who spends a thousand days being well-fed before being killed on the thousand-and-first day.[61] Justin Fox also criticizes the belief in models and especially the belief in efficient markets – a belief that was qualified by Robert Shiller as the "most remarkable error in the history of economic theory."[62]

Derivative products such as Collateralized Debt Obligations (CDOs) can be directly traced as being one of the major factors leading to today's subprime crisis and the greatest financial crisis since the Wall Street crash of 1929. The calculation of risk and value or price for derivatives on the basis of historical time periods was celebrated as a major breakthrough. This advance in financial mathematics was only made possible through the use of the ever more powerful calculating capacity of computers. This made it possible to create many new financial products. It later became apparent that these calculations were in error, and that it was only due to the confidence people had in the ability to calculate them that made these products possible. For example, it was determined that the risk and therefore the price for credit derivatives (Credit Default Swaps) as calculated by Yale Professor Gary Gorton was inaccurate. The confidence and faith in his calculations almost cost AIG its existence and the US government several billion dollars, as it was bailed out to save the financial system in October 2008 and partially nationalized. Gordon blamed the problem on the use of non-conforming data from the current marketplace and unprecedented developments, which deviated from his forecasts based on historical data. But the future is never like the past.

---

[60] Krugman, Paul (2009).

[61] See Taleb (2001, 2007).

[62] See Fox (2009) und Conrad (2010), p. 56.

It is difficult to understand why such an over-confidence in these calculations endured for so long, finally resulting in the subprime crisis, although the LTCM crisis had already illustrated the dangers and weaknesses of these financial calculations. In 2005 there were already warnings against using models for financial calculations based on historical figures.[63] The formulas for option prices (Black & Schools-Formel), which were responsible for the LTCM-crisis, are the best example for the incalculability of the economy. Robert Merton, Myron Scholes and Fischer Black received the Nobel Prize in 1997 for groundbreaking work in Option Pricing Theory. Based on the volatilities of the past, the formulas were developed to calculate prices for rights to sell or buy assets in the future (options). This is apparently an instrument to calculate the future. A hedge fund named Long Term Capital Management (LTCM) wanted to use for speculation, and he hired Robert Merton as a consultant. In 1998 LTCM then lost the investors around 90% of the $4 billion invested, which threatened to trigger a chain reaction on the international finance markets. The issue here is not just the credit taken by LTCM, but also the derivative positions of LTCM as contracting party, with which other finance market actors had protected themselves. Only when the then US central bank president Alan Greenspan intervened personally and pulled together an emergency package of billions from several large banks could the capital market crisis be averted. The second of the hedge funds Merton consulted, named IFC Continuum, closed in 2006. The future was in fact not predictable.[64]

The flaw in the option price theory or risk values such as "value of risk" which were determined on the basis of historical volatility was that future relationships between demand and supply could not fundamentally be accurately depicted. This is how in 2008 Porsche could raise its stake in VW to 74% through the purchase of VW call options, at a much reduced price than if it had bought the shares on the open market. The option price for VW shares did not reflect the actual shortage of shares, which had been calculated on the basis of past price volatility. This miscalculation lead to the share prices being set much too low. The excessive demand for VW shares eventually lead to a short squeeze.

The use of the same seemingly correct risk models led also to a similar investing behavior of the market participants. If the models were wrong all investors came to the same wrong risk assessment, which worsened the subprime crisis. Also the rating agencies used the wrong models to calculate their CDO-ratings. Based on these wrong ratings the investors underestimated the risks substantially and decided all to invest. Therefore the risk models increased the systemic risk and did not decrease it.

Abstract and isolated models of thought are fine in principle. They make it possible to take the complex economy apart into separate connections and thus to allow discoveries about economic processes. Econometrics is thus a valuable ancillary science for economics. There is also nothing to be said against using

[63]"The method of calculation is based upon historic volatility and does not take into account irrational human behaviour, such as panic,... ." Conrad (2005), p. 398.

[64]See Conrad (2005) and Welt-Kompakt dated 08/22/06, p. 15.

mathematics, as long as the effort remains proportional to the usefulness of knowledge gained. The models have unfortunately become so complex however, that they are no longer useful for teaching purposes. The effort required to learn them is greater than the knowledge gained. It is problematic when econometrics, thus the statistics applied to the economy with economic mathematics, is taught as exclusive representation of the only true economics. Without order theory and order politics of order there can be no understanding of the state and economics.

Derivatives as the so-called Collateral Debt Obligations were the trigger and the main reason for the subprime crisis. They are based on complex economic modeling and statistics. Basically we can say that the image of the economy is distorted when only determinist models are applied. More thinking and less calculating would have been much more appropriate. So can the subprime crisis can also be traced back to developments in the economic sciences.

Be that as it may, econometrics, statistics and mathematics have contributed significantly to the continued development of economic science. They deserve recognition, no doubt, but this is no reason for economic science to consist solely of these subjects. At the end of the scientific chain there must be somebody to explain the science of practice and weigh the various theories and approaches against one another on the basis of practical considerations in order to make statements relevant to practices in a comprehensive economic overview. To make statements relevant for practical application the theories and models must be related to the respective practical situation. Only then is it possible to decide what parts of the respective models of thought can be applied. In this highest of disciplines, the relation exists both in theory and in practice, at least within economic science. This requires an analytic, combining intelligence. The considerations must be logically deductive and verbal, since there is no calculability of the economy as a whole. In economic science as a social science mathematic abilities are less important, and the creative approaches to explanation gain importance.

Kahnemann and Tversky found, that the presentation and formulation of questions affects the decision of subjects.[65] In the financial crisis the investment decisions were influenced by the by the wrong ratings and the securitization. The behavior of the lenders was changed. The investors did not question the creditworthiness of the debtors, which would normally be requirement for lending.

Framing can be used to manipulate decisions to the benefit or disadvantage of the decider. For example, you may be more likely to encourage people to take a health check-up by telling them the risks of illness if they fail to get a check-up than by emphasizing the opportunities for early discovery and recovery.[66]

The ratings of the subprime CDOs were based on old data from the US real estate market. Tversky and Kahneman call a behavior focused on old data anchoring. People are biased because they depend too heavily on the first set of data they

[65] See Kahneman and Tversky (1981, 1982, 1984, 1986); Kahneman et al. (1991), pp. 193–206.

[66] See Meyerowitz and Chaiken (1987) and Beck (2014), p. 154.

receive. This data is the "anchor" that distorts the decision.[67] Tversky and Kahneman found also insensitivity to sample size, which is a bias to see patterns in small numbers of results even though more results are needed to regress significant correlations.[68]

The belief in experts was finally criticized after the financial crisis. The complexity of derivatives like the CDO was so high that nobody but the experts of the rating agencies was able to understand their structure and value. Some authors called for the "de-expertizing" of experts.[69]

The wrong ratings of the CDOs were a sign of overconfidence as a subjective favorable judgment of one's self. Subjects regularly overestimate their own knowledge, their control options, their abilities as well as their achievements.[70] Lichtenstein and Fischhoff found that the harder the tasks, the greater the overconfidence. Rating the CDOs was a very complex hard task that only experts were able to perform and understand.[71]

Weinstein tested students and found that they overestimate their positive outcomes and underestimate their negative outcomes. They estimated the likelihood of earning more than $10,000 as their starting salary, 41.5% higher than their fellow students, and the likelihood of a heart attack before the age of 40, 38.4% lower than their peers.[72] **Overconfidence** increases with the difficulty level of the tasks. It is also subject to experts who feel that they are better informed.[73] This is also a problem in economic consulting, which Hayek called the presumption of knowledge. Confirmation bias reinforces the problem.

The confirmation bias describes how people process facts in a way that confirms their own opinions. Contradictory facts are not taken into account or are subordinate.[74] These include:

– Pseudo-diagnostics: Humans tend to favor their own hypotheses rather than weighing them objectively critically against others. Doctors should not commit themselves so early to their diagnosis, for example.[75] The belief perservance bias

[67] See Tversky and Kahneman (1974).

[68] See Tversky and Kahneman (1974), p. 1 and 125.

[69] See Khan (2018), p. 25.

[70] See Metcalfe (1998).

[71] See Lichtenstein et al. (1982).

[72] See Weinstein (1980).

[73] See Angner (2006) and Russo and Schoemaker (1992).

[74] See Wason, Peter C. (1960), Nickerson, Raymond S. (1998), and Beck, H. (2014).

[75] See Doherty et al. (1979).

goes in the same direction: In order not to have to change their opinion, hypotheses are maintained even when they have already been refuted.[76]

Added to this is the illusion of control as an overestimation of one's own influence on processes, such as throwing dice to influence the outcome or selecting a winning ticket. Experiments showed that test takers overestimate their dice skills if they were lucky in the beginning[77] and that test takers are willing to buy the more expensive tickets if they can choose the numbers themselves.[78] Thus, there is a tendency to rate more expensive products as higher quality, although the correlation is very weak. And the willingness to pay a higher price for a product increases when it externally resembles a quality product.

People shy away from change when they cannot assess how they are affected. The status quo is preferred over another alternative (status quo bias). Samuelson and Zeckhauser found that the majority of test subjects do not change their investment portfolio in the case of inheritance. The subjects retained the shares they had inherited or did not buy any shares in cash.[79] In principle, sticking to the status quo can be a rational and efficient approach. Boxall, Adamowicz and Moon found that the status quo bias increases the more complex and time-consuming the decision-making process is.[80] Another explanatory approach is the regret aversion. To revise a decision that has already been made means, on the one hand, that one has to admit to having made a mistake. This generates regret and negative emotions.[81]

This would explain why nobody of the experts corrected or questioned the wrong ratings. The biases show that ratings are not precise or might even be wrong because people make them.

7.2.2.3 Missing Moral Values

The enrichment of managers at the expense of their company and the society was criticized long before the subprime crisis. A scandal is really nothing more than immoral conduct in the eyes of society. Whether we look at top managers just trying to get the most out of the company they have been entrusted with, or manipulating the balance sheets to get rich with stock options or bonus payments at the expense of clueless stockholders, or employees lower down in the hierarchy who try to cheat their colleagues or the market, we are looking at proof that across the globe the economy has to wrest with massive ethical problems. It is worth noting that even model companies, such as Enron, are affected by moral lapses. There are many US

[76] See Ross et al. (1975).

[77] See Langer and Roth (1975).

[78] See Langer (1975).

[79] See Samuelson and Zeckhauser (1988), pp. 12 and Kahneman et al. (1991), pp. 193–206. Beck (2014), pp. 164.

[80] See Boxall et al. (2009) and Beck (2014), p. 167.

[81] See Bell (1982) and Loomes and Sudgen (1982), pp. 805–824.

companies, as well as internationally known investment banks such as Merrill Lynch, Morgan Stanley and Credit Swiss First Boston in the USA and Goldman Sachs, Morgan Stanley and Deutsche Bank in Germany, who have all been accused of stock analyses advocating sales.[82]

The largest bank in the world and the American branch leader Citigroup seems to have had ethical problems as well. The Citygroup head Charles Price addressed his employees with these words: "No one may damage our long-term interests for short-term advantages." He said he would check into "unnecessary risks and unethical behavior" personally if necessary.[83] He prescribed ethics seminars for his employees and had a behavioral code drawn up, and established a department where the employees could anonymously inform the company of unethical behavior. What happened? His predecessor Sandy Weill had set the employees a growth rate target of 15% and seems to have implemented it absolutely. The pressure was apparently so great that the employees, voluntarily or involuntarily, turned to illegal methods to reach the targets. The bank was then only able to avoid lawsuits and the subsequent damage to its image by agreeing to pay out settlements, connected with damage compensation. In 2002 it paid $400 million because Citi analysts portrayed stocks too positively, which Citi investment banking wanted to sell. In 2004 the Citigroup paid $2.65 billion for Worldcom and $70 million to the US Federal Reserve after being accused of lending usury credit and giving credit only in connection with the sale of superfluous insurance. Another accusation was that the bank did not pass on rebates to the customers of their investment funds. In 2004 Citygroup lost their license for private banking in Japan because of abuses of the law against money laundering and market manipulation. In 2005 the US bank supervision forbid Citigroup from any new takeovers until internal rules of ethics had been implemented. In 2005 there were also settlements paid for involvement in the bankruptcies of Global Crossing ($75 million) and Enron ($2 billion). There was also a 4 million British Pound settlement and returned profits of 9.96 million British Pounds for manipulated prices on the London bond market. These are of course just the ethical missteps that were brought to light.[84]

It seems conspicuous that the firms that had seemed to be among the most financially stable for years would wind up in a state of collapse. This is valid for Enron and other firms as well as for Citigroup and the investment banks involved in the subprime crisis. But with an unethical business policy they were only successful in the short term. Long term these firms had financial problems.

The subprime crisis can be considered the epitome of the ethical failure of our modern economy. Everything came together, and many saw in the crisis the final act of our "turbo capitalism", the limitless enrichment of the few at the expense of society, which almost lead to a total collapse of the financial system.[85] The lack of

[82] See Chediak and Escudero (2004), p. 79 and Ogger (2001), p. 103.

[83] Quoted from Capital, 18/2005, p. 54.

[84] See Wirtschaftswoche dated September, 01, 2005, p. 52–58 and Capital, No. 18, 2005, p. 54–56.

[85] See Dahrendorf (2009).

regulation and belief in the self-correcting power of the market was used by a few to take advantage of the situation. The victims were, above all, the socially and economically disadvantaged who were convinced by predatory lenders to buy homes that they could ill-afford and which would lead them to personal bankruptcy, or at worst, homelessness and a life on the streets. This was truly the creation of social misery. Mortgage lenders had to be aware of this, as they were directly involved in working with the subprime borrowers most at risk of default, which should be considered the height of moral irresponsibility. These lenders only gave thought to their personal profit without any consideration for the fate of borrowers. In the end, they were rewarded on the basis of their success in issuing loans. The difficulties that these borrowers would have in repaying these loans were of no consequence to them. For the most part, these borrowers did not have the education or the capacity to understand the nuances of how their mortgages were structured, and lacked the protection of appropriate consumer agencies or law enforcement. All those who knowingly took part in this deception and intentionally inflicted this suffering on unsuspecting borrowers are morally culpable. The Clinton and Bush administrations encouraged lending to subprime borrowers through Fannie Mae and Freddie Mac as part of an ill-conceived social program are also in-part responsible. Also culpable are those who knowingly encouraged this process and profited from the housing and mortgage bubble while helping to finance the ensuing social misery. Noteworthy here are also those bank managers who knowingly gambled with the long-term viability of their banks and the financial system so that they could maximize their profits and bonuses over the short-term. The moral responsibility lies with the financial regulating authorities that tolerated the creation and growth of the real estate bubble and the spread of subprime mortgage products that made it possible. They permitted the creation of a new, unregulated credit market without intervening. In the USA, there were widespread and timely warnings concerning the dangers of a bubble in the real estate, the subprime mortgages and financial innovations that made it all possible.

It is no wonder that societal recognition for managers has dropped to the current low, which the manager's guild should be taking to heart. In a Wall Street Journal survey in 2003, 64% of those questioned said that they do not trust managers. Only one other profession trumped this result. Only 16% of those questioned trusted politicians, and 84% expressed distrust.[86] Other studies determined that managers in the USA and Germany to have a very utilitarian attitude on ethical and moral questions, in particularly among young managers and American economic students. Typical statements included "One has to look after one's own interests," "Morality is just a matter of feelings," or "Sometimes small injustices are necessary in order to reach greater goals."[87] According to a survey among Swiss managers, 75% assume that the market forces automatically provide for an ethically and morally justifiable

[86] See Ergenzinger and Krulis-Randa (2004), p. 4.

[87] See Noll (2002), p. 168.

behavior.[88] It is interesting to note that many managers do not seem to feel comfortable with immoral, unethical conditions. Studies have shown that meanwhile the majority of managers go to work with more or less consciously felt fear.[89]

Studies had already established a very egoistic attitude among American business students in the late 1980s. The behavior is purposeful and opportunistic. Moral reflexivity is severely restricted. Success and continuity are unconditionally the first priority. Typical words are "winning is everything".[90] But this is a global problem. According to a survey among Swiss executives, 75% of managers assume that the market forces automatically provide ethically and morally justified behavior. Another survey among German executives comes to a similar conclusion, inasmuch as 50% assume that their company automatically contributes to the common good through its activities.[91]

According to a survey by GFK market research from 2008, 61% of Germans asked were of the opinion – that sincerity and honesty does not pay – the world is dishonest and people expect to be lied to. And 38% consider it appropriate to lie if it will advance their career.[92]

Ethical problems are increasingly making things more difficult for companies as an internal problem of loyalty. In a study conducted by the German personnel consultation firm Kienbaum, Human Resources managers complain about a generation of applicants with little inclination to fully engage themselves. Nearly every other Head of Human Resources bemoans a lack of social competence. Young people increasingly act to maximize their own benefits. This means, for example, that when they have a question to answer, they consider what answer will be the most advantageous. This generation of streamlined opportunists does not please personnel, because they neither provide the necessary creative input, nor can their supervisors trust them. "The question of what one actually wants to do in five years can hardly be answered. Personnel employees know that employees and companies no longer enter a bond for life. But enthusiasm for a task and the desire of the applicant to do something special is still important to the companies."[93] According to Walter Jachmann, Manager of Human Resources consulting at German Kienbaum, applicants lack backbone and personality:

> Exactly at the time of crisis the company leaders do not get the information they need. No one discusses or contradicts, because everyone just nods and follows the managers.[94]

---

[88] See Ulrich (1993), p. 1173 and p. 1172.

[89] See Noll (2002), p. 168.

[90] See Löhr (1997), p. 198.

[91] See Ulrich (1993), p. 1172.

[92] See Rheinische Post, 04/18/08 and http://de.statista.com/statistik/daten/studie/292/umfrage

[93] Walter Jachmann, Manager of Personnel Consultants Kienbaum, quoted from Handelsblatt dated October 20/21/22 2006, p. 1.

[94] Stefan Tilk, Member of Management at the Bertelsmann subsidiary Arvato Direct Services, quoted from Handelsblatt dated October 20/21/22 2006, p. 1, translated into English.

The internal and external selection processes are also criticized, however. Assessment centers make Human Resources' job easier when evaluating a large number of applicants according to objective criteria in a relatively short amount of time. The tests can be prepared for in advance though, and in order to be successful the candidates must optimize their answers according to predetermined criteria. In these mass tests there is no room for the rough edges of a creative personality. The internal selection processes often reward conformity, making contradiction an unattractive option.[95]

In the meantime, the notion that honesty is stupidity has apparently prevailed not only in the economy, but also across society. It is often said that "one must be able to afford morality". Everyone is his own best friend. Communion and sacrifice are replaced by ruthless utility maximization. According to a survey of CSF market research conducted in 2008, 61% of the Germans surveyed felt that sincerity did not pay off – the world was finally lied to. And 38% thought it would be justifiable to lie if it served their own career.[96]

It is interesting that many managers in immoral unethical conditions do not seem to be able to lie. Studies show that the majority of executives now have more or less consciously felt anxiety at work. The fear of job loss, the fear of making mistakes and the fear of misinformation are dominant here.[97] Fear at the workplace, exaggerated performance pressure and interpersonal competition pressure play an important role in mental illness.[98]

The behavior of bankers did not change significantly after the financial crisis. In 2013, only 36% of Wall Street employees surveyed believed their industry had changed for the better. On the other hand, 52% were convinced that the competition was involved in "illegal or unethical" actions. This information was answered by nearly a quarter of respondents in the "own house experienced" or "first hand" experienced. However, 29% considered unethical or illegal tricks "to be successful," an increase of 17% over 2012 when the study was first conducted. Particularly in the case of younger employees, an ethical attitude seems to be lacking. 36% of young bankers with less than ten years of experience advocated windy tricks, versus 18% of Wall Street veterans with more than 20 professional years. A quarter would be ready for insider trading "if they could earn at least ten million dollars." In the case of the younger colleague, this share even rises to 38%. 17% are convinced "that their bosses look away if they suspect a top performer of insider trading." This is justified by the fact that the income is too low: 26% think that the remuneration plans or bonus structures of their companies are an incentive to betray ethical norms or break the law. This is the case for the younger 31% and the older 21%.[99]

---

[95] See Handelsblatt dated October 20/21/22 2006, p. 1.

[96] See Rheinische Post, 04/18/08 and http://de.statista.com/statistik/daten/studie/292/umfrage (01/22/2010).

[97] See Volk (2000), p. 57.

[98] See Volk (2000).

[99] See Sucharow (2013).

The managers are thus not fulfilling their role model function. The internal company contract for the distribution of work, stress and income is turned upside down, which is rightly felt to be unfair, thus has negative effects on the other employees.

It is difficult to change the business culture in the financial organizations. However, people stick to their ethical internal standards even if this means efforts or sacrificing financial gains.[100] If people are remembered of their honesty-standards, they behave more ethically.[101]

Research shows that a code of ethics only influences manager behavior ethically when the code includes a certification choice. The reason is that the signing of the code increases the moral reasoning in the manager.[102] Thus, employees should sign ethical standards and should be remembered of them during their work. A similar approach is an oath.

In some countries there were attempt so increase the ethical commitment of the employees like the Dutch banking oath initiated by the Dutch Banking Association. As of 2015, all 80,000 bankers and banking staff in the Netherlands had to swear that they will endeavor to maintain and promote confidence in the financial sector, that they will put clients' interests first and take care of shareholders. A breach of the oath can lead to fines, suspension, or even blacklisting.[103]

7.2.2.4 The Importance of Risk Adequate Compensation

Since the Enron, Worldcom and the financial crisis, compensation for bank managers and managers in other public companies have come under intense scrutiny. Compensation has been held responsible for encouraging excess risk-taking, particularly within the financial system. It has been asserted that bonus compensation schemes have caused asymmetries in the treatment of gains and losses, which can lead to excessively risky behavior. The purpose of this chapter is to test this hypothesis.[104] Do unilaterally constructed incentive schemes encourage undue risk-taking? This question is examined with a behavioral experiment using the game roulette. It is used to analyze how unilateral compensation affects risk behavior.

Related Literature

According to principal agent theory (Ross, 1973; Jensen & Meckling, 1976; Nowak 1997) correlating a manager's compensation with either their performance or that of

[100] See Aronson and Carlsmith (1962), pp. 178–182 and Harris et al. (1976), pp. 123–135.

[101] See Mazar et al. (2008), pp. 633–644.

[102] See Ariely (2010), p. 28.

[103] See Khan (2018), p. 10.

[104] See Conrad, Christian A. (2015).

the firm promotes better incentive alignment and leads to higher motivation and thus stronger company values. However, there is an asymmetric imbalance between the term, magnitude and probability of gains and losses in common compensation schemes. Short-term results are rewarded even when these results are later reversed. This encourages risk taking by the employees – agents – at the cost of the company – the principal. The agents undertake actions that generate a high probability of gains in the short-term, while the risk of a larger loss in the longer-term is not taken into consideration, causing the principle to bear all of the long-term risk. A substantial body of literature has emerged to test the relationship between manager compensation and manager behavior and performance.

Figures of the Office of the New York State Comptroller show that bonuses in Wall Street financial institutions continued to register large positive numbers in 2007 and 2008, even while the banks suffered large losses (Sharma, 2012). Surveys by the Financial Stability Forum (2009) showed that over 80% of financial market participants and experts believe that compensation practices played a role in promoting the accumulation of risks that led to the financial crisis. Cuomo (2009) shows that bonuses and overall compensation did not vary significantly even though profits diminished during the financial crisis. Cai et al. (2010) studied the pay structures of banking executives before the financial crisis. They found some problematic practices (such as too much bonus and stock-related compensation). These practices might have encouraged "short-termism" and excessive risk-taking.

Agarwal and Ben-David (2011) results show that the explosion in mortgage volume during the crisis and the deterioration of underwriting standards can be partly attributed to the incentives of loan officers. They studied a controlled experiment conducted by a large bank. The compensation scheme of loan officers was changed from fixed salary to commission-based compensation. Loan officers were 19% more likely to accept loan applications, approved loan amounts larger by 23%, and the loans were 28% more likely to default. The increase in default occurred primarily within the population of loans that would not have been accepted in the absence of commission-based compensation.

However, Gregg et al. (2012) found that the cash-plus-bonus pay-performance sensitivity of financial firms is not significantly higher than in other sectors and concluded that it is unlikely that incentive structures could be held responsible for inducing bank executives to focus on short-term profits. This would mean that we are facing a general compensation problem.

Cooper et al. (2014) found evidence that industry and size-adjusted CEO pay is negatively related to future shareholder wealth changes for periods up to 5 years after payment. Sun reviewed the early executive compensation studies, bonus plan maximization hypotheses and equity-based compensation. Opportunistic management incentives encourage creative earnings management, which may have negative consequences for the company and shareholders. He shows that firms pay a price and its negative impact on shareholders is economically significant (Sun, 2012).

Schotter and Weigelt (1992) use four different compensation schemes to demonstrate that a compensation scheme that induces behavior consistent with lower discount rates is a necessary condition for reconciling divergent time preferences between principals and agents, and that subjects become more myopic in their investment decisions if compensation contracts are incorrectly structured.

Colesa et al. (2006) found that higher sensitivity of CEO wealth to stock volatility encourages riskier policy choices, including relatively more investment in R&D, less investment in PPE, more focus, and higher leverage. They also provide empirical evidence of a strong causal relation between managerial compensation and investment policy, debt policy, and firm risk. Cheating is also influenced by compensation schemes. Gilla et al. (2013) show that exposing workers to a compensation scheme based on random bonuses makes them cheat more but has no effect on their productivity.

Andersson et al. (2013) studied risk-taking on behalf of others in an experiment. The decision makers were facing high-powered incentives to increase the risk on behalf of others through hedged compensation contracts or with tournament incentives. The decision-makers responded strongly to incentives that result in an increased risk-exposure for others. There have also been experimental studies concerning the binary choice task and the study concerning the binary double gamble to explore the predictive validity of dispositional traits and affective states in decision making under risk and uncertainty (Papaeconomou, 2012).

This chapter provides a simple incentive-based experiment regarding unilateral bonus compensation schemes based on the game roulette, which can be easily repeated with the students. There have been several experiments with roulette but with the objective to scrutinize the gambling behavior (Rubio; Hernández & Santacreu) and guessing tendencies (Rubio et al., 2010). The following experiment simulates most common short-term bonus compensation schemes without accountability. They were also the dominating compensation schemes before and during the financial crisis.

Experimental Design Roulette

The purpose of this chapter is to test the hypothesis that unilaterally constructed incentive schemes encourage excess risk-taking. The methodology is to simulate decision- making under asymmetric incentive structures. Therefore an experimental environment similar to the compensation schemes had to be constructed. Roulette has the advantage of clearly demonstrating the probabilities for gains and losses. In the game Roulette the probability of losses is compensated with higher payouts (apart from zero). A higher risk has an equivalent higher payout. In order to simulate behavior with different incentive and risk structures, decision-makers have to be exposed to different remuneration schemes, which is why there were game rounds with different considerations of gains and losses.

Game 5: Roulette

The experiment is started with symmetrical incentive structures. Round A and B have identical incentive structures. Round A serves as a control round for B. Finally in round C a unilateral consideration of the profits takes place and the changes in the betting behavior are recorded. An indicator for higher risk-taking would be a higher capital set even though the winning probability stayed the same.

In round A, the students are able to play Roulette with an initial play capital of €1000. Losses and gains are credited with 100%. The students are asked to check each other's calculations after each game.

In the round B the gambling losses and gains are counted each with 50% and are added to the initial capital of €1000. Thus there were still no conflicting interests and no asymmetries in the treatment of gains and losses. Round B therefore has identical incentive structures as round A. So A is able to serve as a control group for B.

In round C a unilateral consideration of the profits takes place. The set capital is not deducted, if the roulette bet is wrong. Conversely, the payout is credited with 50%, and added to the €1000 of initial capital. The results of the rounds B and C are added, starting from an initial capital of €1000 each and the player with the highest result is rewarded with €10 real money. For this game we chose real money to have a stronger link to compensation in real life. The rules are explained to the students before starting the experiment.

Round C thus corresponds to the unilateral performance-based remuneration of the common bonus-based compensation schemes. Loss and profit incentives are not equally distributed. Losses are borne by the companies and profits are rewarded with bonuses. This simple experiment shows clear results.

Results

The experiment was conducted with 69 students from different Business Bachelor and Master courses at the University of Applied Science HTW at Saarbrücken.[105] The students played 3 rounds Roulette (A, B and C), each with three games. They could bet on red or black, on one of the three thirds of the 36 numbers or on one number. The roulette wheel determined the winning number and color. If it was zero, the game was repeated and not registered. The payouts were distributed according to the probability of winning (x2, x3, x36) and accumulated in each round (Fig. 7.2).

In round C, the sum of the average capital set rose from €1361.88 in round B to €3899.28, by 186%. The highest possible profit (calculated as the product of the set capital and the possible payout) in all three games rose to €30,000.72 (see Figs. 7.3 and 7.4). If you set the maximal possible gain in relation to set capital as a risk measurement indicator, the willingness to take risks increased from 5.05 to 7.69 (see Fig. 7.2). The significantly higher standard deviation in round C shows that some players were more willing to take risks than the average (see Figs. 7.5 and 7.6).

Conclusion

It has been demonstrated that unilaterally constructed incentive schemes encourage excess risk-taking. This would indicate that common bonus-based compensation schemes enhance risk because of the asymmetries in the treatment of gains and losses. Unilaterally constructed compensation schemes were one reason for the financial crisis.

---

[105] See Conrad (2015).

	Round A	Round B	Round C
Average set capital	€1,252.63	€1,361.88	€3,899.28
Average maximal possible gain	€5,946.83	€6,874.49	€30,000.72
Risk as max. possible gain/set capital	4.75	5.05	7.69
Standard deviation average set capital	€779.65	€650.32	€2,408.89
Standard deviation maximal possible gain	€634.21	€9,687.06	€31,585.46

Fig. 7.2 Statistical data

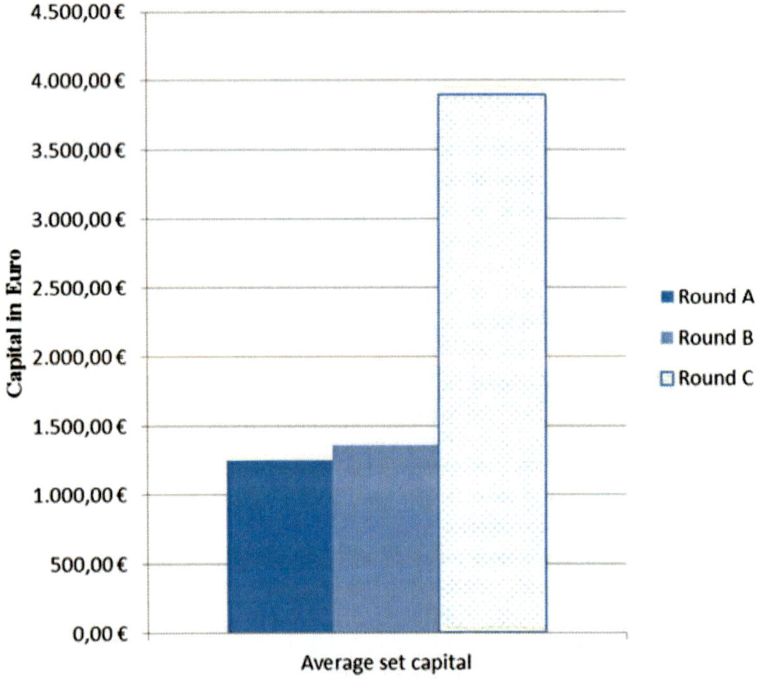

Fig. 7.3 Set capital

The experiment showed that unilaterally constructed incentive schemes encourage excess risk-taking. This would indicate that common bonus-based compensation schemes are not a good idea and in face enhance risk because of the asymmetries in the treatment of gains and losses. In most cases compensation can only decrease down to the base salary while gains from bonuses can be limitless. Short-term results are rewarded even when these results are subsequently reversed. This encourages risk-taking by the employees (agents) at the cost of the company (the principal). They undertake actions that generate a high probability of gains in the short-term while the risk of a larger loss in the longer-term is not taken into consideration, thus

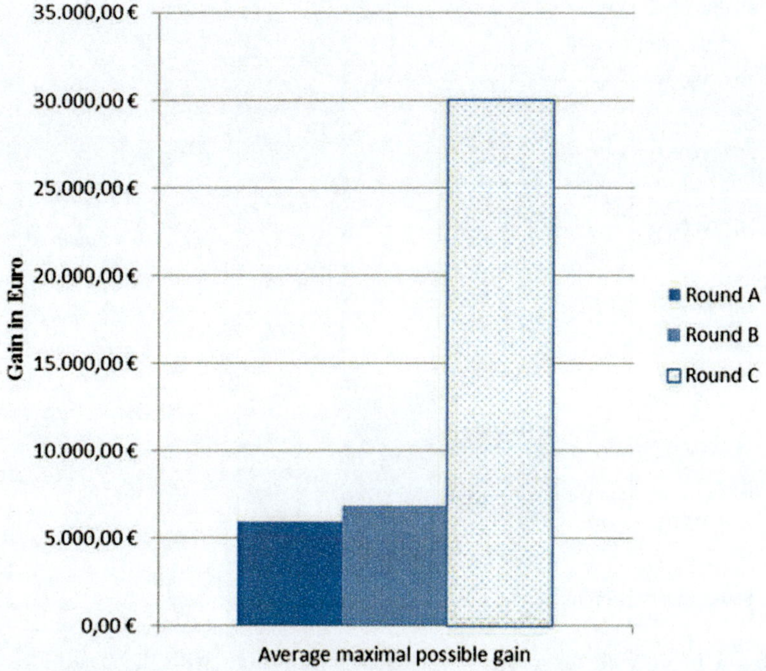

Fig. 7.4 Maximum possible gain

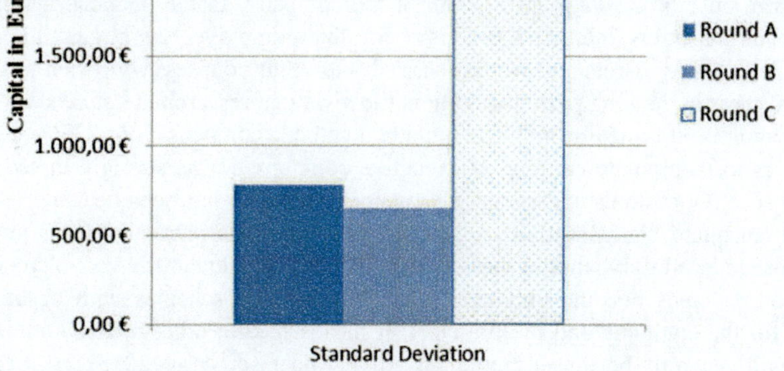

Fig. 7.5 Standard deviation set capital

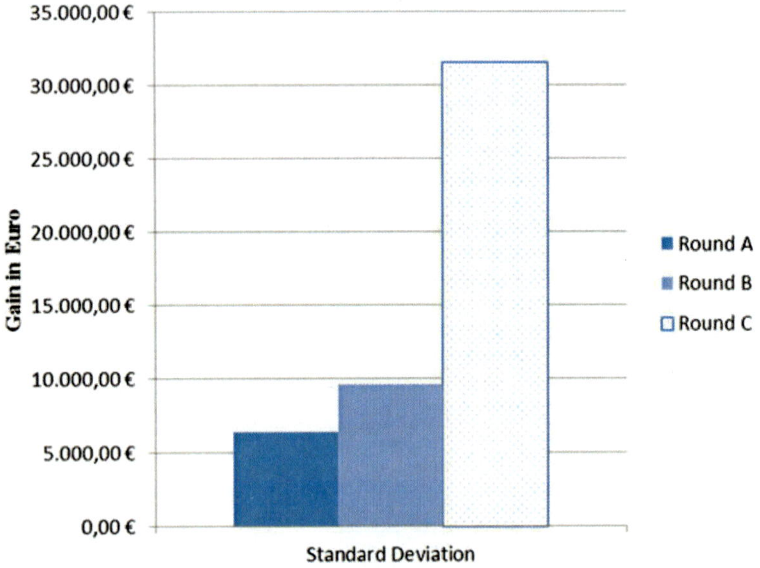

Fig. 7.6 Standard deviation maximum possible gain

becoming a liability to the principal. This does not align with the basic idea of principal-agent theory. Of course a connection between a manager's compensation and a firm or manager's performance will promote better incentive alignment and lead to higher motivation, which increases firm value, but only if losses and profits are remunerated symmetrically.

The existing asymmetries of bonus compensation schemes have led to a divergence of interests between employees on the one hand and the health of financial institutions and other companies at large on the other hand. Compensation packages for CEO's and other managers have gotten out of control. Remuneration and bonuses depend on short-term profitability, which increases share prices in the short-term, but not the long-term health of the company. In the financial system, investment managers increased the risks for their employer by buying highly profitable but risky assets and were rewarded with high bonuses, which led to the financial crisis in the long term. In addition, the review of research literature showed that cheating is promoted by high and unilateral variable compensations. CEOs have incentives to manipulate earnings if executive compensation is strongly linked to performance. Opportunistic earnings management behavior has been detected.

Risk adequate compensation is therefore an important prerequisite for good performance in all risk-handling professions. Without accountability variable compensation schemes become unilateral bonus maximation schemes with negative effects for the company and the principal. It means risking other people's money which will generally be abused (moral hazards) (Andersson et al., 2013).

It is difficult to change the business culture in the financial organizations if the compensation schemes contradict the ethical guidelines. The employees react in the way the company sets the guidelines. If the earning goals cannot be reached with ethical work, unethical methods are applied as the example of Sears has shown. Cheating is also influenced by compensation schemes. Gilla, Prowseb and Vlassopoulosc show that exposing workers to a compensation scheme based on random bonuses makes them cheat more but has no effect on their productivity.[106]

Conclusion
Group adaptation behavior can become market-relevant if market participants have social contact and identify themselves as a group. In the case of the financial crisis there was the common belief in the self-correcting power of the market and the ongoing prosperity and housing price increases. We can call this collective erring.

Kahnemann and Tversky found, that the presentation and formulation of questions affects the decision of subjects. In the financial crisis the investment decisions were influenced by the by the wrong ratings and the securitization. This kind of framing changed the behavior of the lenders. The investors did not question the creditworthiness of the debtors, which would normally be requirement for lending.

The ratings of the subprime CDOs were based on old data from the US real estate market. Tversky and Kahneman call a behavior focused on old data anchoring. People are biased because they depend too heavily on the first set of data they receive. This data is the "anchor" which distorts the decision.[107] Tversky and Kahneman also found insensitivity to sample size, which is a bias to see patterns in small numbers of results even though more results are needed to regress significant correlations.[108]

After the financial crisis the belief in experts was criticized. The complexity of derivatives like the CDO was so high that nobody but than the experts of the rating agencies were able to understand their structure and value.

The wrong ratings of the CDOs were a sign of overconfidence as a subjective favorable judgment of one's self. There was also confirmation bias and regret aversion. Investors processed the facts in a way that confirm their own opinions. This would explain why nobody of the experts corrected or questioned the wrong ratings. The biases show that ratings are not precise or might even be wrong because people make them.

As we have seen unmoral aspiration for enrichment of managers was common in the financial crisis. The bank managers were not fulfilling their role model function. People are influenced in their behavior by their view of the world. Ideas and attitudes, or moral values, must be shown by example and included in education.

Bad examples can ruin common decency as much as it can be dangerous to continually preach thinking in models and maximizing benefit as the only reasonable, rational behavior. The consequence will be that people orient themselves on these behavioral maxims and repress their positive human characteristics such as

---

[106] See Colesa et al. (2006), pp. 431–468 and Gilla et al. (2013), pp. 120–134.

[107] See Tversky and Kahneman (1974).

[108] See Tversky and Kahneman (1974), p. 1 and 125.

sympathy, helpfulness, general willingness to sacrifice and selflessness. Management education in particular must ask itself if it did not indirectly create monster managers; business ethics receives too little attention.

It is difficult to change the business culture in the financial organizations. However, if people are remembered of their honesty-standards, they behave more ethically. Employees should sign ethical standards and should be remembered of them during their work. Finally, it has been demonstrated that unilaterally constructed incentive schemes encourage excess risk-taking. Unilaterally constructed compensation schemes were one reason for the financial crisis.

Comprehension questions

1. Name some causes of the financial crisis.
2. What are the common moral causes of economic crisis?
3. Can you imagine some reasons for the unethical attitude of the managers?
4. What reforms would you suggest to improve the financial system?

7.2.3 The Reforms of the International Financial Market Order

What Follows Why?

After the financial crisis several studies analyzed the risks management practices and came to the conclusion that the investors have underestimated the risks due to products complexity and over-reliance on quantitative analysis (studies by the Financial Stability Forum, the Working Group on Risk Assessment and Capital, the Senior Supervisors Group, the Basel Committee on Bank Supervisions, the International Institute of Finance and the International Monetary Financial Committee) (Voinea & Anton, 2009).

New financial instruments such as derivatives showed their risk potential in the financial crisis. There were also new market participants, whose market influence has grown. By using a qualitative research approach we examine in this chapter the extent to which these two developments affect the economic processes of the market and put financial markets at risk. We also analyze the extent to which the new financial market regulations Basel III and the American Dodd Frank Act are sufficient to limit the systemic risk they cause.

Learning Goals

You should be able to explain what weaknesses of the financial order lead to the financial crisis and what reforms were implemented.

7.2.3.1 Risk and Non-transparency in Derivatives

The bilateral over-the-counter derivatives (OTCs), which are not traded on the stock exchange and therefore not registered, were a central problem in the financial crisis. The supervisory authorities still do not know the exact amount and distribution of the derivatives, which means they cannot know the systemic risk (e.g. the CDS to Greece in the European debt crisis) and cannot intervene. In the financial crisis, the counterparty risks were not properly priced, for example through a reasonable capital securitization. The default of a counterparty or credit could lead to a system risk as a result of contagion, as in the case of Lehman.

Basel III and the Dodd Frank Act provide a framework for trading via central clearinghouses (stock exchanges) as well as standards for a collateral deposit of the CDS seller and a capital backing which the CDS buyer must take to hedge the counterparty risk. The equity requirements of derivatives is determined by comprehensive models; the rating-related bond equivalence approach and the internal Advanced CVA (Credit Value Adjustment) approach, which is based on market data, specifically spreads, have been developed for this purpose (Hofmann, 2011; Deutsche Bundesbank, 2011; Peirce & Soliman, 2016; Giancarlo, 2016). For the remaining OTC derivatives, higher equity requirements apply to counterparty risk, which makes them unattractive to banks. The volume of OTC derivatives is already decreasing (Gaumert et al., 2011; Conrad, 2013a). However, the collateral and the equity capital for the counterparty risk are insufficient to cover the systemic risk of derivatives. The financial crisis has shown very clearly how fast market data can change. If the spreads of the CVA and ratings of the bond equivalence approach change, banks must collateralize the difference.[109]

7.2.3.2 Weaknesses of Risk Indicators and Pricing Methods

Ratings

Uniform ratings are dangerous because all market players are subject to this assessment. If securities such as AAA-rated CDOs prove to be worthless in the financial crisis, asset bubbles can occur, followed by asset crashes. The financial innovations created a false sense of security with their complex mathematical models and AAA ratings. One of the main causes of the subprime crisis was that investors relied on the credit judgments of the rating agencies. The ratings were too good, which meant that the credits were understated with insufficient capital and that during the crisis the valuation adjustments put the creditors at risk.

The Dodd Frank Act decouples the acceptable amount of capital securitization from external ratings. In general, the regulatory and supervisory authorities should remove all references to external ratings and rating agencies from the regulations (Dullien,

[109] See Conrad, Christian A. (2018).

2012). In addition, the Dodd Frank Act subordinates the rating agencies to the SEC. The SEC will regularly monitor the ratings and methods of the agencies and impose fines in the event of infringements, which may include the revocation of licenses. In the financial crisis, rating agencies were not responsible for their valuations. According to the Dodd Frank Act, the rating agencies can be sued for damages by the investors in case of grossly negligent rating errors (*US-Senate*).

The German Council of Experts still sees a risk in wrong or matching external ratings. In the Liquidity Coverage Ratio (LCR) of Basel III, government bonds are equated with cash and in principle the government bonds are weighted lower in the net-stable funding ratio (NSFR). All OECD government bonds and loans are weighted at zero capital, which is what the EU Commission has assumed for the EU member states (European Commission, 2012). As a result, government bonds are preferred by the supervisory regulations, which is why it is assumed that the banks will continue to invest disproportionately in government bonds.

While this preference is desirable for governments, it raises the systemic risk substantially, which does not make sense in view of the present state debt crisis. This preference for government bonds is currently being discussed and has also prompted the Advisory Council to point to the risk of lump risks associated with government bonds. He also proposed foregoing a risk weighting of the claims and advocated large credit limits on government bonds (especially those of one's own state) (Sachverständigenrat, 2011). In the case of bonuses based on equity returns, the zero risk weighting causes moral hazards and discriminates against other loans, such as companies (Schäfer, 2011). In general, risk weighting is an incentive to manipulate ratings.

Value at Risk and Option Pricing Models

The problem with a distorting basis of past values is that it results in other capital market approaches, such as the value at risk (VaR) (Taleb, 2001, 2007), a risk indicator for securities, mainly derivatives, which is based on the historical value changes (volatilities) or assumed distributions of future influencing factors (Conrad, 2010). VaR failed as risk indicator in the financial crisis (Stulz, 2009). VaR models assume that prices correspond to a normal distribution. The occurrence of the financial crisis was incompatible with the assumption of a normal distribution. Such a "fat tail" phenomenon occurs every five to ten years (Crotty, 2009). Actually, the term "value at risk" promises too much and encourages a false sense of security, because the risk is the maximum possible loss and this is usually the capital employed. In order to circumvent the historical limitations of environmental conditions, Basel III prescribes fictitious stress scenarios for the VAR models (Deutsche Bundesbank, 2011). This is a significant improvement, but it should be a general understanding that the future remains unpredictable, and the rating is a very imprecise estimate (Stahl & Conrad, 2000).

The best example of the non-calculability of the economy is the option price formulas (Black & Schools formula). Robert Merton, Myron Scholes and Fischer Black received the Nobel Prize for Breaking Breakthroughs in War Warfare. Building on the volatilities of the past, they developed formulas for the price of buying or selling rights to values that can be exercised in the future (options). It is therefore apparently an instrument with which one can calculate the future, which is why they are also suitable for speculation. A hedge fund hired Robert Merton as a consultant. In 1998, this hedge fund, with the name Long Term Capital Management (LTCM), lost 90% of the $ 4 billion invested and threatened to trigger a chain reaction on the international financial markets.

This was not only about the loans taken by the LTCM, but also by the derivative positions drawn up by the LTCM as a counterparty, which had secured other financial market participants. It was not until the then Federal Reserve president Alan Greenspan personally intervened and created a several billion dollar rescue package, that the capital market crisis could be averted (Single & Stahl, 2000). In 2006, the second Merton advisory hedge fund with the lofty name IFC Continuum closed. So the future could not be calculated.

The weakness of the option price theories or risk indices such as value at risk, which are based on historical volatilities, is that they do not represent the future supply and demand ratios. For example, Porsche was able to buy the majority of VW stock by buying call options more favorably than on the stock market and increased its VW share secretly to 74%. The option prices did not reflect the scarcity of VW shares, as they had been calculated on the basis of past price fluctuations. They were much too low. The demand overhang then led to a short squeeze.

Is Risk Calculable?

Just like the Classic-Neoclassic theory after the Great Depression in 1929, today's economic theory has explanation and justification problems. The statistical models neither foresaw the crisis nor are they now able to explain it. Moreover, the econometric models based on historical figures presumed a safety where there was none, which was in itself one reason for the crisis (Stulz, 2009).

Ratings are estimates of future developments based on past figures. Strictly speaking, the risk of default cannot be calculated because the possible environmental conditions and the probability of their occurrence are not known. Unlike the static experiment of throwing a coin, the basic conditions of random events change constantly. The financial crisis has once again shown how quickly ratings can turn out to be wrong or fall behind events. The risk models thus led to an increase in the systemic risk rather than to a reduction. Nassim Nicholas Taleb wrote about the delusions of control and reliability under which much of Wall Street and many other businesses function. He pointed at the dangers of trusting the "bell-curve" models used by many financial institutions to mitigate risks. He questions the reliance on past historical information and uses the example of the black swan, which nobody expected until its discovery in Australia or the example of the turkey who spends a thousand days being well fed before being killed on the thousand-and-first day (Taleb, 2001, 2007). Justin Fox also criticizes the belief in models and especially the belief in efficient markets – a belief that was qualified by Robert Shiller as the "most remarkable error in the history of economic theory." (Fox, 2009; Malkiel, 2014).

We acknowledge that due to the countless and constantly changing environmental influences and the unpredictable factor of man, only trend forecasts for economic development can be made. Hayek already recognized this. There can be only so-called "pattern predictions" (von Hayek, 1969).

Even after the financial crisis, the principle still applies that the worse the rating the more equity capital needs to be put aside in order to cover the default risk. Oddly, Basel III and the Dodd Frank Act massively increased the capital requirements for banks (Kern, 2010). The proposals of the Basel Committee on Banking Supervision (BCBS), as well as those of the Swiss and British expert groups, called for even higher capital requirements on investors (Sachverständigenrat, 2011). On the other hand, no one can predict how the ratings will change in a crisis and thus also how high the capital requirements will be in order to prevent the insolvency of a system-relevant institution. For example, according to the Basel II criteria, the Swiss UBS had a constant risk-weighted equity ratio of 10%, while the unweighted equity ratio had already fallen to 2% (Sachverständigenrat, 2011).

Basel III tries to solve this problem by a 2.5% additional anticyclical capital buffer (Gaumert et al., 2011). This is a good approach but arbitrary and inconsistent. No one can guarantee that this buffer is sufficient. If credit or default risks are still weighted with ratings, any accuracy that does not correspond to reality is just made up. The financial crisis has shown that ratings are too uncertain as a future prognosis in order to build up the stability of the financial system. The apparent predictability under Basel II led to a dangerous feeling of security. It would therefore be more consistent and risk-averse to forego a risk weighting (Miller, 2016). As in Basel I, the rating should not be decisive for capital adequacy, but all loans should be subject to a flat rate of 8%. Different creditworthiness could then be reflected, as in the periods of Basel I, in the banks' internal risk assessments, and thus in the loan interest rates. A global deterioration of the creditworthiness or an increase in the risks would not, as in the financial crisis, force a higher capital requirement in the short term, which would intensify the crisis. Then, government bonds should also be subject to equity, which seems urgent in view of the current international debt crisis.

7.2.3.3 Introduction of a Separation System

Debt write-offs for banks came mainly from investment banking, both in the financial crises and in the latest state debt crisis. There were also huge bonuses, which were paid out after short-term targets were reached. There should not be long-term credit risks here, which is why this bank is not subject to the credit rules. Bank-internal risk control and monitoring is much lower than in the credit sector. If, therefore, business with credit derivatives and bonds is to be continued in proprietary trading, the credit and default risks from investment banking should be subject to the same internal and external supervision and control. In particular, the rules on equity capital and the treatment of cluster risks must also apply to trading positions. Basel III stipulates that, the banks carry out their own model-based internal risk assessment in the purchase of bonds (securitization positions) and base the price risk in the account books on the basis of the investment portfolio with more equity. However, equity underwriting in the account books is still lower than in the investment portfolios, despite the fact that in the classic corporate and real estate lending businesses there were relatively minor failures in the financial crisis. In addition, the short-term trading positions, unlike corporate loans, are not included in the liquidity indices, which means they do not have to be refinanced. This is difficult to understand in light of the experience gained during the financial crisis when the markets for many trading positions disappeared. After the bankruptcy of Lehman many derivatives could no longer be sold. The failure of Lehman as a major derivative counterparty triggered the system crash. Lehman was too big to fail (Deutsche Bundesbank, 2011; Götzl, 2012).

After the financial crisis fewer and bigger thus even more systemic relevant banks were left in de market (Miller, 2016). The designation of "too big to fail" was introduced in 1998 with the rescue of LTCM by the US Federal Reserve president Greenspan and has been considered irrefutable since then. Here, too, there is a breach of the market-based principle of private liability. This led to negative incentives, so-called moral hazard problems (Conrad & Stahl, 2002a, 2003). The profits from high-risk investments in the financial markets are only limited by a corresponding loss potential. For this, there is only one solution approach: system-relevant banks must be dismantled. Banks must also be able to go bankrupt in order for market incentives to work. Otherwise, a system change takes place moving toward a central administration economy, that is, to socialism. A break-up of the large corporations would also strengthen competition between the banks again.

An alternative approach would be the reintroduction of the separate banking system, i.e. the separation of investment and lending business. This would take account of the different business concepts of investment banking and commercial banking, and would give the financial institutions a non-contradictory objective function. An important argument for a separate bank system is greater risk transparency because processes and risks are handled through markets and are not visible only internally in a universal bank. The supporters of the universal system are opposed to the advantages of combining, scaling and information. However, the extremely high systemic costs of the financial crisis, which had to be borne mainly by taxpayers, are opposed to this (Blum, 2012).

US President Clinton and his Finance Minister Rubin abolished the Glass Steagall Act, and thus the separation system, in 1999. It was originally introduced as a result of the financial crisis in 1929, which was mainly caused by a credit-financed stock bubble. Against the background of the experience in the financial crisis, the reintroduction in the USA or the international introduction of the separation banking system would only be consistent to prevent the transfer of risks from investment banking to credit banks and thus a systemic domino effect of outstanding claims and the transfer to the real economy. Investment banks would no longer be too big to fail and would no longer have to be saved by the state. According to the English Vickers report, the risky investment businesses are no longer allowed for retail banks internally shielded and demarcated within the framework of a ring-fence approach. By 2019, Britain's banks must have ring-fenced their retail banking operations from their parent companies (Sachverständigenrat, 2011; Jenkins, 2017). Like the corresponding American Volcker rule in the Dodd Frank Act, these approaches are not as broad as the Glass Steagall Act (Conrad, 2013a; Krahnen et al., 2017).

The introduction of a separation system would only prevent the risks of investment banking from bleeding into to the retail area of banks, while the debtor and counterparty risk of the investment banking and the accompanying systemic risk would continue. A ban on retail banks financing hedge funds by offering credit – as the Vickers report demands – is a complementary condition sine qua non. A possible total write-off must be considered when banks invest in investment houses, which is why we need a ban on the participation of retail banks in financial institutions with investment risks or at least giving up the value of these holdings. In the Dodd Frank Act the upper limit for investments in investment institutions was set at 3%. These American and English approaches are structurally complementary to Basel III and should therefore be adopted by European governments. The Volcker rule served as a model for the German Separation Act, which came into force on 14 January 2014 (Kern, 2010; Sachverständigenrat, 2011; Conrad, 2013a).

If the pure investment banks only had receivables and liabilities in a separate banking system, all the institutions could theoretically fail without the deposits and loans of the commercial bank system being affected. However, it is precisely the CDS that creates a risk division between all market players, which also entails a risk transfer from the investment banks to the commercial banks. In order to ensure the functioning of a separation system, it would therefore be important to exclude trade of CDSs between these two types of institutes.

7.2.3.4 The Trade-Off Between Yield and Risk and Unilaterally Constructed Incentive Schemes

The high credit risks associated with too little reserve equity also explain the relatively high returns in the financial sector. Between 2002 and 2003, the profits of the financial sector accounted for 40% of domestic corporate profits, and between 2009 and 2011 still 25% (Dullien, 2012). The credit risk of the CDS was not covered by equity as it is with comparable loans, which is why the banks have shown much higher profits in recent years than would have been permissible. When then the bad years came in the form of the subprime crisis, no capital was available to bear the losses. Many speculators had to be bailed out because their failure threatened the financial system. On the other hand, the bonuses were paid in the good years and did not have to be repaid as it turned out that the reported earnings were not sustainable. The financial crisis thus also revealed weaknesses in corporate governance. The bonuses of the companies violated the principle of liability, because only the short-term goal was rewarded. Long-term negative developments were not considered.

An experiment showed that unilaterally constructed incentive schemes encourage excess risk-taking. This would indicate that common bonus-based compensation schemes are not a good idea and in fact enhance risk because of the asymmetries in the treatment of gains and losses (Conrad, 2015). In most cases compensation can only decrease down to the base salary while gains from bonuses can be limitless. Short-term results are rewarded even when these results are subsequently reversed. This encourages risk-taking by the employees (agents) at the cost of the company (the principal). They undertake actions that generate a high probability of gains in the short-term while the risk of a larger loss in the longer-term is not taken into consideration, thus becoming a liability to the principal. This does not align with the basic idea of principal-agent theory. Of course a connection between a manager's compensation and a firm or manager's performance will promote better incentive alignment and lead to higher motivation, which increases firm value, but only if losses and profits are remunerated symmetrically.

The existing asymmetries of bonus compensation schemes have led to a divergence of interests between employees on the one hand and the health of financial institutions and other companies at large on the other hand. Compensation packages for CEOs and other managers have gotten out of control. Remuneration and bonuses depend on short-term profitability, which increases share prices in the short-term, but not the long-term health of the company. In the financial system, investment managers increased the risks for their employer by buying highly profitable but risky assets and were rewarded with high bonuses, which led to the financial crisis in the long term. In addition, the review of research literature showed that cheating is promoted by high and unilateral variable compensations. CEOs have incentives to manipulate earnings if executive compensation is strongly linked to performance. Opportunistic earnings management behavior has been detected.

Risk adequate compensation is therefore an important prerequisite for good performance in all risk-handling professions. Without accountability, variable compensation schemes become unilateral bonus maximation schemes with negative effects for the company and the principal. It means risking other people's money which will generally be abused (moral hazards) (Andersson et al., 2013).

In view of the principal agent problem and the resulting lack of shareholder control, a state intervention seems unavoidable to prevent moral hazard. The Dodd Frank Act offers at least a legal basis to demand that overly generous bonuses be repaid, in the event of a balance sheet correction (Kern, 2010). In addition, many bank managers seem to lack the professional qualification to correctly assess the risks from subprime loans. This also reveals weaknesses in corporate governance, particularly in the case of staff recruitments. Here, the national financial supervisory authorities are called upon to review in particular the experience of the board members in the lending business.

7.2.3.5 Fair Value Loan Valuation

Bank loans are not impaired until they are no longer serviced or permanent deteriorations in the creditworthiness of the borrower exist, which jeopardize the repayment of the loan. One problem, however, is the balance sheet valuation of tradable loans, so-called securitizations, at fair value, i.e. at market value. This was reflected in the financial crisis when the markets for the CDOs had fallen away and the values plummeted. In other words, the fair values were meaningless because of exaggerated values, and they devolved into understated values because of lack of demand and transparency.

The fair value problem reappeared again during the European debt crisis. As the prices of government bonds declined, many European banks needed fresh equity because the price losses resulted in write-offs. US-GAAP and IFRS are aligned to the shareholder's informational needs, which reflect the level of the fair value. A long-term evaluation based on creditor protection and caution would be more appropriate, as it avoids excessive volatility in both revaluations and devaluations (Ballwieser et al., 2009). Market values are determined by supply and demand. This can lead to imbalances that have nothing to do with creditworthiness, or to exaggeration and understatement through herding, that is, irrational human mass behavior (Conrad, 2005). Here, there should be a balance sheet option to suspend the market value on the basis of current internal ratings that can be verified by the bank supervisor, for trading positions such as loans. The IFRSs are to be geared more strongly to long-term values (Ballwieser et al., 2009).

7.2.3.6 Conclusion

The biggest shortcoming of the recent reforms to the stabilization of the financial system, such as Basel III and the American Dodd Frank Act, is that they increase the capital requirements rather than decreasing the risk from the new financial products like derivatives. They do this in order to absorb the increased risk of speculation following the financial market deregulation and the spreading of derivatives, yet this also greatly increases the costs of borrowed capital. This means that growth losses are accepted and the costs of the financial crisis are once again forced upon the general public.

An alternative option to limit systemic risk would be the internalization of systemic risk into market prices. High capital requirements could be renounced if the systemic risks arising from non-regulated financial contractors are correctly priced or reported. It would be feasible to levy a risk tax on transactions with offshore institutions and other counterparties from unregulated financial markets that create a systemic risk but are not subject to the new regulatory requirements. This could be in the form of a flat-rate penalty tax or on the basis of an analysis of the respective systemic risk. In addition, a valuation discount for the claims against these institutions would be required under accounting law.

This would also reduce the problem of the prisoner's dilemma. The cost of the risk posed by these institutions would be internalized and free-rider benefits reduced. This tax could be collected individually by each state, thus without international financial market regulation. This would be in line with the Basel III regulation described above, which provides additional capital requirements for the risk of default for derivatives that are not settled via central counterparties. However, the problem of market influence by speculation with derivatives remains.

It would generally be better to forbid risky and complex financial products than to further increase regulation complexity and the capital requirements as in Basel III and the American Dodd Frank Act. Real-world problems can arise from the investor behavior whenever there are raw materials that fulfill important economic functions, such as foodstuffs. In the case of commodity trading, the position limits should therefore be reintroduced and the leverage of the derivatives restricted. As with medicines, derivatives should be reviewed by their national regulatory authorities for their systemic risk and transparency before they enter the market. Consumer protection should also be considered. No non-transparent derivatives with unlimited risk such as credit-ladder swaps should be permitted.

Comprehension Questions

1. Name the reasons for the financial crisis.
2. What countermeasures have been implemented since then?
3. Do you think that the measures are sufficient to prevent a new financial crisis?

7.3 Speculation in the International Financial Markets

What Follows Why?

One reason for the financial crisis is called speculation with credit derivatives. To what extent is speculation a part of the financial markets? Is it a normal market economy and what are the economic effects? These questions will be answered below.

For some time now, there has been an intensive discussion about the effects of speculation especially with commodities and agricultural product. In the following we examine the effects of speculation based on the most recent research. The following questions will be addressed: Will futures prices and price volatility be influenced by speculation? Would that create false price signals, and if yes, what effects will that have? In specific will there be demand effects for the spot market prices, which would increase the living costs thus could be seen as unethical?

Learning Objectives

You should be able to explain the economic effects of speculation.

7.3.1 *What Empirical Evidence Do We Have About Speculation Influencing Markets?*

Many empirical studies show a relationship between speculation on futures markets and the price development of goods affected on the cash markets, as well as the volatility of prices for goods. Christopher Gilbert shows, for example, the relationship between index-based investments and the prices for foods, and uses it to explain the exorbitant price increases from 2007 to 2008. This connection, and the peak in food prices from 2010 to 2011, was shown by Mario Lagi in a comprehensive model that included surveys for merchants and producers. These papers show that in their respective time frames, speculation caused prices to be about 50% above the level that would have been appropriate for the physical demand and supply. Other researchers from Harvard University and the Federal Reserve Bank of Boston have checked their results. Many other studies arrive at the same conclusions (Deutsche Bundesbank, 2006; Gilbert, 2010; Singleton, 2011; Lagi et al., 2011a, b; Chilto, 2012). Mayer (2009) points out the influence from various types of speculation on commodity prices.

Pies offers a contradictory argument, namely that the prices for commodities also rose within the same time periods, yet they were not the object of index-fund speculation or even traded on futures markets.[110] It cannot be concluded from this however, that there was no effect from index speculation until long-term correlations between these commodities have been examined, eliminating phenomena such as a price transfer substituting non-indexed commodities for indexed commodities (cross-price elasticity). There are also investors who speculate on increasing commodity prices outside of index funds, thus buying non-indexed commodities forward or investing in long futures.

In a study from 2009 the United States Permanent Subcommittee on Investigations concluded that from 2006 to 2008 investments in index funds inflated grain futures prices in relation to the spot prices on the Chicago stock market.[111] This study was contested[112] by another research team (Stoll and Whaley), which was funded by Gresham Investment Management LLC.[113] Stoll and Whaley test index fund inflows for any influence on futures prices. In contrast to other studies, they do not find any significant connection between index fund investments and commodity price increases, however, they only take the large positions reported in the COT

[110] See Pies (2012a), p. 3.

[111] "This Report finds that there is significant and persuasive evidence to conclude that these commodity index traders, in the aggregate, were one of the major causes of "unwarranted changes" – here, increases – in the price of wheat futures contracts relative to the price of wheat in the cash market. The resulting unusual, persistent, and large disparities between wheat futures and cash prices impaired the ability of participants in the grain market to use the futures market to price their crops and hedge their price risks over time, and therefore constituted an undue burden on interstate commerce." Levin et al. (2009), p. 2.

[112] See Stoll and Whaley (2009), p. 65.

[113] The objectivity of this study must be questioned, since financial positions in commodities are key business of Gresham: "Gresham offers several commodity investment programs. Our goal is to provide a responsible way to invest (as opposed to speculate) in the asset class, and to offer our clients the benefits of systematic exposure to a wide range of commodities and commodity groups through the use of commodity futures in Diversified Commodity Portfolios (DCP)." http://greshamllc.com/en/pages.php?s=2 (02/10/2014).

Report and only the positions of index funds into account.[114] Neither did Scott Irwin and Dwight Sanders determine increased prices or increased volatility on futures markets for commodities as a result of investments in indexed commodity funds. In fact, according to their empirical research, the index investments caused decreased price volatility.[115]

Stoll and Whaley also analyzed the development of commodity prices both in and out of the index, finding a weak correlation of between 0.13 and 0.20 in both cases. They found a similarly weak correlation to index commodities for commodity prices outside of the indexes. From these findings they conclude that the index investments had no effect on the prices.[116] Tang und Xiong calculated however, that there was no correlation (less than 0.1) between indexed commodities in the 1990s and early 2000s. The same was true among non-indexed commodities. In 2009 however, the correlation among indexed commodities increased to over 0.5, while the correlation for non-indexed commodities only increased to 0.2.[117] This result can be traced back to the influence of index investments. The prices for indexed and non-indexed commodities developed differently between 2004 and 2008. The indexed commodities increased evenly in that period then fell, which did not reflect fundamental changes in supply and demand, rather in the flows of investment capital. The other commodities developed very differently.[118] The same increase in demand for various products can have differing effects on prices if the supply elasticity differs. The market power on the supply side would also need to be considered, such as the OPEC cartel on the oil market.

Stoll and Whaley also offer the argument that the shifts in futures positions before the phase-out would have led to significant jumps in prices if the index investors had influence over pricing, which was not the case.[119] We can counter however, that the opposing positions must phase-out and be extended as long as we are not talking about a physical delivery that has been agreed upon. Bass points out that the investors keep their demand constant by rolling over their contracts.[120]

At bottom Stoll und Whaley contradict the Subcommittee and do not consider the functionality of futures markets to have been restricted by index investments because only 3% of the contracts from 2005 to 2009 were physically fulfilled, and thus could not have influenced the spot market. This also means that the differences from spot prices are not due to index investments.[121] However this does not mean that the futures prices were not positively influenced, however. 97% non-physically fulfilled contracts indicate a large influence of non-commercial goods.

---

[114] See Stoll and Whaley (2009), p. 66.

[115] See Irwin and Sanders (2010).

[116] See Stoll and Whaley (2009), p. 29 and 65.

[117] See Tang and Xiong (2012), p. 65.

[118] See Tang and Xiong (2012), pp. 55+ and 64+.

[119] See Stoll and Whaley (2009), p. 66.

[120] See Bass (2011), p. 45+.

[121] See Stoll and Whaley (2009), p. 67.

Supporters of speculation offer other causes for the increase in food prices from 2007 to 2008. Irwin and Sanders argue that the greatly increased demand for commodities from China, India and other emerging markets, interruptions in oil production, less demand elasticity in consumers and US monetary policy were all causes of the price increases. Given the negative correlation between the real interest rate and commodity prices, Inamura concludes that too light of a US monetary policy supported the boom in commodity prices.[122] The increased cost of biofuels and weather were given as causes for the increased grain prices.[123] Frenk counters that although the Chinese demand for oil rose by 12% in 2008, Europe and the US entered a recession that brought the international demand for oil down. In fact oil supply increased in the first 6 months of 2008, which makes an increase in oil prices of 50% within the same time period inexplicable.[124] Baffes and Haniotis, like Lagi et al, come to the conclusion from their study that neither the demand from emerging economies nor from biofuel production contributed significantly to the price boom in foods, rather that it was the demand from finance investors.[125] Inamura also considers weather, tensions in the Middle East, and in particular the economic boom in emerging economies (output gap) insufficient to explain the large increase.[126]

In the end the slump in commodity prices after 2008 can only be explained by the lapse in speculation demand resulting from the financial crisis, since all other factors remained constant. The hedge fund manager Masters points out that neither the absolute increases of 2007 and 2010, nor the slump that followed, had been seen before. Such volatility can only be explained by the parallel financial flows, since there were no substantial changes in commodity supply in these time periods.[127]

Inamura found an increasing correlation between commodities and other forms of investment since 2005, and considers it to be an expression of the increased financialization of commodity markets by finance investors. The commodity markets reflect the same liquidity flows in this period as the stock markets.[128] This is indeed an important observation, as the negative correlation is a main reason investors in commodities would diversify and thus reduce the risk of the portfolio as a whole.[129] High futures prices would indicate replenishing stocks and increasing storage capacity. Without high futures prices there would be no sure basis for the

---

[122] See Inamura et al., (2011), p. 5.

[123] See Irwin and Sanders (2010), p. 4+.

[124] See Frenk et al. (2011), p. 45.

[125] See Baffes, John; Haniotis, Tassos (2010). "The demand for grains and oilseeds as biofuel feedstocks has been cited as the main cause of the price rise, but there is little direct evidence for this contention. Instead, index-based investment in agricultural futures markets is seen as the major channel through which macroeconomic and monetary factors generated the 2007–2008 food price rises." Lagi et al. (2011a).

[126] See Inamura et al., (2011), p. 3+.

[127] See Masters (2009), p. 4.

[128] See Inamura et al., (2011), p. 7.

[129] Portfolio theory from Markowitz. See Markowitz (1952).

calculation of profit from commodity stocks, making it purely speculative.[130] The higher future prices are, the higher the assured profits will be. Krugman therefore sees an influence of futures prices on spot prices only via arbitrage, thus a scarcity in spot offers due to stock holding with a view to selling at higher future prices. He only sees this effect with copper and cotton however, not for agrarian products whose stock holding did not increase.[131] For agrarian markets Pies used wheat to determine a decline in stock keeping until 2008. He admits that the data are incomplete however, since private stocks were not registered. Nonetheless, if storage capacities did not increase there is not necessarily anything we can conclude. If the investment costs for new storage capacity are high, futures prices must exceed spot prices for a longer time in order to make the investment worthwhile.

7.3.2 Critique of Methodology

Within the discussion both sides criticize one another's methodological weaknesses in econometric studies based primarily on Granger. Irwin and Sanders' results are criticized based on the fact that the Granger test is not an appropriate method with highly volatile variables, thus distorting results.[132] The problem is of a more fundamental nature, however. If causal variables are not eliminated, false correlations can show up in Granger tests (spurious regression). The same is true for purely coincidental correlations, which can show up particularly in short time periods of observation.

As we have already shown, many speculation proponents argue that the greatly increased demand for commodities from China, India and other emerging economies, interruptions in oil production, less consumer demand elasticity and US monetary policy were all responsible for the price increases. Increased biofuel production and weather were considered to have caused the price increases.[133] If so many factors were truly affecting prices the Granger test would not have been applicable due to multi-causality. The same is true for the effects of weather, since the required stationarity of variables would not be given.[134] Highly volatile variables such as stock prices or commodities were also determined to have insufficient

[130] See Peck (1985), pp. 44–45.

[131] "If high futures prices induce increased storage, this reduces the quantity available to consumers, and it can raise the price. And you can, in fact, argue that something like this has been happening for cotton and copper, where there are apparently large and growing inventories. But for food, it's just not happening: stocks are low and falling." Krugman (2011).

[132] For a critique of Irwin and Sanders see Frenk et al. (2011).

[133] See Irwin and Sanders (2010), p. 4+.

[134] See Schulze (2004), p. 17+ and Hassler (2003), p. 813.

covariant stationarity, thus the requirement for the regression of time series is not met.[135]

Irwin and Sander have been criticized for using lags of one week and not limiting price influences to one week,[136] as well as for using non-representational data. The same is true for the Stoll and Whaley study. The positions of the index funds are not transparent because the DCOT Swap Dealer Data also contains positions from other market participants. The Commodities Futures Trading Commission (CFTC) estimates in fact that only 41% of the positions for crude oil futures belong to the index funds.[137] This represents a general problem. The quality of the data is also questionable, since it is generally based on questionnaires or is incomplete.[138] OTC derivatives were not even required to be posted in the time periods examined. Only after the financial crisis was it decreed that derivatives had to be registered or dealt via clearing houses.[139]

According to the scientists of the Raiffeisen Association the majority of empirical studies show no verifiable connection between stock volumes and the price increase.[140] The NGO WEED disagrees and lists over 100 empirical studies that are critical of speculation.[141] The economic ethicist Pies examined 35 studies and concluded that no negative effect from commodity speculation could be proven.[142]

---

[135] See Pagan and Schwert (1990); Phillips and Loretan (1990); Frenk et al. (2011), p. 45 and http://www.matthias-schlecker.de/kointegrationsanalyse-stationaritaet-und-augmented-dickey-fuller-test (04/04/2014).

[136] See Frenk et al. (2011), p. 47.

[137] See Frenk et al. (2011), p. 47 and Masters and White (2008), p. 33.

[138] "There have been ongoing complaints that the legacy COT trader designations may be inaccurate ... As one example, speculators may have an incentive to self-classify their activity as commercial hedging to circumvent speculative position limits in some markets. But, the CFTC implements a fairly rigorous process – including statements of cash positions in the underlying commodity – to ensure that commercial traders have an underlying risk associated with futures positions. However, in recent years industry participants began to suspect that these data were contaminated because the underlying risk for many reporting commercials was not a position in the physical commodity... Rather, the reporting commercials were banks and other swap dealers hedging risk associated with over-the-counter (OTC) derivative positions." Irwin and Sanders (2012), p. 258. See also Frenk's critique of the Irwin and Sanders study from 2010. See Frenk et al. (2011), p. 48.

[139] See Conrad (2013a, b).

[140] "Ganz im Gegenteil kommt die weit überwiegende Mehrzahl der bis dato zu diesem Thema verfassten empirischen Arbeiten – allerdings ebenfalls auf dem Boden der suboptimalen Terminmarktdatensätze – zu dem Ergebnis, dass kein nachweisbare Kausalzusammenhang zwischen Anlagevolumina und Preisanstiegen besteht." Translation: "Quite the opposite, the large majority of papers written on this topic to date - though also based on suboptimal futures market data sets - come to the conclusion that there no causal connection exists between stock volumes and price increases." Petersen et al. (2012), p. 14.

[141] See http://www2.weed-online.org/uploads/evidence_on_impact_of_commodity_speculation.pdf (Stand 26. November 2013, 04/01/2014).

[142] See Will et al. (2012).

WEED accuses Pies of not examining important studies critiquing speculation and having biased criticism against the methodology used in studies critical of speculation.[143] Irwin reviews the evidence from recent studies and argues that "the growing body of literature fails to find compelling evidence that buying pressure from commodity index investment in recent years caused a massive bubble in agricultural future prices."[144] Both positions are in fact supportable using the empirical studies that have been conducted. One part of the studies shows that speculation has influenced commodity prices and the other part proves the opposite. Again we see here the dilemma and weakness of econometric research. There is no proof of causality, as there can be many factors behind a correlation.

The scientific content of the predominantly Granger-based econometric studies must be questioned. There are fundamental method problems here. Because of the risk of false results, the Granger test is not recommended if the variables under study are extremely volatile, which is the case for commodity prices.[145] For highly volatile variables such as stock prices or commodities, a lack of covariance stationarity was found, which does not provide a condition for regressing time series.[146] Due to innumerable influencing factors on supply and demand, we have a strong multi-causality here in which the individual influencing factors cannot be filtered out precisely. If causal variables have not been extracted, Granger tests can show correlations that are not present (spurious regression). The same applies to purely random correlations, which may arise in particular in the case of short observation periods or incorrect time intervals.[147] Also, weather effects such as those that occur in agricultural products are problematic, because then the necessary stationarity of the variables is missing.[148]

Also, the positions of the index funds are not transparent because the DCOT swap dealer data also contains many positions from other market participants. The Commodities Futures Trading Commission (CFTC) estimates that, for example, crude oil

---

[143] See Henn (2013).

[144] See Irwin, Scott H./Sanders, Dwight R. (2010), p. 1.

[145] See Irwin, Scott H.; Sanders, Dwight R. (2012), p. 258.

[146] See Pagan, A.; Schwert, C. (1990), Phillips, P./Loretan, M. (1990), Frenk, David et al. (2011), p. 45 and http://www.matthias-schlecker.de/kointegrationsanalyse-stationaritaet-und-augmented-dickey-fuller-test (4.04.2014).

[147] See Frenk et al. (2011), p. 47.

[148] See Schulze, Peter M. (2004), p. 17f and Hassler, Uwe (2003), p. 813.

futures accounted for only 41% of positions in index funds.[149] So we also have a general problem here. Likewise, the quality of the data is called into question because they are usually based on interviews or not complete.[150] OTC derivatives did not have to be reported during the investigated periods. Only after the financial crisis was it decreed that they be registered or traded through clearing houses.[151]

Precisely because of such a background, it does not seem to me scientifically founded to derive extreme positions from the existing econometric studies. But this happens again and again, and without logically questioning the results. The absence of a logic-based discussion is a major drawback to current econometric research.

After innumerable studies examining the same thing and coming to different conclusions, it is time to make a change. It is clear that using econometrics proves neither the influence of speculation nor its absence. Additional studies will not change that fact. The two camps of advocates and critics of speculation are still at a draw. Logic should therefore be used as an alternative economic method to analyze the effects of commodity speculation based on known and widely accepted facts.

7.3.3 *The Logic of Speculation*

Stoll and Whaley argue that investment in commodities is no different than invest in stocks, for example. They fail to note however, that the money flowing into commodities is not productive. No production sites are financed, as may be the case with stocks. Commodity investments do not increase the growth of a national economy. There is also no direct offset for scarcities, such as arbitrage and thus making the most of spatial price differences. An investment in commodities is always in the expectation of future price increases and is therefore speculation. Even if the motivation is to diversify a portfolio, the investor still expects increasing commodity prices. Prices may increase due to scarcity, but there are other causes

[149] See Frenk et al. (2011), p. 47 and Masters, M.W.; White, A.K. (2008), p. 33.

[150] "There have been ongoing complaints that the legacy COT trader designations may be inaccurate .... As one example, speculators may have an incentive to self-classify their activity as commercial hedging to circumvent speculative position limits in some markets. But, the CFTC implements a fairly rigorous process – including statements of cash positions in the underlying commodity – to ensure that commercial traders have an underlying risk associated with futures positions. However, in recent years industry participants began to suspect that these data were contaminated because the underlying risk for many reporting commercials was not a position in the physical commodity.... Rather, the reporting commercials were banks and other swap dealers hedging risk associated with over-the-counter (OTC) derivative positions." Irwin, Scott H.; Sanders, Dwight R. (2012), p. 258. See also Frenk's critique of the study von Irwin and Sanders. See Frenk, David et al. (2011), p. 48.

[151] See Conrad, Christian A. (2013a).

such as cost increases and inflation. As the utilization of spatial price differences, speculation can balance out future imbalances between supply and demand if the speculation demand leads to a price increase that signals producers to increase their supply. Such a chain of events is not necessarily the case however, since the future scarcity of goods, thus prices different from current prices, is not assured. In order to divert production in the right direction, the speculators must be better informed than the market, which is not generally to be assumed. The opposite is also a possibility, namely that speculation creates a false signal for production.

Speculating at one's own risk is a fundamental part of a market-based system. New market participants entering both sides of the market through speculation by buying or selling has a stabilizing effect on prices because of the increased liquidity. Gary Cohn, Co-President, Managing Director and CEO of Goldman Sachs New York, argues in favor of allowing non-commercials because where once there were only producers that wanted to sell on futures markets to secure their interests against price fluctuations, now liquidity is available from the other side thanks to non-commercials.[152] With this argument Cohn is forgetting to mention the downstream users of commodities, who are the traditional buyers of commodities and agrarian products on the futures market. In addition, index investors sell differently than speculators because they buy to diversify their portfolios or they want to keep long positions in commodities and risk diversification at a certain proportion to their other stocks. Their profit orientation is also contrary to the downstream users, who want to buy at low prices. Increasing prices attract more investors.[153]

Cheng, Kirilenko and Xiong also show the flip side of liquidity flow. Liquidity flowing in from non-commercials makes the goods dealt on the market fungible, but the 2008 reduction in liquidity put the market under pressure. Emerging markets experienced a similar phenomenon during the Asian crisis of 1997.[154]

Krugman considers speculation to be a zero sum game. Every futures long contract is accompanied by a short contract, which is why he does not see any influence on prices. "Buying a futures contract for oil *does not* reduce the quantity of oil available for consumption; there's no such thing as "virtual hoarding".[155] One must point out however, that the supply and demand on the spot market may not be influenced, but they are on the futures market. Of course a futures contract can only be concluded on the futures market if there is a short position corresponding to the long position, but excess demand will only increase prices until a market participant considers the offset lucrative. In short, if everything else says the same, an additional

[152] See Cohn, Gary, Co-President, Managing Director and COO of Goldman Sachs, New York, Cohn, Gary (2008).

[153] "Traditional Speculators provide liquidity by both buying and selling futures. Index Speculators buy futures and then roll their positions by buying calendar spreads. They never sell. Therefore, they consume liquidity and provide zero benefit to the futures markets." Masters (2009), p. 4.

[154] See Cheng et al. (2012).

[155] See Krugman (2008).

demand for commodities increases prices on futures markets. Even if futures prices do not influence spot prices with a supply scarcity resulting from increased stock holding, it is still possible for expectations to have an influence. Lagi and others have shown this as "... we interviewed participants in the spot market who state unequivocally that they base current prices on the futures market. The use of futures prices as a reference enables speculative bubbles on the futures market to influence actual food prices."[156]

Krugman is correct in that speculation is in principle a zero sum game. What one actor wins, another must lose. In the case of commodity speculation, the speculators can fulfill an important function by buying forward the commodities from downstream users and thus reducing the risk of price changes. In such a case they fill the purpose of insurance, which also a central argument of those in favor of unimpeded speculation.[157] With such an argument however, we must remember that a producer can meanwhile be facing up to 4 speculators and thus speculation goes far beyond simple insurance. The speculators may buy and sell amongst one another,[158] which can lead to an increase of futures prices with excess demand. The index funds invested almost exclusively long until the peak of 2008, which created a great deal of excess demand.[159]

7.3.4 *Price Distortions and Price Manipulation*

Markets can be influenced in many ways by speculation.

> An artificial price influence occurs, for example, through short selling on the supply side. When something is sold that either does not exist or is only lent or bought for which there is no real economic use, supply and demand are artificially altered. The price develops differently than it would to influence supply and demand to the desired extent.[160]

As early as 2010, the share of high-speed trading in US equities trading was approx. 60%. Errors in the computer-aided model algorithms can trigger crashes, such as in 2003 for the shares of the US company Corinthian Colleges. Highly fluctuating prices are an expression of a higher risk, which can deter security-oriented market participants. Short-term mathematical algorithms supersede fundamental long-term value strategies. Such a connection would be conceivable on the stock market. Apart from higher market liquidity, no economic advantage is obvious. On the contrary, a ban on high-frequency trading would stabilize the markets.

---

156 Lagi et al. (2011a, b), p. 5.

157 See Pies and Will (2013), p. 5+.

158 There are empirical studies for this as well, which prove a high degree of trade among finance investors. See Domanski and Heath (2007), p. 65. https://www.bis.org/publ/qtrpdf/r_qt0703g.pdf

159 See Stoll and Whaley (2009), p. 21.

160 See Masters (2009), p. 17.

The impacts of credit default swaps are still contentious. There are the so-called Naked CDS as derivative loan loss insurance without underlying loans. There are those who see a positive effect even in speculative credit default swaps because of the higher liquidity in the market. There are also market participants who believe that the interest rates of the Greek government bonds would be higher if the investors could not insure themselves against a CDS default. However, the Greek Government complained that the betting of hedge funds on Greek bankruptcy over the purchase of CDS would have led to higher margins in Greek government bonds *in the European debt crisis*. Who is right?

If many hedge funds are speculating against European government bonds, for example, they buy the corresponding CDS as a credit default insurance. This leads to an increase in the CDS spreads, which is not only seen as a reflection of the bond yields but is also seen as a risk indicator by the market participants, thus directly and indirectly driving up the price of the bonds. George Soros also sees the CDS 'very critically'. In his opinion, there is the risk of a "bear raid", i.e. a profitable price influence, at CDS due to the asymmetric risk distribution between the buyer (limited risk of loss, value or premiums of the CDS) and the seller (high risk of loss in the event of bankruptcy). A purchase of CDS' increases the borrowing costs of the borrower and thereby improves its credit rating, which in turn increases the value of the CDS'. According to George Soros, this connection together with the short selling of the shares caused the collapse of Lehman, AIG and Bear Stearns (*Soros*, 2009).

The risk of a "bear raid" originates from derivatives because their value is determined by real prices. Due to the theoretically unlimited leverage of derivatives, in small-volume markets it may be worthwhile to influence or manipulate the real price on the market in order to be successful with the derivatives position. This was the basis for the arrangements for Libor and gold fixing between major international banks. Even a collectively coordinated behavior for the manipulation of the courses cannot be ruled out in smaller markets.

Derivatives such as call options affect the cash price if the option holder can insist on physical delivery. Thus in 2008 Porsche was able to purchase VW with call options cheaper than on the stock market and then increase the VW share secretly to 74%. The option prices did not reflect the scarcity of the VW share, since they had been calculated on the basis of past price fluctuations. They were therefore much too low. The demand surplus then led to a short squeeze and a huge increase of the VW price. Option writers must therefore make sure they are at least partially physically secure and inquire about the commodity.

Short selling should generally be banned because someone is selling something they do not own. There is a lot of room for speculative influence. The damage is suffered by the owners who lent the shares.

In a market economy short selling undermines the system because the owners are liable and not the seller. Funds (including ETF funds) should therefore be banned from lending stocks.

7.3.5 Irrationality and Bubble Creation?

As already stated, according to Eugene Fama's fundamentalist efficiency market hypothesis, speculation-induced deviation of futures prices from fundamental data would not be possible because prices always reflect all information rationally. Rising futures prices would therefore only indicate scarcity in the future.[161] However, speculation would not be worthwhile, because the price difference would only reflect the cost of storage. It is often argued that when bubbles form, other than the fundamentals, other market participants form counterparts. This contradicts – as was shown above – the New Behavioral Finance. The empirical investigations of this behavior-oriented research direction confirm the psychologically oriented, non-deterministic explanatory approaches. It turned out that investors perceive and evaluate the information available to them in a very subjective way, and that they do not always maximize the expected benefits in their decisions – contrary to the neoclassical model world.[162] For example, so-called herding can occur, whereby the sociological group orientation of humans dominates. In an uncertain stock-market situation, the investor orients via the other market participants, which the stock market also – at least in the short term – rewarded with rising prices.

Speculation, while exploiting temporal price differentials, can offset future imbalances in supply and demand, for example, where speculative demand leads to a rise in prices that signals producers to increase supply, but this need not be the case as future shortages other than the current prices at arbitrage are uncertain. The speculators must be better informed than the market, but this cannot be assumed. Speculation can therefore also be a non-rational behavior that does not differ from betting and gambling. So the reverse is also conceivable that speculation for the production produces false signals and thus causes bubbles and crashes.

7.3.6 Conclusion

Does speculation have an effect on spot prices that could increase the living costs with unethical effects especially for poor countries? The fact is that financialization has caused new market participants to join commodities and agricultural markets with distinct economic motivations. Because the investors were interested in diversifying their portfolios, massive long positions were built up until the financial crisis. Many billions of dollars thus came into the markets as additional demand. Since the investors did not want the commodities delivered, the additional demand ad a direct influence only on futures markets, not on spot markets. This caused an increase in the secure stock profits that, as long as they were greater than the cost of storage, would

[161] See Gilbert (2010), p. 10.

[162] See Conrad (2005).

lead sooner or later to a scarcity in supply and thus to increased spot market prices. We can therefore assume an influence of futures prices on spot prices if the excess demand on the futures market is high and stays high over a longer time period. If commodity and agriculture producers think futures prices are at a historic high they will sell their production forward, which removes the supply from the future spot market. Increasing prices for end and intermediate goods involving commodities and agriculture product are also possible if the downstream producers secure their positions on futures markets. So we come to the conclusion that speculation influence spot prices of commodities and food prices if it creates a significant excess demand over a significant time period. In this case speculation might be seen as unethical, why regulation is needed.

Many scientists see a distorting market interaction in the restriction of speculation. They see themselves as advocates of liberalized markets, or market-based basic functions. However, the so-called liberalization of the markets around the year 2000 allowed derivatives instruments, which were not market-compliant because they relate to goods or values but do not have to correspond to any real demand or supply. In addition, non-commercial actors were admitted to the market with non-economic but speculative objectives. This has dramatically increased systemic risk.

Only as insurance do derivatives have economic advantages. Derivatives should therefore be permitted only to hedge risks, just before deregulation as a financial instrument, i.e. only in connection with a basic transaction. A corresponding regulation would be an important contribution to the reduction of market influence and systemic risk caused by derivatives. For example, a physical settlement could be prescribed for all derivatives, such as the transfer of the reference security or the corresponding goods. This speculative instrument would be omitted for hedge funds. Speculation would then have to be carried out as before with equity or borrowed capital, thus without the derivatives *leverage*, which would significantly reduce systemic risk.

Behavioral science shows the limits of financial regulation with the help of human beings. The biases show that ratings are not precise or might even be wrong as people make them. The right incentives, thus risk adequate compensation, are more important to induce correct behavior.

In the financial system, investment managers increased the risks for their employer by buying highly profitable but risky assets and were rewarded with high bonuses, which led to the financial crisis in the long term.

Comprehension Questions

1. Explain the economic effects of speculation
2. Is it a normal market economy phenomenon?
3. In your opinion, should speculation with derivatives be limited? How could this be done and what would be the pros and cons?

7.4 Conclusion and Summary: International Financial Markets

Ethical Summary
The subprime crisis can be considered the epitome of the ethical failure of our modern economy. The limitless enrichment of the few at the expense of society, which almost lead to a total collapse of the financial system, was heavily criticized. The victims were, above all, the socially and economically disadvantaged who predatory lenders had convinced to buy homes that they could ill-afford and which would lead them to personal bankruptcy, or even homelessness. There were fines for several banks but not for the managers. They got away with high compensation bonuses and were not held personally responsible. Unilaterally constructed incentive schemes encourage excess risk-taking and they were a cause of the financial crisis. The compensation schemes are still unilateral.

Unfortunately, the moral attitude and behavior of bankers did not change significantly after the financial crisis. It is obvious that the business culture in financial organizations must change. Employees should be required to sign ethical standards or vow an oath and should be reminded of them regularly. A breach of such an oath should lead to fines, suspension, or even blacklisting. It is admittedly difficult to change the business culture in financial organizations if the compensation schemes contradict the ethical guidelines, however.

Behavioral Summary
Investors perceive and evaluate the information available to them in a very subjective way.

We can differentiate between short-term and long-term decisions. Short-term decision-making behavior is about speed. Heuristics and emotions are dominant. Only when individuals consciously think about problems does rational thinking dominate.

New Behavioral Finance Theory shows that investors tend to overestimate their level of in-formation and skills. This is called overconfidence. Overconfidence causes an overestimation of the likelihood that one's decisions will lead to success. In addition, new information is processed and implemented with a delay. This causes an overreaction on the stock exchanges in both directions (overreaction). Price exaggeration and price underestimation occur because the information that contradicts the trend is taken into account too late in the decision-making process. This means that systemic crises like the financial crisis can be explained by human error. Group orientation and adaption (herding) increase the likelihood that all market participants will make the same mistake and therefore cause systemic risk. In the case of the financial crisis, the collective mistake was the common belief in the self-correcting power of the market and the ongoing prosperity and housing price increases. The incorrect ratings of the CDOs were a sign of overconfidence and insensitivity to sample size. Neither was the belief in experts rational. The ratings of the subprime CDOs were based on old data from the US real estate market, a bias that is called anchoring. Status quo bias and regret aversion would explain why none of the experts corrected or questioned the incorrect ratings.

Behavioral science shows the limits of financial regulation due to the actions of human beings. The biases show that ratings are not precise or might even be wrong because people make them.

Speculating at one's own risk is a fundamental part of a market-based system. The biases and the group orientation of investors can lead to collective mistakes in the form of speculation bubbles on the stock market or real estate market.

The Efficient Market Hypothesis has been falsified because the market players are human. Since the psychologically oriented approaches are not deterministic, their drawback is the lack of a uniform universal model conception and the possibility of verification independent of the situation. However, in view of the weaknesses of the classical theory based exclusively on rational behavior, they have considerably enriched financial market theory.

Conclusion

Behavioral science shows that systemic crises such as the financial crisis can be explained by human error. Group orientation and adaption (herding) increase the likelihood that all market participants make the same mistake and therefore create systemic risk. In addition, the financial crisis showed that credit based derivatives coupled with a lack of transparency were leading to a significant concentration of risk. The biggest danger of derivatives is the leverage. If futures are used for speculative purposes for instance, the leverage multiplies artificially the effects of the derivatives on prices (via arbitrage and expectations) and does not reflect an underlying real demand or supply.

We also detected an influence of futures prices on spot prices if the excess demand on the futures market is high and stays high over a longer time period.

Future trading and derivatives should therefore be permitted only to hedge risks, just before deregulation as a financial instrument, i.e. only in connection with a basic transaction. Speculation would then have to be carried out as before with equity or borrowed capital, thus without the derivatives leverage, which would significantly reduce systemic risk.

Thus the biggest shortcoming of the recent reforms to the stabilization of the financial system, such as Basel III and the American Dodd Frank Act, is that they increase the capital requirements rather than decreasing the risk from the new financial products like derivatives. They do this in order to absorb the increased risk of speculation following the financial market deregulation and the spreading of derivatives, yet this also greatly increases the costs of borrowed capital. This means that growth losses are accepted and the costs of the financial crisis are once again forced upon the general public. Unilaterally constructed compensation schemes lead to moral hazard. They encourage excess risk-taking and were one reason for the financial crisis. So compensation schemes should be regulated. Compensation must be limited and balanced.

Comprehension Questions

1. What are the main reasons for the financial crisis?
2. Discuss does speculation belong to the human nature? What are the pros and cons?
3. Do you think that derivatives and manager compensation should be regulated or is this a limitation of positive market forces? Explain your position.

Literature

Agarwal, S., & Ben-David, I. (2011). *The effects of loan officers' compensation on loan approval and performance: Direct evidence from a corporate experiment*. http://citeseerx.ist.psu.edu/viewdoc/summary?doi=10.1.1.365.7234

Agranov, M., & Tergiman, C. (2013). Incentives and compensation schemes: An experimental study. *International Journal of Industrial Organization, 31*, 238–247.

Andersson, O., Holm, H. J., Tyran, J.-R., & Wengström, E. (2013). *Risking other people's money: experimental evidence on bonus schemes, competition, and altruism* (IFN working paper no. 989). www.ifn.se/wfiles/wp/wp989.pdf.

Angner, E. (2006). Economists as experts: Overconfidence in theory and practice. *Journal of Economic Methodology, 13*, 1–24.

Ariely, D. (2010). *Predictably irrational: The hidden forces that shape our decisions*.

Aronson, E., & Carlsmith, J. M. (1962). Performance expectancy as a determinant of actual performance. *Journal of Abnormal and Social Psychology, 65*(3), 178–182.

Baffes, J., & Haniotis, T. (2010, July). *Placing the 2006/08 commodity price boom into perspective* (Policy research working paper No. 5371). The World Bank. http://www-wds.worldbank.org/external/default/WDSContentServer/IW3P/IB/2010/07/21/000158349_20100721110120/Rendered/PDF/WPS5371.pdf

Ballwieser, W., Küting, K., & Schildbach, T. (2009). Fair Value in der Krise. *Der Betrieb*, 04/12/2009, 49 (2009).

Bass, H.-H. (2011). *Finanzmärkte als Hungerverursacher? Studie für die Deutsche Welthungerhilfe e.V.* Bonn. http://www.welthungerhilfe.de/fileadmin/user_upload/Mediathek/Studie_Nahrungsmittelspekulation_Bass.pdf

Beck, H. (2014). *Behavioral economics: Eine Einführung*. Springer.

Behavioral Finance Group. (2000). Behavioral Finance – Idee und Überblick, in: Finanz Betrieb, 5/2000, S. 311–318; O.V., Der wahre Experte weiß nicht nur viel, er weiß auch, was er nicht weiß, in: Handelsblatt dated 4.2.99, p. 29.

Bell, D. E. (1982, September/October). Regret in decision making under uncertainty. *Operations Research, 30*, 961–981.

Blanchard, O. J., & Watson, M. W. (1982). Bubbles, rational expectations, and financial markets. In P. Wachtel (Ed.), *Crises in the economic and financial structure*. Lexington Books.

Blum, U. (2012). Pro Trennbankensystem: Transparente Systematik. *Wirtschaftsdienst, 92*(1).

Blume, L., & Easley, D. (1992). Evolution and market behavior. *Journal of Economic Theory, 58*, 9–40.

Bondt, D., Werner, F. M., & Thaler, R. (1985). Does the stock market overreact? *The Journal of Finance, 40*(3) Papers and Proceedings of the Forty-Third Annual Meeting American Finance Association, Dallas, Texas, December 28–30, 1984. (Jul., 1985), pp. 793–805.

Boxall, P., Adamowicz, W. L. V., & Moon, A. (2009). Complexity in choice experiments: choice of the status quo alternative and implications for welfare measurement. *The Australian Journal of Agricultural and Resource Economics, 53*, 503–519.

Brennan, G., & Buchanan, J. (1985). *The reason of rules*. Cambridge University Press.

Brown, M. E., & Treviño, L. K. (2006). Ethical leadership: A review and future directions. *The Leadership Quarterly, 17*, 595–616.

Cai, J., Cherny, K., & Milbourn, T. (2010). *Compensation and risk incentives in banking. compensation and risk incentives in banking and finance (Research of the Federal Reserve Bank of Cleveland, September 24, 2010)*. https://www.clevelandfed.org:443/Newsroom and Events/Publications/Economic Commentary/2010/ec 201013 compensation and risk incentives in banking and finance apps.olin.wustl.edu/.../BankExecuPayCommentary.p.

Chediak, F., & Escudero, S. (2004). Ethics ratings: the case of five leading U.S. investment banks. In: R. Berndt (Ed.), *Competitiveness und Ethik, Herausforderungen an das Management* (Bd. 11, pp. 77–87). Schriftenreihe der Graduate School of Business Administration.

Cheng, I.-H., Kirilenko, A., & Xiong, W. (2012). *Convective risk flows in commodity futures markets* (Working paper). Princeton University Press. http://www.princeton.edu/~wxiong/papers/RiskConvection.pdf

Chilto, B. (2012, February 24). *Speculators and commodity prices – Redux*. http://www.cftc.gov/PressRoom/SpeechesTestimony/chiltonstatement022412

Cohn, G. (2008). Co-president, managing director and COO of Goldman Sachs. In *Senate hearing* (pp. 110–654). U.PP. Government Printing Office. SUMMIT ON ENERGY. http://www.gpo.gov/fdsys/pkg/CHRG-110shrg45837/html/CHRG-110shrg45837.htm

Colesa, J. L., Danielb, N. D., & Naveenb, L. (2006, February). Managerial incentives and risk-taking. *Journal of Financial Economics, 79*(2), 431–468.

Collin, D. (2006). *Behaving badly*. Dog Ear Publishing.

Conrad, C. A. (2005). Kapitalallokation in der Irrational Exuberance – Erkenntnisse aus Theorie und Praxis. In R. Eller et al. (Eds.), *Handbuch asset management* (pp. 387–406). Schäffer-Poeschel.

Conrad, C. A. (2010). *Morality and economic crisis*. Enron, Subprime & Co., Hamburg: disserta.

Conrad, C. A. (2013a, April). Auf dem Weg zu einer besseren Finanzmarktordnung, in; Bankarchiv. *Journal of Banking and Finance, 61*, 233–241.

Conrad, C. A. (2013b, June). Reformen zur Stabilisierung der Finanzmärkte. *Orientierungen zur Wirtschafts- und Gesellschaftspolitik, 136*, 52–58.

Conrad, C. A. (2014, November). Commodity and food speculation, is there a need for regulation? A discussion of the international research. *Applied Economics and Finance, 1*(2), 58–64.

Conrad, C. A. (2015, November). Incentives, risk and compensation schemes: Experimental evidence on the importance of risk adequate compensation. *Applied Economics and Finance, 2*(2), 50–55.

Conrad, C. A. (2016). The image of man in the economic sciences in light of the financial crisis and recent research results. *Applied Economics and Finance, 3*(1), 95–103.

Conrad, C. A. (2018, March). Weaknesses of financial market regulation. *Applied Economics and Finance, 5*(2), 32–40.

Conrad, C. A., & Stahl, M. (2000a). Wirtschaft, Börsenfieber und Geldpolitik in den USA. *Orientierungen zur Wirtschafts- und Gesellschaftspolitik der Ludwig-Erhard-Stiftung, 85*, 24–32.

Conrad, C. A., & Stahl, M. (Ed.) (2000b). *Risikomanagement an den internationalen Finanzmärkten*. Schäffer-Poeschel.

Conrad, C. A., & Stahl, M. (2002a). Parallels with the 1920s stock market boom and the monetary policy. *Kredit und Kapital, Bd. 35*(4), 533–549.

Conrad, C. A., & Stahl, M. (2002b). Asset-Preise als geldpolitische Zielgröße – das Beispiel der USA. *Wirtschaftsdienst, 82*(8), 486–493.

Conrad, C. A., & Stahl, M. (2003). Geldpolitik und Spekulationsblasen – Das Beispiel der USA. *Österreichisches Bankarchiv, Zeitschrift für das gesamte Bank- und Börsenwesen, 51*(2003), 685–693.

Cooper, M. J., Gulen, H. R., & Raghavendra, P. (2014, October 1). *Performance for pay? The relation between CEO incentive compensation and future stock price performance*. http://ssrn.com/abstract=1572085 or https://doi.org/10.2139/ssrn.1572085

Crotty, J. (2009). Structural causes of the global financial crisis: A critical assessment of the 'new financial architecture'. *Cambridge Journal of Economics, 33*(2009), 563–580. https://doi.org/10.1093/cje/bep023

Cuomo, A. (2009). *No rhyme or reason: The 'heads I win, tails you lose' bank bonus culture.* workplacebullying.org/multi/pdf/Cuomo.pdf

Dahrendorf, R. (2009, July 12). Die verlorene Ehre des Kaufmanns. *Tagesspiegel.* http://www.tagesspiegel.de/wirtschaft/dahrendorf-essay-die-verlorene-ehre-des-kaufmanns/1555814.html

De Bondt, W. F. M., & Forbes, W. P. (1999). Herding in analyst earnings forecasts: Evidence from the United Kingdom. *European Financial Management, 5*(2), 143–163.

Deutsche Bundesbank. (2006, July). Finanzderivate und ihre Rückwirkung auf die Kassamärkte. *Monatsbericht*, 55–68.

Deutsche Bundesbank. (2011). *Leitfaden zu den neuen Eigenkapital- und Liquiditätsregeln für Banken.* https://www.bundesbank.de/Redaktion/DE/Downloads/Veroeffentlichungen/Bundesbank/basel3_leitfaden.pdf?__blob=publicationFile

Doherty, M. E., Mynatt, C. R., Tweney, R. D., & Schiavo, M. D. (1979). Pseudodiagnosticitiy. *Acta Psychologica, 1979*, 111–121.

Domanski, D., & Heath, A. (2007, March). Financial investors and commodity markets. *BIS Quarterly Review*, 53–67. https://www.bis.org/publ/qtrpdf/r_qt0703g.pdf

Donohue, J. J., & Levitt, S. D. (2001, May), The impact of legalized abortion on crime. *The Quarterly Journal of Economics, CXVI* (2), 379–420.

Dullien, S. (2012). Bankenregulierung: Schwindende Statik. *Wirtschaftsdienst, 92*(7), 431–434.

Ergenzinger, R., & Krulis-Randa, J. S. (2004). Anforderungen an das Management unter dem Aspekt von Competitiveness und Ethics in der Gegenwart. In B. Ralph u.a. (Ed.), *Competitiveness und Ethik* (Herausforderungen an das Management, Schriftenreihe der Graduate School of Business Administration Bd. 11, pp. 3–16). Springer.

European Commission. (2012). *Proposal for a regulation of the European Parliament and oft the Council on prudential requirements for credit institutions and investment firms.* COM.

Fedako, J. (2007). *Correlating nonsense*, February 18, 2007. http://antipositivist.blogspot.com

Feldstein, M. (1974, September–October). Social security, induced retirement an aggregate capital accumulation. *The Journal of Political Economy, 82*, 905–926.

Financial Stability Forum. (2009). *FSF principles for sound compensation practices*, 2 April 2009. www.financialstabilityboard.org/wp.../r_0904b.pdf?.

Flood, R. P., & Garber, P. M. (1980). Market fundamentals versus price-level bubbles: The first tests. *Journal of Political Economy, 88*, 745–770.

Fox, L. (2006). *Enron: The rise and fall.* Wiley.

Fox, J. (2009). *The myth of the rational market, A history of risk, reward, and delusion on Wall Street.* HarperBusiness.

Frenk, D., et al. (2011). Review of Irwin and Sanders 2010 OECD report. In Institute for Agriculture and Trade Policy (Ed.) (Ed.), *Excessive speculation in agriculture commodities, selected writings from 2008–2012* (pp. 43–49). http://www.iadb.org/intal/intalcdi/PE/2011/08247.pdf

Froot, K. A., Scharfstein, D. S., & Stein, J. C. (1992). Herd on the street: Informational inefficiencies in a market with short-term speculation. *The Journal of Finance, XLVII*(4).

Gaumert, U., Götz. S., & Ortgies, J. (2011). Basel III – eine kritische Würdigung. *die bank – Zeitschrift für Bankpolitik und Praxis, 2011*(5). http://www.die-bank.de/betriebswirtschaft/basel-iii-2013-eine-kritische-wurdigung

Giancarlo, H. J. C. (2016). Reconsidering the Dodd- Frank swaps trading regulatory framework. In H. Peirce & B. Klutsey (Eds.), *Reframing financial regulation – Enhancing stability and protecting consumers* (pp. 155–179). Mercatus Center, George Mason University.

Gilbert, C. L. (2010). How to understand high food prices. *Journal of Agricultural Economics, 61*(2). http://econpapers.repec.org/article/blajageco/v_3a61_3ay_3a2010_3ai_3a2_3ap_3a398-425.

Gilla, D., Prowseb, V., & Vlassopoulosc, M. (2013, December). Cheating in the workplace: An experimental study of the impact of bonuses and productivity. *Journal of Economic Behavior & Organization, 96*, 120–134.

Gold, G., & Feldmann, P. (2007). *A house of cards – From fantasy finance to global crash*. Lupus Books.

Götzl, S. (2012). *…fokussiert: Baseler Paradoxien*. http://www.gv-bayern.de/Admin/GVB_Module/Druckversion/Druckversion?artikel=73627

Gregg, P., Jewell, S., & Tonks, I. (2012). Executive pay and performance: Did bankers' bonuses cause the crisis? *International Review of Finance, Special Issue: Governance, Policy and the Crisis: Part I, 12*(1), 89–122.

Harris, S. L., Mussen, P. H., & Rutherford, E. (1976). Some cognitive, behavioral, and personality correlates of maturity of moral judgment. *Journal of Genetic Psychology, 128*(1), 123–135.

Hassler, U. (2003). Zeitabhängige Volatilität und instationäre Zeitreihen. In *Wirtschafts-dienst Nr.* 12 (2003), pp. 811–816.

Hayek, F. A. V. (1969). The theory of complex phenomena. In M. A. Bunge (Ed.), *The critical approach to science and philosophy: Essays in honor of Karl R. Popper*. The Free Press of Glencoe, Inc., 1964.

Hayek, F. A. V. (1974). *The Pretence of Knowledge*. Lecture to the memory of Alfred Nobel, December 11, 1974. https://www.nobelprize.org/nobel_prizes/economic-sciences/laureates/1974/hayek-lecture.html

Henn, M. (2013). *Kommentar zum Literaturüberblick zur Spekulation mit Agrarrohstoffen von Will et al., WEED, May 14, 2013*. http://www2.weed-online.org/uploads/kommentar_literaturueberblick_agrarspekulation.pdf

Hermalin, B. E., & Weisbach, M. S. (2007). *Transparency and corporate governance* (pp. 1–26). http://ssrn.com/abstract=958628

Hofmann, C. (2011). *Basel III – Kontrahentenrisiko*. http://www.1plusi.de/dokumente/1_plus_i_fachbeitra

Inamura, Y., et al. (2011). Recent surge in global commodity prices – Impact of financialization and globally accommodative monetary conditions. In *Bank of Japan Review*. 2011 E 2, March 2011. http://www.boj.or.jp/en/research/wps_rev/rev_2011/data/rev11e02.pdf

Irwin, S. H., & Sanders, D. R. (2010). The Impact of Index and Swap Funds on Commodity Future Markets. *OECD Food, Agriculture and Fisheries*. Working Papers, No. 27, Paris 2010. http://ideas.repec.org/p/oec/agraaa/27-en.html

Irwin, S. H., & Sanders, D. R. (2012). Testing the Masters hypothesis in commodity futures markets, in. *Energy Economics, 34*(2012), 256–269. http://ideas.repec.org/a/eee/eneeco/v34y2012i1p256-269.html

Jenkins P. (2017, December 18). Why UK bank ringfences don't make everyone safer. *Financial Times*. https://www.ft.com/content/1d529c3c-e1a6-11e7-a8a4-0a1e63a52f9c

Jensen, M., & Meckling, W. (1976). Theory of the firm. Managerial behavior, agency costs, and ownership structure. *Journal of Financial Economics, 3*(4), 305–360.

Jüttner, J. (1989). Fundamentals, bubbles, trading strategies: Are they the causes of black monday? *Kredit und Kapital, 22*(4), 470–486.

Kahneman, D., & Tversky, A. (1981, January 30). The framing of decisions and the psychology of choice. *Science, 211*, 453–457.

Kahneman, D., & Tversky, A. (1982). The psychology of preferences. *Scientific American, 146*, 160–173.

Kahneman, D., & Tversky, A. (1984). Choices, values and frames. *American Pschologist, 39*(4), 342–350.

Kahneman, D., & Tversky, A. (1986). Rational choice and the framing of decisions. *Journal of Business, 59*(4), 5251–5278.

Kahneman, D., Knetsch, J., & Thaler, R. (1991). Anomalies: The endowment effect, loss aversion and status quo bias. *The Journal of Economic Perspectives, 5*(1), 193–206.

Kern, S. (2010). *US-Finanzmarktreform, Deutsche Bank Research*. Finanzmarkt Spezial, EU-Monitor 77. http://www.db.com/mittelstand/downloads/US_Finanzmarktreform_12_2010.pdf
Khan, A. (2018). *A behavioral approach to financial supervision, regulation, and central banking* (IMF working paper, No. WP/18/178).
Kling, A. (2016). Risk-based capital rules. In H. Peirce & B. Klutsey (Eds.), *Reframing financial regulation – Enhancing stability and protecting consumers* (pp. 13–34). Mercatus Center, George Mason University.
Krahnen, J. N., & Schüwer, U. (2017). Structural reforms in banking: The role of trading. *Journal of Financial Regulation, 3*(1), 66–88. https://doi.org/10.1093/jfr/fjw018
Krugman, P. (2008). Calvo on commodities. *New York Times*, June 21, 2008, http://krugman.blogs.nytimes.com/2008/06/21/calvo-on-commodities/?_php=true&_type=blogs&_r=0
Krugman, P. (2009). How did economists get it so wrong? *New York Times, SEPT, 2*. https://www.nytimes.com/2009/09/06/magazine/06Economic-t.html
Krugman, P. (2011). Speculation and signatures. *New York Times*, February 7, 2011. http://krugman.blogs.nytimes.com/2011/02/07/signatures-of-speculation/
Lagi, M., Bar-Yam, Y., Betrand, K. Z., & Bar-Yarn, Y. (2011a, September). *The food crises: A quantitative model of food prices including speculators and ethanol conversion*. New England Complex Systems Institute. http://necsi.edu/research/social/food_prices.pdf
Lagi, M., Bar-Yam, Y., Betrand, K. Z., & Bar-Yarn, Y. (2011b). *Economics of food prices and crises*. New England complex System Institute. http://arxiv.org/pdf/1109.4859v1.pdf (02/12/2014).
Langer, E. J. (1975). The illusion of control, in. *Journal of Personality and Social Psychology, 32*(2), 311–328.
Langer, E. J., & Roth, J. (1975). Heads I win, Tails it's chance: The illusion of control as a function of the sequence of outcomes in a purely chance task. *Journal of Personality and Social Psychology, 32*(6), 951–955.
Ledgerwood, S., & Taylor, G. (2016). *Enron's California schemes haunt regulators 15 years later*. Risk.net. https://www.risk.net/commodities/energy/2441392/enrons-california-schemes-haunt-regulators-15-years-later. Dated 14th of January 2016 (12/29/2017).
Leland, H., & Rubinstein, M. (1988). Comments on the market crash: Six months after. *Journal of Economic Perspectives, 2*(3), 45–50.
Lichtenstein, S., Fischhoff, B., & Phillips, L. D. (1982). Calibration of probabilities: The state of art to 1980. In: D. Kahneman, P. Slovic, & A. Tversky (Eds.), *Judgment under uncertainty: Heuristics and biases* (pp. 306–334). Cambridge University Press. file:///C:/Eigene%20Dateien2016/Political%20Economy/Material/callibration_probabilities_lichtenstein_fischoff_philips.pdf
Löhr, A. (1997). Die moralische Urteilskraft von Wirtschaftsstudenten: Bemerkungen zum empirischen Forschungsstand. In G. Blickle (Ed.), *Ethik in Organisationen: Konzepte, Befunde, Praxisbeispiele* (pp. 185–208). Verl. für Angewandte Psychologie. isbn:3801710556.
Loomes, G., & Sudgen, R. (1982). Regret theory: An alternative theory of rational choice under uncertainty. *The Economic Journal, 92*(368), 805–824.
Malkiel, B. (2014). *What does the efficient market hypothesis have to say about asset bubbles?* https://www.forbes.com/sites/quora/2014/06/13/what-does-the-efficient-market-hypothesis-have-to-say-about-asset-bubbles/amp/
Markham, J. W. (2006). *A financial history of modern U.S. corporate scandals from Enron to reform*. Sharpe.
Markowitz, H. (1952). Portfolio selection. *Journal of Finance, 12*, 77–91. https://www.math.ust.hk/~maykwok/courses/ma362/07F/markowitz_JF.pdf
Marshall, J. D., Knetsch, J., & Sinden, J. A. (1986). Agents evaluations and the disparity in measures of economic loss. *Journal of Economic Behavior and Organization, 7*, 115–127.
Masters, M. W. (2009). Testimony of Michael W. Masters Managing Member//Portfolio Manager Masters Capital Management LLC before the Commodity Future Trading Commission. http://www.cftc.gov/ucm/groups/public/@newsroom/documents/file/hearing080509_masters.pdf

Masters, M. W., & White, A. K. (2008). *The accidental hunt brothers: How institutional investors are driving up food and Energy prices*. http://www.loe.org/images/content/080919/Act1.pdf (p. 33).

Mayer, J. (2009, October). *The growing interdependence between financial and commodity markets* (UNCTAD discussion paper, No. 195). http://unctad.org/en/Docs/osgdp20093_en.pdf

Mayr, B. (2007). Das ABC der Kreditderivate. In *Treasury log, no. 5, 2007* (pp. 16–19).

Mazar, N., Amir, O., & Ariely, D. (2008), The dishonesty of honest people: A theory of self-concept maintenance. *Journal of Marketing Research*, 45(6), 633–644. Available at SSRN: https://ssrn.com/abstract=979648

Mclean, B. (2001, December 24). Why Enron went bust. *Fortune*, 53–58.

Menkhoff, L., & Röckemann, C. (1994). Noise Trading auf Aktienmärkten. *Zeitschrift für Betriebswirtschaftslehre, 64*(3), 277–295.

Metcalfe, J. (1998). Cognitive Optimism: Self-Deception or memory-based processing heuristic? *Personality and Social Psychology Review, 2*(2), 100–110.

Meyerowitz, B. E., & Chaiken, S. (1987). The effect on message framing on breast-self-examination attitudes, intentions and behavior. *Journal of Personality and Social Psychology, 52*(1987), 500–510.

Miller, S. M. (2016). On simpler, higher capital requirements. In H. Peirce & B. Klutsey (Eds.), *Reframing financial regulation – Enhancing stability and protecting consumers* (pp. 35–59). Mercatus Center, George Mason University.

Mocan, N., & Tekin, E. (2006). *Ugly criminals* (NBER working paper no. 12019, Issued in February 2006). http://www.nber.org/papers/w12019

Muolo, P., & Padilla, M. (2008). *Chain of blame: How Wall Street caused the mortgage and credit crisis*. Wiley.

Nickerson, R. S. (1998). Confirmation bias: An ubiquitous phenomen in many guises. *Review of general Psychology 1998, 2*(2), 175–220.

Noll, B. (2002). *Wirtschafts- und Unternehmensethik in der Marktwirtschaft*. Kohlhammer Verlag.

Nowak, E. (1997). *On investment performance and corporate governance*. Verlag Paul Haupt.

Ogger, G. (2001). *Der Börsenschwindel*. Bertelsmann.

Pagan, A., & Schwert, C. (1990, June). Testing for covariance stationarity in stock market data. *Economics Letters, 33*(2), 165–170.

Papaeconomou, P. (2012). *Individual differences & instance based decision making: Putting "bounded rationality" to the test*. https://www.era.lib.ed.ac.uk/handle/1842/9942

Peck, A. (1985). The economic role of traditional commodity futures markets. In A. Peck (Ed.), *Future markets: Their economic role* (pp. 1–82). American Enterprise Institute for Public Policy Research. http://www.farmdoc.illinois.edu/irwin/archive/books/Futures-Economic/Futures-Economic_preface.pdf

Peirce, H., & Soliman, V. (2016). Rethinking the swaps clearing mandate. In H. Peirce & B. Klutsey (Eds.), *Reframing financial regulation – Enhancing stability and protecting consumers* (pp. 180–224). Mercatus Center, George Mason University.

Petersen, V. J., Herlinghaus, A., Menrad, M. (2012). Risikomanagement auf globalen Agrarmärkten, Deutscher Raiffeisenverband e.V., DZ Bank 2012. http://www.raiffeisen.de/wp-content/uploads/downloads/2012/11/DRV-Brosch-Risiko_10_02.pdf.

Phillips, P., & Loretan, M. (1990). Testing covariance stationarity under moment condition failure with an application to common stock returns, discussion paper no. 947. *Cowles Foundation for Economic Research at Yale University New Haven Conneticut, 1990.*

Pies, I. (2012a). *Wirtschaftsethik konkret: Wie (un)moralisch ist die Spekulation mit Agrarrohstoffen?, Martin-Luther-Universität Halle-Wittenberg: Diskussionspapier No. 2012-15, Halle 2012*. http://wcms.uzi.uni-halle.de/download.php?down=25900&elem=2602684

Pies, I. (2012b). *Lebensmittelpreise: Die Moral der Agrar-Spekulation*. F.A.Z. from 08/31/2012. http://www.faz.net/aktuell/wirtschaft/menschen-wirtschaft/lebensmittelpreise-die-moral-der-agrar-spekulation-11873351.html

Pies, I., & Will, M. G. W. (2013), *Finanzmarktspekulation mit Agrarrohstoffen, Analyse und Bewertung aus wirtschaftsethischer Sicht, Diskussionspapier 2013-24 des Lehrstuhls für Wirtschaftsethik an der Martin-Luther-Universität Halle-Wittenberg, Halle 2013*. http://wcms.uzi.uni-halle.de/download.php?down=32275&elem=2728397

Pies, I., Prehn, S., Glauben, T., & Will, M. G. (2013). *Kurzdarstellung Agrarspekulation* (Diskussionspapier, 2013-2). Martin-Luther-Universität Halle-Wittenberg. http://wcms.uzi.uni-halle.de/download.php?down=27545&elem=2636563

Rasch, S. (1993). Crashs-Naturkatastrophen an den Finanzmärkten? *ZEW-Wirtschaftsanalysen, 1*(3), 269–305.

Ritov, I., & Baron, J. (1992). Status-quo bias and omission-bias. *Journal of Risk and Uncertainty, 1992*(5), 49–61.

Ross, S. A. (1973). The economic theory of agency: The principal's problem. *American Economic Review, 63*(2), 134–139.

Ross, L., Lepper, M. R., & Hubbard, M. (1975). Perseverance in self perception and social perception: Biased attributional processes in the debriefing paradigm. *Journal of Personality and Social Psychology, 1975*, 880–892.

Rubio, Víctor J., Hernández, J. M., Zaldívar, F., Márquez, O., & Santacreu, J. (2010). Can we predict risk-taking behavior? Two behavioral tests for predicting guessing tendencies in a multiple-choice test. *European Journal of Psychological Assessment, 26*(2), 87–94.

Rubio, V. J., Hernández, J. M., & Santacreu, J. *The objective assessment of risk tendency as a personality dimension*. University Autónoma of Madrid. www.uam.es/proyectosinv/psimasd/assessrisk.pdf

Russo, J. E., & Schoemaker, P. J. H. (1992). Managing overconfidence. *Sloan Management Review, 33*, 7–17.

Sachverständigenrat (2011). *Verantwortung für Europa wahrnehmen*. https://www.sachverstaendigenrat-wirtschaft.de/fileadmin/dateiablage/download/gutachten/ga11_ges.pdf

Samuelson, W., & Zeckhauser, R. (1988). Status quo bias in decision making. *Journal of Risk and Uncertainty, 1*, 7–59.

Schäfer, D. (2011). Banken: Leverage Ratio ist das bessere Risikomaß. *DIW Wochenbericht, 46*. http://www.diw.de/documents/publikationen/73/diw_01.c.388897.de/11-46-3.pdf

Schotter, A., & Weigelt, K. (1992, September). Behavioral consequenses of corporate incentives and long-term bonuses: An experimental study. *Managemet Sience, 38*(9), 1280–1298.

Schulze, P. M. (2004). *Granger-Kausalitätsprüfung – Eine Anwendungsorientierte Darstellung, Institut für Statistik und Ökonometrie*. Johannes Gutenberg-Universität Mainz, Arbeitspapier Nr. 28(August 2004).

Schwarz, G. C., & Holland, B. (2002). Enron, WorldCom ... und die Corporate-Governance-Diskussion. In *Zeitschrift für Wirtschaftsrecht*, 23. Vol., 13. September 2002, No. 37, pp. 1661–1672.

Schwarz, N., & Vaughn, L. A. (2002). The availability heuristic revisited: Ease of recall and content of recall as distinct sources of information. In T. Gilovich, D. W. Griffin, & D. Kahneman (Eds.), *Heuristics and biases: The psychology of intuitive judgment* (pp. 103–119). Cambridge University Press.

Schwarz, N., Bless, H., Starck, F., Klumpp, G., Rittenauer-Schatka, H., & Simons, A. (1991). Ease of retrieval as information: another look at the availability heuristic. *Journal of Personality and Social Psychology, 61*(2), 195–202.

Sharma, K. (2012, April). *Financial sector compensation and excess risk-taking – A consideration of the issues and policy lessons* (DESA Working Paper No. 115 ST/ESA/2012/DWP/115). www.un.org/esa/desa/papers/.../wp115_2012.pdf

Shiller, R. J. (1984). Stock prices and social dynamics. *Brookings Papers on Economic Activity, 2*, 457–498.

Shiller, R. J. (2000). *Irrational exuberance*. Princeton University Press.

Shiller, R. (2007). *The subprime solution: How today's global financial crisis happened, and what to do about It*. Princeton University Press.

Shleifer, A. (2000a). *Inefficient markets*. An Introduction to Behavioral Finance.

Shleifer, A. (2000b). Stock prices and social dynamics. *Brookings Papers on Economic Activity, 2*, 457–498.

Shleifer, A., & Vishny, R. W. (1990). Equilibrium short horizons of investors and firms. *American Economic Review, 80*(2), 148–153.

Simon, H. A. (1959). Theories of decision-making in economics and Behavioral science. In *The American economics review. Band 49, Nr. 3, 1.* Januar 1959.

Single, G., & Stahl, M. (2000). Risikopotential Hedge-Fonds – der Fall LTCM. In C. A. Conrad & M. Stahl (Eds.), *Risikomanagement an den internationalen Finanzmärkten* (pp. 379–391). Schäffer-Poeschel.

Singleton, K. J. (2011). *Investors flows and the 2008 boom/bust in oil prices*. http://www.stanford.edu/~kenneths/OilPub.pdf

Sloan, A., & Stern, R. L. (1988). How Vo=VgN(d1) – E/ert N(d2) led to black monday. *Forbes, 25*(1), 55–59.

Soros, G. (2009, March 24). One way to stop bear raids. Credit default swaps need much stricter regulation. *The Wall Street Journal*. https://www.wsj.com/articles/SB123785310594719693

Stahl, M., & Conrad, C. A. (2000). Strategien zur Risikovermeidung an internationalen Finanzmärkten. In C. A. Conrad & M. Stahl (Eds.), *Risikomanagement an den internationalen Finanzmärkten* (pp. 207–221). Schäffer-Poeschel.

Stoll, H. R., & Whaley, R. E. (2009, September). *Commodity index investing and commodity future prices*. Owen Graduate School of Management, 10. http://www.cftc.gov/ucm/groups/public/@swaps/documents/file/plstudy_45_hsrw.pdf

Stulz, R. (2009, March). Six ways companies mismanage risk. *Harvard Business Review*, 86–94.

Stulz, R. M. (2010). Credit default swaps and the credit crisis. *Journal of Economic Perspectives, 24*(1), 73–92.

Sucharow, L. (2013, July). *Wall street in crisis: A perfect storm looming*. Labaton Sucharow's, U.S. financial services industry survey. http://www.secwhistlebloweradvocate.com. (accessed: 28.10.2013).

Sun, L. (2012). Executive compensation and contract-driven earnings management. *Asian Academy of Management Journal of Accounting and Finance, 8*(2), 111–127.

Taleb, N. N. (2001). *Fooled by randomness*. Penguin.

Taleb, N. N. (2007). *The Black Swan; The impact of the highly improbable*. Penguin.

Tang, K., & Xiong, W. (2012). Index investment and the financialization of commodities. *Financial Analyst Journal*, 68(6), 54–74. https://www.princeton.edu/~wxiong/papers/commodity.pdf

The Presidental Task Force. (1988). *Report of the presidental task force on market mechanisms* (Brady-Report). US Government Printing Office.

Treynor, J. (1998). Bulls, beers and market bubbles. *Financial Analysts Journal, 54*(2), 69–74.

Tversky, A., & Kahneman, D. (1974). Judgment under uncertainty: Heuristics and biases. *Science, 185*, 1124–1131.

Ulrich, P. (1993). Unternehmerethos. In Enderle, u.a. (Ed.), *Lexikon der Wirtschaftsethik* (pp. 1165–1175). Herder.

US-Senate. *Brief summary of the Dodd-Frank Wall Street Reform And Consumer Protection Act*. http://banking.senate.gov/public/_files/070110_Dodd_Frank_Wall_Street_Reform_comprehensive_summary_Final.pdf. https://www.dpc.senate.gov/pdf/wall_street_reform_summary.pdf

Voinea, G., & Anton, S. (2009). Lessons from the current financial crisis. A risk management approach. *Review of Economic and Business Studies, 3*(2009), 139–147.

Volk, H. (2000). Verunsicherte Mitarbeiter werden schneller krank. In: *Frankfurter Allgemeine Zeitung vom 18.09.2000*, Nr. 217, p. 37.

Wason, P. C. (1960). On the failure to eliminate hypothesis in a conceptual task. *Quarterly Journal of Experimental Psychology, 1960*, 129–140.

Weinstein, N. D. (1980). Unrealistic optimism about future life events. *Journal of Personality and Social Psychology, 39*, 806–457.

Will, M. G., Prehn, S., Pies, I., & Glauben, T. (2012). *Is financial speculation with agricultural commodities harmful or helpful? – A literature review of current empirical research* (Discussion Paper No. 2012-27, of the Chair in Economic Ethics). Martin-Luther-University Halle-Wittenberg, edited by Ingo Pies. http://wcms.uzi.uni-halle.de/download.php?down=27388&elem=2633683

Williamson, O. E. (1979). *The economic institution of capitalism*. New York 1985.

Woods, T. E. (2009). *Meltdown: A free-market look at why the stock market collapsed, the economy tanked, and government bailouts will make things worse*. Regnery Publications.

Zorita, E. (2006). *Interactive comment on "On the verification of climate reconstructions" by G. Bürger and U. Cubach*. https://www.clim-past-discuss.net/2/S153/2006/cpd-2-S153-2006.pdf

Chapter 8
Business Cycles Theory and Policy

What Follows Why?
Economic fluctuations, above all as fluctuations in demand, are a major problem for people and businesses and can only be influenced to a very limited extent by economic policy. In the following chapter, we will analyze the economic phenomenon and the effects on the economy and show the reasons for cyclical fluctuations.

Learning Goal
You should be able to explain the reasons for cyclical fluctuations.

8.1 The Business Cycles Phenomenon

Real-world non-seasonal fluctuations in aggregate demand are referred to as business cycles. They express themselves in an increasing and decreasing degree of utilization of production potential. We can therefore define economic cycles as follows:

> Economic cycles are fluctuations in the degree of utilization of production potential. They express themselves in cyclical fluctuations of the gross domestic product (measure of the annual output of an economy) by the level required for normal utilization of the productive potential of an economy.

The economy and growth tend to be mutually dependent. The net investment demand becomes growth of the production potential and income for the consumer demand in the following periods. In the narrower sense, therefore, the distinction between economy and growth is artificial. The empirical time series of the national product always contain both growth and economic components.[1] Business cycles

[1] Developments in which the net investments are zero are also conceivable. The production potential would remain unchanged. Fluctuations in the utilization of production potential would be a pure economic phenomenon.

C. A. Conrad, *Economic Systems, Markets and Politics*,
https://doi.org/10.1007/978-3-031-10366-7_8

differ greatly simplified in terms of their qualities, amplitude and temporal cycle length as the distance between two maxima. The actual trends in the gross domestic product show irregular developments, from which a variety of other fluctuations can be filtered out in addition to the stylized sinusoidal cycles.[2]

The fluctuations in the degree of utilization of the production potential entail high welfare-economic costs. In the under-utilization phase, part of the value creation potential is fallow. People are without employment and thus without income and a socially integrating task. Inflation threatens particularly in the boom phase, which is difficult to get under control due to their interdependencies and time lags and causes severe allocation and distribution distortions.[3] An estimate of the economic cost of fluctuations by the National Bureau of Economic Research showed a 2% decline in growth over a 35-year period.[4]

In view of the economic phenomenon, two questions arise from a theoretical point of view: firstly, why are there any changes in the overall economic utilization of production potential and secondly, how can the tendency of sinusoidal development, that is to say, the existence of turning points, be explained. A business cycle theory thus has the task of explaining the causes and relationships of cyclical fluctuations. However, in order to minimize the welfare-economic cost of fluctuations, it should also be able to forecast the development of the national product and derive instruments for smoothing out fluctuations in economic policy from the explanatory notes.

The empirically observed "statistical facts" compiled by SCHEBECK and TICHY[5] 1984 adequately describe the economic phenomenon. Characteristic of the economic cycle are, in particular, the pro-cyclical development of the investment ratio, the nominal wages, the profit share, prices and short-term interest rates, the real wage and the counter-cyclical development of the adjusted wage share.[6] These "stylized facts" should serve in this chapter as a yardstick for assessing the illustrated economic theories: on the one hand, a realistic theory should at least not contradict these facts and on the other hand, a theory that claims to be universally valid should be able to explain many of these facts.

Economic cycles are expressed in cyclical fluctuations in gross domestic product (the measure of the annual output of an economy) around the level required for the normal utilization of the productive potential of an economy (see Fig. 8.1).

After a first upturn (1. phase: expansion, recovery or upswing), there is a boom-like overstrain of existing supply capacities (2. phase: boom or peak) as a result of aggregate demand. The providers respond with it

[2] See Albers (Hrsg.) (1976), pp. 479.

[3] See auch Zarnowitz (1997), pp. 1 and 25.

[4] See Ramey and Ramey (1991).

[5] See Schebeck and Tichy (1984).

[6] See Schebeck and Tichy (1984).

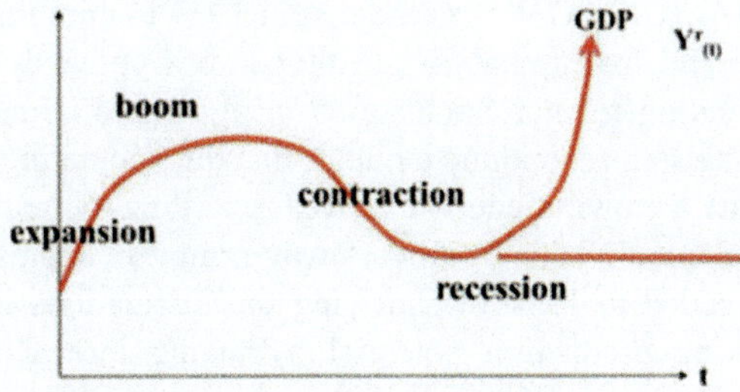

Fig. 8.1 The stylized business cycle

1. Increased use of factors (overtime),
2. Reduction of inventories or increase in order backlog and / or
3. Inflationary price increases.
4. Capacity expansion, new hires

And after a downturn (3. phase: downturn or contraction), there is underutilization of supply capacities due to the cyclical decline in demand.

This is called a recession (4. phase: recession or trough). The most common definition of recession is: at least two consecutive quarters with negative growth, i.e. falling GDP. In this economic phase, numerous insolvencies, mass unemployment and short-time work occur, economic unemployment and usually only small inflationary price level increases.

The heightening of the recession is depression as a persistent stagnation (underutilization of productive capacity) with deflationary tendencies.

Economic Indicators

Leading Indicators: Investment in fixed assets and purchasing managers' index are, for example, a leading indicator relative to GDP, whereas consumption is a lagging indicator (lagging indicator).

8.2 Reasons for Economic Fluctuations from the Economic Theory and Political Economy Conclusions

8.2.1 Dynamic Keynesian Approaches: The Hicks's Super-Multiplier

According to Keynes, fluctuations in autonomous investment, as well as multiplier effects (continued effects of increasing demand) and accelerator effects (increased demand for capacity utilization causes investment), can lead to cyclical fluctuations, as shown below by Hicks's super-multiplier (1950).

SAMUELSON[7] was the first in 1939 to combine the Keynesian Demand Multiplier and Investment Accelerator into a demand-side investment function model, generating regular fluctuations in aggregate demand. However, the drawback of Samuelson's economic model is that the fluctuating gross domestic product does not follow a growth trend, but moves according to the parameter constellation around or to a constant value or moves away from it in explosive fluctuations. HICKS[8] finally succeeded in 1950 in clarifying the fluctuations in the utilization of a constantly growing production potential by taking into account induced and autonomous investments.[9] HICKS (1950) combines a simple consumption function and an accelerator into a dynamic Keynesian approach. The system is in dynamic equilibrium when gross domestic product is growing at the same constant rate as autonomous investment (see Fig. 8.2). Hicks[10] uses the consumption function $C_t = c\ Y_{t-1}$ and the acceleration factor $I^{ind}{}_t = \beta * (Y_{t-1} - Y_{t-2})$. By taking into account induced and autonomous investments $I^{aut}{}_t = A_0 * (1 + w)^t$ [A0: initial value, w: constant growth rate of autonomous investment] HICKs succeeds in explaining fluctuations in the utilization of a constantly growing production potential.

$$Y_t = C_t + I^{ind}{}_t + I^{aut}{}_t = c\ Y_{t-1} + ß(Y_{t-1} - Y_{t-2}) + A_0(1+w)^t \Leftrightarrow$$

$$Y_t = \frac{I^{aut}{}_t}{1 - \frac{c + ßß}{(1+w) + (1+w)^2}}$$

Figure 8.2 shows the autonomous capital expenditures and other development components of the national product, which would develop in the absence of cyclical fluctuations and external disturbances according to the Yt line, i.e. the long-term equilibrium path. This is the imaginary equilibrium path, the real national product, which grows at the same constant rate as the autonomous investments. The induced investments have no capacity effect. YtS, max represents the capacity limit (full employment) and YtD, min of the disinvestment floor. Capacity limit and disinvestment floor are the upper and lower bounds of a tunnel in which growing gross domestic product moves. On the disinvestment basis, investment demand corresponds to the steadily growing autonomous investment.

The actual development of the gross domestic product is an oscillation[11] around the long-term growth path of the gross domestic product. If the gross domestic product in the initial equilibrium at time t0 is in a cyclical upturn due to a positive

---

[7] See Samuelson (1939).

[8] For the Hicks's super-multiplier See Hicks (1950), Tichy (1995), pp. 118, Assenmacher (1998), Teichmann (1997), pp. 11, Wagner (1990), p. 222 and Ott (1963), pp. 196.

[9] i.e. all investments that are not caused by a change in demand, ie long-term investments such as public infrastructure investments and innovations.

[10] See Hicks (1950), Tichy (1995), pp. 11, Assenmacher (1998), Wagner (1990), p. 222 and Ott (1963), pp. 196.

[11] Due to the choice of: $1 < ß < (1 + \sqrt{s})^2$ these are explosive oscillation.

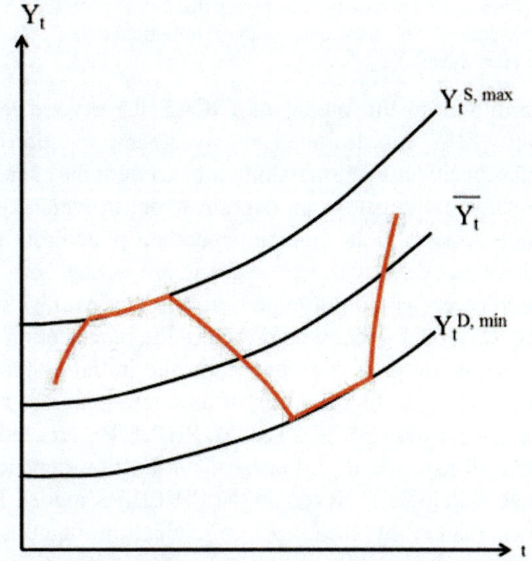

Fig. 8.2 Growth cycles of the Hicks model

exogenous post-crisis shock, it reaches t1 highest value for the time being, which is limited by the growth of production potential (path A). Due to the accelerator context I indt = ß * (Yt-1 – Yt-2), a constant growth rate is a prerequisite for a constant demand. The mere decline in the growth of demand can thus already initiate a downward process. The lower limit of this contractionary process is reached when investment has fallen to the level of failed reinvestment. Induced investment has shrunk to zero as a result of the decline in demand, and gross domestic product growth is determined solely by autonomous investment and pro rata consumption. The upward process is initiated by investment demand induced by the growth of autonomous investment. As soon as Yt + 1 > Yt again, investments are induced.

The biggest shortcoming of this model is the neglect of the monetary side (the investments are not interest-dependent). Price level changes are excluded as an economic determinant. An over-demand has no negative consequences. Furthermore, demand-induced investments have no capacity effect. HICKS, however, highlights the dynamic importance of changes in demand. This makes it possible to explain the sinusoidal fluctuations that can be observed in reality by an increasing gross domestic product growth path. On the other hand, HICKS provides no explanation as to how the growth rate of autonomous investment assumed by him comes about.[12] But he himself admits that the growth rate of autonomous investments does not have to be constant and can even be greatly reduced:

[12] "Public investment, investment which occurs in direct responce to inventions, and much of the 'long-range' investments (as Mr. Harrod calls it) which is only expected to pay for itself over a long period, all of these can be regarded as Autonomous Investment for our purpose." Hicks (1950), p. 59.

> One of the most dangerous things that can happen (and on one occasion, at least surely has happened) is that autonomous investment itself is severely checked by financial breakdown.[13]

Starting from the model of HICKS there were numerous further developments. CHENERY has designed an investment function that depends on both demand and capacity utilization, taking into account the capacity effect of past investments.[14] GOODWIN develops an overall model in which consumer demand consists of an autonomous and an income-dependent part. From the model of GOODWIN arise economic cycles with very realistic properties, with each cycle initiating the following. The cycles do not expire, nor do any explosive oscillations occur – unlike the HICKS model – that would require the introduction of Ceilings. Moreover, the type of oscillation does not depend on the initial conditions or the model coefficients. The missing endogenization of the money market was provided by PHILLIPS and the labor market BERGSTROM. PHILLIPS succeeds in using its model to show the cyclically stabilizing influence of utilization-dependent price changes triggered by wage responses.[15] Based on the PHILLIPS model, BERGSTROM endogenizes the labor market by means of a production function. Corresponding to the profit maximization conditions under perfect competition, the marginal productivity of capital determines the demand for capital, and the marginal productivity of labor determines the demand for labor, which also fixes interest and wage levels. Increases in wages cause ceteris paribus an increase in labor supply, but also a decline in labor demand and thus a decline in gross domestic product. The income decline affects the multiplier.[16]

Conclusion

The policy conclusions that can be drawn from this model are similar to those of the advanced theory of Keynes. The state must compensate for the fluctuations in demand by autonomous demand impulses. Therefore discretionary countercyclical fiscal policy is necessary:

Recession: debt-financed increase in government spending, tax relief
Boom: Government spending cuts, tax hikes

However, HICKS also reveals in its model the sensitivity with which the economy reacts to changes in demand in a dynamic process. Taking into account the now well-known practical recognition and implementation problems of state follow-up taxation, a warning against discretionary political economy can be deduced from this. A one-off (one-period) increase in demand by the state would correspond in the following period (c.p.) to an overall economic decline in demand and thus initiate

[13] Hicks (1950), p. 129.

[14] See Chenery (1952) and Assenmacher (1998), pp. 186.

[15] See Goodwin (1951) and Assenmacher (1998), p. 120ff.

[16] See Bergstrom (1962); Teichmann (1997), p. 17 and Assenmacher (1998), p. 18.

a downward process. At the same time, the model thus highlights the dangers of discretionary cyclical policy management.

8.2.2 *Neoliberal Versus Keynesian, a Synthesis*

The counter-cyclical fiscal policy approach was practiced around the world in the 1960s through the mid-1970s. It was included in the Stability and Growth Act of 1967, which is no longer used. In the government of former Federal Chancellor Schmidt, this policy was also practiced. However, there were significant implementation issues. First of all, there was the problem of correctly interpreting the economic fluctuations. The question of when there was a recession that required an increase in government spending was not clear, as the cycles are not schematic. It then usually took too long for the cyclical measures to be implemented; so that it was often the case that the government's increase in demand did not materialize until the economy was back on the upswing.

However, the crucial problem was the one-sided implementation of the concept of anticyclical fiscal policy. The expansion of public spending in the recession was easy for politicians, but not saving in the boom. In the boom, the ministers want to increase their budgets, as they have "gone without" for years. Politically, cutting spending was not popular in the boom. The politicians feared electoral losses if they cut public spending on their citizens. The consequence of this was that borrowing in the recession was increased by the expansionary fiscal policy, but was not reduced again in the boom. Ultimately, the wide-ranging interpretation of Keynesian depression theory was responsible for the sharp increase in government debt in the 1960s and 1970s.

Monetarism or "Neoliberals" (Supply-Oriented)

As a countermovement to discretionary demand management in the 1960s and 1970s, monetarism, with its main representative Milton Friedman, and neo-liberalism in general, formed an extremely market-oriented economic orientation.

They argued that due to the numerous implementation problems (detection, planning, implementation and impact) and the difficulty of clearly defining the cause responsible for the current economic development, fiscal policy should be used in the short term rather than discretionarily.

Neoclassicism, and in particular quantity theory ($M \cdot v = Y \cdot P$) again became the dominant doctrine. Above all, monetary policy must serve to ensure price stability and may only help cushion external shocks in exceptional circumstances. Real gross domestic product growth cannot be artificially created by an expansionary monetary policy.

The neo-liberals start from the "policy inefficiency hypothesis". Consequently, the influence of politics on the economy must be kept as low as possible. The future environmental conditions are unknown. The market participants therefore make decisions under uncertainty. The state must not further increase this uncertainty by a "non-constancy" of political economy. Rather, what is needed is a binding rule in the form of clear, long-term policy programs, based on a comprehensible system-conforming conception, i.e. a regulatory instead of process policy.

Only in a depression, that is, in a continuing underutilization of production potential for lack of demand, should the state intervene, because otherwise there will be no recovery for the foreseeable future. Clear rules and framework conditions must be created.

The rule-based countercyclical monetary policy remains: In the long term, for example, the ECB orients on production potential, but in the short term also on its utilization or GDP. So in the Recession it lowers the key interest rates and increases the money supply in order to give the economy an expansionary impetus and in the Boom interest rates rise and tightening liquidity to prevent overheating of the economy as well as price increases above its inflation target.

Recession: expansionary monetary policy: $M\uparrow$, $i\downarrow \Rightarrow (p\uparrow), \Rightarrow i\downarrow \Rightarrow I(i)\uparrow$ and
Boom: restrictive monetary policy: $M\downarrow$, $i\uparrow \Rightarrow p\downarrow, \Rightarrow i\uparrow \Rightarrow I(i)\downarrow$

With the neo-liberal orientation, demand-oriented economic policy was replaced by supply-side economic policy. Profit and/or yield expectations of the enterprises returned to the fore, because the creation of jobs over investments should be again supply-oriented and not demand-oriented. The goal of supply-oriented economic policy is therefore to improve investment conditions and increase profit expectations:

1. Increase in competition: a) Reduction of bureaucracy and deregulation b) Privatization of public enterprises c) Degradation of subsidies d) Reduction of public debt
2. Reduction of non-wage labor costs
3. Reduction of social benefits to a minimum, job offers ↑
4. Simple control system with low rates
5. Monetary stability: Orientation of the money supply to the GDP, otherwise inflation results

Political applications (in part): USA Reaganomics, GB Thatcherism, reforms of German Chancellor Schröder "Agenda 2010".

The following overview presents the differences between the Keynesian and neo-liberal economists (see Fig. 8.3).

8.2.3 Technical Progress: The Schumpeter Business Cycle

Characteristic of the starting point of almost all major stock market bubbles is a fundamental real-world economic spark, which establishes a long growth trend. These are product or process innovations that are not a spin off of well-known technologies, but represent exceptional technical advances that result in a sustainable

Neoliberal	Keynsian
Markets tend to balance; they are stable and efficient (market optimists)	Markets and their balances are unstable and inefficient (market pessimists)
Therefore, markets are to deregulate	Therefore, markets have to be regulated
Policy inefficiency hypothesis, rule-binding policy	State must correct market, policy efficiency
Supply conditions for companies are crucial	Demand on the goods markets is crucial
Labor market is largely autonomous	Labor market is derived from the goods markets
Economic framework is crucial, regulatory policy	State intervention is crucial, process politics
Long-term oriented	Short-term oriented

Fig. 8.3 Comparison of Neoliberal and Keynesian

increase in productivity. Often one speaks then of a "new era". Schumpeter (Joseph Alois Schumpeter 1883–1950) speaks of a "creative destruction". The old production processes will be replaced by new, better ones and the economy as a whole raised to a higher level of productivity. The profits of companies using the new technology or producing new products are increasing. A new wave of growth as a discrete business cycle, a sustainable boom of real growth, is emerging. Due to the length of these cycles, they would most likely correspond to the so-called Kondratieff waves. Schumpeter developed his business cycle theory from the two central dynamic competitive functions.

Innovation Function

For the growth process of an economy, the dynamic nature of the competition is of particular importance. Dynamic competition, according to Friedrich August von Hayek, is a search and discovery process.[17] Hayek characterizes competition as a process of discovering facts that would either remain unknown or at least be unused without their existence. For Hayek, competition is above all evolutionary. This applies both to process innovations and to product innovations, whereby an innovation is generally understood to mean the economic realization of an invention, also called invention. In the expectation of an above-average market reward, the entrepreneur is constantly looking for cheaper production processes and new products for which there is potential market demand. To this end, he conducts research at his own risk or evaluates foreign research results economically. The market, and ultimately the consumer or processing producer, decides on the success of a process.

Imitation Function

According to Joseph Schumpeter, competition is a process of innovation and subsequent imitation.[18] The pioneer entrepreneur's successful innovation gives

[17] See von Hayek (1969).

[18] See Schumpeter (1911).

him a competitive advantage in the marketplace over the companies that have retained their old production structure. This competitive advantage results in an above-average profit, which then incites other entrepreneurs to imitate the innovation, or at least forces it to do so if they do not want to be forced out of the market. This leads to a proliferation of new, resource-saving production processes and thus to a comprehensive enforcement of technical progress and, with it, to a growth in production. Innovation and sanctions thus support each other in dynamic competition.

From the innovation function and the imitation function Schumpeter derives his dynamic business theory[19]:

1. **Phase: state of equilibrium**

The prerequisites for a recovery are new productive combinations, with which a far above average profit can be achieved. These productive combinations are so fundamental that they affect the whole economy. This allows:

- Above all, product and process innovations (such as the Internet), fundamental innovations such as the assembly line
- New sources of supply or intermediate consumption
- Development of new markets, e.g. due to the abolition of the "Iron Curtain"
- Organizational corporate reforms (stock corporation etc.)

A dynamic entrepreneur (or inventor) implements this profit potential with the support of a dynamic, risk-taking banker. Both together realize the gain from technical progress (innovation function). By being the first to implement the more productive combinations, they have a temporary monopoly on the market and can reap the pioneering benefits that will lead to Phase 2.

2. **Phase: imitation (upswing and boom)**

The pioneer profits attract many entrepreneurs to imitation (imitation function). They mimic the more productive combinations. For this they have to invest. As there are many who invest, aggregate demand increases. It creates an economic euphoria. The upswing begins. Higher demand will increase the prices and profits of companies, not just in the area of new production combinations. Further investments are encouraged.

$\Rightarrow$ investments (I) st in the area of $\Rightarrow$ prices (P) st in the area $\Rightarrow$ investments (I)
$\uparrow$

[19] See Schumpeter (1939).

3. **Phase: erosion process of pioneer business profits (downturn)**

The high demand leads to rising prices for the precursors. Wages and interest rates, the cost of capital, are also rising, which is why profit margins are falling. After the maturity of the investment, the new offer of imitators comes on the market. The competition and the new offer cause prices to fall. Investments are significantly reduced, which reduces demand and initiates the downturn.

1. Competition of imitators ⇒ prices (P) ↓, profits (G) ↓
2. Rising costs of primary products, labor and capital (interest) ⇒ profits (G) ca ⇒ investments (I) al (interest^D) ↓ prices (P) ↓

4. **Phase: Creative destruction (recession)**

In the recession demand is greater than supply. Production cuts and unemployment are the result. The gross domestic product is falling. The oversupply of new production combinations is pushing companies out of the market with the old non-competitive production processes or products. The companies that have not imitated must apply for bankruptcy. This is how technical progress is enforced. This is a necessary process. Schumpeter speaks of the "elixir of life of capitalism". There is no need for economic policy. On the contrary, a credit-financed fiscal policy would artificially keep uncompetitive companies in the market, which is undesirable.

Schumpeter explains the long cycles caused by fundamental economic changes. A Schumpeterian business cycle would be the boom that occurred in the late 1990s with the Internet boom and the new market that was created, which was followed by a similar downturn, but also left a new economic structure above all in the service area.

The creative product and process innovations, in addition to the positive effect of increasing productivity, still have a negative connotation. On the one hand, as Schumpeter points out, they destroy the old, no longer efficient economic structures, but this also implies structural unemployment.

8.2.4 Overinvestment Theories and Experiments

Overinvestment can also be a cause of economic fluctuations. The key problem for companies is that when making their investment decisions, they do not know how stable the increase in demand is and to what extent competitors are expanding their capacities. As a company, they have to agree on how much each company invests and how much the capacity should be extended. Since such coordination does not exist, companies must approach demand with their production plans. It always comes back to overcapacity and undercapacity. In the upswing, demand is rising (Y^D ↑). As a result, prices and profits rise (p ↑, gains ↑). It is invested (I ↑). There is overcapacity as markets must first coordinate all business plans. Capacities must be reduced again in the adaptation process. Here, too, there are exaggerations, since the capacity reduction as well as the capacity was not coordinated. A similar process in microeconomics is also called pork cycle or cobweb theorem. An example is the overinvestment theory of Karl Marx, which builds on technical progress as a stimulus to the economy.

The overinvestment theory with technical progress by Karl Marx[20] (1818–1883) or the law of the tendency of the rate of profit

Technical progress needs capital for implementation. Marx divides capitalists into owners of the means of production and workers who make a living from their labor. Labor-saving technical progress allows the capitalists higher productivity and thus a higher rate of profit. They invest (accumulation of capital), the demand increases, and the upswing comes. The higher productivity leads to increased competition and thus to a fall in prices and thus also the rate of profit. Labor forces are released by technical progress (impoverishment of the proletariat, formation of an industrial reserve army). As a result, in addition to oversupply, demand is also falling. The dismissed workers can no longer consume anything. It comes to a downturn. The capitalists eliminate each other due to high oversupply in the ruinous competition (recession). The supplier concentration increases (concentration of capital). The rate of profit rises again (upswing) and the process starts from scratch until the collapse of the capitalist system (dictatorship of the proletariat and planned economy) comes.

However, Marx's fears did not materialize in Germany. Through the formation of the unions, the unilateral became a bilateral monopoly on the labor market; the workers no longer competed with each other driving pay down. Strikes were possible. Due to the now balanced distribution of power, the unions can enforce wage increases. Demand increased and there was no sales problem. In addition, product innovation led to a new demand for labor that could be paid for productivity-related wage increases. Existing purchasing power and the re-employed previously released work thus led to an ever-higher level of prosperity.

Overinvestments Caused by Demand and Interest Rates Changes, Evidence from Two Behavioral Experiments

Companies invest if they can make more profit with more production. Increased prices or cost cuts might be reasons for an augmented profit margin and thus trigger investments. This article analyzes the causes of overinvestment and thus investment cycles with two behavioral experiments (experimental simulation, behavioral modeling). Increases in demand and cuts in interest rates are examined as possible causes for overinvestment, which lead to corresponding increases in profits and thus trigger investments. If economic actors make mistakes in managing capacity, overinvestment can result. The problem is that the market participants do not know by how much their competitors are increasing their capacities and the price only reacts once the capacities are on the market. What if the market players systematically make mistakes because they are not behaving rationally or because they do not have all the information, such as the capacity increases of their

[20] See Marx (1864) and Stavenhagen (1969), pp. 157.

competitors? Applying behavioral economics, this essay analyzes the economic behavioral dispositions using models to identify the mistakes actors make in groups (collective error hypothesis). The goal of the chapter is therefore to test if increases in demand can lead to overinvestment due to errors made by market participants and if interest rate cuts can lead to overinvestment due to errors made by market participants

The existing literature and studies are presented and compared to the experiment presented here. Next the experimental design of the study is explained. Finally, the results are present-ed and the conclusions drawn (Conrad, 2022).

Related Literature

It usually takes a while before capacities can be increased when companies invest. The production facilities must be financed, purchased, delivered and integrated into production. Price increases that lead to overinvestment due to delays in expanding supply are primarily seen in the market for raw materials (Humphreys, 2012). Mining projects take five to ten years to complete. Conversely, mine production is difficult to throttle so that the capacities can continue to be used for production as long as the prices are above the variable costs (Glöser-Chowhound et al., 2017).

This is in contradiction to the Efficient Market Hypothesis. This hypothesis assumes that all accessible price-relevant information of the past, present and future are known. The efficient market hypothesis in financial market theory was undisputed until the mid-1980s. Since rational behavior is assumed in principle, irrational behavior or wrong decisions do not influence the price (Sloan & Stern, 1988; Shleifer, 2000a; Menkhoff & Röckemann, 1994; Fama, 1970). However, the spot prices, but also the future prices, can not take into account the investment decisions of the market participants.

Conversely, there is a direction in economics that repeatedly emphasized the difficulties in adapting supply and demand. As early as 1966, Leontief (1966) pointed out that time lags between supply or demand reactions can massively impair the achievement of market equilibrium. This connection found its way into economics as the cobweb theorem (Waugh, 1964; Ezekiel, 1938).

High raw material prices lead to high investments and capacity expansions and low prices lead to low ones, which increases the probability of over- and undersupply. Market expectations play a decisive role in investment decisions (Humphreys, 2012), which is why future prices also have an influence here. These behavior errors in capacity planning were demonstrated in 1992 by Kampmann's market behavior experiments (Kampmann, 1992; Kampmann & Stermann, 1996).

Using experiments with students who played the company, Kampmann and Stermann (1996) obtained an overshoot of production at fixed given prices with a subsequent downward adjustment of production as a recession, i.e. boom and bust cycles. They stated that firms have great difficulties catching up with demand due to production delays and the continuous accumulation of inventory imbalances. Kampmann (1992) found out that the increase of prices apparently induces the firms to further increase output. And Glöser-Chowhound et al. 2017 point out that market participants also need information about the other participants. A balance between supply and demand cannot be achieved even in simple markets (Zame, 2008). Shachat and Zhang (2012) conducted experiments with students with reference to the Cobbweb Theorem and found out "that sellers do a miserable job of making optimal investment decisions. . . ."

Knut Wicksell lays the blame for boom and bust cycles at the doorstep of the monetary policy decision-makers and their inappropriate decisions regarding interest controls (see also Sect. 8.2.7). In the boom the interest rates are too long to low, creating overinvestments as collective error. The reaction of the central bank is too late and too harsh, creating not just the boom but also inadvertently the bust (Wicksell Hypothesis) (Wicksell, 1922, 1968; Grosskettler, 1989).

All these studies show that there appear to be undesirable developments in the markets because not all information is available or correctly applied. The concept of bounded rationality was developed in response to this information problem, implying limited information processing capacities as opposed to complete rationality. A decision that maximizes utility is rationally limited if it takes account of information access and processing (Simon, 1959).

Experimental Design

We want to answer two questions:

A. Can increases in demand due to systematic errors by companies lead to overinvestment or can companies interpret the price signals and collectively manage the expansion of capacity correctly?
B. Could interest rate cuts trigger overinvestment because companies misinterpret higher profit margins and expand capacity?

The purpose of this chapter is therefore to test the two hypotheses:

A. Increases in demand can lead to overinvestment due to errors made by market participants
B. Interest rate cuts can lead to overinvestment due to errors made by market participants

Two behavioral experiments on MS Teams were carried out online with the help of Excel. Increases in demand (game A) and interest rate cuts (game B) were examined as possible causes of corresponding increases in unit profit and thus a trigger for investments.

The two experiments, A and B, were conducted in the summer 2021 and winter semester 2021/22. There were 95 participants in seven groups in game A and 87 students (six groups) in game B, who were participants of different Business Bachelor courses (macroeconomics and political economy) at the University of Applied Science HTW at Saarbrücken, Germany. The task of the students was to invest capital like a manager of a company. The participants were asked to maximize the profit, which is the obligation of a manager as agent for a principal (company owner resp. shareholder). Maximal profit in the group resulted in 10€ real money as variable compensation. The rules were explained to the students before starting the experiment.

Experiments
Game A: The Effects of Increases of Demand on Investments

The goal is to test the following hypothesis: Increases in demand can lead to overinvestment due to errors made by market participants.

The model used was that of a simplified company. Each company (represented by a player) had in the beginning a production capacity (PC) of 500,000 units. The games started with sales (S) of 10 million euros, at a price (P) of 20 euros and cost of 15 euros (C). Thus, the test subjects sold 500,000 goods with their individual company, making a profit (PR) of 2.5 million euros (PR = S – C PC) with an equity (EQ) of 10 million. Each company had to decide on its investment (I). There were delays in expanding the range. For example, investments of 2.5 million euros (two rounds of the game) brought 50,000 increased production capacity in 2 years, or 1 million euros more sales at a price of 20 euros (40% or 50 euros per unit of production capacity, $PC_{t+2} = PC_t + I_t/50$). Investments decreased equity, while profits increased it. Demand and capacities were included in the price. The ratio between demand and capacity was multiplied by the price of the previous period ($P_t = D/PC\ P_{t-1}$). Due to the delayed supply increases, the prices only react to the investments after two rounds. Once production facilities were installed they could no longer be dismantled, so the increase in capacity was irreversible. Whoever had the most equity after 10 rounds won and received 10 euros. The demand was changed and entered by the game master. The game began with a demand equal to supply.

Results
Figure 8.4 shows the increases in demand in rounds 5, 9 and 13. As a result, the prices in Fig. 8.5 increased and with it the average unit profits (UP = PR/PC) in

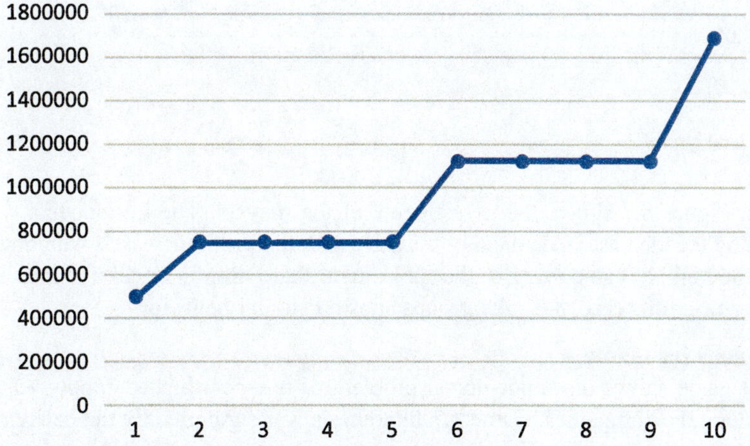

Fig. 8.4 Demand per player in units

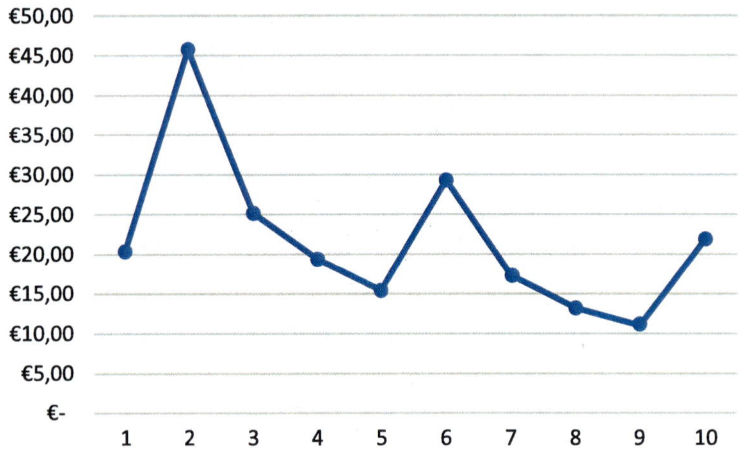

Fig. 8.5 Prices

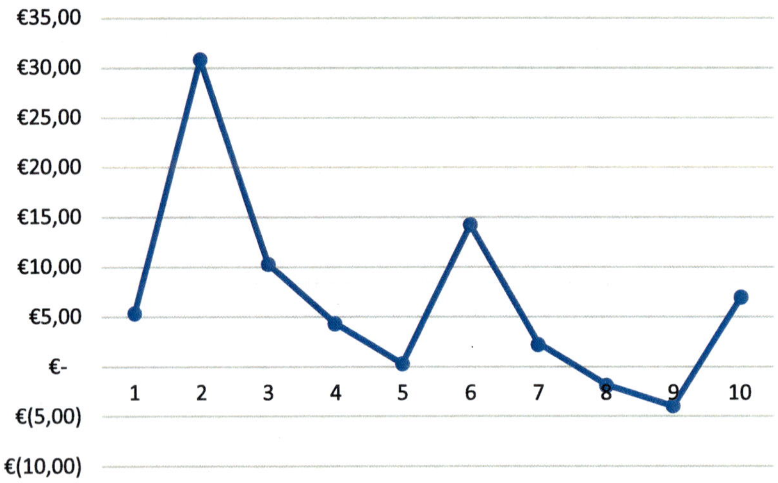

Fig. 8.6 Unit profits

Fig. 8.6. Figure 8.7 shows the investments of the players. The investments were initiated by the increase in demand or the price and unit profit increases, which were always too high, as can be seen in the subsequent sharp drop in prices and thus also average unit profits (Fig. 8.6). All groups showed similar behavior.

Conclusions for Game A

The first game shows the fundamental problem of non-coordinated supply adjustment among the companies. Game A's hypothesis was supported by the behavioral test. The increase in demand led to price increases, which signaled increases in profits. The companies (test subjects) increased their capacities, but did not know

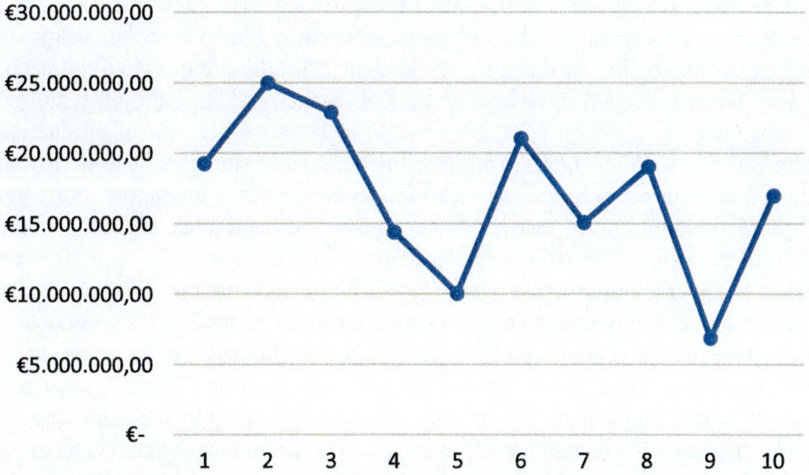

Fig. 8.7 Sum of investments

how much their competitors were increasing their capacities. This led to collective errors. The capacities were increased too much, resulting in investment cycles. First there was an upswing when capacity was being built up and then a downturn when prices fell as a result of overcapacity and companies hardly invested any more.

Assuming a profitable equilibrium, an increase in demand creates an oversupply. And even without an increase in demand, there was a tendency towards overinvestment due to the profitable starting position. The increase compared to the original state, however, clearly shows the influence of the increase in demand. Due to a lack of experience, players tended to over-invest. After the game, the test subjects said that they had underestimated the influence of other market participants on the success of their own investment decisions. In practice, the experience with capacity adjustments should not be much higher than in the Excel games, since managers change in the company and the adjustment processes take years (Thaler, 1989).

Game B: The Effects of Interest Rates on Investments

The aim is to test the following hypothesis: Interest rate cuts can lead to overinvestment due to errors made by market participants.

The model used was that of a simplified company. As before, every company had to make decisions about its investment. Each company (represented by a player) had in the beginning a production capacity (PC) of 500,000 units. New was that the investments were financed by debts. Starting debt capital was 20 million euros. At an interest rate of 5%, the companies paid 1 million euros in interest. The games started with sales (S) of 10 million euros, at a price (P) of 20 euros and cost of 15 euros (C). At a price of € 20, sales were € 10 million. The companies sold 500,000 goods in the first round, making a profit of 1.5 million euros (PR) after deducting the production costs of 15 euros (C) and the 1 million euros in borrowing costs (BC) (PR = S – C PC – BC). Each company had to decide on its investment (I). There were delays in expanding the range. For example, investments of 2.5 million euros (two rounds of the game) brought 50,000 increased production capacity in 2 years, or 1 million euros more sales at a price of 20 euros (40% or 50 euros per unit of production capacity, $PC_{t+2} = PC_t + I_t/50$). The investments directly increased the borrowed capital and the interest to be paid (in addition to the 15 euros production costs per unit), the remaining profit increases the equity. Demand and capacities were included in the price. The ratio between demand and capacity was multiplied by the price of the previous period ($P_t = D/PC\ P_{t-1}$). Due to the delayed supply increases, the prices only react to the investments after two rounds. Once production facilities were installed they could no longer be dismantled, so the increase in capacity was irreversible. Whoever had the most equity after 10 rounds won and received 10 euros. The demand and interest rates were changed by the game master. The game began with a demand equal to supply. The demand was again entered by the game master up to round 6 as equal to supply.

Results

The first round started with 5% interest. The demand had not changed. In the second round the central bank cut interest rates to 2% and in the third round to 0%. The demand was only increased in round 6 (Fig. 8.8). The interest rates were reduced from round 2 (see Fig. 8.9). This led to a sharp increase in investments (Fig. 8.10). The increase in capacity (Fig. 8.11), which was delayed by two rounds, then pulled the price (Fig. 8.12) down, and thus also the average unit profit (UP = PR/PC) Fig. 8.13). All groups showed similar behavior.

The central bank's reaction to possible inflation was also tested. In the sixth round demand increased by 50% (Fig. 8.8). The prices also rose (Fig. 8.12). There was another increase in investments (Fig. 8.10). The central bank reacted too late to the

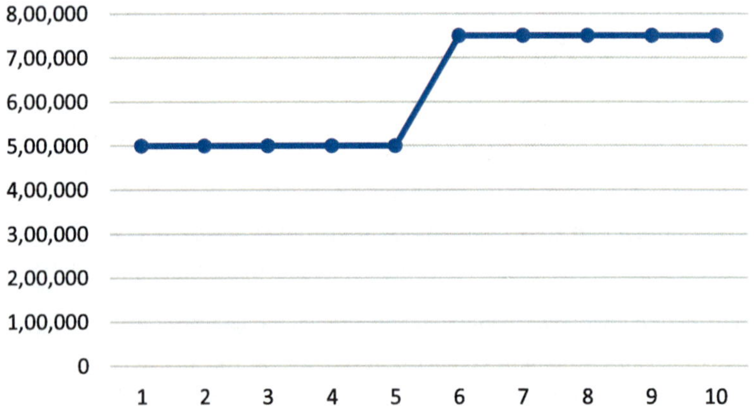

Fig. 8.8 Demand per player

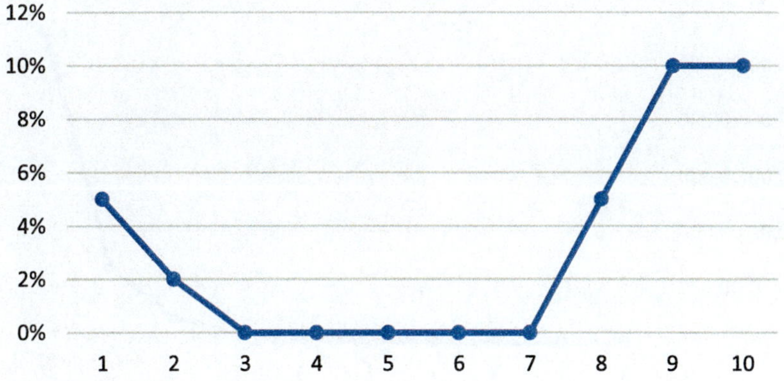

Fig. 8.9 Interest rates

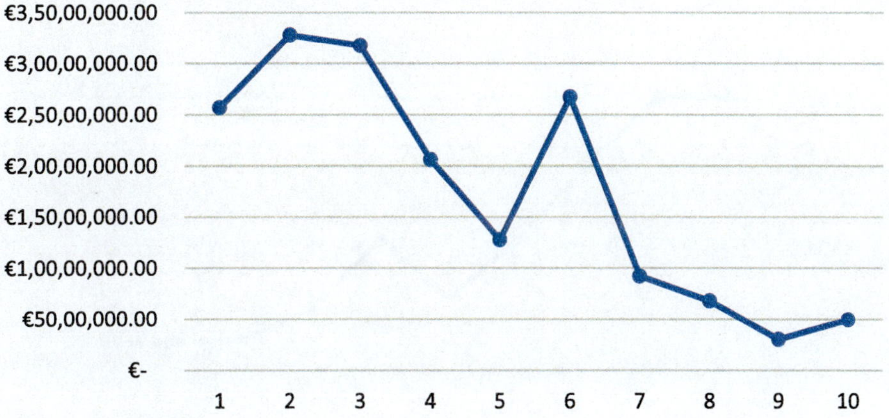

Fig. 8.10 Investments

increased prices (Wicksell assumption) and first raised interest rates to 5% in the eighth round and then to 10% in the ninth and tenth round in order to stop inflation (Fig. 8.12). The higher borrowing costs lead to bankruptcies, as equity dropped massively (Fig. 8.14). It is also interesting that the test subjects barely learned from their mistakes with a tendency to overinvest throughout the game. In practice, there would be a reduction in supply through exit from the market, i.e. bankruptcies.

Conclusion Game B

The experiments confirmed the hypothesis. The interest rate cuts led to unit profit increases. The companies increased their capacities even though prices had not increased. The rate cut thus led to collective errors.

The increase in demand and the associated increase in unit profit also led to overinvestment. The central bank reacted too late and finally raised interest rates too

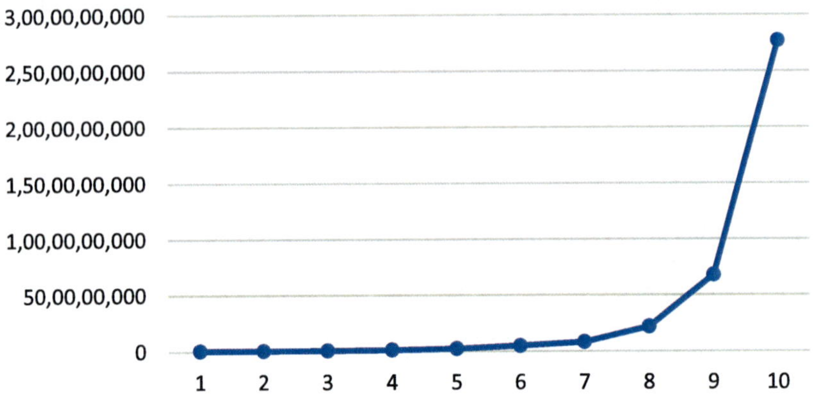

Fig. 8.11 Production capacities

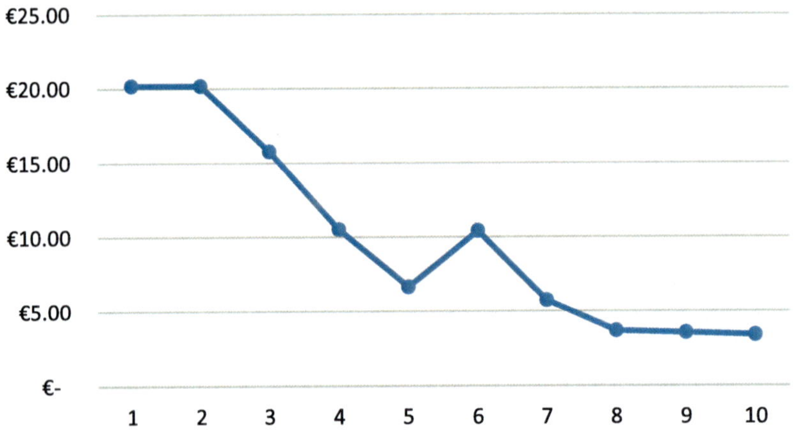

Fig. 8.12 Prices

sharply, resulting in massive bankruptcies because the companies were too indebted during the low interest rate phase. Here, too, there was a collective error. The actors assumed that interest rates would remain low. This phenomenon was seen in the financial crisis. The real estate buyers were unable to pay the interest rates that had risen as a result of the Fed's decision, which ultimately triggered the first loan defaults and thus the crisis (Conrad, 2020).

In game B the participants said that the lack of any borrowing costs had triggered a strong psychological impulse in them to access, i.e. to invest. Apparently similar processes take place as those in discounts or closing out sales.

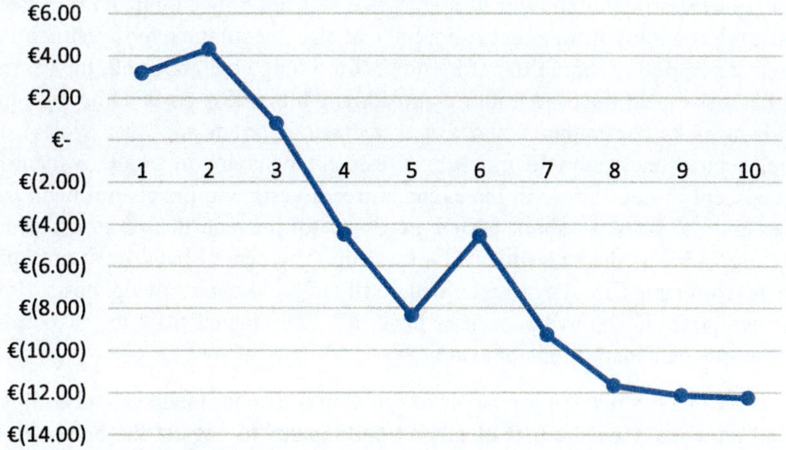

Fig. 8.13 Unit profits

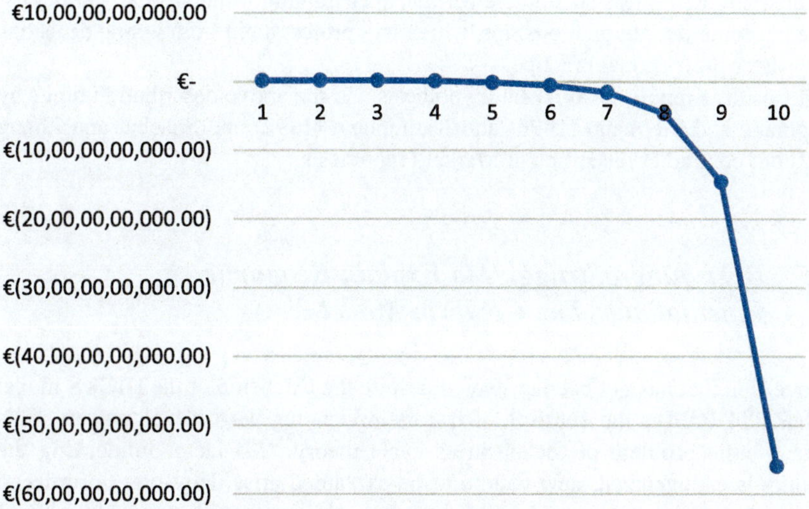

Fig. 8.14 Equity of the companies at the end of each round

Final Conclusion

In our behavioral experiments increases in demand and cuts in interest rates increased unit profits, which led to uncoordinated and thus collectively too high investments. The result was also a misallocation of resources (capital). This made it possible to demonstrate collective errors that led to overinvestment and investment cycles (boom and bust cycles) and which can be relevant to the economy. Central banks and companies should take this into account when making their decisions. The results of our experiments show that interest rate cuts not only stimulate investment to protect the economy from a recession, but can also encourage overinvestment. A low interest rate policy should therefore not last too long and, above all, the central bank must make clear the time limit for subsidizing borrowing costs. Otherwise the central bank risks bankruptcies and a new recession (boom and bust cycles). In addition, central banks should monitor investment behavior in order to identify overinvestment in good time. In the event of overinvestment, the central bank has to raise interest rates at short notice in order to prevent the economy from overheating and thus the subsequent sharp slump. The central bank must not hold inefficient companies in the market with artificially low borrowing costs (low interest rate policy). The overcapacities have to be eliminated from the market so that the supply can adapt to the demand.

The experiments show the fundamental problem of uncoordinated supply adjustment and a tendency on the part of market participants to neglect the behavior of other actors and to underestimate the influence of the market on their own investment decisions (undervalue of external influences). A company can do everything right on an individual economic level, but fail on the macroeconomic one. The games presented are therefore also suitable for manager training. Students can gain experience in economic interrelationships, which will protect them from wrong decisions in their later professional practice.

The results support the Wicksell hypothesis and the above-described findings by Kampmann and Stermann (1996) and Kampmann (1992) and Shachat and Zhang (2012) but contradict the Efficient Market Hypothesis.

8.2.5 *Distribution Struggles to Explain Economic Fluctuations: The Goodwin Model*

The question that has not been answered despite the extension of the HICKS model by BERGSTROM is the question of factors influencing wage developments. This shows a basic problem of the business cycle theory. If a factor influencing the economy is endogenized, new factors to be explained arise. However, in order to maintain the clarity of the model and thus its explanatory value, it is advisable to consider the influencing factors in isolation and to use a new model. The explanation of wage development is dedicated to another model of GOODWIN.

Goodwin developed a model of interdependent, nonlinear differential equations in 1967. In his model, he succeeds in simultaneously explaining the economy, growth and distribution.[21] From his model equations, two sinusoidal oscillations

---

[21] Zum GOODWIN-Modell See Goodwin (1967), pp. 54, Heubes (1986), pp. 86, Kurz (1986), Teichmann (1997), pp. 18 and Wagner (1990), pp. 225.

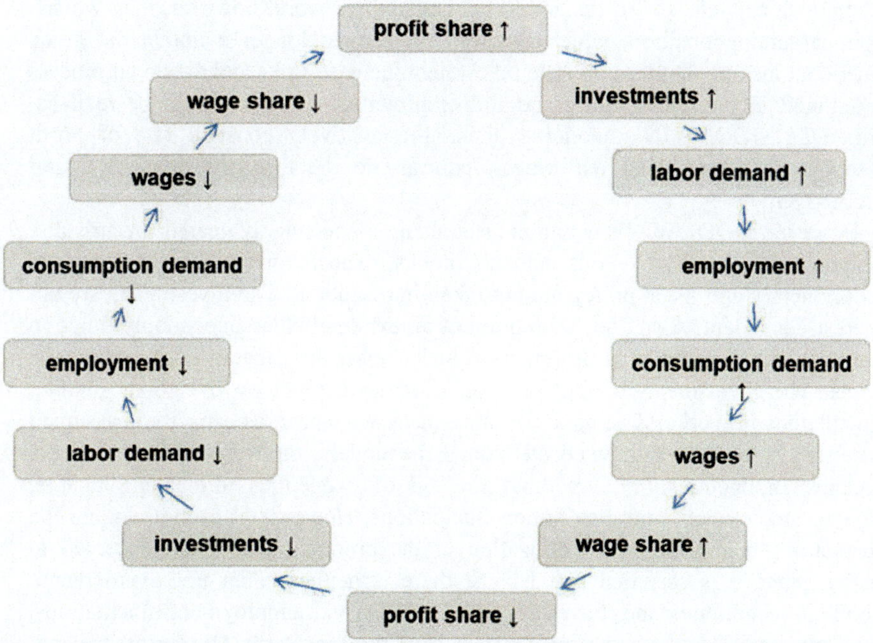

Fig. 8.15 The Goodwin distribution cycle

of the wage share (q, hunter population[22]) and the employment rate (b, prey population) result, which are offset by one phase. A complete business cycle can be modeled (see Fig. 8.15), which also reflects the empirically observed anti-cyclical development of the adjusted wage share and the pro-cyclical development of the profit and investment ratio. According to GOODWIN, his model confirms the instability of capitalist economies identified by MARX. High profits cause entrepreneurs to accumulate capital. Due to the additional demand for work, however, they are worsening their bargaining position, which is why they can no longer maintain the given functional income distribution. The investment increase sinks and the downward process is initiated. Economic stability and full employment can never be realized.

Conclusion

The Goodwin model explains the empirically observed anti-cyclical development of the adjusted wage share and the pro-cyclical development of the profit and investment ratio. According to GOODWIN, his model confirms the instability of capitalist economic systems indicated by MARX. High profits cause entrepreneurs to

[22]The hunter population (wage share) develops with a time lag of one phase, depending on the prey population (employment rate). The term hunter and prey populations comes from the biology that found a similar correlation for predators (e.g., lynxes) and prey (e.g., rabbits) (so-called LOTKA-VOLTERRA equations).

accumulate capital. Due to the additional demand for work, however, they worsen their bargaining position, which is why they can no longer maintain the given functional income distribution. The investment increase sinks and the down process is initiated. Economic stability and full employment can thus never be realized. Moreover, GOODWIN's model explains the relatively constant rate of profit observed with increasing real wages, contrary to the forecasts of MARX and RICARDO.

However, GOODWIN's economic statement is one-sidedly geared towards distribution struggles. Exogenous demand shocks, expectations, price developments and monetary and fiscal policy are not taken into account. The investments are not interest-dependent. Also, the assumption of an extremely classic economy function is unrealistic. The model is designed exclusively for the capacity effect of investments. The investments do not develop a demand effect on the goods market. Fluctuations in workers' demand for labor have no impact, as capacity is assumed to be always full. Given these constellations, the model is far from reality. The model explains endogenously, i.e. without the aid of exogenous influencing factors, growth, employment and distribution fluctuations. However, it cannot explain the fluctuations in the degree of utilization of the production potential observed in reality: since it is assumed that $I = S$, there is neither under nor overdemand. Goodwin economies are therefore pure growth and employment fluctuations. Employment and wage rates are constant over the long term. On the other hand, all absolute sizes grow.

Since, as with HICKS, the state was not included in this model, no direct economic policy conclusions can be derived. In GOODWIN's model, however, the state cannot even be indirectly integrated into the model by exogenously influencing demand. GOODWIN's economic fluctuations are distribution-determined. However, governmental redistribution policy would only slow down economic recovery in this model, due to the reduction in profits and thus in investment. The same applies to the crowding-out of credit-financed expenditure policy, as WOLFSTETTER shows in his model.[23] What is needed are automatisms to mitigate the vibration fluctuations. A progressive taxation of profit would be cyclically damaging. The state is also in demand as a mediator of distribution fights, for example in the form of a concerted action. Due to the assumption of the extremely classic investment function, however, any redirection from profit to labor income slows down the growth process and, at the same time, the economic upturn. Nonetheless, a continuation of the positive growth and employment trends could be achieved if, as a result of the lower employment growth rate, the unions increased their wages less or used the tax revenues on an investment basis. Pure redistribution taxation always reduces growth and employment, unless the workers also save and thus compensate for the reduction in investment of the recipients.

[23] See Wolfstetter (1982) and Assenmacher (1998), S. 229ff.

8.2.6 *Political Economic Cycles: The Political Economic Model of Nordhaus*

The Nordhaus approach goes back to the "New Political Economy". According to the New Political Economy approach, a politician does not maximize the common good, but maximizes their own benefit. Political offices grant this benefit in the form of power, prestige and income. In order to achieve the desired offices, the politician must collect as many electoral votes – one speaks of voice maximization. Positive economic indicators can be used as a political track record and secure voter approval. If the politician starts from the controllability of the economy, he will try to use the instruments at his disposal in such a way that at the time of the election the economic indicators are the best. Already from this behavioral hypothesis can be concluded on the existence of politically induced economic cycles. However, until Nordhaus's economic model was published, the New Political Economy approach lacked the mathematical behavioral model that allowed economic cycles to be endogenously deduced and explained politically initiated business cycles.[24]

The economic indicators used by Nordhaus are inflation and unemployment. Every voter is directly affected by inflation in his role as a goods buyer. Unemployment affects him directly if he loses his job. He may also be indirectly affected if he feels threatened by unemployment, expecting that he could lose his job in the future. Nordhaus cites various reasons for a trade-off between inflation and unemployment. First, low unemployment creates higher aggregate demand, which also affects the price level. Secondly, higher overall demand implies higher strike costs than opportunity costs of lost sales due to lack of production. These cause the employer to accept the wage demands of the workers. In addition, Nordhaus justifies a short-term trade-off with the adaptive reactions of the workers to unemployment and inflation and the consequences on the price level. With high unemployment, they reduce their wage demands. The reduction of production costs leads to a price reduction and, in turn, to a reduction in wage demands. When inflation occurs, the workers realize the real wage reduction late and therefore adjust their wage demands late. The long-term "Phillips curve" L is thus steeper than the short-term "Phillips curve" S (see Figs. 8.16 and 8.17).

As part of the "Phillips curve," the politician can select combinations of inflation and unemployment. However, this only works as long as the money illusion persists. Once the economic subjects have adjusted their expectations, the short-term Phillips curve shifts upward. The politician chooses the maximum vote combination. Citizens 'decisions to re-elect the government are made in response to meeting citizens' expectations: improvements in economic indicators are rewarded with electoral votes. Longer-term improvements and deterioration in the legislature are less significant than recent developments. Consequently, it is maximizing for the ruling party to implement restrictive measures at the beginning of the parliamentary term

[24] See Frey and Lau (1968).

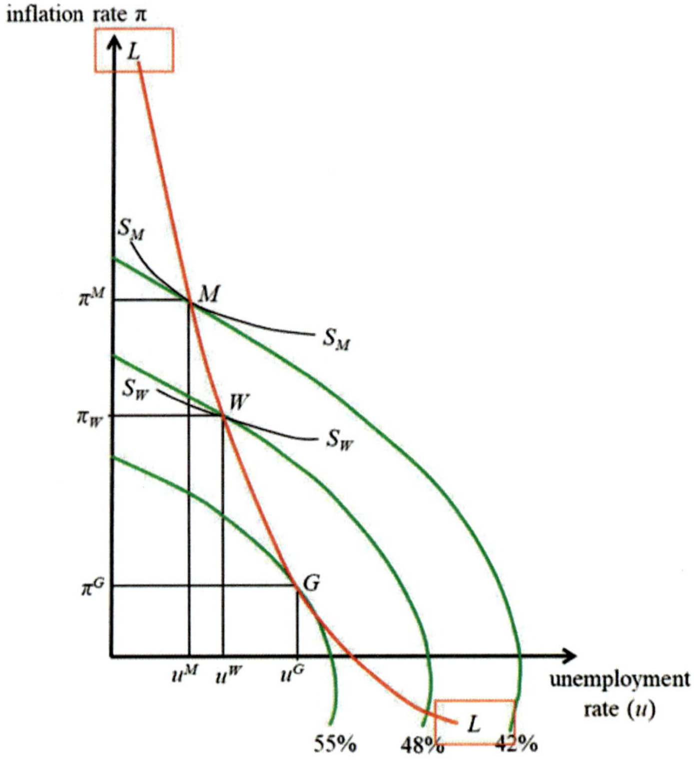

Fig. 8.16 Long-term policy strategies

and expansive measures at the end of the election period. After expansive measures, the short-term Phillips curve shifts from bottom to top. If the government does not pursue a restrictive policy after the election, then before its next re-election, it must increase the inflation rate more than in the first term to reduce unemployment despite higher inflation expectations. The new, worse combination of unemployment and inflation is rated by the electorate with less agreement (measured in electoral votes), which is why the governing party cannot sustain this policy for long. In point E3, the system is in the long-term equilibrium: both expansionary and restrictive pre-election policies would deprive the government of its majority (see Fig. 8.17). After re-election, the government must try to reach the original Phillips curve with the old inflation expectations through a restrictive policy. The discretionary, politically motivated interventions generate business cycles.

NORDHAUS attributes to its political economic model the well-known Phillips curve. As part of the Phillips curve, the politician can select combinations of inflation and unemployment. The politician can deceive the workers in the short term in terms of the inflation rate, which is why they adjust the nominal wages of the inflation rate only delayed and the real wage decreases. As a result, entrepreneurs expand labor demand and thus production. In the short term, the real national product (asymmetric

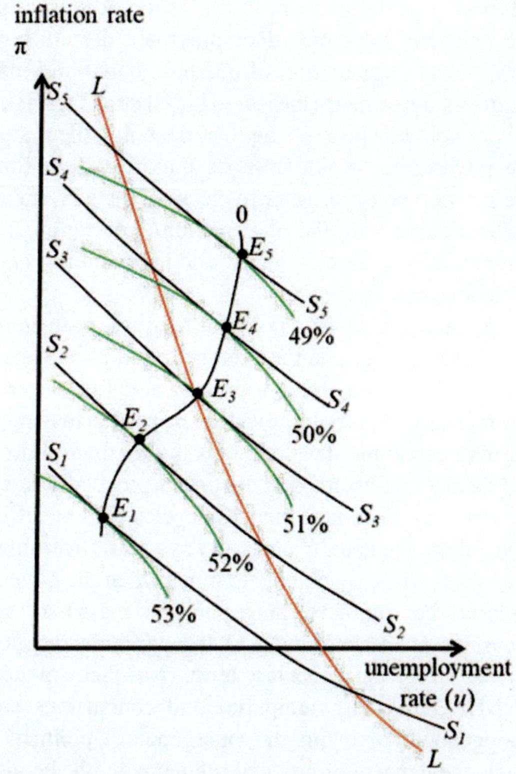

Fig. 8.17 Short-term election result. (Source: Nordhaus, 1975, p. 177 and 179)

time delay / wage-lag hypothesis) increases.[25] However, this only works as long as the money illusion persists. Once the economic subjects have adjusted their expectations, the short-term Phillips curve shifts upward. The politician chooses the maximum vote combination. Citizens' decisions to re-elect the government are made on the basis of meeting citizens' expectations: improvements in economic indicators are rewarded with electoral votes. Longer-term improvements and deterioration in the legislature are less significant than recent developments. Consequently, it is maximizing for the ruling party to implement restrictive measures at the beginning of the parliamentary term and expansive measures at the end of the parliamentary term. After expansive measures, the short-term Phillips curve shifts from bottom to top. If the government does not pursue a restrictive policy after the

[25]NORDHAUS gives different reasons for the trade-off between inflation and unemployment: (1) That a low unemployment rate means that the demand for labor is relatively high, hence the price of labor, the wage that acts as a cost on the general price level. (2) There would be asymmetrical delays (lags) in the effect of changes in the unemployment rate on the general price level because, on the one hand, wage demands are lower in the case of high unemployment and, on the other hand, because an increased inflation rate increases inflation expectations and so that the wage demands of the employees to keep the real wage constant. NORDHAUS concludes that the long-term Phillips curve is steeper than the short-term one. See Nordhaus, (1975), p. 169 f.

election, then before its next re-election, it must raise the inflation rate more than in the first term to reduce unemployment despite higher inflation expectations. The new, worse combination of unemployment and inflation is rated by the electorate with less agreement (measured in electoral terms), which is why the ruling party cannot hold this policy long. On one point, the system is in a long-term equilibrium: the government would lose its majority, both through expansive and restrictive pre-election policies. After re-election, the government must try to reach the original Phillips curve with the old inflation expectations through a restrictive policy. The discretionary, politically motivated interventions generate business cycles according to the election cycles.

In democracies, as a result of the present overemphasis, the average unemployment rate is lower and the average inflation rate above the general welfare optimum (W, see Fig. 8.16) for the present and future generations. Furthermore, the time preference of voters in government politicians suggests a tendency to rate today's positive economic developments higher than future ones. Nordhaus concludes that politicians tend to maximize current prosperity at the expense of wealth for future generations. Nordhaus business cycles also occur in centrally planned economies. Since these are usually one-party systems governing through dictatorship, however, the cycles will only emerge at times when the government needs short-term popular support. For the governing party to maximize voting, to implement restrictive measures at the beginning of the parliamentary term and expansive measures at the end of the parliamentary term. (Nordhaus model).

NORDHAUS' assumptions and conclusions are mostly plausible. The model endogenously explains the emergence of political business cycles and thus highlights the dangers of political influence on the economic process. NORDHAUS has confirmed his theories for Germany, New Zealand and the USA. He identified low political cycles for France and Sweden, whereas the likelihood of political influence on the business cycle was low in the other cases he examined.[26] However, NORDHAUS' model requires a controllability of the economic indicators unemployment and inflation. The macroeconomic fluctuations are not the result of a miscalculation, but of political manipulation. However, this only marginally diminishes the significance of the model since politically induced fluctuations in disorder would only occur more irregularly.

In his fundamental essay NORDHAUS addresses several alternatives that could reduce political fluctuations in the economy. The simplest thing would be to shorten the electoral period to account for the forgetfulness of voters. However, there was a danger that the government would no longer be sufficient for a long-term, strategically oriented policy, and that therefore the policy would only be geared to a short-term perspective. In addition, inefficiencies in the administration would come from the frequent change of government. To refresh the level of information of the voters over and over again, seems to be an unrealistic alternative, given the lack of interest among people in past events (present-day preference). Of particular interest is the

[26] Australien, Kanada, Japan, Großbritannien Australia, Canada, Japan, United Kingdom.

fact that the demand for the political independence of central banks and even finance ministries (in the area of short-term spending decisions) can be derived from this model. However, NORDHAUS sees it as a disadvantage that monetary and fiscal policy is lost as a political instrument to be able to implement the wishes of voters. This statement contains a certain contradiction to the model-immanent critique of politically induced business cycles. Political and economic rationality (utility) are rarely identical. Another alternative would be to reduce the tendency of the Phillips curve, i.e. the short-term trade-off between unemployment and inflation, for example through price and wage freezes or through automatic induction or inflation compensation. Apart from the inflation adjustment, these measures are incompatible with a market-based economic system. They would be market and thus system destroying. Automatic wage inflation or indirect inflation compensation, as with Italian Scala Mobile, would lead to less resistance to inflation and, ultimately, inflation acceleration. For his part, NORDHAUS tends to prevent voter manipulation by exploiting their short-term memory through greater transparency and broader participation in the political decision-making process.

8.2.7 Monetary Policy and the Behavior of the Central Bank as a Reason for Business Cycles

8.2.7.1 The Interest Rate Theorem of Knut Wicksell and Its Support from Behavioral Science

Wicksell (1851–1926) attributes cyclical fluctuations to the wrong decisions of monetary policymakers, i.e. the central banks (at that time still commercial banks) in controlling interest rates.[27] The profitability of investments, the marginal productivity of capital (or internal rate of return), increases due to external factors (due to technical progress).

❶ The central bank does not react or reacts too late (see Fig. 8.18), which is why the internal rate of return (profitability of an investment) is higher than the monetary interest rate. The interest rate of the central bank (i) is therefore lower than the

Fig. 8.18 Upswing due to non-reaction of the central bank

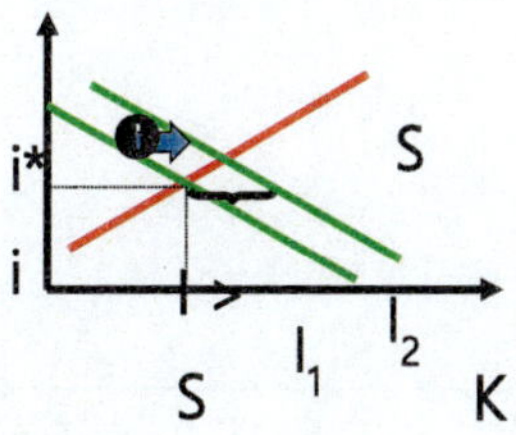

[27] See Grossekettler (1989), pp. 203; Wicksell (1898), pp. 109 and Wicksell (1922), p. 231.

profitability of investments and below the equilibrium interest rate (i *), which would offset supply and demand. There is therefore an over-demand for capital. The result is more investment than savings. The demand shortfall caused by saving is smaller than the additional demand from the companies' investments. Due to the over-demand, it is booming. The central bank does not raise the interest rate, which is why the equilibrium interest rate i * is not reached.

❷ Due to excess demand, the cost of inputs (labor and pre-products) increases, which is why the internal rate of return falls.

❸ Since the aggregate demand is greater than the supply, the price level rises (see Fig. 8.19). As a result of the price increase, the central bank reacts and raises interest rates, which is why the internal rate of interest is now below the interest rate (⇒ equilibrium interest rate i * < i), Which is why investment is now smaller than savings. That the central bank again reacts wrongly and thus triggers the downturn (⇒ I <S ⇒ downturn). The intervention of the central bank in the market thus causes cyclical fluctuations, because the market mechanism is disrupted.

According to Masciandaro, "central bankers are individuals that are subject to the same source of behavioral bias all individuals face."[28]

In 1992, Kahnemann and Tversky determined **loss aversion**. Losses are thus rated more heavily than comparable profits. They also found a non-linear probability estimation. Small probabilities are rated higher than large ones.[29]

Overconfidence is the human tendency to overestimate one's capabilities. Here one can establish a subjective, positive self-judgment. Subjects regularly overestimate their own knowledge, their control options, their abilities as well as their achievements.[30]

People shy away from change when they cannot assess how they are affected. The status quo is preferred over another alternative (status quo bias). Samuelson and Zeckhauser found that the majority of test subjects do not change their investment portfolio in the case of inheritance. The subjects retained the shares they had inherited or did not buy any shares in cash.[31] In principle, sticking to the status

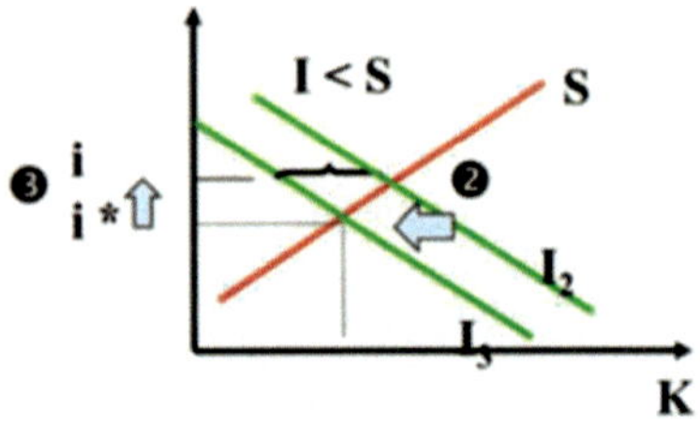

Fig. 8.19 Downturn due to belated reaction of the central bank

[28] Masciandaro, D., F. and Favaretto, 2016.

[29] See Kahneman and Tversky (1981, 1982, 1984, 1986) and Kahneman et al. (1991, pp. 193–206).

[30] See Metcalfe (1998) and Beck (2014), p. 62.

[31] See Samuelson and Zeckhauser (1988), pp. 12, Kahneman et al. (1991), pp. 193–206 and Beck (2014), pp. 164.

quo can be a rational and efficient approach. Boxall, Adamowicz and Moon found that the status quo bias increases the more complex and time-consuming the decision-making process is.[32]

The status quo bias is reinforced by the omission bias.[33] People rate negative results from active actions higher than negative results resulting from non-actions, i.e. omissions. Kahneman and Tversky showed as early as 1982 that the losses on an equity investment are considered to be more negative if they were created through active buying than by neglecting to sell.[34] Ritov and Baron show that parents refrain from vaccination even if the risk of disease is 5/10,000 lower than that of non-vaccination at 10/10,000.[35]

If monetary policy decision-making is subject to biases, including overconfidence and loss aversion, we "can explain monetary policy inertia in setting interest rates" by central banks.[36]

And this would lead so business cycles as Wicksell had described. Status quo bias and omission bias lead to policy mistakes of the central bank. It does not react or reacts too late.

8.2.7.2 The Perverse Elasticity of Credit Offers of Hayek

In contrast, Friedrich August von Hayek (pupil of Wicksell) blames the cyclical overheating for the perverse elasticity of the credit supply, i.e. the uncontrolled development of money supply, in its economic theory.[37] Due to the uncontrolled money creation process there is too much money supply. In the banks' money creation process, these companies pass on the sight deposits of their customers (deposits) to third parties, which creates new sight deposits (see the chapter on monetary policy above). The money will be returned to the bank and can be borrowed again. Hayek calls this unlimited credit a perverse elasticity of the credit supply. Money creation by the banks does not increase interest rates, even though capital demand has increased. Investments are thus greater than savings, which is why the demand on the goods market is greater than the supply ($\Rightarrow I > S$). It creates an upswing. There is an uncontrollable upswing as more money is spent than is saved.

Due to excess demand, the cost of inputs (labor and pre-products) increases, which is why the internal rate of return falls and prices generally rise. Now, lenders are raising interest rates to get inflation compensation, which is why the internal rate

[32] See Boxall et al. (2009) and Beck (2014), p. 167.
[33] See Ritov and Baron (1992), Spranca et al. (1991) and Beck (2014), pp. 168
[34] See Kahneman and Tversky (1982), p. 173.
[35] See Ritov and Baron (1992).
[36] See Masciandaro, D., and F. Favaretto (2014), and Khan, Ashraf (2018), pp. 46.
[37] See von Hayek (1967 [1935]).

of return is now below interest rates and many investments are no longer profitable. There are investment failures and depreciation. The investment demand drops because of saving as a demand failure on the part of the households. The additional demand from companies for investments is not enough to compensate for the drop in demand for savings ($I < S \Rightarrow$ downturn).

Conclusion
Wicksell and Hayek highlight the dangers of central bank intervention. The central banks prevent the natural market mechanism of the money market from balancing out surplus and short supply. This criticism speaks in favor of rule-based monetary policy, which is geared towards the growth of production potential. Only in exceptional cases does the intervention of the central bank in the money market appear justified. If the central bank intervenes, it bears a responsibility for the economic development. The central bank must monitor lending and the speed of money circulation.[38]

8.2.7.3 The Effects on Investment Behavior of Zero Interest Rate Policy, Evidence from a Behavioral Experiment

The Federal Reserve implemented an extreme expansionary monetary policy (Quantitative Easing) and turned to unconventional monetary policy tools such as forward guidance and large-scale asset purchases. The ECB and the central banks of Switzerland, Sweden and Japan went one step further and set their target rates below zero (zero interest rate policy). This monetary policy is controversial and its effects barely researchable, because the influence of monetary policy on the economy cannot be isolated. There are too many additional factors (Nishad Nishad, 2018). The development of growth rates in Japan also raises doubts as to whether there will be positive effects if the zero interest rate policy is applied over a longer period of time. Rather, this policy of cheap money is made responsible for exaggerations on stock markets (Conrad & Stahl, 2002) even including the financial crisis. The allegation is that money is wasted and used for risk-taking if it costs nothing.

Historically, the question is very controversial as to how a central bank can generate real growth through monetary policy instruments. According to monetarism, real gross domestic product growth cannot be artificially generated by an expansionary monetary policy. Friedman and Schwartz used historical time sequences and economic analyses to argue that changes in the money supply had unintended adverse effects, and that sound monetary policy is necessary for economic stability. Hayek and Wicksell even blamed the central bank for boom and bust cycles (Wicksell, 1922, 1898; Hayek, 1935; Friedman & Schwartz, 1969).

Against such a background this chapter examines the effects of interest rate cuts on investment behavior using an experiment. Human behavior is examined in this

[38] See Conrad and Stahl (2003), pp. 685–693.

context. The methodology is to simulate investment decision making under different capital costs. How does the borrower with the borrowed money act in relation to the price of the borrowed capital? They may be bank or non-bank investors. The business banks borrow the money from the central bank and then invest it by lending it to private borrowers just as private investors borrow the money from the banks to invest it, for example, in their own companies, real estate or equities.

The existing literature and studies are presented and compared to the experiment presented here. Next the experimental design of the study is explained. Finally, the results are presented and the conclusions drawn.[39]

Related Literature

"The more money there is the better it is for the economy", is the conclusion of most studies about quantitative easing (Gagnon, 2016) and "the lower the better" is their conclusion for the interest rate. For a long time it was common sense that nominal interest rates cannot fall below zero. This barrier was called the "lower boundary." Scientists have been discussing how to break the Lower Boundary to achieve more economic stimuli since the financial crisis. The arguments for and against a zero-percent policy can be found at Tymoigne (Tymoigne, 2018).

There have been numerous studies about zero interest rate policy, or negative interest rate policy. For example, Cúrdia estimates that in the US, the decline in GDP during the recession would have decreased by half a percentage point if the Fed had lowered the federal funds rate to −0.75% (Cúrdia, 2019). The question arises as to what other consequences follow from subsidizing credits by the central bank. If money is cheap it may be wasted like every other product.

So others argue that low interest rate policy could lead to a buildup of leverage, or asset bubbles by encouraging excessive risk taking by financial market participants (Conrad & Stahl, 2002; Caruana, 2013; Feldstein, 2013; Stiglitz, 2016). Confronted with low interest rates bank and non-bank investors may switch to excessive risk in order to compensate the smaller interest income. (Hannoun, 2015).

The mechanism is called "search for yield". If financial institutions have long-term commitments (such as pension funds and insurance companies) they come under pressure to earn the yield they promised on their liabilities. If they obtain only a low interest return on their assets they might be forced to go in risk (Rajan, 2005; De Nicolò et al., 2010). Unilaterally constructed bonus-based compensation schemes encourage excessive risk-taking and were one reason for the financial crisis (Conrad, 2015).

Empirical studies show (e.g., for Spain, Maddaloni & Peydró, 2010; Ongena et al., 2009) that credit standards tend to loosen when policy rates decline. Maddaloni et al. (2009) show that if overnight rates are lowered credit standards are loosened.

De Nicolò and others (2010) found a negative relationship between the monetary policy rate and ex ante risk taking in a study about US banking policy. The average

[39] See Conrad, Christian A. (2019), pp. 18–27.

internal risk rating by banks and the spread over the federal funds rate decline as monetary policy rate increases. They also test the relation between interest rate to the ratio of the bank's risk-weighted assets to total assets of U.S. commercial banks and bank holding companies using their quarterly financial statements (Call Report filings). They find a strong negative relationship between real interest rates and the riskiness of banks' assets. The relationship is weaker when bank capital is low.

Expansive monetary policies and low interest rates, especially long lasting ones, have been made responsible for credit booms and excessive risk taking. The context is as follows. Lower interest rates lead to higher asset prices and borrower's fortune, in turn allow higher and cheaper lending. Analytical models (Stiglitz & Weiss, 1981), show more risk-taking when interest rates decline and vice versa a reallocation to more quality and safe investments when interest rates rise. The withdrawal leads to less availability of external financing.

Easy and cheap money access encourages greater risk-taking, which leads to asset bubbles. Later crashes of such bubbles could be damaging for the real economy. If they take place in the housing market they may affect balances of credit institutes and thus lead to credit crunches, which affect the real economy severely (Conrad & Stahl, 2002; Claessens et al., 2012; Mian et al., 2015). The cheap central bank money is seen as a reason for the US housing market bubble. The relatively low interest rates in the U.S. during 2001–04 resulted in a rapid increases in house prices and household leverage (Lansing, 2008; Hirata et al., 2012).

Accommodative monetary policy is blamed as one reason for the global financial crisis. Persistently low real interest rates and excess liquidity fueled a bubble as a boom in asset prices and securitized credit and seduced financial institutions into take on increased risk and leverage. Had central banks raised the interest rates earlier and more aggressively and preempted this buildup of risk, the consequences of the burst would have been much less severe (Borio & Zhu, 2008; De Nicolò et al., 2010). Claessens and Kose state that whether and how monetary policy affects risk taking, and thereby asset prices and leverage, remains a subject for further research (Claessens & Kose, 2013).

This chapter details a simple incentive-based experiment regarding investment behavior in relation to borrowing cost based on roulette. There have been several experiments with roulette but with the objective to scrutinize the gambling behavior (Rubio et al., n.d.) and guessing tendencies (Rubio et al., 2010). In 2015 there was a roulette experiment, simulated most common short-term bonus compensation schemes without accountability (Conrad, 2015).

Roulette Experimental Design

The purpose of this chapter is to test the hypothesis that decreasing the interest rate to zero encourages excessive risk-taking in the financial system. The methodology is to simulate investment decision making under different capital costs. Therefore an experimental environment similar to the investment conditions had to be constructed. Roulette has the advantage of clearly demonstrating the probabilities for gains and losses. In the original game (apart from zero) the probability of losses is compensated with higher payouts. A higher risk has an equivalent higher payout.

The experiment was conducted with 107 students from different Business Bachelor courses at the University of Applied Science HTW at Saarbrücken. The students played 3 rounds of Roulette (A, B and C), each with three games. They could bet on red or black, on one of the three thirds of the 36 numbers or on one number. The winning number and color was determined by the roulette wheel. If it was zero, the game was repeated and not registered. The payouts were distributed according to the probability of winning (x2, x3, x36).

The task was to invest borrowed capital like a manager of a company. The participants were asked to maximize the profit the way it is the obligation of a manager to do as agent for a principal (company owner resp. shareholder). Maximal profit in the group resulted in 10€ real money as variable compensation. In order to reduce change in behavior due to learning effects the game consisted of three rounds each with three games. Learning effects should therefore arise early with small influence.

In order to simulate investment behavior with different interest rates thus capital costs, decision-makers were be exposed to three different investment situations. In round A they were allowed to borrow up to 10,000€ (maximum) at 10% interest, in round B at 5% and in round C at 0%. Losses and gains were credited at 100%. The payouts could be reinvested and were accumulated in each round and afterwards the borrowed capital deducted. The results of the rounds A, B and C were added and the player with the highest result was rewarded with €10 real money. The rules were explained to the students before starting the experiment. The students were asked to check each other's calculations after each game. This simple experiment shows clear results.

Results

The sum of the average borrowed capital rose from €5439.93 in round A to €9931.78 in round C, thus by 81.03%. The sum of the average capital set rose from €7211.05 in round A to €14,244.15 in round C, thus by 97.53% (see Figs. 8.20 and 8.21).

How was the risk behavior? The highest possible profit (calculated as the product of the set capital and the possible payout multiple) in all three games rose continuously from €37,483.12 in round A to €98,754.77 in round C, by 163.46% (see Fig. 8.22). The significantly higher standard deviation in round C shows that some players were more willing to take risks than the average (see Fig. 8.23).

If you set the maximum possible gain in relation to set capital as a risk measurement indicator, the willingness to take risks increased by 33.27% from 5.20 in round A to 6.89 in round C (see Fig. 8.24). The same development shows the risk measurement indicator maximal possible gain in relation to the borrowed capital as a risk measurement indicator. The willingness to take risks increased by 46.67% from 6.90 in round A to 10.04 in round C (see Fig. 8.25).

How were the results? How successfully did the investors set their capital? The average gains of round A and B with 10% and 5% interest rate stayed pretty much the same (A: €51.68 and B: €63.60€) whereas in round C the students realized an average loss of €297.66 (see Fig. 8.26).

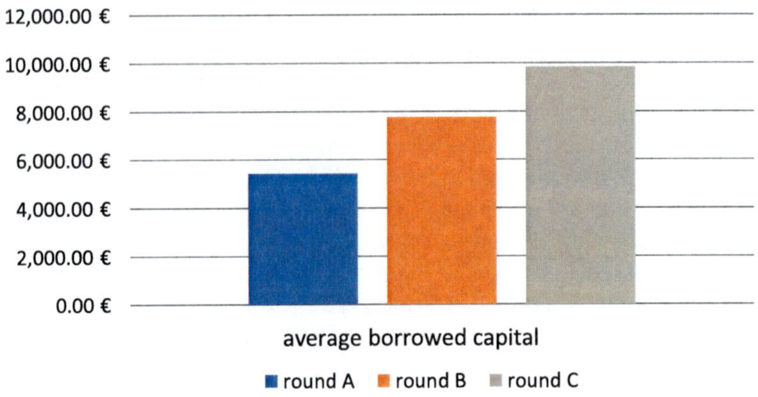

Fig. 8.20 Average borrowed capital

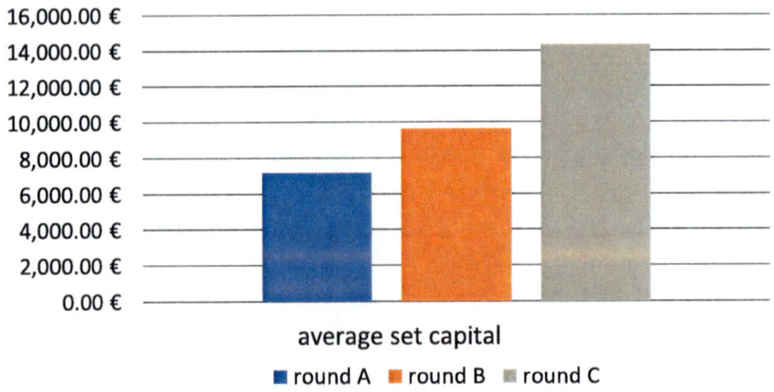

Fig. 8.21 Average set capital

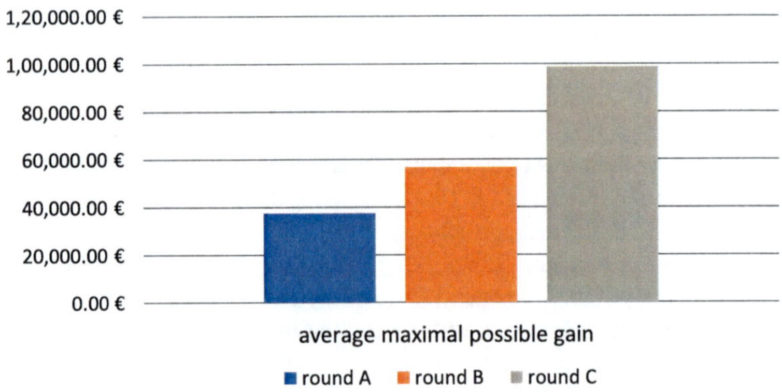

Fig. 8.22 Average maximal possible gain

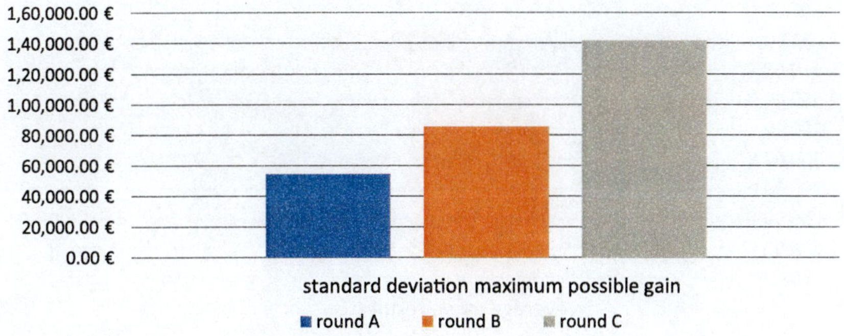

Fig. 8.23 Standard deviation maximum possible gain

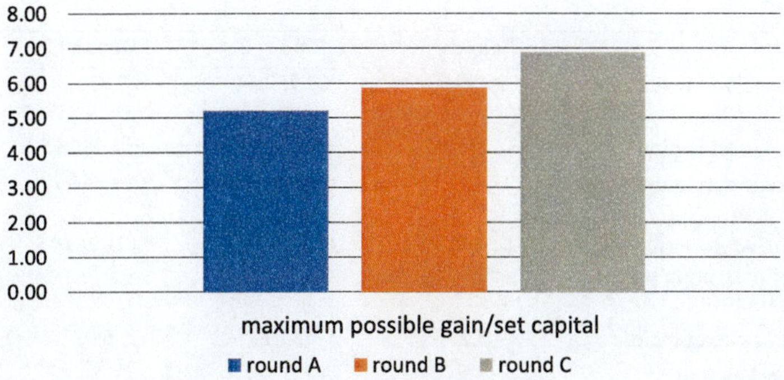

Fig. 8.24 Maximum possible gain in relation to set capital

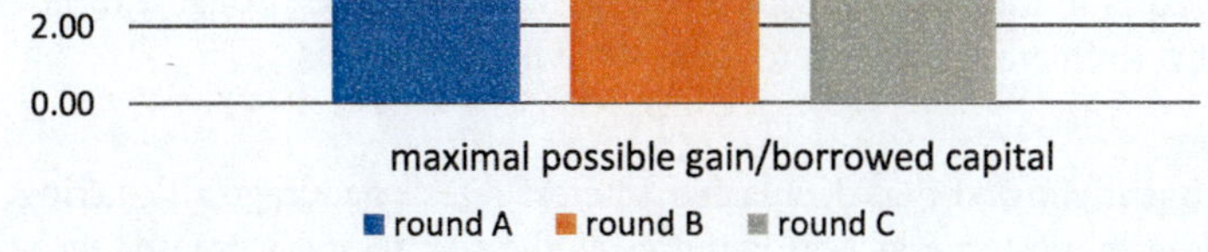

Fig. 8.25 Maximum possible gain in relation to borrowed capital

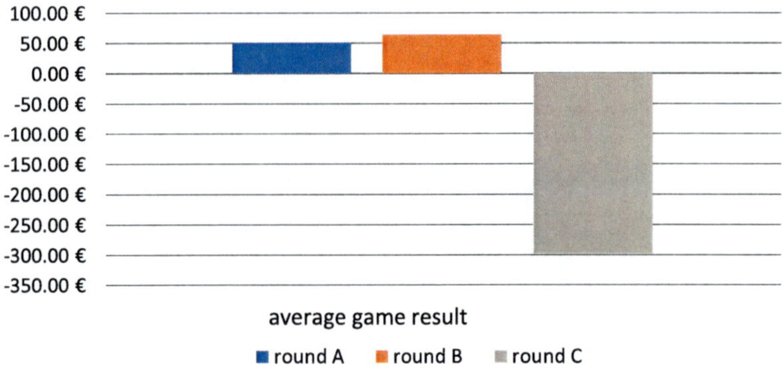

Fig. 8.26 Average game result

	Round A	Round B	Round C
Average borrowed capital	€5,430.93	€7,759.81	€9,831.78
Average set capital	€7,211.05	€9,617.37	€14,244.15
Average maximum possible gain	€37,483.12	€56,466.74	€98,754.77
Standard deviation average maximum possible gain	€54,490.10	€85,157.77	€141,764.15
Risk as max. possible gain/set capital	5.2	5.87	6.93
Risk as max. possible gain/borrowed capital	6.90	7.28	10.04
Average game result, +gain, -loss	€51.68	€63.60	- €297.66

Fig. 8.27 Statistical data

Interestingly, with the decreased interest rate as borrowing costs, the risk taking increases continuously, which means that there are proportional effects of the borrowing costs to the risk behavior (see Fig. 8.27). But the strongest reaction was detected at zero interest rate, where there were no capital costs.

Conclusion

The experiment showed that decreasing interest rates encourage risk-taking. With the decreased interest rate as borrowing costs the risk taking increased weakly but continuously. The risk taking increased strongly when the interest rate reached zero. The experiment showed excessive risk-taking when there were no capital costs. With no capital costs the average result of the game was a net loss, whereas before there was a small profit. It seems that if money is free, human beings react less rationally.

This finding supports the hypothesis that extreme expansive monetary policy with low, zero or negative interest rates encourage financial bubbles and overinvestments or wrong investments in the real economy. Bank and non-bank investors are less prudent and rational the less the capital costs are and extremely irrational and incautious if there are no costs at all.

Decreasing the interest rate to zero encourages excess risk-taking in the financial system. Low interest rate policy could lead to a buildup of leverage, or asset bubbles by encouraging excessive risk taking by financial market participants. Bank and non-bank investors may be encouraged by low interest rates to take excessive risk in their search for profit, which can create asset bubbles on the stock market and housing market. If they are financed by credit, credit crunches and strong economic downturns may follow, which caused the 1929 financial crisis (stock market crash), followed by the great depression and the financial crisis of 2008 (housing credit crisis).

Moreover, it has been demonstrated (see Sect. 8.2.2 and Conrad, 2015) that unilaterally constructed incentive schemes encourage excess risk-taking. This would indicate that common bonus-based compensation schemes enhance risk because of the asymmetries in the treatment of gains and losses. Unilaterally constructed compensation schemes were one reason for the financial crisis.

After the financial crisis many central banks turned to quantitative easing (QE) to support economic growth. In order to reduce long-term borrowing costs they purchased massive and unprecedented amounts of long-term bonds, which created liquidity and decreased the long term borrowing costs. Some central banks even pushed short-term interest rates slightly below zero to stimulate the economy. But the slow recovery, especially in Europe, has raised questions about the benefits of QE bond purchases versus their detriments and whether their effectiveness has reached a limit.

The example of Japan should give pause. Japan is a pioneer of zero interest rate policy and quantitative easing. In 2001 and 2013, the Bank of Japan implemented zero interest rates alongside quantitative easing. Neither managed to stimulate the economy sustainably or to increase inflation (Drozd, 2018). Often when pursuing an inflation target, we forget that we are in a long phase of globalization with falling import prices. In particular, the goods made in China are pushing down prices for many consumer goods.

The question remains as to why the long period of low interest rates in Japan has not led to a second bubble. For a bubble, a constant inflow of liquidity is required, which is financed by loans. After the real estate and equity crash in Japan in the 1980s, Japanese banks still had a lot of bad credit on the books after huge write-offs. They were not recapitalized, so even if they wanted to make the same mistake again, they lacked the equity to real estate and equity loans. Rather, one spoke at that time of a credit crunch, since the Japanese banks and the real economy barely forgave loans for lack of equity, which is why the economy stagnated at a low level. Dell'Ariccia, Laeven and Marquez (2013) showed that the extent of bank capitalization appears to be an important factor for recovery. They found out that facing a lower interest rate, a well-capitalized bank is willing to give more credit, it decreases its monitoring and takes more risk, while a highly levered, a low capitalized bank does the opposite (Dell'Ariccia et al., 2010; Claessens & Kose, 2013).

There are a lot of market distortions due to the market intervention of the central bank apart from the shift to investments with higher yields. If the interest rate is below the inflation rate, there are redistributive effects from creditors to debtors. Insurance companies and pension funds do not have enough earnings to meet their obligations. Money market funds might not earn enough to cover their costs of running. The pension of the population becomes a problem, as the interest income is missing. The effects of a prolonged zero interest rate phase on the financial system has not yet been handled in depth. Banks lack the float profits from loaning their deposits, as well as the margin between investment and lending rate. Negative investment rates are usually not enforceable on the market and neither is a high credit margin if the refinancing rate is zero (Arteta et al., 2016). Lowering the interest rates thus means narrowing net interest margins—the gap between commercial banks' lending and deposit rates. Several studies found a positive relationship between short-term interest rates and net interest margins. A low interest rate environment has the adverse effect on banks' profitability (Claessens et al., 2016; Borio et al., 2015).

The Bank Lending Survey of April 2016 already noted a collapse in European bank profit as a result of low interest rate policy and quantitative easing (Arteta et al., 2016). If the banks lack income, equity is also lacking to lend and to survive new crises. The zero interest rate policy is thus counterproductive. In addition, if the central bank buys corporate and government bonds, it shuts the commercial banks out of this market, especially since it lacks the expertise to manage corporate risk. The financing of enterprises by state organizations is not market-compliant, but characteristic of central administration economies.

All studies assume an interest rate responsiveness to investments. As we know from the Great Depression of 1929, this does not have to be the case. If the expectations of return on investments are negative, interest rates would have to be so negative that they more than offset losses on the investment. But then it would be less risky for companies if they did not invest the money but let it go and take the central bank's negative interest rates as a safe return.

The expectations of the return on investments must not only be negative due to poor economic expectations, they can also be due to a lack of competitiveness. For example, in spite of zero interest rates, nobody would invest in Greek hotels if the comparable Mediterranean holiday in Portugal is much cheaper due to lower labor costs.

Falling interest rates, on the other hand, always affect equity and real estate prices. For one thing, they are the alternative form of investment to bonds and, on the other hand, they can be financed by loans. If the cost of credit decreases, the present value of real estate and equities increases. The demand for shares and real estate and thus also the price will rise. The profits of companies increase due to lower borrowing costs, which also increases the demand for shares and thus the price.

In conclusion, one can say that the side effects of an extremely expansionary monetary policy such as zero interest rate policy, negative interest rate policy or quantitative easing are so great that such an intervention in the markets is only justified in a Keynesian depression situation (Great Depression) as in 1929 and 2008 and only for a limited time. One can only warn against recent suggestions, such as de-bundling cash from electronic currency and making cash depreciate relative to electronic currency, to further reduce key interest rates to negative territory (Assenmacher & Krogstrup, 2018), because the negative effects of these options are not predictable.

8.2.8 The Effects of Money Supply and Interest Rates on Stock Prices, Evidence from Two Behavioral Experiments

What is the impact of interest rate and monetary policy on the stock market? Some studies find a positive impact of expansive monetary policy on stock prices others prove the opposite. The following chapter examines the effects of monetary expansion and interest rate changes on investment behavior on the stock market by illustrating two behavioral experiments with students (Conrad, 2021). In our experiments the increase of money supply and the decrease of interest rates had a direct positive impact on share prices. These findings support the hypothesis that extreme expansive monetary policy with low, zero or negative interest rates encourage financial bubbles on the stock market. To avoid a crash the exit from such a policy must be slow. As happened in 1929, crashes can damage the financial system and the real economy. Central banks must take this into account in their monetary policy.

Introduction

After the financial crisis and now in the Covid-19 crisis many central banks turned to quantitative easing (QE) to support economic growth. In order to reduce long-term borrowing costs, they purchased massive and unprecedented amounts of long-term bonds, which created liquidity and decreased the long term borrowing costs. Some central banks even pushed short-term interest rates slightly below zero to stimulate the economy. But the slow recovery, especially in Europe, has raised questions about the benefits of QE bond purchases versus their detriments and whether their effectiveness has reached a limit. What is the impact of such an expansive monetary policy on the stock market? Empirical studies contradict each other. Some find a positive impact of expansive monetary policy on stock prices others prove the opposite. Against such a background this chapter examines the effects of monetary expansion and interest rate changes on investment behavior on the stock market by illustrating two behavioral experiments with students. In section “Related literature” the existing literature and studies are presented and compared to the experiment presented here. Section “Experimental design” explains the experimental design of the study. Finally, the results are presented (section “Results”) and the conclusions drawn (section “Final conclusion”).

Related Literature
Theoretical Background

A positive correlation between the two variables money supply and stock prices can be interpreted in three different ways. Firstly, there is an ex post correlation when the stock prices increased due to higher productivity in real economy and the central bank provided the money needed to prevent deflation. Secondly, an increase in money supply, e.g. liquidity, leads to portfolio adoptions on the part of the stockholder, to realize the desired proportion of liquidity and assets. The stockholders have more money to buy assets, which leads to an increase in stock prices providing a constant amount of stocks. Thirdly, increased money supply leads to lower interest rates and thereby lowers the discount rate on future cash flows from an enterprise's expected profits. Interest is a main part of production and investing costs of enterprises, therefore lower interest rates means higher profits (International Monetary Fund, 2000a; Baks & Kramer, 1999). In addition, others argue that low interest rate policy could lead to a buildup of leverage, or asset bubbles by encouraging excessive risk taking by financial market participants (Conrad & Stahl, 2002; Caruana, 2013; Feldstein, 2013; Stiglitz, 2016). Confronted with low interest rates bank and non-bank investors may switch to excessive risk in order to compensate the smaller interest income (Hannoun, 2015). The mechanism is called "search for yield". If financial institutions have long-term commitments (such as pension funds and insurance companies) they come under pressure to earn the yield they promised on their liabilities. If they obtain only a low interest return on their assets they might be forced to go in risk (Rajan, 2005; De Nicolò et al., 2010) and purchase stocks instead of bonds. Unilaterally constructed bonus-based compensation schemes encourage excessive risk-taking and were one reason for the financial crisis (Conrad, 2015). However, only one paper examined the effects of interest rate cuts on investment behavior. This behavioral experiment with students showed that decreasing interest rates encourage risk-taking (Conrad, 2019).

The roots of the boom and bust cycle theory go back to Hayek and Wicksell. Friedrich August von Hayek holds the tremendous elasticity of the banking system and the unregulated money supply development responsible for the economy overheating (Hayek, 1976, 1935). Knut Wicksell on the other hand, lays the blame at the doorstep of the monetary policy decision-makers and their poor decisions regarding interest controls (Wicksell, 1922, 1968; Grosskettler, 1989). A set interest level on the capital market below that for the supply and demand balance causes an expansion of the money supply. In specific, the exchange relation of goods to money tips in favor of money. The demand for credit increases because of the low interest level. New current account deposits come into existence through the increased credit. The speed of money circulation increases, and with it the money supply. There is a shift in portfolios, since the value of the investor's liquidity increases relative to the stocks owned. The new money flows into the stock markets and pushes the stock prices ever upwards. Because the interest functions as both an asset yield and a discount factor it brings about an artificial interest reduction in an upswing of the stock price as well as an excessive resource allocation in stock value. This effect can cause the system to overheat. The higher stock prices signify profit potential and represent security to the banks that allows them to grant credit and thus indirectly create money. A self-propagating upward movement is created on the stock market, which supports a boom through excessive liquidity supply from the central banks. Should the central bank reverse interest rate decreases, the same effect in the reverse direction will occur (Conrad, 2000).

Empirical Studies

There are empirical studies about the impact of interest rates on stock market prices. According to Thorbecke (1997), stock prices decline by 0.8% if federal funds rate increases unexpectedly by 1%. Rigobon and Sack (2004) estimated that stock index S&P 500 loses 1.7% because of 3-month rate increases of 0.25% and found a higher effect for Nasdaq index (2.4% decrease).

Trust Kganyago and Victor Gumbo tested the long-term relationship between money market interest rates and stock market returns in Zimbabwe from April 2009 to December 2013. The estimation model controls for money supply growth rate, inflation, volume of manufacturing index, crude oil price and political stability. They found evidence of a strong and statistically significant inverse causal relationship between money market interest and stock market returns (Kganyago & Gumbo, 2015).

The relationship between money supply development and asset prices has been examined in several empirical studies. Using the increase in Japanese stock, art and real estate prices in the second half of the 1980s as an example, empirical studies have shown that the catalyst for the bubble was an expansive monetary policy in conjunction with a productivity increase in the Japanese economy and an higher demand for real estate in Tokyo; all of which expressed itself in more credit given by the banks (Ito & Iwaisako, 1995). In the first half of the 1990s the prices mostly fell back to their original level. Ito und Iwaisako (1995) establish further, that the increase in prices can be explained with fundamental changes in data only until 1987, at which point the bubble took on a life of its own. By Homa and Jaffee (1971) had already found a significant and systematic relationship between stock prices and money supply as represented by deposits and currency. Rozeff (1974) showed that both money supply and M1 aggregate can impact stock prices; a finding which was later supported by Flannery and Protopapadakis (2002). Lastrapes (1998) estimates that stock prices fall off by 2.4% if M1 is reduced by 1%. Safar and Siničáková (2017) prove statistically significant influence of money supply on stock market indices in the US and EU. Pícha (2017) found an influence of money supply on valuation of S&P 500 indices with a 6 month lag. According to the International Monetary Fund further analyses show a positive correlation between the variables money supply and stock prices (International Monetary Fund, 2000b; Baks & Kramer, 1999). However, other studies have come to contradictory conclusions. Black (1987) found that changes in money supply do not influence stock prices. Campbell and Ammer (1993) came to the conclusion that money supply has only minimal effect on stocks prices.

How can these controversial findings be explained? We have fundamental method problems here. The scientific content of the predominantly Granger-based econometric studies has to be questioned. Because of the risk of false results, the Granger test is discouraged if the variables under study are extremely volatile (Irwin & Sanders, 2012). For highly volatile variables such as stock prices, a lack of covariance stationarity was found, which does not provide a condition for the regression of time series (Pagan & Schwert, 1990; Phillips & Loretan, 1990; Frenk, 2011; Schlecker, 2014; Conrad, 2020). Due to innumerable influencing factors on supply and demand, we have a strong multi-causality here in which the individual influencing factors cannot be filtered out precisely. If causal variables are not extracted, Granger tests can show correlations that are not present (spurious regression). The same applies to purely random correlations, which may arise in particular in the case of short observation periods or incorrect time intervals (Frenk, 2011).

Against this background, we decided to analyze the relationship between money, interest rate and stock markets with a behavioral experiment as an alternative scientific method. This should give additional evidence.

Experimental Design

We want to answer two questions:

1. How does the investor react on the stock market if the money supply is changed? Some studies find a positive impact of expansive monetary policy on stock prices while others prove the opposite. However, as most studies show a positive impact we use this as hypothesis.
2. How do the investors react on the stock market if the save interest rate of bonds as an alternative investment is changed and how is the profit of the stock market companies, and therefore also the dividends influenced by the interest rate as cost of borrowed capital? We test the assumption of the portfolio-theory that not only risk but also yield is decisive for the allocation of invested capital.

The purpose of this chapter is to test the hypothesis that:

A. an increase of money supply leads to higher share prices and encourages bubbles with a subsequent crash when money supply is reduced (boom and bust cycle).
B. interest rates influence capital allocation as per the portfolio-theory that capital follows the yield. Thus, bonds are the alternative of shares and vice versa. A decrease in the interest rate should therefore lead to higher share prices and vice versa. Interest rates also influence the cost of capital borrowed from the enterprises. Therefore, lower interest rates lead to higher profits and dividends.

How do the money supply and interest rates affect investment behavior? The methodology was to simulate investment decision making on the stock market under different money supply and interest rates. We conducted two experiments, A and B:

Two experiments, A and B, were conducted in the winter semester of 2019/20 with different groups but were terminated due to the Covid 19 pandemic. There were

56 participants in game A and 43 students in game B, who came from different Business Bachelor courses at the University of Applied Science HTW at Saarbrücken, Germany. Most investment capital is controlled and allocated by agents for third persons. There are family offices, investment firms, fund managers and the managers of companies. The task was to invest capital like an investment agent or a manager of a company. The participants were asked to maximize profit, which is the obligation of a manager as agent for a principal (company owner resp. shareholder). Maximal profit in the group resulted in 10€ real money as variable compensation. The rules were explained to the students before starting the experiment. The students were asked to check each other's calculations after each game.

Game A: Money supply and stocks

Game A aimed to examine how money supply affects the demand for stocks. Apart from stocks, there was only the alternative of holding money as liquidity without interest. The shares did not distribute any dividends.

Students were to invest their money in stocks or hold cash. Ten shares in the fictional corporation Rancom LC with a nominal value of €100 each were added per round. The shares were auctioned every round. The students were informed of the additional amount of money that they had at their disposal each round as a result of the monetary policy of the central bank. They could sell or buy the shares through the lecturer who would auction them off (stock exchange). The highest bids were accepted. The respective maximum price was set as the share price. Sales were served first and settled according to the available bids. Up to round 5 the money supply was doubled. The last two rounds it stayed the same.

Game B: Interest rate and stocks

Game B aimed to examine how interest rates affect the stock's attractiveness as an alternative investment. Two factors affect the investor here. On the one hand, the interest rate is the return on bonds as safe investment, and on the other, it determines the cost of debt and thus also the profit and dividend of the stock corporation. Students were to invest their money in stocks or fixed deposits. There was an initial stock of 0 shares in Rancom LC with a nominal value of €300 (€300 equity and €600 debt). Each round, €1000 were added per player and 10 shares were auctioned off so that stocks and money increased roughly proportionally. The return on capital employed was a constant €60, or 6.67%. The interest rates, which the central bank set as the base rate, were communicated to the students every round. Likewise, the price to earnings ratio and the dividends changed every round in accordance with the change in the cost of debt of Rancom AG. Representing the earnings situation, the students were informed of the dividend yield as a 50% distribution of the profit. Students could invest an amount of money at the relevant interest rate, or sell or buy the shares through the lecturer who would auction them off. The highest bids were accepted. The respective maximum price was set as the share price. Sales were served first and settled according to the available bids. At the end of each round the interest and dividends were added as yield to the invested capital.

These simple experiments show clear results.

Results

Game A: amount of money and stocks

Figure 8.28 shows the development of the money supply and the average bid as share prices and Fig. 8.29 the development of the liquidity on hand (which is the average cash held by the students at the end of each round) and the average share bids of the students. We can see a positive relation between money and share price. In addition, the mere stop of monetary expansion in round 5 created a stock market crash if we look at the average bids which would be relevant for the stock market development. Starting in round 5 we see a slow reaction of the bids. Even though the money supply drops the bids first stay high.

Conclusion game A

In our experiment money supply had a direct positive impact on share prices. The hypothesis was not disproven and seems to be true. Central banks have a strong responsibility for the stock market if they increase the money supply disproportionately to the real production. If there has been an expansive monetary policy followed by increasing stock prices, the exit of this policy must be done slowly, otherwise a crash might follow.

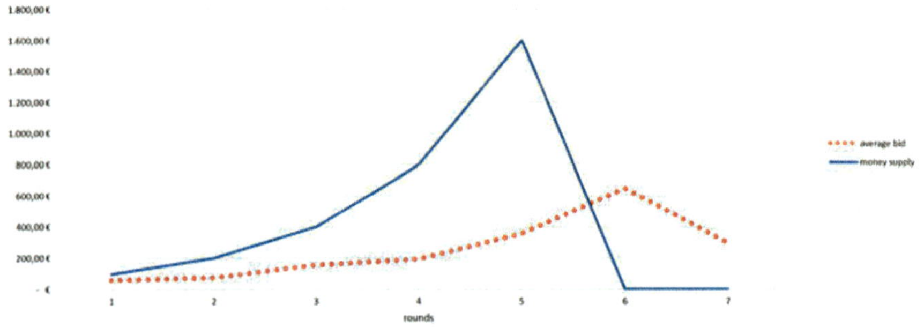

Fig. 8.28 Money supply and average bid

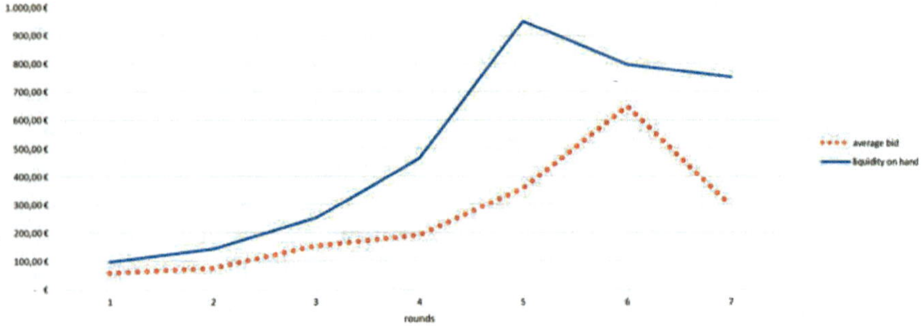

Fig. 8.29 Liquidity on hand and average share bids

Game B: interest rate and stocks

The interest rates were first decreased and then increased (see Fig. 8.30). The dividends were adapted according to the changed-borrowing cost of Rancom LC due to the changes in the interest rate (Fig. 8.31), also the price to earning ratios were adapted (Fig. 8.32).

Share prices were clearly driven by the interest rate reduction, which resulted in higher earnings and dividends (Fig. 8.31). The students adjusted their portfolio according to the changed yield relation between shares and fixed deposits even though the shares were more risky. The sharp increase in interest rates in round 7 led to a stock market crash (see Fig. 8.32) due to quick portfolio adjustments (see Fig. 8.33). And the crash resulted in a strong decrease of the asset value of shares (see Fig. 8.34).

The buying of the shares seemed to be consistent and rational as the dividends and earnings increased. The price to earning ratio shows that the impact of the lower

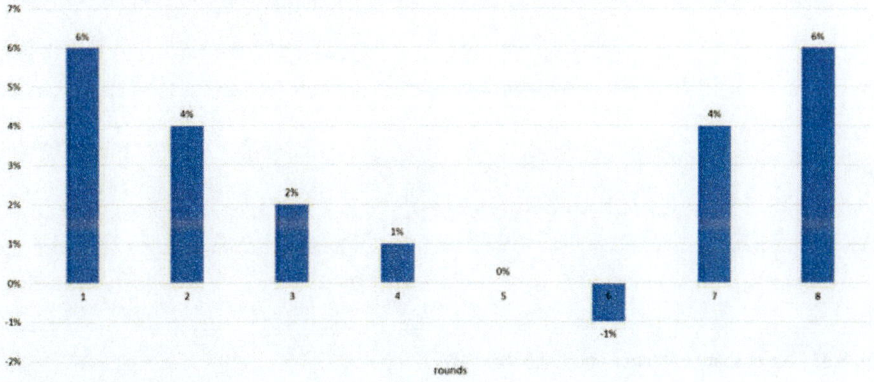

Fig. 8.30 Interest rates

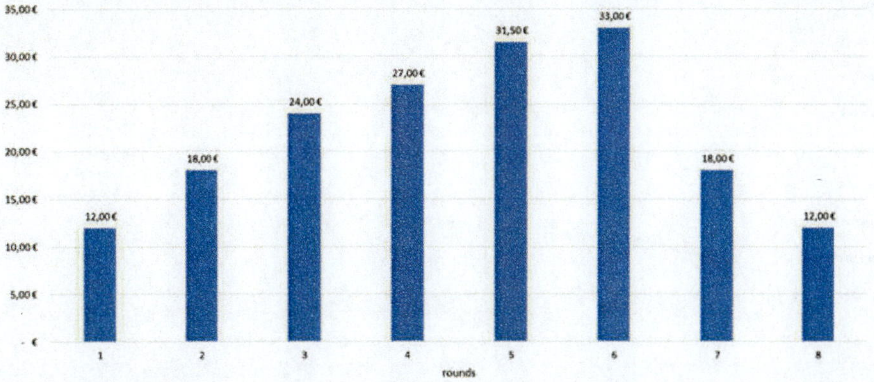

Fig. 8.31 Dividends

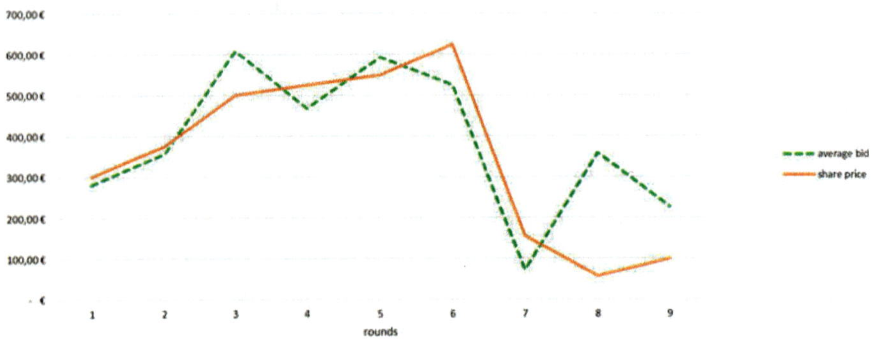

Fig. 8.32 Average bids and share prices

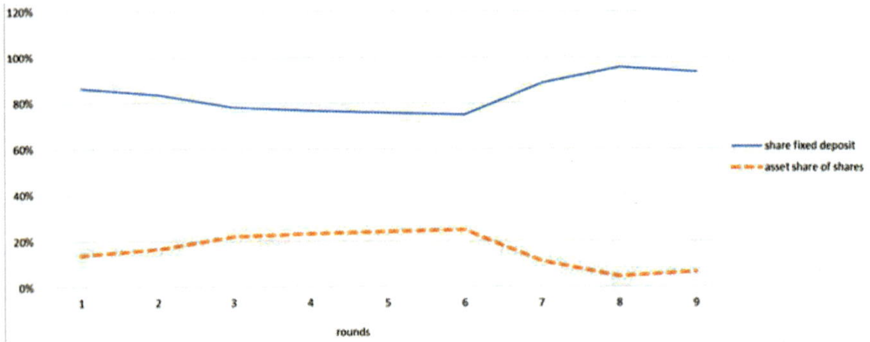

Fig. 8.33 Asset share of shares and fixed deposits

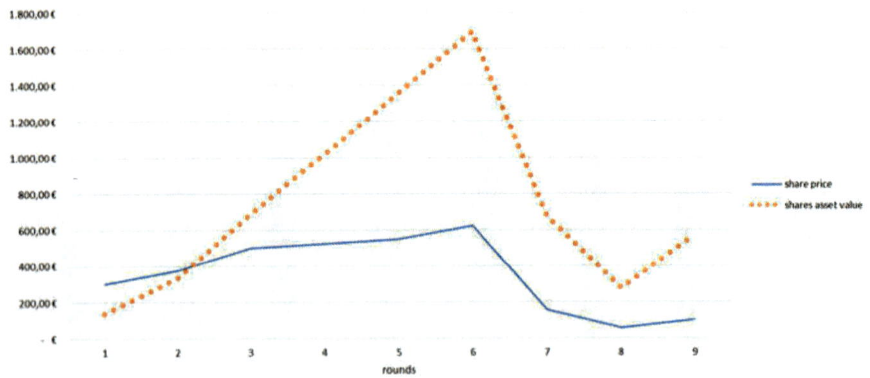

Fig. 8.34 Share prices and the asset value of shares

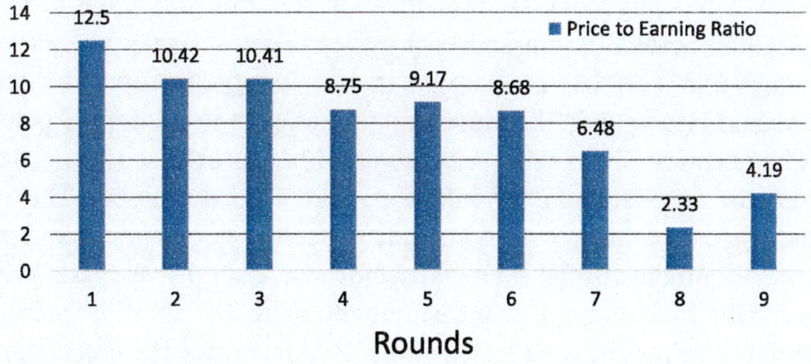

Fig. 8.35 Price to Earning Ratio

interest rates compensated the higher share prices (see Fig. 8.35) as borrowing cost decreased and thus the earnings increased.

Conclusion game B

Our hypothesis was not proven false, as the interest rates influenced the capital allocation according to the portfolio-theory. The students invested in the stocks as assets with higher yields as the interest rate dropped and dividends rose. The higher risk of the shares was not a hindrance. The yield from bonds is the alternative of shares and vice versa. A decrease in interest rate led in the experiment to higher share prices and vice versa. In addition, the interest rates influenced the cost of borrowed capital for the enterprises. Therefore, lower interest rates led to higher profits and dividends.

Share prices were clearly driven by the interest rate reduction, which resulted in higher earnings and dividends. The price to earning ratio is deceptive in that the impact of the lower interest rates compensated the higher share prices even though the profit of the core business activities stayed the same. In our experiments we had an increase in profits of 100% as a reaction to a 66% interest rate reduction, thus an elasticity of 1.5. Thus price to earning ratios are not an adequate pricing tool and cannot help to detect a stock market bubble. The sharp increase in interest rates in round 7 led to a stock market crash due to quick portfolio adjustments. And the crash resulted in a strong decrease of the share asset value.

Final Conclusion

In our experiments the increase of money supply and the decrease of interest rates had a direct positive impact on share prices. All groups show similar behavior and the games may be repeated and reviewed by other scientists in the future. Moreover, the sharp increase in interest rates and the stoppage of money supply increase led to a stock market crash due to quick portfolio adjustments. The crash resulted in a strong decrease of the asset value of shares. Therefore, the central banks must keep in mind that the interest rates do not just influence the investments in the real economy. Boom and bust cycles are a real danger of an expansive monetary policy with low interest rates. If there has been an expansive monetary policy or strong interest rate cuts followed by increasing stock process, the exit from this policy has to be slow to prevent a subsequent crash (boom and bust cycle). Central banks have a responsibility for the stock market if they increase the money supply disproportionately to the real production and intervene in the money market or even in the capital market by a QE-policy. The question if it is wise to do so at all has to be discussed separately.

In addition, the measurement of inflation has to be discussed. The inflation measures used by central banks mainly include consumer goods prices and producer prices. Price developments in the financial sector and asset prices (asset prices) are thus systematically hidden by the measurement method. So it is possible that excessive money production is reflected not in rising prices for consumer goods, but in asset price volatility. If only consumer goods prices are considered, this can lead to unpredictable inflation (Mezger & Stahl, 2001b; Conrad & Stahl, 2002).

Experiment B showed that decreasing interest rates encourage risk taking. The portfolio theory was true in our experiments. Interest rate cuts led to a shift towards shares as an alternative asset with higher yield. The higher risk of the shares was not a hindrance. The mechanism "search for yield" took place. The students reacted to the lower interest rates by taking on risk.

Share prices were clearly driven by the interest rate reduction, which resulted in higher earnings and dividends. The price to earning ratio is deceptive in that the impact of the lower interest rates compensated the higher share prices even though the profit of the core business activities stayed the same. Thus price to earning ratios are not an adequate pricing tool and cannot help to detect a stock market bubble. The valuation indicators for equities would have to be adjusted for the refinancing costs. Even a smooth price-earnings ratio like that of Shiller (CAPE, Cycle-Adjusted Price Earnings Ratio) could be distorted by a prolonged period of low interest rates.

The results of our experiments show that money supply and interest rates not only influence investments in the real economy, they also have a direct impact on the stock markets and tend to favor speculative bubbles. To avoid a crash the exit from such a policy must be slow. As happened in 1929, crashes can damage the financial system and the real economy. Central banks must take this into account in their monetary policy.

8.2.8.1 Case Study: The US Monetary Policy in the Field of Tension of the Stock Market Development

The ECB has pursued an expansive monetary policy since its central bank president Draghi took office. Following the interventions in the context of the financial crisis and the sovereign debt crisis, Draghi tried with an expansionary monetary policy to combat deflation and stimulate economic growth. His program for buying government bonds also served this purpose. Thus, in addition to money being pumped into the market, the banks are forced to lend to companies because of the absence of government bonds as an investment possibility. Furthermore, the purchase of government bonds on the capital market should also reduce the lending rate. The US has also pursued an expansive monetary policy since the crash of the financial crisis but also before (see Fig. 8.36).

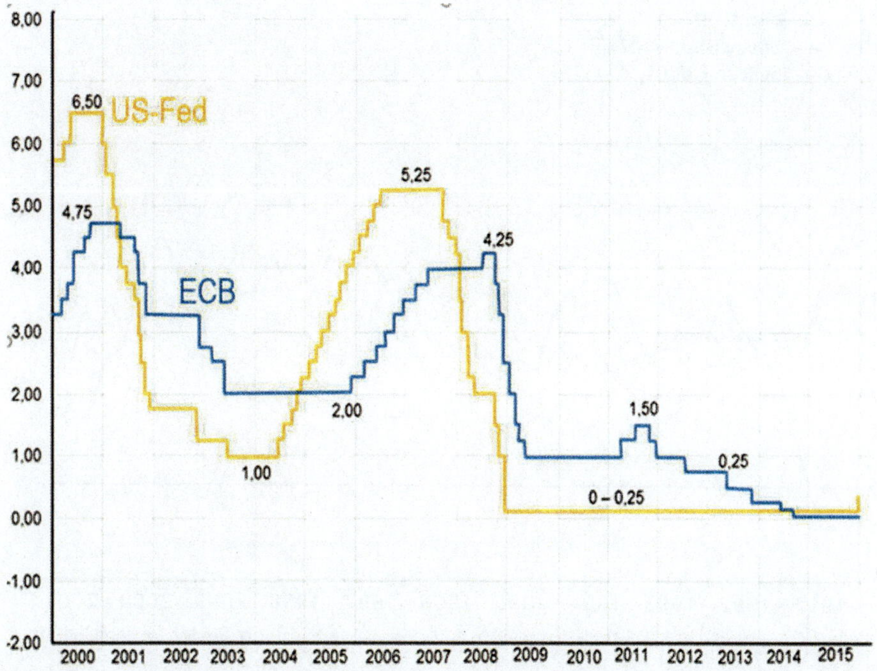

Fig. 8.36 Development of the ECB and US interest rates 2000–2015. (Imprint with friendly permission of finanzen.net GmbH. http://www.finanzen.net/leitzins/)

The following chapter uses the example of the USA to examine the extent to which an expansionary monetary policy can cause speculative bubbles and thus economic fluctuations.

Exercise

Read and discuss the following case study on US monetary policy. To what extent can the monetary policy of a central bank affect assets (asset prices)? Does the central bank have a responsibility here?

The Federal Reserve has been providing ample liquidity with the US economy since 1994 amid the productivity gains of the economic epoch of the time called the "New Economy". The over-proportional growth in money supply in relation to real GDP in recent years (see Fig. 8.37) not only supported the productivity forces of the US economy, but also inflated share prices to an unprecedented degree.

From September 1994 to March 2000, the S&P500 gained more than 250%, giving an annual return of around 25%. The Russian crisis and the subsequent bankruptcy of the hedge fund LTCM[40] in the fall of 1998 proved to be only short-term shifts. Already in the aftermath of the October 1987 crash, Greenspan saved the

[40] See Markus Stahl / Christian Conrad (2000a).

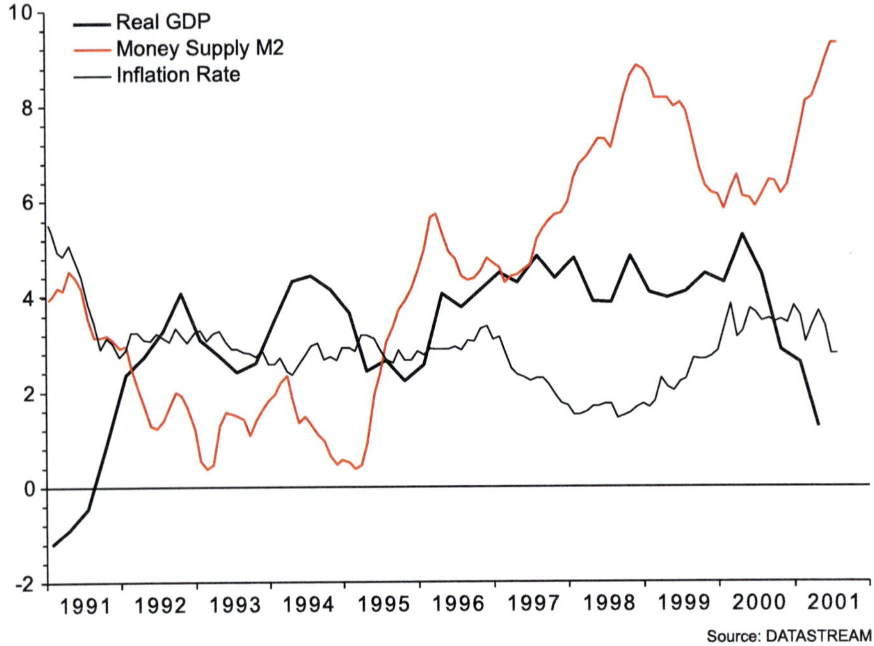

Fig. 8.37 Real growth (bottom right), inflation rate (center right) and money stock M2 (top right)

US stock market with his pragmatic interest rate cuts. In 1998, he managed this for a second time by organizing a rescue operation for the LTCM hedge fund. In addition, he saved the world financial system from a serious crisis. However, the verbal statements and actions of the US Federal Reserve fell wide apart in 1997 and 1998. Already in 1996, Greenspan warned of an "irrational exuberance" when the Dow Jones 30 Industrial Average stood at 6600 points. Just as the development trends of the time of US growth and inflation rates suggested a more restrictive policy, the Fed opted for three cuts in interest rates in the fall of 1998 given the sharp fall in the US stock market. From September 28 to November 17, 1998, the federal funds target rate was reduced by a quarter percent from 5.5% to 4.75% (Fig. 8.38).

It was only these interest rate cuts by the US Federal Reserve Bank that were able to halt the downward process on the stock markets. What could have caused Greenspan to cut interest rates?

We remember the US Federal Reserve's monetary policy in the run-up to the stock market crash of 1929, which was followed by a long-lasting global economic crisis. To what extent American monetary policy contributed to the speculative excess in the twenties and the current stock market upswing, economists divided then as now. It is undisputed that the initial phase of both boom movements was accompanied by an expansionary monetary policy. After 1921, the last year of restrictive monetary policy introduced to combat post-war inflation, the central

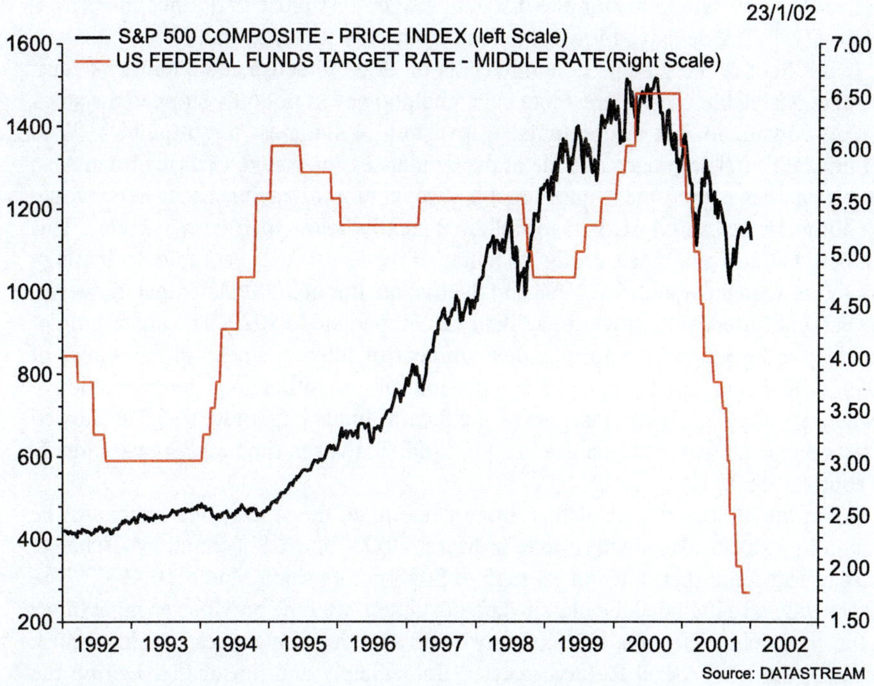

Fig. 8.38 S & P 500 stock index (left scale) and Fed Funds Rate (right scale)

bank lowered the discount rate from 6% in 1921 to 3.5% by mid-1927. For a more restrictive line, there was no reason behind the traditional concept of inflation. The rates of increase in goods prices were consistently below the critical tolerance thresholds. The growth of the money stock M1 developed largely parallel to the real gross domestic product, so that the danger of a pent-up money overhang, which could be steered in the short term on the goods consumption comparatively small. The actual inflation and credit creation, however, took place in the securities sector. Then in 1929 the broker loans reached about 10% of the market capitalization with about 8.5 billion US dollars. When some members of the US monetary system sensed the danger emanating from the securities loans, it was already too late to stop the speculative carousel. When the central bank finally decided to intervene, the three discount rate hikes were no longer enough to slow the speculative movement by a total of 1.5% to the level of 5% in the summer of 1928. This is hardly surprising, given the partially over 10% interest paid on the broker loans, which were mainly fed by industrial companies and foreign banks. Also, Fed Chairman Roy Young's warning that central bank money should not be misused for credit-financed speculation, but is only available for productive purposes, went unheeded, with the US

Federal Reserve finally setting the discount rate on 9 August 1929 once more from 5% to 6%.[41] The decisive blow, as it turned out only 2 months later.[42]

In the light of the global economic crisis of 1929, Greenspan's interest rate cuts are understandable. The interest rate cut signal, however, not only stopped the stock market downtrend, but also stimulated investors' willingness to speculate.[43] With the first rate cut being made outside of the regular session round, Fed Chairman Alan Greenspan has earned the – questionable – reputation of savior, because he would not allow future capital markets to fall dramatically below their current levels. This implicit bailout guarantee really encouraged investors to quadruple technology stocks between the autumn of 1998 and the first quarter of 2000. After that, however, the Federal Reserve (Fed) was in a dilemma comparable to 1929. The unleashing of speculative forces and the furious development of Internet stocks in the winter of 1999/2000 could not be stopped by the interim transition to a more restrictive monetary policy. Only the increase of the federal funds target rate to 6.5% showed effects on the US stock exchanges in April 2000. However, the S&P500 was already at approx. 1500.

As in the 1920s, as part of this interest rate hike, the stock price bubble in the technology stocks also finally broke in March 2000. The US technology exchange Nasdaq lost more than 60% of its high at 5050 points since March 10, 2000. The downswing also included the classic default values. After the previous exaggerations in the consumer sector, the US economy could also threaten a recession. In contrast to 1929, the US Federal Reserve reacted immediately and drastically. During the course of 2001, the Fed downgraded the key rate in eleven steps to 1.75%. From a dynamic point of view, the interest rate reduction trend exceeded the key interest rate cuts in the run-up to the global economic crisis of 1930–1933.[44]

The Fed justifies its very expansionary monetary policy with the growing economic weakness during the course of 2001. It pointed to the decline in consumer confidence and the reluctance of many companies to invest. Added to this was the further deterioration in sentiment related to the terrorist attacks on September 11, 2001. The Fed also openly discussed the weakness of the US stock market and the extent to which investor asset losses could negatively impact their demand. Such comments on monetary policy and the reaction patterns of interest rate policy impressively prove that the stock market development was a key factor in the monetary policy of the US Fed. In contrast to other central banks, the American Fed's goals are not only the price stability, but – among other objectives – the objective of adequate economic growth. The way in which these goals are filled in and weighted according to the respective economic situation is up to the Fed.

---

[41] See Clarke, Stephen (1967).

[42] Die monetären Begleitumstände des Crashs von 1929 untersuchten insbesondere The monetary circumstances of the crash of 1929 examined in particular Temin (1976), and Friedman, Milton / Schwartz, Jacobson (1965).

[43] Conrad, Christian, A./ Schoett, Harry (2000).

[44] See Christian A. Conrad/ Markus Stahl (2000), pp. 25.

In Japan as well, in the mid-1980s, monetary aggregates grew much faster than GDP. With plans for tightening monetary policy already in place, following the global stock crash in October 1987, the Bank of Japan was forced to make its contribution to stabilizing world financial markets by maintaining monetary expansion. While Wall Street and the stock markets in Europe needed more time to digest the price setbacks, the Japanese Nikkei 225 stock index swiftly rose to new highs. From October 1987 to December 1989 it was able to grow again by 80%. At the beginning of 1990, the bubble burst. The Nikkei Index lost almost 70% of the December 1990 level in the following years.[45]

After discussing the influence of monetary policy on assets such as equities in the context of the case study, we will now examine this relationship in more detail.

8.2.8.2 Review of Monetary Policy Objectives

Asset Bubbles as an Indicator of Invisible Inflation

In many cases, as the crisis unfolds, the central bank is forced to mitigate emerging problems in the financial system and the real economy through the printing press and devaluations. The history of money is replete with examples where an inappropriately accommodative monetary policy provided the financial basis for inflation in capital market prices (asset inflation) without rapidly rising commodity prices. The culmination of which was serious crises in the financial system, the undermining of the external and domestic value of the currency and excessive demands on public finances. Already in England in the eighteenth century, a speculative stock price bubble shook the financial markets.[46] Under the leadership of John Blunt, the South Sea Company was mandated to convert government debt and annuity payments into treasury shares with fixed dividend payments.

Although the exact conversion plan was not announced, a run on shares of the South Sea Company began in the spring of 1720. From January to June of 1720, the stock price rose from £ 128 to £ 1050. The entire English stock market was carried away by the speculative fever. The speculative mania was driven by the money creation of the banks, which spent more and more collateral on new securities loans. In France, it was the John Law-based Banque Generale, a forerunner of today's Central Bank, which offered similar services to the French Crown as did the South Sea Company. When Louis XIV died in 1715 he left an extremely high debt of 2.4 billion livre for his successor Louis XV. John Law relieved the royal finances by issuing shares of the Banque Generale and the Mississippi Company against the deposit of government bonds. Speculation in these acts degenerated into a veritable popular movement in the autumn of 1719. Bank John Laws, now renamed Banque Royal, financed speculative excesses by issuing paper notes that were no longer

[45] See Daxhammer and Schmied-Wörle (2000), pp. 45–58.

[46] Or the South Sea Bubble See Chancellor (1999), pp. 58–95.

covered by the bank's gold holdings.[47] In the end, the wealth of stock and paper money owners in England and France had been largely destroyed by the uncontrolled cash of the then still private central banks.[48]

The inflation measures used by central banks mainly include consumer goods prices and producer prices. Price developments in the financial sector and asset prices (asset prices) are thus systematically hidden by the measurement method.[49] So it is possible that excessive money production is reflected not in rising prices for consumer goods, but in asset price volatility. If only consumer goods prices are considered, this can lead to unpredictable inflation. However, price distortions in the financial sector are just as damaging to long-term steady and balanced economic growth as unchecked commodity price inflation. Price distortions in the asset markets can lead to serious misallocations in the real economy and ultimately jeopardize the functioning of the financial system as the central payer and transmission belt of monetary policy.

A stock market boom is supported by an excessive supply of money by the central banks. The parlor game "Monopoly" can serve as a simple example here. After an initially very slow start-up phase with rather low prices for street trains during negotiations between the players, incredibly high amounts for roads are scored in the final phase of the game. The background to this phenomenon is neither the special strategy achievement of the few players who have become rich, nor the luck or misfortune of throwing the dice. The key to the explanation is the universally popular lot-playing field. Passing go gets you 4000 monetary extra units.

The blessings bestowed by "Go" do not mean that the amount of money per player per round is increased by 4000 monetary units. With 5 players and 15 rounds, the money supply increases by 300,000 monetary units. The initial cash amount is 30,000 monetary units per player, so for 5 players a total of 150,000 monetary units. After 15 rounds, the lottery money source now provides more than three times the money supply (150,000 + 300,000 = 450,000). Therefore, one should not be surprised if in bilateral price negotiations between the players on individual streets ever increasing amounts are offered and achieved in the course of the game. The asset price bubble, limited in the original game to the real estate sector, begins to inflate further and further.

The relationship between money supply development and asset prices has been examined in several empirical studies. They show, for example, that in the second half of the 1980s, in addition to increased productivity of the Japanese economy and increased demand for real estate in Tokyo, the sharp rise in prices for Japanese

[47] For the financial scandal of Law, see Kiehling (2000), pp. 19–29.

[48] Gold investments could be successful in such a scenario. See Mezger and Stahl (2001a), pp. 372–378 and Conrad and Stahl (2002).

[49] See Mezger and Stahl (2001b), pp. 15–22.

equities, art and real estate in Japan spurred an expansionary monetary policy. Above all, it expressed itself in increased bank lending.[50]

However, the scientific content of the predominantly Granger-based econometric studies has to be questioned. We have fundamental method problems here. Because of the risk of false results, the Granger test is discouraged if the variables under study are extremely volatile.[51] For highly volatile variables such as stock prices, a lack of covariance stationarity was found, which does not provide a condition for the regression of time series.[52] Due to innumerable influencing factors on supply and demand, we have a strong multi-causality here in which the individual influencing factors cannot be filtered out precisely. If causal variables are not extracted, Granger tests can show correlations that are not present (spurious regression). The same applies to purely random correlations, which may arise in particular in the case of short observation periods or incorrect time intervals.[53]

Different analyses[54] show a positive correlation between the variables, which can be interpreted differently:

1. For example, the productivity of companies could have increased and thus the profits of listed companies and, subsequently, the stock prices. In this case, the central bank would only have expanded the money supply in line with the increase in real production.
2. If the central bank increases the money supply or directly lowers the key interest rate, this may result in a reduction of the long-term interest rate as a discounting factor for the expected corporate profits, which corresponds to a higher present value. As a result, stock prices rise. This connection can easily be illustrated. Apart from the retained profits, the return of a share for a period can be represented as follows[55]:

   1. Yield on exchange profit in% Dividend in%

$$r_k = \frac{p_{t+1} - p_t}{p_t} + \frac{D_{t+1}}{p_t}$$

   2. $= \frac{p_{t+1} + D_{t+1} - p_t}{p_t}$

      [where p is the price of the stock (price) and D is the dividend. t stands for the period].

[50] See Ito, Takatoshi/ Iwaisako, Tokuo (1995).

[51] See Irwin, Scott H./ Sanders, Dwight R. (2012), p. 258.

[52] See Pagan, A./Schwert, C. (1990); Phillips, P./Loretan, M. (1990); Frenk, David u.a., (2011).

[53] See Frenk (2011), a.a.O. p. 47.

[54] See International Monetary Fund, World economic outlook, Washington 2000 and Baks, Klaas/ Kramer, Charles (1999).

[55] See Braley, R. (1983). Actually, all future periods must be included. However, due to the limited real-time forecast horizon, this is not the case here.

In the allocation equilibrium, the stock return must correspond to the alternative investments, including the yield on government securities. It can therefore be regarded as a minimum return, with constant yields and government bonds. Eq. (2) can be solved for pt., i.e. the stock price. You get:

3. $p_t = \frac{p_{t+1}+D_{t+1}}{1+r_k}$

   To increase the informative value of eq. (3), we make two simplifying assumptions. On the one hand, dividends are growing at a constant rate g and on the other hand, the price gains are also constant. As a growth rate of D then g can also be subtracted from the discount factor rk.

4. $p_t = \frac{D}{r_k - g}$

   Consider the constellation rk = 10% (0.1), g = 0.05 and D = $2, we get for pt. = $2 / (0.1–0.05) = $40. With this equation, the effect of an interest rate cut on the price is derived, as well as the rate elasticity. We leave all other numbers unchanged and reduce the interest rate rk by 40% from 10% to 6%. As a result, the price increases $160 (400%) to $200. The interest rate elasticity of the share price is thus 10, an effect that would certainly not have been expected to that extent.

3. Lower interest rates mean lower financing costs for companies, thus increasing their profits, which also leads to a price increase. Assuming that the financing structure of companies consists of 70% debt and 30% equity, an interest rate cut from 5% to 1% as a result of an expansionary monetary policy, assuming an assumed return on equity of 10% would increase the corporate profit by 93.33% (70 x 4% = 2.8, return on equity: 3 + 2.8 = 5.8, calculated with 30 parts of equity capital to 70 parts of debt).

   The valuation indicators for equities would have to be adjusted for the refinancing costs. Even a smooth price-earnings ratio like that of Shiller (CAPE, Cycle-Adjusted Price Earnings Ratio) could be distorted by a prolonged period of low interest rates.

4. Real estate is predominantly financed with debts. A fall in interest rates has a direct effect on the refinancing rates and thus on direct purchasing power. The following applies to a bullet loan:

$$\text{Interest cost} = \text{debt} \times (1 + i/100)^n - \text{debt}$$

Example: If a house cost € 100,000 and the lending rate were 5%, the interest cost would be 100.000 × $(1 + 5/100)^{10}$, or € 162,900. If the central bank now lowers the interest rate to 1%, the interest costs amount to 100,000 × $(1 + 1/100)^{10}$ 110.500 €, which corresponds to a reduction of 30%. The homebuyer can thus afford a 30% more expensive house.

Conversely, the 30% can also be seen as a return potential if you finance an externally leased property with constant rental income.

5. If the money supply is greatly increased, the portfolio of investors shifts in favor of the cash position. Investors want to restore their desired portfolio relation between money and equity investments and therefore demand more shares. The price of shares then rises as well as the price of other goods. This is an expression of inflation because the real productivity of the stock market has remained the same.

We can thus record the following. If the yield on bonds as a competitive investment has a significant impact on stock prices, this also applies indirectly to monetary policy as a determinant of interest. In his business cycle theory, Friedrich August von Hayek[56] has blamed the perverse elasticity of the banking system, that is, the uncontrolled development of money, for the economic overheating. On the other hand, Knut Wicksell[57] attributes them to the wrong decisions of monetary policy makers in controlling interest rates. A fixed interest rate below the equilibrium interest rate on supply and demand on the capital market causes an inflation of the money supply, more precisely a shift of the goods-money exchange relationship in favor of the money. Due to the low interest rate, demand for credit is rising. Increased lending creates new sight deposits. The speed of money and thus also the money supply are rising. As the cash holdings of the investor have risen relative to the securities holdings, portfolio diversification has occurred. The new money flows into the stock markets and drives up the prices. Due to the function of interest rates as the benchmark return and discount factor, an artificial interest rate cut not only causes a rise in stock prices, but also an excessive allocation of resources to stock prices, which can lead to overheating.[58]

In addition, there are self-reinforcement effects: Increased stock prices (and / or real estate prices) signal profit potential and provide collateral for the banks, with which they can operate the credit and thus indirectly the money creation. It comes to a self-reinforcing upward process on the stock market. Refinancing pledges (lender of last resort bailouts) in the event of liquidity squeezes such as those of the International Monetary Fund or the central banks increase the security of speculation and thus support such a development (moral hazard problem). In addition, the low level of interest rates promotes credit-financed equity purchases. However, the bubble can not expand indefinitely, as the price spiral and the rising stock market turnover tie up more and more of the available liquidity. By the time the total money stock is absorbed by the stock market, the market capitalizations of the stocks begin to fall below their own weight. Falling prices trigger further compulsory liquidation in a kind of chain reaction. The crash happens.[59] The same applies to the real estate market.

---

[56] See von Hayek (1929), pp. 81.

[57] See Wicksell (1928, p. 231ff; 1898, p. 101ff) and Grossekettler (1989), pp. 203 f.

[58] See Conrad (2000), pp. 135–146.

[59] See Conrad and Stahl (2000), pp. 24–32.

The Consequences of Asset Bubbles

If high stock prices do not reflect future corporate profits, but rather the exaggerated expectations of a majority of market participants, there may be misallocation of economic resources if companies put out new stocks or bonds at excessive rates and make unprofitable investments. For example, up until March 2000 the bubble on the technology exchanges led to a general over-dimensioning of real investment in this sector.[60] This is where the theories of Hayek and Wicksell take effect. Too much liquidity and a lowering of the interest rate below the equilibrium interest rate encourage speculative bubbles. Overinvestments, which subsequently had to be written off, were also characteristic of the real estate bubble in the USA, Spain and Ireland before the financial crisis. Free money increases your appetite for risk. In addition, investors are taking higher risks in their search for returns due to the lack of alternatives. This was another reason for the financial crisis.

National resources would have been partially misdirected. Investors and lenders would then be faced with significant losses. If the banking system were affected by this industry through high levels of stock ownership or extensive credit exposure to defaults it could lead to crisis developments in the banking industry. Since the credit-forgiveness of the banking system is a direct function of equity, write-offs on equity could lead to growing restrictions on lending. The economy could then suffer from a crippling credit crunch in the banking sector. This situation, for example, was countered by the collapsed stock market bubble in the Japanese economy. At a time when the Bank of Japan forgave money virtually for free, Japanese companies had difficulty obtaining bank loans. There was also a credit crunch as a result of the financial crisis.

The contagion of the real economy through a bursting stock market bubble is – besides going through the banking system (credit crunch) – also via the wealth effect of consumption. If the breezy stock market profits dissipate, only a fiction should be lost. But like all fictions, stock market fictions can also deeply intervene in real economic life. Consumers who have not the slightest fear to spend their budgets months ahead during the bull market in the expectation that they will be able to settle the installments due through stock market profits, have a hard time meeting their obligations after a crash. New acquisitions are unthinkable. On the basis of their securities ownership and the increasing value of their own shares and holdings, entrepreneurs and their companies increasingly borrow on additional investments during the stock market upswing. Overnight they become dubious debtors to whom the bank terminates the loans. It can lead to a vicious cycle of consumer restraint, investment stop, production restrictions, wage losses, mood deterioration and renewed consumer and investment restrictions.

The strength of the wealth effect is shown in the following example: we calculate the consequences of a correction of stock prices by ten percent, assuming a wealth

---

[60] See Stahl (2000a, b).

effect of five percent. Market capitalization of US $16 trillion (US $12.8 trillion, NASDAQ index: US $3.2 trillion) at end of April 2001 such a 10% correction represents a $1.6 trillion asset destruction. Consequently, due to the wealth effect of 5% decline in consumption by $80 billion. Total US private consumption in 2000 was approximately $6800 billion. The wealth effect thus implies a decline in private consumption of about 1.1%. Since consumption in 2000 grew by nominally about 7.8%, this is a very serious order of magnitude. However, the uncertainty band of this estimate is large, since empirical studies put the wealth effect at 2% to 10% of consumption. For a 10% decline in the stock market, the decline in consumption could thus amount to 0.47% (2% wealth effect) or 2.3% (10% wealth effect). Regardless of the exact size of the wealth effect, however, it remains clear that a drastic stock market crash, e.g. 30% is likely to exert a very sustained cyclical effect. Here, the decline in consumption would at best be around 1.5%, but in the pessimistic case almost 7%.[61]

The resource misallocation as a result of an expansionary monetary policy after the bursting of the bubble caused massive loss of assets and economic slumps. In addition to resource misallocation, massive allocative redistributive effects can be identified. They add to the speculative effects of the expansionary monetary policy that monetary policy creates by artificially low interest rates. Even without a negative real rate of return due to inflation, there are massive distributional effects in favor of the debtors to the detriment of the creditors, e.g. savers who can jeopardize the pensions of the population over a longer period of time.

Conclusion

The central banks have to take into account irrational reactions to their monetary policy decisions and counteract the creation of bubbles, especially on the real estate and stock markets. The current objective is that central banks guarantee price stability. In that sense, they would also have to control inflationary risks resulting from the upgrading of equity and a corresponding increase in household consumption. With regard to the recording of the potential for inflation, therefore, consideration should at least be given to measurement that which include a more comprehensive spectrum of prices than the current price trend of the basket of goods. In the case of an intertemporal interpretation of the concept of inflation, in addition to current consumer prices, future price developments – derived from asset price changes – could also be taken into account. Estimates based on the correlation between equity market capitalization and aggregate consumption can be used for this purpose. The central banks would therefore consider a price indicator when considering their monetary policy target, which includes not only current consumer prices but also price developments on the asset markets. As a result, asset price developments would become part of monetary policy governance.

[61] See Conrad and Stahl (2002).

So far, the price development on the stock and real estate markets has not been included in the monetary policy objective. There are reasons for this. Monetary policy, if it wants to remain predictable, can only be based on measurable indicators. However, in contrast to consumer price indices, there are neither empirically recognized values on the overall economic impact of asset price distortions, nor are there any ratios that could indicate any deviation or imbalance. A stock market bubble isn't predictable through empirical-methods because share prices always include expectations about the uncertain, unpredictable future. Ultimately, the central banks cannot determine the fundamentally correct price level of the shares better than the large number of market participants who determine the price level in the markets every day through their buying and selling decisions.

The central bank could also come under pressure if it were accused of destroying equity or real estate assets with its policy, or excessively curtailing the money supply of the real economy and thus slowing down the economy, only to counteract an undetectable stock market bubble. However, the opposite accusation that the central banks represent the interests of the stock exchange investors who see themselves beholden to the US Fed is damaging to the reputation of a central bank.

In principle, a bubble cannot be determined exactly, but it can be suspected. The central bank should first check whether there is a fundamental reason for the exorbitant price growth, which will usually be the case. If the stock exchange in question is an economically representative one, the central bank should, on the one hand, compare the growth rates of the stock market indices with the historical values and, on the other hand, with the current growth of the gross domestic product. If it finds a sustainable historical or relative increase, then the assumption of a bubble is obvious.[62]

Finally, we can record the following recommendations for monetary policy:

1. Potential-oriented, rule-based monetary policy

   As asset prices are mainly driven by expectations and at the same time expectations about future monetary policy play a central role, the most constant, potential-oriented monetary policy is recommended. It contributes significantly to the stabilization of expectations. Orienting the money supply at the development of the gross domestic product and the production potential prevents a money overhang, which in turn makes a stock market bubble no longer possible.
2. Inclusion of asset prices as further indicators of monetary policy governance

   Asset prices should be integrated into the models of the central banks as an "early inflation indicator", so that a rule-based countermeasure is possible. This includes informing the public about the development of the indicators. Investors would anticipate the countermeasures of the central bank in a departure of the indicators and no longer speculate on an increase in prices. This would additionally counteract a bubble.

[62]See Shleifer, Andrei (2000a), Stock Prices and Social Dynamics, in: Brookings Papers on Economic Activity, No. 2, S. 21 and Stahl, Markus/Conrad, Christian A. (2000b), a.a.O., pp. 415–422.

3. No bail-outs

   The rule binding of monetary policy also includes the consistent enforcement of the basic principle of liability and thus a waiver of explicit or implicit bailout promises. If investors can no longer pass speculative risk onto the central bank, this will counteract self-reinforcing speculation. On the other hand, it must be ensured beforehand by the described rule-bound automatisms that there will be no system-endangering asset bubble, which would make a bailout necessary.
4. Flanking monetary policy through measures taken by the banking and stock exchange regulators:
   (a) Reducing the lending rate for equity loans (i.e. the percentage of crediting of shares as collateral for lending) could reduce stock demand in the event of a presumed stock market overheating.
   (b) A prudential increase in safety clearing margins would reduce the leverage effect of derivatives on equity demand.
   (c) Including hitherto unregulated financial market participants, such as hedge funds and offshore banks in financial market supervision and capital adequacy principles would prevent the spread of financial market crises.

Bubbles cannot be prevented with these measures, but they can be counteracted earlier.[63]

8.2.9 *Shocks and Price Rigidities: The New Keynesian Macroeconomics*

Classical theory assumes that prices react quickly and quantities are delayed. However, since an auctioneer who finds an equilibrium price ex ante in a tonneau process does not exist, simultaneous market equilibrium at equilibrium prices is rather the exception than the rule. Empirically, it can be observed that real wages do not fluctuate counter cyclically in the course of the economy, as one would expect. Likewise, in periods of economic underutilization, companies maintain wage levels despite needing less labor. In goods, labor and other markets, prices react only very slowly – in extreme cases in the short term – to supply and demand surpluses.[64] Two major criticisms of the older Keynesian approaches are the incomplete logic of the decision-making and the neglect of the repercussions of quantity rationing on other markets. The New Keynesian Macroeconomics[65] therefore picks up on the Keynesian assumption of fixed prices and wages and takes into account the points of

[63] See Markus Stahl / Christian A. Conrad (2000b), pp. 383–385 and Conrad and Stahl (2002).

[64] See Gerfin and Möller (1980b), p. 201.

[65] Zur Neuen Keynesianischen Makroökonomik See Malinvaud (1977), Barro and Grossmann (1976); Gerfin and Möller (1980a); Gerfin and Möller (1980b); Barro (1971); Clower (1965); Heubes (1991), pp. 65 and Rothschild (1981).

criticism mentioned in the model concept. In the New Keynesian Macroeconomics, neither prices nor wages respond in the short to medium term. Exogenous demand or supply shocks disturb market equilibrium and cause rationing of the opposite supply or demand side, without prices or wages immediately compensating.

The original static model of Malinvaud misled to the conclusion that only an underdose of public demand has negative macroeconomic implications but not an overdose. After all, at least in the short term, there are no demand and supply-determined price changes. Not least because of this, Malinvaud has made his static approach more dynamic in a second model, endogenizing some variables and giving up on fixed prices and wages. The following conditions apply: The job supply is constant. Consumption depends positively on consumption in the previous period and negatively on the unemployment rate. The production function is linearly limitational and is determined by the factors labor (constant, first bottleneck), labor productivity, and production capacity as the second bottleneck and rationing variable. Aggregate demand is composed of consumer demand and investment demand, which is positively affected by a period lagged by both labor returns (labor productivity – real wages) and by capacity utilization. Depending on the real wage and production capacity, four temporary balances emerge, in which the development of real wages depends on the respective regime.

In classical unemployment, real wages fall with the rise in unemployment; with suppressed inflation it rises due to surplus demand in the labor market. Because of the oversupply of Keynesian unemployment, both the nominal wage due to unemployment and oversupply drop the price level, leaving real wages constant. In Walrasian equilibrium, neither nominal wage nor price level change, as no market side is rationed. In the medium term, there are only two stable equilibria in which real wages do not change: the Keynesian regime and the Walrasian equilibrium. In Walrasian equilibrium stability is maintained by balancing a positive labor return effect and a negative capacity under-utilization effect on investment demand. However, an eventual disruption of this balance automatically initiates development into one of the three regimes, which is why the Walrasian equilibrium can not be considered stable, thus leading all combinations to the Keynesian regime in the long term.

For the Keynesian regime, the further development of the GNP depends on the combination of the nominal wage rate and the adjustment parameter of the capital stock. There are two possible developments. In the first case a monotonous approach to a stable equilibrium and in the second more probable case a much longer approach to the stable Keynesian equilibrium with subdued oscillations of the social product around the equilibrium social product, i.e. to cyclical fluctuations until the Keynesian equilibrium is reached. From this point no economic fluctuations can occur or be explained endogenously, which also occurs in the New Keynesian macroeconomics as in the still-to-be analyzed New Classic macroeconomics, namely the persistence problem of how to explain the continuity of cyclical fluctuations, since exogenous shocks must be a part of the explanation. It cannot explain a complete business cycle, which is why both theories in the narrower sense are not among the economic cycle theories.[66]

The pro-cyclical investment and profit rates observed in reality emerge in the model of the New Keynesian macroeconomics as an automatic consequence of changes in the cost-income relations. Prices, wages and interest rates will also behave pro-cyclically, but with a time lag. Although positive shocks can be simulated with the New Keynesian Macroeconomics, it is again a one-time departure from equilibrium followed by a tendency towards a new static equilibrium.

The New Keynesian Macroeconomics result in a new distribution of roles in collective bargaining. According to the New Keynesian Macroeconomics, the responsibility for full employment cannot be attributed either to the collective bargaining parties (entrepreneurs and trade unions) or to the state. The wage bargaining parties must pay attention to wage policies that do not create the situation of classical unemployment, whereas in the situation of Keynesian unemployment the state is obliged to stabilize its policy in the form of an autonomous increase in demand. The flexibility of wages downwards is to be restored by deregulating the labor market (for example by opening clauses). While the New Keynesian macroeconomics approach provides further justification for the need for discretionary government demand-side management, it does not solve the recognition and implementation problems associated with practical economic policy. On the contrary, abrupt exogenous demand shocks require an even faster economic policy recognition and reaction than a permanent underemployment situation.

8.2.10 *Price Adjustment Costs and Information Asymmetries: New Keynesian Macroeconomics*

A number of recent approaches have been developed with the aim of establishing the Keynesian assumption of price rigidity in a microeconomic way. Representing this direction, this chapter presents two causes, price adjustment costs and information asymmetries. If one does not assume imperfect competition, but supply monopolies at least in submarkets, MANKIW and BALL[67]show that price adjustment delays happen when the price adjustment costs are higher than the increased raw material prices due to an expansionary monetary policy. The companies calculate their prices from the outset in such a way that they have enough room for small changes in the inflation rate, in order to avoid a costly price adjustment, be it in advertising leaflets or with excellent goods. Changes in money supply, under this assumption and even rational behavior, can cause a change in the relative price structure, leading to real

[66]Nevertheless, these models explain variations in the utilization of production potential, which is why they are listed along with the other economic theories. See Mankiw (1998) and Assenmacher (1998).

[67]See Mankiw (1985) and Ball and Mankiw (1994).

employment effects. There is also a twofold asymmetry in price adjustments. On the one hand, price adjustments only take place in the case of large changes in the amount of money or changes in inflation, and on the other hand, companies only adjust prices if pricing is worsened as a result of monetary policy because it is expansionary. As a result, the real impact on employment and the social product is greatest if the price reductions of the primary products do not have to be passed on by the companies, that is, if the monetary policy is highly restrictive.

Furthermore, they are expansive and thus have an expansive effect against the drop in investment demand due to the increased level of interest rates.

One criticism of this approach is that the price adjustment costs, but not the adjustment costs of production and employment, are taken into account. In addition, the positive employment effect of the restrictive change in money supply is likely to be more than offset by the negative effect of lower investment demand. Consequently, the value of these models lies above all in the economic justification of the old Keynesian hypothesis that prices are rigid downwards and flexible upwards.[68]

The second central New Keynesian research direction[69] examines the effect of asymmetric information distribution between companies as borrowers and lenders (banks in particular), assuming that companies ration their equity because they cannot find equity investors due to the information asymmetry and consequent higher risk. For employment and production expansion they therefore have to borrow. Since the lenders want to secure their capital on time, so as to withdraw from the company, per this theory they cause bankruptcies earlier than equity investors. The risk of capital loss increases during the recession, which is why credit rationing takes place in this economic phase. This approach explains the empirical pro-cyclical evolution of the pay gap: while labor productivity increases in the recession due to the release of inefficient production factors, there is still an oversupply in the labor market as companies rally due to credit rationing and cannot expand their employment. Restrictive monetary policy may exacerbate the recession because of negative repercussions on lending. On the other hand, an expansionary monetary policy cannot change the long-term equilibrium, since marginal productivity, in turn, determines real wages, with an asymmetry in the effects of restrictive and expansive monetary policy.

Due to the partial non-neutrality of monetary policy, these newer approaches at first sight call for a discretionary economic policy, in particular for an expansive monetary policy in the recession. But they also indirectly show the dangers of mismanagement. Assuming – as the monetarists – unknown or changing time delays in the mechanisms of action, the interventions can increase the economic destabilization due to the asymmetry of effect: An expansionary monetary policy, which will only take effect when the economy is no longer in recession, but in the upswing phase or in the boom causes above all inflation and practically no positive real

[68] See Kugler (1998), S. 32 and Homburg (1996), pp. 60.

[69] See Stiglitz and Weiss (1992) and De Long and Summers (1988) and Homburg (1996), pp. 64.

effects. A subsequent disinflationary policy would be all the more restrictive to social product and employment.[70]

The inclusion of mathematical chaos equations in equilibrium systems (Chaos theory) emphasizes this conclusion. It turned out that, depending on the initial parameter constellation, cyclical as well as chaotic solutions are possible as they move away from equilibrium. However, if in practical economic policy neither the parameter constellation in the initial situation can be determined exactly, nor can the economic policy instruments be precisely dosed, the risk of a malfunction is all the greater.[71]

In the following, the theories are presented and analyzed for their economic policy statements, which, contrary to the Keynesian, non-Walrasian oriented theories, proceed from inherent market stability or an automatic market balance mechanism. Here, essentially, the monetarist theories and the New Classical Macroeconomics are to be ascribed to their further developments.[72]

8.2.11 Adaptive Expectation in Monetarist Theories

The monetarist economic theories are in the narrow sense no economic theories, since they explain only nominal fluctuations in social product, and not real fluctuations in the degree of utilization of the production potential. The two best-known monetarist approaches are those of FRIEDMANN[73] and LAIDLER.[74] FRIEDMANN reinterprets the quantum theory of money by assuming the interest rate as negligible for money demand on the basis of empirical studies. Thus, the nominal income above the money circulation rate is proportional to the monetary development and the circulation rate is a stable function of the inflation rate. The economic agents have a given asset portfolio structure with a real estate income dependent transaction cash demand. The balance is disturbed by an increase in the amount of money that is not perceived immediately by the economic agents, but only late (adaptive expectation). The increase in the monetary balance causes an increase in the cash position of the economic subjects above the desired level. The difference turns directly into consumer demand or first to capital offer and then to investment demand. Given production, only the nominal income increases as a result of the price level increase. The economic agents correct their inflation expectations upwards and

[70]See Kugler (1998), p. 32.

[71]However, the use of nonlinear behavioral functions based on the mathematical chaos theory in neoclassical growth models leads only in exceptional cases to stable solutions, which is why the empirical explanatory content is assessed as very low.

See Teichmann (1997), p. 24.

[72]Conrad (1999), pp. 188–220 and Stavenhagen (1969).

[73]See Friedman (1970), Heubes (1991), pp. 84 and Teichmann (1997), p. 20.

[74]See Laidler (1976a, b), Heubes (1991), pp. 87 and Teichmann (1997), p. 21.

react with a shorter cash duration (higher circulation speed), which leads to a renewed increase in the nominal income (overshooting). Over time, inflation expectations converge to the actual rate of inflation, with fluctuations in nominal income decreasing. Thus, this is a market clearing model or shock reaction model with which no complete business cycle can be simulated. FRIEDMANN seeks to circumvent this limitation by accepting regular monetary shocks. However, FRIEDMANN does not present the real effects of the shocks.

LAIDLER fills this gap by connecting the monetary and real sectors via the Phillips curve. The real income results from the degree of utilization of the labor force potential. The money supply is given exogenously; money demand depends positively on real income and price levels. As with FRIEDMANN, the Phillips curve is based on the assumption of adaptive inflation expectation formation and thus a delayed wage reaction. In the long term, changes in money supply have no effect on the real sector. The old equilibrium with a constant natural unemployment and inflation rate, resulting from the difference between the rate of monetary growth and the growth rate of income, keeps coming up. Short-term, unexpected increases in the money supply cause an increase in the employment level through the wage bill as a result of the illiquidity of the employees. As with FRIEDMANN, the monetary shocks must occur regularly to represent a business cycle. The real sector then responds to expansion or contraction depending on the prevailing expectations.

8.2.12 Determinants of Growth as Economic Factors: The New Growth Theory

The term "New Growth Theory" summarizes various recent theories that seek to endogenize growth-determining factors, thus dissolving the traditional distinction between economic and growth theory.[75] It can be seen – also empirically – that the economic trend influences the growth trend. Based on the efficiency-enhancing effect of Schumpeter's creative destruction, for example, it follows from the approach of AGHION and PAUL[76] that under certain assumptions with the recession's strength and frequency, the growth rate of the social product also increases.

The approaches of the New Growth Theory are concerned with the endogenization of the determinants of innovation waves, fluctuations in the level of technical and organizational knowledge or changes in the capital stock, but not with their effects on economic development as a fluctuation in the degree of utilization of production potential. Based on these approaches, conclusions about

[75] See Ramey, G./ Ramey, V. A. (1995). Business-cycle theory and growth theory have traditionally been treated as unrelated areas of macroeconomics", weshalb vielfach noch davon ausgegangen wird, daß "growth and business-cycle volatility are unrelated." Ramey and Ramey (1995), S. 1138. See also Franz (1999).

[76] See Aghion and Saint-Paul (1993).

political economy can only be drawn indirectly. For example, the approach of SHLEIFER is a warning against restrictive stabilization policy in boom phases, since in this approach companies only realize their investments in times of high demand because, due to the higher contribution margins on the liquidity to implement the invention feature. While a stabilizing restrictive policy would compensate for this pro-cyclical effect, at the same time as reducing aggregate demand, it would reduce innovation, technical progress and hence economic growth.[77]

Also in the model of STIGLITZ (1994), the boom phases have positive feedback on innovation activity. STIGLITZ justifies this with learning effects with high capacity utilization, which stimulate inventions and with the fact that a company will increasingly invest in research and development if it is based on high demand. Moreover, he also supports SHLEIFER's argument that, except for capital market imperfections, companies only have the liquidity needed for research and innovation in boom phases.[78]

The contribution of the New Growth Theory to cyclical policy has so far been low. However, this research direction can be expected to provide significant new insights, especially with regard to the financing effects of discretionary stabilization policy. The state capital demand for deficit spending and alternative tax financing, through their repercussions on companies' innovation activities, directly intervene in the intervene-rational distribution between present and future consumption. Given that firms' innovation activity is positively dependent on profit expectations in a secure environment, a redistributive policy at the expense of corporate profits and an incalculable discretionary economic policy that creates an uncertainty environment should have a negative impact on innovation activity and hence growth.

8.2.13 *Exogenous Change of Political Variables: The New Classical Macroeconomics*

The New Classical Macroeconomics has been developed in numerous publications and goes back to LUCAS (1975), MCCALLUM (1980) and BARRO (1981).[79] The approaches are a response to LUCAS's 1976 criticism of the assumption of constant coefficients within structural econometric models. In view of the systematic change in exogenous political variables that occurs in reality, this is far from reality (LUCAS criticism).[80] In the New Classic Macroeconomics, therefore, the exogenous change in policy variables is a major economic determinant. The New Classical

[77] See Shleifer (1986) and Ramser (1997), p. 200.

[78] See Stiglitz (1994) and Ramser (1997), pp. 221.

[79] To the New Classical Macroeconomics. See Assenmacher (1998, pp. 302), Ramser (1988, pp. 96), Lucas (1975), McCallum (1980), Barro (1981), Tichy (1995, pp. 185), Minford and Peel (1983) and Fischer (1980).

[80] See Lucas Jr (1976) and McCallum (1980).

Macroeconomics can be divided into exogenous and endogenous approaches. The exogenous approaches again differentiate between monetary theories according to the nature of the external economic cause, where the money supply is the exogenous cause, and the real business cycle theories, which regard real shocks as determinative of the economy. The endogenous theories exhibit a nonlinear internal dynamics (intrinsic dynamics, chaos theory) or explain the cycles by means of a modified theory of rational expectations (Sunspot theories).[81]

Demand fluctuations due to wrong adaptation reactions:

The original approach of the New Classic Macroeconomics

The basic assumptions are the existence of a state of equilibrium that always occurs in the long term as well as rational expectations in the sense of a subjective formality. The last point is the difference to the monetarist models, which in principle assume adaptive expectations. The economic agents have a consistent target system and optimize their decisions on the basis of their subjective information about the economic conditions. They use all the information available to them. However, the information is incomplete (asymmetrically distributed), so that an uncertainty prevails. The economic subjects are informed about the fundamental economic connections, d. H. they do not make any systematic mistakes.

Due to the incomplete information about the economic conditions the economic actors are subject to wrong judgments. There are two types of upset: permanent-transitory confusion and absolute-relative confusion. In the case of permanent-transitory confusion, economic agents cannot distinguish whether a change in monetary indicators is permanent or only temporary. On the other hand, if the economic agents cannot see whether relative prices or the entire price level is rising, it is called an absolute-relative confusion. Uncertainty is exacerbated by the assumption of a randomly variable state demand on the submarkets. It follows that only unexpected monetary changes can influence the real variables. Politically initiated changes in the money market give the economic agents complete information. They are therefore anticipated and are ineffective (policy inefficiency hypothesis). Only unsystematic changes in the money supply can cause misperceptions and thus real adjustments.

It is also assumed that market equilibrium always automatically occurs in the long term. Economic fluctuations can therefore only be caused by exogenous factors. Exogenous, staggered, unexpected monetary shocks (e.g. fiscal mismatches, imported inflation at fixed exchange rates, short-term monetary constraints due to international collusion (G7, EMS), etc.) lead to a change in monetary indicators (prices, interest rates). The data changes are misinterpreted by the business entities. The real adaptation reactions of the economic subjects thus triggered differ depending on the underlying type of confusion. An absolute-relative confusion, for example, causes economic agents to increase production [$X = X(p)$], whereas a permanent-transitory confusion can lead to an expansion of investment due to the

[81] See Heubes (1991), pp. 83 and Assenmacher (1998), pp. 301.

lower interest rate. There is a self-reinforcing (cumulative) upward process. After a while, in the case of absolute relative confusion, economic agents recognize that all prices – including those of their primary products – are on the rise, and not just those of their own sales products. They then revise their expansive production decision. In the case of permanent transitive confusion, a correction of the data changes made by the political decision-makers takes place in the medium term. The monetary expansion or interest rate cut is reversed, whereupon the economic agents also correct their decisions. The correction of the decisions triggers contractive effects that initiate a cumulative contracting process.

The New Classical Macroeconomics thus offers a transmission mechanism between the monetary and the real sector and thus also an explanation for the empirically established positive correlation between money supply and real social product. However, the general assumption of the New Classic Macroeconomics of a complete market clearing is critical to question. The wage and price mechanism always works. There is consequently no involuntary unemployment. This hypothesis is in contrast to the empirical short-term wage and price rigidities. Furthermore, in the New Classic Macroeconomics, upset can immediately increase production. That is, either sub-utilization or a time lag of zero must always be assumed, both of which are unrealistic. Also, the assumption of isolated market behavior in terms of absolute-relative confusion seems remote with today's generally available information, especially as economic agents generally operate in several markets at the same time.[82] In general, all pro-cyclical "stylized facts" can be explained with the New Classic Macroeconomics. They occur as a result of confusion in the cumulative upward process. However, using New Classic Macroeconomics, it is not possible to explain economic cycles, but only short-term deviations from equilibrium, which are corrected again (persistence problem). The economic fluctuations as a result of the adjustment reactions lead back to the pareto optimal balance. Another neglected but compelling issue of New Classic Macroeconomics is whether the behavior of economic subjects will not change once they become subject to confusion and thereby suffer monetary losses. It is likely that they will either stop responding or transfer their assets to investments that are not affected by monetary shocks, such as property, plant and equipment.

All in all, however, it can be said that the difficulty of economic theory, whether and to what extent monetary shocks are transferred to the real sector, supports the hypothesis that monetary causes generally have less of an economic impact than real ones.[83]

---

[82] See Assenmacher (1998), p. 309.

[83] In addition, the assessment of the New Classic Macroeconomics on credit-financed fiscal policy should be mentioned. According to the Ricardian equivalence theorem, borrowers are already anticipating the future tax increases necessary for debt service, which is why they do not feel wealthier and therefore no longer consume by issuing government securities. There remains only the demand effect of government spending, which is offset by the future reduction in consumption due to the tax increase. Since the economic subjects also anticipate this and preventively increase their savings rate, this effect is also eliminated. See Felderer, and Homburg (1989), pp. 275. This view is critically questioned. Above all, it is argued that economic subjects will distinguish between the taxes levied during their lifetime and the taxes which the next generation must pay. To discuss the financing effects of government demand increase. See Musgrave et al. (1987), pp. 120.

There are three further unconnected directions, which are classified as neoclassical, Walrasian, the Real Business Cycles models, the Sunspot theories, and the nonlinear models of chaos theory. First, we will analyze the real business cycle approaches that have emerged as a consequence of the criticism of the transmission mechanism from the monetary to the real sector. They reverse causality and see the money supply as a function of real exogenous shocks.[84]

Disturbance of market balance by real exogenous shocks: The Real Business Cycles theories According to the Real Business Cycles approaches, real positive shocks, such as technical progress, longer working hours and foreign direct investment as well as government demand, are the cause of fluctuations in the degree of utilization of production potential. Money making institutions, such as the central bank and the banking system, prompt the monetary adjustment to the new real social product: the real shocks act, whereas the money supply only reacts. Representing the real business cycle approaches, the economically relevant parts of the model of KYDLAND and PRESCOTT[85] will be presented here.

The central component of the model is a stochastic progress function. Technical progress, along with labor and capital, is a factor in a neoclassical production function with constant economies of scale. In maximizing profits, the demand for capital and labor depends on their marginal productivity, to which technical progress has the same effect. For technical progress (λ_{t+1}) is true: $\lambda_{t+1} = p\lambda_t + E_t$; with $0 \leq p \leq 1$ as a coefficient for the effect on the social product. Et, the technology shock variable, is stochastic and autocorrelated according to a first-order Markov process. Et is exclusively random, independent and identically distributed. At $p = 1$ the shocks are transmitted unchecked over time to the social product, at $p = 0$ the shock affects only the period of its onset to the social product. The investment function is positively dependent on technical progress and a stochastic differential equation of first order, which is why, due to the autocorrelation of technical progress, cyclical oscillations can occur which are exacerbated by the investments due to the assumed time lag.

The Real Business Cycles Theory has introduced a new empirical methodology into macroeconomics. Since these models are not suitable as an economic forecasting model due to the exogeneity of their economic causes (persistence problem), we examine whether it is possible to simulate observable economic developments using realistic input variables in reality. This succeeds in an amazing number of cases.[86] However, KYDLAND and PRESCOTT's own empirical examination of the model criticizes stochastic modeling as being adapted to the real social product trajectories until the desired agreement has been reached. Whether the real shocks occurring in reality, apart from exceptions, are sufficiently strong to produce cyclical fluctuations

[84] For the Real Business Cycles theory see Kydland and Prescott (1982), Long and Plosser (1983);, Azariadis and Guesnerie (1986), Ramser (1988), Tichy (1995, pp. 191), Stadler (1994) and Komphardt (1989, p. 213).

[85] See Kydland and Prescott (1982) and Assenmacher (1998), pp. 310.

[86] See Kugler (1998) p. 33.

remains open. In the Real Business Cycles approaches, probability distributions, in this case innovations (i.e. technical progress), explain the course of the business cycle. Again, there is the persistence problem: only with the help of the assumption of repeated, independent, strong, exogenous technology shocks can cyclical fluctuations in employment and demand become apparent. Unfortunately, without a well-founded empirical review, Real Business Cycles theories will remain abstract mathematical models.

Psychological influences on the economy

In addition, in many approaches psychological variables were included as random variables in the New Classical Macroeconomics. So-called "sun-spot variables" are psychological factors that influence expectations of model-related variables, without, however, affecting preferences, technologies or original equipment. It does not matter if these factors have a real impact on economic development. The key is that the economic agents accept this and carry out real transactions. In this way, "sun-spots" (sunspots) can cause cyclical fluctuations.

In the approaches of the New Classic Macroeconomics and the Real Business Cycles as well as in the psychological approaches, the short-term negative real economic effects of misjudgements, expectations and psychological factors are demonstrated with the help of mathematical modeling. They evoke fluctuations in supply and demand, i.e. instability. The monetarist approaches, as well as those of the New Classic Macroeconomics, show that a discretionary monetary policy has no long-term impact on employment, on the contrary. Consequently, for political economy, it can be concluded that the institutional framework (such as that of the financial markets) must be designed so as to minimize the upset and misjudgment of private economic agents.[87] A rule-bound monetary policy must guarantee a constant relation between the quantity of goods and money. EUCKEN's demand for the constancy of economic policy[88] takes on particular significance as a result of these approaches, since the state can also act as a disconcerting factor through discretionary interventions. The New Classic Macroeconomics suggests a stabilization of money and interest rates. On the other hand, the state can deliberately use the mistakes of economic subjects such as the permanent transitory confusion and counteraction in shock situations where overreaction of the economic subjects is to be expected. One example of such a response is the expansive monetary policy that has been implemented in many countries in response to the 1987 stock market crisis. The lower interest rates caused a positive, expansive confusion, which could later be corrected again. The New Classical Macroeconomics emphasizes the importance of "moralsuasion": politicians and other persons with public influence must be aware of the economic impact of their statements. If they spread rumors that give rise to a misjudgment of the economic policy indicators, economic fluctuations will ensue. However, if they explain their policies and pursue them consistently, they can prevent cyclical fluctuations.

[87] See Ramser (1988), pp. 98.

[88] For the necessity of the constancy of economic policy See Eucken (1952), pp. 285.

8.3 Behavioral Approaches to Business Cycles Theory

How do psychological factors affect cyclical fluctuations?

8.3.1 Speculative Bubbles as a Business Cycle Trigger

Speculative bubbles can trigger economic fluctuations through wealth effects and high profits. Corporate interests are valued more by the companies at fair value measurement under ISFR or US GAAP, which increases profits. Household equity assets are also rising and encouraging households to increase their consumption expenditure (wealth effect). Banks are prone to higher lending due to high assets. Here, credit bubbles can arise through credit-financed securities purchases, such as in the world economic crisis of 1929 or credit-financed real estate purchases, as in the case of the US sub-prime financial crisis of 2007. If this development is accompanied by a lax monetary policy, mostly share price and real estate bubbles are created in parallel (as for example with the Japan bubble in the late 1980s). The downturn is triggered by the impairment of loans in the banking system, with only a sufficient inflow of liquidity for the price increase sufficient for the trend break.[89]

Speculative Bubbles is a colloquial phrase commonly used to characterize a strong overvaluation in prices. "A price bubble is a deviation in the price of an asset (gold, foreign currency, stock) from the price consistent with the fundamentals."[90] In the literature, depending on the alleged cause, various names for speculative bubbles like rational and irrational bubbles as well as agency-oriented bubbles, intrinsic bubbles and stochastic bubbles.[91] The distinction between rational and irrational bubbles is artificial, since deviating prices from fundamental data is always irrational. However, according to a broad definition of rationality, all decisions that are confirmed over time are considered rational. With a dynamically growing bubble, however, the yield expectations are always confirmed by rising prices, so that each bubble can be described as rational. Conversely, every bubble – rational in its broadest definition – becomes an irrational bubble after it bursts.

Intrinsic Bubble is when a change in the fundamental sizes is overvalued by the market once and for this reason it does not come to an inflation of the bubble.[92] Agency-oriented bubbles are the result of distorted information processing by investors. This explanatory approach is currently being buoyed by New Behavioral Finance, which will be discussed later. Last but not least, one speaks of stochastic bubbles when there is an auto-accumulating, thus self-reinforcing, psychological overvaluation development. The original price increase may well be fundamentally

---

[89] Stahl and Conrad (2000a), pp. 415–422.

[90] See Santoni and Dwyer Jr (1990, S. 190) and Diba and Grossman (1988), p. 520.

[91] See Bruns (1994), pp. 23.

[92] See Aschinger (1991), p. 271.

justified. The past price increases, however, are forecast by investors as an expectation into the future and overreaching, so that psychological backgrounds dominate the investment decision (Social Dynamics). These exaggerated expectations are repeatedly confirmed by higher prices as a result of the purchases (self-fulfilling prophecies or self-fulfilling expectations) until the bubble bursts.[93]

Bubble expresses the opinion that the overvaluation will not last long – a bubble bursts. In the narrower sense, there can be no overvaluation of a good, since the market price is determined by supply and demand and is always an equilibrium price. The overvaluation must therefore relate to the permanence of the market price.

A dynamic, growing bubble can only arise if the current market price is positively dependent on its expected rise.[94] The goods must not be subject to a temporal decline in value that is greater than the possible increase. They must not spoil or cause excessive storage costs. As a result, equity investments are particularly vulnerable to the formation of speculative bubbles, as their retention costs are low and potential future increases in profit are very high.[95]

8.3.2 *New Behavioral Finance Theory*

As discussed above, it can be observed that investors tend to overestimate their level of information and skills. This is called overconfidence. Subjects regularly overestimate their own knowledge, their control options, their abilities as well as their achievements.[96] Overconfidence causes an overestimation of the probability of success of one's own decisions. People tend to overestimate their own abilities after a series of successes and then take excessive risks. This human weakness underlies the business approach of a shell or cone game. The inexperienced player is initially skeptical, so the game master lets the player win first to lull him into a feeling of safety. Then, when the player thinks he knows how to master the game and the success, the game master tricks, plays faster than before, and thus takes his money away from the player. This human weakness is also effective in a boom when, due to high demand, almost all business decisions and investments are successful. The managers then tend to high self-esteem and invest too much. As a result, the boom will be further increased and the upcoming supply overhang will be even greater if the investments have been realized and the supply comes onto the market.

New information is processed and converted with a delay. This causes an overreaction on the exchanges in both directions (overreaction).[97] There are

[93] See Bruns (1994), p. 25 and Aschinger (1991), pp. 270.

[94] See Flood and Garber (1980), p. 746.

[95] See Ito and Iwaisako (1995), p. 1.

[96] See Metcalfe (1998).

[97] See Behavioral Finance Group (2000); Without Author (1999). See auch Menkhoff and Röckmann (1994), a.a.o., pp. 287 and Shleifer, Andrei (2000b).

exaggerations and understatements in the investments, because the information that contradicts the trend is taken seriously too late in the decisions of the corporate drivers. In the boom, the managers realize too late that now the cost of primary products and wages have increased, other companies have invested or demand has already weakened. They invest too much in expanding their capacities. Conversely, in the downturn, they realize too late that costs have fallen again, demand has stopped falling or suppliers have left the market. They invest too late. The downturn therefore lasts too long.

8.3.3 *Noise Trading Approaches*

A series of psychologically-oriented explanatory approaches emerged called noise trading approaches, where "noise" stands for a disturbance (noise) that causes prices to deviate from the fundamental data, In their models, some noise trading approaches explicitly work with groups of investors who make their decisions on the basis of distorted probability distributions, thus unconsciously behaving irrationally.[98] For example, Shiller models an emotionally charged cyclical stock market demand, with speculative bubbles forming.[99] Imagine that even entrepreneurs are plagued by envy, greed and fear. In the upswing, the entrepreneurs have earned well, now they want more and more and expand too much. The boom is intensified and the downturn afterwards as well. Envy of the success of other entrepreneurs would have the same effect. Conversely, anxiety causes entrepreneurs to not invest in the recession, although the highest profits would be possible here because investment costs, wages and input costs are low.

Bubbles can also be triggered by positive moods of the market participants (price euphoria), which are amplified by feedback (positive feedbacks) and can lead to a rectified mass behavior (so-called herd mentality).[100]

The herd approach can be transferred to the business cycle theory. Even unorthodox, rectified human behavior can trigger business cycles. Fear and panic trigger a downturn, while overconfidence causes an exaggeration, an overshoot in the boom.

The Confirmation Bias describes how people process facts in such a way that they confirm their own opinions.[101] Contradictory facts are not taken into account or are subordinated to the held opinion. Added to this is the illusion of control as an overestimation of one's influence on processes. People shy away from change when they can not assess how they are affected. The status quo is preferred over another alternative (status quo bias). The status quo bias is strengthened by the

---

[98] See Blume and Easley (1992), pp. 9–40.

[99] See Shiller (1984), pp. 457–498.

[100] See Froot et al. (1992), pp. 1461.

[101] See Wason (1960), Nickerson (1998) and Beck, H. (2014).

omission bias. People rate negative results from actions they actively participated in higher than negative results from non-action, ie omission.

If we combine these biases, we can conclude that Managers react too late to the economic indicators which can lead to business cycles. You can also find a status quo in spending behavior. Samuelson and Zeckhauser examined the spending behavior with fictitious companies with test persons. The test subjects were provided with changing business forecasts. With good forecasts, they increased their expenditure, but did not reduce it with poor forecasts which results in overinvestments.[102]

If all market participants behave in the same way with their investment and purchasing decisions, economic cycles emerge. Boni systems can reinforce this by supporting rectified risk-taking behavior.[103] If the actors are only involved in the opportunities and not in the risks, i.e. are not liable for losses but are involved in the profits, this destabilizes the system. Risk-taking overinvestments drive the upswing, while depreciation in the financial system causes the crash and downturn.

For the business cycles, the managers are pessimistic and depressed in the downturn and recession. The opportunities are undervalued and the risks are overstated. The negative emotions are transmitted. Conversely, in the boom the managers are euphoric. Everything succeeds, they sell and earn more than expected. You hear about start-ups, expansion investments and acquisitions. This positive mood is on. Upswing and boom are strengthened.

Tversky and Kahneman call a behavior focused on old data "anchoring". People are biased because they depend too heavily on the first set of data they receive. This data is the "anchor" that distorts the decision.[104] This approach leads us to the general question how future prices influence the behavior of people. Anchoring would mean that the prices signal the future and lead to a corresponding behavior from the economic actors. Take for example the quantitative easing policy of a central bank; its aim is to flatten the interest curve in order to stimulate investments. But if the economic actors see the low interest rates as a sign for a coming recession it will have the opposite effect; they will reduce their investments. This might be a reason why the quantitative easing policy has relatively little effect.

When a central bank tries to communicate its guidance about the future, it influences the expectation of the economic, forcing it to take the biases of the economic actors and behavioral reactions to its wording into account. Using behavioral insights is therefore a key element for influencing the actors towards the central bank's policy goals. A thoughtful, balanced, and selective communication is needed to "anchor" the expectations.[105]

The same is true for the impact of monetary policy, for which the central bank has to take the biases of the economic actors into account. Overconfidence and herding are as dangerous as the belief that the central bank will bail out every investment risk.

---

[102] See Samuelson and Zeckhauser (1988), pp. 22.

[103] See Conrad (2015).

[104] See Tversky and Kahneman (1974).

[105] See Khan (2018), pp. 47.

It is important for the central bank to combine its market interventions with clear signs of termination. An unlimited low interest rate policy can lead to exaggerated positive expectations and thus to speculative overshooting.

According to Masciandaro, "central bankers are individuals that are subject to the same source of behavioral bias all individuals face."[106] But with biases like loss aversion, status quo bias and omission bias a central bank is unable to set interest rates and control the money supply properly.

Behavioral science questions the ability of a central bank or a government to stimulate the economy. It shows that the behavior of people is not rational and not deterministic. This is also the reason, why it cannot supply feasible tools control behavior. Behavioral science shows that only pattern predictions make sense for economics; instruments as incentive management and framework settings only make sense within institutions.

8.4 Conclusion and Summary: Determinants of the Business Cycle

Ethical Summary

There is no direct impact of morality to business fluctuations but we can deduce form the chapters above that morality smoothens economic development. There are studies that support this hypothesis. Chih-Pin Lin a. o. perform a longitudinal analyses covering 155 countries from 1995 to 2015. They discover, that corruption increases the Hodrick-Prescott cyclical volatility of inflation and production in the following 10 years.[107]

Tomoya Suzuki tests the relation between corruption and interest rate shocks and their impact on production. He discovers that the estimated interest rate shock and the corruption level are positively correlated with each other. In addition, the average size of the interest rate shocks is positively associated with the contribution of these shocks to the variability of output growth and with the corruption level.[108]

Behavioral Summary

Man is not Homo Oeconomicus, but – as was presented in Chap. 3. – an irrational and often unsuccessful happiness maximizer, who tries to implement his complex need structure within groups. Stock market fluctuations can be transferred to cyclical fluctuations. However, psychological factors can also have a direct impact on corporate decisions, triggering or intensifying cycles.

[106] Masciandaro, D., F. and Favaretto (2016).

[107] See Chih-Pin Lin et al. (2018).

[108] See Suzuki, T. (2018).

How do psychological factors affect cyclical fluctuations? Speculative bubbles can trigger economic fluctuations through wealth effects and high profits. Here, credit bubbles can arise through credit-financed securities purchases, such as in the world economic crisis of 1929 or credit-financed real estate purchases, as in the case of the US sub-prime financial crisis of 2007.

Overconfidence causes an overestimation of the probability of success of one's own decisions. People tend to overestimate their own abilities after a series of successes and then take excessive risks. This human weakness is also effective in a boom when, due to high demand, almost all business decisions and investments are successful. The managers then tend to high self-esteem and invest too much. As a result, the boom will be further increased and the upcoming supply overhang will be even greater if the investments have been realized and the supply comes onto the market. Overreaction is the case, when new information is processed and converted with a delay. This causes an overreaction on the exchanges in both directions. There are exaggerations and understatements in the investments, because the information that contradicts the trend is taken seriously too late in the decisions of the corporate drivers.

Noise trading approaches can simulate business fluctuations if feelings like envy, greed and fear are implemented. The herd approach can be transferred to the business cycle theory. Even unorthodox, rectified human behavior can trigger business cycles. Fear and panic trigger a downturn, while overconfidence causes an exaggeration, an overshoot in the boom.

The Confirmation Bias describes how people process facts in such a way that they confirm their own opinions.[109] Contradictory facts are not taken into account or are subordinated to the held opinion. Added to this is the illusion of control as an overestimation of one's influence on processes. People shy away from change when they can not assess how they are affected. The status quo is preferred over another alternative (status quo bias). The status quo bias is strengthened by the omission bias. People rate negative results from actions they actively participated in higher than negative results from non-action, ie omission.

With good forecasts, they increased their expenditure, but did not reduce it with poor forecasts which results in overinvestments. If we combine these biases, we can conclude that Managers react too late to the economic indicators which can lead to business cycles.

If all market participants behave in the same way with their investment and purchasing decisions, economic cycles emerge. Boni systems can reinforce this by supporting rectified risk-taking behavior. Risk-taking overinvestments drive the upswing, while depreciation in the financial system causes the crash and downturn.

---

[109] See Wason (1960), Nickerson (1998) and Beck, H. (2014).

Conclusion

If we try to work out an economic-political trend statement of the presented business cycle the following can be stated[110]:

- Long-term national product development is determined by the growth determinants of physical and human capital, including technical progress.
- There is no long-term positive relationship between inflation and employment. On the contrary, the price distortions and the uncertainty of the planning economic agents lead to a reduction of long-term economic growth.
- For the effects of monetary and fiscal policy, the expectations of economic agents are crucial.
- Due to the numerous implementation problems (recognition, planning, implementation and impact) and the difficulty of clearly defining the cause responsible for the respective economic development, fiscal policy should be used on a long-term rather than discretionary basis in the short term.
- Monetary policy must primarily serve to ensure price stability and may only help to cushion external shocks in exceptional circumstances. Real national product growth cannot be artificially generated by an expansionary monetary policy.

The economic-theoretical approaches developed after Keynes complement each other to a much more comprehensive and balanced understanding of the business cycle. They extend the previous models by new economic determinants or a consideration over several periods (dynamization). The most important gain in knowledge that Keynes's economic theory produced is the theoretical proof that fluctuations in the degree of utilization of production potential do not have to be exclusively due to demand, but that supply shocks can also be the cause. This is the merit of the New Keynesian Macroeconomics and New Classical Macroeconomics with its advancements. The shortcoming of these approaches is that they cannot endogenously explain a complete business cycle. They all suffer from the persistence problem and are dependent on exogenous stochastic shocks to simulate cyclical fluctuations. The cyclically acting influences, i.e. the trend component of the time series, are not deterministic here, thus explained, but stochastic, which is less convincing. The explanatory value and thus also the value for the economic education is lower than with the deterministic models. In addition, due to undeterminedness, these models are unsuitable for economic forecasting.

Since many models assume a closed economy, the international economic context is often forgotten in the economic policy debate. This is incompatible with the current framework conditions, as the current globalization discussion shows. With a large share of imports in domestic demand, the effects of a government increase in demand are greatly reduced. The interest-rate sensitivity of investment is also lower in an open economy, since investment in international free capital and goods flows is made where the highest expectations of profitability exist.[111]

---

[110] This is the basic tenor in almost all summaries of the business cycle theory of the last 50 years. See insbesondere Kugler (1998), pp. 34.

[111] See Jaeger (1999, p. 31) and Hesse (1999), p. 39.

The development of the business cycle theory according to KEYNES has above all pointed out the limits of the theory of economics. If the German Stability and Growth Act still testified in 1967 to a belief in the controllability of the economy, then this view is hardly represented today. This applies above all to discretionary demand management. If we want to explain this change of mind, we must search for the causes of the variance in the applied economic theory. What is available to economic researchers as short-term indicators is the statistically aggregated impact of billions of decentralized individual decisions by economic agents coordinated across many different markets. From this sentence, the four unsolvable problems of the applied business cycle theory can be deduced:

1. The multi-causality due to the billions of individual decisions. Only a high abstraction can filter out dominant determinants.
2. Aggregation addresses the structural problems of sectors or anomalies of individual markets, for example due to distortions of competition.
3. The Overlay and Lag Problem: The effects of the many different economic determinants appear superimposed and time delayed.
4. The nondeterminable behavior of human decision makers. This is especially true if you assume irrational behavior. However, KYDLAND and PRESCOTT showed that even with rational behavior, optimal economic governance becomes impossible due to the unpredictable responses of economic agents as a result of the adaptive expectations they have built on previous economic policies.[112]

Most of the newer approaches are based on the "policy inefficiency hypothesis". Consequently, the influence of politics on the economy must be kept as low as possible. The future environmental conditions are unknown. The market participants therefore make decisions under uncertainty. The state must not increase this insecurity by a "non-constancy" of economic policy in addition. Rather, what is needed is a redefinition in the form of clear, long-term policy programs based on a comprehensible, orderly conception, that is, regulatory rather than process policymaking. KYDLAND and PRESCOTT therefore recommend – as does LUCAS – the institutional involvement of politicians in firm codes of conduct, which were chosen by economic theory as being the most appropriate in advance, depending on the economic situation.[113] Politicians are then encouraged within this institutional involvement to explain their goals and instruments to the economic agents, and then to implement them rigorously. Discretionary intervention is acceptable only in those cases where upset already exists and the policy can prevent possible overfunctioning or malfunctioning. Moralsuasion is a suitable instrument in this context. However, in order not to affect the credibility and thus the effectiveness of this instrument, it is restrained in use. The political influence on the economic process must be limited to the minimum (minimum policy). This gain of knowledge

[112] See Kydland and Prescott (1977).

[113] See Kydland and Prescott (1977) and Lucas Jr (1976).

should not be underestimated in its contribution to the recent economic theories of political economy.

The new economic theoretical approaches make a significant contribution to a better understanding of economic developments.[114] They extend the previous models by new economic determinants or a consideration over several periods (dynamization). It turns out that the causes of cyclical fluctuations are much more complex than many Keynesian economists assumed in the 1970s. Although Hicks and the New Keynesian Macroeconomics succeeded in providing a new theoretical foundation for the need for state countercyclical demand management, these models call for a state even more omniscient than Keynesian Demand Management. The new Keynesian-oriented models take into account more influencing factors and developmental interdependencies over a longer period of time. The state must therefore pursue more influencing factors by means of suitable indicators, and detect negative developments even more quickly in order to prevent negative dynamic demand processes, which can initiate a cyclical downward trend. The recognition and implementation problems were, however, already on the basis of the "old" Keynesian theory in the economic policy practice not solvable.[115] The demand of the state in its structure never corresponds to the loss of demand, which severely restricts the effect of government demand increases and, in addition, leads to a crowding out of private demand, which at the same time causes a partial increase in prices. The likelihood of economic policy action seems even greater than under the "old" theories.

All in all, the newer approaches represent the business cycle as a dynamic process that is influenced by many factors. The factors taken up by the theories, with their variety and diversity, point out the complexity of the business cycle and thus also the dangers of influencing economic policy. As a result, economic cycles are no longer controllable, but can be influenced at best.

For practical political economy, therefore, the value of the new economic theories lies above all in pointing out the dangers of discretionary government demand management. The theoretical finding is that economic developments are not controllable due to the unavoidable multicausality and the unpredictable temporal interdependencies. Therefore, automatisms are required that weaken individual procyclical determinants, such as progressive taxation. For economic policy, it follows that the state has to shape the economic framework in such a way that a lack of transparency causes the least possible misjudgment of the economic subjects. Moreover, the state must abstain from intervention so as not to increase the irrationalities. This understanding is mainly due to the New Political Economy and NORDHAUS. The New Classical Macroeconomics also assumes a "Policy Inefficiency Hypothesis". Consequently, the impact of policy influence on the economy is as small as possible. The actions of market participants, especially investors, are future-oriented. The future environmental conditions are unknown. The market

[114] See auch Conrad (1999).

[115] See Berg and Cassel (1992, pp. 163–238).

participants therefore make decisions under uncertainty. The state must not increase this insecurity by "inconsistency" of economic policy. Rather, what is needed is a binding rule in the form of clear, long-term policy programs that are based on a comprehensible, regulatory-compliant concept. Politicians are required to explain their goals and instruments to economic agents and then implement them consistently. Discretionary intervention is justifiable only in cases where upset already exists and the policy can prevent possible overfunctioning or malfunctioning. Moralsuasion is a suitable instrument in this context. However, in order not to affect the credibility and thus the effectiveness of this instrument, it is restrained in its use.

The financing effects of the government's increase in demand have not been integrated into the new economic models. All models are based on a closed economy. Foreign influences are exogenous factors. This is incompatible with the current framework conditions, as the current globalization discussion shows. With a high share of imports in domestic demand, the effects of a governmental increase in demand are greatly reduced. Also, the interest rate responsiveness of investment is lower in an open economy, since investments are made where the highest profitability expectations exist for internationally free capital and goods traffic. Overall, it should be noted that all models directly or indirectly show the dangers of political economic influence. The political influence on the economic process must be limited to the minimum (minimum policy). This is the contribution of the New Economic Theories to Economic Policy. Business cycles are part of economic development.

In the following, we want to summarize the main factors influencing economic development:

1. Market adjustment, marginal vendors are eliminated, profit margin is also increasing due to restructurings, initial recovery
2. Pro-cyclical banks (lending only for positive corporate figures), strengthening the upswing and downswing. The credit policy of banks is pro-cyclical. Companies only get credit for presenting good balance sheets and good economic conditions.[116]
3. Psychology (good and bad mood due to expectations about the future economic development are self-reinforcing, overconfidence)
4. Interdependencies (multipliers and accelerators), reinforcing ups and downs. Keynes: Demand leads to more demand
5. If demand is greater than supply, this will cause investment, which will increase over-subscribers. As the companies cannot assess the demand and also the capacity expansions of the competitors, overinvestments can occur. The reverse process takes place in a downturn when demand is less than supply. $Y^D > Y^S \geq I > S$ and $Y^D < Y^S \geq I < S$.
6. Ripening time of investments, initiating downswing (Schumpeter, overinvestment theory).

[116] See auch zum Kreditverhalten von Banken also on the credit behavior of banks Rottmann and Wollmershäuser (2010).

7. Pro-cyclical profit margin, strengthening ups and downs. Godwin Model ⇨ High profits lead to high investment; low profit leads to few investments
8. Valuations of Assets and Equity Investments, (wealth effect: not only more consumption with more income, but also more wealth ⇨ if the economic agents feel richer, they also spend more), reinforcing ups and downs. Fair value measurement approaches such as IFRS and US GAAP also increase the cycles of valuation fluctuations (mark-to-market and fair value measurement).
9. Downstream wage and price adjustments, introducing turning point.

Comprehension Questions
1. Which economic phases are there?
2. What types of business cycles exist, differentiated by length?
3. Name a leading and a lagging economic indicator.
4. What are three main reasons for economic fluctuations?
5. To what extent can economic fluctuations be caused by monetary policy?
6. Describe the phases of the Schumpeter business cycle.
7. To what extent does psychology play a role in business cycles? Which theories can be used for this?

Literature

Aghion, P., & Saint-Paul, G. (1993). *Uncovering some causal relationship between productivity, growth and the structure of economic fluctuations: A tentative survey* (Working paper no. 4603). National Bureau of Economic Research.

Albers, W., et al. (Eds.). (1976). *Handwörterbuch der Wirtschaftswissenschaften* (Vol. 4). Vandenhoeck und Ruprecht.

Arteta, C., Kose, M. A., Stocker, M. & Taskin, T. (2016). Negative Interest Rate Policies Sources and Implications, *Worldbank Policy Research Working Papers,* 7791, August 2016. http://econ.worldbank.org.

Aschinger, G. (1991). Theorie der spekulativen Blasen. *Wirtschaftsstudium, 20*(6), 270–274.

Assenmacher, W. (1998). *Konjunkturtheorie* (8th ed.). Oldenbourg.

Assenmacher K., Krogstrup, S. (2018). Monetary Policy with Negative Interest Rates: Decoupling Cash from Electronic Money, *IMF Working Paper*, 18/191. https://www.imf.org/en/Publications/WP/Issues/2018/08/27/Monetary-Policy-with-Negative-Interest-Rates-Decoupling-Cash-from-Electronic-Money-46076

Azariadis, C., & Guesnerie, R. (1986). Sunsports and cycles. *Review of Economic Studies, 53*, 725–738.

Baks, Klaas & Kramer, Charles (1999). Global liquidity and asset prices: Measurements, implications and Spillovers. IMF Working Paper 99/168, Washington, International Monetary Fund, 1999.

Ball, L., & Mankiw, N. G. (1994). Asymetric price adjustment and economic fluctuations. *The Economic Journal, 30*, 247–261.

Barro, R. J. (1971). A general disequilibrium model of income and employment. *American Economic Review, 61*, 82–93.

Barro, R. J. (1981). *Money, expectations and business cycles*. Academic.

Barro, R. J., & Grossmann, H. I. (1976). *Employment, and inflation*. Harvard University Press.

Beck, H. (2014). *Behavioral Economics: Eine Einführung* (1st ed.). Springer.

Behavioral Finance Group. (2000). Behavioral finance – Idee und Überblick. *Finanz Betrieb, 5*, 311–318.

Berg, H., & Cassel, D. (1992). Theorie der Wirtschaftspolitik. In *Vahlens Kompendium der Wirtschaftstheorie und Wirtschaftspolitik* (Vol. 2, 5th ed., pp. 163–238). Vahlen.

Bergstrom, A. (1962). A model of technical progress, the production function and cyclical growth. *In Economica, New Series, 29*(116), 357–370.

Black, F. (1987). *Business cycles and equilibrium*. Basil Blackwell.

Blume, L., & Easley, D. (1992). Evolution and market behavior. *Journal of Economic Theory, 58*, 9–40.

Borio, C., & Zhu, H. (2008). Capital regulation, risk-taking and monetary policy: A missing link in the transmission mechanism? *BIS working paper*, 268.

Borio, C., Gombacorta, L., & Hofmann, B. (2015). *The influence of monetary policy on Bank profitability*. Bank for International Settlements, working paper, 514.

Boxall, P., Adamowicz, W. L., & Moon, A. (2009). Complexity in choice experiments: Choice of the status quo alternative and implications for welfare measurement. *The Australian Journal of Agricultural and Resource Economics, 53*, 503–519.

Braley, R. (1983). *An introduction to risk and return* (2nd ed.).

Bruns, C. (1994). *Bubbles und Excess Volatility auf dem deutschen Aktienmarkt*. Betriebswirtschaftlicher Verlag Dr. Th. Gabler GmbH.

Campbell, J. Y., & Ammer, J. (1993). What moves the stock and bond markets? A variance decomposition for long-term asset returns. *The Journal of Finance, 48*(1), 3–37.

Caruana, J. (2013). *Hitting the limits of "outside the box" thinking? Monetary policy in the crisis and beyond*, Official monetary and financial institutions forum lecture (Golden series lecture), https://www.bis.org/speeches/sp130516.htm

Chancellor, E. (1999). *Devil take the hindmost. A history of financial speculation*. Plume.

Chenery, H. B. (1952). Overcapacity and the acceleration principle. *In Econometrica, 20*, 1–28.

Chih-Pin Lin, Chi-Jui Huang, & Cheng-Min Chuang. (2018). Corruption and business cycle volatility: a corporate governance perspective. *Asia-Pacific Journal of Accounting & Economics, 25*(5), 586–606.

Claessens, S. & Kose, M. A. (2013). Financial Crises: Explanations, Types, and Implications, *IMF Working Paper*, 13/28. https://www.imf.org/external/pubs/ft/wp/2013/wp1328.pdf.

Claessens, S., Kose, M. A., & Terrones, M. E. (2012). How do business and financial cycles interact? *Journal of International Economics, 87*(1), 178–190.

Claessens, S., Coleman, N., & Donnelly, M. (2016). Low-for-long interest rates and net interest margins of banks in advanced foreign economies. *Federal Reserve Board, IFDP notes,* April 11.

Clarke, S. (1967). *Central Bank cooperation: 1924–31*. Federal Reserve Bank of New York, Library of Congress Catalog No. 67–17650.

Clower, R. W. (1965). The Keynesian counter-revolution: A theoretical appraisal. In F. H. Hahn & F. Brechling (Eds.), *The theory of interest rates* (pp. 103–125). Macmillan.

Conrad, C. (1999). Entwicklungen der Konjunkturtheorie seit Keynes und ihr Beitrag zur Konjunkturpolitik – eine vergleichende kritische Bewertung. *Konjunkturpolitik, 45*(3), 188–220.

Conrad, C. A. (2000). Theorie und praxis der "speculative bubbles". In C. A. Conrad & M. Stahl (Eds.), *Risikomanagement an den internationalen Finanzmärkten* (pp. 135–146). Schäffer-Poeschel.

Conrad, C. A. (2015). Incentives, risk and compensation schemes: Experimental evidence on the importance of risk adequate compensation. *Applied Economics and Finance, 2*(2), 50–55. https://doi.org/10.11114/aef.v2i4.1053

Conrad, C. A. (2019, July). The effects on investment behavior of zero interest rate policy, evidence from a roulette experiment. *Applied Economics and Finance, 6*(4), 18–27. https://doi.org/10.11114/aef.v6i4.4272

Conrad, C. A. (2020). *Political economy*. Springer-Gabler. https://doi.org/10.1007/978-3-658-30884-1

Conrad, C. A. (2021). The effects of money supply and interest rates on stock prices, evidence from two behavioral experiments. *Applied Economics and Finance, 8*(2), 33–41. https://doi.org/10.11114/aef.v8i2.5173

Conrad, C. A. (2022). The effects of demand and interest rates on investments, evidence of overinvestment from two behavioral experiments. *Applied Economics and Finance, 9*(1), 19–28. https://doi.org/10.11114/aef.v9i1.5452

Conrad, C. A., & Schoett, H. (2000). Das Börsenjahr 1998 – nur knapp vorbei am Crash? In C. A. Conrad & M. Stahl (Eds.), *Risikomanagement an den internationalen Finanzmärkten* (pp. 151–159). Schäffer-Poeschel.

Conrad, C. A., & Stahl, M. (2000). Wirtschaft, Börsenfieber und Geldpolitik in den USA. *Orientierungen zur Wirtschafts- und Gesellschaftspolitik der Ludwig-Erhard-Stiftung, 85*, 24–32.

Conrad, C. A., & Stahl, M. (2002). Asset-Preise als geldpolitische Zielgröße – das Beispiel der USA. *Wirtschaftsdienst, 82*(8), 486–493.

Conrad, C. A., & Stahl, M. (2003). Geldpolitik und Spekulationsblasen – Das Beispiel der USA. *Österreichisches Bankarchiv, Zeitschrift für das gesamte Bank- und Börsenwesen, 51*, 685–693.

Cúrdia, V. (2019). How much could negative rates have helped the recovery? *FRBSF Economic Letter*, 2019–04, February 4, Research from the Federal Reserve Bank of San Francisco. https://www.frbsf.org/economic-research/publications/economic-letter/2019/february/how-much-could-negative-rates-have-helped-recovery/

Daxhammer, R., & Schmied-Wörle, T. (2000). Japan seit 1990: Das schmerzhaft lange Platzen einer Bubble. In C. Conrad & M. Stahl (Eds.), *Risikomanagement an den internationalen Finanzmärkten* (pp. 45–58). Schäffer-Poeschel.

Dell'Ariccia, G., Laeven, L., & Marquez, R. (2010). *Monetary policy, leverage, and Bank risk-taking* (IMF working papers, 10/276). International Monetary Fund. https://www.imf.org/external/pubs/ft/wp/2010/wp10276.pdf

Dell'Ariccia, G., Igan, D., Laeven, L., & Tong, H. (2013). Policies for macrofinancial stability: Dealing with credit booms and busts. In S. Claessens, M. A. Kose, L. Laeven, & F. Valencia (Eds.), *Financial crises, consequences, and policy responses*. IMF. https://www.elibrary.imf.org/view/IMF071/20264-9781475543407/20264-9781475543407/20264-9781475543407.xml?redirect=true

De Long, B. D., & Summers, L. (1988). How does macroeconomic policy affect output? *Brookings Paper on Economic Activity, 2*, 433–480.

De Nicolò, G., Dell'Ariccia, G., Laeven, L., & Valencia, F. (2010). Monetary policy and bank risk-taking. *IMF staff position note*, SDN/10/09. https://www.imf.org/external/pubs/ft/spn/2010/spn1009.pdf

Diba, B. T., & Grossman, H. I. (1988). Explosive rational bubbles in stock prices? *The American Economic Review, 78*(3), 520–530.

Drozd, Lukasz (2018). *The Policy Perils of Low Interest Rates*, Federal Reserve Bank of Philadelphia, Discussion Paper, Q1. https://philadelphiafed.org/-/media/research-and-data/publications/economic-insights/2018/q1/eiq118-policy_perils.pdf?la=en

Eucken, W. (1952). *Grundsätze der Wirtschaftspolitik* (4th unveränderte edition). J.C.B. Mohr.

Ezekiel, M. (1938). The Cobweb theorem. *The Quarterly Journal of Economics, 52*(2), 255–280. https://doi.org/10.2307/1881734

Fama, E. (1970). Efficient capital markets: A review of theory and empirical work. *Journal of Finance, 25*(2), 383–417. https://doi.org/10.2307/2325486

Felderer, B., & Homburg, S. (1989). *Makroökonomik und neue Makroökonomik*. Springer.

Feldstein, M. (2013, September 30). The taper chase. *Project Syndicate*. https://www.project-syndicate.org/commentary/why-the-fed-postponed-the-qe-taper-by-martin-feldstein?barrier=accesspaylog

Fischer, S. (1980). *Expectations and economic policy*. University of Chicago Press.

Flannery, M. J., & Protopapadakis, A. A. (2002). Macroeconomic factors do influence aggregate stock returns. *Review of Financial Studies, 15*(3), 751–782.

Flood, R. P., & Garber, P. M. (1980). Market fundamentals versus Price-level bubbles: The first tests. *Journal of Political Economy, 88*, 745–770.

Franz, W. (Ed.). (1999). *Trend und Zyklus, Wirtschaftswissenschaftliches Seminar Ottobeuren* (Vol. 28). Mohr.

Frenk, D. (2011). Review of Irwin and Sanders 2010, OECD report. In Institute for Agriculture and Trade Policy (Ed.), *Excessive speculation in agriculture commodities, selected writings from 2008–2012* (pp. 43–49) http://www.iadb.org/intal/intalcdi/PE/2011/08247.pdf

Frey, B. S., & Lau, L. J. (1968). Towards a mathematical model of government behaviour. *Zeitschrift für Nationalökonomie, 28*, 355–380.

Friedman, M. (1970). The counter-revolution in monetary theory, London. Deutsch (1973). In P. Kalmbach (Ed.), *Der neue Monetarismus*. Nymphenburger Verlagshandlung.

Friedman, M., & Schwartz, J. (1965). *The great contraction 1929–1933*. Princeton University Press.

Friedman, M., & Schwartz, A. (1969). *A monetary history of the United States*, Princeton University press 1969.

Froot, K. A., Scharfstein, D. S., & Stein, J. C. (1992). Herd on the street: Informational inefficiencies in a market with short-term speculation. *The Journal of Finance, XLVII, 4*.

Gagnon, J. E. (2016). Quantitative Easing: An Underappeciated Success, Peterson Institute for International Economics. *Policy Brief*, PB16–4, APRIL. https://piie.com/system/files/documents/pb16-4.pdf.

Gerfin, H., & Möller, J. (1980a). Neue Makroökonomie. *Wirtschaftswissenschaftliches Studium, 9*, 201–206.

Gerfin, H., & Möller, J. (1980b). Neue Makroökonomische Theorie. *Wirtschaftswissenschaftliches Studium, 4*, 153–160.

Glöser-Chowhound, S., Hartwig, J., Wheat, I. D., & Faulstich, M. (2017). The cobweb theorem and delays in adjusting supply in metals' markets. *System Dynamics Review, 32*(4), 279–308. https://doi.org/10.1002/sdr.1565

Goodwin, R. M. (1951). The nonlinear accelerator and the persistence of business cycles. *Econometrica, 19*, 1–17.

Goodwin, R. M. (1967). A growth cycle. In C. H. Feldstein (Ed.), *Socialism, capitalism and economic growth, essays presented to Maurice dobb* (pp. 54–58). Cambridge University Press.

Grosskettler, H. (1989). Johan Gustav Knut Wicksell. In J. Starbatty (Ed.), *Klassiker des ökonomischen Denkens II* (pp. 191–210).

Hannoun, H. (2015, April 22). *Ultra-low or negative interest rates: What they mean for financial stability and growth*. Speech at the Eurofi High-Level Seminar, Riga. https://www.bis.org/speeches/sp150424.pdf

Hayek, F. A. (1976). *Geldtheorie und Konjunkturtheorie*. Wolfgang Neugebauer. Reprinting of the original from 1929.

Hesse, H. (1999). Korreferat zum Referat K Jaeger, Der Beitrag der traditionellen Theorie zur Erklärung von Trend und Zyklus. In W. Franz et al. (Eds.), *Trend und Zyklus, Wirtschaftswissenschaftliches Seminar Ottobeuren* (Vol. 28, pp. 1–34). Mohr.

Heubes, J. (1986). *Grundzüge der Konjunkturtheorie*. Vahlen.

Heubes, J. (1991). *Konjunktur und Wachstum*. Vahlen.

Hicks, J. R. (1950). *A contribution to the theorie of the trade cycle*. Clarendon Press.

Hirata, H., Kose, M. A., Otrok, C., & Terrones, M. E. (2012). Global house price fluctuations: Synchronization and determinants. In NBER (Ed.), *International seminar on macroeconomics 2012* (Working paper no. 18362). National Bureau of Economic Research. https://www.nber.org/papers/w18362

Homa, K. E., & Jaffee, D. M. (1971). The supply of money and common stock prices. *The Journal of Finance, 26*(5), 1045–1066.

Homburg, S. (1996). Makroökonomik. In A. Börsch-Supan, J. von Hagen, & P. J. J. Welfens (Eds.), *Springers Handbuch der Volkswirtschaftslehre*. Springer.

Humphreys D. (2012). *Mining investment trends and implications for minerals availability* (Polinares Working Paper, 15). Brussels.

International Monetary Fund. (2000a). *World economic outlook*. International Monetary Fund.

International Monetary Fund. (2000b). *World economic outlook, asset prices and the business cycle*.

Irwin, S. H., & Sanders, D. R. (2012). Testing the Masters hypothesis in commodity futures markets, in. *Energy Economics No., 34*(2012), 256–269.

Ito, T., & Iwaisako, T. (1995). *Explaining asset bubbles in Japan*. National Bureau of Economic Research, Working Paper 5358.51.

Jaeger, K. (1999). Der Beitrag der traditionellen Theorie zur Erklärung von Trend und Zyklus. In W. Franz et al. (Eds.), *Trend und Zyklus, Wirtschaftswissenschaftlichses Seminar Ottobeuren* (Vol. 28, pp. 1–34). Mohr.

Kahneman, D., & Tversky, A. (1981). The framing of decisions and the psychology of choice. *Science, 211*(30 January 1981), 453–457.

Kahneman, D., & Tversky, A. (1982). The psychology of preferences. *Scientific American, 146*, 160–173.

Kahneman, D., & Tversky, A. (1984). Choices, values and frames. *American Pschologist, 39*(4), 342–350.

Kahneman, D., & Tversky, A. (1986). Rational choice and the framing of decisions. *Journal of Business, 59*(4), 5251–5278.

Kahneman, D., Knetsch, J., & Thaler, R. (1991). Anomalies: The endowment effect, loss aversion and status quo bias. *The Journal of Economic Perspectives, 5*(1), 193–206.

Kampmann, C. E. (1992). *Feedback complexity and market adjustment: An experimental approach*. PhD thesis, MIT Sloan School of Management, Cambridge, MA.

Kampmann, C., & Stermann, J. D. (1996). *Feedback complexity, bounded rationality, and market dynamics*. Mimeo. Retrieved from http://web.mit.edu/jsterman/www/SDG/feed.pdf

Kganyago, T., & Gumbo, V. (2015). An empirical study of the relationship between money market interest rates and stock market performance: Evidence from Zimbabwe (2009–2013). *International Journal of Economics and Financial Issues, 5*(3), 638–646.

Khan, A. (2018). *A behavioral approach to financial supervision, regulation, and central banking* (p. 46). IMF working paper, No. WP/18/178.

Kiehling, H. (2000). *Kursstürze am Aktienmarkt* (2nd ed.). Dtv Deutscher Taschenbuch.

Komphardt, J. (1989). Konjunkturtheorie heute: Ein Überblick. *Zeitschrift für Wirtschafts- und Sozialwissenschaften, 109*, 173–231.

Kugler, P. (1998). Neuere Entwicklungen in der Konjunkturtheorie. *Allgemeines Statistisches Archiv, 82*, 25–36.

Kurz, R. (1986). Zyklische Wachstum und Verteilung: Das Goodwin-Modell. *WiSu, 86*(6), 305–310.

Kydland, F. E., & Prescott, E. C. (1977). Rules rather than discretion: The inconsistency of optimal plans. *Journal of Political Economy, 85*(3), 473–491.

Kydland, F. E., & Prescott, E. C. (1982). Time to build and aggregate fluctuations. *Econometrica, 50*, 1345–1370.

Laidler, D. (1976a). Inflation in Britain – A monetarist perspective. *American Economic Review, 66*, 467–484.

Laidler, D. (1976b). Inflation – Alternative explanations and policies: Tests on data drawn from six countries. *Journal of Monetary Economics, 4*, 251–306.

Lansing, K. J. (2008). *Speculative growth and overreaction to technology shocks* (Working paper series, 2008–08). Federal Reserve Bank of San Francisco.

Lastrapes, W. D. (1998). International evidence on equity prices, interest rates and money. *Journal of International Money and Finance, 17*(3), 377–406.

Leontief, W. (1966). *Essays in economics. Theories and theorizing*. Oxford University Press.

Long, J. B., & Plosser, C. I. (1983). Real business cycles. *Journal of Political Economy, 91*(1), 29–69.

Lucas, R. E. (1975). An equilibrium model of the business cycle. *Journal of Political Economy, 83*(1975), 1113–1144.

Lucas, R. E. (1976). Econometric policy evaluation: A critique. *Carnegie Rochester Conference Series on Public Policy, 1*(1), 19–46.

Maddaloni, A., & Peydró, J.-L. (2010). *Bank risk-taking, securitization, supervision and low interest rates: Evidence from the euro area and the U.S. lending standards* (Working paper series, 1248). European Central Bank. https://www.ecb.europa.eu/pub/pdf/scpwps/ecbwp1248.pdf

Maddaloni, A., Peydró-Alcalde, J. L., & Scope, S. (2009). Does monetary policy affect Bank credit standards? *Evidence from the Euro Area Bank Lending Survey* https://www.researchgate.net/publication/256000197_Does_Monetary_Policy_Affect_Bank_Credit_Standards_Evidence_from_the_Euro_Area_Bank_Lending_Survey

Malinvaud, E. (1977). *The theory of unemployment reconsidered*. Basil Blackwell.

Mankiw, G. N. (1985). Small menu costs and large business cycles. *Quarterly Journal of Economics, 100*, 529–539.

Mankiw, G. N. (1998). *Makroökonomik* (3rd ed.). Schäffer-Poeschel.

Marx, K. (1864). *Das Kapital: Kritik der politischen Ökonomie. Der Gesamtprozeß der kapitalistischen Produktion*. (Vol. 3, 33. edition, Kap. 1–3). Dietz.

Masciandaro, D., & Favaretto, F. (2014). *Behavioral economics and monetary policy* (BAFFI CAREFIN centre research paper series no. 2015-1).

Masciandaro, D., & Favaretto, F. (2016). Doves, hawks, and pigeons: Behavioral monetary policy and interest rate inertia. *Journal of Financial Stability, 27*, 50–58.

McCallum, B. T. (1980). Rational expectations and macroeconomic stabilization policy. *Journal of Money, Credit and Banking, 18*, 716–746.

Menkhoff, L., & Röckemann, C. (1994). Noise Trading auf Aktienmärkten. *Zeitschrift für Betriebswirtschaftslehre, 64*(3), 277–295.

Metcalfe, J. (1998). Cognitive optimism: Self-deception or memory-based processing heuristic? *Personality and Social Psychology Review, 2*(2), 100–110.

Mezger, M., & Stahl, M. (2001a). Gold – Stabilitätspfeiler in Krisenzeiten. *Die Bank, 5*, 372–378.

Mezger, M., & Stahl, M. (2001b). Neue Erkenntnisse über Inflation und Finanzkrisen. *Orientierungen zur Wirtschafts- und Gesellschaftspolitik der Ludwig-Erhard-Stiftung, 87*, 15–22.

Mian, A. R., Sufi, A., Verner, E. (2015). Household Debt and Business Cycles Worldwide, *NBER Working Paper,* 21581. https://www.nber.org/papers/w21581.pdf

Minford, P., & Peel, D. (1983). *Rational expectations and the new macroeconomics*. Martin Robertson.

Musgrave, R. A., Musgrave, P. B., & Kullmer, L. (1987). *Die öffentlichen Finanzen in Theorie und Praxis* (Vol. 3). UTB.

Nickerson, R. S. (1998). Confirmation bias: an ubiquitous phenomen in many guises. *Review of general Psychology, 2*(2), 175–220.

Nishad Nishad, P. (2018). Effectiveness of Japan's zero and negative interest rate policy, *MPRA paper*, no. 89442. https://mpra.ub.uni-muenchen.de/89442/ MPRA paper no. 89442.

Nordhaus, W. D. (1975). The political business cycle. *Review of Economic Studies, 42*, 169–190.

Ongena, S., Vasso, I., & Peydró, J. L. (2009). Monetary policy, risk-taking and pricing: Evidence from a quasi-natural experiment. In *Discussion paper 2009–31*. Tilburg University.

Ott, A. (1963). *Einführung in die dynamische Wirtschaftstheorie*. Vandenhoeck & Ruprecht.

Pagan, A., & Schwert, C. (1990, June). Testing for covariance stationarity in stock market data. *Economics Letters, 33*(2), 165–170.

Phillips, P., & Loretan, M. (1990). *Testing covariance stationarity under moment condition failure with an application to common stock returns*. Discussion Paper No. 947, Cowles Foundation for Economic Research at Yale University New Haven Conneticut 1990.

Pícha, V. (2017). Effect of money supply on the stock market. *Acta Universitatis Agriculturae et Silviculturae Mendelianae Brunensis, 65*(2), 465–472.

Rajan, R. G. (2005). *Has financial development made the world riskier?* (NBER working paper no. 11728). https://www.nber.org/papers/w11728

Ramey, G., & Ramey, V. A. (1991). *Technology commitment and the cost of economic fluctuations* (Working paper no. 3755). National Bureau of Economic Research.

Ramey, G., & Ramey, V. A. (1995). Cross-country evidence on the link between volatility and growth. *The American Economic Review, 85*(5), 1138–1151.

Ramser, H. J. (1988). Neuere Beiträge zur Konjunkturpolitik: ein Überblick. *IFO-Studien, 34*, 95–115.

Ramser, H. J. (1997). Konjunktur und Wachstum: Der Beitrag der Neuen Wachstumstheorie. *ifoStudien, 43*(2), 211–223.

Rigobon, R., & Sack, B. (2004). The impact of monetary policy on asset prices. *Journal of Monetary Economics, 51*(8), 1553–1575.

Ritov, I., & Baron, J. (1992). Status-quo bias and omission-bias. *Journal of Risk and Uncertainty, 1992*(5), 49–61.

Rothschild, K. W. (1981). *Einführung in die Ungleichgewichtstheorie*. Springer.

Rottmann, H., & Wollmershäuser, T. (2010). *A micro data approach to the identification of credit crunches* (Working paper no. 3159: Monetary policy and international finance). CESifo.

Rozeff, M. S. (1974). Money and stock prices: Market efficiency and the lag in effect of monetary policy. *Journal of Financial Economics, 1*(3), 245–302.

Rubio, V. J., Hernández, J. M., Zaldvíar, F., Márquez, O., & Santacreu, J. (2010). Can we predict risk-taking behavior? Two behavioral tests for predicting guessing tendencies in a multiple-choice test. *European Journal of Psychological Assessment, 26*(2), 87–94. http://www.uam.es/proyectosinv/psimasd/risktaking.pdf

Rubio, V. J., Hernández, J. M., & Santacreu, J. (n.d.). The objective assessment of risk tendency as a personality dimension. *University Autónoma of Madrid* www.uam.es/proyectosinv/psimasd/assessrisk.pdf

Safar, L., & Siničáková, M. (2017). Money supply influence on gross domestic product throughout stock markets in United States and European Union. *Journal of Applied Economic Sciences, 12*(6), 1578–1584.

Samuelson, P. A. (1939). Interactions between the multiplier analysis and the principle of acceleration. *Review of Economics and Statistics, 21*, 235–241.

Samuelson, W., & Zeckhauser, R. (1988). Status quo bias in decision making. *Journal of Risk and Uncertainty, 1*, 7–59.

Santoni, G. J., & Dwyer, G. P., Jr. (1990). Bubbles or fundamentals: New evidence from the great bull markets. In E. N. White (Ed.), *Crashes and panics: The lessons from history*. Wiley.

Schebeck, F., & Tichy, G. (1984). Die "Stylized Facts" in der modernen Konjunkturdiskussion. In G. Bombach, B. Gahlen, & A. E. Ott (Eds.), *Perspektiven der Konjunkturforschung* (pp. 207–224). JCB Mohr.

Schlecker, M. (2014). *Kointegrationsanalyse, Stationarität und Augmented-dickey-fuller-Test*. http://www.matthias-schlecker.de/kointegrationsanalyse-stationaritaet-und-augmented-dickey-fuller-test

Schumpeter, J. A. (1993). *Theorie der wirtschaftlichen Entwicklung* (8th edn., Erstauflage 1911). Duncker und Humblot.

Schumpeter, P. (1939). *Business cycles*. McGraw-Hill.

Shachat, J., & Zhang, Z. (2012, June 21). The *Hayek hypothesis and long run competitive equilibrium: An experimental investigation* (Xiamen University Discussion Paper). https://doi.org/10.2139/ssrn.2089077

Shiller, R. J. (1984). Stock prices and social dynamics. *Brookings Papers on Economic Activity, 2*, 457–498.

Shleifer, A. (1986). Implementation cycles. *Journal of Political Economy, 94*, 1169–1190.

Shleifer, A. (2000a). *Inefficient markets, an introduction to behavioral finance*. Oxford University Press. https://doi.org/10.1093/0198292279.001.0001

Shleifer, A. (2000b). Stock prices and social dynamics. *Brookings Papers on Economic Activity, 2*, 457–498.

Simon, H. A. (1959). Theories of decision-making in economics and behavioral science. *The American Economics Review, 49*(3).

Sloan, A., & Stern, R. L. (1988). How Vo=VgN(d1) – E/ert N(d2) led to black Monday. *Forbes, 25*(1), 55–59.

Spranca, M., et al. (1991). Omission and commission in judgment and choice. *Journal of Experimental Social Psychology, 27*, 76–105.

Stadler, G. W. (1994). Real business cycles. *Journal of Economic Literature, 32*, 1750–1783.

Stahl, M. (2000a) (6. Juni 2000). Die Goldenen Zwanziger im Lichte der Internet Revolution, Chancen und Risiken der Neuen Ökonomie, Die Wirtschafts- und Börsenentwicklung in den USA heute weist große Ähnlichkeit auf mit der Lage vor dem Schwarzen Freitag 1929. Süddeutsche Zeitung, 129.

Stahl, M. (2000b). Die Lektionen des Jahres 1929. In C. Christian & M. Stahl (Eds.), *Risikomanagement an internationalen Finanzmärkten* (pp. 3–20). Schäffer-Poeschel.

Stahl, M., & Conrad, C. (2000a). Die Finanzmärkte im Spannungsfeld der New Economy. In *Wirtschaftsdienst, Hamburgisches Welt-Wirtschafts-Archiv (HWWA), 80.* Jhrg., Juli 2000/VII, S (pp. 415–422).

Stahl, M., & Conrad, C. A. (2000b). Strategien zur Risikovermeidung an internationalen Finanzmärkten. In A. C. Christian & M. Stahl (Eds.), *Risikomanagement an den internationalen Finanzmärkten* (pp. 383–385).

Stavenhagen, G. (1969). *Geschichte der Wirtschaftstheorie*. Vandenhoeck.

Stiglitz, S. E. (1994). Endogenous growth and cycles. In Y. Shinoya & M. Perlmon (Eds.), *Innovation in technology, industries and institutions, studies in schumpeterian perspective* (pp. 121–156). The University of Michigan Press.

Stiglitz, J. (2016, April 13). What's wrong with negative rates? *Project syndicate*. https://www.project-syndicate.org/commentary/negative-rates-flawed-economic-model-by-joseph-e%2D%2Dstiglitz-2016-04?barrier=accesspaylog

Stiglitz, J., & Weiss. (1981). Credit rationing in markets with imperfect information. *American Economic Review, 71*(3), 393–410.

Stiglitz, S. E., & Weiss, A. (1992). Asymmetric information in credit markets and its implications for macroeconomics. *Oxford Economic Papers, 44*(4), 694–724.

Suzuki, T. (2018). Corruption, interest rates and business cycles: Comparison of emerging economies. *Econ Change Restruct, 51*, 303–316.

Teichmann, U. (1997). *Grundriss der Konjunkturpolitik* (5th ed.). Vahlen.

Temin, P. (1976). *Did monetary forces cause the great depression?* Norton.

Thaler, R. (1989). The psychology of choice and the assumptions of economics. In A. E. Roth (Ed.), *Laboratory experimentation in economics. Six points of view* (pp. 99–130). Cambridge University Press. https://doi.org/10.1017/CBO9780511528316.004

Thorbecke, W. (1997). On stock market returns and monetary policy. *The Journal of Finance, 52*(2), 635–654.

Tichy, G. (1995). Konjunkturpolitik (3. edition). Berlin: Springer. Treynor, J. (1998). Bulls, beers and market bubbles. Financial Analysts Journal, 54(2), 69–74.

Tversky, A., & Kahneman, D. (1974). Judgment under uncertainty: Heuristics and biases. *Science, 185*, 1124–1131.

Tymoigne, E. (2018). *On the optimality of a permanent zero central-bank rate: Why were central banks created?* Paper presented at 12th Conference of the Research Network Macroeconomics and Macroeconomic Policies, October 2008. https://www.boeckler.de/pdf/v_2008_10_31_tymoigne.pdf

von Hayek, F. A. (1929). *Geldtheorie und Konjunkturtheorie* (Nachdruck der ersten Auflage von 1929, S. 81 ff). Wolfgang Neugebauer.

von Hayek, F. A. (1935). *Prices and production* (2nd ed.). Kelley (Reprint in The Ludwig von Mises Institute (Ed.). (2008). *Prices & production and other works. F. A. Hayek on money, the business cycle, and the gold standard.* Auburn. https://mises.org/library/prices-and-production. Abruf 28.10.2016).

von Hayek, F. A. (Ed.). (1969). *Der Wettbewerb als Entdeckungsverfahren*. Freiburger Studien.
Wagner, A. (1990). *Makroökonomik* (2nd ed.). UTB.
Wason, P. C. (1960). On the failure to eliminate hypothesis in a conceptual task. *Quarterly Journal of Experimental Psychology, 1960*, 129–140.
Waugh, F. V. (1964). Cobweb models. *American Journal of Agricultural Economics, 46*, 732–750. https://doi.org/10.2307/1236509
Wicksell, K. (1898). *Geldzins und Güterpreise. Eine Studie über den Tauschwert des Geldes bestimmenden Ursachen* (Berichtigter Neudruck der Ausgabe Jena 1898). Scienta Verlag.
Wicksell, K. (1898). *Geldzins und Güterpreise. Eine Studie über den Tauschwert des Geldes bestimmenden Ursachen*. 1968 Scienta (first published Jena 1898).
Wicksell, K. (1922). *Vorlesungen über Nationalökonomie auf Grundlage des Marginalprinzipes: Bd. 2. Geld und Kredit*. 1969. Scienta. (first published Stockholm 1906).
Wicksell, K. (1928). *Vorlesungen über Nationalökonomie, Theoretischer Teil, zweiter Band*. Gustav Fischer.
Wicksell, K. (1968). *Geldzins und Güterpreise. Eine Studie über den Tauschwert des Geldes bestimmenden Ursachen*. Scienta. (first published Jena 1898).
Without Author. (1999). Der wahre Experte weiß nicht nur viel, er weiß auch, was er nicht weiß. *Handelsblatt vom* 4.2.99, S. 29.
Wolfstetter, E. (1982). Fiscal policy and the classical growth cycle. *Zeitschrift für Nationalökonomie, 42*, 375–393.
Zame, W. (2008). General equilibrium (new developments). In S. N. Durlauf & L. E. Blume (Eds.), *The New Palgrave Dictionary of Economics* (2nd ed.). Palgrave Macmillan. https://doi.org/10.1057/978-1-349-95121-5_2354-1
Zarnowitz, V. (1997). *Business cycles observed and assessed: Why and how they matter* (Working paper no. 6230). National Bureau of Economic Research.

Chapter 9
Final Conclusion: Economic Systems, Markets and Politics

The economics, with their focus on a pure objective utility maximization, are far from human reality. Economic sciences are exclusively individually oriented. People decide in a social environment, which is why sociology is at least as important for behavior as psychology. The influence of the group (the company) or society must also be taken into account. All modern societies have institutions and organizations, giving them order, and instilling discipline in their citizens to behave in the manner socially desired. Norms, values and morality are important here, including attitudes towards the political and economic system. The attitudes of people in a society to the economically relevant activities have been paid as little attention by economic science as the existence of general economic knowledge.

Norms that are sanctioned reduce payouts and are critical to decision-making. And the objective benefit is not decisive but the subjectively perceived. However, this is difficult to measure from the outside. However, decision models that build on only objective material utility are misrepresentative and cannot explain many human motives, such as emotions, envy, sense of justice, and compassion. Man is stunted with the homo oeconomicus. It would therefore be more realistic to base the explanation of human behavior on the maximization of happiness as on benefit maximization. Subsequently, recent experimental findings describe humans as social beings and we will then challenge both the economic-scientific behavioral assumption of egoism and benefit maximization. The fact that selfless, or even self-sacrificing, acts exists shows that such an ethic is not unrealistic. This behavior can be explained by a more general theory of maximizing happiness, which is behind theories like the Happiness Theory from Bentham and Mill. Many people are generally good, which is to say they have an ethical disposition. Even behavioral theories have given too little consideration to intrinsic motivations until now. People consciously behave ethically because they understand the importance of such behavior to society, or because they empathize with other people (**enlightened human ethos**).

Human behavior remains not deterministic. If irrational behavior is not the exception, models based on rational behavior can no longer be a rule, but can at

C. A. Conrad, *Economic Systems, Markets and Politics*,
https://doi.org/10.1007/978-3-031-10366-7_9

best describe optimal behavior or average behavior by which the irrational behavior shows deviations. If people do not behave predictably like natural laws, then at best we can set a framework to direct behavior with incentives and sanctions. The economy then consists mainly of institutional regulations, a regulatory framework.

People should be motivated to work happily and efficiently in such a way that they use their skills to maximize the company's participation in the production process. That's how they benefit others. This is best ensured by freedom and competition in decentralized decision-making and market coordination. Quantitative economics should be supplemented in this book by the findings of behavioral sciences.

How are human behavior, culture and human performance related? Is man made for competition? Given the behavior of men, what might be a fair economic system?

Culture is a productive factor as the identity of society. In collectivist cultures, incentives work differently than in individualistic cultures. Productivity can be enhanced if economic policy is geared towards positively assessing performance in society or as a group norm.

Experiments showed that people have a need for self-determination. They want the freedom to take their destiny into their own hands and react to restrictions of this freedom with resistance (so-called reactance). Markets and competition guarantee individual freedom, which is a human desire. This inevitably leads to the desire for free-market freedom and a decentralized organization of the economy. The motives of autonomy and competence show that people actively deal with the challenges of life and want to understand the effects of their actions. Freedom of design and achievement motivation are central human needs. The goal of the individual to be economically productive reflects the need for fair competition in the market economy. The economy can influence the incentives. The rules of the game that lead to rewards or sanctions form the institutional framework for behavior. The state must guarantee the economic freedom of the individual, but must also enable social contact in order to take account of the attachment motivation (motive of social inclusion). In addition, the state structures, especially for the authorities with citizen contact, must be kept accessible and be able to waive regulations and taxation, insofar as they complicate the economic processes for the actor and thus make processes opaque (social inclusion).

What does behavioral science teach about distribution? Altruism and compassion do exist. A limited amount of redistribution can thus be justified, because it enhances welfare. People strive for equal distribution, especially when they identify with other group members. But they reject an equal distribution with different performance of the group members. The performance motivation decreases with equal distribution, which redistributive policy must take into account.. If there is no income, people tend to regard equal distribution as fair. However, the willingness to pay something from earned income is much lower and there is a conflict of interest regarding willingness to perform. The willingness to work with equal distribution for income is very low. It is therefore not advisable to compensate for income differences caused by performance. The purpose of this is to maximize the gross domestic product as a distribution mass. A progressive income tax must not reduce the achievement motivation so much that welfare losses occur. Not only would this not be considered fair, it would also reduce the redistributive mass. In the company, management must consider the employees' strong sense of justice. The distribution of income in the company must be explained to the employees so that it is accepted and the employee remains motivated. In addition, a key task of management is to ensure that the company is also justified among the employees. The same is true for the distribution of income in the society. As the differences between public and non-public behavior show, here too the social norms that can also differ culturally are decisive.

Groups are economically relevant both as companies and as societies of states. People take on roles within groups that influence their behavior. Individuals adapt to the group in order to gain social recognition (social comparison process or aspiring to conformity). The stronger the identification with a group, the more members conform in their behavior and the smoother the coordination of joint actions. Expectations as reliance on the behavior of the other group members are stabilized. The knowledge of belonging to a group leads to behavioral changes, by favoring one's own group members. The enforcement of norms in this case specifically motivates and thus the performance depends positively on the group feeling of belonging, the so-called group cohesion. Norms create moral behavior, as has been shown in experiments. The sanctions to force an individual to comply with the group norms range from the withdrawal of recognition by the group, to mobbing to exclusion. Moods and emotions are transmitted in groups. When communicating positive emotions, the group behaved more cooperatively, and there were fewer conflicts, thus productivity increased. Group adaptation behavior can become market-relevant if market participants have social contact and identify themselves as a group. This is possible in financial centers or online chat platforms, where market participants can exchange their opinions and adapt them to each other. Here too, in the sense of groupthink, false dominant market opinions can arise. This is what New Behavioral Finance calls herding behavior.

Competition within small groups can be counterproductive. In the case of individually identifiable and non-interdependent tasks, however, a productivity-increasing competition was also identified. The individuals try to outdo each other in group performance (social competition, interpersonal competition). It turns out that thanks to this motivational effort, the group performance is well above the sum of the individual performances. Competition between groups increases performance. This corresponds to the market competition between companies as groups. Businesses can thus increase their productivity by increasing group cohesion and ensuring the acceptance of corporate goals.

The performance of groups is influenced by coordination and motivation. On the other hand, social loafing is when the group members limit their performance because they can hide in the group. Decisive here is to make the individual's contribution in the group transparent and to sanction free riding as shown in the public good games. Coordination losses occur when the performance of the individual group members cannot be optimally aggregated, such as in tug of war, if not all use their power simultaneously.

The theory of realistic group conflict has shown the importance of common economic interests and projects for international understanding. Global trade, customs and particularly economic unions can reduce negative attitudes between national groups. Here it is important that the benefits are shared with the group members as well. European integration would be an example of such an approach to international understanding.

An individual can be in conflict with the collective, or other people, and still be dependent on others in the pursuit of their own interests, especially if those interests must be realized in a group. Dependency on other people does automatically limits one's freedom, however. Group-dependent goals cannot be achieved without considering the interests of other group members, which to a certain extent subordinates the individual to the collective, in order to benefit from the group goods. The desirability of the goods, as well as the necessity of individual adaptation, will tend to increase along with the cultural division of labor (emergence). With cooperation society can benefit from division of labor, economies of large scale and specialization. Organized group work allows the combination of individual strengths and allows individual weaknesses to be overcome.

Given human behavior, what might be a fair and functioning economic system? Kant's principles of reason, democracy, and the separation of powers have largely prevailed. Equality, freedom and respect for the rights of others arise from reason. The personality and dignity of man are reflected in human rights. Hume is right to say that the scarcity of goods requires economic activity in the form of labor, which goes hand in hand with deprivation. It is not the desire for organized work that determines occupations, but the shortages or the needs of the people. On a non-performance based income people tend to regard equal distribution as fair. However, the willingness to give up earned income is much lower. And there is a conflict of interest regarding willingness to perform. The willingness to work in equal distribution for income is very low. There can therefore be no need-based justice, but a compensatory social redistribution that protects against unfair acts of fate and makes a humane life possible in the interest of human dignity. The redistribution must be made by others who are willing to do so, otherwise they will emigrate. This requires a social discourse that weighs the balance between sacrifices and needs in a democratic decision-making process, which is supported by all citizens. Justice is an order that is socially accepted. Prerequisite is the freedom to choose between the social roles, i.e. duties and rights. Changes can often be brought about only by revolutions. According to Hayek, society develops evolutionarily. Social market economy increases productivity and the technical development of the economy determines social roles.

Justice results from social discourse. But social decisions are not unproblematic as group decisions. They do not automatically lead to the best decision for a society. The influences on group decisions that cause the informative exchange to be impaired must be prevented because this can lead to decisions that are normative based instead of information based (groupthink).. In addition, even public good games have shown that group interests and individual interests can diverge. Public goods are established only if everyone participates in the financing of that public good, such as a legal system or infrastructure. Individual interests can also directly oppose this, if, for example, a highway is to be built for the community, but to do so a property must be expropriated or lose its value due to external effects. This is why no social rules can arise from individual interests. Individual interests would always try to achieve personal gain, but never weigh the personal interests against other conflicting individual interests and they would never represent the overriding group interests. There must be social discourse about common rules and the form of fairness that the group wants and enforces against individual interests. This results in democracy as the rule of the group. Alternatively, you can hire a third party to represent the common interests, a monarch, but then the group must control the pursuit of common interests.

Even Durkheim and Weber see the need for rules. Civilization is the central strength of humanity. By sharing work in a large group, productivity benefits can be realized. States were founded and "natural rights" were transferred to the state for the organization of this division of labor. The financing and provision of public goods is the central task of the state. These benefits are for anyone who submits to the rule of the state. Recognized institutions must be enforced by the state to protect the individual and enable civilization. Society must agree on morality and give itself group rules. Following the rules of the market maximizes the social return from the division of labor. Imperfect market conditions must be supplemented socially or corrected by the state. Competition limits power and increases freedom, which is seen by humans as a value in itself. The state institutions must provide the framework for economic and social freedom.

Planned economy (central administration economy) considered the abolition of private property and the central coordination of production plans to be two tools with which to better meet the needs of society. However, socialism, or even communism, could not unleash productive forces. The prosperity gap between the capitalist and socialist states became ever greater until the socialist systems collapsed.

Global justice in the sense of equal rights can only exist for public goods, to which all people have the same claim. All other goods were subsumed by settlement and agriculture and then historically fought or defended. Global justice will therefore only be able to refer to behavior towards each other in the sense of universal human rights, with which the rights of others must be respected. Help in times of need will always be voluntary because it is not a public good.

The results of the market correspond only partially to our ideas of what is right, so the social market economy intervenes in the market and affects distribution results. As a social solution to conflictual and non-conflictual games, institutions have established themselves as social rules that are enforced through sanctions. Stabilizing behavioral expectations can prevent damage in conflictual games, while cooperation gains can be safely realized in non-conflictual games. The resulting benefits motivate the individual to join society and submit to the institutions, at least as long as the benefits outweigh the disadvantages. This dynamic is not sufficient to prevent the detrimental effects of human actions.

In the case of market failure, morality would dictate that third parties are not harmed. However, there are also other products that society needs. Inner stability is foremost of these things, understood not only as internal security, but a low crime rate, general harmony among citizens and thus the smooth running of social (also economic) processes. For this, there are many prerequisites: social rules, laws and institutions, and the organizations to enforce them, but they are not enough to bring about a successful society. The institutions and organizations cannot control, monitor and enforce everything. If, on the other hand, no social rules were respected by anyone, the social system would collapse immediately. Where laws and control reach their limit, morality begins. Morality regulates human behavior so as to prevent social harm. Social morality is an important corrective factor in the market economy. In order for a society to function and to develop its productive forces, there is morality as social capital, which has to be in line with the institutions and the economic stage of development. In this context, the attitudes of the people are particularly important for society, thus the community, and social cooperation. The norms, values and morality as well as the attitudes to the political and economic system all play an important role.

In the case of irrational behavior, the state can intervene only in cases in which there are massive health impairments, since irrationality belongs to human nature. Only rarely can a restriction of human freedom be justified. Nudges might be a legitimate instrument for influencing decision-making behavior in favor of the individual as long as the individual is free to decide against them. Framing goes one step further. It manipulates people by presenting information with a slant but claiming it is balanced. Manipulation of free will is not legitimate. The individual must be the one to make any decision when all is said and done. Asymmetric Paternalism is different to framing transparent to the decision maker.

Emotions have a negative connotation for us because they are not rational behaviors, but they can be efficiency enhancing. Short-term decision-making behavior is about speed. Heuristics and emotions are dominant. Only when individuals consciously think about problems does rational thinking dominate.

Corruption acts as a moral hazard, thus as incentives directed against the interests of the company or the community. Only fair competition ensures an optimal allocation of resources and thus efficient overall economic production. Immoral behavior harms society generally, be it within market processes, internal business processes or the erosion of culture. It is particularly important that corruption not become a socially acceptable behavior. The public goods games also show the importance of societal sanctions (norms) and learning/socialization. This means that corruption must be punished directly by the company and the society. The public good games show that cooperative behavior is abandoned if it does not pay to do so. This explains why cheating is contagious. Compliance is determined to a great deal by the corporate culture. Compliance is internally rewarded by good feelings, whereas noncompliance leads to negative feelings.

Politics manages democracy and must remedy the market failure and provide goods. How do politicians behave? What are the motives behind a bureaucracy and, in particular, can it efficiently implement political decisions?

Politicians, bureaucrats and citizens, according to the New Political Economy, like Homo Oeconomicus, maximize their own benefit first, not that of society.

Politicians must therefore be controlled by independent bodies (Federal Constitutional Court) and by institutional guidelines as well as by the press. Each voting procedure has advantages and disadvantages. In addition, as the voting procedures influence the results, it is important to weigh carefully what procedure is chosen. Behavioral science provides new political instruments. Framing is the manipulative representation of information necessary for decision making, as well as the use of extremely disparaging representations of other options in order to force citizens to make decisions to their own detriment. The press in a democracy has the vital task of presenting information so objectively that the citizens can make decisions that are not influenced by specific interests.

Another possibility for manipulation is called shaming. Shaming is the attempt to provoke feelings of guilt in people in order to prevent them from doing certain things. Shaming is only justifiable on the basis of a social discourse that transparently legitimizes the shaming.

What does behavioral science teach about financial markets? New Behavioral Finance Theory shows that investors tend to overestimate their level of information and skills (overconfidence). In addition, new information is processed and implemented with a delay. This causes an overreaction on the stock exchanges in both directions (overreaction). People can collectively err in a group. The group opinion dominates the individual opinion. The individual adopts the group opinion, as already shown in social psychology and sociology (in chapter). This means that systemic crises such as the financial crisis can be explained by human error. For the state this means that it has to take institutional precautions in the form of financial market regulation in order to counteract and mitigate systemic crises. The noise trading approaches show that bubbles can also be triggered by positive moods on the part of market participants (price euphoria), which are reinforced by feedback (positive feedback) and can lead to mass behavior in the same direction (herding).

The financial crisis led to the worst depression since 1929. Only by massive economic programs could worse be prevented. What were the reasons for this epidemic crisis? Were the right reforms implemented or could there be another financial crisis?

After the financial crisis several studies analyzed the risks management practices and came to the conclusion that the investors have underestimated the risks due to products complexity and over-reliance on quantitative analysis. In the case of the financial crisis there was the common belief in the self-correcting power of the market and the ongoing prosperity and housing price increases. We can call this collective erring. In the financial crisis the investment decisions were influenced by the by the wrong ratings and the securitization. Kind of this kind of framing changed the behavior of the lenders. The investors did not question the creditworthiness of the debtors, which would normally be requirement for lending.

The ratings of the subprime CDOs were based on old data from the US real estate market. Tversky and Kahneman call a behavior focused on old data "anchoring". There was also insensitivity to sample size, which is a bias to see patterns in small numbers of results even though more results are needed to find significant correlations. After the financial crisis the willingness to trust experts was greatly reduced.

The complexity of derivatives like the CDO was so complex that nobody besides the experts of the rating agencies was able to understand their structure and value.

None of the experts corrected or questioned the incorrect ratings. The incorrect ratings of the CDOs were a sign of overconfidence.There was also confirmation bias and regret aversion. Investors viewed the facts in a way that confirmed their own opinions. These biases show that ratings are not precise or might even be wrong because people make them.

As we have seen, immoral aspiration for enrichment by managers was common in the financial crisis. Bad examples can ruin common decency as much as it can be dangerous to continually preach thinking in models and maximizing benefit as the only reasonable, rational behavior. The consequence will be that people orient themselves on these behavioral maxims and repress their positive human characteristics such as sympathy, helpfulness, general willingness to sacrifice and selflessness. It is difficult to change the business culture in the financial organizations. However, if people are reminded of their standards of honesty they behave more ethically. Employees should sign ethical standards and should be reminded of them during their employment. Management education in particular must ask itself if it did not indirectly create monster managers; business ethics receives too little attention. Finally, it has been demonstrated that unilaterally constructed incentive schemes encourage excess risk-taking. Unilaterally constructed compensation schemes were one reason for the financial crisis.

New financial instruments such as derivatives showed their risk potential in the financial crisis. There were also new market participants, whose market influence has grown. By using a qualitative research approach we examine in this chapter the extent to which these two developments affect the economic processes of the market and put financial markets at risk. We also analyze the extent to which the new financial market regulations Basel III and the American Dodd Frank Act are sufficient to limit the systemic risk they cause.

The biggest shortcoming of the recent reforms to the stabilization of the financial system, such as Basel III and the American Dodd Frank Act, is that they increase the capital requirements rather limiting the risks of the new financial products like derivatives. It would generally be better to forbid risky and complex financial products than to further increase regulation complexity and the capital requirements as in Basel III and the American Dodd Frank Act.

One reason for the financial crisis is called speculation with credit derivatives. We analyzed the extent to which speculation is a natural and necessary part of the financial markets. Speculation influences spot prices of commodities and food prices if it creates a significant excess demand over a significant time period. In this case speculation might be seen as unethical, which is why regulation is needed.

Many scientists see a distorting market interaction in the restriction of speculation. They see themselves as advocates of liberalized markets, or market-based basic functions. However, the so-called liberalization of the markets around the year 2000 allowed derivatives instruments, which were not market-compliant because they relate to goods or values but do not have to correspond to any real demand or supply. In addition, non-commercial actors were admitted to the market with non-economic but speculative objectives. This has dramatically increased systemic risk. More regulation is needed, yet behavioral science shows the limits of financial regulation due to the nature of human beings. The biases show that ratings are not precise or might even be wrong because people make them. Right incentives, thus risk-adequate compensation, is more important for achieving the right behavior.

In the financial system, investment managers increased the risks for their employer by buying highly profitable but risky assets and were rewarded with high bonuses; leading to the financial crisis in the long term. The compensation schemes have to be regulated. Bonuses must be limited and managers must partake in the risk.

Economic fluctuations, above all as fluctuations in demand, are a major problem for people and businesses and can only be influenced to a very limited extent by economic policy.

The nondeterminable behavior of human decision makers and the multi-causality due to the billions of individual decisions are the key problems of business cycle policy. This is especially true if you assume irrational behavior. However, KYDLAND and PRESCOTT showed that even with rational behavior, optimal economic governance becomes impossible due to the unpredictable responses of economic agents as a result of the adaptive expectations they have built on previous economic policies.[1]

Most of the newer approaches are based on the "policy inefficiency hypothesis", which calls for the influence of politics on the economy to be kept as minimal as possible. The future environmental conditions are unknown. The market participants therefore make decisions under uncertainty. The state must not increase this insecurity by a "non-constancy" of economic policy.

All in all, the newer approaches represent the business cycle as a dynamic process that is influenced by many factors. The variety and diversity of factors addressed by theories point out the complexity of the business cycle and thus also the dangers of influencing economic policy. This perspective holds that economic cycles are no longer controllable, but may be influenced. All models directly or indirectly show the dangers of political economic influence. The political influence on the economic process must be limited to the minimum (minimum policy). This is the contribution of the New Economic Theories to Economic Policy. Business cycles are part of economic development. Due to the numerous implementation problems (recognition, planning, implementation and impact) and the difficulty of clearly defining the cause responsible for the respective economic development, fiscal policy should be used on a long-term rather than discretionary basis in the short term.

What is needed is a redefinition in the form of clear, long-term policy programs based on a comprehensible, orderly conception, that is, regulatory rather than process policymaking. Discretionary intervention is acceptable only in those cases where there is already upset in the system and the policy could prevent possible overfunctioning or malfunctioning. Moralsuasion is a suitable instrument in this

[1] See Kydland and Prescott (1977).

context. However, in order to maintain the credibility and thus the effectiveness of this instrument, it is used sparingly. The political influence on the economic process must be limited to the minimum (minimum policy). This gain of knowledge should not be underestimated in its contribution to the recent economic theories of political economy.

How do psychological factors affect cyclical fluctuations? Man is not Homo Oeconomicus, but - as was presented in Chap. 3 – an irrational and often unsuccessful happiness maximizer, who tries to implement his complex need structure within groups. Speculative bubbles can trigger economic fluctuations through wealth effects and high profits. Here, credit bubbles can arise through credit-financed securities purchases, such as in the world economic crisis of 1929 or credit-financed real estate purchases, as in the case of the US sub-prime financial crisis of 2007. Stock market or real estate fluctuations can therefore be transferred to cyclical fluctuations.

If all market participants behave in the same way with their investment and purchasing decisions, economic cycles emerge. Boni systems can reinforce this by supporting rectified risk-taking behavior. Risk-taking overinvestments drive the upswing, while depreciation in the financial system causes the crash and downturn.

Psychological factors can also have a direct impact on corporate decisions, triggering or intensifying cycles. Overconfidence causes an overestimation of the probability of success of one's own decisions. Overreaction happens when new information is processed and converted with a delay. This causes an overreaction on the exchanges in both directions. There are exaggerations and understatements in the investments, because the information that contradicts the trend is taken seriously too late in the decisions of the corporate drivers. Emotions trigger business cycles. Managers are depressed in the downturn and recession. Conversely, in the boom the managers are euphoric. The negative emotions are transmitted. With noise trading approaches business cycles can be explained by the transference of emotions, which are contagious. Fear and panic trigger a downturn, while overconfidence causes an exaggeration, an overshoot in the boom.

A confirmation bias exists when contradictory facts are not taken into account or are subordinated to the opinion held. Added to this is the illusion of control as an overestimation of one's influence on processes. People reject any change when they can not assess how they are affected (status quo bias). With good forecasts they increase their expenditure, but do not reduce it with poor forecasts' which results in overinvestments. If we combine these biases we can conclude that managers react too late to the economic indicators which can lead to business cycles.

Overconfidence and herding are as dangerous as the belief that the central bank will bail out every risk of the investments, so it is important that the central bank combines its market interventions with clear signs of termination. An unlimited low interest rate policy can lead to exaggerated positive expectations and thus to speculative overshooting. Applying the behavioral concept of anchoring on monetary policy would mean that a low interest rate policy could have negative effects. If the economic actors see the low interest rates as a sign for a coming recession a low interest rate policy will have a negative effect on investments. Behavioral science generally questions the ability of a central bank a government to activate the economy. The expectations of economic agents are crucial to the effects of monetary and fiscal policy. Thus monetary policy must primarily serve to ensure price stability and may only help to cushion external shocks in exceptional circumstances. Real national product growth cannot be artificially generated by an expansionary monetary policy. Together with the insights from business cycle theories we can conclude that there is no long-term positive relationship between inflation and employment. On the contrary, price distortions and the uncertainty in the planning of economic agents lead to a reduction of long-term economic growth. Long-term national product development is determined by the growth determinants of physical and human capital, including technical progress.

For practical political economy, therefore, the value of the new economic theories is mostly in pointing out the dangers of discretionary government demand management. The theoretical finding is that economic developments are not controllable due to the unavoidable multicausality and the unpredictable temporal interdependencies. Therefore, automatisms are required that weaken individual procyclical determinants, such as progressive taxation. For economic policy, it follows that the state has to shape the economic framework in such a way that lack of transparency causes the least possible misjudgment of the economic subjects.

The following section summarizes the main insights of this book.

Classical economics only regards the individual as a utility maximizer and derives human behavior in the economy from this, but humans are social animals. This book takes a broader approach that looks at the economic actor both individually and as part of a group. This results in new insights into behavior. In civilization man cannot maximize only his utility, but must do so in dependence with others. In addition, behavioral science shows that humans are inclined to have a moral compass. They have a limited willingness to help others and usually do not maximize their benefits indefinitely at the expense of third parties. The group influences the behavior of the individual by attempting to achieve its own goals through compulsion to conform, which can conflict with the goals of the individual. The individual, in turn, strives to be recognized by the group and prefers his own group members. Here the individual finds himself in a constant conflict between his personal goals and those of the group. This leads to the following conclusions for economics:

1. Morality enhances productivity

In a moral environment, people are more motivated and cooperative. They are more likely to share information and work together. In particular, the distribution of group success among the group members, which is perceived as fair, is decisive for their commitment. Morality has to be worthwhile. The state has to ensure the individual advantage of ethical behavior in society with ethical institutions. Managers in a company have the same function. Free riders must be dealt with. This also applies to the redistribution of group output among group members. It must be perceived as fair or people will no longer participate in the public goods created by the collaborative production in the group. The added value from emergence through division of labor and cooperation in the group can no longer be realized if individuals refuse to cooperate. Man is socially oriented but not exclusively. People pursue their own goals through the group but are not willing to completely sacrifice their individual benefit to maximize the collective group benefit. Against this background socialism and communism cannot function on the basis of common property.

2. Competition must follow fair rules

Competition takes place between and within groups. In the economy, companies and states form groups. In the case of cooperative tasks however, competition does not increase productivity. In the case of cooperation, states and companies can increase productivity by promoting group cohesion and group identification. Joint tasks for states can increase identification, reduce conflicts on a global level and thus increase productivity. For individual tasks the focus should be on the individual's performance. Compliance with rules (institutions) is crucial for the participation and commitment of the individual in competition. Only a competition based on performance that is perceived as fair can increase productivity. Performing well must be worthwhile for the individual. An equal distribution with different levels of performance is not accepted, but redistribution to needy group members in the sense of social security usually is.

Freedom of design and achievement motivation are human needs. They are thus overarching goals of the state, which the state must take into account in its organization and institutions. This inevitably leads to the desire for market freedom and a decentralized organization of the economy.

3. Political power must be limited institutionally

If people are motivated by the threat of deprivation, a welfare state must not set the guaranteed subsistence level too high. Otherwise productivity falls when people are cared for without working. A basic income without benefits cannot work. On the other hand, in order to generate growth for a prosperous industrialized country, it may be necessary to allow immigration in areas where the labor is needed, since the local population is no longer motivated to achieve for more wealth. When people do not behave rationally to their advantage, the state has the task of supporting them in their decisions to their advantage through nudges and precautionary regulations (asymmetrical paternalism). However, the limited rationality and weaknesses in information processing must not be exploited to the detriment of the citizens. Framing as the manipulative representation of information necessary for decision making, as well as the use of extremely disparaging representations of other options in order to force citizens to make decisions to their own detriment must be rejected. Rather, in a democracy the press has the special task of presenting the information so objectively that the citizen can make a decision that is not influenced from outside. The short-term and long-term advantages and disadvantages of alternative decisions must be made transparent to the citizen. Because some people are motivated to act solely to achieve more power, institutional precautions such as the separation of powers, mutual control of state organizations and the subordination of political power to a constitution are required in order to limit the political power of the individual.

In conclusion, human behavior cannot be predetermined, which is why only pattern prediction (Hayek) is suitable for economics. Irrational behavior must also be included in economics. Economics is only related to reality as a social science, thus behavioral science makes an important contribution. Incentives and sanctions are decisive for human behavior, which is why institutional economics is of particular importance. People are also social animals (company, nation). That is why ethics, especially fairness for people, plays a major role in the decisions they make and is the basic prerequisite for achieving productivity gains from human coexistence.

Literature

Kydland, F. E., & Prescott, E. C. (1977). Rules rather than discretion: The inconsistency of optimal plans. *Journal of Political Economy, 85*(3), 473–491.

Solutions to the Exercises

To Chap. 3: The Functioning of Market and Competition

Competition functions
Assign the examples below to the respective competition functions.

1.
⇒ Innovation and imitation function
2.
⇒ Steering function
3.
⇒ Liberty function
4.
⇒ Control function
5.
⇒ First allocation function and adaption function
6.
⇒ Sanction function
7.
⇒ Adaption function (and steering function)
8.
⇒ Second allocation function
9.
⇒ Distribution function, incentive function und innovation function
10.
⇒ Distribution, incentive function und innovation function
11.
⇒ Incentive function (distribution function)

C. A. Conrad, *Economic Systems, Markets and Politics*,
https://doi.org/10.1007/978-3-031-10366-7

To Chap. 6: Traits of the Political Systeme

Solution Voting Rules Berlin versus Bonn

	146 x 3 = 438	222 x 2 = 444	289 Σ 1.171
	222 x 3 = 666	265 x 2 = 530	170 Σ 1.366
	289 x 3 = 867	170 x 2 = 340	198 Σ 1.405

Fig. 6.7 Solution transfer task voting rules